North Carolina Hiking Trails

Third Edition

Allen de Hart

APPALACHIAN MOUNTAIN CLUB BOOKS
BOSTON, MASSACHUSETTS

Cover Photograph: *Oconoluftee Overlook, Great Smoky Mountains National Park.* Dedra Murphy
Book & Cover Design: Carol Bast Tyler
All photographs by the author unless otherwise noted.

Copyright © 1982, 1988, 1996, by Allen de Hart. All rights reserved.

Published by the Appalachian Mountain Club, 5 Joy St., Boston, MA 02108.

Distributed by the Globe Pequot Press, 6 Business Park Rd., PO Box 833, Old Saybrook, CT 06475.

THIRD EDITION

Library of Congress Cataloging-in-Publication Data
De Hart, Allen.
    North Carolina hiking trails / Allen de Hart. — 3rd ed.
        p.   cm.
    Includes bibiliographic references (p.   ) and indexes.
    ISBN 1-878239-48-1 (pbk.   : alk. paper)
    1. Hiking—North Carolina—Guidebooks. 2. Trails—North Carolina—Guidebooks. 3. North Carolina—Guidebooks. I.Title.
GV199.42.N66D4   1996
917.56—dc20   95-52825
                                                                                CIP

The paper used in this publication meets the minimum requirements of the American National Standard for Information Sciences—Permanence of Paper for Printed Library Materials, ANSI Z39.48–1984.∞

**Due to changes in conditions, use of the information
in this book is at the sole risk of the user.**

Printed on recycled paper using soy-based inks.

Printed in the United States of America.

10 9 8 7 6 5 4 3 2 1   96 97 98 99 00 01

Contents

To the volunteers who design, construct, and maintain the hiking trails in North Carolina.

Acknowledgments

The third edition of this book has been made possible by the assistance of many resource personnel of the forests and parks, professional outdoor sports and recreation specialists, hikers, and college and university students. Those who assisted me in accumulating data, double-checked research material, planned the logistical needs, and spent relentless days of field work deserve grateful acknowledgment. Our work was mitigated by having the original research manuscripts and maps from the 1980–1981 research of Kay Scott, former state trails coordinator, and her supervisor, Jim Hallsey, assistant chief of planning and special studies section of the Division of Parks and Recreation.

By 1986 an additional library of trail information had been accumulated for the second edition. Recognition of faithful hiking friends such as Alan Householder, Todd Shearon, and Kevin Bighannitti was made at that time. Additional information came from the Division of Parks and Recreation by Susan Currie, trails coordinator; Bynum Riggsbee, visitor service director; Mike Dunn, interpretive and education director; and Jim Hallsey again, who had been promoted to chief of operations. Others whose work became part of the second edition were Harry Baker, landscape architect for the Blue Ridge Parkway; Melinda Waldrep, landscape architect of the national forests in North Carolina; and Joseph Smith, assistant chief ranger of the Cherokee area of the Great Smoky Mountains National Park.

Although research is part of every year between editions, there are public employees who give special attention when we approached the final preparation of this third edition. From the national forests' staff is Melinda MacWilliams, who provided updated lists and commentary on forest trails. Others in the four national forests are as follows: Laurene Hillman, ranger, and Holly Jenkins, recreation manager of the Croatan National Forest. From the Nantahala National Forest are Glenn McConnell, ranger, Jim Burchfield, trail and wilderness technician, and Frank Findley, forester (Cheoah District); Erin Bronk, ranger, Chad Boniface, recreation forester, and Judy Green, acting resource assistant (Highlands District); Charles Miller, ranger, and Terry Dickey, forestry technician (Tusquitee District); Michael Wilkins, ranger, and Joe Nicholson, recreation specialist (Wayah District). From the Pisgah National Forest are Kimberly Brandel, ranger, Joseph Fore, forestry technician, and Tanya Henderson, forester and recreation assistant (French Broad District); Mike Anderson, ranger, and Phillip Kromer, supervisory forester (Grandfather District); Art Rowe, ranger, and Sue Elderkin, forestry technician and recreation specialist (Pisgah District); Paul Bradley, ranger (Toecane District); and from the Uwharrie National Forest, Tamara Malone, ranger, and Kelly Cagle, forestry technician.

Third edition trail information has been from Jean Cashin of the Appalachian Trail Conference; Burt Kornegay of the Bartram Trail Society; Karen Wade, superintendent, and Don De Foe, assistant director of resources of the Great Smoky Mountains National Park; Will Orr, landscape architect, and Lisa Jameson, resource management specialist, of the Blue Ridge Parkway; and Russell Berry Jr., superintendent of Cape Hatteras National Seashore.

Assistance from the state's Division of Parks and Recreation came from Darrell McBane, trails coordinator, and from regional trail specialists Dwayne Stutzman (mountains), Beth Timson (piedmont), and Tom Potter (coastal). Assisting with maps and information of the county and municipal trail systems and greenways are Alice Webb, parks planner and landscape architect (Cary); Guillo Rodriguiez, planner (Durham); Bonnie Kuester, director, and Jim Sykes, resource manager (Greensboro); John DeKemper, park planner (Mecklenburg County and Charlotte); Victor Lebsock, park and greenway planner (Raleigh); Chris O'Keefe, planner (New Hanover County); and Judy Hunt, principal planner (Winston-Salem and Forsyth County).

The list of families and friends who provided food and shelter during the years of three editions is too numerous for this space, but among those who provided a consistent home away from home were Drs. Frank and Doris Hammett and Mr. and Mrs. Kenneth Ayala (Waynesville); Mr. and Mrs. Bruce Phillips (Jacksonville); Dr. and Mrs. Lee Copple (Highlands); Mr. and Mrs. Barry (Kay Scott) Rosen (Morganton); and Mr. and Mrs. R. M. Collins (Pilot Mountain). I am also indebted to many hikers and backpackers who were part of a continuous team to assist me in the snows of winter, heat of summer, and at times of risky conditions. I am particularly indebted to Alan Householder, who assisted in locating new trails and exploring abandoned trails, and to Ron Barlow and his son Eric of Cleveland, who researched trail conditions, road names, and signs. In recognition, the others are Hill Allen, Robert Ballance, Frank Barringer, Mike Batts, Mike Beaman, Kevin Bighannitti, Tom Boles, Tom Bond, Peyton Bonner, John Borum, Jimmy Boyette, Chris Bracknell, Jeff Brewer, Andy Britt, Tony Butler, Richard Byrd, Cathy Carter, Dean Carter, Richard Caviness, Kim Caudle, John Chess, John Chesson, Lori Clark, Sherry Clark, Gale Clayton, Joe Cohn, Steve Cosby, Brian Cox, Paula Crenshaw, John Culbertson, Susan Currie, Mike Daley, Jerry Dickerson, Tony Droppleman, Bill Flournoy, Greg Frederick, Larry Gibbons, Dave Giesen, Fess Green, Todd Gregory, Travis Griffin, Geoff Haas, Robert Hall, Jim Hallsey, Rusty Hamilton, Heath Hamrich, Tom Harris, Bill Hatch, Rudy Hauser, Tate Hayman, Kellie Heath, Lisa Helm, David Hicks, Carl Hill, Neil Hine, Patrick Hobin, Van Hockett, Alan Householder, Mike Hudson, Steven Hughes, Bryan Jackson, Lloyd Jacobs, Jeff Jeffries, Tim Jenkins, Joel Johnson, Randy Johnson, Billy Jones, Jeff Jones, Tom Key, Steve King, Hans Kirsch, Sherri Lanier, John LeMay, John Lentz, Jack Lewis, Jason Mason, Darin Matthews, John Matthews, Ray Matthews, Taylor Mayo, Darrell McBane, Fuki Miyoshi, Hazel Monroe, Charles Moore, Roger Moore, Lenny Murdock, Lisa Myers, Arch Nichols, Billy Norris, Les Parks, Dennis Parrish, Reggie Ponder, Allen Poole, Jay Price, Fletcher Raiford, Georgette Ray, Mark Roberts, Mike Sanderson, Chuck Satterwhite, Brooks Savage, Kay Scott, Ed Seagroves, Greg Seamster, John Shaffner, Todd Shearon, John Shelton, Brad Shuler, Alison Sipfle, Brad Smith, Joe Smith, Scott Smith, Eddie Sori, Steve Strader, Dwayne Stutzman, Gigi Sugg, Allen Tharrington, Dave Thompson, Kenneth Tippette, Doug Wassum, Mark Waters, Buster White, Harold White, Travis Winn, and Kevin Zoltek.

I express my special appreciation to the editorial staff of Appalachian Mountain Club Books: former editor Arlyn Powell (who suggested and worked with the first edition); his successor, Michael Cirone, who followed with support; and Gordon Hardy, current editor and publisher, for his guidance of the third edition.

Introduction

The tempered light of the woods is like a perpetual morning...
—Ralph Waldo Emerson

Elizabeth Hair, a former chair of the Mecklenburg County Commissioners, said in 1986 that "I believe in trails even if I do not hike them." Her statement was in support of greenways in the city of Charlotte and its environs, but to those listening to her at a statewide trails meeting, it could mean any trail. The word trail, spoken as a noun, is easy to believe in. It has a pleasant sound; its synonyms are satisfying: path, walkway, passageway, lane. Trails go somewhere, to surprises and challenge, to a feeling of freedom and independence, to musing and to fantasy, to physical exercise, and to accomplishing a goal. Perhaps along the way you will find the perpetual mornings described by Emerson in *Essays* (1844).

This book provides a description in part or in detail of nearly 1,000 trails covering more than 3,500 miles. Immensely diverse, it describes trails to suit every preference. There are long backcountry trails in the wilderness for mystery, "silence and whispers," "sudden radiances," and "idle aires," as Fiona MacLeod wrote in *Where the Forest Murmurs*. Or you can take short walks for magnificent views of sunsets over the Smokies on the *Waterrock Knob Trail,* or in the "land of waterfalls" follow the *Whitewater Falls Trail,* or listen to the "talking trees" on the Holmes State Forest trails, or walk an estuarian boardwalk on the *Cedar Point Tidewater Trail,* or appreciate the *Wolf Creek Trail* for the physically disabled in the Nantahala National Forest. Each of the state's trails is distinctive, unique, with its own ambiance, almost a personality. They all deserve superlatives, but I have restrained my descriptions so that you may have plenty of surprises. I have hiked all these trails at least once, some of them many times, and the *Greencroft Lake Trail* more than once a week since 1963. Rehiking always brings a new experience. John Burroughs, a hiking friend of John Muir, said, "Follow the path you took yesterday to find new things." I have found many new things in observing the process of succession, in the changes of the seasons, and wildlife habitats. I found trails that were manicured, neatly blazed, frequently used, remote and wild, or clean but natural. In contrast some were eroded, neglected, mutilated by ATVs, or covered with US Forest Service (USFS) timbering slash. In addition to the natural forest duff, there are trails with soft grass, pea gravel, wood chips, clay, sand, sawdust, rocks, brick, asphalt, and cement. Walking these trails again for the third edition of this book I learned more about their history, about the people who constructed them, their animal and plant life, and the cities and towns and countryside around them. For me it was an extraordinary field trip, a valuable natural history classroom. It was a long journey of reality, like the state's motto, *Esse quam videri* (to be rather than to seem).

Some of the trails have more distinctive features than others. For example, four of the longest singular trails are the *Appalachian Trail* (305.1 mi), the *Bartram Trail* (71.1 mi), the *Cape Hatteras Beach Trail* (75.8 mi), and the *Lakeshore Trail* (41.8 mi). The *Mountains-to-Sea Trail*, when completed, will be the state's longest. In contrast there are short trails such as *Black Camp Gap Trail* (66 yd), on the Heintooga Rd, 3.6 mi off the Blue Ridge Parkway at mp 458.2; *Gwyn Memorial Trail* (91 yd) at mp 298.6 on the Blue Ridge Parkway; and *Rob Taylor Trail* (80 yd) also on the parkway at mp 433.8. The highest trail is *Mt Mitchell Summit Trail*, and the highest changes in elevation are the *Noland Divide Trail* (4,155 ft) and the *Baxter Creek Trail* (4,142 ft), both in the Smokies. The trail with views of all 49 mountain peaks over 6,000 ft in the state is the *Crabtree Bald Trail*. The lowest trail elevation is the *Cape Hatteras Beach Trail*.

THE FIRST TRAILS

Some archeologists claim that American Indians were living in the area that is now North Carolina as long ago as 5000 B.C. during the Archaic period. They base their claim on excavations in Rowan, Stanly, Montgomery, and Orange Counties. The Woodland period, the first 1500 years A.D., shows the development of pottery, agriculture, and burial ceremonies. By the time of Spanish and English explorations, it is estimated the region had about 25 tribes in an aboriginal population of 30,000. The tribes constituted three major linguistic families: the Algonquin in the coastal area of the Albemarle and Pamlico Sounds (which included the Hatteras Indians); the Iroquoian, including tribes E of Raleigh to Beaufort County and all of the Cherokee in the mountains; and the Siouan tribes, including such groups as Catawba, Occaneechi, Keyauwee, and Waxhaw in the central area of the state.

The Indian trails developed from the paths made by animals to their food and water sources. As nomadic life changed to more permanent settlements with the advent of agriculture, the trails became major routes between communities for communication and trade. These trails were used also for warfare between the tribes and exploration by the Europeans, and later some trails became colonial roads. The 1928 trail map by W. E. Myer shows a remarkable similarity in trail location to some of the current superhighways. For example, I-85 follows part of the *Lower Cherokee Trading Path* in South Carolina and the *Occaneechi Path* from Charlotte to Petersburg. The *Saponi Trail* was a route much like the US-29 route from Greensboro to Charlottesville, and I-77, from Charlotte to Columbia on the *Occaneechi Path*. The *Catawba Trail* went NW from near Spartanburg, through Asheville, and on to Kentucky to join what became the *Daniel Boone Trail* (that was from the Yadkin River Trading Fort near Salisbury to Boonesborough, Kentucky). From an area near Lake Keowee in South Carolina, the *Tuckalcechee Trail* wove through the mountains to the Tennessee River and into Tennessee. A multiple-trail intersection was at Wilkesboro. The *Occaneechi Path* on its route from the *Old Cherokee Path* passed near Morganton to the *Occaneechi Path* near Hillsborough; the *New River Trail* went N into Virginia and West Virginia; the *Northern Trail* went S to join the *Cherokee Trading Path* near Spartanburg; and the trail that became the *Daniel Boone Trail* passed through from Salisbury on its route to the Cumberland Gap at the boundary of Tennessee, Virginia, and Kentucky. (Here it joined what was earlier called the *Warrior's Path* and later the *Wilderness Trail*).

The first known contact of Europeans with the Indians was in 1524 when Giovanni da Verrazzano, in the service of France, explored the coastline between areas now known as Wilmington and Kitty Hawk. In 1540 the daring Spanish explorer Hernando de Soto left Florida on his long march to the Mississippi. It was May 21 when he arrived in Xualla, a large village inhabited by the Saura tribe between the Saluda and Broad Rivers in what is now South Carolina. De Soto's route across the Appalachians has been disputed, but most studies indicate that he followed a trail across the Blue Ridge Mountains near present-day Highlands and Franklin and to Guasili (the mouth of Peachtree Creek at the Hiwassee River, 3 mi E of what is now Murphy). The Saura tribe must have had a trail from Xualla (in what is now Greenville County, South Carolina) to what is now the Asheville area, because the Cherokee name for Swannanoa means "trail of the Saura" or Suali (pronounced "Shualla" by the Spaniards). In 1566 another Spanish exploratory force, led by Juan Pardo, followed the trail that de Soto had traveled from Charleston to Xualla (called Joaro by Pardo), where they built a fort to make their excursions into the hills and mountains of the Appalachians.

English exploration on the Indian paths began in early July 1584 when Captains Philip Amandas and Arthur Barlowe went ashore in the Pamlico Sound (about 20 mi from an island called Roanoak). They stayed two months with friendly Indians who fed them fruits and white corn and "braces of fat bucks, conies, hares, fish, the best in the world." A year later, almost to the day, another English expedition of 108 arrived with Thomas Hariot, the first scientist-historian to visit the Indians. They stayed for nearly a year and in the process followed numerous trails and rivers. One trail led to a "great lake," Paquipe (Lake Mattamuskeet). But the year ended in warfare with the natives. The next expedition, July 22, 1587, became the historic "lost colony" of Roanoke Island. Following the English establishment of Jamestown in 1607, the trails into North Carolina began with John Pory in 1622. He made a 60-mi "fruitful and pleasant" overland journey to the Chowan River. In 1650 Edward Bland went to the Roanoke River, and in 1654, Nathaniel Batts established a permanent residence by the Chowan River (near present-day Winton).

Another explorer ("father of Piedmont explorers") was a German physician from Virginia, John Lederer, who in 1670 was sent by Sir William Berkeley into the heart of the Carolinas. Riding a horse, he and his Indian guide followed the "Trading Path" (*Occaneechi Path*) to Suala (mentioned by de Soto). Lederer followed an eastern return route on his two-month excursion. He kept a detailed diary of his journey (much like current *Appalachian Trail* hikers, with the exception that it was written in Latin). In 1671 Thomas Batts followed a trail to the headwaters of the New River from the *Occaneechi Path,* and in May 1673 James Needham, Gabriel Arthur, and an Indian guide left Petersburg, followed the *Occaneechi Path* to the Catawba River, and journeyed west on a trail to Hickory Nut Gap by Chimney Rock. (Needham was slain by Indians on his second journey.)

In 1700, John Lawson, surveyor general for the North Carolina colony, began a 1,000-mi journey on the trails from Charleston, South Carolina, into the Piedmont and out to the coast of North Carolina. He kept a lengthy diary that was published in England as *Lawson's History of Carolina.* Understanding and generally sympathetic to the natives, he and his friend Baron Christoph von Graffenried (founder of New Bern) were captured upstream on the Neuse River by the Tuscarora in 1711. A few days after Lawson's torture and execution, the baron's ransom offer was accepted for his freedom. He was led "two hours" from the village (near Contentnea Creek, E of present-day Snow Hill) and sent home on foot (about 40 mi).

Other colonial trailblazers were pioneer explorer Daniel Boone, Methodist circuit rider Bishop Francis Asbury, and naturalist William Bartram. Boone, who lived near the Trading Fork of the Yadkin River (N of Salisbury), began an expedition with a party of six in 1767 to explore Kentucky. Twice captured and twice escaped, he returned in 1771, but started on another expedition in 1773 (see chapter 10, section 3). From 1771 to 1816 Bishop Asbury was the champion of equestrians. He covered 275,000 mi over the pioneer trails from New England to South Carolina, and his circuit included 60 trips across the Appalachians. On November 29, 1810, he wrote in his famous diary that "our troubles began at the foaming, roaring stream [Cataloochee Creek] and losing ourselves in the wood," but they arrived safely at their destination in present-day Clyde (see chapter 7, *Asbury Trail*). In 1775, when Bartram was on his 2,500-mi journey from Pennsylvania to Florida and back, he followed a "trading path" into the Cherokee territory on "serpentine paths of verdant swelling knolls...and fragrant strawberries, their rich juice dying my horse's feet" (see Chapter 2, *Bartram Trail*).

HOW TO USE THIS BOOK

This completely revised third edition is divided into 16 chapters that cover the national forests (Croatan, Nantahala, Pisgah, and Uwharrie); the national parks and refuges; the state parks, forests, and historic sites; city and county parks; private and college properties; and a progress report on the *Mountains-to-Sea Trail*. Each chapter and section has an introduction to acquaint you with the location of and access to the properties, addresses and telephone numbers for information, and the nearest support services. If not in the main introduction, this information will be shown in a specific section where trails are concentrated. An appendix provides you with names and addresses of clubs and organizations that can assist you in your planning. It is recommended that allied maps be secured in your advance planning and that some familiarity be developed with the topography of the area to which you are going. This will enable you to plan better for your transportation, seasonal needs, and hiking and camping supplies. This book is designed to be carried in a side pocket of your backpack or in a large pocket of your jacket. Maps in an attached pocket outline the general location of the trails.

Format for Trail Descriptions: The trails are described either numerically (all USFS trails are described from the lowest to the highest number, the official method of USFS inventories), or alphabetically, or from areas to areas. In the national forests the descriptions may be described from SW to

NE, but in the Smokies in the opposite direction. Exceptions are made when trail proximity or connections are an advantage to your planning options.

Title and Number: The trail name is from the most current source, but references may indicate that it was formerly known by another name. Some trails will carry a double name because they run jointly for a distance. An example is where the *Mountains-to-Sea Trail* runs jointly with an original trail. The first number nearest the title is the USFS trail number, listed in parentheses, the official number assigned by the USFS on its trail inventories and maps. It is significant because it is on all the US Geological Survey (USGS) maps modified for USFS use—the topo map you should use in the national forests. This is the same number that you will see on special maps (examples are the Linville Wilderness or Joyce Kilmer/Slickrock Wilderness) created by the USFS. Additionally, you may see the trail number on commercial maps. If the number is absent, the USFS has not assigned a number or the number may have been deleted from its inventories. Each district or national forest should have its own group of numbers, but unfortunately you will find that the assignments in North Carolina are set at random (with trail inventories from 1 through 700). The exception is the Croatan National Forest, with all numbers in the 500 range. A few major or interstate trails will carry the same number through all districts, regardless of the national forest. Examples are the *Appalachian Trail* (#1), the *Bartram Trail* (#67), and the *Overmountain Victory Trail* (#308). Following the USFS number, or the trail name outside the national forests, are capital letters to indicate trail traffic: foot (F), bike (B), horse (H), wheelchair (W), interpretive (I), or other (O). These are the official USFS codes used on its transportation inventory. The second number on the page, at the outside margin in bold type, is a numeric assignment by the publishers of this book for the purpose of matching trails in the book to the pocket maps. These numbers also are listed in the index to serve as an easy locator reference.

Mileage: The trail length is always within the nearest 0.1 mile (with the exception of short trails that may be described in yards or feet). All numbers followed by *mi* (mile/s) indicate the distance from one trailhead to another. If the mileage is followed by *round-trip* or *backtrack*, it means the distance is a loop (perhaps using a road route) or doubled by returning on the same route. When a group of trails is used for a combined or connecting mileage, the length will be followed by *combined* to indicate the total mileage of multiple routes. I used a 400 Rolatape measuring wheel (which registers each foot) on all the trails.

Connecting Trails: Where a single trail is listed with a number of connecting trails, some of the trails may be covered in more detail under another heading. If so, they will be enclosed in parentheses. Although reading about a connecting trail may create a temporary break in your train of thought, a return to the main description usually will start with the words *to continue* or *continuing ahead*. The objective is to give you flexibility on how far you wish to hike before backtracking, making a loop, or staying on the main trail. If continuing, you can ignore the paragraphs in parentheses, but the information will be available if you change your mind.

Difficulty: Trails are described as *easy* (meaning the trail has a gentle grade, may be short, and does not require a rest stop); *moderate* (with a greater change in elevation or rough treadway that requires some exertion and likely rest stops); or *strenuous* (with the need for some skill over rough treadway, high or steep elevation change, exertion, and perhaps frequent rest stops). Elevation changes on strenuous trails are usually listed.

Special Features: Some of the trails have features that are more distinctive, unique, unusual, rare, or outstanding than trails in general. This listing will follow "Length and Difficulty" or "Connecting Trail" and will precede "Trailhead and Description." The word *scenic* is frequently used as synonymous with impressive, bucolic, unspoiled, panoramic, or pleasant to experience. I have made an effort to avoid using superlatives for every trail, even when I may have felt it was deserving. I found beauty in all the trails; you probably will also, but I have left some mystery for your judgment.

Trailhead: Where possible, access to a trailhead is described from the North Carolina official highway map. More specifically, I have used county and city maps. Because the USGS or the USGS-FS (Forest Service) topographic maps are not as easily or quickly attainable, they are not emphasized but are listed either after the introductory paragraphs or at the end of the trail description. The nearest city, town, or community is usually cited; otherwise roads by title and number and their junctions are listed. If the trailhead has more than one access option, the easiest and nearest is described first.

Description: Trail descriptions are determined by trail length, usage, features, history, connective value, difficulty, and book space. Most of the trails are described as *main* or *primary* (blazed, marked, or maintained). Some are *primitive* (the opposite of primary), and others are as follows: *side* or *spur* (a shorter route or to a point of interest); *multiple* (used by horses, bikers, hikers, or vehicles); *jeep* (mainly old forest or hunting roads); *manway* or *wilderness* (exceptionally primitive, grown up, or obscure); *special* (used for special populations, such as the physically handicapped). A *gated* trail may be a foot trail for pedestrians during a protective season for wildlife that is open to both hikers and vehicles at other times, and a *seeded* trail is usually a former logging road planted with grass for soil stabilization. There are numerous paths used by hunters and fishermen that may be called *fisherman's* trails or *hunter's* trails in both public and private game lands. Some of the mountain trails are used as *ski* trails in wintertime. Other trails may be described as *recreational* (jogging, exercise, fitness); *historic* (emphasizing heritage, historic districts, historic sites); and *nature* (interpretive, botanical, kiosk displays).

Address and Access: The addresses and telephone numbers are your most immediate source of additional information about the trail area and trail conditions. They are listed at the end of an introduction or description. The access explains how to arrive at either the address or at campgrounds, parks, or special places administered by the address source.

Support Facilities: To assist you in planning for your food supply, gasoline and vehicle services, and accommodations, the nearest stores are listed at large or major groupings of trails. The nearest (or most amenable to hikers) commercial campgrounds are listed, particularly in areas where public campgrounds do not have full services or hot showers. Motels are listed for some areas.

Maps: An official North Carolina highway map is essential. Although you may be familiar with the area, you may need to give someone clear directions about where you will be or how you are to be picked up after a long hike. The map is available at service stations, Chambers of Commerce, and free from the North Carolina Department of Transportation, PO Box 25201, Raleigh, NC 27611; 919-733-7600. Detailed county maps are available from county courthouses, local Chambers of Commerce, and statewide from the N.C. Dept of Transportation for a nominal cost. City maps are available from city newsstands and bookstores and Chambers of Commerce for a small charge. Additionally you may wish to contact the state's Division of Travel and Tourism, N.C. Dept of Commerce, 430 N. Salisbury St, Raleigh, NC 27611; 919-733-4171 (in Raleigh) or 800-847-4862 (toll-free elsewhere) for information on county or city vacation attractions and services. If you plan to hike in a wilderness area, a topographical map and compass are necessary. They could save your life in a crisis or if you are lost. (If you plan to order topo maps, the address is Branch of Distribution, USGS, Box 25286 Federal Center, Denver, CO 80225. Because you must pay in advance, write for a free N.C. Map Index and order form. Allow two to four weeks for delivery.) For immediate needs contact a local outdoor-sports store or blueprint company.

The best source for acquiring the USGS-FS maps (which show the forest boundaries and the trails with numbers) is National Forests of North Carolina, Post and Otis Sts, (PO Box 2750), Asheville, NC 28802; 704-257-4200. Also ask for a revised list (most recent dates of publication) of the USFS forest and wilderness maps. State parks and county and city parks also have maps of their areas. Contact the main offices (addresses in chapters 9, 10, 11, 12, and 13). For a map of the Great Smoky Mountains National Park, contact the main office address listed in chapter 7.

Signs, Blazes, and Markers: It would be ideal if all trails were signed and blazed. Because they are not, it is suggested that you carefully follow the directions in this book. If there are signs, they are usually at the trailheads, and blazes are usually painted on trees at eye level at irregular intervals. An exceptionally large number of trails in the national forests have neither. One district, Grandfather, in the Pisgah forest has 200 mi of trails, none of which (except the *MST*) is blazed. As a result I have described the trails with emphasis on other landmarks—rock formations, flora, bridges, streams, and unique points of interest, for example. (Do not expect to see signs or markers in any of the wilderness areas. That is in keeping with the wilderness milieu.) Vandalism results in the loss of numerous signs. You will find more signs in the Great Smoky Mountains National Park (GSMNP) and state parks than in the national forests, but many of the trail-distance signs in the GSMNP are not correct. The USFS trail numbers and the assigned numbers in this book for the map references will not be seen on trail posts, trees, or other markers. The *AT* blaze is a white 2x6-inch vertical bar, with same-size blue blazes indicating a spur (often to water) or an alternate route. The *Bartram Trail* blaze is yellow, the same size as the *AT,* and the *MST* blaze is a white dot, three inches in diameter. Alternate *MST* trails may be blue. You will see a wide range of other colors where there is a color-coded trail system, such as the Pisgah district in chapter 3, section 3. The USFS boundary line has bright red markings, and some trees for timbering may have blue, white, green, or yellow markings.

Plants and Animals: North Carolina has 89 species of ferns and more than 3,500 species and varieties of other vascular plants. Flowering plants account for nearly 3,000 of these, with 313 species native only to the mountains, 183 species in the Piedmont, and 469 species in the coastal plains. Many others grow in two or all the regions. A recommended sourcebook for the botany-oriented hiker is *Manual of the Vascular Flora of the Carolinas* by Radford, Ahles, and Bell. Another book is *Wild Flowers of North Carolina* by Justice and Bell.

Two pocket-size books on trees are *Common Forest Trees of North Carolina* by the North Carolina Department of Natural Resources, Division of Forest Resources, and *Important Trees of Eastern Forests* by the USFS. There are some exceptionally beautiful areas of gardenlike displays in all the national forests and in the GSMNP. I have described their locations throughout this book, but I have avoided a description of areas with the most rare species. The *USFS Land and Resource Management Plan (1986–2000)* lists 31 endangered species that are in the Nantahala and Pisgah forests and 13 in the Croatan and Uwharrie forests. Emphasis has been given some plants, with the botanical name in parentheses. After the first mention of the botanical name, it is not used again. The most common rhododendron (one of nearly 20 species) is the *Rhododendron maximum,* called rosebay or great laurel, with light pink and whitish blossoms. It is the source of massive thickets or slicks in the mountains. *Rhododendron catawbiense,* called mountain rosebay or purple laurel, is seen in both the mountains and a few scattered counties in the Piedmont. Craggy Gardens on the Blue Ridge Parkway and Roan Mountain have superb examples. Most of the other species are called azalea, and I have made that distinction where they appear prominently. My listing is according to what I saw at a particular time of the season. Your hike may offer others.

Wildlife is likely to be seen on any day's hike, particularly in parks, refuges, and forests where wildlife is protected and hunting forbidden. Your best chance is to know the animals' watering and feeding places and look for them early or late in the day. Also, walk softly, talk at low decibels, and leave the dogs at home. In the Nantahala and Pisgah forests alone, there are about 400 vertebrate species. There are 138 species of reptiles and amphibians, 442 species of mollusks, and 418 species of fish. There are 12,000 species of *Arthropods,* some of which (such as mosquitoes, "no-seeums," chiggers, mites, ticks, and flies) welcome your visit on the trails. Your chance of hearing, or perhaps seeing, birds is good. A recommended book is *Birds of the Carolinas* by Potter, Parnell, and Teulings. Other books are *Amphibians and Reptiles in the Carolinas and Virginia* by Martof, Palmer, Bailey, Harrison, and Dermid; *Mammals of North Carolina* by Brimley; and the Golden Press pocket-size guideooks on butterflies and moths, spiders, and fishes. (See bibliography.)

HEALTH AND SAFETY
Accidents happen to the most cautious hiker, and even a minor mishap can ruin an otherwise pleasant journey. To minimize risk and to maintain good health, some suggestions (more critical in the backpacking backcountry) are

listed below. Although you may wish to hike alone, the park and forest officials (who must make plans for a rescue) encourage you to have one or more companions to reduce the danger of hypothermia, poisonous snake bites, injury from a fall, and being lost or sick. Someone in the group should carry a first-aid kit with water purifier, moleskin, assorted band-aids, antibiotics, disinfectant ointment, prescription pills for severe pain, simple painkiller, gauze pads, adhesive tape, tweezers, biodegradable soap, sunburn ointment, insect repellent, medicine for an upset stomach, and your personal medical prescriptions. A basic safety package would include waterproof matches, maps, compass, emergency freeze-dried food, a whistle, a 75-ft rope, a knife (preferably *Swiss*), flashlight (preferably one with krypton bulbs), and a windproof hooded jacket. Your guide or outdoor-store consultant may recommend more or less. You may wish to read *Medicine for the Outdoors* by Auerbach during your planning. Another book is *Practical Outdoor Survival* by McDougall. (See Bibliography.)

Hypothermia, a major cause of death for outdoor recreationists, is caused by the lowering of body heat. It can be fatal even in the summertime. Sweaty and wet clothes lose about 90 percent of their dry insulating value, and windchill increases the danger. The best lines of defense are to stay dry; get out of the wind, rain, or snow to avoid exhaustion; and know the symptoms and treatment. The symptoms are uncontrollable shivering; vague, incoherent speech; frequent stumbling, and drowsiness. The victim may be unaware of all of these. Treatment for mild impairment is to place the victim in a dry place, in dry clothes, and in a warm sleeping bag, and give warm drinks (no alcohol). Try to keep semiconscious victims awake, warm the head and face, provide person-to-person warmth, and evacuate to an emergency hospital as quickly as possible.

If you become lost, use the universal distress signal of three of anything—shouts, whistles, light flashes, or smoke signals. Do not panic, stay in one place, make a fire and stay warm, conserve your food, drink plenty of water, and climb a tree if it will help determine your location. After a reasonable time without rescue, find a valley and follow its water sources downstream. Someone has said that to be safe in the forest "use your head first and if things go wrong remember to *keep* it." Some off-trail hikers are using global positioning system (GPS) equipment to rescue themselves, or cellular telephones for location or rescue assistance.

Lightning is another danger. Some precautions are to stay off sharp prominent peaks, avoid standing under a cliff or in a cave entrance, avoid seams or crevices on rocks, and avoid standing under prominent trees or other tall objects. Squat down and insulate yourself from the ground if possible. Also, do not stay on a beach or in a boat or cross a stream or marsh. Anything metal, including your pack frame, should be removed from your body.

Some precautions to take when crossing a stream include unfastening your backpack bellyband, keeping your boots on (or using your spare pair), always facing upstream, keeping your balance with a steady pole, and avoiding rapids.

You should carry pure drinking water and use only water officially designated safe by the forest or park. My listing of springs and clear streams in this book does not mean the water has been tested. Properly boiling the water remains one of the best ways to be safe, or use a pump water purifier. For the health of you and others, particularly those downstream, camp at least 100 ft away from streams. Human waste should be 300 ft away from a campsite or stream and should be buried if vault toilets are not available. Another rule is to carry out all trash. A few other suggestions are not to hike at night, be sure your boots fit to avoid blisters, and use care with fires, knives, or firearms if hunting. Firearms are prohibited in national, state, and local parks, but are allowed for hunting in specific areas of national forests and wildlife refuges. If you have questions contact the local sheriff's office and the state's Wildlife Resource Commission (license) at 919-662-4370. (In 1995 the N.C. legislature passed a law allowing concealed weapons. A permit is necessary; there are restrictions.)

TRAIL COURTESY

The majority of hikers say they choose trails to encounter the natural environment and to get away from people, particularly crowds. That desire may be realized on remote and infrequently used trails, but privacy is declining with an increase in trail usage throughout North Carolina. Multiuse trails create the most immediate response because hikers must move aside to permit horse, bike, and motorized traffic to pass. Most hikers turn and stop to see what margins are required. On paved trails, the hiker confronts higher-speed bike traffic and in-line skaters. Equestrians should avoid any speed beyond the horse's walking stride, and bikers should slow down to prevent spooking the horses. Horses usually can be heard, but bikers are more silent and should sound a bell or a whistle to hikers. Both equestrians and bikers should dismount when crossing bridges.

For long-distance hikers the question of courtesy becomes more intense at shared campsites, shelters, and campgrounds. Tired and hungry, the main concerns are to have peace and quiet sans radios and television. (Cellular telephones offend some hikers; others consider them a lifesaver in an emergency.) At most campgrounds or shelters there is an unwritten code of early curfew for rest and sleep. Irritations flair easily when offending hikers leave toothpaste suds from dental care at the spring, or worse when body bathing is done at the spring. More offensive is the hiker who does not bury solid human waste. Another breach of courtesy is leaving trash and unburnable materials at the firesite or elsewhere. Strangers may be sensitive to random photography of them; gaining permission is advisable. Owners who insist on taking pets (almost always dogs) should respect the issues of leashing and control.

HIKING GEAR

Where possible it is wise to purchase the best quality of hiking gear to ensure durability and comfort. Professional or experienced hikers can give you advice on this topic. The options for hiking equipment become more diverse each year. For the environmentally conscious hiker there are now choices in ecogear recycled fibers. Before you purchase, I recommend you examine *Backpacker* magazine's annual "Buyer's Guide," published in March. The guide covers packs, tents, sleeping bags and pads, boots, water filters, stoves, lighting, repairs, and more. The magazine also reviews such other essentials as food and clothing in other random months. Colin Fletcher's *The Complete Walker III* is an excellent guide on equipment and how to prepare for a "house on your back." Choose equipment stores nearest you in case you must make exchanges or need advice. If you order, there are a number of reliable companies, some of which are L. L. Bean, 800-221-4221; Campmor, (catalog) 800-230-2151, (order) 800-226-7667; Cabela's, 800-237-4444; and REI, 800-426-4840.

FUTURE TRAILS

In the pages ahead are descriptions of many trails, some constructed more than a century ago. Others are so new they are in the process of being constructed. In addition to this comprehensive list are future trails existing in dreams and on master-planning maps. Although the legendary masterwork is the *Appalachian Trail,* which passes 305.1 mi through the state, the *Mountains-to-Sea Trail (MST)* will eventually surpass the *AT* in distance. It will rival the *AT* also in scenic value because of its track, from Clingmans Dome (6,643 ft) at the Tennessee state line NE along the Blue Ridge Mountains (340 mi). (See chapter 16.)

Connecting trails already exist and others are planned, such as a connection to the *Palmetto Trail* (South Carolina's mountains-to-sea trail) S of Brevard. Others are the *Northern Peaks Trail*, N of Boone, to the *Carolina Creeper Trail* (rail-trail), which connects with the *Virginia Creeper Trail* (rail-trail) and the *AT* S of Damascus, Virginia. In the Pisgah ranger district of the Pisgah National Forest, the most visited of any district in the state's national forests and having the largest number of trails, more trails are planned for construction. (See chapter 3, section 3.) The *MST* and its alternate trail passes through this district. Another long rail-trail is the *American Tobacco Trail* from the city of Durham SE. Two other potential long rail-trails are the *Pender County Trail* and the *Roanoke Valley Trail*. Small town landmarks are being emphasized, such as the *Wendell Historic Trail* in Wendell.

The fastest growth in the number of trails in the past 10 years has been in multiuse greenway systems. This effort will continue, probably at an increased rate. Examples of trails developed and on the drawing boards are Mecklenburg County (Charlotte area), Triad area of Winston-Salem/High Point/Jamestown/Greensboro; and Research Triangle area of Chapel Hill/Durham/Raleigh/Cary. Another city, Jacksonville, has nearly 40 trails planned or under construction. With the passage of the Parks and Recreation Trust Fund by the 1995 state legislature that allocated 56.25 percent of the funds to improving the quality of state parks, a 15 percent allocation was made for local governments to apply for grants. This will increase the number of parks and potential trails in communities across the state. For more information on the development and progress of future trails in North Carolina, write or call me at Louisburg College, Box 3058, Louisburg, NC 27549; 919-469-2521 or 919-496-4771.

PLANNING YOUR TRIP

Your checklist for getting started should include the choice of dependable companions and appropriate trails; choice and purchase of your equipment, maps, food, gear, and supplies; contacts with the forest or park headquarters for weather conditions and safety hazards, and permits (if required); and plans for daily or round-trip mileage, campsites, and vehicle parking or shuttles. After parking your vehicle at the trailhead, be sure it is locked and that all valuables are stored in the trunk (better yet, left at home). Some of the shuttle-service contacts available near the *Appalachian Trail* are: Jack Coriell (704-369-6820; Franklin); Agnes Murray (704-586-8861; Bryson City); Charlie Watts (704-479-2504; Fontana); and Worley Edwards (615-743-5617;

Erwin, Tenn.). Descriptions of where to park at the trailheads are included in this book. Also, throughout the book I have indicated what areas require permits for camping and have explained how the permits can be acquired.

Ostensibly you wish the trail and the campsites to be natural and clean. You can help in keeping them desirable by avoiding impact. That means no-trace camping—removing all litter, trash, and garbage; erasing evidence of campfire; never digging trenches; refraining from using overused campsites, and avoiding shortcutting switchbacks.

In planning your trip you may wish to include other outdoor sports. For whitewater sports and mountain climbing contact the Nantahala Outdoors Center, 133077 Highway 19W, Bryson City, NC 28713; 704-488-2175. For horseback-riding trails and camps contact Horse Commodity Coordinator, Extension Horse Husbandry, Dept of Animal Science, NCSU, Box 7523, Raleigh, NC 27695; 919-737-2761. Cross-country skiing information is available from the National Ski Patrol, Cataloochee Ski Area, Maggie Valley, NC 28751; 704-926-0285.

Concerning emergencies, the following numbers are in addition to a call to the local 911 operator: the N.C. Wildlife Resources Commission for boating accidents, missing persons, fishing and game laws, 800-662-7137; for toxic poisons, Carolina Medical Center, 800-848-6946; Blue ridge Parkway (BRP), for emergencies, 800-727-5928; or national forests, 704-257-4264 for fires and 911 for emergencies.

To assist you in your planning, I have listed in the appendix information on the state's AT clubs, the addresses of other clubs, some US and state government agencies, state citizens' groups, and some organizations whose primary interest is hiking.

Many hikers before you have described their hiking experiences as a time to "hear myself think," "get acquainted with my soul," "have a psychological holiday." Henry David Thoreau hiked "for absolute freedom and wildness." The American Hiking Society describes it as "brushing past a thousand life forms, beckoning,/ leading you onward to new sensations and discoveries around the bend./ In that moment when you are on a trail,/ your mind is free to roam,/ to observe, to daydream./ All extraneous concerns drop away…"

Now that you have this guidebook in hand and are preparing for the trails, I hope you will become active also in preserving the natural resources by joining an organization whose mission is to protect and maintain the trails. And, I hope that you enjoy hiking the trails as much as I have enjoyed hiking and describing them. Welcome to the trails of North Carolina.

Abbreviations

In an effort to save space in this book, abbreviations are used wherever possible. The majority are part of everyday usage.

AMC	Appalachian Mountain Club	NF	National Forest
AT	Appalachian National Scenic Trail	NP	National Park
		NPS	National Park Service
ATC	Appalachian Trail Conference	NW	northwest
ATV	all-terrain vehicle	ORV	off-road vehicle
B	bicycle trail	R	right
BRP	Blue Ridge Parkway	Rd	Road (used in proper names)
BT	Bartram Trail	rec	recreation/al
ca	circa	RR	railroad
CCC	Civilian Conservation Corps	RS	ranger station
CMC	Carolina Mountain Club	rte	route
DEHNR	Department of Environment, Health, and Natural Resources	S	south
		SC	South Carolina primary toad
E	east	sec	section
elev	elevation	SE	southeast
F	foot trail	SR	state secondary road
fac	facilities	sta	station
FR	forest road	svc	service/s
FS	forest service	SW	southwest
ft	foot/feet	tel	telephone
GSMNP	Great Smoky Mountains National Park	TIS	Transportation Information System
H	horse trail	topo	topographic map
I	interstate highway	TVA	Tennessee Valley Authority
jct	junction or intersection	US	federal highway
L	left	USFS	United States Forest Service
mi	mile/s	USGS	United States Geological Survey
mil	million	USGS-FS	United States Geological Survey-Forest Service
mp	milepost (usually on the BPR)		
MST	Mountains-to-Sea Trail	W	west
Mt	Mount (used in proper names)	W	wheelchair trail
Mtn	mtn/s Mountain, mountain/s	YACC	Young Adult Conservation Corps
N	north	YCC	Youth Conservation Corps
NC	state primary road	yd	yard/s
NE	northeast	4WD	four-wheel drive

PART I

Trails in the National Forests

*It is the policy of Congress that the national forests are established
and shall be administered for outdoor recreation, range, timber,
watershed, and wildlife purposes.*
—Multiple-Use Sustained Yield Act of 1960

There are four national forests in North Carolina with a total of 1,238,344 acres: Nantahala (526,061); Pisgah (504,181); Croatan (159,102); and Uwharrie (49,000). This is an increase of 20,987 acres since 1988. Land acquisition by the United States Forest Service (USFS) is determined by financial allocations and adjoining land availability. Current acquisitions are generally limited to exchanges of tracts more beneficial to the USFS. Among the few ongoing acquisition programs are the *Appalachian Trail* corridor and the Chattooga River watershed.

As one of the state's major natural resources, and as a recreational source for more than 20 million visitors annually, the forests continue to be of vital public interest. In 1987 about 65 million board feet (mmbf) of timber was harvested (from a proposed 73 mmbf); a proposal was made for 45 mmbf in 1993; and by 1994 an amendment to the Land and Resource Management Plan proposed an annual harvest of 34 mmbf. Clear-cutting would be reduced from about 4,500 acres in 1975 to about 240 acres annually by 1995 in the Nantahala and Pisgah forests. Public interest in additional recreational facilities has increased steadily in the past ten years. Within the forests are 76 developed recreational areas (such as campgrounds, picnic areas, and boat ramps), and 51 special-interest areas where timber is not cut or vehicular traffic allowed (such as Joyce Kilmer Memorial Forest, Looking Glass Rock, and Linville Gorge). The forests have 477 trails with a total of 1,653 miles. Add the desirable gated forest roads, and hikers have more than the distance of the *Appalachian Trail* (2,157.8 mi) on which to hike, roam, and explore. Of inestimable value in the forests are the 1,885 identified plant species and 645 species of vertebrates, including the fish species.

The state is the birthplace of professional forestry management, initiated in 1892 when George Vanderbilt employed Gifford Pinchot (1865-1946) to manage the Vanderbilt Forest at Biltmore near Asheville. Pinchot (born in

Simsbury, Connecticut) graduated from Yale University in 1889 and studied forestry at the Ecole Nationale Forestiere in France. His success at Biltmore Forest prompted Vanderbilt to purchase an additional 120,000 acres, a section of which later became a nucleus of Pisgah National Forest, established in 1916. In 1895 Carl Schenck, a renowned German forester, succeeded Pinchot, and Pinchot was made a member of the National Forest Commission to work out the plans of the US Forest Reserve Act authorized by Congress in 1891. Pinchot headed the Department of Agriculture's Forestry Division from 1898 to 1910 (under three US presidents) while holding a professorship of forestry at Yale University. During this period he was influential in the establishment of the US Forest Service in 1905. By 1908 he had become chairman of the National Conservation Commission. Although his stay in North Carolina was only a few years, his pioneering philosophy of forestry laid the foundation not only for Dr. Schenk's first forestry school in America, but also for the shaping of USFS policy since. "National Forests exist today because the people want them. To make them accomplish the most good the people themselves must make clear how they want them run," Pinchot said in 1907. This statement has proven true many times both in Congress (25 acts) and in the nation's 133 national forests.

Among the congressional acts that affect North Carolina's national forests are the Weeks Law (1911), which authorized the purchase of lands for timber production; the Multiple-Use Sustained Yield Act (1960), which reemphasized the basic purpose of forests to protect natural resources and to serve the public's varied recreational interests; the Wilderness Act (1964), which established a system of preserving areas from all timber cutting and mining and development; the National Trails System Act (1968), which established a protective system of national recreational and scenic trails (such as the *Appalachian Trail*); the National Environmental Policy Act (1970), which required all federal agencies to prepare reports on the environmental impact of all planned programs and actions in formal Environmental Impact Statements (EIS); the Forest and Rangeland Renewable Resources Planning Act (RPA) (1974), which required the USFS to prepare long-range programs of forest administration, roads and trails, research, and cooperative programs; and the National Forest Management Act (NFMA) (1976), which required full public participation in the development and revision of land management plans and periodic proposal of a Land and Resource Management Plan (hereafter referred to as the Plan) by the national forests. Each new congressional act and each new national forest chief alters the directional policies of the USFS. That is the way Pinchot predicted it. Silviculturists who once read the public mind to emphasize timbering, mining, hunting, and fishing now find a public demanding additional parking space and campgrounds, trails for mountain biking, and less timber cutting and road building. This trend is illustrated by statements in 1994 from the new USFS chief, biologist Jack Wood Thomas. He said, "I plan to implement ecosystem management, develop new knowledge, synthesize research, and apply it to management of natural resources." His policy would gradually phase out clear-cutting, balance multiple uses, and prioritize environmental protection of soil, water, plant, and wildlife.

These goals area also addressed by the current (1995) forest supervisor for North Carolina forests, Randle G. Phillips. Not only does he support the policies of Thomas, he has stated his position in *Highlights of the Land and Resource Management Plan, Amendment 5* for the 1994 Nantahala and Pisgah National Forests. "Our new Plan fosters old growth forests, habitat for neotropical birds and biodiversity; the provision of wood product supply that is sustainable and cost-effective over time; and focusing on maintaining the forests' natural beauty."

Land use planning itself is not a new exercise for the USFS. The agency has engaged in planning of national forest uses since its establishment in 1905. But the planning process has changed as the public's interest and expectations have changed. At present there are two levels of planning: the forestwide Land and Resource Management Plan, which is strategic in nature, and the project plans typically made at each ranger district prior to activities actually taking place in the forest. The forestwide plan is designed to make the following decisions: (1) establish forestwide multiple-use goals and objectives for all resources; (2) establish standards and guidelines for management activities; (3) establish management areas and management area objectives (somewhat similar to a county zoning ordinance); (4) designate lands suitable for timber production and establish an upper limit on the amount of harvest per decade; (5) make recommendations for wilderness; and (6) establish monitoring and evaluation requirements.

Now there is a focus on involving the public throughout the planning process. The public is involved in reviewing data, discussing issues and concerns, and reviewing draft plans. Members of the public may be included on field trips, invited to workshops and focus group meetings, or may participate by submitting written comments. For example, in 1994 the supervisor's office for the state's Nantahala and Pisgah National Forests plan received more than 2,500 letters that identified more than 8,000 distinct categories of concern. The major categories were forest timber-cutting policy, recreation and wetlands, ecosystem management, forest road construction, and general recommendations. Results of the plan become a dynamic document, subject to even further amendment and specifically revised within a 10- to 15-year cycle.

The second level of planning takes place at the ranger district prior to an actual management project taking place. This provides another opportunity for public involvement. Involvement at the project level is just as important as it is at the forestwide level. For example, the forest-wide plan may give general directions about building trails, but the decision to actually build a specific trail at a specific place, or to maintain it, is the responsibility of the district. Likewise, while the forestwide plan decides which areas will allow timber harvest, the district makes a project decision to actually build a particular logging road and the method of harvesting. Public involvement can affect these decisions.

To learn more about the current goals and objectives and management philosophy for the four national forests in North Carolina, you can request a copy of the latest forestwide plans from the USFS supervisor's office in Asheville (address at the end of this introduction). To keep informed about the projects the ranger districts are planning, you may request to be put on the mailing list for the "Schedule of Proposed Actions" that is sent out periodically to interested parties. (These addresses are listed at the end of each introduction in chapters 1 through 4.) The USFS guidelines on trail maintenance are described in appendix G of the forestwide plan.

Part of the forests' planning process is to evaluate the designated and potential wilderness areas. The USFS began an evaluation process for the Croatan and Uwharrie National Forests in 1995; the Nantahala and Pisgah plan begins in 1997.

There are 11 wilderness areas—six in the mountains, one in the Piedmont, and four in the coastal area—for a total of 103,276 acres. Trails in these areas are described in the next four chapters. Camping permits in the wilderness areas are not required except in the Linville Gorge Wilderness (see details in chapter 3, section 2). Legislation has been introduced in Congress for additional wilderness areas, but the bill has not made it past a Senate committee. For example, Lost Cove and Harper Creek areas in the Grandfather Ranger District were chosen for congressional approval more than 10 years ago.

Wilderness management takes its guidelines from the Wilderness Act of 1964, whose purpose is to preserve and protect natural environments, and to provide a wilderness experience for its users. As a result, a wilderness area is considerably different from other forest lands. Hikers need to be aware of the contrasts. Among the differences are that no timber is harvested in wilderness areas. Recreational usage is allowed but not promoted with blazes, signs (except at boundaries or trailheads), campsites, or shelters. Construction of reservoirs, electrical power projects, transmission lines or roads is prohibited. Any facility, however primitive, is there only to protect natural resources and user safety. All forest usage of wilderness is by nonmotorized means, and power tools are not used for maintenance (if any maintenance is done at all) of the trails. (Exceptions are allowed for the USFS to deal with health and safety issues, fire suppression, and insect or disease control.)

The USFS has prescribed a few set policies for hikers and other wilderness users. Basics include no trace camping, and the regular rules of "pack it in, pack it out" apply. You should be familiar with the brochure "Leave No Trace Land Ethics" offered free by the USFS and National Park Service. The maximum group size is usually ten (or may be restricted to six in some locations). Campsites should be at least 100 ft from springs and other water sources, and wood for the fires should be from dead or down trees. The feeding of wildlife, particularly bears, is prohibited. Other suggestions are for you to plan and prepare well in advance to meet nature on its terms. Be in good health, choose one or more companions, file a trip plan to leave with your family or with the ranger in case of emergency. Complete a checklist of backpacking gear, clothing, food, medication, flashlight, waterproof matches, first-aid kit, and other essentials. Carry a compass and topo maps (named at the end of each trail description in this book), and a wilderness map (if such exists from the ranger's office). Boil or treat all water for consumption. Use biodegradable soap. Know the symptoms of and how to treat hypothermia (see "Health and Safety" in the introduction of this book). Avoid holidays or popular weekends. Walk quietly to prevent disturbing the wildlife. The USFS advises against cross-country or bushwhacking trips unless you are experienced or have wilderness survival skills. Careful planning with consideration of the above guidelines should prevent you from becoming lost or injured, and save the cost of search and rescue teams.

Hunting and fishing are allowed in the national forests, including the wilderness areas, but are restricted in recreational areas and some special areas. Licenses are required by the N.C. Wildlife Resources Commission, which determines and sets seasons, bag limits, and other regulations for wildlife and fish management. The commission also regulates private game lands that have been leased for public use. Some wilderness properties may be near or adjoining the national forests.

The USFS supervisor's office in Asheville and each district ranger's office maintain a trail list under the heading of "Transportation Information System" (TIS). It lists each trail's name (not by alphabet but by ascending USFS trail numbers), road or trail termini, mileage to the nearest one-hundredth, USFS modified topographical maps, difficulty, surface type, primary management objective, national trail type, user opportunity, prohibitions, maintenance responsibility, maintenance level, traffic volume, and traffic classification. The classification uses (F) for foot trails, (B) for bicylce trails, (H) for horse trails, and (W) for wheelchair trails. Because this information is coded, a code identification list is necessary for usage of the TIS for trails.

A lack of funding and staff within the USFS results in primitive conditions on many of the trails. Volunteer citizens' groups are helping the USFS. An example is the Cherry Point and Carteret Wildlife Club: It builds boardwalks and maintains the *Neusiok Trail* (USFS #503) in the Croatan National Forest. There's also maintenance by adopt-a-trail projects in the Grandfather Ranger District of Pisgah National Forest on *Heartbreak Ridge Trail* (USFS #208) and *Star Gap Trail* (USFS #209) by Camp Woodson; and construction and maintenance on the *Mountains-to-Sea Trail* (USFS #440) by Carolina Mountain Club, Balsam-Highlands Task Force, and Central Blue Ridge Task Force in the Nantahala and Pisgah National Forests. Other volunteer groups also maintain the *Appalachian Trail* (USFS #1). (See chapters 5 and 16 and the appendix for organizational support groups.)

Hikers may notice a difference in trail length and signage between the USFS descriptions and descriptions in this book. An explanation may result from USFS relocations, partial closures, extensions, distance estimation, and measuring methods. The author's most recent measurements with a measuring wheel were in 1994–95.

Some hikers find the unmaintained trails appealing and challenging. If you are interested in such trails not described in this book, you may wish to contact the district ranger's office before traipsing on questionable routes. Take a USFS modified forest service map with you. The current maps of specific areas in wilderness are also helpful. Request a list of the maps available for purchase from either the district offices or the forests' headquarters in Asheville. Usually the cost for each map is between $3 and $5.

Information: Forest Supervisor, National Forests of North Carolina, Post Office Bldg, Post and Otis Sts, (PO Box 2750), Asheville, NC 28802; 704-257-4200. For general information call 919-662-4381; for game laws and management call 919-733-7291; for licenses call 919-662-4370; for violations of boating, fishing, or hunting laws call toll free 800-662-7137 (a 24-hour service every day of the year); and for hunting and fishing accidents or the disappearance of a person, call emergency 911 or the local police or sheriff's office. Address: North Carolina Wildlife Resources Commission, 512 N Salisbury St, Raleigh, NC 27611.

1. Croatan National Forest

The trail is like wild grapes
Sweet pure raw nature ....
—*Neusiok Trail* by Todd Shearon

The history of the Croatan National Forest, the most coastal of North Carolina's four national forests, and the most truly coastal E of the Mississippi River, began in 1933 when a purchase unit was established. In 1935, 77,000 acres were acquired. Today it encompasses 159,102 acres. The forest is almost totally surrounded by the Neuse, Trent, White Oak, and Newport Rivers. Bogue Sound and Bogue Banks separate its southern border from the Atlantic Ocean.

The name of Croatan comes from the Algonquin Indian word for "council town." Today, however, its coastal environment is used for year-round recreation. Within the forest are 95,000 acres of pocosin, which is a Native American word meaning "swamp on a hill." Actually, pocosin is a layer of organic topsoil that has resulted from a series of physiographic and biological changes occurring within the last 9,000 years. A wet upland bog with black organic muck, pocosin varies in depth from inches at the edge to several feet in the central area. It has high acidity, dense vegetation, and no drainage pattern in low sections. In 1984, 31,221 acres of pocosin were designated by Congress as wilderness areas that represent a unique estuarian ecosystem. The largest of these is Pocosin (11,709 acres), a tract between NC-24 and Great Lake area. Others are Sheep Ridge (9,297 acres), bordered on the SE by beautiful Great Lake and Long Lake; Pond Pine (1,685 acres), between the Pocosin and Sheep Ridge areas; and Catfish Lake South (8,530 acres), between Maysville on NC-58 and Catfish Lake.

Adjoining this priceless forest is the US Marine Corps Air Station at Cherry Point US Naval Reservation. As a result of this proximity, the Corps has proposed twice, in 1986 and 1994, to establish a combat training air base in wetlands surrounded by wilderness. Both proposals failed when objections were filed by conservationists with the help of the Southern Environmental Law Center.

Hunting (both big and small game), fishing (both salt- and freshwater), boating, swimming, water-skiing, camping, picnicking, and hiking are popular in the Croatan. Catfish Lake and Great Lake are within the USFS boundaries. They have yellow bullheads, fliers, and black crappie. Brice Creek has catfish, bluegill, redbreast sunfish, largemouth bass, black crappie, yellow perch, bowfin, and gars. White Oak River and Hadnot Creek have striped mullet, chain pickerel, flounder, and croaker in addition to species found in Brice Creek. Although lake fishing is usually poor because of high acidity, the saltwater fishing is popular at the lower end of the Neuse River and in the saltwater marshes. Other activities include oystering, crabbing, and flounder gigging.

More than 90 species of reptiles and amphibians have been discovered in the forest. Among them are the spotted turtle (*Clemmys guttata*); Mabee's salamander (*Ambystoma mabeei*); the more rare tiger salamander (*Ambystoma tigrinum*); and the longest snake in the forest, the eastern coachwhip (*Masticophis flagellum*). Poisonous reptiles are the cottonmouth, eastern diamondback rattlesnake, timber rattlesnake, Carolina pigmy rattlesnake (*Sistrurus miliarius*), and copperhead. The bays, swamps, marshes, and creeks provide a haven for migratory ducks and geese. Such birds as egrets, including the snowy egret; flycatchers; woodpeckers; woodcocks; hawks, including the marsh hawk; osprey; and owls are plentiful, too. Among the threatened or endangered species are the red-cockaded woodpecker (*Picoides borealis*), American alligator (*Alligator mississipiensis*), and the bald eagle (*Haliaeetus leucocephalis*).

Large stands of pines—pond, loblolly, and longleaf—are in the forest. Common hardwoods are oaks (including laurel [*Quercus laurifolia*], bluejack, and blackjack), yellow poplar, sweet and tupelo gums, swamp cypress (*Taxodium distichum*), American holly, and maple. Wildflowers—bright red pine lily (*Lilium catesbaei*), orchids, gaillaria, and nine species of insectivorous plants—are profuse. Shrubs include titi, fetterbush, gallberry, wax myrtle, and honeycup.

Recreational areas are Pinecliff (open April 1 through October 30), Brice Creek, Cahooque Creek, Fishers Landing, and Haywood Landing (open year-round). No fees are charged. Two campgrounds, Cedar Point and Neuse River, described below, have daily-fee camping.

The district has eight trails listed on its inventory (TIS), all of which are classified as hiking trails. But in recent years 1.0-mi *Hunter Creek Trail (USFS #505)*, near the S edge of Pond Pine Wilderness, is used for 4WD vehicles and is not maintained for hiking. Also on the list is *Old Bear Trail (USFS #150)*, a 0.5-mi dead-end off FR-121-D (S of Croatan). It was closed in 1986. *Morton Field Lake Trail (USFS #504)*, a 3.5-mi pocosin area between FR-3012 and FR-126 (W of Great Lake), is not maintained. A more recent trail casualty is unique *Sheep Ridge Trail (USFS #513)*, a 3.6-mi route through a pocosin of insectivorous plants (pitcher, round-leaved sundew, butterworts, and bladderworts). The entire trail was burned during the Fish Day Fire of the spring/summer of 1994. Access to this area is in a remote location at the SW edge of Sheep Ridge Wilderness. For walking along the forest roads by dredged canals, use the following directions. From US-70 in Croatan turn on Catfish Lake Rd (SR-1100) at the Croatan Presbyterian Church and drive straight to FR-152; turn L. The first 0.5 mi is accessible by passenger car, but the next 1.0 mi may require either 4WD vehicle or walking. At the end of FR-173 and jct with FR-3103 is an area for observing the pocosin wilderness. In the future the district plans new trails or trail extensions elsewhere in the forest.

ADDRESS AND ACCESS: Maps and additional information are available from the District Ranger, Croatan National Forest, 141 E Fisher Ave, New Bern, NC 28560; 919-638-5628. Access is 7.3 mi SE of New Bern on US-70, at the jct with E Fisher Ave, L.

SUPPORT FACILITIES: There are facilities for camping and other activities in the Croatan National Forest at the Neuse River Recreation Area (no hookups) and Cedar Point Campground (with electrical hookups). Access to the Neuse River Recreation Area from the ranger's office is 2.0 mi SE on US-70 and L on SR-1107 for camping and L on SR-1107 0.5 mi NW of the ranger's office on US-70 R on FR-141 to Fishers Landing. On the SW side of the NF is Cedar Point Campground near Swansboro. From the jct of NC-58/24, go N on NC-58 for 0.6 mi, and L onto SR-1114 to FR-153-A. A nearby commercial campground is Tommy's Campground on NC-24 E at 301 Cedar Point Blvd, 1.0 mi W of the jct of NC-58 and NC-24; 919-393-8715. Another camping area is Whispering Pines Campground: From the jct of US-70 and NC-24, go W 10.0 mi on NC-24 (near the community of Ocean); full svc, rec fac; open year-round; address is 25 Whispering Pines, Newport, NC 28570; 919-726-4902.

CEDAR POINT RECREATION AREA (Carteret County)

The Cedar Point Recreation Area has facilities for boating, camping (with hookups), drinking water, fishing, nature study trails, picnicking, flush toilets, and warm showers.

ACCESS: From the jct of NC-58/24 E of Swansboro, go 0.6 mi N on NC-58 to the entrance to Cedar Point, L on SR-1114. Go 0.5 mi to a L on graveled FR-153-A. Parking area is located 0.8 mi on the road near White Oak River.

Cedar Point Tideland Trail (USFS #502) (F)   1

LENGTH AND DIFFICULTY: 1.4 mi, easy

SPECIAL FEATURE: viewing blinds for shorebirds

TRAILHEAD AND DESCRIPTION: From the parking area follow the trail signs and cross the first of six boardwalks at 0.1 mi. This beautiful natural area is where seawater mixes with the freshwater of White Oak River in a tidal estuary. Here are dark bronze cordgrass, marsh elder *(Iva frutescens)*, and succulents such as leafless glasswort (*Salicornia europaea*). This species of glasswort has green stalks which turn red in late summer. Other plant species are star-shaped flowering sea purslane (*Sesuvium portulacastrum*), sea oxeye (*Borrichia frutescens*), and sweet bay magnolia. In this tranquil marsh visitors may see osprey, great blue heron, and snowy egret. Pass the first of two blinds for viewing birds and other wildlife at 0.4 mi. The second viewing blind is at 0.6 mi. Cross fire road, the last boardwalk at 1.1 mi, and return on a loop trail to the parking lot at 1.4 mi. The trail is well graded through pine and hardwoods and includes 0.3 mi of cypress boardwalks in a marshland estuary. The trail is a national recreation trail, initially listed as the *Chautauqua Trail*. (*USGS-FS Map:* Swansboro)

PINECLIFF RECREATION AREA (Craven County)

The Pinecliff Recreation Area is on the S side of the Neuse River (within sight of the ferry to Minnesott Beach). It has facilities for drinking water, fishing, picnicking, and sanitary stations. It is the N trailhead for the *Neusiok Trail* that extends 20.9 mi S to the Newport River in Carteret County. If hiking the trail when the Pinecliff entrance gate is closed, park and walk 0.2 mi to the picnic area. The district plans to create a loop off the *Neusiok Trail* from the Pinecliff Recreation Area S/SW for a day hike.

ACCESS: From the jct of US-70 and NC-101 in Havelock turn L on NC-101 and go 5.3 mi to the jct of NC-101 and NC-306. Turn L on NC-306,

Neuse River Ferry Rd, and go 3.3 mi to FR-132. Turn L on an unpaved road and go 1.7 mi to Pinecliff Recreation Area.

2 *Neusiok Trail (USFS #503) (F)*

LENGTH AND DIFFICULTY: 20.9 mi, moderate

SPECIAL FEATURES: Neuse River beach, estuaries, pocosins

TRAILHEAD AND DESCRIPTION: The *Neusiok Trail* was designated part of the *Mountains-to-Sea Trail* system in May 1990. The best sections for backpacking and primitive camping on the *Neusiok Trail* are between the Neuse River and NC-306, between NC-101 and Billfinger Rd, and S of the Alligator Tram Rd. Camping is impossible in the dense vegetation along Deep Creek Rd. Hiking is preferable in the winter months to avoid insects, heat, and snakes. Insect repellent is recommended. All water for drinking and cooking must be carried. Long trousers, high boots, watchful eyes, staying on the trail, and sleeping in tents are precautions against poisonous snakes. All trash must be packed out.

From the parking area at Pinecliff enter the picnic area, turn L to pass the sanitary facilities into the woods, and follow white blazes to a boardwalk at 0.3 mi. If the boardwalk is underwater, go R to the beach and continue upriver. Follow up the Neuse River beach among scenic swamp cypress groves and Spanish moss. Ahead can be seen the Cherry Point US Marine Corps Air Station. At 1.4 mi leave the beach, ascend the steps, and follow an erratic path through hardwoods and pine. Glimpses of Hancock Creek can be seen through the trees, R, at 2.0 mi. Pass L of a bog cove at 2.3 mi, cross a swamp at 2.7 mi on a boardwalk. (This and the next two boardwalks have been constructed by the Cherry Point and Carteret Wildlife Club.) Pass R of a USFS road at 2.9 mi. Cross a boardwalk through another swamp among palmetto (*Sabal minor*) at 3.1 mi. Make a sharp L at 3.6 mi to avoid a wide swamp, but cross a boardwalk over it and a tributary to Cahooque Creek at 4.4 mi. Turn R on an old field road bordered with loblolly pine at 4.5 mi and enter a swamp with a boardwalk at 5.3 mi. Follow the edge of a hardwood timber cut and cross two boardwalks at 5.6 mi and 5.7 mi. At 6.0 mi is a grove of large beech and holly. For the remainder of this section follow an old road through pines and reach a gated road at NC-306 at 6.6 mi. (NC-101 is 2.0 mi R; on NC-306 and FR-132, L, it is 2.7 mi for a return to the Pinecliff picnic area.) At the jct of the *Neusiok Trail* and NC-306 (E side) is a small parking area for hikers.

Cross the road and follow a footpath through dense undergrowth and tall pine. At 6.9 mi cross a boardwalk and follow an old field road bordered with loblolly and pond pine. At 8.2 mi turn sharply R onto an old forest road. Cross FR-136 (which goes 1.0 mi out to NC-101) and continue through the forest. At 8.6 mi begin an 0.8-mi section of tall oak and pine and patches of sensitive fern (*Onoclea sensibilis*). Reach NC-101 at 9.4 mi (R: 6.8 mi back to the Pinecliff picnic area on NC-101 and NC-306. L: 2.1 mi to North Harlowe store with groceries, gasoline, and telephone).

Cross NC-101 and enter a beautiful open forest of longleaf pine. Scattered undergrowth is yaupon, bracken, beard grass, blueberry, and Christmas fern. Cross a 300-ft boardwalk at 10.2 mi to a hardwood forest. A 150-ft boardwalk is at 10.7 mi. (Here is a jct where the trail continues L through a pine forest, a timber cut area, a section of dense undergrowth, and scattered insect-eating plants. The blazes are faint or nonexistent in sections. Exit at Billfinger Rd [FR-147] after 2.0 mi.) A better route from the boardwalk is straight for 0.1 mi to Billfinger Rd. Turn L and follow it for 1.4 mi to jct with the route mentioned above. Go 0.2 mi farther on Billfinger Rd to jct with Little Deep Creek Rd (FR-169) at 12.4 mi. (To the L on Little Deep Creek Rd it is 1.1 mi N to NC-101 at North Harlowe. Lilly Lodge #803 is at the W corner of the road jct; the grocery store is E.)

Turn R on Little Deep Creek Rd (FR-169) and hike S on the road (the *Neusiok Trail* route) for 1.9 mi to where the trail turns L off the road at 14.3 mi. From the road cross a short footbridge to enter a dense forest of loblolly pine, wax myrtle, bays, maple, titi, sweet gum, greenbrier, and yellow jessamine. Trail blazes are small metal tags nailed to trees. After 0.8 mi begin to follow L of a small canal; pass a damp area, a drain into Money Island Swamp, at 15.6 mi. After another 0.2 mi enter a more open area with small pines and switch cane. At 16.4 mi turn E to parallel Alligator Tram Rd (FR-124) for 0.5 mi to the road crossing at 16.9 mi. (The road is gated to the R [W] where it accesses the Weyerhaeuser Paper Company, and to the L [E] the road is 1.8 mi to SR-1155. North from there it is 1.3 mi to a jct with NC-101; S from there it is 2.3 mi to the community of Mill Creek and jct with SR-1154.)

After crossing Alligator Tram Rd, cross a short canal footbridge to enter a dense area of undergrowth for 0.6 mi. Enter into an open longleaf pine forest at 17.5. Follow an old road, used frequently by hunters, through sections of switch cane, pitcher plants, bracken, and other ferns. Cross two small drains of Mill Creek at 18.5 mi and 18.9 mi. Pass a trash dump, leave the old road, and descend slightly to cross Mill Creek Rd (SR-1154) (also called Newport Rd or Orange St) at 19.3 mi.

Look for the trail sign and white blazes, and follow through hardwoods and pines for 1.6 mi; reach the Newport River parking area and S terminus of the trail at 20.9 mi. It is 1.1 mi on FR-181 back to Mill Creek Rd (SR-1154) and 5.5 mi L (W) on Mill Creek Rd to Newport. It is 0.2 mi R (E) to the community of Mill Creek. From there it is 3.5 mi N to NC-101. (*USGS-FS Maps:* Cherry Point, Newport)

ISLAND CREEK AREA (Jones County)

ACCESS: In a separate N tract of the forest, this area can be reached from Pollocksville, jct of US-17 and Beauford Rd E to Island Creek Rd. Drive E on Island Creek Rd for 5.5 mi to the Island Creek parking area, L. If coming S on US-17/NC-55 into New Bern, after crossing the New River bridge, turn L on US-70 Bypass, cross the Trent River bridge, and turn R onto SR-1004 to follow it 8.0 mi. If coming E on US-70 (divided four-lane) into New Bern, cross the other Trent River bridge and take the first ramp R. Go under the bridge (N) to US-70 Bypass and turn L. Make an immediate L again onto SR-1004, and go back under the bridge (S). Follow SR-1004 for 8.0 mi.

3 *Island Creek Trail (USFS #509) (F)*

LENGTH AND DIFFICULTY: 0.6 mi, easy

SPECIAL FEATURES: climax forest, limestone base

TRAILHEAD AND DESCRIPTION: (Plans are to expand the designated trail up the entire length of Island Creek. This would add about 2.5 mi of trail to the existing loop.) From the parking area follow the sign into a picturesque and unusual natural history area in a virgin forest that has progressed through plant succession stages to a beech climax forest. On a base of limestone the flora and fauna are unique to eastern North Carolina. Large beds of Christmas fern form a ground cover with tall oaks, hickories, pines, and cucumber trees. The Trent Woods Garden Club of New Bern has assisted the USFS in developing the trail, and its 146 acres have been registered as a natural area by the N.C. Natural Heritage Program. (*USGS-FS Map:* Pollocksville)

2. Nantahala National Forest

I beheld with rapture and astonishment . . . a world of mountains piled upon mountains.
—William Bartram

The Nantahala National Forest, the state's largest (526,061 acres), is a vast area of mountain ranges, waterfalls, lakes, and rivers in the southwest corner of the state. In 1981 the Balsam–Bonas Defeat Land Purchase added 40,000 acres in Jackson County. Congress declared in Public Law 98–11 that the area would be designated the Roy Taylor Forest in recognition of congressman Taylor's affection and respect for the mountains, forests, and streams of western North Carolina and for his "sustained efforts to protect areas especially suited to outdoor recreation and the enjoyment of nature and to assure public access thereto." While serving 16 years as a Congressman, Taylor was a member of the Committee on Interior and Insular Affairs and chairman of the Subcommittee on National Parks and Recreation.

There are three wilderness areas in the Nantahala National Forest: Joyce Kilmer/Slickrock (13,132 acres) in the Cheoah District, Southern Nantahala (12,076 acres) in the Wayah District, and Ellicott Rock (3,930 acres) in the Highlands District. Within the Joyce Kilmer/Slickrock area is the Joyce Kilmer Memorial Forest, a 3,800-acre sanctuary of virgin timber and pristine wilderness splendor. No other forest in the state can compare to its large groves of tulip trees (yellow poplar).

Established in 1920, the Nantahala National Forest received its name from a Cherokee word meaning "land of the noonday sun," an appropriate description for the many narrow gorges that receive the sun's direct rays only at midday. In the 8-mi-long Nantahala Gorge, mostly in Swain County, the precipitous gorge walls tower 2,000 ft. Other deep chasms are Tuskasegee, Wolf Creek, Cullasaja, Chattooga, and scores of deep north-side coves.

Nantahala is also a land of hundreds of waterfalls. Whitewater Falls, south of Sapphire, is considered to be the highest cascading river (411 ft) in

Panthertown. Allen de Hart

eastern America. Cullasaja Falls, west of Highlands, is similar to Whitewater Falls, with cascades thundering 250 ft into the gorge. Other spectacular falls are Dry Falls, Bridal Veil Falls, and Glen Falls near Highlands, Rainbow Falls south of Sapphire, and Toxaway Falls near Sapphire. Ten major rivers flow through the forest. The turbulent Chattooga is a National Wild and Scenic River, with headwaters in the Highlands Ranger District, and a 4.5-mi section of the Horsepasture River near Sapphire has also been made a part of the National Wild and Scenic Rivers system.

The Nantahala region is also a land of precious stones—ruby, sapphire, garnet, and amethyst. Wildlife roams its forest—deer, wild hog, fox, bear, mink, and raccoon. It is home for at least 38 species of birds, including grouse, turkey, hawks, and owls. First investigated by William Bartram in 1776, its plant life is a botanist's dream. All the hardwoods and conifers common to the southern Appalachians are found here. Rare and endangered species of flowering plants are hidden in countless vales and rock crevices or can be found blooming on fertile slopes.

Previous to the coming of Europeans, the forests of the Nantahala were the home of the Cherokee Indian Nation, whose domain was mainly from western Virginia to Alabama. Their famous Chief Junaluska was born and lies buried in the Nantahala. During different periods the Cherokee were both enemy and ally of the early settlers. For example, the Cherokees fought side by side with the troops of Gen Andrew Jackson against the Creek Indians at the Battle of Horseshoe Bend in 1814. Chief Junaluska later said, "If I had known that Jackson [US president, 1829–37] would drive us from our homes, I would have killed him that day at the Horseshoe." When the Supreme Court upheld the rights of the Indians after Georgia attempted to evict them, President Jackson is reported to have remarked, "John Marshall has made his decision; now let him enforce it." In 1838 President Jackson's successor, President Martin Van Buren, ordered Gen Winfield Scott to enforce the provision of a fraudulent 1836 government treaty the Cherokees signed for a move west of the Mississippi (now Oklahoma). The removal in the winter of 1838–39 of approximately 17,000 Cherokees was a shameful "Trail of Tears," and 25 percent died during the march. The Reverend Evan Jones of South Carolina described the exodus as "multitudes...allowed no time to take anything with them...their houses were left prey to plunder."

It is estimated that 1,000 Cherokees fled to the mountains, mainly in the area of Swain, Jackson, and Haywood Counties. One of those who fled was Tsali, who accidentally killed a soldier on the march. General Scott promised that all the other Indians in the mountains would be permitted to remain if Tsali and two family escapees would surrender and be executed for the soldier's death. The military kept its promise and the Cherokee descendants today are part of the Qualla Reservation, the largest Indian reservation east of the Mississippi. (See *Tsali Trail* in this chapter, the Great Smoky Mtns National Park in chapter 7, and the Cherokee Arboretum and *Lake Junaluska Trail* in chapter 14.)

The history of the Cherokee is vividly portrayed in the summer outdoor drama "Unto These Hills" in the Mountainside Theatre in Cherokee, late June to late August. For information contact Cherokee Tribal Travel and Promotion, PO Box 465, Cherokee, NC 28719; 704-497-9195.

The four districts of the Nantahala National Forest are:

Cheoah Ranger District, USFS, Rte 1, Box 16-A, Robbinsville, NC 28711; 704-479-6431. (From Robbinsville go 1.0 mi W on US-129; turn L on SR-1116.)

Highlands Ranger District, USFS, 2010 Flat Mtn Rd, Highlands, NC 28741; 704-526-3765. (From Highlands go 2.0 mi E on US-64 and turn L on Flat Mtn Rd for 2.0 mi.)

Tusquitee Ranger District, USFS, 201 Woodland Dr, Murphy, NC 28906; 704-837-5152. (Across the Hiwassee River at the first traffic light L from jct of US-19/219 and US-64.)

Wayah Ranger District, USFS, 8 Sloan Rd, Franklin, NC 28734; 704-524-6441. (Turn at first R off US-64 W from US-64 and US-441/23 S jct.)

Because the old and new *Bartram Trail* traverses all four districts, it is described first.

4 *Bartram Trail (71.1 mi; USFS #67) (F)*
(Sections 1 and 2 are in Macon County; section 3 is in Swain County; and section 4 is in Graham and Cherokee Counties.)
    CONNECTING TRAILS:
        (Hurrah Ridge Trail) (USFS #004)
        (West Fork Trail) (USFS #444)
        (Scaly Mountain Trail) (USFS #67A)
        (Trimont Trail) (No USFS #)
        (Appalachian Trail) (USFS #001)
        (Jones Knob Trail) (USFS #67B)
        (Whiterock Mountain Trail) (USFS #67C)
        (Piercy Creek Trail) (No USFS #)
        (Laurel Creek Trail) (USFS # 19F)

The *Bartram Trail* is named in honor of William Bartram (1739–1823), the first American-born naturalist to receive international fame for his botanical research. Born in Philadelphia, Bartram's expeditions in the southeastern states traversed at least 28 counties in North Carolina, 3 of which are Macon, Cherokee, and Graham. The exact route of his expedition is not known, but the North Carolina Bartram Trail Society and the Nantahala National Forest staff have jointly planned the trail to run as close to the original area he explored as is feasible in the Nantahala forest. Crossed in places by private property, the trail is continuous when using gravel and paved roads. Generally running E to W, it provides some remote areas where may be seen bear, deer, turkey, grouse, and numerous songbirds such as tanagers, towhees, and the Carolina junco.

From Oconee State Park in South Carolina the yellow-blazed *Bartram Trail* traverses NW over Long Mtn, turning SW as it crosses the Chattooga River into Georgia's Chattahoochee National Forest near Earl's Ford for a 37.4-mi route to North Carolina. At Warwoman Dell near Clayton, Georgia, it goes N to Rabun Bald (4,696 ft). From there it is 4.2 mi to FR-7, near the North Carolina state line and the southern entrance into the Nantahala National Forest. It is at this point that the description of the trail begins. Some suggested campsites and water sources are described along the trail, and support systems are listed at the end of each section. The North Carolina Bartram Trail Society has divided the trail route into seven sections, each with a detailed map and trail description. Map #1 includes a trailhead at Beegum Gap, near Rabun Bald, in Georgia. Former map #7 is now called the *Bartram Trail Western Extension* and a new #7 map will be designed for a section from Beechertown to the NW terminus at the *Appalachian Trail*, near Cheoah Bald. (For descriptive purposes in this book, the distance has been divided into four sections, with a description from the SW to NW.) In addition to the hiking trail, the society has included a 11.0-mi canoe trail in its trail system from Otto downriver to Franklin on the Little Tennessee River. For information about the trail maps, relocations, canoe trail, and available vehicle shuttle service, contact the society at Rte 3, Box 406, Sylva, NC 28779; 704-293-9661, or PO Box 1214, Cullowhee, NC 28723; 704-293-3999. The society publishes a newsletter, has a membership, and holds regular and special meetings to which the public is invited. The Bartram Trail Conference is located at 3815 Interstate Court, Suite 202A, Montgomery, AL 36109; 205-277-7050. For information on the *Bartram Trail* in South Carolina see *Hiking South Carolina Trails* by Allen de Hart, Globe Pequot Press, PO Box 833, Old Saybrook, CT 06475.

1: Chattahoochee National Forest to Wallace Branch

LENGTH AND DIFFICULTY: 31.2 mi, moderate to strenuous (elev change 3,023 ft)

SPECIAL FEATURES: vistas from Scaly Mtn, Jones Knob, Whiterock Mtn, Fishhawk Mtn, and Little Tennessee River Valley

TRAILHEAD AND DESCRIPTION: This section is in the Highlands District of the Nantahala National Forest. From the jct of NC-106 and US-64/NC-28 in Highlands, go S on NC-106 for 6.8 mi to Scaly Mtn jct with Hale Ridge Rd (SR-1625) and turn L. Proceed for 2.6 mi and turn L on Chattahoochee FR-

7. After 1.1 mi park near the trailhead sign.

Ascend N through hardwoods, buckberry, and rosebay rhododendron on a well-graded trail built by the YCC and blazed yellow. Cross log bridges at 0.1 mi and 0.6 mi, and skirt a timbered area. Skirt E of Osage Mtn at 0.9 mi and cross a ridge at 1.1 mi. Ascend and descend on the graded trail between coves and streams that are tributaries of Overflow Creek, crossing footbridges at 1.5 mi, 1.7 mi, 2.1 mi, and 2.4 mi. (At 2.5 mi pass jct with *Hurrah Ridge Trail*, R. It goes for 0.6 mi, leading to Blue Valley Rd, FR-79.) Continue under a heavy canopy of rosebay rhododendron, large oaks, and white pines. (At 2.9 mi pass jct of *West Fork Trail*, R; it travels for 1.0 mi, leading to Blue Valley Rd, FR-79.) Begin ascent to NC-106 at 3.1 mi, and reach the scenic landscape of Osage Mtn, Blue Valley, and Little Scaly Mtn from Osage Mtn Overlook at 3.6 mi. Cross the highway, climb steeply at a power line and through open woods of oak and locust damaged by fire. At 4.0 mi, 35 yd L, is a small waterfall, a natural shower. Rock-hop a cascading stream above the falls, pass through rhododendron thickets, ascend steeply, and turn sharply R onto a fire road at 4.4 mi. Continue the ascent for scenic views of Georgia, Osage Mtn, Blue Valley, and Little Scaly Mtn. At 5.0 mi jct with the *Scaly Mountain Trail* (USFS #67A), L, a spur trail that ascends 0.5 mi to scenic Scaly Mtn (4,804 ft). (The North Carolina Bartram Trail Society is planning a trail relocation from Scaly Mtn N to Hickory Gap to avoid Hickory Gap Rd [SR-1621] and private land.) Follow the old fire and timber road around the mtn into a timber clear-cut and a garden of flame azalea, rhododendron, laurel, and wildflowers that reaches a peak of color the second week in June. At a road jct, keep L (R is to a TV relay station). At 6.2 mi jct with Hickory Gap Rd (SR-1621); turn L. (It is 1.1 mi, R, on Hickory Gap Rd to Broadway Gap and Turtle Pond Rd [SR-1620] for a jct with NC-106. On NC-106 L it is 2.4 mi to Glen Falls and the town of Highlands.)

Hike the Hickory Gap Rd for 2.5 mi, past an open area named Lickskillet, and reach Hickory Gap at 8.7 mi. The road is rough and passes through private properties. From Hickory Gap descend L on the road to the NF boundary and then climb steeply to a ridge top and rock outcrop for E views of the Turtle Creek area and, on clear days, views of Whiteside Mtn, Shortoff Mtn, and Balsam Mtn. Reach a clear-cut area of Jones Gap at 9.7 mi; here are panoramic views of Balsam Mtn (E), Plott Balsams (NE), Smoky Mtns (N), and Blue Ridge Mtns (S), particularly on clear days. Continue on a seeded trail, pass outcroppings, and take the E slope of Jones Knob (4, 622 ft) where a blue-blazed spur, *Jones Knob Trail* (USFS #67B), L, leads to the top for 0.3 mi. Arrive at Whiterock Gap at 10.5 mi. Here are good campsites and a spring is nearby, E. Skirt E of Whiterock Mtn, but a blue-blazed spur, *Whiterock Mountain Trail* (USFS #67C), L, ascends 0.3 mi to the top for outstanding vistas of Tessentee Valley in the S and Nantahala range of mountains in the W. Cliffsides, three species of rhododendron, laurel, orchids, and other wildflowers, and a combination of conifers and hardwoods make this area incredibly scenic. Proceed to the ridge and summit of Little Fishhawk Mtn. A short and steep blue-blazed spur trail to the R ascends to the top of Fishhawk Mtn (4,748 ft) at 11.7 mi. (At the summit is a commemorative plaque for William Bartram by the North Carolina Bartram Trail Society.) Continue to Wolf Rock at 13.6 mi, and begin a descent on a ridge, W, with switchbacks, to an old orchard at Doubletop Fields at 15.2 mi. Between here and Cedar Cliff, in a saddle, is a trail jct. The current *Bartram Trail* route turns L (S) on switchbacks to the headwaters of Buckeye Creek and to Buckeye Creek Rd (SR-1640) at 18.2 mi. (At the saddle the Bartram Trail Society plans to reroute the trail to the NW side of Cedar Cliff and descend to the Pinnacle and to Gray Gap before descending to a new trailhead at Hickory Knob Rd (SR-1643).

From here to the Wayah Ranger District office in Franklin it is 12.2 mi on paved secondary roads through the beautiful Little Tennessee River Valley. Follow SR-1640 for 0.6 mi to a jct with the Tessentee Rd (SR-1636). After 2.2 mi is a jct with Hickory Knob Rd (SR-1643) where the trail turns R (N). At Hickory Knob Church turn L on Clark's Chapel Rd (SR-1646) at 22.6 mi. At 24.6 mi cross a bridge over the Little Tennessee River to Teague Rd (SR-1651) and to Wide Horizon Rd (SR-1652). After a parallel with the river, turn NW and at 27.9 mi cross US-441 to SR-1152 and SR-1154 before arriving at the Westgate Plaza shopping center at 29.0 mi. Continue by crossing under US-64 for a turn L (W) on SR-1463. After 0.2 mi turn R (N) on Sloan Rd (SR-1153) and walk another 0.2 mi to the Wayah Ranger District headquarters, R, at 29.4 mi. The trail continues 0.1 mi to cross Old Murphy Rd (SR-1442) (also called Old US-64). Follow Pressley Rd (SR-1315) and a narrow unpaved road for 1.7 mi to a parking area at Wallace Branch. (*USGS-FS Maps:* Scaly Mtn, Rabun Bald, Prentiss, Franklin)

SUPPORT FACILITIES: Highlands: groceries, svc sta, tel, restaurants, sport supplies; Town House (hotel), Main St, open June–October; 704-526-2790. Franklin: shopping centers and supply stores; Franklin Hotel, 223 W Palmer St, 1 block W on US-23/64/441/NC-28, open May–October; 704-524-4431. The Pines Campground, 6.0 mi W on US-64 from jct of US-441/64 in Franklin, full svc, including laundry; open year-round, 590 Hayesville Hwy, Franklin, NC 28734; 704-524-4490.

2: *Wallace Branch to Beechertown*

LENGTH AND DIFFICULTY: 34.0 mi, moderate to strenuous (elev change 2,333 ft)

SPECIAL FEATURES: Wayah Bald, Nantahala Lake, surge chamber area

TRAILHEAD AND DESCRIPTION: This section with yellow blazes is in the Wayah District of the Nantahala National Forest and is a national recreation trail for the first 17.6 mi (dedicated May 18, 1985). To approach the trailhead from the Franklin Bypass (US-64), go S of Franklin to the jct of US-441/23 and US-64. Proceed W on US-64 to the Wayah Ranger District sign at 1.0 mi, and turn R on Sloan Rd (SR-1153). Go 0.3 mi (Wayah Ranger District Office, R) to jct with Old US-64 and Pressley Rd (SR-1315). Cross Old US-64 (also called Old Murphy Rd, SR-1442) and continue 1.7 mi on Pressley Rd to its end and park at the Wallace Branch parking area.

Cross the stream on a footbridge and hike through a young forest with scattered mature poplars and oaks. Cross a cascading stream R at 0.1 mi and cascades L on Wallace Branch at 0.3 mi. Enter a white pine stand at 0.4 mi and cross an old road at 0.5 mi. (The former *Bartram Trail* turned R and followed through a white pine forest, a good campsite area, for 0.7 mi to the Trimont Ridge.) Cross a small stream and ascend on the NE side of the ridge. Reach the ridge crest at 0.8 mi, and continue on the slope to jct with the old *Trimont-Bartram Trail* at 1.3 mi. Turn L and follow the ridge W. (To the R it is 0.4 mi to the jct of the former *Bartram Trail,* R, and the old *Trimont Trail,* which leads to private land and a residential area in Franklin to the E at 4.1 mi. Motorcyclists, bikers, and horseback riders use the trail in this area. At 1.6 mi pass S of Bruce Knob, turn sharply R, and reach a gap at 1.8 mi. Begin a long ascent, steep in spots, along the ridge spine. Reach the crest at 2.3 mi, then descend to Locust Tree Gap at 2.5 mi. Traverse a large black cohosh (*Cimicifuga racemosa*) garden. Ascend and skirt S of Wilkes Knob (3,800 ft) at 3.2 mi. Descend and ascend over knobs for 2.1 mi, and reach a gravel road at 5.3 mi. Continue on the ridge, skirt the N side of the knob, and descend and ascend over knobs for another 2.2 mi; reach a grazing road at 7.5 mi. Follow the grazing road for 0.1 mi, then turn L and leave the old road at 7.7 mi; ascend at a sharp R. Along the ascent are trillium, doll's eyes (*Actaea pachypoda*), maidenhair fern (*Adiantum pedatum*), wild orchids, and bee balm (*Monarda didyma*). Hardwoods include hickory, locust, and oak. At 8.0 mi skirt the S side of a knob in a horseshoe shape and ascend from a plateau at 8.6 mi. A deep and dangerous rock fissure is near the L of the trail at 9.2 mi, near a sharp R. Reach an old lodge and a grassy field at 9.6 mi. Follow an old road to jct with the *AT* at 10.0 mi. (At this point a 57.0-mi loop can be made by using the *AT* and the *Bartram Trail* to their other jct at Cheoah Bald. See section 3 below.) Turn L, follow the *AT* through chestnut oak, laurel, and azalea to Wayah Bald observation tower (5, 342 ft) at 10.2 mi. Views are outstanding, particularly E. (Wayah is a Native American word for "wolf.") It is 4.3 mi on the gravel road to Wayah Gap and paved SR-1310.

Follow the yellow and white blazes into the forest, R, and descend through yellow birch, conifers, and rhododendron, with Canadian violets and other wildflowers. At 11.9 mi pass the old jct of the *AT* and *Bartram Trail*. A campsite area and spring are on the R at 12.0 mi. Turn R off the *AT* at 12.1 mi onto McDonald Ridge W of Wine Spring Bald. Enter an open grazing field of orchard grass and clover at 12.4 mi. Blazes are infrequent. Follow a seeded road through two more grazing fields for 1.7 mi, and then reach Sawmill Gap and FR-711 at 14.1 mi. Turn L from the gate, go 30 yd, turn R on a seeded road, and ascend. At 14.6 mi turn L on a bank and follow to the crest of a rocky ridge. Follow the ridge up and down from cols for 1.8 mi. There are partial views of Nantahala Lake. Descend; at 17.6 mi, near a small stream, R, reach paved SR-1310 at the lakeside (L it is 7.1 mi to Wayah Gap and the *AT*).

Turn R on SR-1310; arrive at the Lake Side Camp Store at 18.2 mi. (The store has groceries, sports supplies, snack shop, gasoline, telephone; open year-round.) Turn L, immediately past the store. Descend on a gravel driveway and cross Lee Branch into a young poplar forest. Reach an old woods road, fork R, and enter a white pine grove at 18.7 mi. Leave the old road at 19.3 mi onto a foot trail among loosestrife (*Lysimachia lanceolata*) and white snakeroot (*Eupatorium rugosum*). Cross a ridge, return to old road, and enter a stand of white pine at 19.5 mi. Leave old road on a footpath that curves around the ridge on a level contour; lake views, L, are through the trees. At 20.3 mi turn sharply L by tall poplar and descend on an old woods road. Pass through a rhododendron grove and through a patch of colicroot (*Aletris farinosa*). Pass a view of the Nantahala Lake Dam at 20.7 mi and enter another old road for a view of a deep chasm, L. Bear L at a road fork, pass an abandoned dump truck, descend on three switchbacks, pass under a power line, and arrive at a gravel road at 21.2 mi (road R goes 0.9 mi to SR-1401). Ahead, follow an old road across the Nantahala River (low flow here), and turn R at a locked cable gate. Follow the private road downstream, pass cascading stream in Lambert Cove at 21.4 mi and a spring, L, at 22.4 mi. Pass under a large penstock from Whiteoak Dam at 23.3 mi, cross a wood bridge over Dicks Creek to SR-1401, and cross the road to the entrance of Apple Tree Group Camp at 23.4 mi. (To reach Beechertown by vehicle from this point, drive E on SR-1401 across the bridge and immediately turn L on FR-308. Go 3.2 mi to jct with SR-1310; turn L and arrive at US-19 after another 4.1 mi.)

Continuing on the *Bartram Trail*, cross the rail fence near the Apple Tree Group Camp sign and go 0.2 mi to the old Piercy Creek Rd. Turn R, follow downstream, pass campsites C and D. (Sections of the *Bartram Trail* now follow the *Nantahala Trail* blazed in blue.) At 25.3 mi cross Walnut Creek and Poplar Creek at 25.7 mi. (R it is 0.2 mi to the Nantahala River and FR-308). Ascend on a S slope, cross a ridge, and follow a N slope around Turkey Pen Cove at 27.0 mi. At 27.9 mi turn R, downstream, and reach the confluence with Piercy Creek at 28.1 mi. Cross the stream and jct with the blue-blazed **9** *Piercy Creek Trail*. (It descends 1.5 mi along the stream to the creek's confluence with the Nantahala River. Rock-hopping or wading is necessary, but after a heavy rain the passage may be difficult or impossible. The best place to cross may be upriver for about 250 ft. After crossing to paved SR-1310, it is 1.7 mi L (N) to the Nantahala River launch site in Beechertown.) Continue L on the *Bartram Trail* and follow an old road through a white pine forest and good campsites. Reach jct, L, with the blue-blazed *Laurel Creek Trail* at 28.4 mi. (*Laurel Creek Trail* goes 1.5 mi to jct with the blue-blazed *Apple Tree Trail* where a L turn provides a return to Apple Tree Group Camp after another 1.1 mi. See section 4 of this chapter.) Continue upstream in a white pine forest on a pleasant old road with switchbacks. At 28.8 mi cross a small stream where trail is arbored with rhododendron. At 29.4 mi turn sharply R on a footpath. (Ahead the *Nantahala Trail* continues 0.5 mi to Sutherland Gap and jct with the blue-blazed *London Bald Trail,* another loop option for a return to Apple Tree Group Camp.) On the footpath follow along the slope and curve around spur ridges. Pass a spring at 29.8 mi, ascend, and curve around another spur ridge E of Rattlesnake Knob (4,052 ft) at 30.2 mi. Slopes have hot-tempered yellow jackets and plenty of rattlesnake orchids. Other wildflowers on the banks of rich soil are meadow rue (*Thalictrum clavatum*), galax (*Galax aphlla*), flowering raspberry (*Rubus odoratus*), blue-bead (*Clintonia borealis*), sweet cicely (*Osmorhoza claytonii*), and Indian pipe (*Monotropa uniflora*). Some of the trees are oak, birch, white pine, rhododendron, basswood, and butternut (*Juglans cinerea*). Shrubs include bladdernut (*Staghylea trifolia*), rhododendron, and laurel. At 30.8 mi follow an old woods road for 0.3 mi. At 31.4 mi reach the crest of the ridge and the boundary of the Nantahala Power and Light Company (NPLC). Spectacular views are to the Snowbird Mtns and the Nantahala Gorge and N toward Cheoah Bald. Descend on 10 switchbacks to the NPLC surge chamber at 31.8 mi. Descend on the well-graded NPLC access road for 1.6 mi to a L turn down an embankment. Keep L on a gravel road and pass a house. Arrive at paved Nantahala River Rd (SR-1310) at the USFS Nantahala River launch site in Beechertown, and jct with US-19 at 34.0 mi. Here is drinking water, comfort station, and a good location for vehicle shuttle, but camping is not allowed. Support facilities are described below. (*USGS-FS Maps:* Franklin, Wayah Bald, Topton, Hewitt)

SUPPORT FACILITIES: On US-19 L (SW) it is 1.5 mi to Brookside Campground with full svc (including hot showers, laundry, and grocery store), rec fac, open all year, fully operational May 1 through October 1. Address: Box 93, Topton, NC 28781; 704-321-5209. On US-19 R (NE) it is 8.5 mi to Wesser and the Nantahala Outdoor Center for hiking and outdoor sports supplies, restaurant, groceries, motel. Address: US-19 W, Box 41, Bryson City, NC 28713; 704-488-2175.

3: Beechertown to Cheoah Bald

LENGTH AND DIFFICULTY: 5.9 mi, strenuous (elev change 3,043 ft)

SPECIAL FEATURES: Ledbetter Creek Gorge, Cheoah Bald

TRAILHEAD AND DESCRIPTION: This section is in the Cheoah Ranger District of the Nantahala National Forest. In 1995 this new section had not been completed. Therefore, at the time of publication for this third edition, the following description is based on parts of the trail constructed or flagged. The route adds a new dimension to the natural beauty of the *Bartram Trail* because of the wilderness character of the Ledbetter Creek Gorge.

From the Nantahala River launch site and parking area at the jct of Ball Rd (SR-1310) and US-19/74, follow US-19/74 R (N) on the shoulder. In the beginning is a state highway marker indicating that near this area William Bartram met Cherokee chief Atakullakulla in May 1776. After 0.9 mi on the highway, cross to ascend an embankment at Ledbetter Creek. Cross the railroad near the cascading creek and begin 1.4 mi of switchbacks to rejoin the creek and an old RR grade logging route. Cross the main stream and tributaries among rhododendron, conifers, and southern hardwoods for 1.0 mi before ascending a steep slope to the E. Begin switchbacks and reach the headwaters of Ledbetter Creek at 4.9 mi. Turn W and ascend out of the gorge to Bellcollar Gap. Ahead is a jct with the *AT* at 5.6 mi. To the R it is 0.3 mi for an ascent to Cheoah Bald (5,062 ft), a scenic lookout and the W terminus of the *Bartram Trail*. (From here it is 7.0 mi E on the *AT* to Wesser and US-19/74. To the W on the AT it is 4.3 mi to Stecoah Gap and NC-143.) (*USGS-FS Map:* Hewitt)

SUPPORT FACILITIES: (See Wesser in preceding section.)

4: Beechertown to Tatham Gap (Western Extension)

LENGTH AND DIFFICULTY: 11.5 mi, moderate to strenuous (elev change 2,116 ft)

SPECIAL FEATURES: Johanna Bald, remoteness

TRAILHEAD AND DESCRIPTION: This section is in the Cheoah District of the Nantahala National Forest. The following description is a former route of the *Bartram Trail,* now referred to as a western extension. It is not maintained by North Carolina Bartram Trail Society and may not have maintenance from the Cheoah Ranger District either. (If its name is changed, it may be called the *Johanna Bald Trail.*) Meanwhile, consult the district ranger's office about the trail's condition. It officially begins at Tulula Gap on US-129. A vehicle approach from Beechertown is to take US-19 S for 2.5 mi to Topton and turn R on US-129 for 2.1 mi to the trailhead, L, across the road jct with Campbell Rd (SR-1200). However, a bushwhacking foot route is described below that involves private property. Hikers are advised to respect the private-property signs. Cross US-19 between two power lines, visible from the Nantahala River launch site. At 0.1 mi cross the Southern RR and ascend steeply (more than 500 ft elev gain in 0.3 mi) in a hollow. Reach an abandoned Graham County RR and platform at 0.4 mi with outstanding views of the Nantahala Gorge. Reach a gravel road that leads to paved Campbell Rd (SR-1200); turn L and reach US-129 at 0.6 mi. Parking space is severely limited on US-129 in a dangerous curve. (It is 11.0 mi W on US-129 and 1.1 mi on SR-1116 to the Cheoah Ranger District headquarters.)

Begin at the trailhead (S side of US-129). Ascend gradually and at 0.3 mi enter a burned open slope with new growth, berries, and wildflowers. Cross a footbridge at 0.4 mi, reenter the young forest, and reach Snowbird Mtn on the ridge crest at 0.7 mi. Curve around a knoll at 1.3 mi, and return to the ridge at 1.6 mi. At 2.0 mi follow the Graham-Cherokee county line. (For the next 5.0 mi there are long sections of the trail where timber cutting has destroyed the trail, and trees with blazes are missing. Where in doubt, stay on the major ridgeline. There are not any good campsites on the ridge.) Reach Jutts Gap (3,700 ft) at 5.1 mi, ascend on switchbacks S of a knob, and skirt the S side of Little Bald (4,300 ft) at 6.3 mi. At 8.5 mi reach Teyahalee Bald (Johanna Bald) Lookout Tower (4,716 ft), with TV and radio transmitting stations. From Johanna Bald hike on FR-423B, rough and rocky in places, as it winds down the mtn for 3.0 mi to Tatham Gap (3,645 ft) at 11.5 mi. To the L is Andrews and to the R is Robbinsville. Descending to Robbinsville it is 3.3 mi on gravel FR-423 before Long Creek Rd (SR-1110). It is another 2.5 mi to the jct of Kilmer Rd (SR-1127) near the large lumber company in Robbinsville. A turn R through the town on SR-1127 is an additional 1.5 mi to US-129. Some of the vegetation in this section includes oak, birch, red maple, hemlock, wild cherry, sourwood, dogwood, azalea, rhododendron, chestnut sprouts, pine, hickory, striped maple, locust, and a wide variety of wildflowers. (*USGS-FS Maps:* Hewitt, Robbinsville, Andrews)

SUPPORT FACILITIES: In Robbinsville there are shopping centers, restaurants, supply and service stores, PO, motel, and medical personnel.

From Tatham Gap to Porterfield Gap, a distance of 10.5 mi, is the remaining unmaintained western extension of the former *Bartram Trail* route. The Bartram Trail Society's original plans were to route the trail across the Snowbird Mtns to connect with trails in the Cherokee National Forest in Tennessee. Among the reasons for the society's abandonment of the western extension are that the trail passed over private property outside the Tusquitee and Cheoah Ranger Districts, lack of membership in the area to construct and maintain the trail, and that Bartram probably never explored farther than Sweetgum in the Tulula Creek Valley E of Robbinsville. Because some hikers may wish to follow the old route across a wild, rugged, and isolated area, the following description is provided. The trail is strenuous not because of high elev gains on the ridgeline, but because of obscure routing, summer growth, and difficult routes up the Snowbird Mtns to Porterfield Gap. Access is across the road from the end of section 4 in Tatham Gap, described above. The trail crosses a number of significant points of flat areas and near high peaks along the main ridge. Forest trees are chiefly hardwoods of oak, birch, beech, and maple. Wildflowers are prominent; deer and grouse are the major wildlife. At 3.0 mi reach Walker Field (4,015 ft). Skirt S of Old Billy Top (4,120 ft) at 4.6 mi and reach Cozad Gap (3,360 ft) at 7.0 mi. At 10.1 mi ascend to skirt S of Rocky Spring Top (3,791 ft) and descend on a rough treadway to Porterfield Gap (3,462 ft) at 10.5 mi. For hikers who do not wish to backtrack to Tatham Gap, the two exits from Porterfield Gap are described below.

The N exit, down the mtn and partially by Wolfpen Branch, is 1.0 mi on an old jeep road to Little Snowbird Creek, where it jct with a rough road used by owners of private summer homes in Long Bottoms. Follow the road for 2.3 mi downstream, where it becomes Little Snowbird Rd (SR-1115). Here the road is gravel for 4.9 mi, and paved for another 5.0 mi to jct with Kilmer Rd (SR-1127). A turn R (E) is another 5.2 mi to downtown Robbinsville on SR-1127. Another exit from Porterfield Gap is down the mtn, S, on old logging roads mainly on USFS property along Allman Creek for 2.8 mi to jct with Allman Creek Rd (SR-1378). After 0.6 mi jct with Hyatt Creek

Rd (SR-1379), a paved road, for 0.8 mi into the town of Marble and US-19/129. Before either route is chosen, it is recommended that the hiker carry USGS-FS topo maps of Marble and Santeetlah Creek and a compass. (*USGS-FS Maps:* Andrews, Marble, Robbinsville, Santeetlah Creek)

SUPPORT FACILITIES: (See information above in section 4.)

SECTION 1: CHEOAH RANGER DISTRICT

The Cheoah Ranger District has 120,110 acres with Lake Santeetlah in the center. On the N boundary is the Little Tennessee River, which is also the S boundary of Great Smoky Mtns National Park, but the river is dammed for the entire distance by Calderwood Lake, Lake Cheoah, and Fontana Lake. The S boundary is rimmed by the remote Snowbird Mtns, and its W border is more remote along the Tennessee line that fronts the Cherokee National Forest. Also in the W is the 14,900-acre Joyce Kilmer/Slickrock Wilderness Area, with its NW corner in Tennessee. Some of the most spectacular mtn views are in this district, particularly from the *AT* as it ascends to Cheoah Bald (5,062 ft) from Wesser and crosses the Fontana Dam after 25.2 mi. Other panoramic views are from Wauchecha Bald (4,368 ft), Johanna Bald (4,716 ft), and Hangover Mtn (4,170 ft).

There are five recreational areas, all of which provide developed family campgrounds (except the Joyce Kilmer Memorial Forest, but Horse Cove is nearby). The Tsali area is described under *Tsali Trail*, and Cheoah Point and Horse Cove are described under the *Kilmer/Slickrock Trails*. Cable Cove is near Fontana Lake, 4.5 mi E on NC-28 from Fontana Village. Rattler Ford Group Campground (reservations required) is by Santeetlah Creek near the entrance to the Kilmer Memorial Forest. The national forest outside the campgrounds is also available for "primitive camping" unless the area is posted closed (such as for boating, picnicking, trailheads, or administrative sites). The Kilmer/Slickrock Wilderness Area is protected by regulations and general etiquette as described in the introduction to this chapter.

The construction of the Tellico-Robbinsville Scenic Highway, under the direction of the Federal Highway Administration, provides a paved-road access from Santeetlah Gap jct with SR-1127 to Tellico Plains in Tennessee. The highway dramatically affects the trail system in the area. For example, *Cedar Top Trail* #61 and *Hooper Bald Trail* #60 are both impacted heavily. Maintenance has ceased on the remaining sections of the trails and their descriptions are omitted. The new road provides fast access to *King Meadows Trail* at Hooper Bald and to *Big Snowbird Trail* from Big Junction. There is an improved access route to Strawberry Knob and the *Fodderstack Trail* #94 (Tenn.) with completion of the highway. But the road has mutilated and scarred the mtns with some artificial walls where grass or trees can never grow, and where the wilderness qualities are destroyed forever. Conservationists tried for many years to prevent its construction.

There are two special-interest trails at the Cheoah Ranger Station. The *Camp Santeetlah Historic Trail* (USFS #152) begins at the parking area. Fol- **10** low the signs on the paved trail that switchbacks up the hillside into a forest of hemlock, pitch pine, poplar, hickory, ferns, laurel, and trailing arbutus. Along the way are history markers, one of which indicates that the trail was dedicated August 13, 1983, "in honor of the men who served the Civilian Conservation Corps (CCC) and their lasting contributions to our nation's national forests," specifically Camp NCF-24, Co 3447, that opened here in 1934 and closed in 1941. Reach an observation deck at 0.4 mi; backtrack. Or, continue ahead on the *Cheoah Trail* (USFS #143). It is a 2.3-mi loop, a **11** timber-management interpretive trail with signed timber stands and exam ples of timber management. Timber cuts and silvicultural work are demon strated on the slopes facing Santeetlah Lake. Another trail, the *Massey Branch Fitness Trail,* is 0.5 mi E of the ranger station on Massey Branch Rd **12** (SR-1116). The loop trail is 0.7 mi with 14 exercise stations on a wood-chip treadway under white pine, oak, and maple. It has an excellent view of part of Santeetlah Lake after the 120-yd climb to an easy route.

ADDRESS AND ACCESS: District Ranger, Cheoah Ranger District, Rte 1, Box 16-A, Robbinsville, NC 28711; 704-479-6431. From Robbinsville go 1.0 mi W on US-129 and turn L on Massey Branch Rd (SR-1116) for 1.1 mi to the ranger station. District Ranger, Tellico Ranger District, Cherokee National Forest, Ball Play Rd, Tellico Plains, TN 37385; 615-253-3094.

TSALI RECREATION AREA (Graham and Swain Counties)

The Tsali Campground and Fishing Access Area provides a ramp for boating, fishing in Fontana Lake, water skiing, camping (with showers and flush toilets), horseback riding, mountain biking, picnicking, nature study, and hiking. From the Tsali Campground to the lake is a 0.5-mi footpath, *Mouse Branch Trail* (USFS #153). The area is named in honor of the Cherokee Indian Tsali (Charlie), who escaped with his family from the "Trail of Tears" (see introduction to this chapter) to the Smoky Mtns. In the escape a US Army soldier was accidentally killed. Gen Winfield Scott asked Will Thomas, a Cherokee friend, to find Tsali and tell him that if he would surrender and pay the penalty of death, all the other Cherokee who had escaped the march to

Oklahoma (approximately 1,000) would be permitted to remain. Tsali replied, "I will come. If I must die, let it be by our own people." Tsali, his oldest son, and his son-in-law were executed by a three-member Cherokee firing squad here at the old stockade.

ACCESS: From the jct of NC-28 and US-74/19 in Lauada, go W on NC-28 for 6.6 mi to the Tsali Campground sign, R, and on FR-521 descend 1.6 mi to the parking area.

13- *Tsali Horse Trail (18.5 mi: USFS #38); Thompson Loop Trail (7.4 mi;*
15 *USFS #152); Mouse Branch Loop Trail (5.3 mi; USFS #153) (F, B, H)*

LENGTH AND DIFFICULTY: 31.2 mi combined, easy to moderate

SPECIAL FEATURES: lake views, wildlife, wildflowers

TRAILHEAD AND DESCRIPTION: Access to all trails begins at the parking lot intersection. The popular *Tsali Horse Trail* consists of a W loop and an E loop of the peninsula. A forest road cuts through the center with Graham County W and Swain County E. The E loop has two spur trails to provide connections for making choices of three loops with lesser distance. The large parking area at the main trailhead was constructed in 1994 to accommodate an increase in trail users. On two adjoining peninsulas are the *Thompson Loop Trail* and *Mouse Branch Loop Trail,* also multiple-use trails. Although hikers may use the trails at any time, there is a schedule for horses and mountain bikes. In 1996 the following list was on a sign between *Thompson Loop Trail* and the entrance road to the campground: *Thompson Loop Trail* and *Mouse Branch Loop Trail* for equestrians on Sunday, Monday, Wednesday, and Friday; for bikers on Tuesday, Thursday, and Saturday. On the *Tsali Horse Trail* bikers have Sunday, Monday, Wednesday, and Friday; equestrians have Tuesday, Thursday, and Saturday. Bikers must wear helmets and other appropriate safety gear. Night biking and horse riding are considered unsafe.

The *Tsali Horse Trail* has a well-graded treadway, connects to the campground, and has hitching racks and observation points along the peninsula. There are dips and curves in and out of more than 40 coves. Wildlife includes deer, raccoon, fox, squirrel, hawks, woodpeckers, and songbirds. Vegetation is that of the lower-slope (less than 2,000 ft elev) Appalachian hardwood forest. Most of the forest is open with light understory, but often there are small patches of berries, sumac, sourwood, and laurel. There are scattered hemlock, scrub and white pine, and poplar. Wildflowers include sunflower, cone flower (*Rudbeckia hirta*), downy false foxglove (*Aureolaria virginica*), horsemint (*Collinsonia canadensis*), wild phlox, soapwort, gentian, orchids, henbit, and violets. Because the trail has multiple options in choosing loop distances, details are not described here. A signboard at the entrance indicates distances and connection choices. Without options for the other two trails, their description is as follows.

From the parking area cross the road intersection to *Thompson Loop Trail* sign. Descend 134 yd, cross stream, and turn L. Ascend among hardwoods, rhododendron, laurel, fetterbush, holly, and hemlock. Woodpeckers and songbirds are prominent. Reach the ridge top at 0.8 mi and after 0.1 mi turn L on a logging road. Turn R at 1.3 mi and 1.5 mi. At 2.4 mi is an excellent view of Fontana Lake and the Great Smoky Mtns beyond. To the R a dedication sign is to David Thompson of the Cheoah Ranger District. Leave the road and begin a footpath at 2.8 mi. At 3.9 mi turn R to wind in and out of coves. Views of the lake and Murphy Branch are possible in the wintertime, and where there are open oak forests, views are noticeable in other seasons. Follow an old road at 5.7 mi, cross a number of streamlets and jct with *Mouse Branch Loop Trail*, L, at 6.8 mi in a gap. (The *Thompson Loop Trail* continues through the gap and follows a road for the remainder of the distance.)

The *Mouse Branch Loop Trail* ascends on an old road to the top of the ridge at 0.3 mi. Here are views of the lake, L, and the peninsula on which is the *Thompson Loop Trail*. Turn R at a fork in the road at 1.2 mi, and R again at 1.7 mi. The trail becomes a foot trail. At 2.9 mi the hillside has been timbered and burned, but a cove has been left uncut at 3.1 mi. Cross a small stream at 4.0 mi, followed by views of Mouse Branch, L. Ascend from a cove on an old logging road at 5.1 mi; rejoin *Thompson Loop Trail* at 5.3 mi, turn L on the frequently used road. It is 0.6 mi to the parking area. (*USGS-FS Map:* Noland Creek)

SUPPORT FACILITIES: One of the nearest commercial campgrounds is Lost Mine Campground, 8.0 mi SW on US-74/19 from the jct of US-74 and NC-28. Turn off at the sign, across the road from the Nantahala Outdoor Center, and proceed for 1.0 mi L up Silvermine Rd. Full svc, rec fac. Open March 15 through October 31; 704-488-6445. Bryson City, with restaurants, motels, and shopping areas, is 12.0 mi E of Tsali Recreation Area.

PANTHER CREEK AREA (Graham County)

Panther Creek Trail (USFS #68) (F)

16

LENGTH AND DIFFICULTY: 8.0 mi round-trip, moderate

TRAILHEAD AND DESCRIPTION: From the jct of NC-28 and Panther Creek Rd (SR-1232) at Panther Creek Bridge and backwater of Fontana Lake (2.0 mi W of Tsali Campground on NC-28), drive up SR-1232 beside Panther Creek for 2.3 mi to the parking area. (To the L of the parking area is the former 2.5-mi *Grassy Gap Trail,* L of woods road that goes up Cook Branch. It is an access to the *AT* at Grassy Gap [3,050 ft], but is no longer maintained by the USFS.) *Panther Creek Trail* forks R from the parking area and follows Shell Stand Creek, crossing Whiteoak Branch at 1.4 mi and approaching Reid Branch at 1.8 mi. Jct with *Reid Branch Trail* (USFS #155) is on the R. (The *Reid Branch Trail* ascends N for 0.5 mi to FR-410, which exits to Panther Creek Rd. It is no longer maintained by the USFS.) Continue on *Panther Creek Trail,* L, up Shell Stand Creek in a forest of oak, maple, birch, rhodo-dendron, and scattered hemlock. Reach the trail's terminus at 4.0 mi near the confluence of Deep Creek and Whiteoak Creek, an excellent area for backpack camping. Backtrack. (*USGS-FS Maps:* Hewitt, Wesser)

FONTANA VILLAGE AREA (Graham County)

17 *Lookout Rock Trail (USFS # 40) (F)*

LENGTH AND DIFFICULTY: 2.0 mi round-trip, moderate

TRAILHEAD AND DESCRIPTION: From the SW end of Fontana Village on SR-1246, near the last cottages, look for Lookout Rock signs across a T intersec-tion. Ascend gradually up a slope on the R side of a stream. Cross the stream at 0.5 mi and reach by switchbacks the former *AT* at 1.0 mi. The trail is now the *Yellow Creek Mountain Trail* from Tapoco W to Walker Gap E. (A loop hike could be made here by following *Yellow Creek Mountain Trail* L for 1.6 mi to Walker Gap [3,450 ft] and the current *AT.* Turn L on the *AT* and descend for 2.7 mi to NC-28, near Fontana Lake Dock. Turn L on NC-28 and go 2.5 mi to Fontana Village for a complete loop of 7.8 mi.) (*USGS-FS Map:* Fontana Dam)

18- *Lewellyn Cove Nature Trail (0.7 mi; USFS #50); Fontana Village Trail*
19 *(0.9 mi; USFS #157) (F)*

LENGTH AND DIFFICULTY: 1.6 mi combined, easy

TRAILHEAD AND DESCRIPTION: From Fontana Village entrance road and Fontana Texaco sta, drive 1.4 mi E on NC-28 to the parking area. A well-graded and heavily used loop trail is across the highway. Fifty indigenous trees and shrubs are labeled with botanical and common names. A visitor's trail connecting with Fontana Village, the *Fontana Village Trail,* runs from the stream in Lewellyn Cove for 0.9 mi. (Other planned connections will run to the golf course and swimming pool area.) (*USGS-FS Map:* Fontana Dam)

YELLOW CREEK MOUNTAIN AREA (Graham County)

Yellow Creek Mountain Trail (USFS #48) (F)

LENGTH AND DIFFICULTY: 9.3 mi, strenuous (elev change 2,350 ft)

CONNECTING TRAILS:
  (*Lookout Rock Trail*)
  (*AT*)

TRAILHEAD AND DESCRIPTION: In Tapoco (14.5 mi W from Robbinsville on US-129) at the jct of US-129 and Rhymers Ferry Rd (SR-1247) (which leads 8.5 mi to NC-28 in Fontana Village), park in a small area on US-129. Walk 30 yd on SR-1247 and cross Meadow Branch on a footbridge. (This blue-blazed trail is infrequently hiked, but because of its scenic beauty, it deserves more attention. One disadvantage is its lack of water sources. Until 1947 it was the circuitous route followed by the *AT* between the Smokies and the Cheoah Mtns. It was reopened in 1971 by the Boy Scouts of Tapoco, Troop 415.) Climb steeply up the switchbacks through rhododendron, scrub pine, white pine, dogwood, laurel, and witch hazel (*Hamamelis virginiana*). Follow the ridge for 0.6 mi and a burned S slope to reach Bearpen Gap at 1.4 mi under a power line. Along the route are splendid views of the Cheoah River Valley and Hangover Lead. Banks of wildflowers are profuse—trailing arbutus, coral bell, goldenrod, and Devil's shoestrings (*Tephrosia virginiana*) in clusters of pink wings and yellow standards (the latter plant contains rotenone, an insecticide ingredient). (At Bearpen Gap a loop trail can be made by following an unnamed trail L to Rhymers Ferry Rd, SR-1274, at Jenkins Grocery. Turn L and follow the road to the trailhead at 3.0 mi.) Continue on the *Yellow Creek Mountain Trail* up the mtn, using care to avoid other trails and woods roads, to Old Yellow Creek Rd (also called Oldfield Gap Rd, SR-1249) at 1.8 mi. Cross the road, L, and ascend an embankment to follow a ridge of oak, pine, sourwood, and laurel. Continue on the ridge, ascending and descending over knolls to a steep climb at 3.1 mi. Reach Kirkland Gap (2,800 ft) at 5.6 mi and Green Gap (3,455 ft) at 7.8 mi. *Lookout Rock Trail* is L of the gap. (It descends 1.0 mi to the SW corner of Fontana Village, connecting with SR-1246.) Arrive at Walker Gap (3,450 ft) at 9.3 mi to join the current route of the *AT*. Backtrack or take the *AT* N for 2.7 mi to NC-28. Another route would be to take the *AT* S to Yellow Creek Gap at Tuskeegee Rd (SR-1242) for 3.7 mi. Vehicle switching would be necessary. (*USGS-FS Maps:* Fontana Dam, Tapoco)

JOYCE KILMER/SLICKROCK WILDERNESS AREA (Graham County, North Carolina; Monroe County, Tennessee)

The Joyce Kilmer Memorial Forest, of which 3,840 acres are in the Little Santeetlah Creek watershed, and the Slickrock Creek watershed, with 11,060 acres, together form two basins separated by a ridge between Stratton Bald and Haoe Lookout. The Smokies are N across the Little Tennessee River, and the Cherokee National Forest in Tennessee is to the W. Filled with virgin timber, the Kilmer Memorial was established by Congress in 1936 to honor the famous author of "Trees," Alfred Joyce Kilmer, a soldier who was killed in World War I at the Battle of Ovreq. The Belton Lumber Company started cutting the virgin timber up the Little Santeetlah Creek in 1890, but before it reached the huge trees in what is now the Kilmer Memorial Forest, the company went bankrupt and the trees were spared. In 1936 the USFS also purchased the Slickrock Creek basin from the Babcock Lumber Company of Pennsylvania, which had cut more than 70 percent of the timber in the watershed.

This wilderness is rich in both flora and fauna. Hundreds of species of shrubs, wildflowers, vines, ferns, mosses, lichens, and herbaceous plants form the understory. Rhododendron, laurel, and flame azalea are also abundant. Trees include poplar, hemlock, sycamore, basswood, oak, maple, birch, and beech. Animal life includes wild hog, fox, bear, deer, raccoon, mink, and other smaller mammals. Two species of poisonous snakes—the copperhead and the timber rattler—are in the area. In addition to the songbirds, the wilderness has grouse, wild turkey, owls, hawks, and raven. Under specific state laws, hunting and fishing are allowed in the wilderness by the N.C. Wildlife Resources Commission, Division of Game, as described in the introduction to this chapter.

SUPPORT FACILITIES: For the Slickrock Creek Wilderness Area, the closest USFS campground is Cheoah Point on Santeetlah Lake, 8.6 mi E on US-129 from the Cheoah Dam bridge and *Slickrock Creek Trail* parking area in Tapoco. Enter the campground on Old US-129 (SR-1146). Facilities include campsites, tables, grills, drinking water, comfort stations, and picnic area. (From the campground it is 7.0 mi E on US-129 to Robbinsville.) From the Cheoah Dam bridge it is 2.2 mi N on US-129 (near jct with NC-28) to a motel, restaurant (with mountain recipes), groceries, gasoline, and telephone. Address: Crossroads of Time, Deals Gap, Tapoco, NC 28780; 704-498-2231. Also, from the Cheoah Dam bridge 0.4 mi E on US-129 turn L on Rhymers Ferry Rd (SR-1247) for 1.3 mi to Jenkins Grocery. A USFS campground for the Kilmer Wilderness Area is Horse Cove, 0.2 mi on FR-416 across Kilmer Rd (SR-1127) from the

Kilmer Memorial Forest and picnic area entrance. Facilities at Horse Cove are the same as for Cheoah Point. Groceries, motel, and shopping centers are 13.4 mi E on Kilmer Rd (SR-1127) to Robbinsville.

SLICKROCK ACCESS: There are two road access points for the Slickrock Wilderness Area trails. One is at the S side of the US-129 bridge over Calderwood Lake, below Cheoah Dam, and the other is at Big Fat Gap, via FR-62, 2.2 mi SE from the Cheoah Dam bridge on US-129 and 7.0 mi W from jct with US-19/74. FR-62 is closed to vehicles from late December to mid- or late March because of weather conditions.

Slickrock Creek Trail (13.0 mi; USFS #42); Hangover Lead Trail (5.3 mi; USFS #56) (F)   **21-22**

CONNECTING TRAILS ON SLICKROCK CREEK TRAIL
- *Ike Branch Trail (2.1 mi; USFS #45)*   **23**
- *Nichols Cove Trail (2.9 mi; USFS #44)*   **24**
- *Big Fat Trail (1.5 mi; USFS #41)*   **25**
- *Slickrock Creek Spur Trail (0.7 mi; USFS #42A)*   **26**
- *(Haoe Lead Trail)*

CONNECTING TRAILS ON HANGOVER LEAD TRAIL
- *(Haoe Lead Trail)*
- *Deep Creek Trail (3.9 mi; USFS #46)*   **27**
- *Locust Ridge Trail (0.8 mi; USFS #401)*   **28**
- *Big Fat Trail (1.5 mi; USFS #41)*
- *Windy Gap Trail (1.3 mi; USFS #400)*   **29**
- *Yellowhammer Gap Trail (1.7 mi; USFS #49)*   **30**
- *Ike Branch Trail (2.1 mi; USFS #45)*

TOTAL LENGTH AND DIFFICULTY: 26.5 mi combined, moderate to strenuous (elev change 4,150 ft)

SPECIAL FEATURES: fishing, Lower Falls, Hangover outcroppings

TRAILHEAD AND DESCRIPTION: The greatly contrasting *Slickrock Creek Trail* and the *Hangover Lead Trail* run N-S and can easily be connected with short trails at either end to form a major loop into the Slickrock Wilderness Area basin and E rim. Additional trail loops are possible into the Tennessee section of the wilderness for the W rim to make a complete rim loop of approx 26.6 mi. Sections of the wilderness are rugged and remote with minimum trail signing and generally without blazes. Hikers are advised to take adequate food and clothing, rain gear (there are thunderstorms almost daily in the summer), tent, stove (frequently the wood is wet), topo maps, and compass. Although there are plenty of water sources on all the basin and mountainside trails, water is absent or intermittent on the rim trails. (Drinking water from Slickrock Creek should be boiled or treated.) Wilderness rules and regulations apply on all the trails, and hikers are reminded to follow the "no-trace" policy of hiking and camping. Slickrock Creek is an excellent brown trout stream.

From the parking area at the S side of the Cheoah Dam bridge follow the *Slickrock Creek Trail* sign into the woods and parallel Calderwood Lake on a wide scenic trail. At 0.7 mi jct with *Ike Branch Trail,* L (described on the return route). Plant life in the vicinity includes poplar, birch, maple, hemlock, fetterbush, jewelweed (*Impatiens capensis* and *pallida*), sweet cicely, and wild hydrangea (*Hydrangea arborescens*). At 0.8 mi cross a footbridge; at 1.0 and 1.4 mi cross boardwalks over a precipice. A pink rhododendron (*Rhododendron minus*) grows here and frequently (with other species) in the entire Slickrock basin. At 1.6 mi cross another bridge over a precipice and turn L to the mouth of Slickrock Creek. Pass the edge of the lake backwater and arrive beside the pools and cascades of Slickrock Creek at 1.9 mi. Follow upstream on sections of an old RR grade. (This was the access route of the Babcock Lumber Company of Pittsburgh, which cut 70 percent of the virgin forest in the gorge between 1915 and 1922. It had to cease logging when Calderwood Lake was constructed.) Rocky treadways, rock walls, wildflowers, and cascades make this section of the trail scenic. Rock-hop or wade the creek at 2.7 mi into Tennessee and reach the Lower Falls at 3.0 mi. Continue upstream and cross the creek again at 3.5 mi to a jct with *Ike Branch Trail* at 3.7 mi. Good campsites are in this area. To complete this first loop turn L on *Ike Branch Trail* up Yellowhammer Creek in a forest of poplar, sycamore, basswood, rhododendron, and ferns. Ascend; at 4.2 mi jct with *Yellowhammer Gap Trail* (which leads to *Nichols Cove Trail,* R, at 4.3 mi.). (The *Hangover Lead Trail* is described on the longer return loops.) Pass through an area of oak, pine, buckberry, flame azalea, and huckleberry on a dry ridge at 4.6 mi. Cross another ridge at 4.9 mi and descend into a deep hollow of hemlock, poplar, and rhododendron. Cross a stream four times and descend on an exceptionally steep slope by a ravine. Reach the N terminus of *Ike Branch Trail* and jct with *Slickrock Creek Trail* at 5.8 mi; turn R and return to the parking area for a total of 6.5 mi.

For a second and longer loop continue upstream on the *Slickrock Creek Trail* from the jct with the *Ike Branch Trail* at 3.7 mi. Cross a small tributary before fording Slickrock Creek into Tennessee at 4.0 mi. At 4.2 mi reach the jct with *Stiffknee Trail* (USFS #106) at the state line. (*Stiffknee Trail* goes W up Little Slickrock Creek for 3.3 mi to Farr Gap and jct with *Fodderstack*

Trail [USFS #95]. The *Stiffknee Trail* could be a route to *Fodderstack Trail* for a complete hike of the rim by using *Fodderstack, Stratton Bald, Haoe,* and *Hangover Lead Trails* for approx 26.6 mi. A major problem with such a loop is the lack of water on the basin's rim.) Continue upstream for 0.2 mi to jct with *Nichols Cove Trail,* L, after fording Slickrock Creek in the process. Here the hiker has a choice of following *Nichols Cove Trail* to rejoin the *Slickrock Creek Trail* after 2.8 mi to *Big Fat Trail,* or follow *Yellowhammer Trail* off *Nichols Cove Trail* to *Ike Branch Trail* and return for a loop of lesser distance. If *Nichols Cove Trail* is chosen, ascend in a narrow scenic passage of waterfalls and cascades, hemlocks, ferns, and rhododendron. Cross the stream six times and at 0.9 mi jct with *Yellowhammer Gap Trail,* L. (The 1.7-mi *Yellowhammer Trail* ascends gently NW and crosses a number of small drains from the Hangover Lead. The trail weaves in and out of coves in a forest dominated by oak, poplar, birch, and rhododendron. At 1.8 mi jct with *Ike Branch Trail* and the *Hangover Lead Trail.* A turn R on the *Ike Branch Trail* continues NW for a return to US-129 and a loop of 9.5 mi.) Continue ahead on the *Nichols Cove Trail,* pass signs of former human habitation at rock piles and terraces, tombstones, and once cleared fields at 1.3 mi. Begin a steep ascent at 1.8 mi to reach a ridge nose where a L curve goes to the ridge crest. At 2.3 mi jct with *Windy Gap Trail,* L (F). (It descends 1.3 mi from *Hangover Lead Trail.*) Begin to descend at 2.4 mi. After 0.3 mi of a steep descent, reach a level area, cross Big Fat Branch, and jct with *Big Fat Trail* at 2.9 mi. There are good campsites here. To the R it is 150 yd to *Slickrock Creek Trail,* and to the L on *Big Fat Trail* it is 1.5 mi up to Big Fat Gap. (The *Big Fat Trail* ascends to switchbacks at 0.2 mi and follows mainly on the S side of the stream, steeply in sections. Cross the stream at 0.9 mi, shift S to cross a tributary, and follow switchbacks to reach Big Fat Gap parking area and FR-62 at 1.5 mi. At the Fat Gap parking area, a L turn on the *Hangover Lead Trail* for 2.4 mi to a jct with *Ike Branch Trail,* R, will lead back to US-129 in Tapoco for a loop of 11.6 mi.

If choosing to hike the *Slickrock Creek Trail* instead of the *Nichols Cove Trail,* continue upstream on remnant sections of the old RR grade and cross the stream to the Tennessee side at 4.7 mi. Enter a rocky section at 5.2 mi and pass through a narrow canyon at 5.4 mi. Cross Wildcat Branch, a tributary, curve around the nose of two spur ridges, and cross back into North Carolina at 6.2 mi. (For the next 0.2 mi the area is good for camping.) Cross the creek again at 6.4 mi and at 6.6 mi (the last crossing from Tennessee) below Wildcat Falls. Cross Slickrock Creek and reach the confluence of Slickrock Creek and Big Stack Gap Branch and *Big Stack Gap Trail* (USFS #

139), R, at 7.3 mi. (The *Big Stack Gap Branch Trail* goes 1.8 mi upstream to a cross-trail with *Fodderstack Trail* and *Crowder Creek Trail* # 48 in Cherokee National Forest.) Cross a tributary at 7.5 mi and Slickrock Creek again to reach the jct with *Nichols Cove Trail* at 7.9 mi. A third loop option can be made here by returning to US-129 on either *Nichols Cove, Yellowhammer,* and *Ike Branch Trails* for a total of 13.8 mi or climbing the *Big Fat Trail* to jct with *Hangover Lead* and *Ike Branch Trails* N for a total of 14.1 mi.

For the fourth and final loop option, continue upstream and ascend to the nose of a spur ridge to cross Buckeye Branch at 8.2 mi. Ascend gradually and cross two more drains before crossing Hangover Creek at 9.0 mi, the last generally level area for camping within the next 4.0 mi. At 9.6 mi the trail forks. (Ahead is a 0.7-mi dead-end trail to the cascading confluence of Slickrock Creek and Naked Ground Branch.) At the fork, turn sharply L on a W slope and curve around the ridge to cross a tributary that flows into Hangover Creek. For the next 2.9 mi ascend on switchbacks (where some sections are overgrown) on a steep ridgeline, but cross a tributary four times before reaching the major ridge knoll. The forest in this area is mixed hardwoods, rhododendron, and scattered conifers. Reach a trail crossroads at 13.0 mi with *Haoe Lead Trail* and *Naked Ground Trail* (4,850 ft). (With a vehicle shuttle, trail connections can be made to all trails described below in the Kilmer basin. The *Haoe Lead Trail* connects R, 0.5 mi, with the *Stratton Bald Trail*.) Follow the *Haoe Lead Trail* L for 0.8 mi along the ridgeline to jct with a shortcut R of the *Haoe Lead Trail* and 0.1 mi farther for another jct of the *Haoe Lead Trail,* R, and the beginning of the *Hangover Lead Trail,* L, at Haoe Lookout (5,249 ft) at 13.9 mi. (Here the *Haoe Lead Trail* goes down the mtn for 5.1 mi to Kilmer Rd.) The Hangover Lookout (the site of a former fire tower) has limited vistas. Proceed on the *Hangover Lead Trail,* descend easily to Saddle Tree Gap, and jct with the *Deep Creek Trail,* R, at 14.0 mi. (The *Deep Creek Trail* descends to join the *Haoe Lead Trail* described below.) Ahead at this point is a 0.3-mi dead-end spur to prominent rocks and cliffs for the most panoramic and spectacular viewing of the Slickrock Wilderness Area. Dense rhododendron landscapes the rocks. Back on the *Hangover Lead Trail* descend in a forest of beech and birch to curve W of a knoll. Return to the ridge at 14.8 mi. Begin steep descent and enter a virgin hemlock forest at 15.2 mi. (Damp, often foggy, and dark serpentine-shaped roots in rhododendron thickets may offer the fantasy of a descent into the land of *The Hobbit*.) Begin a gradual descent at 15.4 mi and follow the trail through oak, red- and green-striped maple, birch, sassafras, hemlock, and flame azalea to the edge of the ridge. At 15.8 mi is jct R with

Locust Ridge Trail. It descends steeply 0.8 mi to FR-62, 0.9 mi E of Big Fat Gap. Descend steeply on six switchbacks at 16.6 mi and reach Big Fat Gap parking area at 16.8 mi. (The large public parking area is popular with both hikers and hunters.) To the L the 1.5 mi *Big Fat Trail* descends to connect with the *Slickrock Creek Trail,* and the 1.3-mi *Windy Gap Trail* descends to jct with *Nichols Cove Trail.* To the R FR-62 winds down the mtn for 7.0 mi to US-129, 2.2 mi SE of Tapoco. Cross the parking area and ascend steeply on an old woods road into a hardwood forest with scattered conifers to the summit of Cold Spring Knob (3,480 ft) at 17.2 mi. Follow the dry ridge on a moderate and gradual descent to the summit of Caney Ridge (2,800 ft), which rises from the E, at 18.3 mi. Among hardwoods, huckleberry, and buckberry descend to Yellowhammer Gap (2,520 ft) and jct with *Ike Branch Trail* at 19.1 mi. Turn R, descend to jct with *Slickrock Creek Trail,* turn R, and return to the parking area at US-129 at the Cheoah Dam bridge for a total loop of 21.4 mi. (*USGS-FS Maps:* Tapoco, Whiteoak Flats)

KILMER ACCESS: There are two road routes to the Kilmer section of the Kilmer/Slickrock Wilderness Area. One paved road entrance is from Robbinsville. Drive 1.0 mi W of Robbinsville on US-129, turn L on Massey Branch Rd (SR-1116) toward the ranger station. At 4.3 mi turn R on Kilmer Rd (SR-1127), pass the jct with the new Tellico-Robbinsville Scenic Highway, and descend to a crossroads with Santeetlah Rd (FR-416) at 13.4 mi. The Kilmer Memorial Forest and picnic area entrance road is L for 0.6 mi. The other route, 7.2 mi E of Tapoco on US-129, begins at the jct with Old US-129 (SR-1147). Drive 0.5 mi to Santeetlah Rd (SR-1134), which becomes FR-416 on a gravel road, and reach the crossroads with SR-1127 at the entrance to the Kilmer picnic area after 6.0 mi.

Haoe Lead Trail (6.5 mi; USFS #53) (F)   **31**

CONNECTING TRAILS:
Deep Creek Trail (3.9 mi; USFS #46)
Jenkins Meadow Trail (1.8 mi; USFS #53A)   **32**
(Hangover Lead Trail)
(Slickrock Creek Trail)
(Naked Ground Trail)
(Stratton Bald Trail)
TOTAL LENGTH AND DIFFICULTY: 12.2 mi combined, moderate to strenuous
SPECIAL FEATURES: Deep Creek cascades, Haoe Lookout area
TRAILHEAD AND DESCRIPTION: From the crossroads of Kilmer Rd and

Santeetlah Rd, described above, drive up (W) Kilmer Rd (also called Wagon Train Road, SR-1127) for 5.4 mi to a large parking area, R. Park here for entrance across the road to the *Haoe Lead Trail*. (Up the road it is 0.2 mi to the Maple Springs observation area and the cul-de-sac end of this previously controversial road that conservationists stopped from **33** penetrating the Slickrock area. The *Maple Springs Observation Trail* (USFS #71) is a 220-yd paved scenic loop [designed for wheelchair access] that provides N views of the Cheoah River Valley, Yellow Creek Mtn, and the Great Smoky Mtns.)

Ascend the graded *Haoe Lead Trail* (constructed by the YACC in 1979) in a forest of hardwoods and white pine. At 0.5 mi reach a ridgeline and cross to the N slope in a rocky area. At 0.8 mi is water, L. Jct R at 1.1 mi with *Deep Creek Trail*.

(*Deep Creek Trail* begins in a rocky area. Ferns are prominent with wildflowers that include umbrella-leaf [*Diphylleia cymosa*], crested dwarf iris, black and blue cohosh, and twisted-stalk [*Streptopus roseus*]. Trees include basswood, hemlock, birch, and buckeye. Cross small streamlets, pass large rock formations at 0.7 mi and 1.1 mi. Pass a second-growth forest at 1.6 mi and reach cascading Deep Creek at 2.1 mi. Cross a footbridge to an old timber road and turn L. [To the R is the former entrance to the *Deep Creek Trail*, 2.5 mi downstream to FR-445 which forks from FR-62, the route to Big Fat Gap. Entrance remains possible on this route though sections are overgrown.] Ascend steadily into the Hudson Deaden Branch area through rhododendron, hemlock, and hardwoods, and more steeply on switchbacks to jct at 3.9 mi with the *Hangover Lead Trail* in Saddle Tree Gap [5,120 ft], the boundary of the Kilmer/Slickrock Wilderness Area.) (To the R it is 90 yd to the fork where the *Hangover Lead Trail* goes L and a 0.2-mi spur route, R, ascends to panoramic views at Hangover Mtn. The L fork of *Hangover Lead Trail* ascends 0.2 mi to the Haoe Lookout [5,249 ft] and jct L with *Haoe Lead Trail*. A return can be made here on the *Haoe Lead Trail* for a total loop of 9.2 mi.)

To continue on the *Haoe Lead Trail* from the NE jct with the *Deep Creek Trail*, ascend steadily to Rock Creek Knob and follow W on the main ridgeline. Turn on a S slope and at 3.3 mi cross the Kilmer/Slickrock Wilderness boundary and jct with the N trailhead of *Jenkins Meadow Trail* at 3.6 mi.

(The *Jenkins Meadow Trail*, #54A, descends SE on a slope to join a ridgeline and wilderness boundary at 0.7 mi, and at 1.8 mi ends at a jct with *Naked Ground Trail*. It is another 0.9 mi L on the *Naked Ground Trail* to SR-1127.)

Continue on the *Haoe Lead Trail* up the slope and to the main ridgeline to a more level area known as Jenkins Meadow. Pass through dense groves of rhododendron and ascend steeply to Haoe Lookout at 5.1 mi and jct with the *Hangover Lead Trail,* R. (From here a loop of 9.2 mi can be made by reversing the route described above for the *Deep Creek Trail.*) Continue L from the lookout, descend, follow narrow ridge crest at 5.6 mi, and at 6.0 mi arrive at the jct with *Slickrock Creek Trail,* R, and *Naked Ground Trail,* L. Ahead the *Haoe Lead Trail* ascends its final 0.5 mi to a jct with the *Stratton Bald Trail* and the boundary of the wilderness area at 6.5 mi. (To the R the *Stratton Bald Trail* goes 1.8 mi to the *Fodderstack Trail,* #95, in the Cherokee National Forest, and L it descends for 6.7 mi to SR-1127.) Backtrack, or use a connecting trail. (*USGS-FS Maps:* Big Junction, Santeetlah, Tapoco, or Joyce Kilmer/Slickrock Wilderness and Citico Creek Wilderness [Nantahala and Cherokee National Forests] trail map)

Naked Ground Trail (5.7 mi; USFS #55); Stratton Bald Trail (8.5 mi; USFS #54) (F)

CONNECTING TRAILS:
   (*Jenkins Meadow Trail*)
   (*Haoe Lead Trail*)
   (*Slickrock Creek Trail*)
   Wolf Laurel Trail (0.6 mi; USFS #57)
TOTAL LENGTH AND DIFFICULTY: 14.2 mi combined, strenuous (elev change 3,220 ft)
SPECIAL FEATURES: wildlife and wildflowers on Horse Cove Ridge
TRAILHEAD AND DESCRIPTION: These two trails can make a 13.2-mi loop: the first provides a study of the Little Santeetlah Creek drainage, and the second provides a major observation of Horse Cove Ridge high above the eastern flow of both the Little Santeetlah and Santeetlah Creeks. Park at either the space assigned at the Kilmer picnic area entrance on SR-1127 and *Naked Ground Trail* E trailhead or at the Rattler Ford Group Campground entrance across the bridge S of *Stratton Bald Trail* on SR-1127. It is 0.4 mi between the two parking options.

If beginning on the *Naked Ground Trail,* ascend on switchbacks to the ridge crest and jct with *Jenkins Meadow Trail,* R, near a spring. (*Jenkins Meadow Trail* is a 1.8-mi connector that ascends from here to *Haoe Lead Trail* described above.) Follow the slope, L, cross a small stream at 1.4 mi and at 1.7 mi. At 1.8 mi is the old trail that connected with the Kilmer picnic area, a route that is now closed. At 1.9 mi jct with an alternate trail. The

L route crosses the Little Santeetlah and follows through a damp and dense forest of rhododendron, tall hemlock, and tulip poplar. It rejoins the R alternate after 0.6 mi. Cross Adamcamp Branch at 2.9 mi on a footbridge, and cross five more streams before beginning the final ascent; last dependable water is at 4.8 mi. Begin the first of 14 switchbacks at 4.9 mi in a forest of oak, yellow birch, and flame azalea. Arrive at Naked Ground Gap and end of *Naked Ground Trail* at 5.7 mi, and jct with *Haoe Lead Trail*, R and L. Here is a popular campsite and outstanding views of the Little Santeetlah Creek drainage. Across the gap is the S trailhead of the *Slickrock Creek Trail*.

To continue the loop, turn L and ascend 0.5 mi on the *Haoe Lead Trail* at 6.2 mi. (To the R the *Stratton Bald Trail* goes 1.8 mi to its W-end jct with *Fodderstack Trail*, #95, in the Cherokee National Forest.) Turn L and descend on a ridge with four switchbacks. Among the oaks and yellow birch are flame azaleas (which usually bloom here in late July), blue-beads, Indian cucumber-root (*Medeola virginiana*), and moosewood (*Viburnum alnifolium*). At 6.8 mi jct with blue-blazed 0.6-mi *Wolf Laurel Trail*, R. (It descends gradually to FR-81F in a level area of Wolf Laurel basin. To reach this trail by road, take SR-1127 E from the Kilmer entrance road for 2.3 mi to Santeetlah Gap. Turn R and go 6.7 mi to Fork Ridge Rd [FR-81F], R for another 3.0 mi on a narrow 4WD road.) At 7.5 mi is a timber road, R, that leads to FR-81F. Wildlife is often seen here. Continue on ridge through sections of open forest. Some of the understory vegetation includes flame azalea, huckleberry, bladdernut, and mountain laurel. At 8.9 mi are scenic views E and S. Pass a large rock overhang at 9.8 mi. At 11.4 mi pass ruins of an old cabin, and at 11.5 mi a scenic forest slope, L. At 11.7 mi leave the wilderness boundary; at 12.4 mi cross a number of small streams with footbridges and descend into a grove of hemlock, white pine, great laurel, rhododendron (*Rhododendron arborescens*), and white honeysuckle to parallel Santeetlah Creek. Reach SR-1127 at 12.9 mi and turn L to follow SR-1127 for 0.3 mi to the parking area (or R 0.1 mi to Rattler Ford Group Campground parking area). (*USGS-FS Maps:* Big Junction, Santeetlah Creek, Tapoco)

37 - *Joyce Kilmer Memorial Trail (1.2 mi; USFS #43); Poplar Cove Loop Trail*
38 *(0.7 mi; USFS #58) (F)*

LENGTH AND DIFFICULTY: 1.9 mi combined, easy

SPECIAL FEATURES: virgin forest, historic memorial

TRAILHEAD AND DESCRIPTION: From the parking area of the Joyce Kilmer Memorial Forest and picnic area at the end of FR-416 from SR-1127, follow the trail signs and ascend alongside cascading Little Santeetlah Creek to cross a footbridge. Log seats for rest and contemplation are along the national recreation trail in this primeval forest of mosses, rhododendron, hemlock, yellow poplar, fetterbush, trillium, cohosh, wood sorrel, and crested dwarf iris. At the jct with *Poplar Cove Loop Trail* is a sign that indicates Alfred Joyce Kilmer was born in New Brunswick, New Jersey, December 6, 1886, and killed in action in France, July 30, 1918. The grove of yellow poplar is the most spectacular feature on the trails; many are 16 to 22 ft in circumference and over 120 ft tall. Cross another footbridge over Little Santeetlah Creek on the return loop to the parking lot. (*USGS-FS Map:* Santeetlah Creek)

SNOWBIRD MOUNTAIN AREA (Graham County)

Snowbird Loop Nature Trail (USFS #55) (F)   **39**
LENGTH AND DIFFICULTY: 0.5 mi, easy

TRAILHEAD AND DESCRIPTION: From Cheoah district office go SW on Massey Branch Rd (SR-1116) for 2.3 mi to jct with Kilmer Rd (SR-1127) and turn R sharply on SR-1127. Go 1.3 mi to Snowbird picnic area before crossing Snowbird Creek bridge for parking. A well-graded nature trail follows Snowbird Creek upstream, across the road. Circle up the slope for a return in a beautiful forest of hemlock, holly, rhododendron, cucumber tree, oak, maple, and exceptionally large sassafras trees. (*USGS-FS Map:* Robbinsville)

Big Snowbird Trail (10.7 mi; USFS #64) (F)   **40**
CONNECTING TRAILS:
    Snowbird Mountain Trail (10.6 mi; USFS #415)   **41**
    Sassafras Creek Trail (2.5 mi; USFS #65)   **42**
    Middle Falls Trail (1.0 mi; USFS #64A)   **43**
    Burntrock Ridge Trail (1.7 mi; USFS #65A)   **44**
    Mitchell Lick Trail (1.5 mi: USFS #154)   **45**
TOTAL LENGTH AND DIFFICULTY: 26.3 mi combined, moderate to strenuous
    (elev change 2,739 ft)
SPECIAL FEATURES: RR history, remote, waterfalls
TRAILHEAD AND DESCRIPTION: Three major trails begin at Junction, the end of FR-75, deep in the enchanting backcountry of the Snowbird Mtns. The *Big Snowbird Trail* follows Snowbird Creek up and through the watershed for a gain of 2,600 ft to Big Junction at the Tennessee state line. The *Snowbird Mountain Trail* rejoins the *Big Snowbird Trail* near the top of the basin but follows a high ridge route on the S. *King Meadows Trail* also follows a high ridge route but is N of the basin: it ends at Hooper Bald after a 2,700-ft

elev gain, and can be connected with the other two trails by the 1.5-mi *Mitchell Lick Trail*. These trails provide loop options, but scarce water sources on the ridges limit convenient campsites. A rugged and remote area, it was once the home of Cherokee who found security here from the "Trail of Tears." Early white pioneers prospected for minerals and set up scattered grazing farms, but it was the timbering of the virgin forests of chestnut, poplar, and hemlock from 1928 to 1942 that severely altered the environment. Now healing from the scars of the Buffalo-Snowbird RR, you will see historic signs of both the old RR and pioneer life on the high plateaus. Access is as follows:

From the jct of US-129 and Kilmer Rd (SR-1127) in Robbinsville, go 3.3 mi to jct with Massey Branch Rd (SR-1116), from which it is 2.3 mi R to Cheoah district office, and bear L at the fork on SR-1127 for 2.2 mi to jct with Little Snowbird Rd (SR-1115). Turn L on SR-1115 and go another 2.2 mi to jct with Hard Slate Rd (SR-1121). Turn a sharp L at jct and continue for 1.0 mi to a bridge over Snowbird Creek. Look for "Dead End" sign and "One Way" sign on R at bridge over Little Snowbird Creek. This is Big Snowbird Rd (SR-1120), which becomes FR-75. Proceed on this gravel road for 6.0 mi to the Junction parking area, a total of 13.7 mi from Robbinsville and 12.7 mi from Cheoah district office.

Begin the trail on an old RR grade that crosses a number of earthen hummocks and goes under large poplars and maples. At 0.2 mi *Snowbird Mountain Trail* begins on the L. Continue on the *Big Snowbird Trail* on the old RR grade and L of cascading Snowbird Creek. The understory is composed of rhododendron, wild hydrangea, and sweet pepperbush; the forest trees are hemlock, birch, basswood, poplar, and cucumber tree. At 2.8 mi reach the jct of *Sassafras Creek Trail*, L, 250 yd beyond Sassafras Creek. (This trail is an alternate to the *Big Snowbird Trail*. If you choose this trail, ascend on an old RR grade for 0.7 mi to Sassafras Falls. After 0.1 mi beyond the falls, leave the old RR grade and turn R on *Burntrock Ridge Trail*. It goes 1.7 mi to jct with *Big Snowbird Trail*. [An old trail continues upstream and forks after 0.1 mi, the L going up Fall Branch for 1.0 mi, the other, *Sassafras Creek Trail*, up Sassafras Creek for 2.2 mi, and both to jct with the *Snowbird Mountain Trail*. Both may be abandoned and unmaintained.] Climb steeply on *Burntrock Ridge Trail* to Burnt Rock Ridge at 2.0 mi, descend to the mouth of Littleflat Branch, and rejoin *Big Snowbird Trail* at 2.5 mi.)

Continuing on *Big Snowbird Trail* and on an old RR grade, pass L of Big Falls at 3.9 mi. Reach an alternate trail, *Middle Falls Trail*, at 4.0 mi. (This trail, R, near Mouse Knob Branch, ascends steeply for 0.2 mi, and then descends gradually to the *Big Snowbird Trail* after 1.0 mi. It is an alternate that avoids 11 fordings of Snowbird Creek, which may be impossible to cross during high water.) If continuing on the *Big Snowbird Trail,* cross the creek frequently and arrive at beautiful Middle Falls and its large pool at 5.1 mi. At 5.3 mi the *Burntrock Ridge Trail* jct is L, at the mouth of Littleflat Branch.

After a few yd *Middle Falls Trail* rejoins *Big Snowbird Trail,* R. The *Big Snowbird Trail* continues to Upper Falls at 6.3 mi. Follow the trail past Meadow Branch, Rockbar Branch, a number of unnamed tributaries, Bearpen Branch, and two more tributaries before leaving the main stream, L, at 8.7 mi. Ascend steeply to jct with *Mitchell Lick Trail* at 9.0 mi. (*Mitchell Lick Trail* is a 1.5-mi connector to *King Meadows Trail* described below.) Follow the *Big Snowbird Trail* L, and at 9.3 mi jct with *Snowbird Mountain Trail,* L. (The *Snowbird Mountain Trail* is described below.) Continue the ascent along the Graham/Cherokee county line to the ridge top, the Tennessee–North Carolina boundary, and turn R at 9.8 mi. Follow the ridge NE, ascend to a knob and then to scenic Laurel Top (5,317 ft) at 10.3 mi. At 10.7 mi reach the end of the trail at Big Junction at Tellico Plains–Robbinsville Scenic Highway. It is approximately 11.5 mi NE to a jct with SR-1127 at Santeetlah Gap. A turn R (SE) on SR-1127 to SR-1115 and to FR-75 is about another 16.0 mi to the trail's origin as described. (See access above.) Backtrack, or return on one of the other two major trails, or arrange a vehicle switch to the Tellico Plains–Robbinsville Scenic Highway at Big Junction.

To hike the green-blazed *Snowbird Mountain Trail,* begin at the *Big Snowbird Trail,* L, 0.2 mi from Junction (as described above). On a graded trail cross two streams lined with birch, poplar, sassafras, spicebush (*Linders benzoin*), hemlock, rhododendron, and violets. Pass Wildcat Branch cove and reach Deep Gap (3,340 ft) at 1.3 mi. Turn R, ascend to Wildcat Knob on Sassafras Ridge at 2.5 mi, and continue to descend and ascend over and around knolls. At 3.2 mi is a USGS benchmark on a knoll (3,830 ft) and an old trail intersection (R to Snowbird Creek and L to Juanita Branch). At 5.0 mi reach Bee Gap (4,040 ft), where a faint trail, R, descends along Falls Branch to Sassafras Falls and the *Sassafras Creek Trail.* Continue traversing on gradual and sometimes steep grades through scattered grassy fields, hardwoods, laurel, flame azalea, and rhododendron. At 6.7 mi pass an old trail (*Sassafras Creek Trail,* which may be abandoned) R that leads 2.2 mi down Sassafras Creek to *Sassafras Creek Trail* and *Burntrock Ridge Trail* at Sassafras Falls. Ascend to Pantherflat Top (4,680 ft) at 8.5 mi and dip to a gap before ascending Dillard Top (4,680 ft) at 9.0 mi. The trail's end and jct with *Big Snowbird Trail* is at 10.6 mi. Return options include backtracking or descending on *Big Snowbird*

Trail for 9.3 mi to make a 20-mi loop to Junction parking area or taking *Mitchell Lick Trail* to jct with *King Meadows Trail* for 1.8 mi and a loop back to Junction for 18.4 mi. Another option is to continue on *Big Snowbird Trail* for 1.4 mi to jct with Tellico Plains–Robbinsville Scenic Highway. (*USGS-FS Maps:* Big Junction, Marble, McDaniel Bald, Santeetlah Creek) (Snowbird Area Trail Map, from the district ranger's office, is recommended.)

46 *King Meadows Trail (USFS #63) (F)*

LENGTH AND DIFFICULTY: 6.0 mi, strenuous (elev change 2,740 ft)

CONNECTING TRAIL:

(*Mitchell Lick Trail*)

TRAILHEAD AND DESCRIPTION: This yellow-blazed trail may be overgrown for the first 3.0 mi. (On some maps the entrance trailhead for *King Meadows Trail* and parts of its route from FR-75 in Junction may be different from the description below.) At the end of FR-75, at Junction, follow the *Big Snowbird Trail,* pass the jct with the *Snowbird Mountain Trail,* L, at 0.2 mi, and go upstream for another 0.2 mi to jct with the *King Meadows Trail,* R. (There may not be any signs here.) Cross Snowbird Creek and begin the ascent of Firescald Ridge (L of Owlcamp Branch). At 1.0 mi reach the ridge of the Snowbird Creek Divide in a hardwood forest. Continue the ascent, and at 1.9 mi make a long curve around a high knoll to reach Deep Gap (also known as Twin Oaks Gap) at 2.8 mi. Intersect with an old sled road, R and ahead, that was used by early settlers of the mountain plateaus. Continue ahead, ascend steeply, curve around Bee Knob, and arrive at King Meadows at 3.7 mi at the E knob. Pass through a partially grassy area formerly cleared of trees by early settlers. Ascend for 1.1 mi, leave the ridge, and pass over a saddle in the main curve around Queen Ridge at 5.1 mi. Enter a small gap and ascend to a more level area and jct with *Mitchell Lick Trail,* L, at 6.1 mi. (The *Mitchell Lick Trail,* an old jeep road, connects to the Snowbird trails described above. It descends to cross Sarvis Branch at 0.4 mi, follows Flat Ridge before descending to cross Snowbird Creek in a forest of hemlock and hardwoods, and reaches *Big Snowbird Trail* at 1.5 mi.) Ahead on the *King Meadows Trail* it is 0.4 mi to Hooper Bald (5,429 ft), the trail's end, and former jct with *Hooper Bald Trail.* Exit at the Tellico Plains–Robbinsville Scenic Highway. Backtrack, or have a second vehicle. It is approximately 10.0 mi NE on the highway to SR-1127 at Santeetlah Gap. A turn R (SE) on SR-1127 to SR-1115 and to FR-75 is about another 16.0 mi to trail's origin. (See access above.) (*USGS-FS Maps:* Santeetlah Creek, Big Junction)

SUPPORT FACILITIES: The nearest USFS campground (no hookups) is Horse

Cove, across from the entrance to the Joyce Kilmer Memorial Forest. It is 7.2 mi W on Kilmer Rd (SR-1127) from the jct with Little Snowbird Rd (SR-1115). Motels, shopping centers, restaurants, and other services are available in Robbinsville.

NOLTON RIDGE AREA (Graham and Swain Counties)

Bear CreekTrail (USFS #62) (F)   **47**

LENGTH AND DIFFICULTY: 6.4 mi round-trip, moderate to strenuous (elev change 1,820 ft)

TRAILHEAD AND DESCRIPTION: From the jct of US-129 and US-19/74 in Topton, take US-129 W for 4.1 mi to Bear Creek Rd (SR-1201) and turn R. (It is 7.6 mi ahead on US-129 to Robbinsville.) Cross over an old railroad, pass a log cottage and mobile home on the L, enter the edge of the forest, and park. Follow the road through a young forest of mixed hardwoods, hemlock, poplar, rhododendron, tag alder, laurel, yellow root, and a wide variety of ferns and flowers along the creek. At 0.3 mi cross an old bridge onto a seeded road. At 0.7 mi cross Dee Branch, and cross Bear Creek at 0.9 mi. From this point on, the trail is on the R side of Bear Creek, but it crosses Cherry Branch at 1.7 mi. Ruins of a few old houses are near the trail. The trail dead-ends at 3.2 mi at FR-259 near the Graham and Swain county line. (It formerly continued 4.8 mi farther to Sassafras Gap at the *AT*. But its current end is near enough to the new section of the *Bartram Trail* in Ledbetter Creek area that a connection could be made. The *Bartram Trail's* NW terminus is Cheoah Gap on the *AT*. See the *Bartram Trail* description in the beginning of chapter 2.) (*USGS-FS Map*: Hewitt)

CHEOAH MOUNTAIN AREA (Graham County)

Wauchecha Bald Trail (8.3 mi; USFS #47); Cody Gap Trail (0.4 mi; USFS #156) (F)   **48-49**

LENGTH AND DIFFICULTY: 8.7 mi combined, strenuous (elev change 2,425 ft)

SPECIAL FEATURES: rugged and remote

TRAILHEAD AND DESCRIPTION: From Robbinsville, jct of US-129 and NC-143, go W on US-129 for 7.0 mi and turn L on SR-1146 at Cheoah Point Campground. Follow a sign for 0.7 mi to the campground and park near the entrance where a blue-blazed trail begins at a telephone pole. Go up the ridge through white pines for 0.2 mi to US-129. Cross the highway, climb steeply under a power line, and reach Cheoah Mtn ridge at 0.7 mi. Leave the ridge at 1.8 mi, cross a stream at 2.2 mi, and return to the ridge at 2.7 mi.

Cross an old road at 2.8 mi. Vegetation is mixed hardwoods, rhododendron, hemlock, and laurel. Formerly called *Old Roughy Trail*, it lives up to its name in some of the knoll climbs. Descend slightly from the ridge and cross Hazelnut Spring at 4.2 mi. Continue to ascend and follow the S slope of the ridge at a number of points. Reach Locust Licklog Gap at 5.2 mi, and Haw Gap at 6.2 mi. At 6.9 mi there is a jct with a partially used FR, L. (It descends 4.0 mi to Yellow Creek Gap at Tuskeegee Rd [SR-1242] and jct with the *AT.*) Continue ahead to Wauchecha Bald (4,385 ft), the site of a former fire tower, at 7.1 mi. Here is a jct with the original *Wauchecha Bald Trail* (USFS # 47). Follow the trail for another 0.7 mi to a fork. The trail bears R for 0.5 mi to the *AT,* S, and at the fork the *Cody Gap Trail* bears L for 0.4 mi to the *AT,* N. Backtrack, or use the *AT* N for use of a second vehicle. (It is 2.4 mi N on the *AT* from Cody Gap to Yellow Creek Gap and Lower Tuskeegee Rd [SR-1242] between US-129 W and Tuskeegee community on NC-28 E.) (*USGS-FS Maps:* Robbinsville, Fontana Dam)

SECTION 2: HIGHLANDS RANGER DISTRICT

The Highlands Ranger District almost doubled its size when the 40,000-acre Balsam–Bonas Defeat lands were acquired in 1981, and named the Roy Taylor Forest in 1982. A scenic observation overlook in his honor is at mp 433.8 on the BRP. Congress appropriated $13.4 million for the purchase, identified by the USFS as probably the largest single holding suitable for the forest system in the eastern part of the nation. The new property, all in Jackson County, adjoins the Blue Ridge Parkway on the N boundary of the district. Mead Lake and Wolf Creek Lake, 90 mi of streams, and eight waterfalls are in the tract. Headwaters of Tanasee Creek, Wolf Creek, Caney Fork, and Moses Creek drain into the scenic Tuckasegee River from high ridges such as Rich Mtn and Coward Mtn. Among the peaks that are about a mile high are Coward Bald (5,187 ft), Gage Bald (5,574 ft), Charley Bald (5,473 ft), and Rich Mtn (5,583 ft).

In 1988 the Panthertown Valley tract was purchased for $8 million. Its 6,295 acres extend S of the Bonas–Defeat Area to include the headwaters of the Tuckasegee River and to the rim of Blue Ridge, a high range of the Tennessee Valley Divide. Owned by Liberty Life Insurance Company, the tract was placed on sale in 1986 without a buyer until Duke Power Company purchased it in 1988. Duke Power sold it to The Nature Conservancy with the exclusion of a transmission power corridor from the NW to the SE. Negotiations followed with congressional approval of the addition to the Nantahala National Forest.

A wider range of the district's 113,000 acres is in the SE corner of Macon County. Its boundaries extend to the Georgia state line and the Chattahoochee National Forest, and the South Carolina state line and the Sumter National Forest. Its western border is with the Wayah district, but E of Franklin. A wilderness area, the 3,030-acre Ellicott Rock Wilderness Area covers a rugged and beautiful area of the Chattooga River in a tri-state tract. Some of the state's major waterfalls are in the district. They include the highest, 411-ft Whitewater Falls; Dry Falls; Cullasaja Falls; Rainbow Falls; and Flat Creek Falls. A major mountain attraction is Whiteside Mtn (4,930 ft), 5.0 mi E of Highlands. Its sheer rock face is considered to be among the highest in eastern America. Another scenic mtn is Yellow Mtn (5,127 ft) with abundant wildflowers and blueberries. The district's major trail is the *Bartram*, which enters from Georgia S of Osage Mtn and ascends to the high country of Scaly Mtn, Whiterock Mtn, and Fishhawk Mtn before descending to Hickory Knoll Creek. The district's major recreational areas are Cliffside Lake and Vanhook Glade Campground (open April 1–October 31, no hookups), 4.5 mi W of Highlands on US-64. Camping is prohibited at Whiteside, Cullasaja Gorge, Cliffside, Whitewater Falls, and Balsam Lodge.

Hunting and fishing are allowed in the district except from May 1 to October 1. Panthertown Valley is a bear sanctuary. Mountain biking is allowed on specific trails in Panthertown Valley, Round Mtn, Little Yellow Mtn Gap, Blue Valley, Stewart Cove, Moss Knob, and Brush Creek. Wilderness is off-limits to bikers, but all gated forest roads are available unless otherwise posted. Equestrians may contact the district office for both special trails and regular multi-use hiking trails. There are also specific locations for ORV trails. Special trails for the physically disabled are at Balsam Lodge, Whitewater Falls, and fishing pier at Cliffside. The district's foot trail system does not have blazes except the *Bartram*, *Mountains-to-Sea*, and *Foothills Trails*. There are not signs at trailheads, but some trail networks have map display boards. The district has some abandoned trails, and at least 20 trails on its TIS inventory are either overgrown or in a planning stage of usage. *Henson Gap Loop Trail* (USFS #471) (2.7 mi), *Henson Branch Trail* (USFS #473) (2.5 mi), and 5.3 mi of *Blue Valley Loop Trail* (USFS #470) will be used for hikers and equestrians. A few trails are new; for example *Chattooga Cliffs Trail*, an extension upstream from the *Chattooga River Loop Trail*. The district has free maps and brochures available for recreational interests.

The district has 18.3 mi of the *Bartram Trail* (USFS #67) from FR-52 W to Buckeye Creek Rd. In addition, there are spur trails *Scaly Mountain Trail* (0.7 mi, USFS #67A) and *Jones Knob Trail* (0.3 mi, USFS #67B). (See *Bar-*

tram Trail description at the beginning of this chapter.) It has 12.9 mi of the *Mountains-to-Sea Trail* (USFS #440) from Old Bald Ridge as the BRP boundary E to BRP boundary at Haywood Gap. It has an additional access by the *Bearpen Gap Trail* (0.7 mi, USFS #442) from the parking area of Bearpen Gap on the BRP. (See *Mountains-to-Sea Trail* in chapter 16 for details.)

ADDRESS AND ACCESS: District Ranger, Highlands Ranger District, USFS, 2010 Flat Mtn Rd, Highlands, NC 28741; 704-526-3765, 2.0 mi E from Highlands on US-64 and on Flat Mtn Rd (N) 2.0 mi.

CLIFFSIDE LAKE AND VANHOOK GLADE RECREATION AREAS
(Macon County)

Cliffside Lake and Vanhook Glade recreation areas provide camping with 20 sites (no electrical hookups), picnicking, fishing, swimming, nature study, and hiking on interconnecting trails. Vegetation in the area includes a mature forest of hemlock, white pine, oak, maple, rhododendron, buckberry, and numerous species of wildflowers. Fish are chiefly rainbow and brook trout. In 1995 a fishing pier opened for the physically handicapped. (*USGS-FS Map*: Highlands)

ACCESS: In Highlands at the jct of US-64 and NC-28, proceed NW on US-64/NC-28 for 4.4 mi to the Cliffside entrance. Go 1.4 mi on FR-57. The Vanhook Glade Campground is on the highway 0.2 mi before the Cliffside entrance.

53- *Clifftop Vista Trail (1.5 mi; USFS #2A); Potts Memorial Trail (0.5 mi;*
56 *USFS #2B); Clifftop Nature Trail (1.1 mi; USFS #2F); Vanhook Trail (0.3 mi; USFS #2C) (F)*

LENGTH AND DIFFICULTY: 3.4 mi combined, easy to moderate

TRAILHEAD AND DESCRIPTION: From the parking area at Cliffside Lake go W on the road across Skitty Creek for a few yd, where the *Clifftop Vista Trail* begins at a sign. Go either R or L to the summit of the ridge. If R, pass or take as a side trail the *Potts Memorial Trail* to a white pine plantation. Continue in a circular direction and reach a gazebo at 1.8 mi, where views are provided of Flat Mtn and the Cullasaja River basin (and the Highlands Sewage Plant). Here is a jct with the *Clifftop Nature Trail* that goes R or L. To the R, the trail ends at FR-57, 0.4 mi from the Vanhook Glade Campground. To the L, it winds down the mtn on switchbacks to the point of origin at the parking area. The trail passes through trees and shrubs in a mixed hardwood forest with an understory of sourwood, buckberry, sweet pepperbush (*Clethra acuminata*), and dogwood. The *Vanhook Trail* is a connector trail from the Vanhook Glade Campground for 0.3 mi NW to FR-57 and another 0.6 mi on the road to Cliffside Lake.

Cliffside Loop Trail (0.8 mi; USFS #2); Homesite Road Trail (1.4 mi; USFS #443); Skitty Creek Trail (0.3 mi; USFS #2E) (F) **57-59**

LENGTH AND DIFFICULTY: 2.5 mi combined, easy

TRAILHEAD AND DESCRIPTION: From the parking area at Cliffside Lake walk to the loop on the road and circle the lake, or join the *Homesite Road Trail* for a longer hike. At the Cliffside Lake Dam follow Skitty Creek for a few yd before turning E through a hardwood forest. At an old road on which there are private homes, turn R and reach a gate at 1.4 mi at US-64. Dry Falls is R, 0.4 mi on US-64, and Bridal Veil Falls is L, 0.4 mi on US-64. Backtrack, or follow US-64, R (NW) for 0.2 mi to *Skitty Creek Trail*, R, and return via FR-57 to the lake area.

Dry Falls Trail (USFS #9) (F) **60**

LENGTH AND DIFFICULTY: 0.1 mi, easy

TRAILHEAD AND DESCRIPTION: From the parking area on US-64/NC-28 (1.0 mi E of the Cliffside Lake entrance), follow the signs and descend to the 70-ft waterfall with a trail running underneath. Rare plants are in the area, watered by a constant mist from the updraft in the Cullasaja Gorge (in Cherokee "cullasaja" means honey or sugar water). The surrounding stone is schist and gneiss, between 500 million and 000 million years old.

CHINQUAPIN MOUNTAIN AND GLEN FALLS AREA (Macon County)

Chinquapin Mountain Trail (3.2-mi round-trip; USFS #3); **61-**
Glen Falls Trail (2.8-mi round-trip; USFS #8) (F) **62**

LENGTH AND DIFFICULTY: 6.0 mi combined, moderate to strenuous

TRAILHEAD AND DESCRIPTION: From the jct of US-64 and NC-28/106 in Highlands, go SW on NC-106 for 1.7 mi to a sign for Glen Falls Scenic Area. Turn L and proceed on a gravel road for 1.0 mi to the parking area. Follow the *Chinquapin Trail* sign; bear R at the fork with *Glen Falls Trail*. Descend, cross East Fork a number of times, and pass through hardwoods, conifers, and rhododendron. Rock-hopping is necessary at some of the stream crossings. At 0.5 mi reach a jct with other access points from NC-106. Ascend gradually on switchbacks, pass a spur trail to views of Blue Valley, and reach the summit of Chinquapin Mtn (4,160 ft) at 1.6 mi. Back-track. (Or, continue along the top of the ridge and start to descend. At a T intersection and sign turn R and make a short loop before intersecting with trail up Chinquapin Mtn. There are not any blazes but several signs directing hikers to scenic overlooks and the trail back to Glen Falls parking area.)

For the *Glen Falls Trail* follow the same directions as above to the parking area. Enter the trail by following gray blazes and bear L. (To the R is the *Chinquapin Mtn Trail*.) Descend steeply through mixed hardwoods past three major cascades. Spur trails lead to impressive views from the main trail. Descend to FR-79C, Blue Valley Rd, at 1.4 mi. Return by the same route, or use a second vehicle placed on Blue Valley Rd, off NC-28, near the Georgia state line. (It is SR-1618 before it becomes FR-79C). (*USGS-FS Map:* Highlands)

WEST BLUE VALLEY AREA (Macon County)

63- *West Fork Trail (0.9 mi; USFS #444); Hurrah Ridge Trail (0.6 mi; USFS*
64 *#4) (F)*

LENGTH AND DIFFICULTY: 1.9-mi round-trip and combined, moderate

TRAILHEAD AND DESCRIPTION: These two nonblazed spur trails form a loop with the yellow-blazed *Bartram Trail*. From US-64 and NC-28 jct in Highlands, take NC-28 S for 6.0 mi to Blue Valley Rd (SR-1618), which becomes FR-79. Turn R on SR-1618 and go 6.0 mi to West Fork of Overflow Creek to park. Begin with the *West Fork Trail* on the R before crossing Overflow Creek; ascend on a rocky and frequently wet trail for 0.9 mi to the *Bartram Trail*. (On the *Bartram Trail*, R, it is 0.7 mi to Osage Mtn Overlook at NC-106.) Turn L on the *Bartram Trail* and go 0.4 mi. Turn L again on *Hurrah Ridge Trail*. (The *Bartram Trail* continues on for 2.9 mi to Hale Ridge Rd, FR-7.) Descend on the *Hurrah Ridge Trail* through a dry area with mixed hardwoods and hemlock and cross Overflow Creek to the parking area. Other vegetation on the trail is rhododendron, laurel, white pine, ferns, and wildflowers. (*USGS-FS Maps:* Highlands, Scaly Mtn)

CHATTOOGA RIVER AREA (Jackson and Macon Counties)

65- *Bad Creek Trail (3.1 mi; USFS #6); Fork Mountain Trail (6.4 mi) (F)*
66 LENGTH AND DIFFICULTY: 12.6-mi round-trip; combined, easy to strenuous
CONNECTING TRAILS:
    (*Ellicott Rock Trail*)
    (*Chattooga Trail*)
    (*East Fork Trail*)

SPECIAL FEATURES: Ellicott Wilderness Area, historic markers

TRAILHEAD AND DESCRIPTION: From the jct of US-64 and NC-28 in Highlands, drive SE on Main St, which becomes Horse Cove Rd (SR-1603) for 4.6 mi down the mountain to the end of the pavement and a jct with Bull Pen Rd (SR-1178). Turn R and go 3.0 mi to the bridge over the Chattooga River and continue for 2.7 mi to a small parking area and signboard for *Bad Creek Trail*, R. (The Ellicott Wilderness Area is now 100 ft from the Bull Pen Rd. The trail is no longer maintained.) Follow the faded-brown-blazed trail through a forest of hemlock, white pine, and laurel on an old forest road. Cross a stream at 0.2 mi and enter a rhododendron grove. Turn R at 0.6 mi, reach a ridge crest at 0.8 mi, curve L on the ridge slope, but return to the ridge at 1.3 mi. Reach the former Ellicott Wilderness Area boundary at 1.4 mi. Turn R from an old road to a foot trail in beds of galax and huckleberry. At 1.8 mi the Chattooga River is audible; jct with the *Fork Mountain Trail* at 1.9 mi, L. Continue ahead and descend on 10 switchbacks to a grove of large hemlock by the Chattooga River at 3.0 mi. (Here is a jct with the E terminus of *Ellicott Rock Trail* requiring a river fording.) Proceed downstream for 0.1 mi to Ellicott Rock where a simple "NC" has been chiseled. Ten ft downstream is Commissioner Rock, the true intersection of North Carolina, Georgia, and South Carolina. Carved on this rock is "LAT 35 AD 1813 NC+SC." Both rocks are named for surveyors who first surveyed the state lines. Backtrack, or continue downstream in South Carolina on the *Chattooga Trail* for 1.8 mi to jct with *East Fork Trail*, which ends at the Walhalla Fish Hatchery after 2.4 mi. (See chapter 1, section 1 in *Hiking South Carolina Trails*, listed in the bibliography of this book.)

The *Fork Mountain Trail* (also known as *Sloan Bridge Trail*) leaves the *Bad Creek Trail* in North Carolina but after 265 yd enters South Carolina and follows a well-graded trail that weaves in and out of more than 20 coves and as many spur ridges. Blazed a rust color, it follows a S-side slope in hardwoods and laurel. Cross a small stream at 0.5 mi and at approx 0.8 mi reenter North Carolina. Pass a rock formation at 1.0 mi, and at 1.2 mi and 1.4 mi cross the dual forks of Bad Creek where the rocks are moss covered, the hemlocks tall, and the fetterbush thick. Pass a huge yellow poplar at 1.5 mi (near the reentry to South Carolina) and another large poplar at 2.0 mi. Indian pipe and pink lady slippers are along the trail. Cross an old woods road at 2.5 mi and a ridge crest at 3.0 mi. Enter an arbor of laurel at 3.3 mi for 0.3 mi. Pass through a fern glen in an open forest and enter a grove of exceptionally large hemlocks and poplars to cross Indian Camp Branch at 3.9 mi. At 5.2 mi cross a ridge into a beautiful open forest of hardwoods.

Cross Slatten Branch at 5.7 mi near good campsites. Walk through an unforgettable virgin grove of rhododendron and laurel and cross more small streams. Arrive at SC-107 at 6.4 mi. It is 0.1 mi, R, across the East Fork of the Chattooga River bridge to the Sloan Bridge picnic area. (At the E corner of the picnic area is the *Foothills Trail* described below.) If using a second vehicle for the return to the *Bad Creek Trail* entrance in North Carolina, drive N on SC-107 for 1.7 mi and turn L on Bull Pen Rd (SR-1100) for 2.6 mi. (It is 6.3 mi on SC/NC-107 N to Cashiers.) (*USGS-FS Map:* Cashiers)

67 Slick Rock Trail (USFS #11) (F)

LENGTH AND DIFFICULTY: 0.2-mi round-trip, easy

TRAILHEAD AND DESCRIPTION: Follow the directions given above from Highlands, turn R on Bull Pen Rd (SR-1178), go 0.7 mi, and park on a narrow road shoulder, R. An unmarked trail ascends for 0.1 mi to a large rock formation with scenic views W into the Chattooga River basin. A wide variety of mosses and lichens grow in the apertures. This scenic spot was the site for the filming of *The Mating Game.* (*USGS-FS Map:* Highlands)

68 Ellicott Rock Trail (USFS #431) (F)

LENGTH AND DIFFICULTY: 7.0-mi round-trip, moderate

SPECIAL FEATURE: Ellicott Wilderness Area

TRAILHEAD AND DESCRIPTION: From Highlands follow the directions given above, turn R on SR-1178, and go 1.7 mi. (Pass primitive Ammons campsite on the R at 1.1 mi.) Turn R onto a parking spur with a trail sign. Hike an old road with an even grade for a gradual descent to Ellicott Rock Wilderness Area boundary at 2.0 mi. The trail begins as a set of steps to discourage ATVs because motorized vehicles and mountain biking in wilderness areas are prohibited. The forest is mainly hardwoods with mixed sections of hemlock. At 3.0 mi bear L off the old road, descend steeply, and reach the Chattooga River at 3.5 mi. (There are two descents into the gorge. The straight, longer trail is recommended. The shorter trail, L, has a number of large deadfalls.) To locate Ellicott Rock, a survey marker for the North Carolina–South Carolina–Georgia state boundaries, ford the river (wading is always necessary, and impossible during high water), and go downstream for approximately 0.1 mi. Exploratory trails in the area can be confusing, and another rock, Commissioner Rock (10 ft downstream from Ellicott Rock), is the true boundary jct of the three states. Commissioner Rock bears the inscription "LAT 35 AD 1813 NC+SC." Both of these rocks were named for early surveyors of the state lines. The vegetation in this area is mixed hardwoods with scattered pine, hemlock, and thick rhododendron. Backtrack, or hike out on the 3.1-mi *Bad Creek Trail* described above. (*USGS-FS Maps:* Highlands, Cashiers)

Chattooga River Trail (0.7 mi; USFS #432); Chattooga River Loop Trail (1.0 mi; USFS #433); Chattooga Cliffs Trail (3.5 mi)

LENGTH AND DIFFICULTY: 1.7 mi (loop); 3.5 mi (linear); moderate

TRAILHEADS AND DESCRIPTION: None of these trails is the same as the *Chattooga Trail* in South Carolina and Georgia downstream. To access the first two trails follow the directions given above from Highlands, turn R on Bull Pen Rd (SR-1178) at the paved end of Horse Cove Rd, and drive 3.0 mi to park at the one-way Chattooga River bridge. Enter the trail by an information board and sign honoring the YCC. To the R the cascading river has huge boulders, large potholes, sandbars, and pools. Trees on the trail are oak, maple, white pine, beech, and hemlock. There are two species of rhododendron. Ascend on switchbacks among dense forest understory. Cross a small stream at 0.4 mi and reach a jct, L, with the *Chattooga River Loop Trail* at 0.7 mi.

(Ahead and upriver begins the *Chattooga Cliffs Trail*. Under construction in 1995 and 1996, it parallels the river, crosses Holly Branch at 0.6 mi, and jct with an access trail, L, at 1.0 mi. To the E of the trail are Chattooga Cliffs on the W side of Bull Pen Mtn. [The 1.2-mi access trail follows an old road for moderate walking among wildflowers and ferns to a ridge and saddle at Whiteside Cove Rd, SR-1606. On the road it is 0.8 mi L, SW, to the jct with Bull Pen Rd and Horse Cove Rd. On the R, NE, it is 2.7 mi to the *Chattooga Cliffs Trail's* N trailhead at the Whiteside Cove Cemetery. The N trailhead is also accessible from NC-107 in Cashiers SW on Whiteside Cove Rd for about 3.9 mi.] Continuing upriver the *Chattooga Cliffs Trail* at 1.5 mi will cross a bridge, lowered in place by helicopter, at Norton Mill Creek. Cascades on the creek and a rushing flumelike section of the Chattooga River make this one of the trail's highlights. At 1.8 mi the trail will cross an old road and soon begin to ascend away from the Chattooga Cliffs. Near the trail's end it descends to a gap S of the cemetery.)

To complete the *Chattooga River Loop Trail*, ascend and parallel the *Chattooga River Trail* for a return to Bull Pen Rd. At 0.3 mi enter an old logging road and reach a large parking area above Bull Pen Rd at 0.8 mi. To the R is an access to Bull Pen Rd for vehicles, but to the L is a narrow trail that descends to the *Chattooga River Trail* and 90 yd R to the bridge and completion of the loop. (*USGS-FS Maps:* Highlands, Cashiers)

WHITEWATER RIVER AREA (Transylvania and Jackson Counties)

72 *Whitewater Falls Trail (USFS #437)*

LENGTH AND DIFFICULTY: 2.0 mi round-trip, easy

SPECIAL FEATURES: Whitewater Falls, geology

TRAILHEAD AND DESCRIPTION: From the jct of US-64 and NC-281 in Sapphire, take NC-281 (formerly SR-1171) for 8.6 mi S to the Whitewater Falls Scenic Area. Turn L for 0.3 mi to a parking area with views of Lake Jocassee. (Camping or use of alcoholic beverages is not allowed within the area surrounding the parking area, trails, and Whitewater Falls.) Hike for 0.2 mi on a paved trail to an overlook of the spectacular 411-ft Upper Whitewater River Falls. (The trail is user-friendly for the physically disabled to the overlook.) (The *Foothills Trail* crosses here; see below.) Turn L at the overlook to Tongue Rock L at 100 yd. Follow an old road to the river at 0.6 mi, ford it (unless the water is too high for safety), and go upstream for another 0.4 mi. Backtrack. Picnicking is allowed but no camping in the area. (Use extreme care in exploring downstream because lives have been lost at the falls.) Vegetation in the area includes white pine, hemlock, oak, maple, thimbleberry, rhododendron, and woodland sunflowers. (*USGS-FS Map:* Cashiers)

73 *Foothills Trail (USFS #436) (F)*

LENGTH AND DIFFICULTY: 4.0 mi, moderate to strenuous (elev change 1,240 ft)

SPECIAL FEATURES: Whitewater River Falls, hemlock forest

TRAILHEAD AND DESCRIPTION: The white-blazed 85.2-mi *Foothills Trail* passes through the Highlands district for 4.0 mi from its trailheads in Oconee State Park and Jones Gap State Park in South Carolina. From the W, entrance is necessary at the Sloan Bridge picnic area on SC-107, 8.0 mi S of Cashiers. Begin on the E side of the highway and ascend gently the W slope of the Chattooga Ridge. After 1.0 mi leave Sumter National Forest and enter North Carolina. After 0.3 mi begin a switchback, reach a ridge crest for partial views of Lake Jocassee, and start a decline. At 0.7 mi descend steeply. Reach the gap between Grassy Knob and Round Mtn at 1.1 mi in a setting of ferns, rhododendron, and wildflowers. Turn R at 1.3 mi on an old woods road, cross a small stream, and parallel a tributary of Whitewater River. At 2.3 mi turn sharply R, off the old woods road, and on a footpath ascend to NC-281 at 2.5 mi. (It is 7.8 mi L on NC-281 to the town of Sapphire, and 0.8 mi R to the Whitewater Falls Scenic Area.) Cross the road and guardrail for a descent to the bank of the Whitewater River. Follow an old road jointly with the *Whitewater Falls Trail* to the main overlook of Upper Whitewater Falls at 3.0 mi. (To the R is a paved [wheelchair-accessible] 0.2-mi trail to the parking area, which has rest rooms.) Follow the white-blazed *Foothills Trail* down the steps; after the first 100 steps is another superb view of the 411-ft falls and cascades. Descend steeply and cross the river on a new steel bridge, lowered there by helicopter in 1993. Cross Corbin Creek (where the bridge was lost to flooding in 1994, but should be replaced by the time this book is published), and enter a damp evergreen understory of tall hemlock. Leave North Carolina at 4.0 mi. Backtrack, or continue downstream to a campsite at 5.1 mi (6.1 mi if including the first 1.0 mi in South Carolina). The *Foothills Trail* turns sharply L, but a spur trail leads downstream to a gravel road for 0.5 mi to the Lower Falls—a dangerous area anytime and extremely so when wet or slippery (*USGS-FS Map* for this description: Cashiers). The *Foothills Trail* returns to North Carolina for 2.5 mi in the Highlands Ranger District before continuing on its route E through properties of the Duke Power Company. (For a detailed description of the *Foothills Trail* see *Hiking South Carolina Trails* by Allen de Hart, Globe Pequot Press; 800-243-0495; and *Guide to the Foothills Trail* by the Foothills Trail Conference, Box 3041, Greenville, SC 29602; 803-232-2681.)

HORSEPASTURE RIVER AREA (Transylvania County)

Horsepasture River Trail (F)   **74**

    LENGTH AND DIFFICULTY: 2.8 mi round-trip, moderate to strenuous

    SPECIAL FEATURE: outstanding series of waterfalls

    TRAILHEAD AND DESCRIPTION: On October 27, 1986, this 435-acre tract officially became part of the National Wild and Scenic River system. Earlier the area was threatened by an out-of-state power company that planned to destroy the water flow of the magnificent falls. Local conservationists immediately began a grassroots campaign, and legislators and state and federal organizations and agencies saved the Horsepasture River Falls.

    From the jct of US-64 and NC-281 in Sapphire (10.1 mi E of Cashiers), turn S on NC-281 and go 1.8 mi to a parking area on the L side of the highway by the Horsepasture River. Climb down any of a number of steep rocky spurs to the main trail downstream and pass Drift Falls at 0.1 mi. The ungraded trail requires considerable back and neck bending as it passes through a rugged concourse of rhododendron and rocks. Each trail spur provides outstanding views of waterfalls. Cross a small stream at 0.3 mi and reach Turtleback (also called Umbrella) Falls at 0.4 mi. At 0.6 mi Rainbow

Falls thunders 150 ft into a deep pool, spraying a mist against the canyon walls to form a rainbow when the sun is right. On the high side of the trail wildflowers grow in profusion. A creek crosses the trail at 1.0 mi. Ascend for 240 yd and bear sharply R to descend again to the riverside at Stairway Falls at 1.4 mi. Backtrack. (Beyond this point extreme care should be used in the 0.8-mi treacherous descent to Windy Falls, an extraordinary group of falls and cascades.) (*USGS-FS Map*: Reid)

YELLOW MOUNTAIN AREA (Macon and Jackson Counties)

75 *Yellow Mountain Trail (USFS #31) (F)*

LENGTH AND DIFFICULTY: 9.4 mi round-trip, strenuous (elev change 1,047 ft)

SPECIAL FEATURE: vistas from Yellow Mtn summit

TRAILHEAD AND DESCRIPTION: From the jct of US-64 and NC-28 in Highlands, proceed E on US-64 for 2.6 mi to Buck Creek Rd (SR-1538, also called Cole Mtn Rd), and turn L. (From Cashiers W on US-64 it is 7.4 mi to Buck Creek Rd.) Go 2.2 mi to Cole Gap (4,200 ft) and park on the L side of the road by FR-4535; trail sign is R. The nonblazed trail ascends gradually on an old woods road through hardwoods and abundant wildflowers. Orchids, trillium, false foxglove, Solomon's seal, hellebore, starry campion, and a number of rare species such as wolfsbane (*Aconitum reclinatum*) and grass-of-Parnassus (*Parnassia asarifolia*) line the trail. After 0.4 mi, narrow spur trails, L, extend a few yd to the Western Cliffs for scenic vistas of Round Mtn and Panther Mtn. There is a small spring at 0.6 mi, R. Reach Cole Mtn (4,600 ft) at 0.9 mi, descend gradually, and begin a steep climb on switchbacks to Shortoff Mtn at 1.4 mi. Skirt S of the first peak for scenic views. Descend to gap and ascend S of second peak (5,000 ft); descend, and at 2.0 mi bear L (N) of the third peak to follow along the Jackson-Macon county line. Descend to a gap at 2.5 mi, and ascend to Goat Knob (4,640 ft) at 2.7 mi. Descend steeply, join an old road, turn R, and reach Yellow Mtn Gap at 3.2 mi. Continue on the graded trail up switchbacks bordered by laurel, rhododendron, berries, and hardwoods to the summit of Yellow Mtn (5,127 ft) at 4.7 mi. Spectacular views from Yellow Mtn are of Standing Indian, Whiterock Mtn, and Albert Mtn. The old fire tower was reconstructed in the 1990s and in 1992 was recognized as a national historic lookout. Part of it is locked and used for two-way radio transmissions. The rock formations are composed mainly of gneiss. Backtrack. (*USGS-FS Maps*: Highlands, Glenville)

76 *Silver Run Trail (USFS #435) (F)*

LENGTH AND DIFFICULTY: 0.2 mi round-trip, easy

TRAILHEAD AND DESCRIPTION: From Cashiers at the jct of US-64 and NC-107, take NC-107 S for 4.0 mi and park on the L side of the highway. Descend on a graded trail into a damp forest of rhododendron, hemlock, and poplar. Cross a stream on a log footbridge to beautiful 30-ft Silver Run Falls, wading pool, and small beach. It is part of the headwaters of the famous Upper Falls of the Whitewater River described above. Backtrack. (*USGS-FS Map:* Cashiers)

EAST FORK AREA (Jackson County)

Whiteside Mountain Trail (USFS #70) (F) 77

LENGTH AND DIFFICULTY: 2.0 mi, moderate

TRAILHEAD AND DESCRIPTION: A national recreation trail, it was completed in 1974. From Cashiers go W on US-64 to the Jackson and Macon county line, and turn L on Wildcat Ridge Rd (SR 1600). Go 1.0 mi to the Whiteside Mtn sign, L, into a parking area. (From Highlands jct of US-64/NC-28, go E on US-64 5.4 mi and turn R on SR-1600.) From the parking area begin the hike up steps. Ascend on a (formerly gray-blazed) trail to the ridge at 0.2 mi and turn L. At 0.7 mi reach Devils Point, the summit (4,930 ft), for magnificent views of the Chattooga River Valley, Timber Ridge, Blackrock Mtn, Yellow Mtn, and Terrapin Mtn. Follow the precipitous edge of sheer cliffs, 400 to 600 ft high, to an overlook at 1.1 mi. Begin the descent on an old road to the parking area to complete the loop. The granite landmark is composed of feldspar, quartz, and mica. Vegetation consists of oak, birch, maple, rhododendron, laurel, flame azalea, sweet pepperbush, abundant wildflowers, and scattered conifers. (*USGS-FS Map:* Highlands)

PANTHERTOWN VALLEY AREA (Jackson County)

The Panthertown Valley area has a honeycomb of old RR grades and logging roads constructed in the past century. Some are completely filled with forest growth and not passable, others are partially filled with young trees and expansive ground covers of blueberry bushes and greenbriers. A few roads, more recently used but now closed to vehicular traffic, are the sources for trails described ahead. In 1996 the USFS had not completed an inventory of potential trails for the valley area or the Flat Creek drainage, which was formerly owned by Liberty Life Insurance Company before the purchase of the Panthertown Valley tract. Use of old roads on the high elevations of Blue Ridge, the S and SE boundary, W at Laurel Knob, E to Hogback Mtn and Toxaway Mtn Lookout, is particularly uncertain because of residential

development. Hikers will discover a number of paths cut through the underbrush either to connect roads (trails) or to open potential loops. The paths
have been made by volunteer citizens, who sometimes were not authorized
to make these changes. It is recommended that hikers who plan to leave the
old roads where evidence of usage is in question should have both topo
maps and a compass. (Request Big Ridge and Lake Toxaway USGS modified
maps from the district office. Maps dated 1946 are not satisfactory.)

Purchased in 1988, the 6,295-acre Panthertown Valley tract is one of the
most unique natural areas in North Carolina. There are upland bogs, outcroppings, grassy meadows, rare botanical sites, 20 miles of mtn trout
streams, and elevations ranging from 3,000 ft to 4,777 ft. Because this valuable tract is now protected, thanks to congressional help and the wisdom of
The Nature Conservancy, the property has been recommended as a national
natural landmark. Users will find the valley and the rim of the ridges around
it offer solace, challenge, education, and recreation. If the user has only one
choice, walk down the road from Salt Rock Gap for 0.3 mi to the first ledge
on the L and watch the sunrise over the valley or the sunset cast color and
shadows on the fissures and crevices of Big and Little Green Mtns.

78- *Salt Rock Gap Trail (0.8 mi; USFS #448) (F, H); Deep Gap Trail (1.1 mi;*
85 *USFS #449) (F); Panthertown Creek Trail (1 mi; USFS #450) (F, H);*
Sassafras Gap Trail (5.5 mi; USFS #448A) (F, B); Greenland Creek Trail
(2.2 mi; USFS #451) (F, B); Schoolhouse Falls Trail (0.1 mi; USFS #462)
(F); Hogback Mountain Trail (2.9 mi; USFS #453) (F, H); Big Green
Mountain Trail (1.2 mi; USFS #469) (F, H)

SPECIAL FEATURES: scenic valley, cliffsides, waterfalls, plant life, geology,
    fishing

TRAILHEADS AND DESCRIPTION: From US-64 (1.9 mi E of Cashiers) turn N
on Cedar Creek Rd (SR-1120) and ascend 2.2 mi to turn R on Breedlove Rd
(SR-1121). Drive 3.5 mi to the end of the road at a USFS gate and information sign. (Other accesses are described below.)

Salt Rock Gap Trail descends on a gravel road. At 0.3 mi is a cliffside with
sweeping E views of Panthertown Valley. Particularly impressive are views of the
Big Green Mtn (nearest) and Little Green Mtn (beyond) granite walls. Bristly
locust, sweet-shrub, mosses, and wildflowers border the trail in a forest of hardwoods and pines. At 0.6 mi is a jct, R, with *Deep Gap Trail.*

(*Deep Gap Trail* is an easy walk on the mountainside to follow upstream
alongside Frolictown Creek. After 0.1 mi past pines is a grazing field bordered with autumn olive, an apple tree on the L, and pink lady slippers on

the R side of the road. The road slightly descends to a jct with *Panthertown Creek Trail*, L, at 0.3 mi. Continue ahead 0.1 mi to rock-hop Frolictown Creek at the top of a waterfall. From here the trail gently ascends to the forest boundary. Within 80 yd from the creek crossing, the trail passes through an incredible carpet of galax under tall hardwoods. After another 0.7 mi the trail ends at a locked forest gate in Deep Gap. Backtrack to *Panthertown Creek Trail*, R. After 0.3 mi rock-hop Panthertown Creek near the W wall of Big Green Mtn. [To the immediate L is a 0.4-mi unnamed shortcut downstream to an extraordinary cascade with sloping rock formations in pastel colors, a wide pool, and white sandbars. The arbored trail connects with *Hogback Mountain Trail*, described below.] Continue upstream on the *Panthertown Creek Trail*. After 90 yd, R, is a large roofed shed and grassy meadow for camping. Other campsites are upstream under tall pines toward the granite wall of Big Green Mtn. At 1.1 mi the trail ends at the creekside. Backtrack. [An observant hiker may notice a blue-flagged unnamed and unauthorized connector trail L, NE, which ascends a hollow for 0.5 mi to jct with *Big Green Mountain Trail*, described below.])

If continuing on the *Salt Rock Gap Trail* and passing the *Deep Creek Trail* jct, descend 0.2 mi to a four-way trail intersection. Here is the end of *Salt Rock Gap Trail*. To the L is *Sassafras Gap Trail*, whose NE trailhead is on Rock Bridge Rd (SR-1140) outside Panthertown Valley; ahead is *Greenland Creek Trail*, whose E trailhead is at Cold Mtn Rd (SR-1301); and to the R is *Hogback Mountain Trail*, which descends at a boundary gate on Hogback Mtn.

To hike the *Hogback Mountain Trail* turn R, descend through pines, pass flat and grassy sites for camping near the white sand pathway, and cross an old bridge over Panthertown Creek at 0.3 mi (1.1 mi from the parking area at the Salt Rock Gap parking area). This area is sometimes flooded and debris may be washed against the birch, rhododendron, and bush honeysuckle. (Immediately to the R, after crossing the bridge, is the 0.4-mi shortcut trail, mentioned above, to a scenic spot on Panthertown Creek. Go upstream 0.1 mi among rhododendron to the waterfall and large pool.) Backtrack. To continue on the *Hogback Mountain Trail* follow the grassy road ahead. After 0.1 mi there is a wildlife clearing on the L, and the old road is darkened by dense white pine. Running cedar is part of the forest floor. Peaceful and serene, this section has only the soughing sound of the pines. At 0.9 mi on the trail cross a small stream and begin to ascend. Pass a grassy road, L, and ascend steeply among yellow and black birch, maple, and oak. Reach a grassy four-way old road intersection at 1.7 mi. (To the L the old road goes 1.2 mi to the USFS boundary and a private road. It follows a generally even contour and passes the headwaters of Greenland Creek.)

(To the R of the intersection is *Big Green Mountain Trail*. It follows a grassy old road among hardwoods, passes an old road, R, and enters a clearing at 0.5 mi. It descends to a saddle at 0.7 mi [where on the L is the jct of the 0.4-mi unnamed shortcut up from *Panthertown Creek Trail*]. Follow straight ahead on the old road to a knoll, slightly descend, and reach a fork at 1.1 mi. [To the R the trail ends after 100 yd in a cul-de-sac.] To the L from the fork is a 0.1-mi access to a breathtaking view from the W face of Big Green Mtn. Scrub pine, mountain laurel, heather, and mosses cling to the precipitous granite. Backtrack to *Hogback Mountain Trail*.)

To continue on the *Hogback Mountain Trail*, turn R at the four-way jct and begin to ascend. The forest is chiefly cherry, oak, birch, maple, and scattered pines. Blueberry is the dense understory, and a few pink shell azaleas are on the higher elevations. At 2.2 mi turn W and ascend a knoll. Descend to cross a stream with a hollow log culvert in a rhododendron thicket. At 2.9 mi is a locked USFS gate at the E base of Little Hogback Mtn; the current end of the trail is at a residential development. Backtrack to the *Salt Rock Gap Trail* intersection with *Greenland Creek Trail*. On the way back and after crossing the old bridge at Panthertown Creek, hikers may see a shortcut trail to the R. (It goes through a grove of white pine and grazing fields for 0.2 mi to *Greenland Creek Trail*.)

Follow the old road of *Greenland Creek Trail* past a small cascade, L, and into a boggy area at 0.2 mi. After passage through a white pine grove, reach a scenic area on the R at 0.8 mi. Here is a low waterfall where white sheets of water flow into the valley's largest pool. An open-sided but roofed shed is near the pool. At 0.9 mi turn R to cross an old bridge over Panthertown Creek. Immediately to the L is a 30-yd path to the confluence of Panthertown Creek and Greenland Creek, whose waters become the Tuckasegee River. Follow an eroded road upstream with Greenland Creek on the L, and cross an old bridge at 1.4 mi. To the R, on either side of the bridge, is the 0.1-mi *Schoolhouse Falls Trail*. The waterfall and pool is one of the valley's most attractive and popular places to visit. To return to the *Greenland Creek Trail*, either backtrack or ascend 0.1 mi to the L for rejoining the road. (After 120 yd from this access there is an unauthorized shortcut of 130 yd up an embankment to avoid a switchback in the road.) Follow the road to the top of the mountain for 0.5 mi to reach the end of the trail at a locked USFS gate and small parking area at 2.2 mi (3.0 mi from Salt Rock Gap parking area). Vehicle access here from US-64 at Lake Toxaway is N on NC-281 for 0.9 mi to a turn L (W) on Cold Mtn Rd (SR-1301) for 5.6 mi.

For hiking the *Sassafras Gap Trail* from the jct of *Salt Rock Gap Trail*, *Hogback Mountain Trail*, and *Greenland Creek Trail*, ascend slightly on an old road that is below the S wall of Blackrock Mtn. The road is parallel E with the *Greenland Creek Trail* but higher on the mountainside. Pass R of a cliff-side at 0.4 mi, and at 1.6 mi begin a turn N and then W among coves filled with rhododendron and mountain laurel. Ascend gradually to the E base of Blackrock Mtn at 2.5 mi. Turn E on the old road, slightly descend, and turn N again to cross Honeycamp Branch at 3.3 mi. From here pass E of Sassafras Mtn (4,430 ft). (Hikers may see exploratory trails that ascend to Blackrock Mtn or Sassafras Mtn. These routes lead SW along the crest to access Salt Rock Gap and the parking area for a loop. An example is a narrow path beginning at the L side of the gate at the Salt Rock Gap parking area. It ascends to a ledge of Salt Rock and follows some old roads for 1.0 mi to Blackrock Mtn. Hardwoods, wildflowers, ferns, and pink shell azaleas are distinctive along the way. A topo map or advice from the district ranger's office is recommended.) Reach Sassafras Gap at 3.9 mi. From here and beyond Rattlesnake Knob are views (particularly good in the wintertime) of Tuckasegee River basin, Cold Mtn (S), and Shelton Pisgah Mtn (E). Pass through saplings of birch and sassafras and blueberry bushes. At 4.8 mi the trail follows former FR-4661, now grass seeded and constructed with Cowetta drains. Among hardwoods, rhododendron, and pine descend to tank traps at Rock Bridge Rd (SR-1140). (Parking space for one vehicle in 1996.) Vehicle access here from NC-381 is 0.8 mi, 9.5 mi S to US-64 at Lake Toxaway, and 1.5 mi N on NC-281 to Tanasee Creek Reservoir and Tanasee Creek Rd. (*USGS-FS Maps*: Big Ridge, Lake Toxaway)

(At the *Sassafras Gap Trail* trailhead on Rock Bridge Rd, described above, the road is an access to two other trails, both in a planning stage. To reach the first, drive 0.8 mi farther W on Rock Bridge Rd to the top of a ridge at a road jct. Here Rock Bridge Rd ends, but FR-4662 continues ahead. To the L is a private road, but between it and FR-4662 is *Flat Creek Trail* [USFS #447] [F, **86** H]. The trail follows an old road. To reach the second trail, drive down the mountain on FR-4662 for 2.2 mi to a dead end. Hike across logs of a former bridge over Flat Creek. [An old road to the R goes W 0.5 mi to private property at a saddle.] Inconspicuously the *Rocky Knob Trail* [USFS #446] [F, H] **87** enters slightly L into rhododendrons. Both trails are about 3.0 mi long and connect about 0.6 mi S of Rocky Knob. A loop could be formed of about 11.2 mi if using FR-4662 as a connector.) (*USGS-FS Map*: Big Ridge)

BONAS DEFEAT AREA (Jackson County)

There are a few unofficial trails in the Bonas Defeat area of the Tuckasegee River Gorge, Wolf Creek Gorge, and the Tanasee Creek basin. The area is scenic, rugged, and remote. Because there are pockets of private property (particularly along NC-281), Lake Toxaway, Sam Knob, and Big Ridge USGS (modified for FS use) maps are recommended to determine boundary lines. (Also, contact the ranger's office at 704-526-3765 if you have questions.) Two exciting routes are described below.

Access to the Tuckasegee River Gorge from the W is by NC-281 from its jct with NC-107 in Tuckasegee (SE of Cullowhee) E 14.2 mi to Phillips Store, R, but park on the L near the old store. (From the E take NC-281 from US-64 [8.0 mi W of Rosman], and drive 11.2 mi to the Phillips Store.) If walking to

88 *Tuckasegee Gorge Trail* (USFS #438) (F) from the store, request permission from the store owner (or, if closed, the nearest neighbor) to walk over private property. (Or you may enter the gorge from a private driveway 0.2 mi W of the store on NC-281. Permission there should be requested from the landowner, whose house is off the curve, S. This road route is 2.0 mi W to the powerhouse for access to the gorge, L.) If going across the fence in front of the store, cross the pasture to the SW corner at 0.2 mi. Cross a barbed-wire fence and descend to a road. Pass a water gauging station, follow a pathway through the forest by Tanasee Lake, and reach another road. Follow the road, but take a sharp L to the lake at 0.5 mi. Climb down to the spillway and descend on rock layers below the dam. Descend with care by twisting around boulders, rock-hopping, and avoiding a fall into hundreds of water-carved potholes. (The area can be extremely dangerous. Nonslip shoe soles are a necessity. Avoid sections with red markings.) After passing Slickens Creek and Doe Branch mouths, L, the Bonas Defeat Cliffs loom upward, L. (The legend of Bonas Defeat is that a hunting dog named Boney chased a deer to the cliff edge; the deer jumped sideways, missing the cliff, but Boney dived over it, meeting his defeat.) Continue the descent to the powerhouse. Backtrack, or follow the gravel road (described above). At the first fork, take a R and return to the next fork near the dam. Bear L and return on the entrance route for a strenuous round-trip of 4.0 mi.

Less known than the Tuckasegee, the Wolf Creek Gorge also has soft spots in the rocks where the rapids have shaped the design. Access is to follow the directions as given above for the Tuckasegee River Gorge, except the

89 *Wolf Creek Gorge Trail* (USFS #439) (F) is W, 1.5 mi from the old Phillips Store, and 0.5 mi W of the Wolf Creek Dam. Park at the Wolf Creek Baptist Church. Descend on a clear footpath behind the church and bear slightly L and down (across an old road) at 0.1 mi. At 0.4 mi reach Wolf Creek, whose fury has sculpted bowls and fissures, pools, and waterfalls. Huge hemlock, birch, white pine, and oak tower over rhododendron, laurel, ferns, and wildflowers. Return on the same route for a round-trip of 1.0 mi. (Wolf Creek flows SW for 1.4 mi to a confluence with the Tuckasegee River at the powerhouse. A descent to the river can also be made on Pioneer Lodge Rd [SR-1139] by going 0.3 mi W on NC-281 from the church.) (The *Wolf Creek Gorge Trail* is on USFS property, except the church lot and a section below the falls near the mouth of the creek at Tuckasegee River.)

BALSAM LAKE AREA (Jackson County)

Robinson Trail (0.3 mi; USFS #477); Wolf Creek Trail (0.3 mi; USFS #478); Malonee Trail (0.6 mi; USFS #476) (F, W)

90-92

LENGTH AND DIFFICULTY: separate trails, round-trip, easy
SPECIAL FEATURES: scenic, wildlife, access for disabled
TRAILHEADS AND DESCRIPTION: These trails are part of Balsam Lake Recreation Area, acquired by the USFS in 1981. The Balsam Lake Lodge is rented to the public for educational and recreational meetings. Up to 16 overnight guests have accommodations. Lodge is open from March 1 to November 31. Call the district office for information. The *Robinson Trail* is a nature trail whose access can be either in front of the lodge at steps to the lake or to the S side by a wide gravel route for the disabled. A sheltered fishing and boat dock is at the Balsam Lake Dam. Part of the trail has wildflowers and overhanging rhododendron.

The other trails are at the N end of the lake in a recreational area that has sheltered picnic tables, rest rooms, and a grassy playing field. The *Wolf Creek Trail*, constructed in 1992 with financial assistance from private organizations and volunteers, is an exceptional trail for the physically disabled. It is easy for wheelchairs to be positioned on spur trails to watch Wolf Creek splashing toward the lake. There are galax, painted trillium, white violets, and ferns under birch, hemlock, and rhododendron. Nearby, and also from the parking area, is the *Malonee Trail*. It is flat, crosses Wolf Creek on a bridge, and winds through large trees at the lake's edge on the E side. Fishing is allowed from extended piers. Access is from NC-107 E on NC-281 for 9.2 mi to Little Canada. Turn L on Charlie's Creek Rd (SR-1756) for 4.0 mi to the lodge entrance, R. It is 0.6 mi farther to Balsam Lake Recreational Area. (If from NC-215 it is W 5.0 mi on Charlie's Creek Rd.) (*USGS-FS Map:* Sam Knob)

SECTION 3: TUSQUITEE RANGER DISTRICT

The Tusquitee (the Cherokee word for "where the water dogs laughed," based on a legend of thirsty, talking water dogs) Ranger District is the state's most western district and the largest—158,348 acres—in the Nantahala National Forest. Mainly in Cherokee County, its NW corner adjoins the Unicoi Mtns and the Cherokee National Forest in Tennessee. Its N border is with the Cheoah Ranger District along the ridgeline of the Snowbird Mtns. On the E boundary is the Wayah district and a small connection with the Georgia state line in the SE. Three major TVA lakes, the Hiwassee and Appalachia in Cherokee County and Chatuge in Clay County, provide large areas for fishing and other water sports. The largest of the lakes, Hiwassee, is 22.0 mi W of Murphy. It was completed in 1940 at the cost of $23 million. In addition to the Unicoi Mtn range, the Chunky Gal Mtn range in the SE, and the Tusquitee Mtn range in the center, there are outstanding areas for wildlife and natural beauty. The Fires Creek Wildlife Management Area with Fires Creek running through its basin and the *Rim Trail* circling its rim to Tusquitee Bald (5,240 ft) is the most distinctive and eminent area. Within the rim is a network of diverse hiking, bicycling, and horseback riding trails. Its 14,000 acres are a bear sanctuary, but other game hunting and trout fishing are allowed The district's other major trail is the *Chunky Gal Trail,* a NW-SE route from Tusquitee Bald to the *AT* in the Wayah Ranger District. The Tusquitee Ranger District has 40.0 mi of trails for motorbikes and ATV usage.

The district has two USFS-developed campgrounds: Jack Rabbit at Lake Chatuge and Hanging Dog at Lake Hiwassee. Both places have camping, picnicking, day hiking, and fishing with boat-launching facilities. Other recreation areas are Cherokee Lake picnic area off NC-294, SW of Murphy, and Bob Allison, a primitive camping and picnic area N of the community of Tusquitee, which is NE of Hayesville.

ADDRESS AND ACCESS: District Ranger, Tusquitee Ranger District, USFS, 201 Woodland Drive, Murphy, NC 28906; 704-837-5152. The office is across the Hiwassee River at the first traffic light, L (S), from the jct of US-19/129 and US-64.

FIRES CREEK AREA (Clay County)

The 16,000-acre Fires Creek watershed has three recreational sites, one of which is a picnic area at Leatherwood Falls. The primitive campgrounds are at Huskins Branch Hunter Camp near the Fires Creek entrance, and Bristol Camp, 4.0 mi up Fires Creek Rd (FR-340) from the Leatherwood Falls parking area. Other sites for camping are along the creeks and roads. No camping is allowed in designated wildlife openings. Bristol Camp is divided into two areas, one of which is a developed horse camp. The horse camp has tables, fire rings, and corrals. (Reservations and a fee may be necessary.) The other camp has a vault toilet and drinking water, shared by both camps. Fishing for rainbow, brook, and brown trout is allowed according to North Carolina Game Lands regulations. Bear hunting and use of ORVs are prohibited. Hunting for wild turkey, deer, and grouse is permitted in season. Both the copperhead and the timber rattler are in the sanctuary. Among the bird species are woodpeckers, warblers, owls, hawks, towhees, and doves. Vegetation includes all the Southern Appalachian hardwood species and six species of pine. Rhododendron and laurel slicks are commonplace, and wildflower species number in the hundreds. The area is considered ideal for backpacking. The longest trail, the *Rim Trail*, traverses the boundary on a high, elongated rim for 25.0 mi with spur trails down to the basin. Some sections are restricted to hikers only, and other sections are used by both equestrians and hikers. All trails in the basin are used by both except *Leatherwood Falls Loop Trail*, *Trail Ridge Trail*, *Shinbone Ridge Trail*, *Bristol Cabin Trail*, and *Omphus Ridge Trail*, which are limited to hiking. The district is in the process of creating additional trails on some of the old RR grades or older trails similar to *Bald Springs Trail* (USFS #78).

ACCESS: At the jct of US-64/NC-69 in Hayesville go W on US-64 for 4.9 mi, and turn R on Lower Sweetwater Rd (SR-1302). (From Murphy go E 9.2 mi on US-64 from US-129/19.) Follow SR-1302 for 3.7 mi and turn L on a gravel road, Fires Creek Rd (SR-1344). After 1.7 mi enter the gate and reach Leatherwood Falls parking area and picnic ground after 0.3 mi.

SUPPORT FACILITIES: The nearest store with groceries and gasoline is at the jct of US-64/SR-1302 described above. Hayesville has other supply and service stores, and the commercial campground with the longest season is Ho Hum Campground, 8.0 mi E of Hayesville on NC-175 and 3.5 mi N of Hiawassee (Georgia). It is open March 15–November 15, full svc, rec fac; 704-389-6740. Also see Chatuge Lake Area below. Murphy has shopping centers, restaurants, and motels, and Hayesville and Hiawassee have motels.

Rim Trail (USFS #72) (F, partial H)   **93**
LENGTH AND DIFFICULTY: (25.0 mi, easy to strenuous, elev change 3,390 ft)

CONNECTING TRAILS:

94	*Cover Loop Trail* (0.3 mi; USFS #74, easy)
95	*Leatherwood Falls Loop Trail* (0.7 mi; USFS #73, easy)
96	*Phillips Ridge Trail* (3.3 mi; USFS #388, moderate, elev change 815 ft)
97	*Trail Ridge Trail* (2.7 mi; USFS #382, strenuous, elev change 1,425 ft)
98	*Shinbone Ridge Trail* (1.5 mi; USFS #80, strenuous, elev change 1,349 ft) (Chunky Gal Trail)
99	*Far Bald Springs Trail* (1.9 mi; USFS #389, strenuous, elev change 1,490 ft)
100	*Bald Springs Trail* (3.0 mi; USFS #78, strenuous, elev change 2,120 ft)
101	*Little Fires Creek Trail* (3.1 mi; USFS #386, strenuous, elev change 2,145 ft)
102	*Bristol Cabin Trail* (1.2 mi; USFS #76, moderate)
103	*Omphus Ridge Trail* (1.3 mi; USFS #75, strenuous, elev change 1,000 ft)

SPECIAL FEATURES: Leatherwood Falls, heath balds, scenic

TRAILHEAD AND DESCRIPTION: Water is infrequent on the *Rim Trail*, but four springs are usually dependable and are described below. Signs and blazes are sparse. (At the picnic area is 0.3-mi paved *Cover Loop Trail*, accessible for the physically disabled to observe Fires Creek.) Begin R of the parking area, and follow a blue blaze across the arched bridge into a white pine stand. Turn L of the comfort station at 0.1 mi, curve L to Leatherwood Falls over an elevated bridge, and jct with the *Leatherwood Falls Loop Trail* at 0.3 mi. (The *Leatherwood Falls Loop Trail* turns L and skirts the mountainside through rhododendron and hardwoods with occasional views of the falls. The trail descends to the FR at 0.6 mi for a L turn to cross the bridge, and a return to the parking area at 0.7 mi.) Turn R on the *Rim Trail*, reach FR-6176 at 0.4 mi, take a sharp turn R up the bank at 0.6 mi, and follow switchbacks. Join and rejoin old logging roads. At 1.6 mi there is a jct with the old trail on the ridge; bear R. Pass through an experimental forest section of hardwoods, and begin a steep rocky ascent at 1.8 mi. Reach a plateau at 2.0 mi, and an intermittent spring at 2.2 mi. Ascend on switchbacks constructed by the YACC in 1980 to another ridge crest on the Cherokee/Clay county line at 3.2 mi. A horse trail comes in from the L to join the *Rim Trail*. Keep R and follow the old road W of Shortoff Knob to a spring on the L at 3.3 mi, and cross Big Peachtree Bald (4,186 ft) with Peachtree Valley to the L at 4.4 mi. Follow the rim with Valley River on the SE and a precipitous edge on the NW to Will King Gap at 5.4 mi.

(To the R is 3.3-mi *Phillips Ridge Trail*, a horse/hiker trail, which descends gradually to the E before turning S after crossing the headwaters of Laurel Creek. It follows a logging road, first to enter coves on the W side of Phillips Ridge, but then crosses the ridge to descend for a crossing of Hickory Creek at 2.3 mi. After another mile it reaches a trailhead in a sharp curve at Laurel Creek. From here it is 0.5 mi downstream to a jct with *Rockhouse* **104** *Creek Trail*, L, another horse/hiker trail that ascends NE for 2.3 mi to *Trail Ridge Trail* and the *Rim Trail*. At the confluence of Laurel Creek and Rockhouse Creek is FR-340A, an 0.8-mi access from Fires Creek Rd [FR-340], 1.7 mi from Leatherwood Falls parking area.) At 5.7 mi on the *Rim Trail* are occasional N views of the Chestnut Flats to the drainage. Follow a contour grade until an ascent to Big Stamp Lookout (4,437 ft) is reached at 7.9 mi. The trail skirts the summit, but an access route of 0.2 mi to the top is on the S side. Views are limited because the fire tower has been dismantled.

(The access route, FR-427, R, descends 4.0 mi to Long Branch Rd. From there, R, it is 1.0 mi to Fires Creek Rd, and R 6.1 mi to Leatherwood Falls parking area. After 0.1 mi on the descent is *Rockhouse Creek Trail*, R, a horse/hiker route on an old forest road for 2.3 mi along Rockhouse Creek to FR-340A. After another 0.2-mi descent on the access road from the *Rim Trail*, the *Trail Ridge Trail* begins, R. It is a 2.7-mi blue-blazed hiker trail that descends steeply on rough Trail Ridge. At 2.2 mi are unique weathered or carved bowls in the rocks and surveyor's bench marks. The trail reaches Fires Creek Rd a few yd N of Bristol Camp. From here it is 4.0 mi W on Fires Creek Rd to the Leatherwood Falls parking area.)

Continue along the rim, with exceptionally steep drops on the N side; pass at 9.1 mi a faint trail descending N, the *McClellan Creek Trail*. Ascend and descend over knobs—Whiteoak Knob, Defeat Knob, Beal Knob. (Soon after Beal Knob is an unnamed horse/hiker trail, R, that descends S on a ridge between the tributaries of Short Branch. It crosses the toe of Sassafras Ridge and Long Branch to access the terminus of FR-340 and the SW terminus of *Shinbone Ridge Trail*.) After Beal Knob, the *Rim Trail* is for hikers only to Tusquitee Bald. Ascend to Sassafras Knob (4,650 ft) at 12.3 mi. Skirt S of Weatherman Bald (4,960 ft) at 12.9 mi and reach the boundary of Cherokee, Macon, and Clay Counties at County Corner at 13.6 mi (5,149 ft). A sign indicates the boundary, but the bears may have chewed all or parts of the sign. Here is a good open grassy spot for a campsite. (To the L [N] is the unmaintained *Old Road Gap Trail* that descends 1.6 mi to a FR, and L 1.1 mi to Junaluska Gap Rd [SR-1505]. Left on SR-1505 it is 3.5 mi to Andrews.) A spring is on the *Shinbone Ridge Trail*, 65 ft SE from a small grassy area at Country Corner on the *Rim Trail* and 140 ft R in a rhododendron grove. The spring is small but is usually dependable. It has water usually during a dry summer.

(From the spring the blue-blazed *Shinbone Ridge Trail* gradually descends on Shinbone Ridge in and out of grassy paths for 0.5 mi. In a scenic forest of white pine, hemlock, hardwoods, ferns, and flame azalea, there are views through the trees of Sassafras Ridge N and the Fires Creek watershed S. Descend steeply; a clear-cut is L at 1.2 mi. At 1.5 mi descend on steps to a timber road. There is space for three vehicles on a level area in the ridge grove. From here, L, it is 10.2 mi down the mountain on Fires Creek Rd to Leatherwood Falls parking area.)

Continue ahead on the *Rim Trail* to a spur trail, L, at 14.7 mi. (The spur leads 0.1 mi to views from Signal Bald, named for the Cherokee usage of smoke signals. From Signal Bald the spur extends another 0.1 mi to Tusquitee Bald [5,240 ft] and makes a jct with the *Chunky Gal Trail* along the way. The *Chunky Gal Trail* is described below.) Descend from Tusquitee Bald and rejoin the *Rim Trail*. Another horse trail, 1.9-mi *Far Bald Springs Trail*, is planned here to descend R (W) to jct with FR-340. Here also the *Rim Trail* becomes a horse/hiker trail for 2.3 mi. After 0.2 mi to rejoin the *Rim Trail* from Tusquitee Bald there is a small saddle and a water source. Reach Potrock Bald (5,215 ft) at 16.1 mi. Here is a good campsite with vistas of Chatuge Lake and beyond into Georgia. Potrock received its name from small and large "bowls" appearing to have been carved by the Indians or the weather. A good spring is on the R at 17.1 mi.

On a gentle grade reach Matlock Bald (4,949 ft) at 17.2 mi. Ahead the rim edge on the S drops steeply. (Just before Johnson Bald [4,949 ft] a 3.0-mi horse/hiker trail, *Bald Springs Trail*, is planned to descend R. Its valley terminus is on Fires Creek Rd [FR-340] W of Mule Flat Bend, and about 6.0 mi E of Leatherwood Falls parking area.) Continuing on the *Rim Trail* for about 0.7 mi there is a jct with another horse/hiker trail, R. It is 3.1-mi *Little Fires Creek Trail*. (It descends steeply partly on an old forest road to exit on FR-340, 0.3 mi NE of Bristol Camp.) From here to the end of the *Rim Trail* usage is for hikers only.

Ascend Chestnut Stomp Knob (4,400 ft) at 18.4 mi. From here continue the descent to Shearer Gap, Cold Spring Gap, and finally to Carver Gap (2,996 ft) at 22.3 mi. (*Bristol Cabin Trail* jct is here; it descends R for 1.2 mi to Bristol Camp on Fires Creek Rd.) After 0.4 mi farther on *Rim Trail*, *Omphus Ridge Trail* jct R. (Both of these trails leave Fires Creek Rd 2.0 mi apart and connect with the *Rim Trail* 0.4 mi apart. They provide an excellent 4.9-mi loop trail combination from Bristol Camp. From the *Omphus Ridge Trail* jct on Fires Creek Rd, it is 2.0 mi on the road SW to Leatherwood Falls parking area.)

From the *Omphus Ridge Trail* jct, continue on the ridge and enter a rhododendron arbor before crossing Graveyard High Knob at 23.6 mi.

Descend and level off slightly at 23.9 mi, take an old road R, and follow the N side of the main ridge at 24.7 mi. Continue to descend to a small cove and leave the forest at a new timber road at 24.8 mi. Follow the road L to Fires Creek Rd for 0.1 mi, turn L, and go another 0.1 mi to the Leatherwood Falls parking area at 25.0 mi. (*USGS-FS Maps:* Andrews, Hayesville, Topton)

CHUNKY GAL MOUNTAIN AREA (Clay County)

Chunky Gal Mtn is a high, remote, 8.0-mi ridge that averages 4,500 ft in elev from the Tennessee Valley Divide of the Blue Ridge Mtns NW to Shooting Creek Bald. It has three major gaps, the lowest of which is Glade Gap (3,679 ft). Through it passes the celebrated US-64 from Manteo to Murphy, the state's longest highway (569.0 mi). The legend of Chunky Gal Mtn is that a plump Indian maiden fell in love with an Indian youth of another tribe in another valley. To break up the romance her parents banished the young brave, but she deserted her family and followed him over the mtn that bears her sobriquet. Access to the mtn is described below under the *Chunky Gal Trail.*

> SUPPORT FACILITIES: The nearest towns for supplies are E 17.4 mi on US-64 to Franklin and W 16.0 mi to Hayesville. The nearest campgrounds are the Chatuge Lake Area (described below), or the Standing Indian Area, 7.5 mi E, and described in detail in section 4 of this chapter.

Chunky Gal Trail (USFS #77) (F)   105

> LENGTH AND DIFFICULTY: 21.7 mi, moderate to strenuous (elev change 2,160 ft)

> SPECIAL FEATURES: gemstones, isolated, wild herbs

TRAILHEAD AND DESCRIPTION: This trail has exceptional potential for an extended backpacking trip. It is a connector trail between the *AT* at the Southern Nantahala Wilderness Area and the *Rim Trail* on the E rim of the Fires Creek basin. Access to either end is by foot: 2.9 mi using the *AT,* or 2.8 mi using the *Shinbone Ridge Trail* and the *Rim Trail.* Whichever route you choose, the minimum hiking distance is 27.3 mi. To extend the excursion, more than 10.0 mi of the *Rim Trail* can be used, or long distances on the *AT.*

On US-64, 2.0 mi W of Rainbow Springs, or 0.3 mi W of the Macon/Clay county line, turn L on unmarked gravel FR-71. Follow the narrow, winding road for 5.4 mi to Park Gap and 1.4 mi farther to its jct with the *AT* in Deep Gap. Here is a parking and picnic area. From here begin the hike S on the graded *AT* section; ascend steeply, cross outcrops, and cross a footbridge at a water source at 1.2 mi. Circle the Yellow Mtn ridge crest at 1.6 mi and descend to Wateroak Gap at 2.1 mi. Ascend to the ridge, skirt

NW of Big Laurel Mtn (5,100 ft), descend, and reach a jct with the blue-blazed *Chunky Gal Trail* R at 2.9 mi (4,700 ft).

Follow the trail along Chunky Gal Mtn ridge for 0.7 mi to a scenic escarpment L (W) with views of Ravenrock Ridge and the Muskrat Branch basin. Shooting Creek Knob can be seen NW beyond the valley. Follow a ridge spine in a forest of oak, birch, hemlock, rhododendron, laurel, and wildflowers. The escarpment contains quartz, garnet, and olivine. Descend steeply to Bear Gap at 1.5 mi. Ascend steeply to a high unnamed knob and descend to Grassy Gap at 2.3 mi. Deer are frequently seen here. For the next 1.3 mi ascend and descend across four knobs and saddles and jct R with an old trail, *Riley Cove Trail,* at 3.6 mi. Continue ahead to climb Riley Knob (4,480 ft) at 4.4 mi. Descend and begin switchbacks at 5.0 mi. Cross a woods road and at 5.2 mi exit to US-64 in Glade Gap. (It is 6.8 mi W to Shooting Creek and 16.0 mi to Hayesville. To Franklin, E, it is 17.4 mi.)

Cross US-64, turn L on old US-64, and turn R on an old jeep road at 5.4 mi. Pass under the powerline, cross Glade Branch on a footbridge, and on switchbacks pass under the power line again. (Avoid the shortcuts that have been made under the power line.) Jct with an old road at 5.6 mi. Turn R and ascend on Chunky Gal Mtn with a combination of old roads and footpaths for 12 switchbacks before a more gradual contour at 6.4 mi. Enter a rhodo-dendron tunnel at 7.1 mi, pass large boulders, and at 7.9 mi jct with a faint trail ahead. (The faint trail leads to Shooting Creek Bald [5,010 ft], also called Boteler Peak.) The R turn makes a radical change in direction, but descend N on the ridge and pass through a natural garden of laurel, flame azalea, and ferns. At 8.7 mi pass R of a clear-cut, reenter the forest, and exit at another clear-cut at 9.1 mi. Columbine (*Aquilegia canadensis*), sundrops (*Oenothers fruiticose*), spiderwort (*Tradescantia virginiana*), and flame azalea grow in profusion here, and in the forest are a variety of herbs collected by the mountain residents under permits from the USFS. After another section in the forest and another clear-cut, turn L on an old woods road at 9.3 mi. Skirt around the ridge and descend to a jct with a FR in Perry Gap at 10.3 mi. (It is 4.0 mi R [E] down the mtn to Buck Creek and US-64.) Continue ahead, N, on a gated FR through a clear-cut to Tate Gap at 11.4 mi. Leave the road, follow on an old jeep road on the ridge with knobs for 1.9 mi where a sharp L (W) is made for a steep descent to Woods Rd (SR-1307), also called Tusquitee Rd, in Tusquitee Gap at 13.9 mi. (SR-1307 is an access S for 3.7 mi to a paved road and jct with the Tuni Gap Rd described below.) Cross the road, ascend NW to a spur ridge of a peak at 14.3 mi. Curve around another spur and descend steeply to a gap at 15.0 mi. Pass old roads, ascend to the ridge crest, and skirt W of an unnamed knob. Leave the main ridge and descend to follow rippling spur ridges and coves with banks of galax, fire pink, and trailing arbutus to a trail jct at 17.3 mi. Here is a relocation: the *Chunky Gal Trail* turns sharply L. (Ahead the trail goes to Tuni Gap and ends.) Descend on a poorly designed and constructed trail to the Bob Allison Camp. At 17.5 mi reach an old road; turn L, and leave, R, at 17.6 mi into a partial clearing. Reach an old RR grade at 17.7 mi, cross two streams on a rough RR grade, and rock-hop the Big Tuni Creek at 18.0 mi. Enter the edge of the campground and go upstream through a stand of hemlock and poplar for a jct with FR-400 at 18.2 mi. The Bob Allison Camp has a vault toilet, drinking water, picnic tables, and a grassy area for camping. (The camp can be reached from Hayesville Town Square by following the Tusquitee Rd [SR-1307] NE for 8.7 mi to the end of the pavement. Continue L [N] for 4.3 mi on Mosteller Rd [SR-1311], which becomes FR-400, to the camp, 0.8 mi S of Tuni Gap.)

On FR-400, turn R and cross the cement bridge over Big Tuni Creek to enter L a scenic area with cascades. Follow the blue blazes on a relocated trail that is rough, steep, and rocky. Part of the trail is not well graded and follows a wet treadway. Timber cuts affect its direction. After 1.2 mi turn L and ascend steeply on switchbacks to Dead Line Ridge. Curve around a knoll to follow a narrow ridge that ends in a gentle saddle between Signal Bald R and Tusquitee Bald (5,240 ft) L, an elev gain of 2,160 ft at 21.5 mi. Both peaks have outstanding scenery and Tusquitee provides views of Shooting Creek Bald SE, Wine Spring Bald E, Chatuge Lake S, and Nantahala Lake NE. Exit to the *Rim Trail* at 21.7 mi. Backtrack to Allison Camp or use the *Rim Trail* for egress. (*USGS-FS Maps:* Rainbow Springs, Shooting Creek, Topton)

CHATUGE LAKE AREA (Clay County)

The Jackrabbit Mountain Recreation Area has 103 camping sites, picnic facilities, boating, swimming, skiing, lake fishing, nature study, and hiking. Comfort stations and warm-water showers are available. Both the campgrounds and the swimming area are usually open from the first week of May to the end of October. (The nearest commercial campground is Ho Hum Campground on NC-175 near the entrance to Jackrabbit Mtn Campground. It is open from March 15 to November 15. Full svc, rec fac; 704-386-6740.)

ACCESS: Entry to Jackrabbit is from US-64 jct with NC-175 (4.7 mi E of NC-67 jct in Hayesville). Go S on NC-175 for 3.4 mi, turn R at

Jackrabbit on Philadelphia Rd (SR-1155), and proceed 1.2 mi to the campground.

107 *Jackrabbit Mountain Scenic Trail (USFS #384) (F)*

LENGTH AND DIFFICULTY: 2.4 mi, easy

TRAILHEAD AND DESCRIPTION: Follow the trail sign R of entry to a blue-blazed trail through generally open forest of white oak, sourwood, and pine. Cleared spots provide views of Chatuge Lake. Reach the crest of a ridge at 0.6 mi, cross wooden bridge near a spring at 1.3 mi, pass the edge of Chatuge Lake at 1.6 mi, and reach the boat ramp parking area at 2.1 mi. Return to the camping area and parking lot at 2.4 mi. (*USGS-FS Map:* Shooting Creek)

HIWASSEE LAKE AREA (Cherokee County)

Located on Lake Hiwassee, Hanging Dog Recreation Area has 69 campsites, a picnic area with tables and grills, and boat launching facilities for fishing, boating, and skiing. Flush toilets are available, but there are not any showers. The area is usually open from April 1 to the end of October, but one camping area for tent camping is open all year with a small fee. It is section D with a vault toilet and hand water pump. Other sections are A and C on the R, and B (with D) on the L when entering. (One of the nearest commercial campgrounds is Mr. Piper's Campground, Rte 6, Box 100, Murphy NC 28906; 800-520-5567. Full svc, excellent rec fac. Open all year.)

ACCESS: From downtown Murphy, at the jct of Tennessee St and Valley River Ave (Business US-19), take Tennessee St W (it becomes Brown Rd, SR-1326) and drive 4.4 mi to the campground sign, L, and go 1.1 mi to the entrance.

108 *Ramsey Bluff Trail (USFS #81) (F)*

LENGTH AND DIFFICULTY: 2.1 mi combined, easy

TRAILHEAD AND DESCRIPTION: The trail can be made into a loop by beginning at the end of the loop road in section B. There is an interpretive segment in between here and an exit to FR-652 in section D. To continue, turn L on FR-652 and walk to the upper boat ramp. Turn R near the corner of the parking area and go N through sections C and A to exit on FR-652 near the entrance to section B. On an even-grade terrain the forest has oak, pine, sourwood, dogwood, maple, birch, ferns, and wildflowers. (*USGS-FS Map:* Murphy)

SECTION 4: WAYAH RANGER DISTRICT

The Wayah Ranger District has 133,894 acres of which 12,076 are in the Southern Nantahala Wilderness Area. The W side of the district is within the Macon County line where it borders the Tusquitee and Cheoah districts. Its NW boundary extends into Swain County to Fontana Lake and includes an isolated section of the Cowee Mtns at the jct of Swain, Macon, and Jackson Counties. The Highland District is E and the Georgia state line and the Chattahoochee National Forest is the S boundary. The AT goes NW for 51.7 mi on the Nantahala Mtn range from Deep Gap to Wesser at the Nantahala River. Some of the magnificent peaks on the AT are Standing Indian Mtn (5,490 ft), Albert Mtn (5,280 ft), Siler Bald (5,216 ft), Cooper Bald (5,249 ft), Rocky Bald (5,180 ft), and Wayah Bald (5,336 ft). In addition to the AT, another long trail, the *Bartram Trail,* passes through the district for 21.1 mi. The wilderness boundary surrounds the AT in the Standing Indian Area and at the headwaters of the Nantahala River. Adjoining the wilderness boundary in the NE is Coweeta Experimental Forest.

The district has nine recreational areas: Standing Indian with a campground, picnic and fishing areas; Wayah Crest picnic area; Nantahala Gorge with fishing and water sports facilities; the Apple Tree Group Campground (requires reservation); Wayah Bald and Arrowwood Glade picnic areas; and Almond Point, Alarka, Greasy Branch, and Wilderness Marina serving as boating sites at Fontana Lake.

The district's 48 trails are color blazed except the ones not maintained and used mainly by hunters. Examples are *Wildcat Trail* (2.5 mi; USFS #14) **109** (F), accessible from US-441/23 (between Otto and Norton communities) on Norton Rd (W) to FR-751, L (W), and to the trailhead at the end of the road. Another hunters' trail is *Cullowhee Trail* (7 mi; USFS #370) (F). The **110** W trailhead is at private property, but the NE access is from NC-107 and Speedwell Rd (SR-1001) 1.3 mi SE on NC-107 from the main entrance of Western Carolina University) for a turn R on SR-1001; go 6.4 mi to park in a small area on the L of the highway. Cross the road into a stand of white pine. Kirby Knob is reached at 1.5 mi, and Sheep Knob is at 2.8 mi. Timbering may have blocked some of its passage. Other hunters' trails are described near Wayah Bald near the end of this section. Hiking trails are blazed blue, the AT white, and the *Bartram Trail* yellow. At the time this edition went to press there were not any designated mountain bike trails.

All horse trails in the district are blazed orange. *Big Indian Loop Trail* is described ahead. It and three other horse trails are on the same road, FR-67,

111 for easy access. Access to *Blackwell Gap Loop Horse Trail* (4.2 mi; USFS #366) (F, H) is at FR-67B near the Backcountry Information Center at Standing Indian Campground. Its other access is 1.8 mi farther upriver on FR-67 to
112 FR-7282, L. This also is the trailhead access for *Hurricane Gap Loop Horse Trail* (4.3 mi; USFS #36) (F, H), which circles Hurricane Creek to the end of FR-67 in the shadow of Albert Mtn. Another equestrian trail is *Thomas*
113 *Branch Loop Horse Trail* (3.7 mi; USFS #375) (F, H) 0.4 mi farther upriver on
114 FR-67, L, at a horse camp. *Camp Shortcut Trail* (0.5 mi; USFS #36B) (F, H), is a connector between the horse camp and *Blackwell Gap* and *Hurricane Gap* horse trails to avoid using FR-67.

> ADDRESS AND ACCESS: District Ranger, Wayah Ranger District, USFS, 8 Sloan Rd, Franklin, NC 28734; 704-524-6441. From the jct of US-441/23 and US-64 in Franklin, go W on US-64 for 1.0 mi and turn R on SR-1153 at the sign and go 0.3 mi.

NANTAHALA LAKE AREA (Macon County)

Access to all the trails in this area can begin at the Apple Tree Group Camp. The camp received its name from the fruit trees that once grew near Apple Tree Branch, the route of the Cherokee Indians between areas that are now Franklin and Robbinsville. At least two distinguished travelers passed this way. It is likely that Atakullakulla, "Little Carpenter," a Cherokee peace chief known to British royalty, met the famous botanist William Bartram in this location. (See the *Bartram Trail* description in the beginning of this chapter.) The camp is designed for group tent camping at four campsites, two of which serve 25 people and two of which serve 50 people; they are signed A through D. Water, sanitary facilities, and hot showers are provided. Reservations are necessary from the ranger's office. (*USGS-FS Map:* Topton)

> ACCESS: From Wesser on US-19 go SW to Beechertown Power Station. Turn L on SR-1310, follow up the river for 4.4 mi to FR-308, R, at a horseshoe curve. Go 3.1 mi on FR-308 to a jct with Dicks Creek Rd (SR-1401). Turn R, cross the bridge, and turn R to the camp entrance. From Franklin on US-64, go W 3.8 mi to Wayah Gap sign R and follow SR-1310 W 18.6 mi to Andrews Rd (SR-1400), which becomes SR-1401, L. Go 2.4 mi to the camp entrance, R. From Andrews take the Junaluska Rd (SR-1505) and go 12.5 mi E to the camp entrance, L.

115 *Apple Tree Trail (USFS #19B) (F)*
> LENGTH AND DIFFICULTY: 2.2 mi, strenuous (elev change 1,640 ft)
> CONNECTING TRAILS: *Junaluska Gap Trail* (4.3 mi; USFS #19, moderate) (F)

Junaluska Gap Trail (4.3mi; USFS #19, moderate) (F) **116**
Diamond Valley Trail (0.9 mi; USFS #19D, easy) (F) **117**
Laurel Creek Trail (1.5 mi; USFS #19F, easy) (F) **118**
(London Bald Trail)

TRAILHEAD AND DESCRIPTION: Park across the road from Apple Tree Branch and follow the blue blazes R of the branch on an old road. Cross the branch and pass a jct with the blue-blazed Junaluska Gap Trail L at 0.3 mi.

(On the *Junaluska Gap Trail* skirt E of the mtn, curve SW with SR-1401 on the L to jct with the white-blazed *Diamond Valley Trail* at 1.6 mi. Continue on an even grade through mixed hardwoods, hemlock, and rhododendron, occasionally going in and out of small coves to jct with *Hickory Branch Trail* at 3.0 mi. [*Hickory Branch Trail* is a 1.3-mi connector trail between this point and the *London Bald Trail*.] Cross Matherson Branch at 3.5 mi, and jct with the *London Bald Trail* at 4.2 mi. Turn L to the highway, SR 1401, in Junaluska Gap at 4.3 mi. Backtrack, or make a loop with the *London Bald Trail*, or use a vehicle shuttle.)

Continue on the *Apple Tree Trail*, cross the stream again at 0.7 mi, and then pass a faint road jct. Proceed on a gradual grade through a forest of oak, elm, white pine, beech, sassafras, silver bell (*Halesia carolina*), laurel, rhododendron, and numerous wildflowers. At 1.1 mi pass a jct with the blue-blazed *Laurel Creek Trail*, R.

(*Laurel Creek Trail* is similar to *Diamond Valley Trail* in that access and exit are dependent on other trails. On the *Laurel Creek Trail* descend, first on a slight ridge in hardwoods, and then into a deep dense grove of rhododendron along Piercy Creek and to the mouth of a tributary, L, at 1.5 mi. A loop trail at the jct with the *Bartram Trail* [formerly the *Nantahala Trail*], R, requires another 5.5 mi of hiking to the campground. A turn L for 1.5 mi connects with the *London Bald Trail* to form a loop back to the camp for 5.9 mi.)

Continue ahead on the *Apple Tree Trail* to the white-blazed *Diamond Valley Trail* jct at 1.4 mi, L.

(Descend on the *Diamond Valley Trail* for 0.9 mi, following Diamond Valley Creek to a jct with the *Junaluska Gap Trail* in a clearing at SR-1401 and Dicks Creek. Backtrack, or return L on the *Junaluska Gap Trail* for a loop total of 4.2 mi.)

On the *Apple Tree Trail* reach the summit of a knob at 1.7 mi. Climb steeply on a second knob, reach the summit of a third peak SE of London Bald, and reach a jct with the blue-blazed *London Bald Trail* at 2.2 mi. Backtrack, or turn L to follow the *London Bald Trail* for 6.2 mi out to Junaluska Gap and SR-1401, or turn R and follow the *London Bald Trail* for 2.8 mi to its NE terminus at Sutherland Gap and jct with the *Nantahala Trail*. A return loop to the campground can be made from here on the *London Bald Trail* R and the *Nantahala/Bartram Trail* for a total of 9.3 mi. (See *Nantahala Trail* below.)

119 *Nantahala Trail (USFS #19E) (F)*

LENGTH AND DIFFICULTY: 6.5 mi, moderate

CONNECTING TRAILS:
(*London Bald Trail*)
(*Laurel Creek Trail*)
(*Bartram Trail*)

TRAILHEAD AND DESCRIPTION: Except for the last 0.5 mi W on this trail, it is now the *Bartram Trail*. It requires either backtracking for a total of 13.0 mi, or connecting with other trails such as the N trailhead of *London Bald* in Sutherland Gap, or *Laurel Creek Trail* (1.5 mi E from Sutherland Gap) on the *Bartram Trail* as described above. (See the beginning of chapter 2 for details of the *Nantahala/Bartram Trail* from Apple Tree Group Camp.)

120- *London Bald Trail (9.0 mi; USFS #19C) (F); Hickory Branch Trail (1.3*
121 *mi; USFS #19A) (F)*

LENGTH AND DIFFICULTY: 10.3 mi combined, strenuous (elev change 1,360 ft)

CONNECTING TRAILS:
(*Junaluska Gap Trail*)
(*Apple Tree Trail*)
(*Nantahala Trail*)

TRAILHEAD AND DESCRIPTION: This trail requires either backtracking for a total of 18.0 mi, or hiking a lesser distance by using a connecting trail to a second vehicle. Ascend on switchbacks of a timber road to a L turn on the S slope of a ridge to reach the crest at 0.8 mi. Slope L off the ridge, parallel the Macon/Cherokee county line, and turn NE at the headwaters of Pine Branch at 1.5 mi among oak, pine, maple, laurel, and hemlock. From here the trail weaves in and out of fern-covered coves on a generally level contour of about 4,000 ft elev. Pass through a saddle on a spur ridge at 3.1 mi. At 3.7 mi jct L with a spur trail to the ridge crest and NE end of FR-6166A. Continue from a cove and jct R at 3.9 mi with *Hickory Branch Trail* on a ridge.

(The *Hickory Branch Trail* follows the ridge crest but soon curves E to descend and cross the headwaters of Hickory Branch. From there it ascends to a knob before descending to cross Hickory Branch again. After another crossing of the branch among rhododendron and tall trees, it jct with *Junaluska Gap Trail* at 1.3 mi.)

Continuing on the *London Bald Trail*, slightly ascend to the S shoulder of Hickory Knob at 4.4 mi. Begin a long curve in a cove before turning L on a ridge. Switchbacks follow in the ascent to the E side of London Bald at 6.2 mi. Here is a jct R with *Apple Tree Trail*. (It descends 2.2 mi to the campground.) The trail continues on a moderate contour until Piercy Bald, where it descends rapidly on the main ridge to switchbacks. At 7.4 mi jct R with FR-7082. It descends to jct with *Apple Tree Trail, Branch Trail*, and *Diamond Valley Trail*.) The *London Bald Trail* continues to descend, crosses small knobs, and drops to Sutherland Gap at 8.9 mi. It turns R and after 0.3 mi jct with the *Nantahala Trail*. Backtrack, or take the *Nantahala Trail* and the *Bartram Trail* for another 6.5 mi to the campground. (*USGS-FS Map:* Topton)

STANDING INDIAN AREA (Macon County)

The Standing Indian Campground, a FS facility, has camping and picnic sites that are open all year. Reservations are not required except at the adjoining Kimsey Creek Group Camp. Water and sanitary facilities are provided, but there are not any electrical or sewage hookups. A special parking area for hikers and backpackers has been constructed at the Backcountry Information Center on FR-67/2 (0.2 mi L of the campground and picnic entrance gate). The Nantahala River, which flows through the campground, is a popular trout stream. The campground is exceptionally well landscaped in an area where the Ritter Lumber Company had its main logging camp for the Upper Nantahala basin. Downstream, at Rainbow Springs, the company had a double-head rig band saw mill to process huge trees. Although timber harvesting has continued in the area since it was first purchased in the 1920s, the upper headwaters are now protected by the 12,076-acre Southern Nantahala Wilderness Area. The *AT* wraps around the S and E ridge of the basin and provides a master connecting route for the ascending trails. Forest vegetation in the area includes all the Southern Appalachian hardwoods, with groves of pine and hemlock. Bear, deer, turkey, grouse, fox, squirrel, raccoon, hawks, and owls are part of the wildlife.

The Cherokee Indian legend of Standing Indian Mtn is that a Cherokee warrior was posted on the mountaintop to warn the tribe of impending danger from an evil winged monster that had carried off a village child. Beseeching the Great Spirit to destroy the monster, the tribe was rewarded with a thunderstorm of awesome fury that destroyed the beast, shattered the mountaintop to bald rubble, and turned the warrior into a stone effigy, the "standing Indian," in the process.

ACCESS: From the jct of US-64 and Old US-64 (0.4 mi E of the Nantahala

River bridge in Rainbow Springs and 12.0 mi W from Franklin) take Old US-64 for 1.8 mi to Wallace Gap and turn R on FR-67/1.

Support Facilities: A commercial campground, The Pines RV Park, is 5.0 mi W from Franklin on US-64. Full svc, open all year, address: 490 Hayesville Hwy, Franklin, NC 28734; 704-524-4490.

122 Pickens Nose Trail (USFS #13) (F)

Length and Difficulty: 1.4 mi round-trip, easy

Special Features: rock climbing area, nature study

Trailhead and Description: From the Backcountry Information Center drive 8.7 mi on FR-67 up the mtn to a parking area, L (0.7 mi beyond the AT crossing in Mooney Gap). Hike across the road and ascend before leveling on a rocky ridge. The first vistas, E-S, are at 0.3 mi, but the vistas W-S at 0.7 mi at Pickens Nose (5,000 ft) are exceptionally scenic. The Chattahoochee National Forest is S and the Betty Creek basin is down 2,000 ft from the top sheer cliffs. A beautiful area any season with all the evergreens, June is particularly colorful with laurel, rhododendron, azalea, black locust, and Bowman's root (*Gillenia trifoliata*). (*USGS-FS Map:* Prentiss)

123 Bearpen Gap Trail (USFS #22) (F)

Length and Difficulty: 4.8 mi round-trip, strenuous (elev change 1,200 ft)

Trailhead and Description: From the Backcountry Information Center drive 3.2 mi on FR-67 to the trail sign and parking area. (Parts of this trail have been relocated because of a timber sale.) Enter the forest L of a locked gate, hike 0.2 mi to a logging road, and take the R fork. Follow the road, and at 1.0 mi take the R fork to curve around a ridge. At 1.9 mi cross the last stream near a large quartz rock in a hemlock grove. Galax, blue-beads, and wood betony are along the trail. Ascend steeply in a mixed forest; at 2.4 mi reach the AT on gated FR-83 (Ball Creek Rd) in Bearpen Gap. (Across the road it is 0.3 mi up a steep and rocky path to Albert Mtn [5,280] fire tower for the most panoramic views in the Standing Indian Area. Backtrack to the *Bearpen Gap Trail* or take the AT N 3.1mi to *Long Branch Trail* and 1.9 mi down to the information center, or S on the AT for 6.3 mi to *Timber Ridge Trail*, R, which descends 2.5 mi to FR-67, and another 1.6 mi on the road to the W trailhead of *Bearpen Gap Trail* and parking area for a loop of 12.8 mi.) (*USGS-FS Maps:* Prentiss, Rainbow Springs)

124 Kimsey Creek Trail (USFS #23) (F)

Length and Difficulty: 7.4 mi round-trip, moderate

Trailhead and Description: From the Backcountry Information Center follow the blue-blazed trail to the picnic area, cross the Nantahala River bridge, follow *Park Creek Trail* N for 0.1 mi, and turn L at *Kimsey Creek Trail* sign. Skirt E of the mtn and follow a gradually ascending grade up Kimsey Creek. Three wildlife grazing fields are on this route. At 2.6 mi pass the confluence with Little Kimsey Creek; reach Deep Gap and the *AT* at 3.7 mi. Backtrack, or go L on the *AT* for 2.5 mi to Standing Indian (5,499 ft) and return L on the *Lower Ridge Trail* to the campground and picnic area for a total circuit of 9.7 mi. (*USGS-FS Map:* Rainbow Springs)

Lower Ridge Trail (USFS #28) (F)

LENGTH AND DIFFICULTY: 7.8 mi round-trip, strenuous (elev change 2,105 ft)

SPECIAL FEATURE: views from Standing Indian

TRAILHEAD AND DESCRIPTION: This is a frequently used and exceptionally steep trail to the top of Standing Indian. There are views of the Nantahala basin on its ascent. Begin at the Backcountry Information Center parking area, follow the blue-blazed trail to the campground road, cross the bridge over the Nantahala River, and turn L to begin the trail. Go up the riverside and cross a road and footbridge over Kimsey Creek at 0.2 mi. Cross another stream at 0.5 mi. At 1.0 mi begin a series of switchbacks in a forest of hardwoods, hemlock, and colorful patches of trillium and hepatica. At 1.5 mi reach the ridge crest and follow the ridge L to arrive on top of a knob at 1.8 mi. Descend to John Gap at 2.1 mi. Skirt W of a knob, reach another gap, skirt W of Frog Mtn, and reach Frank Gap at 3.1 mi. Continue a steep ascent and jct with the *AT* at 3.9 mi for a spur climb of 0.2 mi to Standing Indian (5,499 ft). Here from rock outcroppings are magnificent views of the Blue Ridge Mtns and the Tallulah River Gorge running into Georgia. Backtrack, or loop back to camp on the *Kimsey Creek Trail*, going R on the *AT* for 2.5 mi at Deep Gap for a return at 10.3 mi; or go L on the *AT* for 3.5 mi to *Beech Gap Trail*, turn L, and descend for 2.8 mi to FR-67 at a parking area (4.0 mi from the Backcountry Information Center parking area, the point of origin). (*USGS-FS Map:* Rainbow Springs)

Big Laurel Falls Trail (0.6 mi; USFS #29) (F); Timber Ridge Trail (2.5 mi; USFS #20) (F) 126-127

LENGTH AND DIFFICULTY: 6.2 mi round-trip combined, easy to moderate

SPECIAL FEATURES: scenic area at Big Laurel Falls

TRAILHEAD AND DESCRIPTION: From the Backcountry Information Center parking area drive 4.7 mi on FR-67 to joint trailheads of *Big Laurel Falls Trail* and *Timber Ridge Trail*. The blue-blazed *Big Laurel Falls Trail* goes R

NANTAHALA NATIONAL FOREST 81

and crosses a footbridge over Mooney Creek in a forest of hemlock, yellow birch, and rhododendron. Follow an old RR grade arbored with rhododendron, curve L around Scream Ridge, and follow to the base of Big Laurel Falls at the confluence of Kilby Creek, Gulf Fork, and Big Laurel Branch at 0.6 mi. Backtrack. For the *Timber Ridge Trail* follow the blue blazes L from FR-67, ascend steeply on switchbacks, and skirt L of Scream Ridge in an area of rhododendron, birch, ferns, and cohosh. Cross an old forest road on the ridge at 0.7 mi and begin a descent through large beds of galax. Rock-hop Big Laurel Branch at 1.0 mi. Ascend to Timber Ridge and go through fern beds with a canopy of oaks. Reach the *AT* at 2.5 mi, 0.5 mi W of the *AT* Carter Gap Shelter. Backtrack. (*USGS-FS Maps:* Prentiss, Rainbow Springs)

128 *Mooney Falls Trail (USFS #31) (F)*

LENGTH AND DIFFICULTY: 0.2 mi round-trip, easy

TRAILHEAD AND DESCRIPTION: From the Backcountry Information Center go up FR-67 for 5.5 mi to roadside parking for Mooney Falls. Hike 0.1 mi through a tunnel of rhododendron and laurel to a cascading fall on Mooney Creek. Remains of a fallen American chestnut tree are at the falls and on the ground are prominent wildflowers. Backtrack. (*USGS-FS Map:* Prentiss)

129- *Park Ridge Trail (3.2 mi; USFS #32) (F); Park Creek Trail (4.8 mi; USFS*
130 *#33) (F)*

LENGTH AND DIFFICULTY: 8.0 mi round-trip combined, moderate to strenuous (elev change 880 ft)

CONNECTING TRAILS:
(*Lower Ridge Trail*)
(*Kimsey Creek Trail*)

TRAILHEAD AND DESCRIPTION: These trails connect at both the N and S trailheads to form a loop. From the Backcountry Information Center parking area follow signs and blue blazes through rhododendron and hemlock to cross a footbridge over Wyant Branch at 0.1 mi. On the paved campground road, turn L, cross the Nantahala River bridge, and jct L with the *Lower Ridge Trail*. (The 3.9-mi *Lower Ridge Trail* is a scenic route to the *AT* and Standing Indian Mtn.) Turn R and follow an old RR grade. At 0.3 mi jct with the *Kimsey Creek Trail*, L. (The 3.7-mi *Kimsey Creek Trail* goes upstream to Deep Gap and a jct with the *AT*.) At 0.4 mi jct with the *Park Ridge Trail*, L. Ahead on the old RR grade is the *Park Creek Trail*. If choosing the *Park Ridge Trail*, ascend, cross a small stream, and skirt E of Bee Tree Knob from a cove. At 1.0 mi arrive at a gap and ascend Middle Ridge in a hardwood forest.

Leave the ridge at Penland Gap at 2.9 mi and reach FR-71/1 at Park Gap picnic and parking area at 3.2 mi. To the R is a jct with *Park Creek Trail*. (FR-71/1 goes L for 1.4 mi to Deep Gap and the *AT*, and R for 5.4 mi to US-64, 2.4 mi W of US-64/Old US-64 jct at Rainbow Springs.)

To follow the *Park Creek Trail* from N to S continue downstream of the Nantahala River after leaving the *Park Ridge Trail*. After 0.2 mi a narrow footpath leaves the old RR grade, L, and parallels the old RR grade for 0.9 mi. Either route can be hiked, but the footpath appears to be in need of more use by hikers; it is also a high-water route. The small dam on the river at 1.2 mi is constructed to permit upstream migration for spawning trout. Reach Park Creek at 1.6 mi and cross on a footbridge. Follow up the cascading Park Creek where the trail is flanked by mixed hardwoods, hemlock, rhododendron, ferns, mossy rocks, and profuse wildflowers. At 2.6 mi cross a small stream and ascend gradually on the E side of the slope to cross two more streams before beginning switchbacks at 4.5 mi. Reach FR-71/1 and the Park Gap picnic and parking area at 4.8 mi. Backtrack or return on the *Park Ridge Trail*. (*USGS-FS Map*: Rainbow Springs)

Big Indian Loop Trail (8.0 mi; USFS #34) (F, H); Beech Gap Trail (2.8 mi; USFS #35) (F) **131-132**

LENGTH AND DIFFICULTY: 10.8 mi combined, moderate to strenuous (elev change 910 ft)

TRAILHEAD AND DESCRIPTION: From the Backcountry Information Center drive 2.8 mi on FR-67 to the parking area and signs for *Big Indian Loop Trail* and Big Indian Rd (FR-67/A). The trail is designated a horse trail, but it is used by hikers, bikers, fishermen, and hunters. Begin at the footbridge across the Nantahala River. Turn R and then curve L around a knoll for 0.5 mi to a fork near a tributary to Big Indian Creek. Choose the L fork if taking the shortest route to *Beech Gap Trail*. On a generally level contour proceed through a forest of oak, maple, poplar, hemlock, and rhododendron to cross Big Shoal Branch, followed by a L turn to cross Big Indian Creek at 1.1 mi. Parallel the river in an ascent, then move away from the river in a steep approach at 1.8 mi (where a spur trail descends L 0.6 mi to FR-67). Reach a knoll on Indian Ridge at 2.1 mi, and after 0.3 mi farther arrive at Kilby Gap. Ascend steeply before leveling off at the jct with *Beech Gap Trail* at 2.8 mi. It goes ahead, S; the *Big Indian Loop Trail* turns sharply R, NW.

(The *Beech Gap Trail* weaves around the base of Blue Ridge through a forest of hardwoods, laurel, and flame azalea to cross a streamlet flowing to Kilby Creek in a deep cove at 0.6 mi. Then it makes a longer curve around a toe of Blue Ridge to jct with the *AT* at Beech Gap at 1.1 mi. Backtrack, or follow the *AT* L (N) for 2.5 mi to jct with the *Timber Ridge Trail*. It begins L and descends 2.5 mi to the parking area at Mooney Creek and FR-67. From here it is 1.9 mi down FR-67 to the *Big Indian Loop Trail* parking lot.)

If continuing on the *Big Indian Loop Trail* from the *Beech Gap Trail* jct, the trail at first ascends on the NE slope of Blue Ridge to a curve at 3.1 mi. For the next 2.0 mi through hardwoods, laurel, and rhododendron slicks, the elev stays slightly above the 4,600-ft contour. At the greater change it is 4,800 ft NW and above Deadening Knob. After approaching the S slope of *Upper Trail Ridge,* the trail begins to descend rapidly at 5.4 mi to the headwaters of Nichols Branch. After a switchback and crossing of Nichols Branch, the trail turns E, then S, on a return to the fork for a completion of the loop. Turn L for a return to the parking lot at FR-67 at 8.0 mi. (*USGS-FS Map:* Rainbow Springs)

133 Long Branch Trail (USFS #86) (F)

LENGTH AND DIFFICULTY: 3.8 mi round-trip, moderate

TRAILHEAD AND DESCRIPTION: From the parking area at the Backcountry Information Center go E across the road and climb gradually to a partial lookout of the Nantahala basin at 0.6 mi. Pass through a forest of hemlock, yellow birch, maple, and wildflowers, and cross a horse trail and grazing field with strawberries at 1.5 mi. At 1.7 mi cross Long Branch, which has remnants of an old RR grade. Cross a seeded road, begin a steep climb at 1.8 mi, and at 1.9 mi reach the *AT* on the main ridge line. Backtrack, or make a loop by hiking R on the *AT* for 3.4 mi to Albert Mtn, described above, and jct with the *Bearpen Gap Trail* for a descent to FR-67 for 2.4 mi. Hike downstream on FR-67 for 3.2 mi to the point of origin for a total of 10.9 mi. (*USGS-FS Map:* Rainbow Springs)

134 John Wasilik Memorial Poplar Trail (USFS #30) (F)

LENGTH AND DIFFICULTY: 1.4 mi round-trip, easy

TRAILHEAD AND DESCRIPTION: From Wallace Gap on Old US-64 go 0.4 mi on the Standing Indian Campground road, FR-67, to Rock Gap. Follow the trail sign to a graded trail through an impressive and significant stand of yellow poplar and cherry to the second largest yellow poplar in the US (26.1 ft in circumference and 9.0 ft in diameter). An early Wayah district ranger, John Wasilik, has been remembered by naming the poplar in his honor. (*USGS-FS Map:* Rainbow Springs)

WESSER AREA (Swain and Macon Counties)

Wesser Creek Trail (USFS #26) (F)

LENGTH AND DIFFICULTY: 3.5 mi, strenuous (elev change 2,227 ft)

TRAILHEAD AND DESCRIPTION: This blue-blazed trail is part of the former white-blazed *AT*, which was relocated in 1980 to avoid highway traffic and a residential district. At the jct of US-19 and Wesser Creek Rd (SR-1107), drive up SR-1107 for 1.7 mi and turn L to a parking area. Hike 0.4 mi to cross Wesser Creek in a grassy meadow near the old shelter. Ascend on switchbacks and join the roadway in sections to cross a small stream at 1.5 mi. At 1.7 mi cross another small stream and leave the road to a graded trail with switchbacks. In a forest of hardwoods ascend steeply in sections and at 3.5 mi jct with the new route of the *AT*. A spring is to the L. Backtrack, or take the *AT* for an extended hike. To the L it is 0.7 mi to Wesser Bald (4,627 ft) for panoramic vistas of the Nantahala Mtn range from the newly constructed Wesser Bald platform. Beyond the peak it is 1.4 mi to Tellico Gap and Tellico Rd (SR-1365). If taking the *AT* N, it is 4.8 mi of undulating trail to the A. Rufus Morgan Shelter and another 0.8 mi to US-19 and the Nantahala Outdoor Center by the Nantahala River. (*USGS-FS Map:* Wesser)

WAYAH BALD AREA (Macon County)

A. Rufus Morgan Trail (USFS #27) (F)

LENGTH AND DIFFICULTY: 1.0 mi round-trip, moderate

TRAILHEAD AND DESCRIPTION: From US-64 and US-441/23 jct S of Franklin, go W on US-64 for 3.8 mi. Turn R at sign for Wayah Bald, and go 0.2 mi to sign for Lyndon B. Johnson Conservation Center at jct of Old US-64 and SR-1310. Turn L and go 4.1 mi to FR-388 and turn L. Proceed for 2.0 mi on a gravel road and park at the trail sign, R. Ascend on switchbacks through open woods of tall poplar, cucumber tree, maple, oak, and birch, with ferns and wildflowers banking the trail. Deer may be seen on the trail. Cross a stream at 0.2 mi and reach the lower cascades of Left Prong of Rough Fork at 0.4 mi. Continue on the trail to the base of the upper falls at 0.5 mi. Backtrack.

(The trail is named in honor of the Rev. Albert Rufus Morgan, 97 years old when he died in Asheville, February 14, 1983. Affectionately called the "Modern Moses" and "Uncle Rufus," no one has ever loved the mountains, and the *AT* in particular, more than he. He was founder of the Nantahala Hiking Club in 1950. One of his favorite peaks was Mt LeConte in the Smokies; he climbed it 172 times, the last on his 92d birthday. "He was a poet, a priest, and a great friend of the Appalachian Trail," wrote Judy Jenner in a tribute to him in the *Appalachian Trailway News (ATN)*, May/June 1983. She also wrote a feature story on him in the Nov/Dec edition of *ATN*, 1979.) (*USGS-FS Map:* Wayah Bald)

137- *Wilson Lick Trail (0.2 mi; USFS #369) (F); Wayah Bald Trail (0.3 mi;*
138 *USFS #374) (F, W)*

LENGTH AND DIFFICULTY: 1.0 mi round-trip, easy

TRAILHEADS AND DESCRIPTION: From the jct of Boardtree Rd (FR-380) and Ball Rd (SR-1310) continue up the mountain on SR-1310 to Wayah Gap. Turn R (N) on gravel FR-69. In addition to two short trails from the road, there are two longer unblazed hunters' trails. At 0.5 mi, R, at a parking area
139 is 1.5-mi *Shot Pouch Trail* (USFS #17). An unmaintained hunters' trail, it crosses the *AT* and goes L on the slope of a ridge to cross Shot Pouch Creek before continuing to a dead end. Farther up the road after 0.8 mi is the blue-blazed *Wilson Lick Trail* on the R. It ascends to the *AT*. Continuing up the road for 0.3 mi is FR-69B on the L. Turn or walk from here to a hairpin
140 curve, the S trailhead for 3.5-mi *Rocky Bald Trail* (USFS #18). An unmarked and unmaintained hunters' trail, it crosses the *AT* and follows a ridge before descending to the E side of Rocky Bald. It exits at FR-711 at a hairpin curve on a ridge. (Vehicle access to this exit from the community of Kyle is to turn off Whiteoak Rd onto FR-711 and ascend 3.9 mi to the ridge.) Beyond the jct with FR-69B, continue to a parking area at Wayah Bald (5,342 ft). Follow paved *Wayah Bald Trail* to a tower for spectacular views of Trimont Ridge E and Nantahala Mtns S. (*USGS-FS Map:* Wayah Bald)

3. Pisgah National Forest

"Go up to the top of Pisgah... look at the land with your own eyes..."
—Deuteronomy 3:27

In the 1994 Land and Resource Management Plan of the Nantahala and Pisgah National Forests, 17 special-interest areas (18,458 acres of the forest's total 495, 979 acres) are described in the Pisgah National Forest. Such designated areas are set apart from land for "timber production and not available for use by vehicles." Although not classified as wilderness under the Wilderness Act of 1964, the protection has some of the same characteristics for protecting the natural environment. These areas may consist of unusual geological formations, botanical and wildlife concentrations, bog locations, heath balds, and old-growth forests. Because of the selections, the public is better served. Some of these special-interest places are described in this chapter.

There are three wilderness areas: Middle Prong (7,900 acres) and Shining Rock (18,500 acres) in the Pisgah Ranger District and Linville Gorge (10,975 acres) in the Grandfather Ranger District. Two others in the Grandfather district, Lost Cove and Harper Creek, were proposed by the mid-1980s, but Congress has not acted. The wilderness areas, watershed, and streams provide protection for the many species of wildlife common to the Appalachian region. More than 200 species of plants have been found in the Roan Mtn area alone, and 39 of 55 species of wild orchids in the state are found in the Pisgah. Dominant trees are oak, birch, maple, and poplar. Conifers range from shortleaf pines to red spruce and fragrant fir. Primary among the fish is the brook trout, often stocked in the cascading tributaries. Deer among the big game and squirrel among the small game are the most plentiful.

Pisgah National Forest is the oldest of the state's four national forests. Its irregular boundaries encircle four districts—Pisgah in Buncombe, Haywood, Henderson, and Transylvania Counties; Grandfather in Avery, Burke,

Caldwell, McDowell, and Watauga Counties; Toecane in Avery, Buncombe, Madison, Mitchell, and Yancey Counties; and the French Broad in Haywood and Madison Counties.

The Pisgah is a natural world unto itself with the Blue Ridge Parkway dividing it, the *AT* on its border with Tennessee, and such extraordinary natural attractions as Looking Glass Rock and Falls, Mt Pisgah, Bald Mtn, Roan Mtn Gardens, Table Rock, Hawksbill Mtn, Harper Creek Falls, Sliding Rock, Shortoff Mtn, Upper Creek Falls, Black Mtns, and Big Lost Cove Cliffs. It is also the site of a number of historic firsts. Gifford Pinchot, hired by George Vanderbilt to manage his vast Biltmore Estate, initiated the first forest man-

Upper Creek Falls. Allen de Hart

agement program here in 1892, and six years later Carl A. Schenck opened here the first school of forestry in America, the Biltmore Forest School. (Reconstructed and named the Cradle of Forestry, it is located in the Pisgah Ranger District on US-276.) After Vanderbilt's death in 1914, the area was sold to the US government and in the process became one of the first tracts of the Pisgah National Forest. The first property purchased under the federal Weeks Act of 1911 was 8,100 acres on Curtis Creek in the Grandfather Ranger District.

Pisgah has 40 recreational areas for fishing, picnicking, nature study, hiking, and camping. Some of the areas are designed for primitive camping and have limited facilities to protect the ecology. A directory of these facilities may be requested from one of the addresses below. The *Mountains-to-Sea Trail* (*MST*), planned and under construction from Clingmans Dome to Nags Head since the early 1980s, will incorporate a number of trails already on the NF inventory plus new trails through the Pisgah National Forest from the Rough Butt Bald area to the Beacon Heights area (see chapter 16).

The four districts of the Pisgah National Forest are as follows:

French Broad Ranger District, USFS, PO Box 128, Hot Springs, NC 28743; 704-622-3202. (On Bridge St, US-25/70, in Hot Springs.)

Grandfather Ranger District, USFS, Rte 1, Box 110-A, Nebo, NC 28761; 704-652-2144. (At NE corner of I-40, Nebo exit 90, and Harmony Grove Rd.)

Pisgah Ranger District, USFS, 1001 Pisgah Highway, Pisgah Forest, NC 28768; 704-877-3350. (From jct of US-276/64 and NC-280, N of Brevard, 2.0 mi W on US-276.)

Toecane Ranger District, USFS, PO Box 128, Burnsville, NC 28714; 704-682-6146. (On US-19 Bypass in Burnsville.)

SECTION 1: FRENCH BROAD RANGER DISTRICT

The French Broad Ranger District has 80,335 acres, some of which are the most rugged and isolated terrain in the Appalachians. Its boundaries are almost exclusively in Madison County, with the NE corner of Haywood County adjoining. Its W boundary is flanked by the Cherokee National Forest in Tennessee. Along most of this border is 66.0 mi of the *AT* on high, scenic, and remote ridges and peaks such as Big Butt (4,838 ft); Camp Creek Bald (4,844 ft), the district's highest; Rich Mtn (3,643 ft); Bluff Mtn (4,686 ft); Walnut Mtn (4,280 ft); Max Patch Mtn (4,629 ft); and Snowbird Mtn

(4,263 ft). Sparse population in Madison County allows this beautiful area to remain a tranquil and natural place to love and visit. Hunting, fishing, and running the white water of the French Broad River are popular sports in the district. The varied flora is an enticement to any botanist. An example is described below in the *Laurel River Trail* section.

The recreation areas and points of interest in the district are Rocky Bluff (campground and picnic area: described below); Silver Mine (group campground and picnic area: see *Pump Gap Trail* below); Murray Branch Picnic and Canoe Launch Site (see *River Ridge Trail* below); Harmon Den (dispersed use and day-use area: see description below). The designated horse trails are in the Harmon Den Area, and a designated bike trail is 5.4-mi *Mill* **141** *Ridge Bike Trail* (also open to hikers). To access the bike trail drive 3.4 mi E of Hot Springs on US-25/70 (under the *AT* bridge), turn L on forest road, and turn L again to cross the highway on the bridge. Follow the road to its end at a parking area. The trail has scenic views, particularly of the Laurel River Gorge. Another biking trail is *Laurel River Trail*, described below.

During the early 1990s the district began an expansive effort to reopen some of its overgrown trails (*Green Ridge Trail* is an example); relocate parts of others (*Hickey Ridge Trail* is an example); build new ones (see *River Ridge* **142** *Trail*); and to develop a new access to *Whiteoak Flats Trail* (USFS #286). These efforts and the efforts for environmental protection of the Shelton Laurel Creek backcountry and game land are indications of good leadership and service to the public. The district ranger's office has maps and information on trails and other recreational activities in the district. For information on rafting and canoeing outfitters in Hot Springs contact Madison County Chamber of Commerce, 704-689-9351; for warm natural mineral baths at the Hot Springs, 704-622-7676.

ADDRESS AND ACCESS: District Ranger, French Broad Ranger District, USFS, PO Box 128, Hot Springs, NC 28743; 704-622-3202. The office is on US-25/70 in the center of Hot Springs.

SUPPORT FACILITIES: Because Rocky Bluff Campground does not have hookups or showers, a nearby commercial facility is Hot Springs Campground; 704-622-7676. It is located upriver between the French Broad River and the RR in Hot Springs. It has hot showers (arrangements can be made for natural mineral baths), primitive campsites, and sites with hookups. For *AT* hikers the Hiker Hostel (maintained by the Jesuits of the Catholic Church) is located in Hot Springs. Address: Hiker Hostel, PO Box 7, Hot Springs, NC 28743; 704-622-7366. In Hot Springs are a motel, restaurants, grocery store, and service stations.

SHELTON LAUREL BACKCOUNTRY AREA (Madison County)

Fork Ridge Trail (USFS #285) (F)

LENGTH AND DIFFICULTY: 4.0 mi round-trip, strenuous (elev change 1,610 ft)

TRAILHEAD AND DESCRIPTION: This yellow-blazed trail is also known as *Big Creek Trail*. From the jct of US-25/70 and NC-208, follow NC-208 up Big Laurel Creek for 3.5 mi to jct with NC-212 at Belva. Turn R on NC-212 and proceed for 10.7 mi to Big Creek Rd (SR-1312), which forks L at Carmen Church of God. Follow SR-1312 for 0.7 mi where the pavement ends at a fire warden station. Continue for another 0.6 mi on a gravel road and enter Pisgah National Forest where the road becomes FR-111. After 1.0 mi farther reach parking space, L, at Wildcat Hollow Creek's confluence with Big Creek.

From the R side of the parking area ascend gradually on a well-graded slope that runs E of Fork Ridge. Reach the ridge crest at 0.7 mi. Forest flora consists of hardwoods, with the lower elev having rhododendron and buck-eye, and the higher elev having laurel, flame azalea, and copious patches of large, sweet, highbush blueberries. Spots of wintergreen, dwarf iris, and galax furnish a ground cover. The wildlife includes bear, deer, turkey, grouse, and chipmunk. After reaching a ridge sag at 0.9 mi, ascend steadily, sometimes steeply, on switchbacks to jct with the *AT* at 2.0 mi. (It is 0.2 mi R on the *AT* to the Jerry Cabin Shelter.) Backtrack, or make a 9.2-mi loop with a R (E) on the *AT* for 4.3 mi to a jct with the 3.9-mi *Green Ridge Trail* and a return on FR-111 (see below). (*USGS-FS Maps:* Greystone, Flagpond)

Green Ridge Trail (USFS #287)(F)

LENGTH AND DIFFICULTY: 3.9 mi, strenuous (elev change 2,420 ft)

SPECIAL FEATURES: underground creek, remote, wildflowers

TRAILHEAD AND DESCRIPTION: From the jct of NC-208 and NC-212 at Belva, turn on NC-212 and proceed 10.7 mi to the Carmen Church of God. Turn L at the fork of Big Creek Rd (SR-1312) and go 1.3 mi to the Shelton Sawmill, R. Cross Dry Creek at the FR-111 sign and park in a small area, or turn R if FR-3509 is not gated. Cross the creek and after 1.0 mi leave the gravel road onto an old forest road. Cross the creek repeatedly on a yellow-blazed trail. Forest vegetation is ironwood, poplar, white pine, hemlock, oak, and birch. Both spring and summer wildflowers are exceptionally profuse; they include starry campion, bee balm, trillium, orchids, twisted-stalk, hellebore, meadow rue, Indian-physic, and phlox. Among the forest animals are bear, bobcat, turkey, grouse, owls, chipmunk, and the timber rattlesnake. The creek goes underground in places, appearing dry; thus its name. (Some of the mountain residents have a number of ghost stories about this hollow.) At 1.4 mi the old road ends and the trail begins across the creek. Cross small cove streams in switchbacks at 1.7 and 1.8 mi. Waterfalls are R at 1.9 mi. Curve L and continue to ascend on a well-graded trail that may have borders of nettles. After ascending the slope of Green Ridge, reach the top in a flat area and jct with the AT at 3.9 mi. Backtrack. The jct may not be signed, but it is 4.4 mi R to Devil Fork Gap on the *AT* to NC-212, and L on the *AT* for 4.3 mi to the jct with *Fork Ridge Trail* (see *Fork Ridge Trail* above). (*USGS-FS Maps:* Greystone, Flagpond)

145 *Pounding Mill Trail (USFS #297) (F)*

LENGTH AND DIFFICULTY: 6.4 mi, strenuous (elev change 2,764 ft)

CONNECTING TRAILS:

146   *Hickey Fork Trail* (2.3 mi; USFS #292) strenuous (F)

147   *White Oak Trail* (2.2 mi; USFS #293) strenuous (F); *(AT)*

SPECIAL FEATURES: logging history, remote, Camp Creek Bald

TRAILHEAD AND DESCRIPTION: From the jct of US-25/70 and NC-208, take NC-208 for 7.2 mi to a bridge over Little Laurel Creek. Sixty yd beyond is a USFS gated road, R. On the L of the highway is limited shoulder parking. (If needing to turn around, continue around the curve to turn around at a former service station.) Follow an easy treadway on a winding logging road on the ridge side. Below, on the R, is Pounding Mill Creek with an old road paralleling it on the other side (the former *Pounding Mill Trail*). On the trail are white pine, hemlock, rhododendron, laurel, dog hobble, and ferns. Cross a cascading tributary at 1.1 mi and at 1.9 mi rock-hop Pounding Mill Creek. Here in a grassy area is the remains of a former sawmill. Buttercups, trillium, and waterleaf grow in the damp grounds nearby. Cross the cascading creek twice more, pass through beds of poison ivy, and enter a more open forest with tall hardwoods. At a small waterfall leave the creek and begin a steep ascent. Reach Pounding Mill Gap at 3.4 mi. (To the R is a 0.7-mi old woods road to Angelico Knob [3,429 ft]. An overgrown road descends to connect with Duckmill Rd [SR-1308].) Continue a steep ascent to Seng Gap at 4.0 mi, and jct with yellow-blazed *Hickey Fork Trail* R.

(The *Hickey Fork Trail* descends into a gorge and follows the West Prong of Hickey Fork. From its upper reaches the trail descends rapidly along a scenic stream for 0.9 mi to reach a spectacular flume and waterfall. At 1.0 mi cross a tributary with a flume, R. Descend steeply to pass another flume on the creek, L, and at 1.2 mi cross other small tributaries in a gorge of hemlock, poplar, and rhododendron. At 1.8 mi rock-hop the creek, turn

L, ascend, reach a ridge top, descend, and reach an old RR grade. Cross a bridge over the East Prong of Hickey Fork and ascend steps to FR-465. Turn R 75 yd to gate and parking area. Access to this point from Belva intersection of NC-208 and NC-212, take NC-212 6.9 mi [0.3 mi past a store on the R] to Hickey Fork Rd [SR-1310] L. It is 1.2 mi farther to the parking area.)

Continuing on the *Pounding Mill Trail* ascend steeply and at 4.7 mi jct with *White Oak Trail*, R, in Seng Gap.

(The *White Oak Trail* descends to cross the headwaters of Hickey Fork at 0.1 mi, then drops deeply into a damp and dark hollow at 0.4 mi. In a rocky hardwood forest with groves of rhododendron and tall hemlock, the trail approaches a waterfall, R, at 0.6 mi. Descend steeply and proceed around a ridge [scenic views in the wintertime] to switchbacks. At 1.5 mi is a jct with a forest road, R, but turn L among laurel. There is a jct with a logging road at 2.0 mi; keep R; a clear-cut is L. Descend and arrive at FR-465 at a cul-de-sac among rhododendron, roadside patches of coltsfoot, and tall poplar, the end of the trail. From here it is 1.3 mi R, with scenic East Prong of Hickey Fork paralleling L, to the parking area at *Hickey Fork Trail* described above.)

On the *Pounding Mill Trail* ascend to a natural spring (may be seasonal) at 4.9 mi. Ascend steeply on Seng Ridge, but level out at 5.1 mi. The last water source is at 5.3 and 5.6 mi. At 6.4 mi the *AT* crosses the trail in a rhododendron grove. (To the L the *AT* is 6.2 mi S to Allen Gap at NC-208, and 13.9 mi N to Devil Fork Gap at NC-212.) Ahead a 0.2-mi spur trail steeply ascends to the top of Camp Creek Bald (4,844 ft) at the Tennessee state line. From a lookout tower are fantastic views W of the Cherokee National Forest, and into the Tennessee Valley, N and E, is the chain of Bald Mtns, and SW to the Great Smoky Mtns. (*USGS-FS Maps:* Greystone, Hot Springs, White Rock)

HOT SPRINGS AREA (Madison County)

Shut-in Creek Trail (USFS #296) (F) 148

LENGTH AND DIFFICULTY: 4.0 mi round-trip, easy

TRAILHEAD AND DESCRIPTION: From Hot Springs drive W on US-25/70 for 2.7 mi to Upper Shut-in Creek Rd (SR-1183) and turn L at a store. Go 2.3 mi to a small parking area on the N side of the Shut-in Creek bridge. Follow an old jeep road, SE, and upstream of the East Fork of Shut-in Creek, in a hollow. Frequently rock-hop the stream and its small tributaries. Other sections of the trail are wet from mountain seepage. Liverwort covers some of the rocks. At 1.0 mi pass through a beautiful meadow of clovers, asters, daisies, and other wildflowers. Deer have been seen here. Enter a white pine stand and at 1.7 mi a hemlock stand. Ascend to ruins of a pioneer homestead at 1.8 mi. Jct with the *AT* and FR-3543 at 2.0 mi in Garenflo Gap. Backtrack. (L it is 6.6 mi on the *AT* to Hot Springs, and R it is 3.5 mi to Bluff Mtn [4,686 ft].) (*USGS-FS Maps:* Lemon Gap, Paint Rock)

149- *Jack Branch Trail (2.4 mi; USFS #299) (F); River Ridge Loop Trail (1.3*
150 *mi; USFS #281) (F)*

LENGTH AND DIFFICULTY: 6.1 mi combined, round-trip, easy to strenuous (elev change 1,400 ft)

TRAILHEAD AND DESCRIPTION: From US-25/70 at the end of the French Broad River bridge in Hot Springs, turn on Paint Rock Rd (SR-1304). Follow downriver for 4.1 mi to end of pavement, and continue another 0.3 mi on a gravel road. Park L by the river, across from Bartley Island. Enter the trail near a sign and follow a blue-blazed trail on an old road in a deep ravine up the E slope, away from Jack Branch, for 0.1 mi. The forest flora includes mixed hardwoods with hemlock, rhododendron, fetterbush, and buffalo nut (*Pyrularia pubera*) in the lower elev, and chestnut oak, laurel, and pines in the upper elev. At 0.4 mi leave the damp area and reach a ridge crest at 0.5 mi. (Plans by the district are to construct a short connector trail, L, on the ridge to *River Ridge Loop Trail*.) Follow the ridge in a generally xeric environment with patches of wintergreen, trailing arbutus, blueberries, and azalea. At 0.9 mi turn NW, follow an upgrade in and out of tributary coves of Murray Branch to 1.9 mi, and begin a NE ascent through old fields with views of French Broad River Valley. Reach the Tennessee state line and Cherokee NF in a gentle gap at FR-422 at 2.5 mi. Backtrack. (Primitive trails lead L for 1.9 mi to Bearpen Gap and *Ricker Branch Trail* into Tennessee, and R for 3.5 mi to Rich Mtn Lookout Tower and the *AT*.)

For the *River Ridge Loop Trail* trailhead continue downriver 0.7 mi from *Jack Branch Trail* on SR-1304 to Murray Branch Rec Area (mainly for picnicking near the French Broad River). Park on the L. Walk across the road to the R side of a small stream at the trailhead. Ascend 0.2 mi to a fork in the loop. Turn R through white pines, and arrive at the ridge rim for a beautiful view of the river, R. (Before turning L to return, a connector trail may have been constructed R to connect with *Jack Branch Trail*.) Turn L at 0.7 mi to follow an old road for a return to Murray Branch Rec Area. (*USGS-FS Map:* Hot Springs)

151- *Pump Gap Trail (5.5 mi; USFS #309) (F); Lover's Leap Trail (0.6 mi;*
152 *USFS #308) (F)*

LENGTH AND DIFFICULTY: 7.1 mi combined, round-trip, moderate to strenuous

TRAILHEADS AND DESCRIPTION: From the N side of the French Broad River bridge on US-25/70 in Hot Springs, curl under the bridge on Lover's Leap Rd for 0.3 mi to the FS boundary gate and parking area at Silver Mine Creek. Begin *Pump Gap Trail* (loop) whether on the road upstream to the campground, or jointly with the orange-blazed *Lover's Leap Trail*, which ascends on the R near the gate. After 0.2 mi the *Pump Gap Trail* descends L to the campground area and the *Lover's Leap Trail* turns sharply R. (It climbs 0.4 mi to a jct with the *AT* and a remarkable vista of the French Broad River, the town of Hot Springs, and Spring Creek Mtns beyond. From this rocky precipice is a drop of 500 ft and part of a Cherokee Indian romance legend. Backtrack, or descend on the *AT* to the river and return to the parking area for a loop of 1.6 mi. If following the *AT* L [N] from Lover's Leap it is 1.9 mi to Pump Gap, where a return on the *Pump Gap Trail* makes a loop of 4.0 mi to the parking area.)

On the yellow-blazed *Pump Gap Trail* pass the Silver Mine Campground and follow upstream among hemlock, tulip tree, rhododendron, and fetterbush. Pass two former explosive storage bunkers, R. Cross tributaries of Silver Mine Creek five times and at 1.0 mi jct with the return trailhead of the loop, L. Ascend through evergreens and at 1.5 mi intersect with the *AT* in Pump Gap, an area with tall hardwoods and hemlock. Cross the *AT*, gradually descend, make a sharp L away from Pump Branch at 2.1 mi. Ascend two switchbacks around a dry mtn side where banks of wintergreen and trailing arbutus grow. Turn L on a ridgeline at 2.3 mi. Cross, or briefly follow, a few old logging roads before an ascent to cross the *AT* again at 3.1 mi. After 100 yd, R, is the grave site of Lucinda Daniel. Start a descent into a beautiful cove of hemlock, rhododendron, and cascades at 4.3 mi. Complete the loop at 4.5 mi, turn R, and return to the parking lot at 5.5 mi. (*USGS-FS Map: Hot Springs*)

Laurel River Trail (USFS #310) (F, B)

LENGTH AND DIFFICULTY: 6 mi round-trip, easy

SPECIAL FEATURES: RR history, exceptional diversity of plant life

TRAILHEAD AND DESCRIPTION: Park at the jct of US-25/70 and NC-208 in the parking area, near dumpsters, on the E side of Big Laurel Creek (1,600 ft). Enter on a private gravel road, descend slightly, and bear R to a fork at 0.1 mi. Arrive at a private dwelling and a gate at 0.2 mi. Follow an old RR grade with vertical cliffs L and white-water rapids R. Pass a spring at 0.4 mi L and a burley tobacco barn L at 0.7 mi. Cross the Pisgah National Forest boundary at 0.9 mi. On a yellow-blazed trail unsurpassed for riverside beauty, pass a series of rapids at 1.2 mi. Turn L at 2.9 mi to Runion, logging and mining settlement of the past. Reach the Southern RR tracks and the French

Broad River at 3.0 mi. Backtrack.

In the spring and summer of 1977 and 1978, the N.C. Natural Heritage Program of the Department of Natural Resources and Community Development made a botanical study of this 3.0-mi trail. The discovery of more than 250 species of vascular plants was an overwhelming surprise. Five species listed as threatened or endangered were found. Among them are alumroot (*Heuchera longiflora*), wild rye grass (*Elymus riparius*), saxifrage (*Saxifraga caroliniana*), and a species each of phacelia and corydalis. Bluebells, Dutchman's pipe, orchids, and soapwort (*Saponaria officinalis*) were among the common wildflowers. (*USGS-FS Map:* Hot Springs)

ROCKY BLUFF RECREATION AREA (Madison County)

The Rocky Bluff Recreation Area provides camping, picnicking, hiking, nature study, and fishing in Spring Creek. The area is open usually from mid-April to mid-December. It has flush toilets, lavatories, and water fountains but no showers. The campground is on a high ridge under tall white pines and oaks and has cement tables, grill, and graveled tent sites. The area was formerly a residential settlement with farms and a school.

ACCESS: From Hot Springs go S on NC-209 for 3.3 mi.

154- *Spring Creek Nature Trail (1.6 mi; USFS #312) (F); Van Cliff Trail (2.7*
155 *mi; USFS #313) (F)*

LENGTH AND DIFFICULTY: 4.3 mi combined, easy to strenuous

TRAILHEADS AND DESCRIPTION: From the S edge of the center of the Rocky Bluff Recreation Area (3.3 mi S of Hot Springs on NC-209), follow the trail sign and descend gradually on the yellow-blazed *Spring Creek Nature Trail.* At 0.5 mi arrive at a vista of Spring Creek near a large rock formation. Turn L for 65 yd and then turn R to follow a well-graded and scenic trail around the mtn on the L side of the cascading stream. At 1.2 mi turn L and begin an ascent on an old road to the campground and picnic area. Flora includes white pine, hemlock, fetterbush, basswood, oak, liverwort, and abundant wildflowers.

For the more strenuous *Van Cliff Trail,* follow the yellow blazes SW from the S edge of the center of the picnic area on a grassy road. At 0.1 mi turn R over a rocky treadway (with poison ivy) and climb to NC-209 at 0.3 mi. Turn L on the highway for 50 yd and go R on an old road. Ascend, sometimes steeply, R of cascading Long Mtn Branch. At 0.7 mi turn sharply L over the branch and follow another old road; hike the N side of the ridge. Forest trees consist of white pine, hemlock, basswood, oak, and hickory. Parts of the trail have running cedar, cancer root (*Conopholis americana*), and Indian pipe (*Monotropa uniflora*). Make a sharp L over a stream in a cove at 0.9 mi. Reach the top of a ridge at 1.3 mi, and begin a descent into a rocky ravine at 1.6 mi. Follow an old road and switchbacks to NC-209 at 2.2 mi. Cross the highway and descend steeply, turn sharply R among boulders at 2.4 mi, cross Long Mtn Branch at 2.5 mi, and return to the campground at 2.7 mi. (This trail is also known as the *Long Mountain Branch Trail*.) (*USGS-FS Map:* Spring Creek)

HARMON DEN AREA (Haywood County)

The Harmon Den Area is an excellent place for dispersed usage. Although there are not any developed campgrounds, primitive campsites are along FR-148. Users must follow "no-trace" and "carry in, carry out" camping rules. Hunting, fishing, and horseback riding are also popular activities. At the jct of FR-148 and FR-148A is a display board with an area trail map and guidelines for day use. No overnight camping is allowed here. Among day-use activities are hiking the scenic *AT*, forest roads, and the equestrian trails. Significant to this area are five horse trails (F, H), one of which (*Cherry Creek Trail*) is described below. The others are *Buckeye Ridge Trail* (5.4 mi; **156** USFS #304), accessed on SR-1182 S of jct at *AT* crossing; *Cherry Ridge Trail* **157** (1.6 mi; USFS #300), accessed on SR-1182 or on FR-148; *Cold Springs Trail* **158** (3.6 mi; USFS #302), accessed at jct of FR-148 and FR-3526; and *Robert Gap* **159** *Trail* (2.5 mi; USFS #303), accessed at jct of FR-148 and SR-1182. See access description to FR-148 under *Cherry Creek Trail* below.

Cherry Creek Trail (USFS #300) (F, H)   **160**

LENGTH AND DIFFICULTY: 2.5 mi, moderate to strenuous (elev change 1,350 ft)

TRAILHEAD AND DESCRIPTION: From the jct of I-40 and FR-148, Harmon Den, exit 7, and 7.0 mi E of the Tennessee state line, drive up the mtn on FR-148 for 4.4 mi to the S trailhead in a curve at Cherry Creek. (Because the trail has a 1,350-ft elev gain, the N trailhead may be preferred with a vehicle switch.) Continue up the mtn on FR-148 for 1.8 mi to take a L on Max Patch Rd (R-1182) and go 1.6 mi to jct with the *AT* at the state line. (To the R the *AT* leads 0.8 mi to the grassy bald of Max Patch Mtn [4,629 ft]. If you have not hiked this priceless natural wonder, do not leave until you experience its awesome panoramic beauty. It is the "crown jewel of the Appalachian Mountains," wrote Bob Proudman. Dedicated July 9, 1983, as part of a 5.0-mi relocation of the *AT*, it is the result of 14 years of work and negotiations by Arch Nichols and the Carolina Mountain Club, USFS, and others.) Begin the *Cherry Creek Trail* on the *AT* (S), but after 0.2 mi leave the *AT*, L, at a blue blaze. In a forest of oak, hemlock, flame azalea, galax, and blue-bead, reach a logging road at 0.7 mi. Turn L and then R after 75 yd. Descend into a pristine forest of large hemlocks and rock formations with leafy lichen at 1.1 mi. Cross a stream at 1.5 mi and pass cascades at 2.0 mi. At 2.3 mi reach a timber road, turn R for 50 ft and then L. On the W side of Cherry Creek descend to FR-148 at 2.5 mi. (*USGS-FS Map:* Lemon Gap)

161- *Rube Rock Trail (4.3 mi; USFS #314) (F); Groundhog Creek Trail (1.9*
162 *mi; USFS #315) (F); Appalachian Trail (2.9 mi; USFS #1) (F)*

LENGTH AND DIFFICULTY: 9.7 mi combined, round-trip, strenuous (elev change 1,840 ft)

TRAILHEADS AND DESCRIPTION: From I-40, exit 7, described above for *Cherry Creek Trail*, drive up FR-148 to FR-148A, L, just before the Harmon Den parking lot. Drive up FR-148A 1.3 mi to Browns Gap and intersect the *AT*. Park here. Follow the *AT* S 0.6 mi to jct with the *Rube Rock Trail*, L. (It is 2.3 mi on the *AT* to Deep Gap, from which a return on the loop is made.) The trail descends on the E side of the ridgeline of Harmon Den Mtn for 0.5 mi before easing out on the crest. After a knob, it descends to a jct with FR-358A (which is also a horse trail) at 0.9 mi. Turn R, follow it 0.5 mi, turn L off the road, and continue the descent to a tributary of the Rube Rock Branch at 1.4 mi. Criss-cross the stream and at 2.2 mi cross the main branch among tulip tree, hemlock, and rhododendron. Cross the branch twice more to the slopes of a side ridge of Harmon Den Mtn. Descend steeply in hardwoods and laurel to Tom Hall Branch, where the traffic sounds of I-40 can be heard at 3.3 mi. Turn W around a toe of the ridge to enter the hollow of Rube Rock Branch. Cross the branch again, curve around the toe of Hickory Ridge to more I-40 sounds, and go N to jct with *Groundhog Creek Trail*. (To the L it is 0.5 mi out to a field, FR-3522, and a gate at a dead-end I-40 ramp, 5.9 mi W from the welcome center and rest area. No parking is allowed at the ramp or forest gate.)

Ascend the hollow of *Groundhog Creek Trail* through tulip tree, maple, hemlock, and birch. At 0.9 mi cross Chestnut Orchard Branch, followed by Ephraim Branch. At 1.7 mi reach Groundhog Creek Shelter, a stone shelter with five bunks. A spring is nearby. Continue ahead for 0.2 mi to reach the *AT* at Deep Gap (also called Groundhog Creek Gap). A loop can be made R to join the *Rube Rock Trail* after 2.3 mi on the *AT* for a return loop of 9.7 mi. (On the *AT* at Deep Gap it is 5.6 mi NE to Max Patch Rd [SR-1182], and 7.8 mi SW to Pigeon River and I-40.) (*USGS-FS Map:* Waterville)

SECTION 2: GRANDFATHER RANGER DISTRICT

The Grandfather Ranger District with 186,735 acres is partially in McDowell, Burke, Caldwell, and Avery Counties. The Linville Gorge Wilderness Area, in the center of the district, is in Burke County and has 10,975 acres that protect the natural environment of the Linville River and its divides. Two other wilderness areas, Lost Cove and Harper Creek, are proposed in the Harper Creek Area of Caldwell and Avery Counties. The district's W boundary is the Blue Ridge Parkway, and a section of the Toecane Ranger District adjoins in the SW near Mt Mitchell. Among the outstanding localities for scenic beauty are Table Rock, Hawksbill Mtn, Shortoff Mtn, the three cliffs of Lost Cove, the major waterfalls of Harper and North Harper Creeks, and Wiseman's View. There are five picnic areas: Barkhouse on NC-181; Mulberry NW of Lenoir; Old Fort W of Old Fork; Table Rock NW of Morganton; and Woodlawn on US-221 (see the next paragraph). Two picnic and camping areas (without hookups) are at Curtis Creek, N of Old Fork and off US-70 NW, and Mortimer, SE of Edgemont and off NC-90.

The district has 70 trails on inventory, some of which have been abandoned because of overgrowth and lack of use. Trails are not blazed (with the exception of the *MST*); thus, hikers should have a map of the district (two specific ones are Linville Gorge Wilderness Area and Harper Creek Area). One of the shortest and most popular trails is *Wiseman's View Trail* (0.2 mi; USFS **163** #224) (F, W). It is the only paved trail suitable for wheelchair usage and is accessible on Kistler Memorial Highway, 3.8 mi from NC-183 in the community of Linville. The longest trail, *Wilson Ridge Trail* (14.7 mi; USFS #269) (F, **164** B), is primarily used by bikers. A number of backcountry forest roads are used by equestrians. Combining a number of established trails, including 8.0 mi of new trail for a total of 46.5 mi, is the *MST*. It goes through the district from the *Overmountain Victory Trail,* W of Linville Gorge rim NE to Beacon Heights near Grandfather Mtn (see *MST* in chapter 16). There is an exercise trail, the 14-station loop *Woodlawn Trail* (0.5 mi; USFS #220), at the Woodlawn Picnic **165** Area, 6.5 mi N of Marion on US-221, where the *MST* crosses from Woods Mtn W to an unfinished point E at the North Fork of the Catawba River.

ADDRESS AND ACCESS: District Ranger, Grandfather Ranger District, USFS, Rte 1, Box 110-A, Nebo, NC 28761; 704-652-2144, exit 90 (Nebo–Lake James) on I-40.

OLD FORT PICNIC AREA (McDowell County)

166 *Young's Ridge/Kitsuma Peak Trail (USFS #205) (F, B)*

LENGTH AND DIFFICULTY: 4.2 mi, moderate to strenuous (elev change 1,565 ft)

TRAILHEAD AND DESCRIPTION: (This trail includes the former *Kitsuma Peak Trail* and the *Young's Ridge Trail* and is also used by mountain bikers.) In Old Fork on US-70 at the jct with Catawba Ave, go W 0.3 mi on US-70 and turn R on Mill Creek Rd (SR-1407). Drive N 3.0 mi and turn L into the Old Fort Picnic Area, L. Park and follow the trail upstream on the L through a ravine dark with heavy hemlock shade. (On the R there is a 0.5-mi loop trail near Swannanoa Creek.) Goats beard (*Aruncus dioicus*) grows on the damp banks. Follow the switchbacks to the ridge top at 0.9 mi. Turn R and continue W up and down knobs to Kitsuma Peak (3,195 ft) at 3.6 mi. Views of Greybeard Mtn and Mt Mitchell Wildlife Management Area are impressive. Descend on switchbacks to an open path by a fence on the N side at I-40 at 4.0 mi. Turn R and at 4.2 mi reach a parking overlook at Ridgecrest. (Access from I-40 is Ridgecrest, exit 66.) (Overlook gate usually closed at 8:00 PM. Check with the Blue Ridge Baptist Conference Center across the street from the gate for information on parking.) (*USGS-FS Maps:* Black Mtn, Old Fort)

HEARTBREAK RIDGE AREA (McDowell County)

167- *Heartbreak Ridge Trail (4.5 mi; USFS #208) (F); Star Gap Trail (1.5 mi;*
168 *USFS #209) (F)*

LENGTH AND DIFFICULTY: 6.0 mi combined; strenuous (elev change 2,928 ft)

SPECIAL FEATURES: Glass Rock and Licklog Knobs, scenic, remote

TRAILHEADS AND DESCRIPTION: The N trailhead access is at BRP milepost 354.7, and the S trailhead is at Brookside Baptist Church on Graphite Rd (SR-1408). Access to the church from Old Fort is W on Old US-70 to Mill Creek Rd (SR-1400), R. After 2.2 mi it turns R on Graphite Rd. The church is 0.2 mi farther, R. There are not any signs or blazes.

If hiking from the N trailhead, park on a grassy flat shoulder of the BRP (but do not leave vehicles here overnight). Cross the road and enter an inconspicuous opening in dense rhododendron. After 0.1 mi is Hemphill Spring, 40 ft L from skeletal roots of an American chestnut. At 0.2 mi jct with a pioneer road at a beech tree in a flat area. (Across the road is the abandoned *Glass Rock Knob Trail* [6.0 mi; USGS #226]. It drops precipitously on switchbacks with scattered quartz and mica into a gorge with cascades and multiple tributaries to Mill Creek. Its S trailhead is closed at private property NW of Graphite community.)

On the pioneer road turn L, ascend to 4,840 ft, then descend to a wildlife clearing with remnants of a farm disk at 0.5 mi. Keep L at the trail fork, and go 0.1 mi to another trail fork. *Heartbreak Ridge Trail* goes R at a sign "Adopt-A-Trail, Camp Woodson." (The pioneer road to the L becomes an overgrown trail for an isolated exploratory route to Iron Mtn, a ridge that parallels Heartbreak Ridge. The route skirts Rocky Mtn, crosses *Star Gap Trail* after about 3.5 mi, and then follows FR-4030 about 6.5 mi to exit at Curtis Creek Rd [SR-1227] 1.5 mi NW of US-70 and 1.8 mi E from RR tracks in Old Fort. Modified USGS topo maps Montreat and Old Fort should be used for this exploratory route.)

After a few yd from the *Heartbreak Ridge Trail* adoption sign there is an overlook, R, into Mill Creek Gorge and the Pinnacle (5,665 ft) to the NW. Descend on a well-maintained trail through chestnut, oak, maple, laurel, and scattered patches of witch hazel and galax. At 1.2 mi turn sharply L (avoid ATV route ahead). Continue descending to a twin knob at 2.1 mi. From a saddle ascend to Licklog Knob (3,225 ft) at 4.1 mi. Descend to a saddle at 4.5 mi to jct with *Star Gap Trail*. (Ahead is an abandoned section of *Star Gap Trail* that drops to Jarrett Creek, ascends to Star Gap, and descends to private property at Newberry Creek.)

Turn R on *Star Gap Trail* and descend on 20 switchbacks for 1.0 mi to a campsite. In the descent are oaks, black gum, laurel, two species of rhododendron, and banks of meadow rue, bloodroot, and yellow violets. Follow an old forest road downstream to rock-hop Pritchard Creek at 1.1 mi, cross Southern RR at 1.3 mi, and after 100 yd turn L off the old road for a descent to a meadow at Brookside Baptist Church at 1.5 mi, the end of the trail. (See access description above.) (*USGS-FS Maps:* Montreat, Old Fort)

CURTIS CREEK RECREATION AREA (McDowell County)

Recreation activities here are camping (with vault toilets and hand water pump), picnicking, fishing, and hiking. A natural spring is at the Snooks Nose trailhead. The area is historic because it is part of the first 8,100-acre tract purchased under the 1911 Weeks Act. The tract is dedicated to Dr. Chase P. Ambler (1865–1932) of Asheville for his efforts to establish the national forests.

ACCESS: From I-40 exits 72 and 73 at Old Fort, go 0.2 mi into town, turn R on US-70, and go 1.0 mi to jct, L, on Curtis Creek Rd (SR-1227), which becomes FR-482. After 5.1 mi from US-70, reach the campground.

SUPPORT FACILITIES: A year-round commercial campground in the area is

Triple C Campground, 6.0 mi N on NC-80 from its jct with US-70, NW of Marion. Full svc, swimming pool. Address: 1666 Buck Creek Rd, Marion, NC 28752; 704-724-4099. Service stores in Old Fort; motels and shopping centers are in Marion.

169 *Snooks Nose Trail (USFS #211) (F)*

LENGTH AND DIFFICULTY: 4.0 mi, strenuous (elev gain 2,800 ft)

SPECIAL FEATURE: views of Iron Mtn range and Newberry Creek watershed

TRAILHEAD AND DESCRIPTION: At the S entrance to the campground (near old rock post of former CCC camp) enter on the old road (a natural spring is R in the hemlocks); curve in a cove; rock-hop a stream at 0.3 mi in a forest of hemlock, poplar, birch, and beech; and ascend steeply. At 0.7 mi reach a spur ridge, level off, then ascend steeply again, R, off the old road (trail direction is vague here). Reach a ridge crest, turn L at 1.2 mi. Pass R of a large cliff at 1.3 mi and reach an outcropping with vistas at 2.0 mi, after a number of switchbacks. A religious testimony about the mountains is lettered on the rocks. Continue along the ridge crest, ascend to Laurel Knob (4,325 ft) without views at 3.0 mi. In a forest of galax, laurel, and rhododendron reach a gap at 3.4 mi. Ascend steeply to the Green Knob Overlook and a sign about the USFS on the Blue Ridge Parkway (mp 350.4) at 4.0 mi. Backtrack or use second vehicle up to the BRP from the campground on FR-482. (*USGS-FS Map:* Old Fort)

170 *Hickory Branch Trail (USFS #213) (F)*

LENGTH AND DIFFICULTY: 4.0 mi round-trip, moderate to strenuous (elev change 1,100 ft)

SPECIAL FEATURES: primitive, waterfalls, wildlife

TRAILHEAD AND DESCRIPTION: There are two campground trailheads. One ascends the hillside by the hand water pump, the other from the lower end of the campground on a FR. They join 0.6 mi up Hickory Branch. From the pump ascend to the ridge, descend, and follow an old woods road upstream to a ravine wash and jct with the other route. If using the FR route, rock-hop Curtis Creek on the FR but leave the road at the end of the meadow at a holly tree and a beech tree. Go upstream, cross the branch, and join the other route near cascades and pools in the ravine. Hemlocks and rhododendron are prominent. At 0.8 mi reach the confluence of streams, cross the L fork, and ascend L of scenic cascades. After 11 switchbacks through laurel, blueberry, and turkey grass reach the ridge top in a saddle at 2.0 mi. Backtrack. (The *Leadmine Gap Trail* [USFS #212] goes L but is obstructed with forest growth. The old open trail R leads down to Mackey Creek.) (*USGS-FS Map:* Old Fort)

Mackey Mountain Trail (USFS #216) (F)   **171**

LENGTH AND DIFFICULTY: 8.0 mi, moderate to strenuous (elev gain 2,115 ft)

SPECIAL FEATURES: bear sanctuary, remote

TRAILHEAD AND DESCRIPTION: The NW access to this trail is at the jct of Curtis Creek Rd (FR-482) and Sugar Cove Rd (FR-1188), 4.4 mi up from the Curtis Creek Campground on FR-482 and 1.8 mi down the mtn on FR-482 from BRP mp 333. The trail is not blazed, but the orange bear sanctuary markers make good directions for the first 5.0 mi. Water is infrequent or nonexistent on the ridgeline. Begin at the road jct and ascend an embankment or follow the old road R through rhododendron and oak to the W slope of the ridge. In addition to the bear, grouse, and turkey habitat, yellow-jacket nests are commonplace on the trail banks. At 1.0 mi switch to the E side of the ridge, but soon return to follow across a long knob and to a narrow ridge before ascending Narrow Knob (3,440 ft) at 2.8 mi. Follow a narrow rim, then a level area to skirt W of Mackey Mtn (4,035 ft) at 4.0 mi and jct with an old trail, R. Continue ahead along the ridge, ascend to a knob (3,960 ft), and descend to a trail jct at 6.2 mi, R. *Greenlee Mountain* **172** *Trail* (USFS #222) descends 2.0 mi to Maple Hill Rd (SR-1414). Turn L on the *Mackey Mountain Trail* and descend, partially on steep woods roads among virgin poplar. Follow switchbacks (difficult to follow in places) and cross a dry streambed at 6.7 mi. Bear R at an old road jct at 7.5 mi. Leave the forest boundary at 7.6 mi, cross Deep Cove Creek, go 160 yd, turn a sharp L, cross the creek again, go 35 yd, and turn R on an old road at 7.8 mi. Exit from the trees in the center of two private driveways. Go across the bridge over Clear Creek to a small parking area on public Clear Creek Rd. (If parking here, use caution not to block the gated road upstream or to drive across the private bridge to park.) A second vehicle is advisable. It is 2.6 mi downstream on Clear Creek Rd (SR-1422) to US-70, and R 5.4 mi on US-70 to Curtis Creek Rd, R. (*USGS-FS Maps:* Old Fort, Marion W)

WOODS MOUNTAIN AREA (McDowell County)

Woods Mountain Trail (USFS #218) (F)   **173**

LENGTH AND DIFFICULTY: 10.6 mi round-trip, moderate

CONNECTING TRAIL:

(*Woods Mountain Access Trail*, moderate)

Armstrong Creek Trail (2.5 mi; USFS #223, strenuous, elev change 1,420 ft)   **174**

SPECIAL FEATURES: chinquapin patches, remote, vistas

TRAILHEAD AND DESCRIPTION: (This trail is also the *MST*, which has a white circle blaze.) Park at the Buck Creek Gap jct of NC-80 and BRP mp 344.1, on the E side. Follow a sign up the BRP svc road (*Woods Mountain Access Trail*) that parallels the BRP for 0.7 mi to Hazelwood Gap, the beginning of the *Woods Mountain Trail*. Turn R on the trail, opposite a large white oak, and skirt S of the knob. After 0.2 mi jct with *Armstrong Creek Trail*, L in a small gap.

(The *Armstrong Creek Trail* is primitive but passable in its steep descent on switchbacks to the headwaters of Armstrong Creek at 0.7 mi. In a forest of oak, birch, poplar, hemlock, and rhododendron, it parallels the creek generally, but crosses it eight times and crosses some small drains. Reach a cul-de-sac in the road at the Armstrong Fish Hatchery at 3.0 mi. Ingress here is up Armstrong Creek Rd [SR-1443] for 4.5 mi from NC-226A, 7.4 mi SE of Little Switzerland.)

On the *Woods Mountain Trail* the ridge becomes a narrow spine covered with blueberries, turkey grass, laurel, and chinquapin. Dominant trees on the trail at this point are oak and pitch pine. Scenic views of Table Rock, Hawksbill, Mt Mitchell, Green Knob, and Armstrong Valley are found. Other views along the ridge include Mackey Mtn and Lake Tahoma. Descend to a saddle of oak, hemlock, and laurel at 1.0 mi. At 1.7 mi the trail slopes on the N side of the ridge in an arbor of rhododendron and galax. There are more views L (N) from an outcrop at 3.2 mi. Particularly attractive is a stand of tall hemlock after a saddle at 3.8 mi. Ascend steeply on a rocky ridge at 4.2 mi where for the next 0.2 mi are impressive views L (N) of Grandfather Mtn, Hawksbill, and Table Rock. At 5.1 mi jct with an old road, R and L. To the L it is 0.3 mi to the site of the former Woods Mtn Lookout Tower (3,646 ft). Backtrack, or follow the *MST* R down the mtn for 7.9 mi to US-276, 0.1 mi S of the Woodlawn Roadside Park parking lot. (See chapter 16.) (*USGS-FS Maps:* Celo, Little Switzerland)

SUPPORT FACILITIES: (See Curtis Creek Rec Area.)

LINVILLE GORGE WILDERNESS AREA (Burke County)

The Linville Gorge Wilderness Area has 10,975 acres of wild, rugged, and scenic terrain. It is a distinct challenge to the climber, hiker, camper, and naturalist. Its boundaries are on the canyon rims. Its west side is near the Kistler Memorial Highway (SR-1238), a gravel road on Linville Mtn. The E boundary extends from Jonas Ridge to the S base of Shortoff Mtn. The wilderness does not include the famous Linville Falls, 0.3 mi upstream from the N boundary. (The Falls are part of the NPS described in chapter 6.) For 14.0 mi through the wilderness, the Linville River's white water cascades in a descent of 2,000 ft. Major escarpments rise on the river's walls. The wilderness is rich in both plant and animal life. There are five species of rare plants, four species of rhododendron, and virgin forests in the deep coves. Among the flowering plants are sand myrtle (*Leiophyllum prostratum*), red chokeberry (*Sorbus arbutifolia*), azalea, turkey beard, bristly locust, yellow root, silverbell, orchids, ninebark, and wild indigo (*Baptisia tinctoria*). The major species of animals are deer, bear, squirrel, raccoon, grouse, turkey vulture, hawks, owls, and brown and rainbow trout. The poisonous snakes are the timber rattler and the copperhead. Free permits from the USFS are required for camping in the gorge only on weekends and holidays from May 1 through October 31. Time limit in the gorge is three consecutive days and two nights, one weekend permit per month per visitor, and group size not to exceed 10. No-trace camping is the rule. Permits may be obtained at the ranger's office in Nebo M–F, 8:00–4:30, or by mail (see address in the introduction). Also, permits are available in person at the Linville Falls Visitor Center, open April 15 to November 1, 9:00–5:00. Access to the center is 0.5 mi S on Kistler Memorial Highway (SR-1238) from NC-183, 0.7 mi E from its jct with US-221 in Linville Falls.

The *Linville Gorge Trail* is the major trail; its traverse is in the gorge, paralleling the river on the W side. Seven short but steep access trails descend from Kistler Memorial Highway (SR-1238) along the W rim. (Another trail, the 0.2-mi *Wiseman's View Trail*, is only an overlook into the gorge. It is 3.8 mi from NC-183.) The E rim has two short access trails from FR-210, but other trails on the E rim connect with each other. There are some trail signs at access points to the gorge, but inside the wilderness the trails are not blazed or signed. The use of a recent topo map or the Linville Gorge Wilderness Map is recommended. (*USGS-FS Maps:* Linville Falls, Ashford)

SUPPORT FACILITIES: Campgrounds, motels, restaurants, svc sta, and small grocery stores are at Linville Falls on US-221 and NC-183 jct.

Linville Gorge Trail (USFS #231) (F)   **175**

LENGTH AND DIFFICULTY: 11.5 mi, strenuous (elev change 2,025 ft)
CONNECTING TRAILS, WEST RIM:

180	*Sandy Flats Trail* (1.0 mi; USFS #230, strenuous, elev change 900 ft) (F)
181	*Conley Cove Trail* (1.4 mi; USFS #229, strenuous, elev change 930 ft) (F)
182	*Pitch-In Trail* (1.4 mi; USFS #228, strenuous, elev change 1,760 ft) (F)

CONNECTING TRAILS, EAST RIM:
   (*Devil's Hole Trail*)
   (*Spence Ridge Trail*)

SPECIAL FEATURES: rugged, geology, scenic

TRAILHEAD AND DESCRIPTION: All the trails on the W rim can be used as loops with SR-1238 as a connector. A vehicle switch is another option. The nearest and easiest access to the Linville Gorge is on the *Pine Gap Trail* on SR-1238, 0.9 mi from the jct of NC-183 and SR-1238 (0.7 mi from the US-221/NC-183 jct in Linville Falls). From the parking area descend easily into the gorge and at 0.7 mi jct with the *Bynum Bluff Trail*, R. To the L is a short spur to views of the canyon, and the *Linville Gorge Trail* begins ahead. (The *Bynum Bluff Trail* ascends 1.0 mi, steeply at first, to a parking area on SR-1238, 1.5 mi from NC-183). Descend in a forest of hardwoods, hemlock, and dense rhododendron. At 1.2 mi jct with the *Cabin Trail*, R. (The 0.8-mi *Cabin Trail* is a primitive spur that is extremely steep and rough to SR-1238, 1.9 mi from NC-183.) At 2.0 mi on the *Linville Gorge Trail* jct R with the *Babel Tower Trail* at a cliffside for overlooks of a horseshoe bend and river rapids. (The *Babel Tower Trail* ascends 1.2 mi to a parking area on SR-1238, 2.7 mi R to NC-183. It is a popular route with switchbacks, but generally a scenic ridge route. It is 1.1 mi S on SR-1238 to Wiseman's View.)

Continue the descent on a slope near the river for excellent views of the gorge at 2.5 mi. At 3.4 mi pass the jct L with the *Devil's Hole Trail*. (The 1.5-mi *Devil's Hole Trail* may be difficult to locate, but it crosses the river at a less steep area than usual and follows up Devil's Hole Branch to a ridge between Sitting Bear Mtn and Hawksbill Mtn to exit at FR-210.) At 3.7 mi are scenic views of Hawksbill Mtn. At 3.8 mi is a spring, and a campground, and a jct R with *Sandy Flats Trail*. (The *Sandy Flats Trail*, primitive and steep, ascends 1.0 mi to SR-1238, 3.7 mi S of NC-183.) Reach *Spence Ridge Trail*, L, at 4.6 mi. (*Spence Ridge Trail* fords the river and ascends for 1.7 mi on switchbacks to a level area and then the rim's parking area on FR-210, described below.) Continue downriver and at 5.5 mi jct with *Conley Cove Trail*, R. (The *Conley Cove Trail* ascends on a well-graded route through a forest of oak, pine, cucumber tree, silverbell, and wildflowers. At 1.0 mi is a water source and a

183 few yd farther is a primitive trail jct, L. [The unmaintained route is *Rock Jock Trail*, USFS #247, which follows above the escarpment for 2.8 mi.] Pass a cave and on switchbacks reach SR-1238 at 1.4 mi, 5.3 mi from NC-183.) The

Linville Gorge Trail continues 100 yd downriver to a swimming hole and a large open outcropping with views of the Chimneys and Table Rock on the E rim. Other views follow. Cross a small branch at 6.8 mi. The next 2.0 mi of the trail and the river have a mild decline. Jct with the *Pitch-In Trail,* R, at 9.1 mi. (The *Pitch-In Trail* ascends 1.4 mi with excellent views of the gorge, particularly of Shortoff Mtn, to SR-1238, 7.3 mi R to *Pine Gap Trail.* To the L on SR-1238 it is 2.3 mi to the *MST* and the Pinnacle 0.2 mi off the road E, and 0.8 mi farther to the trailhead and parking area R (W) of the *Overmountain Victory Trail.* Down the mtn on SR-1238 it is 4.1 mi to NC-126, from where it is 16.0 mi E to Morganton and 10.2 mi W to I-40 at the Nebo exit.)

The *Linville Gorge Trail* follows an old jeep road and passes through grassy glades under tall poplar and elm. At 10.9 mi is a good swimming hole. In a few yd wade the river in a flat area and reach the wilderness boundary at private property at 11.5 mi. Backtrack.

Devil's Hole Trail (1.5 mi; USFS #244) (F); Jonas Ridge Trail (4.4 mi round-trip; USFS #245) (F); Hawksbill Mountain Trail (1.4 mi round-trip; USFS #217) (F); Spence Ridge Trail (1.7 mi; USFS #233) (F); Table Rock Gap Trail (1.6 mi; USFS #243) (F); Little Table Rock Trail (1.2 mi; USFS #236) (F); Table Rock Summit Trail (1.4 mi round-trip; USFS #242) (F) **184-190**

LENGTH AND DIFFICULTY: 13.2 mi combined and round-trip, moderate to strenuous (elev change from 520 ft to 1,340 ft)

SPECIAL FEATURE: exceptional vistas

TRAILHEADS AND DESCRIPTION: These short trails are grouped because they have an access from FR-210 on the E rim; two of them descend to connect with the *Linville Gorge Trail.* A longer trail that follows the rim, *Shortoff Mountain Trail,* is described below separately. From the jct of NC-183/181 at Jonas Ridge go S on NC-181 for 3.0 mi to the Old Gingercake Rd (SR-1264) and turn R. At 0.3 mi turn L, at the first fork, on Gingercake Acres Rd (SR-1265), which becomes FR-210. At 2.6 mi reach a small parking space, R, for access to the *Jonas Ridge Trail* and *Devil's Hole Trail.* Ascend for 240 yd on a path that may be divided to approach the same ridge crest to *Jonas Ridge Trail.* (A turn L is 0.6 mi on a primitive path up the ridge to Hawksbill Mtn and jct with *Hawksbill Mountain Trail.*) Turn R and after 280 yd jct with the primitive *Devil's Hole Trail,* L. (Ahead up the ridge *Jonas Ridge Trail* dead-ends on Gingercake Mtn at 1.6 mi, but not before a steep climb on Sitting Bear Mtn and past huge rock formations.) Descend steeply (1,160 ft elev change) on *Devil's Hole Trail* among rhododendron, large hemlock, and chestnut oak in the cove. Cross rocky sections of the streambed and arrive at a cliff top at

1.4 mi. Climb down to the river at 1.5 mi. If planning to connect with the *Linville Gorge Trail* on the mountainside across the river, cautiously look for the safest rock formation on which to rock-hop or be prepared to wade the river. Otherwise, backtrack.

Drive down FR-210 another 1.3 mi and park L for the *Hawksbill Mountain Trail*, R (W). Ascend steeply on Lettered Rock Ridge through laurel and rhododendron arbors to a trail jct at 0.5 mi. Turn L. (The R trail follows the ridge for an access L to rock climbing and N for 0.7 mi to SR-210 at Devil's Hole access.) Reach the rocky summit (4,020 ft) of Hawksbill Mtn at 0.7 mi at the E boundary of the wilderness. Vistas are superior. Mountain ash and blueberry bushes are colorful in autumn. Backtrack.

The rim access to *Spence Ridge Trail* is another 1.0 mi on FR-210 to the parking area, R and L. A frequently used route, the first 0.2 mi is level and arbored with rhododendron. At 0.4 mi curve R in a jct and descend. (Ahead on the old road is a primitive trail, *Little Table Rock Trail*, which descends to a curve L and crosses a small stream at 0.3 mi. It ascends on a spur ridge, descends to a small drain, and ascends a very steep grade through white pine and hemlock. At 1.1 mi it reaches the top of Little Table Rock. A campsite and vistas are R. To the L is another primitive route, *Little Table Rock Trail*, to a water source at 160 yd. Ahead is a jct with *Table Rock Summit Trail* at 1.2 mi and an access to *Table Rock Gap Trail*, L.) Continue on the *Spence Ridge Trail*. Descend on switchbacks to a jct across the river with the *Linville Gorge Trail* at 1.7 mi.

At the parking area for the *Spence Ridge Trail*, the *Table Rock Gap Trail* follows an old road S for 0.4 mi to a cul-de-sac and jct with the *MST*. Turn R, ascend steeply, and after two switchbacks in a rhododendron slick reach a jct with the *Table Rock Summit Trail*. Backtrack, or use the *Table Rock Summit Trail*, L, for a 0.4-mi ascent to the top, or take a R 100 yd for an option to descend on the *Little Table Rock Trail* described above, or continue on the *Table Rock Summit Trail* for 0.3 mi to the Table Rock Picnic Area and parking lot.

For vehicle access to the Table Rock Picnic Area, drive ahead on FR-210 for 1.1 mi to FR-210B. Turn R and go 2.9 mi to the picnic area (passing an entrance to the Outward Bound School and climbing steeply the last mile). The picnic area has a vault toilet but no water source. Camping is not allowed here. Follow the *Table Rock Summit Trail* N on white-blazed *MST*. Jct with the *Little Table Rock Trail*, L, at 0.3 mi. Pass the *Table Rock Gap Trail* 100 yd ahead, and ascend on six rocky switchbacks to the summit (3,909 ft) at 0.7 mi with magnificent views and a 360-degree panorama.

Shortoff Mountain Trail (USFS #235) (F)

191

LENGTH AND DIFFICULTY: 11.2 mi round-trip, strenuous (elev change 1,048 ft)

SPECIAL FEATURES: The Chimneys, vistas of Linville Gorge

TRAILHEAD AND DESCRIPTION: This trail is also the *MST*, and it skirts the E rim of the wilderness except at the Shortoff Mtn area, which is in the wilderness. From the S edge of the Table Rock Picnic Area (described above), follow the trail on a gentle path to an open ridge of chinquapin, blueberry, and bracken at 0.4 mi. Pass W of the Chimneys (3,557 ft), an area of fissures, irregular spires, and overhangs, to the ridge return at 0.8 mi. Descend steeply to a cliff with a view of Table Rock and a deep watershed at 1.3 mi. Descend to Chimney Gap (2,509 ft) at 1.8 mi. At 2.1 mi in a saddle, R, is the obscure and primitive 1.3-mi *Cambric Ridge Trail,* which dead-ends at the **192** river). At 2.3 mi is an intermittent spring, L (60 yd from the trail) in a grove of galax and rhododendron. Ascend and descend, reach a knob at 2.7 mi, turn R at 3.0 mi at an old trail jct, and soon follow an old jeep road. At 5.0 mi pass a natural wildlife water hole. Turn R at an old road jct at 5.4 mi to reach the precipitous edge of Shortoff Mtn (3,000 ft) at 5.6 mi. Here are exceptionally scenic views of the gorge and both rims. Vegetation includes hemlock, spruce, blueberry, oak, and bristly locust. South 0.1 mi on the trail is a usually dependable spring in a gulch. Backtrack or continue ahead on the *MST*. (The *MST* descends to an old road R and crosses the Linville River for a climb to the Pinnacle and jct with SR-1238. See chapter 16.) A private road access from NC-126 on the Old Wolf Pit Rd should not be used. The parking sign on the 1986 wilderness map is in error, according to George Cook, former district ranger.

Brushy Ridge Trail (USFS #232) (F)

193

LENGTH AND DIFFICULTY: 4.0 mi round-trip, moderate

TRAILHEAD AND DESCRIPTION: This is an isolated trail in the wilderness that does not connect with any of the other trails. Access is on a private residential road and parking space is limited to two cars. (The private area should be respected by not parking off the road space anywhere else, or blocking any driveway.) To access, follow the Old Gingercake Rd (SR-1264) (as described above) 0.3 mi from NC-181 and turn R. After 0.9 mi on the L are two driveways close together; take the second one and after 0.2 mi in a curve park on the small space to the R. An old forest road slightly descends SW of the curve to follow an easy treadway for 1.2 mi, where it becomes a footpath. Begin a descent and at 1.3 mi are spectacular views of the gorge, R. In a rocky descent to 1.6 mi are equal views downriver of Hawksbill, Table

PISGAH NATIONAL FOREST 109

Rock, and the Babel Tower. On an overgrown rocky route are both Canadian and American hemlock. Reach a knob with stereophonic sounds of the river at 2.0 mi. Backtrack. (*USGS-FS Map:* Linville Falls)

NORTH CATAWBA AREA (McDowell County)

194 *Overmountain Victory Trail (USFS #308) (F)*

LENGTH AND DIFFICULTY: 3.5 mi, moderate

TRAILHEAD AND DESCRIPTION: In celebration of the bicentennial (1780–1980) of the "Overmountain Men," this yellow-blazed trail was planned, constructed, and designated a national historic trail in 1980. During the American Revolution, when Col Patrick Ferguson of the Loyalist Army sent word to the frontier mountain men that he would destroy them, the men responded by mustering a troop of 1,000 from Virginia, Tennessee, and North Carolina to seek out Col Ferguson, who was killed at the Kings Mountain battle in South Carolina. Marching for 12 days from Sycamore Shoals in Tennessee, the men passed along this route on September 30, 1780. (See introduction to section 4 of this chapter.) East access is on the Kistler Memorial Highway (SR-1238), 0.8 mi S from the Pinnacle and 4.1 mi N from NC-126. From the parking lot follow an old wagon road through a forest of white pine, laurel, and hardwoods. Cross a small stream at 0.3 mi and the Yellow Fork at 1.0 mi in thick rhododendron. At 1.5 mi cross a FR (accessible by vehicle 1.9 mi N from the trailhead on SR-1238). Descend gradually on a grassy road through hardwoods. Pass two grazing fields, L, and reach a flat ridge at 3.1 mi. A water source is R. Reach the W terminus at a FS gate, trail sign, and paved Old Linville Rd (SR-1560), L and R, at 3.5 mi. Bridge Branch is R in a residential area. (About 0.1 mi of this exit is private property. However, receive permission from Bertie Edwards by calling 704-756-4766 after 10:00 A.M.) It is 2.5 mi, R (N), on SR-1560 to a jct with US-221 in Ashford. (*USGS-FS Map:* Ashford)

WILSON CREEK AREA (Avery, Burke, and Caldwell Counties)

This large area has a network of more than 25 trails. They are concentrated in the deep valleys and gorges from the foldings of metamorphic rock that runs NW to SE from the Blue Ridge Mtn crest to the hill country W of Lenoir. From S to N the drains that flow E are Steels Creek; Upper Creek; Harper Creek; North Harper Creek; Lost Cove Creek; and the major basin, Wilson Creek. In the center of the area is Mortimer Recreation Area, the only family campground (no hookups), but commercial full-svc campgrounds are near the NF boundary. Mortimer has facilities for picnicking, camping, fishing, and hiking. The 4.5-mi double-loop *Thorps Creek Trail* (USFS #279) (F) at the edge of the campground may not be maintained because of forest-fire damage. The campground is the location of a former CCC camp. The area also has two other picnic sites, Barkhouse on NC-181 and Mulberry N of Lenoir. Mortimer is now a ghost area; once nearly 1,000 residents worked here at the Riddle Lumber Company or other plants. Major forest fires devastated the mtns in 1916 and 1925, and floods washed away the town in 1916 and 1940. The rough but scenic state road that provides access to the community was constructed on an old RR grade in 1950. Streams are stocked with trout; the forests have bear, turkey, deer, grouse, raccoon, skunk, and squirrel. Rattlesnakes and copperheads are also in the area. The forests are chiefly birch, oak, hickory, poplar, hemlock, white pine, laurel, and rhododendron. The area is well-known for its Brown Mtn Lights, a mysterious flickering light that according to legend is the spirit of a Civil War slave with a lantern looking for his master.

ACCESS: To reach Mortimer Recreation Area from Morganton go 10.5 mi N on NC-181 to jct R on Brown Mtn Beach Rd (SR-1405, also called Collettsville Rd) at Smyrna Baptist Church. Go 5.0 mi on SR-1405 to SR-1328, L at the Mortimer sign. Go 4.5 mi to jct across the Wilson Creek bridge and turn R. After another 4.5 mi reach the campground. From Collettsville go SW on Adako Rd (SR-1337) for 2.2 mi and turn R at the Mortimer sign to follow the directions above.

SUPPORT FACILITIES: Two commercial campgrounds in the area are Steels Creek Park, 704-433-5660, 1.2 mi N on NC-181 from Smyrna Baptist Church, and Daniel Boone Family Campground, 704-433-1200, 1.7 mi N on NC-181 from Smyrna Baptist Church, approx 13.5 mi N of Morganton. Full svc, rec fac; open April 1 to late fall. A small general store is at the corner of NC-90 and Wilson Creek Rd (SR-1328) at Mortimer Rec Area, and another store is about 2.6 mi S on SR-1328. A store with snack food is on NC-181, in Jonas Ridge, 0.8 mi S from the jct of NC-181/183. Motels and restaurants are at the jct of US-221 and NC-183 in the community of Linville Falls. Morganton and Lenoir have shopping centers, restaurants, motels, and hospitals.

Lower Steels Creek Trail (2.9 mi; USFS #238) (F); Upper Steels Creek
Trail (2.9 mi; USFS #237) (F)

LENGTH AND DIFFICULTY: 5.8 mi combined, moderate

SPECIAL FEATURES: waterfalls, fishing, wildlife

TRAILHEADS AND DESCRIPTION: These trails can be connected with 1.8 mi on FR-2128 for a total of 7.6 mi. To reach the upstream trailhead of the *Lower Steels Creek Trail*, turn off NC-181 on FR-2128 (9.6 mi S of NC-181/183 jct in Jonas Ridge and 4.4 mi up the mtn from SR-1405 at Smyrna Baptist Church), and drive 2.1 mi to jct with an old forest road, L. Park and walk on the road for 0.2 mi to a gate and descend to Steels Creek at 0.5 mi. Rock-hop, pass a fish barrier, L, and at 0.8 mi leave the road L into a grazing field. Reenter the forest at 0.9 mi and rock-hop the creek. Immediately rock-hop again and follow a path through white pine, birch, and ironwood. At 1.2 mi rock-hop the creek, L (watch for a N.C. Wildlife Commission trout sign on a white pine facing the stream, otherwise you may miss the crossing). Rock-hop again at 1.4 mi and pass through a clear-cut. (Passage may be difficult here because of timber slash and overgrowth to the next stream crossing.) Cross the stream at 1.6 mi (either on a log bridge or by wading). Enter a rhododendron canal with orange-fringed orchids (*Habenaria ciliaris*) in sunny spots. At 2.0 mi turn L at remnants of an old log cabin and ascend gently on an old road to NC-181 at 2.9 mi. Descend the embankment. (There are not any trailhead signs here, but one landmark to watch for is the end of a guardrail across the road from the trailhead, 0.3 mi up the mtn from the National Forest sign and 0.2 mi down the mtn from FR-4095.) Backtrack or use a second vehicle 1.7 mi up the mtn to FR-2128, L.

For the *Upper Steels Creek Trail* follow the same route to FR-2128, but pass the parking area for the *Lower Steels Creek Trail* and drive 1.8 mi farther to a parking area at the road terminus. Hike upstream on a jeep road to creek cascades at 0.2 mi. Rock-hop the creek and jct with the white-blazed *MST* after 75 yd. Turn R, ascend through a rhododendron thicket with rapids and pools, R. Pass a waterfall at 0.6 mi. At 0.9 mi turn sharply L, ascend steeply to an old RR grade, and at 1.3 mi pass through an ideal camping area of tall trees and grassy grounds. Enter a grazing field and reach a FR, R. Cross Gingercake Creek and Steels Creek to follow under tall poplar and white pine. At 1.9 mi rock-hop the creek and again at 2.0 mi. Follow a well-graded FR to a ridge top at 2.8 mi and at 2.9 mi leave the *MST* (which goes R). Continue ahead for 120 yd to a locked FR gate and jct with FR-496. Backtrack or take FR-496, R, for 1.3 mi to NC-181, then R to FR-2128. (*USGS-FS Map:* Chestnut Mtn)

198 *Upper Creek Falls Trail (USFS #268B) (F)*

LENGTH AND DIFFICULTY: 1.6 mi, strenuous

TRAILHEAD AND DESCRIPTION: From the Barkhouse Picnic Area on NC-181, drive N 0.8 mi to the parking lot, R. (From the jct of NC-181/183, drive S, down the mtn, 4.1 mi to the parking lot, L.) This popular loop and scenic trail begins at the side of the parking lot. Follow it through hardwoods, laurel, and rhododendron; descend on switchbacks; and arrive at the top of Upper Creek Falls at 0.4 mi. There are huge boulders and pools upstream. Rock-hop the creek into more rhododendron and descend steeply among rocks, mosses, and ferns to cross the creek again at 0.7 mi. Ascend, pass under a large overhanging rock, and climb switchbacks to the side of the parking lot at 1.6 mi. (*USGS-FS Map:* Chestnut Mtn)

Greentown Trail (5.7 mi; USFS #268) (F); Greentown Short-cut Trail (1.2 mi; USFS #268A) (F) 199-200

LENGTH AND DIFFICULTY: 6.9 mi combined, strenuous (elev change 1,268 ft)
CONNECTING TRAILS:
(MST)
(Raider Camp Trail)

TRAILHEADS AND DESCRIPTION: The trailhead is on the E side of NC-181 (across the road from FR-496), 0.4 mi S of Barkhouse Picnic Area. Follow an old logging road (white-blazed *MST*) and descend into a cove. At 1.0 mi reach Upper Creek, but go upstream to cross at 1.2 mi; turn R. At 1.8 mi jct with *Greentown Short-cut Trail*, R, near the mouth of Burnthouse Branch. (*Greentown Short-cut Trail* descends in a gorge on the E side of Upper Creek to the scenic Lower Upper Creek Falls at 0.7 mi. Exit at a parking area to FR-197 at 1.2 mi. FR-197 descends to FR-982, R to NC-181, 4.0 mi S from the *Greentown Trail* entrance.) Continue on an old eroded road; reach an old parking and primitive campsite at a jct, R, with FR-190 at 3.8 mi. Bear L, make a long curve to a saddle with forks at 4.5 mi. Avoid the forks, go straight (from Burke County to Avery County), and descend. At 4.9 mi take the L fork; reach *Raider Camp Trail* at 5.7 mi. (*Raider Camp Trail*, described above, goes L for 0.2 mi to South Harper Creek Falls and *Harper Creek Trail*, and R for 2.6 mi to jct with the E trailhead of *Harper Creek Trail*. (*USGS-FS Map:* Chestnut Mtn)

Phillips Branch Trail (USFS #278) (F) 201

LENGTH AND DIFFICULTY: 1.9 mi, moderate
SPECIAL FEATURES: waterfalls, scenic gulch

TRAILHEAD AND DESCRIPTION: Park in a cove on Wilson Creek Rd (SR-1328), 2.2 mi S of Mortimer Rec Area. On an unsigned trail ascend steeply for 60 yd to an old RR grade, turn L, and at 0.4 mi climb steeply to the top of Phillips Creek Falls. Cross the creek, continue ascent in a gorge with tall hemlock and white pine. Curve R from stream confluence, ascend to old logging road, and turn L. Reach a saddle at 1.4 mi, cross old roads, and descend rapidly into a scenic gulch with dense fetterbush and rhododendron. Cross Raider Creek to good campsites and jct R and L with *Raider Camp Trail* at 1.9 mi (between two large poplars with initials "R.J."). Backtrack, or make a loop by turning R. Go 0.3 mi to jct with *Harper Creek Trail,* turn R and follow it to SR-1328. Turn R on SR-1328 and follow it downstream to the point of origin at 4.3 mi. (*USGS-FS Map:* Chestnut Mtn)

202 *Harper Creek Trail (USFS #260) (F)*

LENGTH AND DIFFICULTY: 6.3 mi, strenuous (elev change 1,000 ft)

CONNECTING TRAILS:

203   *Yellow Buck Trail* (2.1 mi; USFS #265, moderate) (F)
204   *Raider Camp Trail* (2.8 mi; USFS #277, moderate) (F)
      (*MST*)
      (*Simmons Ridge Trail*)
205   *North Harper Creek Trail* (4.5 mi; USFS #266, strenuous, elev change 1,320 ft) (F)
206   *Persimmon Ridge Trail* (2.7 mi; USFS #270, moderate) (F)
207   *North Harper Creek Access Trail* (1.0 mi; USFS #266A, easy) (F)
208   *North Harper Creek Falls Trail* (1.3 mi; USFS #239, moderate) (F)

SPECIAL FEATURES: waterfalls, fishing

TRAILHEAD AND DESCRIPTION: If using the E trailhead at Wilson Creek, the combination of Harper Creek and North Harper Creek trails is shaped like a crooked Y with North Harper forking R. An advantage for using one or both of these trails is to create options for eight loop routes from modest to more challenging lengths. All but *Simmons Ridge Trail* are in the proposed Harper Creek Wilderness Area. The clear rushing streams have sculpted the metamorphic rocks in falls, flumes, and pools. Trout are stocked and the NCWRC requires artificial lures. The two main trails follow the stream banks and cross the creeks frequently. Under normal weather conditions all fording can be rock-hopping. Water snakes and copperheads are seen sunning in the summer, and brilliant cardinal flowers (*Lobelia cardinalis*) bloom on wet grassy islands in late summer. Trail access routes connect from SR-1328 (E), FR-464 (N), and FR-85 (W).

Begin the *Harper Creek Trail* at a narrow parking area on Wilson Creek Rd (SR-1328), 1.4 mi S of the Mortimer Rec Area. Ascend gradually on a well-graded trail to a ridge crest and jct, R, with *Yellow Buck Trail* at 0.4 mi. (The *Yellow Buck Trail* ascends steeply on an old skid road for 0.7 mi to slope W of Yellow Buck Mtn [2,470 ft] and continues on a gentle route with white pine and bristly locust [*Robina hispida*] to jct with the *Persimmon Trail,* L, at 1.8 mi.

Ahead it is 0.3 mi to FR-464, the trail's end, and 4.0 mi E on FR-464 to Mortimer.) Continue on the *Harper Creek Trail* on a wide clear woods road to a jct, L, with *Raider Camp Trail* at 1.3 mi. The *Harper Creek Trail* turns R.

(The *Raider Camp Trail*, also the white-blazed *MST*, goes 135 yd to cross Harper Creek, turn L, and jct with *Phillips Creek Trail*, L, at 0.3 mi. The trail follows up Raider Creek through good campsite areas 0.7 mi before ascending on an eroded old road to a ridge crest and crossroads at 2.0 mi. It goes straight to follow a level and scenic woods road in an open forest to jct with *Greentown Trail*, L, at 2.6 mi. Turn R at the jct and descend to a cliff for views of the spectacular 200-ft waterfall and cascades known as South Harper Creek Falls. Continue on switchbacks to cross Harper Creek and intersect with *Harper Creek Trail* at the top of the falls at 2.8 mi. *Harper Creek Trail* goes L for 1.1 mi to its terminus on FR-58 and R downstream for 3.9 mi to its first encounter with *Raider Camp Trail* and back to SR-1328 for a loop of 9.3 mi.)

To continue on *Harper Creek Trail* from the first encounter, turn R, ascend gently for 0.1 mi to a spur route, and go another 0.2 mi to views of the scenic Harper Creek Falls and pool. Continue on the main trail, also the white-blazed *MST*, and pass the falls on a precipitous slope. Rock-hop the creek three times before a jct at the mouth of North Harper Creek, R, at 3.4 mi. *North Harper Creek Trail* ascends 4.5 mi to FR-58 and is described in more detail below. Continue on the *Harper Creek Trail* where the treadway becomes rough in some sections. At 4.1 mi cross a tributary in a forest of hemlock, hardwoods, and rhododendron. At 5.2 mi arrive at the spectacular 200-ft falls and cascades known as South Harper Creek Falls. A few yd beyond the top of the falls jct L with *Raider Camp Trail*, described above, for a reverse loop. Curve R at the nose of a ridge and ascend for 0.1 mi to an easy grade through oak, maple, and laurel and reach FR-58 at 6.3 mi, the W trailhead. Across the road is the S trailhead of *Simmons Ridge Trail*, described below. On FR-58, L, it is 0.5 mi to private property (the early settlement of Kawana), and R on FR-58 it is 0.5 mi to the W trailhead of *Persimmon Ridge Trail*. Here is another potential loop route, using *North Harper Creek Trail*, for a return total of 12.8 mi to SR-1328.

At the confluence of Harper and North Harper Creeks the *North Harper Creek Trail* starts upstream, R, and at 0.5 mi it intersects with *Persimmon Ridge Trail*, L and R.

(*Persimmon Ridge Trail*, L, is a steep ascent W for 0.1 mi to a ridgeline. Ascend gradually to a knob [2,785 ft] at 1.7 mi and drop to FR-58 on a woods road at 2.1 mi. It is 0.5 mi L on FR-58 to the W trailhead of *Harper Creek Trail* and 3.0 mi R on FR-58 to the N trailhead of *Simmons Ridge Trail*.

The E section of *Persimmon Ridge Trail* leaves North Harper Creek and ascends 0.6 mi to a jct with *Yellow Buck Trail*. A turn L is 0.3 mi to FR-464; a turn R on *Yellow Buck Trail* would provide a loop of 8.1 mi back to SR-1328.)

Continue on the *North Harper Creek Trail;* rock-hop the creek three times while passing through a flat area for campsites at 0.6 mi and by a deep pool, flumes, and ferns at 1.4 mi. At 1.8 mi jct with *North Harper Creek Access Trail* (also called *Clearcut Trail*), R. (*Clearcut Trail* is a well-graded, scenic, open-woods access route of 1.0 mi from FR-464, 5.4 mi from Mortimer.) Cross the creek a number of times and reach another campsite at 3.1 mi. At 3.3 mi, L, is Chestnut Cove Branch Falls, and at 3.4 mi is jct, R, with a dubious trailhead of *North Harper Creek Falls Trail.* An ax mark on a tulip poplar, L, is a simple sign.

(The *North Harper Creek Falls Trail* ascends 0.3 mi on an erratic manway to a logging road. Follow the road through dense blackberry patches and saplings, and bear L at another old road to reach FR-464 at 1.3 mi. It is 1.3 mi R to *North Harper Creek Access Trail* and L on FR-464 1.9 mi to FR-58.)

Continue up *North Harper Creek Trail*, ascend steeply through rhododendron to a large, high rock formation, L. Cross the creek and arrive at the base of an exceptionally beautiful North Harper Creek Falls at 3.6 mi. Ascend on switchbacks to the top of the falls for another scenic area of cascades and pools. Cross the creek to campsites, turn L, ascend, cross the creek three more times, the last at 4.4 mi. Reach the W terminus of the trail at 4.5 mi. Left on FR-58, it is 0.4 mi to *Simmons Ridge Trail,* and R on FR-58 it is 0.2 mi to FR-464. Here is a primitive campsite and picnic area. It is 8.6 mi R on FR-464 and NC-90 to Mortimer Rec Area, and L it is 4.5 mi to jct of NC-181/183 in Jonas Ridge. For the NC-181 access route, go 2.5 mi L on FR-464 to Long Ridge Baptist Church, turn L on SR-1518, and go 0.5 mi. Turn R on SR-1471, go 0.8 mi to jct with NC-181 and BRP, and turn L on NC-181 for 0.7 mi to jct of NC-181/183. (*USGS-FS Maps:* Chestnut Mtn, Grandfather Mtn)

209 *Simmons Ridge Trail (USFS #267) (F)*

LENGTH AND DIFFICULTY: 5.2 mi, moderate

SPECIAL FEATURES: RR grade, wildlife

TRAILHEAD AND DESCRIPTION: Access is described above from NC-181 to the W trailhead of *North Harper Creek Trail.* From that trailhead on FR-58 go 0.4 mi to a small parking space, L, but the trailhead is R at a large cucumber tree. (Passage may be difficult on the trail for a section because of timber slash and overgrowth.) Ascend 90 yd to a ridge and follow an old logging road in a hardwood forest to the top of Headquarters Mtn (3,970 ft) at 1.4

mi. Descend to a gated dirt FR (R, 0.4 mi to old Jonas Ridge Rd [SR-1518, also called Mortimer Rd]. Left, SR-1518 becomes SR-1401 in Burke County and leads 2.1 mi to NC-181 in Jonas Ridge. Right, SR-1501 is 0.7 mi to Long Ridge Baptist Church and R to FR-464.) Cross the dirt road and descend to join an old RR grade at 2.8 mi. Follow it for the remainder of the trail through a forest of oak, locust, maple, laurel, and rhododendron. Exit at FR-58 at 5.2 mi. Ahead is the W trailhead of *Harper Creek Trail* described above. On the R it is 0.5 mi to private property and the South Fork of Harper Creek. It is 3.5 mi L to the N trailhead of *Simmons Ridge Trail*. (*USGS-FS Maps:* Chestnut Mtn, Grandfather Mtn)

Big Lost Cove Cliffs Trail (1.2 mi; USFS #271) (F); Little Lost Cove   **210-**
Cliffs Trail (1.3 mi; USFS #271A) (F); Darkside Cliffs Trail (0.5 mi;   **212**
USFS #272) (F)

LENGTH AND DIFFICULTY: 5.7 mi, round-trip combined, moderate

SPECIAL FEATURES: geology, spectacular vistas

TRAILHEADS AND DESCRIPTION: These three trails do not connect but are grouped because of proximity and similarity. The easiest access is from NC-181, 0.7 mi N of jct with NC-183. Turn R on SR-1471 and go 0.8 mi, turn L on SR-1518 and go 0.5 mi, and turn R at Long Ridge Baptist Church on FR-464. Descend 2.0 mi to a narrow parking edge in a sharp L curve. The trail ascends 0.4 mi in laurel and rhododendron with ground cover of wintergreen (*Gaultheria procumbens*) to an old jeep road. Descend to the cliffs at 1.2 mi for a grand 180-degree view of Lost Cove, Grandfather and Grandmother Mtns, and the BRP. Drive down FR-464 for 1.1 mi to W trailhead of *Little Lost Cove Cliffs Trail*. Park R, and ascend on an old jeep road. At 0.6 mi is the first of a number of spurs for a 360-degree view of Grandfather Mtn, Timber Ridge, Wilson Creek basin, Harper Creek basin, Hawksbill Mtn, and Blowing Rock area. Descend to FR-464 on a gated jeep road at 1.3 mi. Drive down FR-464 another 0.6 mi to *Darkside Cliffs Trail*, L, but park R of road. Walk this easy 0.5-mi route first through hardwoods and then rhododendron and pitch pine for superb views of the Wilson Creek basin, Blowing Rock area, and Grandfather Mtn range. Backtrack. On FR-464 it is 6.1 mi down the mtn to NC-90 and to Mortimer Rec Area. (*USGS-FS Map:* Grandfather Mtn)

Timber Ridge Trail (1.5 mi; USFS #261) (F); Lost Cove Trail (7.5 mi;   **213-**
USFS #262) (F); Hunt-Fish Falls Trail (0.8 mi; USFS #263) (F)   **215**

LENGTH AND DIFFICULTY: 9.8 mi combined, moderate to strenuous

SPECIAL FEATURES: wildlife, waterfalls, vistas

TRAILHEADS AND DESCRIPTION: These trails connect as a group and are within the proposed Lost Cove Wilderness Area. The N access (described first) is on FR-981 and the S access is on FR-464. From the Mortimer Rec Area go 2.0 mi W on NC-90 to the S edge of Edgemont and turn L on FR-981. Drive 4.0 mi to a parking space, L, before crossing the bridge of Gragg Prong, opposite FR-192. (Ahead on FR-981 it is 0.4 mi to Roseborough and Roseborough Rd, SR-1511. It goes 4.5 mi up the mtn to the BRP and Linville.) Hike across the bridge, turn L on a short jeep road, and begin the *Lost Cove Trail* (also the white-blazed *MST* route) at the downstream corner of a small meadow. Rock-hop Gragg Prong four times in the first 2.0 mi. At 1.0 mi jct with a spur trail, R, that ascends gradually to *Timber Ridge Trail* for 0.4 mi. At 1.2 mi are falls, sunbathing rocks, pools, and campsites in a forest of white pine, oak, laurel, hemlock, and rhododendron. Pass a high falls at 1.5 mi, jct with *Timber Ridge Trail,* R, at 2.3 mi near convergence with Lost Cove Creek. Rock-hop Lost Cove Creek and reach the high cascades L and three-tiered Hunt-Fish Falls, R, at 3.0 mi, an excellent fishing and sunning area. (The *Hunt-Fish Falls Trail* ascends L steeply, 0.8 mi on switchbacks to FR-464 for a S access. This access is 1.7 mi W from Mortimer Rec Area on NC-90 to FR-464, L, and 3.1 mi farther up the mtn to the trailhead parking area, R.) Cross Lost Cove Creek above the falls and turn L, upstream. (A number of side trails to campsites are confusing with a spur trail that goes R to *Timber Ridge Trail.* If using the spur trail as a shortcut, look for the spur with the most usage. After 0.6 mi, steeply, it jct with the *Timber Ridge Trail.* A turn R will connect with the E trailhead at Cragg Prong; a L turn is 0.4 mi to its original W jct with *Lost Cove Trail.*)

Continue upstream on the *Lost Cove Trail,* but the trail may be overgrown enough to make it difficult to follow for the next 1.7 mi in its crisscross passage of the stream. At 4.3 mi, L is Little Lost Cove Creek and falls. Turn R, cross the creek, and ascend on switchbacks to jct with an old trail, L, at 5.4 mi. Turn R (SE), curve around Bee Mtn, and follow the ridge to the W trailhead of *Timber Ridge Trail* at 6.4 mi. It goes ahead; *Lost Cove Trail* makes a sharp turn L. At 6.5 mi descend into a huge natural amphitheater landscaped by nature with ferns, rocks, wildflowers, and a spring. At 7.5 mi return to the parking area. (*USGS-FS Map:* Grandfather Mtn)

216- *Wilson Creek Trail (6.6 mi; USFS #258) (F); Wilson Creek Access Trail*
218 *(1.4 mi; USFS #258 A) (F); White Rocks Trail (0.8 mi; USFS#264) (F)*
  LENGTH AND DIFFICULTY: 8.8 mi combined, moderate to strenuous
  SPECIAL FEATURES: remote, fishing, wildlife, rugged

TRAILHEADS AND DESCRIPTION: These primitive trails combine to provide two accesses NW and two SE. Signs and blazes are absent except unofficial markings by hikers or fishermen. Wading is necessary at some of the fordings, particularly downstream. For the SE trailheads, from Mortimer Rec Area, drive N on NC-90 through Edgemont, cross *Wilson Creek Trail* trailhead, L, at 4.0 mi. Parking area is small. Another 1.5 mi up the mtn on FR-45 is the *White Rocks Trail* trailhead, L (it is an 0.8-mi shortcut down Bark Camp Ridge to jct with the *Wilson Creek Trail* at the mouth of Laurel Mtn Branch). Begin the *Wilson Creek Trail* by ascending Bark Camp Ridge in a forest of oak, white pine, and laurel. Curve L of a knob, descend, and in a cove cross Crusher Branch at 0.8 mi. Ford the creek twice and jct with *White Rocks Trail* at 1.8 mi. Cross Laurel Mtn Branch and ford the creek frequently in the next 3.0 mi. Campsites are good at Turkey Branch and Flat Land Branch. At 4.8 mi reach the confluence of Andrews and Wilson Creeks. Between them, in a fork, *Wilson Creek Trail* turns R at red paint marks and the *Wilson Creek Access Trail* proceeds ahead. (If following the *Wilson Creek Access Trail,* rock-hop Andrews Creek a number of times and reach the convergence with Stackrock Creek, R, at 0.8 mi. In a rhododendron thicket are scenic cascades and pools. Arrive at a grazing field at 1.2 mi, turn R, and follow a gated old road to FR-192 at 1.4 mi [6.2 mi from FR-45]. It is 1.0 mi L to Old House Gap and 2.6 mi R to Edgemont Rd [SR-1514].) The main *Wilson Creek Trail* is overgrown, but you may follow the red markers up Wilson Creek to its jct with an alternate route. Cross Wilson Creek immediately after forking R from *Wilson Creek Access Trail,* pass two huge rock overhangs, cross the creek twice more, and at 0.5 mi reach a frequently used campsite. Two signs are on trees in memory of Mike Borders and J.C. Bryant, both killed in a vehicular accident. There are two routes out from here. The roughest is to go 390 ft upstream in a manway to a rocky island and a paint marker. Cross the creek at a cucumber tree and the mouth of Bee Branch. Turn sharply R and follow red "B.B." initials on a poplar to an old RR grade. Follow the "B.B." and white markers to the convergence of Wilson Creek and Little Wilson Creek, R. Ascend an old RR grade between the creeks but leave the grade at 0.4 mi. Pass through a rhododendron grove and exit by a campsite at FR-192 at 0.6 mi (5.9 mi from FR-45 entrance). The other option is to follow the jeep road at the memorial campsite. After 0.8 mi jct with an old logging road. Turn L and follow to FR-192 at 1.3 mi. From here it is 0.3 mi L to the Little Wilson Creek Access, and 1.9 mi farther to *Wilson Creek Access Trail.* To the R it is 0.6 mi to the Edgemont Rd (SR-1514). From this jct it is 4.1 mi L to US-221 (0.5 mi E of the BRP); R on

SR-1514 it is 5.8 mi down the mtn to FR-45 and the SE trailhead of *Wilson Creek Trail*. Along FR-45 are two other isolated trails described below.

219- *Woodruff Branch Trail (2.4 mi; USFS #256) (F, B); Bill Crump Trail (1.2*
220 *mi; USFS #257) (F)*

LENGTH AND DIFFICULTY: 4.8 mi round-trip, easy

TRAILHEADS AND DESCRIPTION: These trails do not connect, but both have trailheads on FR-45 within 1.6 mi of each other and are old roads closed to vehicular use. (The *Woodruff Branch Trail* is designated for mountain bicycle use.) For access go N from Edgemont on SR NC-90, which becomes FR-45 for 4.7 mi (pass *Wilson Creek Trail* access at 2.0 mi) to *Woodruff Branch Trail*, R. Cross hummock (also called "tank trap") and follow pleasant seeded road across Barn Ridge, and descend to a parking area near the mouth of Woodruff Branch at Anthony Creek to Anthony Creek Rd (SR-1362) at 2.4 mi. Backtrack, or use a second vehicle 2.1 mi NW to Gragg on FR-45, R, for 4.5 mi (SE) on Globe Rd (SR-1516), which becomes SR-1362. The *Bill Crump Trail* is 1.6 mi up FR-45 from the *Woodruff Branch Trail*. A rarely used trail, it descends S and crosses Cary Flat Branch in a young forest of laurel, hemlock, and oak. It drops to the nose of a hill and dead-ends at a private road. Backtrack. (*USGS-FS Maps:* Grandfather Mtn, Globe)

THUNDERHOLE CREEK AREA (Caldwell and Watauga Counties)

221- *China Creek Trail (2.6 mi; USGS #250) (F,B); Thunderhole Falls Trail*
222 *(0.1 mi; USGS #253) (F)*

LENGTH AND DIFFICULTY: 5.4 mi, round-trip, moderate

SPECIAL FEATURES: Thunderhole Falls, cascading stream, wildlife

TRAILHEADS AND DESCRIPTION: Access is on gravel Globe Rd (SR-1367) 3.4 mi S of Blowing Rock from S Main St (also US-321B). Parking space is R (W) at FR-4071. (If approaching from Collettsville it is 15.6 mi on NC-90 to Anthony Creek Rd [SR-1632]. Turn R and go 1.0 mi to turn R on Globe Rd; ascend for 4.4 mi to access L [W]). There are not any signs or blazes at the parking area or on the trail or forest road.

From the parking space follow FR-4071 over tank traps (where a forest gate has been removed). Descend and at 0.4 mi turn L off the road to a pioneer road and reach a flat area among walnut, poplar, and wildflowers. Wildlife includes deer and raccoon. Rock-hop or wade Thunderhole Creek at 0.8 mi, cross the creek another three times, and at 1.5 mi cross China Creek to a fork in the old road. A turn L is on the *Thunderhole Falls Trail*. It ascends 0.1 mi among rhododendron to a combination flume and waterfall. Backtrack to the fork and proceed upstream by China Creek. At 1.8 mi cross FR-4071 (a low-water cement bridge is R on the road). Cross the creek twice and at 2.2 mi cross a small tributary, Long Branch. After three more creek crossings reach a tributary to the R, the ending of the trail at 2.6 mi. (There is a trackable route to the L, which follows up China Creek to the Moses H. Cone Memorial Park of the BRP, but the route's N passage may be on private property. The USFS lists the N terminus at Mayview Park in Blowing Rock.) Backtrack. If using FR-4071 for a return to the Globe Rd, it is 2.5 mi from the low-water cement bridge to Globe Rd. (*USGS-FS Maps:* Globe, Boone)

SECTION 3: PISGAH RANGER DISTRICT

This district of 156,103 acres and historic distinction is the flagship of the state's NF districts. It is the most popular, attracting approximately 5 million visitors annually. "What we do is for the public and for future generations," said Art Rowe, the district ranger, reflecting the philosophy of the area's first forest manager, Gifford Pinchot. The district is a hiker's mecca with more than 375 mi of trails, most of which are blazed in white, red, orange, blue, or yellow (except in the two wilderness areas, where blazes or maintenance are not provided). At each trailhead and connection is a sign with the trail's name, its color, and logos for its usage (foot trail, bike, or horse), difficulty, and direction. Hikers have an exceptionally wide choice of trails—for ecological study and forest history; on steep rocky balds, dry ridges, and in remote forested canyons and coves; into the backcountry for solitude; and by creeksides and waterfalls.

In the preceding districts the order of trail description has followed the order of USFS trail inventory numbers (as seen on USGS maps) from lowest to highest. This district is treated differently because of its exceptionally long list of trails. I have divided the trails into 12 groups according to trail proximity, disregarding both the USFS numerical order in its TIS and the additional trail numbers printed on the district's alphabetized map. However, it is important for the user to acquire the district trail map for not only knowing the topographical trail outline, but by looking closely, for seeing the USGS quad map numbers reproduced alongside the trail in a parallelogram.

All trails that loop or that can be connected are described together. Isolated or singular trails are described in the introduction of the area. One trail is particularly different. It is *Mount Pisgah Trail* (1.3 mi; USFS #355) (F), **223** whose access is from Mt Pisgah parking lot at mp 407.6 of the BRP (see chapter 6). The trail begins at a sign, soon enters the national forest, and begins a strenuous climb at 0.4 mi. After a rocky ascent on switchbacks it reaches the summit (5,721 ft) at an observation deck. The panoramic views include Pigeon River Gorge and Shining Rock Wilderness.

The district's longest trail, *Art Loeb Trail* (30.0 mi), is described as a single area; the *Mountains-to-Sea Trail* (62. 0 mi) is not described separately because it jointly follows other named trails most of its distance (see chapter 16). (By the time this edition is published, the Carolina Mountain Club will have completed the *MST* Connector [11.6 mi] from the *Art Loeb Trail* crossing of FR-816 NE to jct with *Buck Spring Trail* off US-276. The connector may become the mainline *MST* with the Davidson River route becoming the *MST* Alternate.)

Descriptive grouping in this district is generally from W to E, first covering the two wilderness areas and a pocket of trails around the Black Balsam Knob between the wildernesses—all on the N side of the BRP. On the S side of the BRP the descriptions begin with Courthouse Creek Area, followed by Upper Davidson River, Lower Davidson River, Avery Creek, Pink Beds, South Mills River, Laurel Mtn, North Mills River, and Bent Creek, the latter the most eastern on the NW side of the BRP.

The district has exceptionally strong public relations with volunteer groups in trail maintenance and recommendations. The largest and most historical is the Carolina Mountain Club for foot trails. An active bike group is the Blue Ridge Bicycle Club and an active equestrian group is the Pisgah Trailblazers. Other maintenance groups are Balsam-Highlands Task Force, Haywood Knolls, Pisgah Hikers, and Wilderness Rangers. The district has nearly 25 proposed new trails, most in the Looking Glass Rock complex. At press time of this book at least 6 proposed trails had been adopted by the Blue Ridge Bicycle Club for maintenance.

Recreational facilities provide four family campgrounds: Davidson River, the largest, across the Davidson River from the ranger station; Lake Powhatan in the Bent Creek Experimental Forest near the French Broad River, off NC-191 near the BRP; North Mills River, W of North Mills; and Sunburst on NC-215, N of the BRP at Sunburst. There are three group camps that require reservations: Upper and Lower Cove Creek, near the US Fish Hatchery; North and South White Pines, on FR-477 near the ranger station; and Kuykendall, off US-64 between Rosman and Brevard. Picnic areas are Coontree, Pink Beds, Looking Glass Rock, and Sycamore Flats, all on US-276 between the BRP and Brevard, and Stony Fork on NC-151, S of Chandler. Primitive and roadside camping and picnicking are indicated at appropriate signs throughout the district. Among the major natural attractions are Looking Glass Falls, Looking Glass Rock, and Sliding Rock, all on US-276 W of the ranger station; Courthouse Creek Falls off NC-215 NW of Rosman; and Mt Pisgah off the BRP. Other attractions are the US Fish Hatchery off US-276 NW of the ranger station and the Cradle of Forestry in America N of Sliding Rock on US-276. The district has two wilderness areas—Middle Prong (7,900 acres) and Shining Rock (18,500 acres), both NW in the district; and Bent Creek Experimental Forest (where a number of state champion trees may be observed) at the N edge of the district. The district has numerous streams for fishing, game animals for hunting, old roads and trails for equestrians and mountain bikers, routes for cross-country skiing, and domes for rock climbers. (Inquire at the ranger station for information on native trout fishing.) Swimming is at Lake Powhatan off NC-191, and observation/water play areas are at Sliding Rock and Looking Glass Falls, both on US-276 W of the ranger station. There is a 79.0-mi scenic byway auto loop in the district and vicinity. (Request a free brochure for its route.)

The district boundaries are N at the French Broad River near and S of Asheville, W with the Highlands District of the Nantahala National Forest, S by the Toxaway River area, and E by US-64 and NC-280. Sections are in Buncombe, Henderson, Transylvania, and Haywood Counties, and through the district runs the BRP. The district is named after Mt Pisgah (5,721 ft). According to legend the peak was named after the Biblical mtn Pisgah where Moses saw the "promised land" by the Rev. James Hall, an Indian-fighting Presbyterian chaplain who was in the area in 1776 with Gen Griffith Rutherford's expedition against the Cherokee. Another legend is that George Newton, a Presbyterian teacher-minister gave it the name. The district originated when George W. Vanderbilt acquired more than 125,000 acres upon which was constructed Biltmore Estate, a reproduction of a sixteenth-century large French chateau. (Biltmore is not part of the current Pisgah National Forest.) His vast forests, which included Mt Pisgah (earlier owned by Thomas Clingman, for whom Clingmans Dome is named), were first managed by conservationist Gifford Pinchot and later by Carl A. Schenck, the famous German forester. It was Schenck who established the Biltmore Forest School in 1898, the birthplace of scientific forestry in America (see Pink Beds Area in this section). After Vanderbilt's death in 1914, his heirs sold tracts of the forest in 1917 to the US government for forest preservation.

ADDRESS AND ACCESS: District Ranger, Pisgah Ranger District, USFS, 1001 Pisgah Highway, Pisgah Forest, NC 28768; 704-877-3350. Access is 1.6 mi W on US-276 from the jct of US-276/64 and NC-280, N of Brevard.

224 *Art Loeb Trail (30.0 mi, USFS #146) (F)*

LENGTH AND DIFFICULTY: Section I, 12.2 mi, strenuous; Section II, 7.0 mi, strenuous; Section III, 7.0 mi, moderate; Section IV, 3.8 mi, moderate to strenuous (elev change 4,084 ft); 33.0 mi total if *Cold Mountain Trail* is included

CONNECTING TRAILS:
(MST)
(North Slope Loop Trail Connector)
(Cat Gap Trail)
225 *Cedar Rock Trail (0.9 mi; USFS #124, strenuous) (F)*
(Butter Gap Trail)
(Farlow Gap Trail)
(MST Connector)
226 *Art Loeb Spur Trail (0.6 mi; USFS #108, easy) (F)*
227 *Ivestor Gap Trail (4.3 mi; USFS #101, easy) (F)*
(Graveyard Ridge Trail)
(Shining Creek Trail)
(Old Butt Knob Trail)
228 *Cold Mountain Trail (1.5 mi; USFS #141, strenuous, elev change 1,025 ft) (F)*

SPECIAL FEATURES: Pilot Mtn, Black Balsam Knob, Shining Rock Wilderness, geology, vistas, wildlife, wildflowers

TRAILHEAD AND DESCRIPTION: The *Art Loeb Trail*, designated a national recreation trail in 1979, is named in honor of the late Arthur J. Loeb, a hiking enthusiast and dedicated leader of the Carolina Mountain Club. The trail is the district's longest and most challenging. Its elev gain from the Davidson River to Black Balsam Knob is 4,084 ft, or 2,926 ft if ascended from the Daniel Boone Boy Scouts Camp. It undulates between cols and peaks with rapturous vistas. Although the full trail can require much exertion if backpacked S to N, it is divided into four sections with connecting or loop trails to allow for modest excursions and easier vehicle shuttle. For the first 18.0 mi the white circle blaze is for the *MST*, jointly followed by a white rectangular blaze for the *Art Loeb Trail*. It is rarely marked in its passage through the Shining Rock Wilderness. The trail passes through an exceptional variety of hardwoods and conifers, heath gardens, wildflowers, and shrubs. Mammals common to the area are bear, deer, gray fox, red and gray squirrels, rabbit, chipmunk, and woodchuck. Among the songbirds are Carolina junco, winter wren, nuthatch, scarlet tanager, warblers, and vireos. Snow buntings are seen in the winter. Other birds in the area are hawks, owls, turkey, grouse, raven, and woodpeckers.

Section I: From the Pisgah Ranger Station go E 0.3 mi to the Davidson River Campground sign (1.3 mi W from US-276/64, NC-280 jct). Turn, and before the bridge turn L into the *Art Loeb Trail* parking lot. Walk downstream 0.2 mi to the swinging bridge. Cross the swinging bridge over the Davidson River, turn L, and follow white blazes on a river plain through bee balm, coneflowers, and virgin oak and poplar. Cross a footbridge at 0.5 mi. Turn R on a grassy road for 50 ft before turning L up steps. Begin an ascent W on the Shut-In Ridge. Ascend through rosebay rhododendron and reach the crest at 2.9 mi. Descend to Neil Gap at 3.3 mi. At 3.7 mi jct R with the yellow-blazed 1.3-mi *North Slope Loop Trail Connector,* which descends for 2.0 mi to the Davidson River Campground parking lot; it is described above in the Davidson Rec Area. Climb to Chestnut Knob (3,840 ft), and descend to Cat Gap and a double trail jct at 6.3 mi. (The *Cat Gap Trail* goes R [NE] for 2.2 mi to the Fish Hatchery on FR-475 [a section formerly called *Horse Cove Trail*], and the *Cat Gap Trail* goes L [NW] for 2.5 mi for a loop to the same exit.) At 6.9 mi in Sand Gap, pass the *Cedar Rock Trail,* R, that ascends 0.3 mi to Cedar Rock Mtn (4,056 ft). (Cedar Rock Mtn is a partially exposed massif with exceptional views, but it can be dangerous for climbing in wet or icy weather, or on slick pine needles.) Cross a stream at 7.0 mi, circle S of Cedar Rock, and reach an A-frame shelter at 8.6 mi. Two streams are nearby. Ascend to Butter Gap at 8.8 mi, a jct of seven roads and trails. (*Butter Gap Trail* descends R [N] for 2.7 mi to join *Cat Gap Trail* for 0.8 mi for an exit to the Fish Hatchery on FR-475. The *Cedar Rock Trail* goes R [E] for 0.5 mi to the summit.) Continue ahead, L, on the ridge through open woods of hickory, oak, maple, locust, and sourwood with an understory of huckberry. Reach the summit of Chestnut Mtn, cross FR-471 at 11.6 mi, reach the summit of Rich Mtn at 11.8 mi, and descend to Gloucester Gap (3,250 ft) and Davidson River Rd (FR-475) at 12.2 mi. (To the R, FR-475 descends 6.7 mi to jct with US-276, and L for 2.7 mi to jct with NC-215 via SR-1321. Also at Gloucester Gap is FR-471, which goes SE for 8.2 mi on Cathey Creek Rd to US-64 at Selica. Another road here is FR-229, which ascends NW from Gloucester Gap for 2.5 mi to a parking area near Deep Gap.) (*USGS-FS Maps:* Pisgah Forest, Shining Rock)

Section II: Cross FR-475, ascend, cross FR-229 at 12.8 mi and again at 13.8 mi. Begin strenuous multiple switchbacks on Pilot Mtn and reach the summit (5,020 ft) at 14.4 mi. Vegetation is chinquapin, bush honeysuckle (*Diervilla sessilifolia*), laurel, blueberry, and chestnut oak. Hundreds of ladybird beetles have been seen here. Views are outstanding. Descend on switchbacks through yellow birch and other hardwoods to Deep Gap, follow FR-229 for 0.1 mi, and reach an A-frame shelter at 15.2 mi. A spring is 75 yd NW of the shelter. Climb Sassafras Knob with a ground cover of galax and wood betony and an understory of laurel, mountain ash, and azalea. Descend to Farlow Gap at 16.1 mi and jct with *Farlow Gap Trail.* (The blue-blazed *Farlow Gap Trail,* described above, goes 3.1 mi to *Daniel Ridge Trail,* which goes down the mtn to Davidson River Rd [FR-475].) Ascend to Shuck Ridge through oak, beech, and spruce. Reach BRP mp 421.2 at 17.6 mi. Turn L on the road and go 90 yd to trail steps up an embankment. Ascend on an exceptionally steep treadway with steps to the crest and jct with the *MST,* L and R, at 18.0 mi. (The *MST* leaves the *Art Loeb Trail* L and goes 3.2 mi to NC-215 and beyond. To the R an alternate route of the *MST* goes 1.1 mi on the *Art Loeb Trail* before turning off, R, on a new 11.6 mi route to *Buck Spring Trail.* See chapter 16.)

On a narrow trail through fir and spruce pass Silvermine Bald and reach FR-816, the end of Section II, at 19.1 mi. To the R it is 0.8 mi to the BRP. To the L it is 0.3 mi to a water source and at 0.5 mi the Black Balsam parking area, a popular base for hikes to a variety of surrounding trails. From here the 0.6-mi *Art Loeb Spur Trail* ascends to Black Balsam to jct with the *Art Loeb Trail.* The *Ivestor Trail* goes W on a broad old RR grade for 4.3 mi to jct with the *Art Loeb Trail* at Ivestor Gap and again at Shining Rock Gap. It is used more than any other access trail by hikers and backpackers to the Shining Rock Wilderness. It is also used by blueberry pickers, birders, equestrians, and hunters who use the wilderness boundary at Ivestor Gap from August 15 to January 2. Springs are at 0.9 mi and 1.6 mi. (*USGS-FS Maps: Shining Rock, Sam Knob*)

Section III: Cross FR-816 and jct with *MST Connector* (which goes NE for 11.6 mi to join the *Buck Spring Trail* and *MST*). Ascend through a heath bald area to jct L at 19.5 mi with the *Art Loeb Spur Trail.* Reach the grassy scenic summit of Black Balsam Knob (6,214 ft), the highest peak in the district, at 19.6 mi. Continue N on the ridge to Tennent Mtn (6,046 ft) at 20.8 mi. (The mtn is named in honor of Dr. G. S. Tennent, an early leader in the Carolina Mountain Club.) Descend and follow an old road entry to Ivestor Gap and the E boundary of the Shining Rock Wilderness at 21.5 mi. (R is *Graveyard Ridge Trail,* which connects after 0.2 mi with *Grassy Cove Trail* before the *Graveyard Ridge Trail* goes 3.2 mi farther E to the BRP, mp 418.8.) Contact here is with the *Ivestor Trail,* which continues to parallel the W side of the ridge toward Shining Rock Gap. The *Art Loeb Trail* skirts the E shoulder of Grassy Cove Top. At 22.7 mi reach Flower Gap and skirt E of Flower Knob on an old RR bed through an arbor of beech with bush honeysuckle, purple *Habenaria* orchids, and sundrops in sunny places. A spring is R at 23.1 mi. Proceed to Shining Rock Gap at 23.3 mi, an overused camping area and trail terminal. (The *Ivestor Trail* ends here after collecting the traffic from Fork Mtn Trail and *Little East Fork Trail* from the W. This is the W terminus for the *Shining Creek Trail* and the *Old Butt Knob Trail*, both separately but steeply ascending from Big East Fork at US-276.) Ahead are the white quartz outcrops (less pretentious than some visitors expect, but geologically venerable) that have given the area its name. It is easily reached in 0.2 mi partially by the *Old Butt Knob Trail*. (Overuse camping has damaged the thick stands of laurel, bristly locust, fetterbush, blueberry, and fly poison). (Hikers are requested to protect the environment and read the material on "No-Trace Use" on the back of the Pisgah District Trail Map.) Continue the *Art Loeb Trail* on an old RR bed N of Shining Rock Gap to a spur trail R at 23.8 mi (which leads 0.5 mi to *Old Butt Knob Trail*). Reach Crawford Creek Gap at 23.9 mi, leave the old RR grade, and ascend to Stairs Mtn (5,869 ft) at 24.1 mi. Enter a red spruce grove at 24.9 mi, and pass through the scenic Narrows where painted trillium and a number of rhododendron species create color and fragrance at 25.2 mi. At 25.6 mi and 25.7 mi are two magnificent views of the W Fork of the Pigeon River Valley, Lickstone Ridge, and Great Balsam Mtn. Descend to Deep Gap, an open grassy area with scattered locust at 26.2 mi. (Ahead is the 1.5-mi *Cold Mountain Trail*, which ascends to a dead end on the summit of Cold Mtn [6,030 ft]. Halfway up the ascent is a spring. Backtracking is required.) (*USGS-FS Maps:* Cruso, Shining Rock, Sam Knob)

Section IV: The *Art Loeb Trail* makes a 90-degree turn L for its descent into the lush headwaters of Sorrell Creek. The first seepage is at 26.9 mi, and at 28.0 mi are cascades, campsites, and part of a copious display in a mixed hardwood forest of such wildflowers as saxifrage, umbrella leaf, lady slipper, golden Alexander, and trillium. At 28.9 mi leave the ridge crest of laurel and descend on switchbacks to the trail's N terminus and parking area at the S edge of the Daniel Boone Boy Scouts Camp at 30.0 mi. If leaving vehicles here it is necessary to inform the Boy Scouts Camp director. Access here is on Little East Fork Rd (SR-1129), which goes 3.8 mi downstream to NC-215 (13.0 mi L [S] to the BRP and 5.3 mi R [N] to US-276). (*USGS-FS Maps:* Cruso, Waynesville)

MIDDLE PRONG WILDERNESS (Haywood County)

In 1984, a wild, remote, and rugged 7,900-acre section of the district officially became the Middle Prong Wilderness. Its boundary is NC-215 (E), the

BRP (S and W), and near the toe of Big Beartrail Ridge (N). In the center of the wilderness is long Fork Ridge, whose waters drain E into the W Fork of the Pigeon River and W into the Middle Prong of the W Fork at Sunburst. Sunburst was a lumber town for the Champion Paper Company in the early 1900s. It had more than 10 camps harvesting the huge hemlock, chestnut, and poplar. Although the forest is recovering, parts of old RR and skid grades and logging equipment remain scattered in the Middle Prong area. Wildlife includes bear, deer, red and gray squirrel, turkey, and grouse, and Middle Prong has native brook trout. Rich lush coves are full of wildflowers, and large sweet blueberries are prominent on the grassy meadows of Fork Ridge and its E escarpment. Old roads and old trails provide numerous man-way options, but none of them is blazed, marked, or signed. Two of the longer and better known trails are described below. Access to them is easy, but once in the wilderness it is advisable to have a topo map and compass or hike with experienced companions familiar with the similar ridges and coves. A developed base camp can be Sunburst Rec Area. It has campsites with water and toilets and a picnic area.

ACCESS: Sunburst Rec Area is on NC-215, 8.6 mi W from the BRP, and 9.6 mi S from US-276 near Woodrow. Access on the BRP is described below.

SUPPORT FACILITIES: The nearest groceries and services are in Woodrow, with full provisions and services 5.0 mi W from Woodrow to Waynesville.

229- *Haywood Gap Trail (5.8 mi; USFS #142) (F); Buckeye Gap Trail (4.0 mi;*
230 *USFS #126) (F)*

LENGTH AND DIFFICULTY: 13.8 mi, combined and round-trip, strenuous (elev change 2,468 ft)

TRAILHEADS AND DESCRIPTION: From the S end of Sunburst Campground hike 1.6 mi upstream W of Middle Prong on FR-97 and ascend two switchbacks. On the third major curve leave FR-97, L, and follow a primitive route across Little Beartrap Branch. Enter the wilderness boundary to campsites near the mouth of Big Beartrap Branch, R, at 2.7 mi. Rock-hop the Middle Prong at an area once called the "cattle crossing." Cross Camp Two Branch and at 3.4 mi jct with the *Buckeye Gap Trail*. At this point either trail can be ascended to jct with the *MST*, which can be used for a connector to return here after 8.0 mi. If taking *Haywood Gap Trail*, cross the Grassy Ridge Branch and follow the main stream for 2.2 mi to Sweetwater Spring (W side of trail). From here it is 0.2 mi to Haywood Gap (5,225 ft) and BRP mp 426.5. Turn L on the *MST*, which has routed wood signs, and go 1.8 mi on a graded footpath to jct with the *Buckeye Gap Trail* on an old RR grade. (The *Buckeye Gap Trail* access here is out 0.2 mi across a small stream to Rough Butt Bald Overlook [mp 425.4], elev 5,300 ft. If vehicle is left on the BRP overnight, the BRP ranger should be informed at 704-456-9530, weekdays 9:00–4:30.) Turn L on the *Buckeye Gap Trail* and follow jointly with the *MST* for 1.0 mi where Buckeye Creek is crossed in a rhododendron grove. The forest also has birch, beech, cherry, maple, and scattered fir and spruce. After 75 yd ahead, the *MST* turns sharply R up the slope, but the *Buckeye Gap Trail* continues on the old RR grade with numerous seeps. Descend gradually and after 1.5 mi from the *MST* turn abruptly L off the old RR grade. (For exploratory hikers who wish to follow part of the old and obscure 7.0-mi *Green Mountain Trail* [(USFS **231** #113], bushwhack R [E] approx 0.4 mi up to scenic Fork Ridge anywhere along the 1.5-mi stretch after leaving the *MST*.) Descend steeply to cross Grassy Ridge Branch and rejoin the *Haywood Gap Trail* at 4.0 mi. Turn R downstream and return to the Sunburst Rec Area. (*USGS-FS Map:* Sam Knob)

SHINING ROCK WILDERNESS (Haywood County)

To emphasize connecting trail options from the East Fork (parallels US-276) and West Fork (parallels NC-215) of the Pigeon River and from the BRP (S) into the Shining Rock Wilderness (N), the following 18 trails are grouped under the title of Shining Rock Wilderness. Because the longest section of the *Art Loeb Trail* is in the Davidson River area, it and three other connecting trails have been described earlier in this chapter. Also, the *MST* is described in chapter 16. All the trails connect directly with or have trail access to the *Art Loeb Trail*, the area trail most impacted by visitors. Among the least used trails are *Little East Fork, Fork Mountain, Fire Scald Ridge, Old Butt Knob,* and *Cold Mountain.* All trails are for foot traffic only. The highest concentration of people is at the Black Balsam parking area at the end of FR-816 (1.2 mi from BRP mp 420.2). Four official trails (and one created by hikers) fan out from the parking area. Camping permits are not required in the Shining Rock Wilderness, and in 1982 the FS established a "volunteer ranger program" to educate and monitor the public on "wilderness ethics." Group size is limited to 10, and fires are prohibited. Nevertheless, high-impact camping remains a problem. (See "Wilderness Experience" in the introduction to part I.) Five trails are found exclusively in the Shining Rock Wilderness: *Big East Fork, Cold Mountain, Grassy Cove, Old Butt Knob, Shining Creek,* and almost all of *Little East Fork.*

232 *Little East Fork Trail (USFS #107) (F, H)*

LENGTH AND DIFFICULTY: 5.0 mi, strenuous (elev change 2,312 ft)

TRAILHEAD AND DESCRIPTION: From the jct of NC-215 and the BRP go N 13.0 mi on NC-215 to Little East Fork Rd (SR-1129) and turn R (5.3 mi S from US-276 and turn L). Proceed 3.8 mi to the parking area past the Daniel Boone Boy Scouts Camp, R. Hike up the road a few yd, cross the Little East Fork of the Pigeon River bridge, and turn L through Boy Scout camps named for a variety of Indian tribes. Follow an old RR grade, rough in sections, for the entire distance. The river has numerous cascades and pools. The forest is mainly hardwood with groves of hemlock and rhododendron in the lower elevations and spruce with birch near the top. Enter the NF at 0.3 mi, and cross Cathey Cove Creek. At 1.0 mi enter the Shining Rock Wilderness. Cross Hemlock Branch at 1.3 mi and at 2.8 mi cross the Little East Fork. The gradient increases, but follow switchbacks for the remainder of the route to jct at 5.0 mi with *Ivestor Gap Trail.* Left it is 0.4 mi to Shining Rock Gap and connection with the *Art Loeb Trail,* and R it is 3.9 mi to the Black Balsam parking area. (Using the *Art Loeb Trail,* N, a loop of 12.1 mi can be made for a return to Camp Daniel Boone.) (*USGS-FS Maps:* Sam Knob, Shining Rock, Waynesville)

233- *Fork Mountain Trail (6.2 mi; USFS #109) (F); Fire Scald Ridge Trail*
234 *(1.1 mi; USFS #111) (F)*

LENGTH AND DIFFICULTY: 7.3 mi combined, strenuous (elev change 2,620 ft)

TRAILHEADS AND DESCRIPTION: From the BRP/NC-215 jct in Beech Gap, descend N on NC-215 8.4 mi to parking space, R, beside the river (0.2 mi before the Sunburst Rec Area). Because the footbridge has been washed away, rock-hop or wade (river may be impassable with high water) the West Fork of the Pigeon River. After crossing, immediately turn R, go upstream for 0.4 mi, cross and turn L at the mouth of Turnpike Creek, and turn sharply R to leave the stream at 0.8 mi. Ascend on switchbacks to a narrow gap on the Fork Mtn ridgeline at 2.0 mi. (The old timber road L is 0.4 mi to High Top [5,263 ft].) Turn R and follow an old road (except in a few relocations), undulate on knobs but leave the ridge to skirt E of Birdstand Mtn at 3.2 mi. The forest is chiefly hardwoods with laurel, rhododendron, blueberries, and ferns. At 4.7 mi, in a shallow gap, jct with the primitive *Fire Scald Ridge Trail,* R.

(The *Fire Scald Ridge Trail* W access is from NC-215. [This trail may be so overgrown it may be difficult to follow. USGS modified forest map (Sam Knob) may be essential.] From the BRP described above, descend 5.3 mi to a narrow space for parking against a rock wall, L, on a curve. Cross the road, climb over the guardrail, and descend steeply through wildflowers, tall basswood, poplar, and locust to the rapids of the West Fork of the Pigeon River at 0.1 mi. If the river is high, crossing can be made on double steel cables. Across the river climb an exceptionally steep trail, faint in most places, to a fork on the old skid road at 0.3 mi. Bear R or L for climb to *Fork Mountain Trail*. If L, follow up the stream for a short distance and climb the slope 0.8 mi for a rapid, rugged, 1,240-ft elev gain. If R, ascend gradually on spur ridges for 0.8 mi and make a curve up Fire Scald Ridge for another 0.6 mi to rejoin the trail at *Fork Mountain Trail*, a total loop of 2.8 mi. Some of the vegetation is sweet pepperbush, arrowwood, rhododendron, and liverwort.)

Continue ahead on the *Fork Mountain Trail* and skirt E of the ridge for the final mile to reach *Ivestor Gap Trail* at 6.2 mi. (It is 1.7 mi R to the Black Balsam parking area, and 0.5 mi L to Ivestor Gap and connections with the *Art Loeb Trail*.) (*USGS-FS Maps*: Sam Knob, Shining Rock, Waynesville)

Big East Fork Trail (3.6 mi; USFS #357) (F); Grassy Cove Trail (3.2 mi; USFS #362) (F)

235-236

LENGTH AND DIFFICULTY: 6.8 mi combined, moderate to strenuous (elev change 2,256 ft)

SPECIAL FEATURES: scenic river, fishing

TRAILHEADS AND DESCRIPTION: At the BRP/US-276 jct in Wagon Rd Gap, descend W on US-276 2.9 mi to the Big East Fork parking area, L. Hike up US-276 (across the Big East Fork bridge) 0.1 mi and turn R at the *Big East Fork Trail* access. Follow an old road that becomes an old RR grade. At 0.4 mi jct R with a 0.2-mi spur connector to *Shining Creek Trail* (on the other side of the river.) Ahead the trail forks L at 0.5 mi. (The R fork is a dead-end side trail to a waterfall and pool.) At 1.1 mi pass a rocky area with rapids, white azalea, and cinnamon ferns. At 1.3 mi leave the river and ascend on the slope, rock-hop Bennett Branch, and return to the riverside at 1.8 mi. For the next 1.8 mi follow the scenic riverside where the loud rattle of king-fishers can be heard over the roar of the rapids. Excellent camping and fishing locations are along the way, and scenic flumes and clear pools are frequent. The forest is mostly birch, hemlock, rhododendron, maple, poplar, buckeye, and wildflowers. At 3.6 mi reach the end of the *Big East Fork Trail* at Bridges Camp, a frequently used campsite. Rock-hop or wade the East Fork of the Pigeon River to begin the *Grassy Cove Trail*. (A USGS-FS topo map [Shining Rock] may be necessary for hikers to locate and follow this trail.) (The continuing trail on the S side of the river is a fisherman's trail. There are not any signs or blazes for the *Grassy Cove Trail*.)

Across the river, follow *Grassy Cove Trail* steeply upstream on the N side of Grassy Cove Prong, a splashing stream with moss-covered rocks. At 0.9 mi leave the stream and veer R up a steep hollow of birch, hemlock, and poplar to a level area on Grassy Cove Ridge at 1.7 mi. Continue the ascent and end the trail at the jct with the Graveyard Ridge Trail at 3.0 mi. (The *Graveyard Ridge Trail* goes L 3.2 mi to its S end and jct with the *Graveyard Fields Trail* at the BRP. Ahead the trail gently ascends 0.2 mi to its N end at a jct with the *Art Loeb Trail* and *Ivestor Gap Trail* in Ivestor Gap. It is 1.7 mi N on the *Art Loeb Trail* for a return loop on either the *Shining Creek Trail* or the *Old Butt Knob Trail* described below.) (*USGS-FS Map:* Shining Rock)

237- *Shining Creek Trail (4.1 mi; USFS #363) (F); Old Butt Knob Trail (3.6*
238 *mi; USFS #332) (F)*

LENGTH AND DIFFICULTY: 7.7 mi combined, strenuous (elev change 2,556 ft)

CONNECTING TRAILS: *(Art Loeb Trail); (Ivestor Gap Trail)*

SPECIAL FEATURES: vistas from outcroppings

TRAILHEADS AND DESCRIPTION: At the BRP/US-276 jct in Wagon Rd Gap, descend W on US-276 2.9 mi to the Big East Fork parking area, L. At the end of the parking area follow the unblazed *Shining Creek Trail* through a clearing, and at 0.3 mi turn R at a fork. (The L fork is a spur trail that goes to the East Fork of the Pigeon River, where wading or rock-hopping is necessary to jct with the *Big East Fork Trail*. The best approach to this trail is to follow the directions described above under *Big East Fork Trail*.) Ascend on switchbacks to a small saddle, Shining Creek Gap, at 0.7 mi, and jct R with unblazed *Old Butt Knob Trail* in a rhododendron thicket.

(The *Old Butt Knob Trail* ascends on the extremely steep Chestnut Ridge in sections of dense rhododendron, laurel, oak, and chestnut saplings to a knob at 1.5 mi. Follow an easier grade for the next 0.5 mi to Old Butt Knob and pass outcroppings along the way for scenic views of Shining Rock Wilderness. Descend to Spanish Oak Gap in a forest of oak, birch, and maple. Ascend to Dog Loser Knob and more off-trail vista points at 2.8 mi. Descend gradually to Beech Spring Gap and a spring, L, at 3.0 mi. Ascend on switchbacks to Shining Rock [5,940 ft], the highest point of the trail, and curve L [S] to Shining Rock Gap at 3.6 mi. Here is a jct with the *Art Loeb Trail, Ivestor Gap Trail,* and *Shining Creek Trail*.) There are not likely to be any signs here. Hikers may need USGS-FS topo map (Shining Rock).

To continue on the *Shining Creek Trail*, descend from Shining Creek Gap to the bank of Shining Creek in a forest of hemlock and mixed hardwoods at 1.0 mi. Follow large boulders upstream on the steep R and flumes, cascades, and pools, L, in the creek. Among abundant wildflowers cross Daniels Cove

Creek at 2.0 mi, and at the confluence of the N and S prongs of Shining Creek, stay R. Follow the streamside in a forest of tall hickory, oak, and birch, and at 3.1 mi cross at a stream fork to begin a steep climb on a ridge slope. On switchbacks enter sections of rhododendron, beech, spruce, and moss beds to reach Shining Rock Gap at 4.1 mi. Jct here with *Art Loeb Trail, Ivestor Gap Trail,* and *Old Butt Knob Trail.* A return loop on the *Old Butt Knob Trail* totals 8.4 mi to the parking area. (*USGS-FS Map:* Shining Rock)

BLACK BALSAM KNOB AREA (Haywood County)

At a SE corner between the Middle Prong Wilderness (W side of NC-215) and Shining Rock Wilderness (E side of NC-215) and the BRP on the S side, is a triangular section of the district that is distinctly different. It is a plateau with fields of wildflowers, knobs, and balds with Black Balsam Knob (6,214 ft) the highest in the district. From grassy slopes and rocky coves is drainage into the headwaters of both forks of Pigeon River. Both the *Art Loeb Trail* and the *Mountains-to-Sea Trail* intersect here. In this place of scenic beauty among windswept rocks, grasses, and spruce is also a fragile environment. There are endangered species of wildlife and plants and it deserves protective usage. Those who use the Black Balsam parking lot for access into the Shining Rock Wilderness will need not only to know how to use and be safe in the backcountry, but to have a district map for planning any long-range journeys on unmaintained trails described above.

Flat Laurel Creek Trail (3.7 mi; USFS #346) (F, B, H); Little Sam Knob Trail (1.3 mi; USFS #347) (F) **239-240**

LENGTH AND DIFFICULTY: 5.2 mi, combined, easy
CONNECTING TRAILS:
  (MST)
  (Ivestor Trail)
  Art Loeb Spur(/Black Balsam) Trail (0.6 mi; USFS #108, easy) (F)
SPECIAL FEATURES: Scenic views of Sam Knob and Fork Ridge
TRAILHEADS AND DESCRIPTION: At the BRP/NC-215 jct in Beech Gap, descend N on NC-215 0.8 mi to parking area, R, to begin the orange-blazed *Flat Laurel Creek Trail* (formerly called *Sam Knob Trail*), which can be used for cross-country skiing. Rock-hop Bubbling Spring Branch and follow an old RR grade with borders of bush honeysuckle, rhododendron, cherry, maple, blackberry, blueberry, and gentian. Cross a cement bridge at 0.7 mi where a 125-ft cascade is R. At 1.6 mi are scenic views of Mt Hardy, Fork Ridge, and the gorge of the West Fork of the Pigeon Valley. Spectacular

views of Sam Knob (6,130 ft) begin at 1.8 mi, and at 2.0 mi, L, near a landslide are scenic views of Flat Laurel Creek cascades and pools. Campsites are 0.3 mi farther in a flat area near Flat Laurel Creek, as are three routes to the Black Balsam parking area. Two routes are across the creek and the other route follows the old RR grade. (The routes across the creek are described first.) To continue on the *Flat Laurel Creek Trail,* rock-hop the creek in a rhododendron grove and reach a trail fork in a flat area. Turn L and cross a streamlet, follow any of a number of camp trails up to a large wildlife field with scenic views, L, of Sam Knob. Bear R, and ascend easily in the field to an old logging road at 2.7 mi. Follow the road to a gate and pass the rest rooms to the Black Balsam parking lot.

The second route is from the fork, mentioned above. Veer R on an open field path that ascends casually 0.8 mi to the SW corner of the Black Balsam parking lot. (Some hikers call the path the *Goldenrod Trail* for the magnificent exhibition of *Solidago* species that bloom in late September. It is a time when the fall colors come early to these gentle hillsides, mile-high meadows, and heath balds, all covered with the xanthous and ochre of goldenrod, purples of asters, and crimson of the blueberry bushes.)

The third route is the original *Flat Laurel Creek Trail,* which begins on the old RR grade where the *Sam Knob Trail* turned L. Follow the wide trail 180 yd to rock-hop a tributary and jct, R, with the *Little Sam Knob Trail* at 0.4 mi. At 0.8 mi rock-hop Flat Laurel Creek in an area of scattered spruce, mountain ash, and blackberries. Cross culverts for other small streams in an easy scenic approach to Black Balsam parking area at 1.4 mi. (The *Ivestor Gap Trail* begins here, N, on an old RR grade, and the *Art Loeb Spur/Black Balsam Trail* ascends E to jct with the *Art Loeb Trail.* On FR-816, S, it is 1.3 mi to BRP mp 420.2.)

The yellow-blazed *Little Sam Knob Trail,* mentioned above, follows an old RR grade through a forest of spruce, birch, and rhododendron and open spots with thornless blackberry (*Rubus canadensis*) SE of Little Sam Knob (5,862 ft). Rock-hop a tributary at 0.4 mi, ascend to a jct with an unnamed trail, L, turn sharply R, and follow an old RR grade on the W slope of Chestnut Bald Ridge. At 0.8 mi is a scenic view of Mt Hardy; enter a ravine from a former RR trestle; and jct with the *MST* at 1.3 mi. (It is 1.0 mi L to jct with the *Art Loeb Trail* and 2.2 mi R to NC-215. The latter could form a 7.0-mi loop to the beginning of the *Sam Knob Trail* on NC-215.) (*USGS-FS Map:* Sam Knob)

241- *Graveyard Fields Trail (3.2 mi; USFS #358) (F); Graveyard Ridge Trail*
242 *(3.4 mi; USFS #356) (F, B, H)*

LENGTH AND DIFFICULTY: 6.6 mi combined, easy to moderate

SPECIAL FEATURES: Yellowstone Prong waterfalls

TRAILHEADS AND DESCRIPTION: (The *Graveyard Fields Trail* is also called *Yellowstone Falls Trail*.) On the BRP at the Graveyard Fields Overlook mp 418.8 (5,120 ft), begin on a paved trail through dense rhododendron. Descend to a rocky area and bridge over the Yellowstone Prong of the East Fork of the Pigeon River at 0.2 mi. Cross and turn R for a trail to the Second Falls at 0.3 mi. Backtrack to the bridge, but stay on the N side of the stream for a jct with *Graveyard Ridge Trail*. (There may be a relocation of the *Graveyard Ridge Trail* farther upstream because of erosion.)

(The *Graveyard Ridge Trail* follows an old logging road that ascends gently 0.4 mi to Graveyard Ridge, but quickly curves to follow the S slope. [This route may be relocated.] At 1.5 mi, hiking N, cross Dark Prong Gap and intersect the *MST Connector* [E of Black Balsam Knob]. Cross the headwaters of Dark Prong, curve E at the base of Tennent Mtn in a forest of birch, rhododendron, and spruce, and jct with *Grassy Cove Trail*, R, at 3.2 mi. Turn sharply L and reach Ivestor Gap at 3.4 mi to jct with the *Art Loeb Trail*.)

Continuing on the *Graveyard Fields Trail*, after another 0.6 mi jct L with a return loop but continue ahead for 0.5 mi to the scenic Upper Falls. Return for a complete loop at 3.2 mi. (Yellowstone is named from the yellow mosses, lichens, and minerals on the rocks. The area received its name from moss-covered fallen spruce trunks and stumps that resembled a graveyard. The trunks were destroyed by a fire in November 1925 that burned 25,000 acres of prime timber.) (*USGS-FS Map:* Shining Rock)

COURTHOUSE CREEK AREA (Transylvania County)

Beetree Trail (USFS #612) (F, B)   243

LENGTH AND DIFFICULTY: 1.8 mi, strenuous (elev change 1,330 ft)

TRAILHEAD AND DESCRIPTION: From the jct of the BRP in Beech Gap (mp 423.2) and NC-215 descend S 1.9 mi on NC-215 to a small parking area in curve. (To the R is a 300-yd trail to a spring in Cold Spring Gap, the headwater of Beetree Fork.) For an easy descent enter the blue-blazed trail on the L (E) side of the road and descend through hardwood and laurel on Big Fork Ridge to a knoll at 0.3 mi. Leave the ridge on a S slope and descend on switchbacks to the stream among cove hardwoods and hemlock. Crisscross the stream on a flat section of the trail to exit on the E side of the NC-215 bridge. From here it is 3.3 mi up the road to the N trailhead. (It is 0.4 mi farther S on NC-215 to the entrance, L, to *Summey Cove Trail,* described below, and another 1.1 mi farther S on NC-215 to jct with FR-140, L, the entrance road to the E trailhead for *Summey Cove Trail*. Ahead on NC-215 is it 10.2 mi to US-64.) (*USGS-FS Map*: Sam Knob)

244 *Courthouse Creek Trail (USFS #128) (F)*

LENGTH AND DIFFICULTY: 1.8 mi, strenuous (elev change 1,880 ft)

TRAILHEAD AND DESCRIPTION: There are three accesses to FR-140: (1) From the jct of the BRP in Beech Gap (mp 423.2) and NC-215 descend SE 6.6 mi on NC-215 to Courthouse Creek Rd (FR-140); turn L. (2) From US-64 and NC-215 jct in Rosman, drive N 10.2 mi on NC-215; turn R. (3) From US-276 (3.5 mi NW of the ranger station) turn L on Davidson Creek Rd (FR-475), which becomes McColl Rd (SR-1327), for 8.0 mi to NC-215. Turn R on NC-215 and drive 2.6 mi to FR-140; turn R. Follow gravel FR-140 for 0.9 mi, veer L, and continue 3.0 mi to a parking area at the road's end. The creek is part of the headwaters of the French Broad River. The trail may be blazed blue, but unmaintained. Ascend steeply upstream, L, by cascades and flumes. Cross the scenic stream at least twice, depending on stream erosion. There are remnants of an old RR grade at 0.5 mi. At 0.6 mi bear R at creek's fork, and at 0.8 mi ascend steeply L of a large cascade. Through a rocky and rough gorge, climb steeply to the jct of an unmarked trail at 1.7 mi (used by mtn climbers to the Devil's Courthouse wall), turn L, and ascend to the Devil's Courthouse parking overlook at BRP mp 422.4. Vegetation on the trail includes dense fetterbush and rhododendron, black cohosh, birch, buckeye, white snakeroot, oak, and red spruce. (*USGS-FS Map*: Sam Knob)

245- *Summey Cove Trail (USFS #129) (F, B); Courthouse Falls Trail (USFS*
246 *#130) (F)*

LENGTH AND DIFFICULTY: 2.3 mi combined, moderate

SPECIAL FEATURES: Courthouse Falls, wildflowers

TRAILHEADS AND DESCRIPTION: Follow the same directions described for access to *Courthouse Creek Trail*, except follow FR-140 for 3.1 mi (0.8 mi before road's end) and park on the R. The trail is unsigned and unblazed. The first trail, which is the orange-blazed *Courthouse Falls Trail*, begins at the bridge and follows and old road downstream. At 0.2 mi, L, is a narrow path (with sections of steps) that descends 0.1 mi to a pool at the scenic Courthouse Falls. Continue on the old road to campsites at Mill Station Creek at 0.5 mi; turn L, cross the creek. Ascend in a forest of poplar, basswood, hemlock, and buffalo nut. Curve R at the ridgeline at 1.0 mi and descend gently to good campsites in Summey Cove at 1.3 mi. Cross the stream and ascend Big Fork Ridge; descend in a hardwood cove with numerous wildflowers, including orange fringe orchids that bloom in mid-August. Arrive at NC-215, the S trailhead, at 2.1 mi. (It is 5.4 mi R to Beech Gap at the BRP, and 1.2 mi L to FR-140.)

UPPER DAVIDSON RIVER AREA (Transylvania County)

Across Pilot Mtn and Sassafras Knob, E from Courthouse Creek, are Laurel, Shuck, Daniel Ridge, Cove, and Caney Bottom tributaries, which form Davidson River. Along the spine of Pilot Mtn and other peaks, weaves the N-S flow of the *Art Loeb Trail* in ascents and descents. Three trails in this area rise to make connections with it. On its high warm rocks are ladybugs and gnarled windblown chestnut oaks hovering over tight patches of buckberry. To the N of the large cove is the mile-high BRP on the Eastern Continental Divide. In addition to wild trout, the streams below this ridge are stocked with brook, brown, and rainbow trout for catch and release. Within 3.0 mi of the river's forming, the crystalline clear rushing river flows between Looking Glass Rock on the N side and John Rock on the S side. Both are granite massifs whose trails to the top bear their names. Here in this sunny, but often easily flooded, valley are waterfalls, fish hatchery, timber history, group campgrounds, and seven trails looping skyward. Access to the area is on FR-475, which begins W off US-276, 3.5 mi W of the ranger station. Two short rock-climbing access trails to Looking Glass Rock are 0.7-mi *Slick Rock Falls Trail* (USFS #117) (F), and 0.4-mi *Sunwall Trail* (USFS #601) (F). Both are blazed yellow, and both are accessible on the E side of FR-475B, which begins N from FR-475, 0.1 mi W of the fish hatchery.

247-248

ACCESS: From the jct of US-276/64 and NC-280 (N of Brevard) drive 1.2 mi NW on US-276 and turn L at the campground sign.

SUPPORT FACILITIES: At the access jct listed above there is a motel, restaurant, camping and fishing supplies, laundry svc, svc sta, and grocery. A large shopping center with national chain stores is here.

Daniel Ridge Loop Trail (4.0 mi; USFS #105) (F, B); Farlow Gap Trail (3.2 mi; USFS #106) (F, B)

249-250

LENGTH AND DIFFICULTY: 10.2 mi combined round-trip, moderate to strenuous (elev change 1,924 ft)

SPECIAL FEATURES: cascades for sliding, Shuck Ridge Creek waterfalls, geology

TRAILHEADS AND DESCRIPTION: From the ranger station go 3.5 mi W on US-276, turn L on Davidson River Rd (FR-475), and go 4.1 mi to FR-137, R, and park. Cross the cement bridge at the pool and sunbathing rocks. At 0.1

mi turn L off the main road. Follow upstream to the site of a former fish hatchery and fork in the trail. The L route is near the river with campsites, pools, and sliding rocks. The R route follows an old RR grade and rejoins the other trail at 1.2 mi at a pool and campsite. Turn R to another RR grade; jct with the blue-blazed *Farlow Gap Trail* at 1.8 mi.

(The *Farlow Gap Trail* goes upstream 250 ft to cross the Right Fork of the Davidson River. Ascend gradually on an old road and cross Fork River Ridge Creek at 1.4 mi. Curve around Daniel Ridge and ascend to the top of scenic Shuck Ridge Creek waterfall at 2.2 mi. Ascend steeply to pass an old mica mine at 2.7 mi and reach Farlow Gap and jct with the *Art Loeb Trail* at 3.2 mi. [To the L the *Art Loeb Trail* ascends Sassafras Mtn, dips to a saddle, and ascends mile-high Pilot Mtn for exceptionally scenic views.] Vegetation at the gap is mainly maple, oak, and birch. Backtrack to *Daniel Ridge Loop Trail*.)

Continuing on the *Daniel Ridge Loop Trail* follow the red blazes through a young forest and on an old road to wildlife grazing fields. After 0.5 mi the trail curves around a knob before descending on switchbacks to FR-5046 at 3.1 mi. Cross the road and descend the NE side of the ridge to close proximity with a stream and jct with FR-5046 at 3.6 mi. Turn R and follow the road to the point of origin at 4.0 mi. (*USGS-FS Map:* Shining Rock)

251- *Caney Bottom Loop Trail (4.6 mi; USFS #361) (F, B on the W side);*
252 *Caney Bottom Extension Trail (0.7 mi; USFS #340) (F, B)*
LENGTH AND DIFFICULTY: 6.0 mi combined, round-trip, easy to moderate
TRAILHEADS AND DESCRIPTION: At the jct of US-276 and Davidson River Rd (FR-475), follow FR-475 upstream (past the state fish hatchery) for 3.5 mi to a parking area, L. Cross the road to the gated entrance road of Cove Creek Group Camp. Cross a footbridge over Cove Creek at 0.1 mi. At 0.3 mi is a waterfall, R, and at 0.4 mi is a trail sign, L. Leave the road, ascend, and bypass the group camp area on a trail heavily used by bikers. In a hemlock grove at 0.8 mi are good campsites. Other vegetation along the trail includes oak, poplar, locust, maple, and laurel. Cross a footbridge over Cove Creek to jct with the loop portion of the trail. If going R, pass a rock formation at 1.2 mi, L, and a waterfall, R, at Caney Bottom Creek. Follow an old RR grade that parallels Caney Bottom Creek and pass a high cascading waterfall at 1.5 mi. At 2.1 mi jct with the blue-blazed *Caney Bottom Extension Trail*, R. (The extension goes easily up the ridge for 0.7 mi to jct with FR-225, a dead-end road to Cove Creek, L, but R is an access road to FR-475B near Looking Glass Rock.) Continue on the *Caney Bottom Loop Trail* by turning L to cross a footbridge. At 2.4 mi the trail is on an old RR grade that it follows on a

gradual descent for nearly 1.8 mi. Along the way, in a mixed hardwood forest, the trail passes high above a waterfall, L, at 3.8 mi. Return to the loop jct at 4.2 mi for an exit to the point of origin. (*USGS-FS Map:* Shining Rock)

Long Branch Trail (2.5 mi; USFS #116) (F, B); Cemetery Loop Trail (1.2 mi; USFS #341) (F, B)   **253-254**

LENGTH AND DIFFICULTY: 3.7 mi combined, easy to moderate

TRAILHEADS AND DESCRIPTION: At the jct of US-276 and FR-475 (3.5 mi W from the ranger station), drive 5.4 mi on FR-475 to a small parking area for *Long Branch Trail,* L. (It is 0.1 mi beyond the trailhead for *Cemetery Loop Trail.*) Follow the orange-blazed trail in a slight descent to parallel Long Branch. At 0.4 mi jct with yellow-blazed *Cemetery Trail,* L, which leads to a former pioneer settlement and the McCall Cemetery. (It slopes around a low hill to follow at 0.8 mi an old wagon road to FR-475. A turn L up the road makes the 1.2-mi loop.)

Continuing on the *Long Branch Trail,* cross Long Branch and weave in and out of cove hardwoods and rhododendron to ascend a short ridge. Descend to cross FR-5095 at 1.8 mi. After another easy walk descend steeply to cross Searcy Creek. Ascend and jct with Butter Gap Trail at 2.5 mi (described ahead). Backtrack, or with a second vehicle go L another 1.5 mi on *Butter Gap Trail* and *Cat Gap Loop Trail* to exit at the fish hatchery for a total of 4.0 mi. (The use of *Butter Gap Trail,* R, for 2.0 mi to Butter Gap at the *Art Loeb Trail,* R, and 3.4 mi on the *Art Loeb Trail* to Gloucester Gap returns you to FR-475. A turn R with a descent of 0.7 mi on FR-475 to the entrance of Long Branch is a loop of 8.6 mi.) (*USGS-FS Map:* Shining Rock)

Cat Gap Loop Trail (USFS #120) (F, B partial)   **255**

LENGTH AND DIFFICULTY: 4.7 mi, strenuous

CONNECTING TRAILS:

   Butter Gap Trail (2.7 mi; USFS #123, moderate) (F, B)   **256**

   Cat Gap Bypass Trail (0.6 mi; USFS #120A, moderate) (F)   **257**

   (Art Loeb Trail)

   John Rock Trail (1.8 mi; USFS #365, moderate) (F)   **258**

SPECIAL FEATURES: wildlife, wildflowers, scenic John Rock

TRAILHEAD AND DESCRIPTION: (Usage of the *Cat Gap Loop Trail* provides access to four loop options.) At jct of US-276 and FR-475, go 1.5 mi on FR-475 to the state fish hatchery, L, and to the parking area. (Visitors are welcome at the hatchery where 60,000 trout are raised annually.) To access *Cat Gap Loop Trail* from the parking area, pass between the bulletin board and education center building to cross a gated vehicle bridge over Cedar Rock Creek. Bear R on this frequently used orange-blazed trail in a forest of cove hardwoods, hemlock, and running cedar. Cross a footbridge at 0.3 mi. Ascend, pass R of cascades and pools. Jct with the blue-blazed *Butter Gap Trail*, R, at 0.8 mi in Picklesimer Fields.

(The *Butter Gap Trail* is an optional loop. It follows an old RR grade, crosses Grogan Creek at 0.4 mi, and follows upstream on the W side through a forest of mixed hardwoods, hemlock, and rhododendron. At 0.7 mi it jct with orange-blazed *Long Branch Trail* (which goes W for 2.5 mi to FR-475). The *Butter Gap Trail* passes cascades, and at 1.1 mi a waterfall. At 2.1 mi the trail becomes steep at the headwaters of the creek, and at 2.7 mi it reaches the trail terminus and jct with the *Art Loeb Trail* in Butter Gap. Here are multiple trails and roads. [The spur trail, L, ascends 0.5 mi to Cedar Rock Mtn with outstanding views. Ahead the *Art Loeb Trail* descends 0.2 mi to an A-frame shelter, and 2.3 mi farther on the *Art Loeb Trail* is a jct with *Cat Gap Loop Trail* in Cat Gap to make a loop back to the fish hatchery for 8.5 mi.])

Continue upstream on the *Cat Gap Loop Trail* among blueberries, yellow root, spicebush, white pine, and oak. At 1.9 mi jct L with orange-blazed *Cat Gap Bypass Trail* to Horse Cove Gap. (This beautiful 0.6-mi trail follows a wide old RR grade through tall hardwoods, scattered hemlock, and fern beds. Songbirds are prominent. If using this route the loop back to the parking area is 4.3 mi.) Continue an ascent on the *Cat Gap Loop Trail* among dense laurel to Cat Gap (3,350 ft) at 2.5 mi and jct with the *Art Loeb Trail*. Here are two white oaks with unique knobs on their trunks. Turn L on the *Cat Gap Trail*, first to descend on a slope, then down the ridge to a jct in Horse Cove Gap with *Cat Gap Bypass Trail*, L, the yellow-blazed *John Rock Trail* ahead, and the continuance of *Cat Gap Loop Trail*, R.

(The scenic *John Rock Trail* ascends steeply to a knoll among hardwoods, laurel, indigo bush, and buckberry, descends to a saddle, and up to John Rock at 0.7 mi. [The monolith is part of 435 acres protected as a special interest area.] Descend and to the L is exposure to the granite dome where views are of the fish hatchery, Davidson Valley, Looking Glass Rock, and the range of BRP mtns. [Because of water oozing from the edges of mosses and laurel, the rock can be slippery.] Continue descending to a level wet area among rhododendron before descending on the E slope of John Rock. Rejoin *Cat Gap Loop Trail* after 1.8 mi.)

If continuing R on the *Cat Gap Loop Trail* from Horse Cove Gap, descend steeply on rocky treadway. Jct with the *John Rock Trail*, L, at 3.4 mi.

Descend, pass sections of wild geraniums, mayapple, blue and black cohosh, and maidenhair ferns. Rock-hop Horse Cove Creek and follow an old flat RR grade. Cross small streams and a major footbridge over Cedar Rock Creek for a return to a field at 4.6 mi and parking area at the fish hatchery at 4.7 mi. (*USGS-FS Map*: Shining Rock)

Looking Glass Rock Trail (USFS #114) (F)   **259**

LENGTH AND DIFFICULTY: 6.2 mi round-trip, strenuous (elev change 1,369 ft)

SPECIAL FEATURES: scenic granite dome, rock climbing

TRAILHEAD AND DESCRIPTION: From the jct of US-276 and FR-475, go 0.4 mi on FR-475 to a parking area, R. Ascend steadily on the yellow-blazed trail that has numerous switchbacks for the first 1.8 mi. A frequently used trail, it is eroded in sections on the steep E slope. Pass through a mixed hardwood forest with scattered Carolina hemlock (*Tsuga caroliniana*) and an understory of laurel. At 2.7 mi arrive at the edge of the N face; ascend to the highest point and trail terminus (3,969 ft) at 3.1 mi. Here is the NW face with magnificent views of the Pisgah National Forest and the BRP areas. The dome is not protected with guardrails and is dangerous when wet or icy. Backtrack. (*USGS-FS Map*: Shining Rock)

Case Camp Ridge Trail (USFS #119) (F)   **260**

LENGTH AND DIFFICULTY: 3.1 mi round-trip, strenuous (elev change 1,100 ft)

TRAILHEAD AND DESCRIPTION: From the ranger station go W on US-276 8.6 mi, turn L on Headwaters Rd (FR-475B), and proceed 0.8 mi to Case Ridge Gap for parking. Ascend R on the blue-blazed *Case Camp Ridge Trail* through a forest of oak, laurel, hemlock, locust, buckberry, and blueberry to a gap at 0.2 mi. (To the L a new trail is being constructed; it will ascend W to gated FR-5045 and S trailhead of 1.3-mi blue-blazed *Seniard Ridge Trail* **261** [USFS #609] [F]. It ascends steeply on switchbacks to the BRP between mp 417 and mp 418. Access to FR-5045 is off FR-225, which is off FR-475B farther S from the *Case Camp Ridge Trail* trailhead.) At 0.5 mi reach the ridgeline where there are excellent views of Looking Glass Rock when the leaves are off the trees. Ascend on switchbacks, pass ruins of an old house at 1.3 mi, and arrive at BRP mp 415.9. Backtrack. (*USGS-FS Map*: Shining Rock)

LOWER DAVIDSON RIVER AREA (Transylvania County)

Hardly more than 1.0 mi E from the US Fish Hatchery in Upper Davidson River Area is the mouth of Looking Glass Creek and an intersection with US-276. With the creek's sparkling wild trout waters it widens the Davidson

River in its 5.0-mi passage to the forest boundary at the intersection of US-276/64 and NC-280 in the unincorporated town of Pisgah Forest. When entering the district from this intersection on US-276 you are on a Forest Heritage national scenic byway. After the first 0.4 mi is Sycamore Flats Picnic Area, L, followed by a parking area on the riverbank, L, for the *Sycamore Cove Trail*, R. At 1.2 mi is the entrance, L, to Davidson River Recreation Area, the district's largest and most popular campground. It has 161 sites (mainly shaded by the forest) for tents, RVs, and motor homes. There are grills, tables, group water sources, flush toilets, and hot showers (no hookups). Activities are mainly hiking and fishing, and tubing in the summer. A fee campground, it is usually open all year on a first-come basis. (Reservations can be made by a seven-day advance call to 800-280-2267.) E of the campground is the Schenck Civilian Conservation Center.

Farther W 0.4 mi on US-276 is the entrance, R, to the Pisgah Ranger Station and Visitor Center (adjoined R by a maintenance work center). Farther upriver are the English Chapel, L (across the river bridge), and on US-276 the Coontree Picnic Area, L. After 3.5 mi from the visitor center on US-276 begin an ascent to Looking Glass Falls, R, and beyond to Sliding Rock Recreation Area, L. In this grand entrance to the district's busy headquarters hub are two long-distance trails and eight loop trails from diminutive to lengthy multiloops.

Two loop trails begin at the visitor center parking area. The *Andy Cove Nature Trail* (USFS #288) (F), a national recreation trail constructed by the YCC, is a 0.6-mi loop that has interpretive stations, some on an elevated walkway. At 0.2 mi is a swinging bridge over a deep ravine. After crossing Andy Cove Branch and more boardwalks among hemlocks and rhododendron, it makes a jct with the 1.5-mi *Exercise Trail* (USFS #344) (F) in a grove of tall white pine. If going R, cross US-276 and the bridge over Davidson River at 0.2 mi, turn L of the English Chapel, and exit at Davidson River campground bridge. Turn L, cross the bridge, turn L on a fishing road, and go 230 ft before leaving the road. Cross US-276 again and return to the visitor center parking lot.

At the campground, a good base for day hikes, is the 3.7-mi *North Slope Loop Trail* (USFS #359) (F, B partial) entrance. It begins at a parking lot 0.1 mi L, after the main campground entrance. Orange-blazed, the trail passes the amphitheater to an old timber road. It curves in and out of coves on the N side of North Slope Ridge. Cove hardwoods, ferns, and wildflowers are dominant. At 2.1 mi cross a small stream and jct with yellow-blazed *North Slope Connector Trail* (USFS #149) (F). (It ascends steeply on switchbacks for

1.3 mi to connect with the *Art Loeb Trail* on the N side of Stony Knob. Backtrack, or use the *Art Loeb Trail* L for a return to its trailhead at the swinging bridge over Davidson River near the campground for a loop of 7.5 mi.) Continuing on the *North Slope Loop Trail* turn R, and at 2.5 mi turn R to pass S of the English Chapel. Switchback on an old road to bypass a section of the campground before returning to point of origin. (*USGS-FS Maps:* Pisgah Forest, Shining Rock)

An isolated short linear trail is *Moore Cove Trail* (USFS #318) (F). **266** Access is 1.0 mi W of Looking Glass Falls on US-276. Park near a bridge, R (between the highway and the creek). The yellow-blazed trail may begin down steps across the bridge and up the stream bank (construction is under way; look for sign). Follow an old RR grade; cross Moore Branch three times on footbridges among rhododendron. Reach 45-ft Moore Branch cascades at 0.7 mi. Backtrack. (*USGS-FS Map:* Shining Rock)

Coontree Loop Trail (USFS #144) (F, B) **267**

LENGTH AND DIFFICULTY: 3.7 mi, strenuous (elev change 1,160 ft)
CONNECTING TRAILS:
(*Bennett Gap Trail*)
TRAILHEAD AND DESCRIPTION: From the ranger station go W on US-276 for 3.0 mi to park at the Coontree Picnic Area parking lot, L. Cross the road to the blue-blazed *Coontree Loop Trail* entrance. Follow upstream through ironwood, poplar, birch, and oak. At 0.2 mi is the loop fork. If taking the R prong, follow an old road by a stream through ferns, wildflowers, and rhododendron. Ascend to Coontree Gap (2,960 ft) at 1.2 mi and jct with the red-blazed *Bennett Gap Trail*, R and L. (The *Bennett Gap Trail* goes 0.9 mi R through a forest of hardwoods and hemlock on a N slope for a descent to Avery Creek Rd [FR-477] at a low bridge.) Turn L and follow both trails for 0.5 mi; turn L on *Coontree Loop Trail* and descend steeply on switchbacks to Coontree Creek. Follow it downstream, crossing it at least twice (depending on erosion) in a gradual descent. Rejoin the loop at 3.5 mi. (*USGS-FS Map:* Shining Rock)

Sycamore Cove Trail (USFS #143) (F, B) **268**

LENGTH AND DIFFICULTY: 3.2 mi, moderate
CONNECTING TRAILS:
(*Art Loeb Trail*)
(*MST*)
Grassy Road Trail (1.1 mi; USFS #364, easy) (F, B) **269**

TRAILHEAD AND DESCRIPTION: Although a loop, there are two trailheads. Because of the popularity of this trail and the heavy traffic on the highway, the district prefers parking at the *Art Loeb Trail* parking lot. It is accessible off US-276 immediately L (before crossing the bridge) after entrance to Davidson River Campground (0.2 mi E of the ranger station). Walk downriver to the *Art Loeb Trail* trailhead and swinging bridge, R (and the *MST* R and L). Turn L, cross a small stream and US-276 to enter the trail (whose other exit is 0.2 mi R on US-276). Pass under tall poplar, sycamore, and hemlock where spicebush and ferns provide a fresh forest smell. At 0.5 mi cross a stream on a log bridge and reach a jct where the *MST* forks L at 0.6 mi. Ascend R on the *Sycamore Cove Trail* among white pine to jct with *Grassy Road Trail*, L, at 0.7 mi. (The orange-blazed 1.1-mi *Grassy Road Trail* is a former logging road. It has sunshine and wildflowers and is a connector to *Thrift Cove Trail*, *MST*, and *Black Mountain Trail*.)

Curve R and ascend among white pine, later under rhododendron arbors. At 1.5 mi reach the highest area of the trail, turn S, and follow an old road on the slope of the ridge. Laurel and rhododendron are prominent. Descend gradually to a stream and turn R at 2.8 mi. Under hemlock, beech, and poplar pass spicebush, fetterbush, mandrake, club moss, and ferns. Descend steeply; cross the stream six times before an exit at US-276. It is 0.3 mi L (E) to Sycamore Flats Picnic Area, and 150 ft R (W) to roadside parking. Another 0.2 mi upriver is back to the other trailhead. (*USGS-FS Map:* Pisgah Forest)

270 *Black Mountain Trail (USFS #127) (F, B)*
LENGTH AND DIFFICULTY: 7.8 mi, strenuous (elev change 2,086 ft)
CONNECTING TRAILS:
271   *Thrift Cove Trail* (3.8 mi; USFS #603) (F, B)
   (*MST*)
272   *Pressley Cove Trail* (1.2 mi; USFS #112) (F)
   (*Turkey Pen Gap Trail*)
273   *Buckhorn Gap Trail* (N) (1.7 mi, S 2.9 mi; USFS #103) (F, B, H)
   (*Club Gap Trail*)
   (*Avery Creek Trail*)
   (*Buckwheat Knob Trail*)
SPECIAL FEATURES: wildlife, wildflowers, views from Clawhammer Mtn
TRAILHEAD AND DESCRIPTION: On US-276, 0.2 mi E of the ranger station, park outside the fence of the district work center in a paved parking lot or grassy area. Follow the trail sign upstream on an old timber road. At 0.2 mi jct

R with the red-blazed *Thrift Cove Trail,* another timber road. (The *Thrift Cove Trail,* used mainly by bikers, crosses Thrift Creek and ascends a ridge for 0.2 mi to an open area and jct with the *MST,* R. For the next 230 ft the *MST* follows the road to a turn, L, down in the gorge. Ahead, up the ridge, continues *Thrift Cove Trail,* and to the R is easy orange-blazed 1.1-mi *Grassy Road Trail* (USFS #364) (H, B), appropriately named. [Its NE terminus is with *Sycamore Cove Loop Trail.*] The *Thrift Cove Trail* follows a ridge or its shoulder to the headwaters of Thrift Creek where the trail crosses at 2.4 mi. Here it turns S to jct and follows the *Black Mountain Trail* to *Thrift Cove Trail's* origin.)

Continuing on the *Black Mountain Trail* there is a jct at 0.5 mi with the *MST,* R. (The *MST* goes R on a separate trail to join part of *Sycamore Cove Loop Trail* to a crossing of US-276. From there it jointly runs with the *Art Loeb Trail* to the BRP area, but from here it follows jointly on the *Black Mountain Trail* before leaving it on the N side of Rich Mtn ridge. See chapter 16.) Continue ascending steeply in Thrift Cove on the old road, cross the creek four times, and at 1.4 mi pass an old road R, which is the *Thrift Cove Trail.* At 1.8 mi the road becomes more of a path. Ascend steeply to Hickory Knob at 2.4 mi, and descend to Pressley Gap at 2.9 mi. Here is FR-5099 R and L. Access to *Pressley Cove Trail* is L, 0.2 mi down the road.

(The orange-blazed *Pressley Cove Trail* descends in an arbor of laurel. Cross a small stream at 0.4 mi, descend steeply on a S slope with scenic views of the cove, L. Pass through hemlock and beech. Reach a grazing field at Avery Creek Rd [FR-477] at 1.2 mi. It is 126 yd, L, to the bridge over Avery Creek (and jct with E trailhead of *Bennett Gap Trail* described below), 1.4 mi to US-276, and 0.5 mi, L, on US-276 to the ranger station. Right on FR-477 it is 0.3 mi to a parking area at Clawhammer Rd [FR-5058], R. The road can be used as an access to Buckhorn Gap and *Black Mountain Trail.*)

From Pressley Gap on the *Black Mountain Trail* follow the ridge on sections of old logging roads, and at 3.9 mi jct with *Turkey Pen Gap Trail,* R. Here is a small spring in a forest of large oak and hickory with beds of hay-scented and cinnamon ferns. (The *Turkey Pen Gap Trail* follows a ridgeline E for 5.5 mi to Turkey Pen Gap and FR-297 off NC-280.) To continue on the *Black Mountain Trail* ascend to skirt W of Black Mtn peak in arbors of rhododendron and laurel to rejoin the ridge at 4.2 mi. Descend steeply and follow a narrow ridge to reach a rock overhang at 4.4 mi. Ascend to Clawhammer Mtn (4,140 ft) at 4.6 mi. From the outcroppings are superb views of Pilot Mtn, Looking Glass Rock, and NW to Pisgah Ridge. Blueberries, rhododendron, and galax are prominent. Descend steeply to Buckhorn Gap (3,520 ft) at 5.7 mi to cross the orange-blazed *Buckhorn Gap Trail* in an old RR grade cut. The cut is now a gravel and improved forest road. To the R (N) it is 0.6 mi on the road before the *Buckhorn Gap Trail* leaves the road R. It descends on switchbacks to jct at 1.7 mi with *South Mills River Trail* on Grassy Ridge. On the S side of the gap the gravel road descends 1.0 mi to a 0.1-mi spur off the R, but the trailhead for *Buckhorn Gap Trail* is farther down the mtn, S, and to the R. The *Buckhorn Gap Trail* ends at *Avery Creek Trail* (see Avery Creek Area below).

Continue on *Black Mountain Trail* up log steps from Buckhorn Gap. After 0.3 mi, R, is the Buckhorn Gap Shelter with bunk beds. A spring is nearby. Ascend on the ridge. Pass coves with cinnamon ferns and ascend on switchbacks to SW slope of Soapstone Ridge. At 6.6 mi reach the crest of Rich Mtn in an oak-hickory forest. At 6.8 mi, L, is a rock outcrop with views of the Avery Creek drainage. The *MST* leaves the trail at 7.0 mi, R, near a large oak, and descends on an old forest road to the Pink Beds (see chapter 16). Continue on the *Black Mountain Trail,* which is an old woods road with woodland sunflowers, mountain mint, and wood betony. Descend to Club Gap at 7.8 mi, the end of *Black Mountain Trail.* Here is an intersection with *Buckwheat Knob Trail* ahead; *Club Gap Trail,* R; and *Avery Creek Trail,* L (see Avery Creek Area below). (Access to US-276 is on *Club Gap Trail* for 0.8 mi. Descend on an old woods road with switchbacks to FR-477, 0.3 mi R to US-276 near the entrance to the Cradle of Forestry.) (*USGS-FS Maps:* Pisgah Forest, Shining Rock)

AVERY CREEK AREA (Transylvania County)

Only 0.6 mi W upstream on US-276 from the ranger station is the mouth of Avery Creek at Davidson River. Here is the S entrance of FR-477, which parallels the creek NW before ascending on a crooked journey to a high ridge before crossing Bennett Gap. It then descends to exit near the Cradle of Forestry in America. Up this narrow road in a narrow valley are North and South White Pine Group Camps (tents only, no vehicles except horse trailers with sleepers are allowed). Avery Creek drops 1,186 ft from its headwaters to the Davidson River, thus creating many cascades and waterfalls. Native trout are in the creek's pools. To the valley's NE is Black Mtn; FR-5088 winds N from Avery Creek Rd to Buckhorn Gap and Buckhorn Shelter at *Black Mountain Trail;* and off *Buckhorn Gap Trail* is Twin Falls. Coves have dense gardens of ferns, wild geraniums, white snakeroot, and tall tulip trees. Two short trail loops are formed with *Avery Creek Trail.*

274 *Avery Creek Trail (USFS #327) (F, B)*
LENGTH AND DIFFICULTY: 3.2 mi, strenuous (elev change 1,340 ft)

SPECIAL FEATURES: waterfalls, wildlife, wildflowers

TRAILHEAD AND DESCRIPTION: Access to the NW trailhead of *Avery Creek Trail* is on yellow-blazed *Club Gap Trail,* whose trailhead is 0.3 mi L on Avery Creek Rd (FR-477) after it leaves US-276 at the S edge of Cradle of Forestry. *Club Gap Trail* ascends 0.8 mi on an old road with switchbacks to Club Gap. On the L is the NW trailhead of *Black Mountain Trail;* ahead is *Avery Creek Trail;* and to the R is *Buckwheat Knob Trail.*

The blue-blazed *Avery Creek Trail* descends steeply on a W slope of the rim among upland hardwoods. It passes under a power line at 0.4 mi and 0.9 mi; it follows switchbacks to an old RR grade near Avery Creek at 1.1 mi. In a forest mix of hemlock, poplar, and rhododendron the trail passes excellent campsites. Wildflowers are profuse at openings under the power line. At 2.2 mi jct with *Buckhorn Gap Trail,* L.

(The orange-blazed *Buckhorn Gap Trail* [S] begins on the N side of Avery Creek under a power line opening with a grassy meadow and sparse saplings. The trail enters a deep, damp, and dense forest on the E side of Henry Branch, but crosses it twice. Tall cove hardwoods give depth to the gorge. At 0.7 mi jct with yellow-blazed *Twin Falls Trail* [USFS #604] [F], a **279** 0.4-mi spur to a scenic waterfall. From this area the *Buckhorn Gap Trail* leaves its N direction and turns E to the option of two exits at Clawhammer Cove Rd [FR-5058]. The first forks L to meet the road at 1.4 mi [1.0 mi L and up the road to Buckhorn Gap]; the second forks R, turns S, and meets the road at 2.0 mi [1.6 mi L and up the road to Buckhorn Gap].)

The *Avery Creek Trail* continues down Avery Creek, hugging its banks, but after 0.3 mi it divides with *Avery Creek Trail (Upper)* following R a wide and easy forest road 0.7 mi to exit at a small parking area on FR-477, and *Avery Creek Trail (Lower)* going L to cross a footbridge over the creek. If going L continue downstream on an old RR grade among hemlock, rhododendron, and fetterbush. At 0.3 mi are cascades on the creek, R, and a small waterfall on a tributary, L. At 0.4 mi are more cascades and a flume, R. At 0.6 mi jct with orange-blazed *Clawhammer Cove Trail,* L.

(The *Clawhammer Cove Trail* moves away from Avery Creek and turns N on an old RR grade to parallel Clawhammer Cove Creek. The beauty of the cove is in the open forest of high poplars and acres of dense ferns spreading throughout the stream area and up the mountainside. At 0.7 mi rock-hop the stream and ascend. To the L, for 100 yd is a waterfall. Turn SE, ascend on an old woods road, and reach FR-5085 at 1.1 mi among clusters of poplar and maple. Backtrack.)

On the return to *Avery Creek Trail (Lower),* turn L and follow it on a footbridge to an old roadbed for 0.2 mi where it ends at FR-477. On FR-477, R, it is 0.3 mi up the road to the parking area for *Avery Creek Trail (Upper),* and 4.6 mi farther to US-276 near Cradle of Forestry. To the L, down the mtn, it is 0.3 mi to a horse camp and stable and FR-5085, L. After another 2.0 mi FR-477 exits at US-276 0.5 mi W from the ranger station.

(The yellow-blazed *Buckwheat Knob Trail* begins at Club Gap, ascends, and passes under a power line. It reaches Buckwheat Knob at 0.5 mi. It then descends to a shallow gap, crosses another knob, and descends partially on a jeep road to the trail's end in Bennett Gap at Avery Creek Rd [FR-477]. Across the road begins red-blazed *Bennett Gap Trail,* described below. To the R on FR-477 it is 2.3 mi to US-276 near the Cradle of Forestry, and L it is 2.3 mi to the SE end of *Avery Creek Trail.*) (*USGS-FS Maps:* Shining Rock, Pisgah Forest)

280 *Bennett Gap Trail (USFS #138) (F, B)*

LENGTH AND DIFFICULTY: 2.9 mi, strenuous (elev change 1,191 ft)

CONNECTING TRAILS:

  (*Buckwheat Knob Trail*)

281 *Perry Cove Trail* (1.2 mi; USFS #151, strenuous) (F, B)

  (*Coontree Gap Trail*)

  (*Pressley Cove Trail*)

TRAILHEAD AND DESCRIPTION: Access to the NW trailhead of *Bennett Gap Trail* is on Avery Creek Rd (FR-477) 2.3 mi from US-276 at the Cradle of Forestry (8.0 mi NW on US-276 from the ranger station). The trail begins on the S side of the road in Bennett Gap (3,516 ft). (Across the road, N, is the S trailhead of *Buckwheat Knob Trail.*) Ascend E on a ridgeline of hardwoods and turn SE. Ahead are occasional views of Avery Valley, L, and Looking Glass Rock and Pilot Mtn, R. At 0.8 mi begin a descent to Saddle Gap where a jct with *Perry Cove Trail* is L.

(The red-blazed *Perry Cove Trail* descends rapidly from upland hardwoods to cove hardwoods. At 0.5 mi it begins to follow Perry Cove Branch to its confluence with Avery Creek. It exits at FR-477 near a horse stable and FR-5058, 0.5 mi NW on FR-477 from the E exit of *Bennett Gap Trail.*)

To continue on the *Bennett Gap Trail,* ascend on the NE slope of Coontree Mtn for a jct with *Coontree Loop Trail* at 1.1 mi. *Coontree Loop Trail* goes R to US-

276, but at this point jointly follows *Bennett Gap Trail* for 0.6 mi in a descent to Coontree Gap. (Here *Coontree Loop Trail* turns R to exit at Coontree Picnic Area on US-276.) *Bennett Gap Trail* forks L (E) and starts descending on the dark shoulder of the ridge to FR-477 at 2.9 mi. Spring wildflowers are prominent among the coves, and rosebay rhododendron are among poplar, oak, and hemlock. At FR-477 it is 126 yd L (over the low bridge) to *Pressley Gap Trail* trailhead, R. The trail enters a patch of wildflowers and autumn olive. Downstream on FR-477 it is 1.4 mi to US-276, 0.5 mi W of the ranger station. (*USGS-FS Maps:* Shining Rock, Pisgah Forest)

PINK BEDS AREA (Transylvania County)

The Pink Beds is an unusual forested upland bog with an average altitude of 3,250 ft. It extends more than 5.0 mi between the E slopes of the Pisgah Ridge and the W slopes of Soapstone Ridge and Dividing Ridge. The headwaters of the South Fork of Mills River converge here. Its name most likely has come from the dense pink rosebay rhododendron and laurel common throughout the area. Other sources may be the pink rock formerly quarried in the region or the masses of wild pink phlox and pink roses among the fern meadows. A gravel forest road and trails give access into its floral displays and near its numerous serpentine streams. On US-276 is the Cradle of Forestry Discovery Center and nearby is Pink Beds Picnic Area. Yellow Gap Road (FR-206) from US-276 to North Mills River Rec Area goes through the Pink Beds.

Two loop trails originate at the Forest Discovery Center's main building. The *Biltmore Forest Campus Trail* (USFS #006) (F, W) is a 0.9-mi easy, paved, **282** national-recreation loop trail that provides a historic tour of the buildings of the Biltmore Forest School. It was founded by Carl A. Schenck, a German forester employed by George Vanderbilt to manage his vast forest empire. Schenck became the father of American forestry management because of his work here from 1897 to 1909. The school opened in 1898, and had 367 alumni before closing in 1914. In 1968, Congress passed the Cradle of Forestry in America Act, which established 6,400 acres commemorating a natural national historic site. The *Forest Festival Trail* (USFS #319) (F, W) is **283** also a paved, easy, 1.0-mi interpretive loop trail that features exhibits of forestry management and logging equipment, based on Dr. Schenck's Biltmore Forest Fair of 1908. From the parking area there is an access to the N trailhead of *Club Gap Trail,* which makes a S jct with *Black Mountain Trail,* described in the Davidson River Area. The Forest Discovery Center is open from the first of May to the end of October, daily, 10:00 AM to 6:00 PM. A small fee is charged for entrance. (For information call 704-877-3130.)

ACCESS: From BRP mp 412, descend E on US-276 for 3.8 mi, or from Brevard jct of US-64/276 follow US-276 W for 12.0 mi.

284 *Pink Beds Loop Trail (USFS #118) (F, B)*
LENGTH AND DIFFICULTY: 5.0 mi, easy
CONNECTING TRAILS:
   (MST)
   (South Mills River Trail)
TRAILHEAD AND DESCRIPTION: On US-276 (0.2 mi W of the Cradle of Forestry entrance) enter the Pink Beds Picnic Area and parking lot. At the NE end follow the trail sign, descend to cross Pigeon Branch and to a meadow where the trail begins its loop at 0.1 mi. Turn R, follow the orange blaze into a hemlock grove with soft duff, and cross a number of tributaries of the South Fork of the Mills River on footbridges. Most of the treadway is on an old RR grade and can easily accumulate standing water in rainy seasons. At 1.6 mi jct with the white-blazed *MST* (L on the *MST* it is 0.3 mi to the N side of the *Pink Beds Loop Trail*). After 75 yd the *MST* veers R on its route to join the *Black Mountain Trail*. Continue ahead downstream in a natural garden of tall ferns, white azaleas, fox grapes, and pink wild roses at 1.9 mi. Turn sharply L at 2.7 mi at a jct with a Pink Beds connector trail to the *South Mills River Trail,* R. (It is 0.9 mi downstream to the gauging sta and FR-476 described in the South Mills River Area.) Follow an old RR grade in sections of open forest of oak, poplar, birch, and pine, and cross Barnett Branch on footbridge 120 yd before a jct with the *MST* at 3.8 mi. (R it is 0.5 mi to FR-1026, and L it is 0.3 mi to the S side of the trail loop.) Continue ahead and return to the meadow and point of origin at 5.0 mi. (*USGS-FS Maps:* Pisgah Forest, Shining Rock)

285 *Buck Spring Trail (S) (USFS #104) (F)*
LENGTH AND DIFFICULTY: 6.2 mi, moderate (elev change 1,200 ft)
TRAILHEAD AND DESCRIPTION: On US-276 (2.3 mi E from the BRP and 1.3 mi W from the Pink Beds Picnic Area) park on the N side of the highway. Follow the trail sign on a gently graded footpath. Cross Bearwallow Branch at 0.3 mi, the first of 13 streams on this scenic trail that winds in and out of coves and around 10 ridges on a gradual ascent to the Pisgah Inn. At 0.9 mi jct with *MST Connector*, L, and at 1.1 mi jct with the white-blazed *MST*, R, which jointly runs with the trail for the remainder of the route. (The 11.6-mi *MST Connector* goes SW to connect with the *Art Loeb Trail* at FR-816.) At 4.3 mi begin a steeper ascent to where two long switchbacks reach an old

RR grade at 5.9 mi. On a level area with superb vistas of the Pink Beds and Black Mtn, arrive at the Pisgah Inn at 6.2 mi. The *MST* continues (see chapters 6 and 16). (*USGS-FS Maps:* Shining Rock, Cruso)

SOUTH MILLS RIVER AREA (Henderson and Transylvania Counties)

South Mills River forms in the Pink Beds, and on its circuitous route it flows through a rugged, remote, gorge-like valley between two long ridges out to join the North Fork near the town of Mills River. On the N side are peaks and ridges such as Funneltop, Rich, Grindstone, and Buttermilk. On the S side are Soapstone, Clawhammer, Black, and Sharpy. From them flow numerous tributaries that, like the river, have native trout. Wildlife in the forest includes bear, deer, grouse, turkey, raccoon, fox, owls, hawks, and many species of songbirds. The area is considered one of the best for equestrian traffic—more than 40.0 mi of trails, plus another 10.0 mi on gated forest roads. At least eight loops can be formed for trail users. There are four access routes to the interior of this challenging area: One from NC-280 on Turkey Pen Rd (FR-297), described first; South Mills River Rd (FR-476) off Yellow Gap Rd (FR-1206) from US-276; *Bradley Creek Trail* off FR-1206, 4.5 mi W from North Mills River Rec Area; and Clawhammer Cove Rd (FR-5058) off Avery Creek Rd (FR-477), whose access is from US-276.

South Mills River Trail (USFS #133) (F, B, H)   286

LENGTH AND DIFFICULTY: 12.0 mi, easy to moderate

CONNECTING TRAILS:

    (*Turkey Pen Gap Trail*)

    (*Vineyard Gap Trail*)

    (*Bradley Creek Trail*)

    Mullinax Trail (1.2 mi; USFS #326, easy) (F, B, H)   287

    Poundingmill Trail (1.5 mi, USFS #349, easy) (F)   288

    Wagon Road Gap Trail (0.7 mi; USFS #134, moderate) (F)   289

    Cantrell Creek Trail (1.9 mi; USFS #148, moderate) (F, B, H)   290

    (*Squirrel Gap Trail*)

    (*Buckhorn Gap Trail*)

    (*Pink Beds Loop Trail*)

SPECIAL FEATURES: fishing, forestry history, wildlife

TRAILHEAD AND DESCRIPTION: From the jct of US-276/64 and NC-280 near Brevard, proceed NE on NC-280 5.0 mi to Henderson/Transylvania county line. Turn L between private homes on Turkey Pen Rd (FR-297) and drive 1.2

mi on a narrow gravel road to a parking area in Turkey Pen Gap, a source of multiple trailheads for both hikers and equestrians. To the L begins the *Turkey Pen Gap Trail;* to the R begins *Vineyard Gap Trail.* Ahead (on a continuation of the FR) is the *Bradley Creek Trail* beginning at a gate, and on a footpath (L of the gate) is the E trailhead of the *South Mills River Trail.* This remarkable trail stays almost exclusively in sight and sound of the fast-moving South Fork of Mills River, whose headwaters are in the Pink Beds and the E slope of the BRP Pisgah range. Although high peaks, such as Black Mtn (4,286 ft) on the S and Funneltop Mtn (4,266 ft) on the N, rise from the gorge, they are never seen from the trail's forested route. The trail crosses the river 13 times, 9 of which must be forded. Because crossing the river can be difficult or impossible after heavy rains, alternate routes or plans are advised. The route basically follows an old RR grade that evokes historical fantasies of the way it was a century ago. A hiker has written "visitation is only by ghosts" on a sign at the chimney of the former Cantrell Creek Lodge. It is a multiple-use trail for horses, bikers, hikers, and trophy trout anglers, and short sections are used by ATV riders. In addition to some of the less used connecting trails, there are numerous old logging roads that offer hikers solitude.

Begin the *South Mills River Trail* by descending on a heavily used footpath to the river at 0.4 mi, cross the swinging footbridge, and ascend to an old road (R and L) at 0.6 mi. Turn L and follow a S slope of maple, poplar, birch, and rhododendron. At 0.7 mi jct with *Mullinax Trail,* R. (The *Mullinax Trail* follows an old seeded road that is rough in places and is used both by hikers and equestrians to the jct with *Squirrel Gap Trail* at 1.2 mi. A 5.0-mi loop can be made from this point by going L on the *Squirrel Gap Trail* 0.7 mi to turn R on the 1.8-mi *Laurel Creek Trail,* another R on the *Bradley Creek Trail,* and a final R at the E-end jct with the *Squirrel Gap Trail.*)

At 2.0 mi jct R with the *Poundingmill Trail.* (The *Poundingmill Trail* follows the Poundingmill Branch upstream and follows sections of old logging roads. At 1.5 mi jct with the *Squirrel Gap Trail* on Poundingstone Mtn after a steep ascent from the branch. It is 0.8 mi R on *Squirrel Gap Trail* to jct R with *Mullinax Trail.*)

Continue on the *South Mills River Trail,* pass a wildlife field, R, at 2.7 mi, and cross the South Mills River on a swinging footbridge at 2.2 mi. At 3.1 mi jct with the *Wagon Road Gap Trail.* (The *Wagon Road Gap Trail* is an orange-blazed foot trail that ascends 0.7 mi on a steep and sometimes rocky treadway in Big Cove to jct with the *Turkey Pen Gap Trail* in Wagon Road Gap. It is 2.5 mi L on the *Turkey Pen Gap Trail* to Turkey Pen Gap parking area.)

At 3.7 mi cross the South Mills River on a swinging footbridge. Enter a large grassy meadow with tall poplar and oak. Rock-hop Cantrell Creek at 3.9 mi and arrive at the remnants of Cantrell Creek Lodge in a meadow at 4.0 mi. Only a chimney with a double fireplace remains; the lodge was moved in 1978 to the Cradle of Forestry on US-276. A few yd N, at the edge of the forest, is the S terminus of the *Cantrell Creek Trail*. (This is the trail route to follow for avoiding the eight fordings of the South Mills River in the next 4.7 mi. It ascends gradually upstream 1.9 mi to a jct with *Squirrel Gap Trail*, but along the way at 1.0 mi, L, is the *Horse Cove Gap Trail*, a 0.8-mi connector that shortens the route from 5.4 mi to 3.8 mi to the *South Mills River Trail* at Wolf Ford.)

To continue on the *South Mills River Trail*, cross the meadow of wild-flowers at Cantrell Creek Lodge site, ascend a low hill, and return to the riverside. Follow the old RR grade and wade the river eight times before a jct with the blue-blazed *Squirrel Gap Trail*, R, at 8.7 mi at a swinging foot-bridge over the South Mills River. To the R is the former South Mills River Rd (Wolf Rock Rd) (FR-476), now unmaintained but an alternate route (USFS #133A). To the L the *South Mills River Trail* begins its ascent on switchbacks to go in and out of coves on the NE slope of Clawhammer Mtn. (At its jct with *Buckhorn Gap Trail*, there is an access to FR-5058, which connects with Avery Creek Rd [FR-477] and out to US-276, 0.5 mi W of the ranger station.) After leaving the jct with the *Buckhorn Gap Trail* it descends on switchbacks to rejoin the former FR-476.

If hiking the alternate route, and after 0.1 mi, leave the old road R, in a curve, and follow a footpath across Clawhammer Creek. Pass scenic High Falls, cascades, and pools in a forest of hemlock, rhododendron, and fetter-bush. Rock-hop or wade the river at 9.4 mi. Cross West Ridge Branch at 9.7 mi. At 10.2 mi jct with the main *South Mills River Trail*, which crosses N of a large horseshoe curve in the river. Arrive at the parking area of Wolf Fork Rd (FR-476) at 11.1 mi. Here is a water-level gauging sta, built in 1935. (It is 1.3 mi N on FR-476 to Yellow Gap Rd [FR-1206] and another 3.3 mi L to US-276 near the Pink Beds Picnic Area.) The trail continues upstream on a beau-tiful footpath among laurel, ferns, fetterbush, and white azalea. Cross the river on a log bridge (which may be washed away) at 11.8 mi and a small log bridge into a flat area of ferns in the approach to a jct with the orange-blazed *Pink Beds Loop Trail* at 12.0 mi. (*USGS-FS Map*: Pisgah Forest)

Bradley Creek Trail (5.1 mi; USFS #351) (F, B, H); Squirrel Gap Trail (7.5 mi; USFS #147) (F, B, H partial)   **291-292**

LENGTH AND DIFFICULTY: 12. 6 mi combined, one-way, moderate to strenuous

TRAILHEADS AND DESCRIPTION: From Turkey Pen Gap parking area (see access to *South Mills River Trail* above). Enter the gate and descend 0.4 mi to the river where the *South Mills River Trail* goes upstream. Fork R on the *Bradley Creek Trail* and ford the river at 0.8 mi (the county line). Continue downstream to where the old road forks L and the other, *Riverside Trail*, fords the river. (The yellow-blazed *Riverside Trail* goes 3.1 mi downstream. It is used mainly by equestrians who must ford the river at five crossings and often on muddy treadway. The trail ends at a jct with the *Vineyard Gap Trail* near an old homestead site in a grassy flat area.)

The *Bradley Creek Trail* takes the L fork at the river and ascends gradually to Pea Gap. It descends to and crosses Pea Branch for a jct L with the E terminus of *Squirrel Gap Trail* at 1.7 mi. Continue R and follow Pea Branch downstream to Bradley Creek where the trail crosses Case Branch at 2.2 mi and jct with *Vineyard Gap Trail*, R. Hike upstream parallel with Bradley Creek, but cross it a number of times. In wet weather there is frequent seepage from the mountainsides and the tributaries. At 3.4 mi jct L with yellow-blazed *Laurel Creek Trail*. (It serves as a 1.8-mi connector up Laurel Creek to *Squirrel Gap Trail* near Poundingstone Mtn.) Pass a jct with FR-5051, which winds up the W side of Queen Creek Mtn to Yellow Gap on the Yellow Gap Rd (FR-1206). Ahead on the *Bradley Creek Trail* is Bradley Creek Reservoir. From here the trail continues another 1.5 mi to its N terminus in a hollow at Yellow Gap Rd (FR-1206), 4.5 mi W of North Mills River Rec Area. Backtrack or have a second vehicle.

To access the *Squirrel Gap Trail* follow the *Bradley Creek Trail* from Turkey Pen Gap parking area for 1.7 mi before leaving it, L. Begin the blue-blazed *Squirrel Gap Trail* up Pea Branch; after 0.7 mi jct with *Mullinax Trail*, L. (The *Mullinax Trail* is an easy 1.2-mi yellow-blazed route to *South Mills River Trail*.) The *Squirrel Gap Trail* turns R and passes through Mullinax Gap for a jct, R, with *Laurel Creek Trail* at 1.4 mi on the N side of Poundingstone Mtn. After 260 yd jct L with the *Poundingmill Trail*. (The orange-blazed 1.5-

mi *Poundingmill Trail* is for hiker traffic only to the *South Mills River Trail*.) Continue ahead, first on the ridge of Laurel Mtn and then on the N slope through a forest of hardwood, laurel, and rhododendron. Pass through Laurel Gap (3,480 ft), the trail's highest point, and where, if you do not see a squirrel, you may hear a chipmunk. Follow the S slope of Rich Mtn in and out of coves. Jct L with red-blazed *Cantrell Creek Trail* and Cantrell Creek crossing at 4.0 mi. In a forest of oak, maple, hemlock, and hickory, reach the jct L with the orange-blazed *Horse Cove Gap Trail* (an 0.8-mi connector to the *Cantrell Creek Trail*) at 5.4 mi. Cross the headwaters of Laurel Brook and pass through Squirrel Gap (3,320 ft) at 6.7 mi. Descend gradually to Glady Branch waterfalls, L, at 7.3 mi. Reach the trail's terminus at 7.5 mi at a jct with the *South Mills River Trail*. Backtrack, or exit upriver on the *South Mills River Trail* for 2.4 mi to the parking area for FR-476 if a second vehicle is used. (*USGS-FS Map:* Pisgah Forest)

Turkey Pen Gap Trail (USFS #322) (F, B) 296

LENGTH AND DIFFICULTY: 5.5 mi, strenuous
CONNECTING TRAILS:
  (*Wagon Road Gap Trail*)
  (*Black Mountain Trail*)

TRAILHEAD AND DESCRIPTION: From Turkey Pen Gap parking area at the end of FR-297, ascend L on steps (W) to a dry ridge with blue blazes. Reach Simpson Gap at 0.7 mi. At 1.1 mi begin a 0.4-mi climb on switchbacks to Sharpy Mtn. Descend moderately in an oak forest with an understory of laurel, rhododendron, blueberry, and ground patches of galax. Arrive at Wagon Rd Gap and *Wagon Road Gap Trail*, R, at 2.5 mi. (The orange-blazed *Wagon Road Gap Trail* descends rapidly 0.7 mi to jct with the white-blazed *South Mills River Trail*.) Ascend to McCall Mtn. Descend to Deep Gap at 4.0 mi. Continue on the ridge and enter Muleshoe Gap at 4.7 mi (N of Horse Knob). Begin a 0.8-mile ascent to a jct with the *Black Mountain Trail* (S of Black Mtn peak, 4,286 ft) at 5.5 mi. (It is 1.8 mi N on the *Black Mountain Trail* to *Buckhorn Gap Trail*, where a R turn offers a potential 18.8-mi loop by using the *South Mills River Trail*. It is 3.9 mi L on the *Black Mountain Trail* to the ranger station on US-276.) (*USGS-FS Map:* Pisgah Forest)

Vineyard Gap Trail (USFS #324) (F, B) 297

LENGTH AND DIFFICULTY: 3.3 mi, moderate

TRAILHEAD AND DESCRIPTION: From Turkey Pen Gap parking area at the end of FR-297, ascend on steps R (E) on a dry ridge, and at 0.2 mi bear R on the ridge.

Follow the ridgeline, but descend to a damp hollow before ascending to another ridge. Descend to Vineyard Gap and turn L. (The trail ahead follows Forge Mtn ridge to private property.) Descend on a spur ridge and ford South Fork of Mills River at 2.3 mi. Pass the mouth of Bradley Creek and follow Bradley Creek upstream. Twice wade or rock-hop the stream in a forest of hardwoods, hemlock, and rhododendron. Arrive at campsites and a crossing of Bradley Creek to *Bradley Creek Trail* at 3.3 mi. Backtrack or follow *Bradley Creek Trail* for 2.2 mi to Turkey Pen Gap parking area. (*USGS-FS Map*: Pisgah Forest)

LAUREL MOUNTAIN AREA (Transylvania and Henderson Counties)

Separating the South Mills River Area from the Laurel Mtn Area is gravel FR-1206 running from US-276 near the Cradle of Forestry E for nearly 12.0 mi to North Mills River Rec Area, and 5.2 mi beyond on paved North Mills River Rd (SR-1345) to NC-191. Five trails ascend N from FR-1206, three of which can connect with the *Buck Spring Trail* at Pisgah Inn and Campground on the BRP. From the W slopes of Pilot Rock and Forked Ridge are unforgettable views into the Pink Beds and Funneltop Mtn (4,226 ft). Parking space is small at all the trailheads on FR-1206.

298- 301 *Thompson Creek Trail (2.4 mi; USFS #602) (F); Pilot Rock Trail (3.6 mi; USFS #321) (F, B); Laurel Mountain Trail (7.4 mi; USFS #121) (F, B, no biking at BRP); Laurel Mountain Connector Trail (0.3 mi; USFS #110) (F, B)*

LENGTH AND DIFFICULTY: 13.7 mi combined, one-way, strenuous (elev change 2,078 ft)

SPECIAL FEATURES: Pilot Rock monolith, rock outcrops, wildlife, wildflowers

TRAILHEADS AND DESCRIPTION: The trails connect near the BRP, but the first three all have different trailheads on Yellow Gap Rd (FR-1206). One desirable loop can be made at Little Bald Mtn, but all other attempts require road walks on FR-1206. Access to *Thompson Creek Trail* on FR-1206 is 3.1 mi from US-276 (0.4 mi W of the Pink Beds Picnic Area) to the W side of the creek, L. Ascend gradually 0.5 mi to cross a tributary among rhododendron, hemlock, and poplar. Here the trail begins a steady ascent on a ridge with the tributary and Thompson Creek, R. After 1.0 mi on the ridge curve R to a descent and crossing of the creek's headwaters at 1.6 mi. Here are ferns, mosses, rhododendron, and hardwoods. Ascend to the spine of Dividing Ridge where on the E side is a jct with *Pilot Rock Trail* at 2.4 mi.

To the L *Pilot Rock Trail* ascends to the top of Little Bald Mtn (5,280 ft) in the BRP property at 0.5 mi. It descends to jct with *Buck Spring Trail* where, if turning L, you reach Pisgah Inn parking lot at mp 408.6 at 1.2 mi.

If ascending *Pilot Rock Trail* from FR-1206, 0.9 mi E from the Thompson Creek trailhead, park in a cove at Grassy Lot Gap. Ascend the orange-blazed trail on the N side of the road into a forest of poplar, beech, locust, and oak. Cross small Bradley Creek after 100 yd, pass through a young forest, and begin switchbacks on a well-graded trail at 0.4 mi. At 0.9 mi are exceptionally scenic views of the Pink Beds, South Mills River Valley, and Funneltop Mtn (4,266 ft) from Pilot Rock. Ascend a ridge on switchbacks among beds of galax and trailing arbutus and groves of laurel and chestnut oak. At 2.3 mi jct with a 0.3-mi side trail (*Laurel Mountain Connector Trail*), R, that connects with *Laurel Mountain Trail*. After 0.2 mi ahead on *Pilot Rock Trail*, jct with the *Thompson Creek Trail*, L.

Blue-blazed *Laurel Mountain Trail* forms a dry crescent on the S shoulder of Laurel Mtn. It begins on FR-1206 and ends also on the *Buck Spring Trail* near the BRP terminus of *Pilot Rock Trail*. From the jct of US-276 and Yellow Gap Rd (FR-1206) (0.4 mi W of the Pink Beds Picnic Area), drive 8.5 mi to the trailhead L, but park on the R side of the road. (It is 0.2 mi ahead to Yellow Gap, and a descent of 3.1 mi to North Mills Rec Area. Beyond on North Mills River Rd [SR-1345] it is 5.2 mi to NC-191, 0.9 W of the community of Mills River.) Ascend over hummocks on an old roadbed and follow through a former clearcut of young oak, poplar, locust, and hemlock. Ascend gradually around a round knob at 0.8 mi. At 1.3 mi is a wide cove on a level contour. After another two coves the trail follows the contour line on the S slope of Black Mtn, a knobby triangular ridge top unseen from the trail. Reach Rich Gap at 2.7 mi with views in the wintertime of North Mills River Valley. Continue to a sharp curve on a steep ridge, return to coves S of Rich Gap Mtn, and reach Johnson Gap at 4.4 mi. Winding in and out of coves the trail curves in Sassafras Gap at 5.2 mi and straight through Good Enough Gap at 5.6 mi. The trail ascends on switchbacks on the ridge crest to Turkey Spring Gap at 6.4 mi and jct with *Laurel Mountain Connector Trail*, L. (The 0.3-mi connector allows for a good hiking or biking loop of 2.5 mi with *Pilot Rock Trail*, *Laurel Mountain Trail*, and *Buck Spring Trail*.) Continue ahead on the E slope of Little Bald Mtn in oak, birch, laurel, and rhododendron on switchbacks into the BRP boundary. Jct with the *Buck Spring Trail*, R and L, at 7.4 mi (see chapter 6). It is 0.3 mi R to the BRP Buck Spring Overlook parking area, mp 407.7, or L 0.8 mi to Pisgah Inn. Backtrack or use a second vehicle. (*USGS-FS Map:* Dunsmore Mtn)

Pilot Cove/Slate Rock Creek Trail (4.3 mi; USFS #320) (F, B) Pilot Cove Loop Trail (2.1 mi) (F, B) 302-303

LENGTH AND DIFFICULTY: 6.4 mi, combined, moderate

SPECIAL FEATURES: rock outcrops, wildlife, wildflowers

TRAILHEADS AND DESCRIPTION: South of Laurel Mtn is a pair of trails that rise and fall from wet coves to dry windblown ledges. Access to them from US-276 (0.4 mi W of the Pink Beds Picnic Area) is 5.2 mi on Yellow Gap Rd (FR-1206) (1.2 mi E of *Pilot Rock Trail* trailhead on FR-1206). Enter the trail on the R side of the stream in Pilot Cove. After 0.2 mi is jct with yellow-blazed *Pilot Cove Loop Trail*, R. Continue on the blue-blazed *Pilot Cove/Slate Rock Creek Trail*, cross a log footbridge in a laurel thicket, and enter an open flat area. At 0.5 mi cross the stream on a log bridge where fern beds are expansive. Ascend, pass through a growth of saplings, cross an old overgrown logging road at 1.0 mi, and ascend steeply. Trailing arbutus and gold star are among the wildflowers. Grouse may be heard on the ridges. Arrive at the top of Slate Rock Ridge and jct with the N end of *Pilot Cove Loop Trail* at 1.3 mi.

(If following the *Pilot Cove Loop Trail* ascend to a higher ridge among laurel and descend on switchbacks to a saddle at 0.8 mi. After another 0.1 mi come to a rock dome with weather-sculpted bowls. Here are outstanding views SW of the Pink Beds, S to Funneltop Mtn, and NW to the BRP range. Laurel, mosses, wildflowers, and table mountain pine (*Pinus pungens*) cling to the rock crevices. Ascend to another knoll among chestnut oak at 1.3 mi, after which begin a descent on switchbacks. Return to the main trail at 2.1 mi.)

Continuing on the *Pilot Cove/Slate Rock Creek Trail* descend 85 yd to cross a trickling stream. At 1.6 mi cross Slate Rock Creek at a tributary confluence (where for the trail's remaining 2.7 mi follows an old RR grade). Cross small tributaries and pass frequent cascades among rhododendron patches. At 2.4 mi enter a more open forest with tall poplar, maple, oak, and scattered hemlock. Ferns and wildflowers are profuse. Cross two more tributaries near each other, followed by a crossing of the creek at 3.6 mi. Cross the creek again at 3.9 mi, and exit at FR-1206 (near a concrete bridge) at 4.3 mi. It is 1.6 mi R (W) on FR-1206 to Pilot Cove, the other trailhead. (*USGS-FS Map:* Dunsmore Mtn)

NORTH MILLS RIVER AREA (Henderson County)

In a huge cove, much like the headwaters of Davidson River, the North Fork of Mills River receives its drainage from more than 30 tributaries, all funneled into an outlet between Seniard Mtn in the N and Little Rich Mtn in the S. At the pass is North Mills River Rec Area with a campground, and it is where FR-1206 ends and North Mills River Rd (SR-1345) begins. The river and paved SR-1345 parallel E to SR-191 and the town of Mills River. Along the way the South Fork of the river and North Fork coverge. Separating these forks in the W are high mtns such as Funneltop, Rich, Grindstone, and Queen Creek. On the W and N side of the valley is the BRP from Little Pisgah Mtn N to Truckwheel Mtn. In this area are turkey, bear, deer, grouse, squirrel, quail, and many species of cove and ridgeline hardwoods and wildflowers. Wild trout waters are upper Big Creek, Middle Fork, and Fletcher Creek. Trail and road users will notice scattered wildlife fields in the area. The fields are maintained by the North Carolina Wildlife Resources Commission. One forest road, Wash Creek Rd (FR-5000) runs through the area. It begins at the campground off FR-1206 and winds up the E side of Wash Creek to Bent Creek Gap at the BRP (mp 404), where it becomes Bent Creek Gap Rd (FR-479), which descends to Lake Powhatan.

All the trails in the system are linear, but with the use of forest roads there can be at least nine loops. The hub for the options is at the *Trace Ridge Trail* parking lot. Also here are gated Hendersonville Reservoir Rd (FR-124) and FR-5097, both essential for loop plans. One trail, for hikers only, is on the E side of Wash Creek Rd. It is *Bad Fork Trail* (USFS #323), a strenuous **304** 1.8-mi orange-blazed path whose S trailhead is 0.5 mi up FR-5000 from the jct with FR-124. The N trailhead is on the BRP exit to FR-5000. Because of its steepness a second vehicle may be a good choice for hiking down the trail. If so, descend gradually at first on a woods road, then drop 650 ft in elevation to a damp cove with rhododendron. Cross Bad Fork at 1.2 mi. On an old road the decline decreases in a beautiful forest of tall poplar, hickory, maple, ferns, rock formations, and cascades.

Bear Branch Trail (1.3 mi; USFS #328) (F, B, H); Wash Creek Trail (0.8 **305-** *mi; USFS #606) (F, B, H); Trace Ridge Trail (3.1 mi; USFS #354) (F, B,* **313** *H); Spencer Gap Trail (1.6 mi; USFS #600) (F, B); North Mills River Trail (1.6 mi; USFS #353) (F, B, H); Fletcher Creek Trail (2.4 mi; USFS #350) (F, B, H); Spencer Branch Trail (2.3 mi; USFS #140) (F, B, H); Middle Fork Trail (2.0 mi; USFS #352) (F, B, H); Big Creek Trail (4.9 mi; USFS #102) (F, B, H)*

TOTAL LENGTH AND DIFFICULTY: 20.0 mi combined, one-way (additional distances on the roads), easy to strenuous (elev change 2,581 ft)

TRAILHEADS AND DESCRIPTION: From the jct of NC-191/280 in the community of Mills River, drive N 0.9 mi to North Mills River Rd (SR-1345), L (W) at the North Mills River Rec Area (Campground) sign. Drive 5.0 mi on SR-1345 to the edge of the campground and turn R on Wash Creek Rd (FR-5000). Drive 2.0 mi, turn L on Hendersonville Reservoir Rd (FR-142), cross a cement low-water bridge, and at 0.5 mi reach a parking area and gated roads. All of the above trails can be accessed from this point.

To use *Bear Branch Trail* go back to FR-5000, cross the road, and climb the hummock and follow the easy blue-blazed route to near the branch's headwaters. Jct with FR-5001; either backtrack or return on FR-5001 to FR-5000 and turn L to point of origin.

For yellow-blazed *Walsh Creek Trail,* go 0.4 mi back toward FR-5000 and turn R. It parallels Wash Creek on a flat and easy old timber road for 0.8 mi to a gap. Turn on a S extension of *Trace Ridge Trail* and return to the parking lot after 0.5 mi. Or, from the gap descend 0.4 mi to jct with *North Mills River Trail* in a wildlife field.

The scenic blue-blazed *North Mills River Trail* goes upriver, sometimes fording it. Mainly a horse trail, hikers have to wade the river, which is likely over the knees. The trail's NW terminus is at FR-142 in a grassy meadow. It is 0.6 mi R on FR-142 to the parking lot.

Orange-blazed *Trace Ridge Trail* begins N (R of the gated FR-5097) from the parking lot on an old forest road. Follow a dry ridgeline after first skirting W of the first knob, but ascend and descend on all the other knobs. Along the way are oak, maple, white pine, dogwood, locust, laurel, and azalea. Descend to a gap at 2.7 mi and jct with *Spencer Branch Trail,* L. Ascend steeply and at 3.0 mi jct with *Spencer Gap Trail,* R. Ascend another 0.1 mi to the BRP (mp 401.8, 0.1 mi W of Beaverdam Gap Overlook). Backtrack to *Spencer Gap Trail.*

The blue-blazed *Spencer Gap Trail* for hikers and bikers goes E on generally level treadway on the S side of Ferrin Knob and below the BRP. At 0.7 mi it crosses a small tributary of the headwaters of Wash Creek, then descends on switchbacks to an old logging road at 1.3 mi. Here it turns L and reaches FR-5000 in a sharp curve, 1.6 mi down the mtn from Bent Creek Gap of the BRP. Backtrack, or descend on FR-5000 for 2.0 mi to the entrance for *Trace Ridge Trail* parking lot. If not backtracking on the *Trace Ridge Trail* or the *Spencer Gap Trail,* the *Spencer Gap Trail* can be chosen as an option for 4.0 mi (2.5 mi on the *Spencer Branch Trail* and 1.5 mi on FR-142) back to Trace Ridge parking lot.

Access to the *Fletcher Creek Trail* and the *Spencer Branch Trail* is on gated FR-142 (L of the gated FR-5097 at the parking lot). Descend to the N edge of the North Fork of Mills River at 1.0 mi, pass cascades of Long Branch, R. At 1.2 mi is the *Fletcher Creek Trail* trailhead, R. (Ahead on FR-142 it is 0.3 mi to the trailheads of *Spencer Branch Trail* and *Big Creek Trail* at the Hendersonville Reservoir.) Turn R off FR-142 on blue-blazed *Fletcher Creek Trail* (an old road) and ascend. Achieve a minor crest on the slopes of Coffee Pot Mtn after 0.6 mi. Begin a slight descent and reach the confluence of Middle Fork and Fletcher Creek and good campsites at 1.1 mi. Jct with *Spencer Branch Trail,* R and L.(To access *Middle Fork Trail* cross Fletcher Creek, bear L a few yd on *Spencer Branch Trail,* before turning R up *Middle Fork Trail* as well as by the stream itself. See *Middle Fork Trail* below.) Turn R and follow jointly 0.2 mi with *Spencer Branch Trail* and *Fletcher Creek Trail* to a trail fork. If taking *Fletcher Creek Trail,* cross the creek and follow an old RR grade in a forest of hardwoods, hemlock, and rhododendron. Pass two wildlife clearings and end at FR-5097. Backtrack or follow FR-5097, L, to *Middle Fork Trail* for a return to *Spencer Branch Trail* or R on FR-5097 to *Spencer Branch Trail.*

After leaving the fork with *Fletcher Creek Trail,* the *Spencer Branch Trail* continues upstream, E of Fletcher Creek, until the stream's confluence with Spencer Branch. Ahead the trail crosses Spencer Branch three times before crossing FR-5097 at 0.6 mi. After another 0.5 mi upstream veer R and ascend for 0.3 mi to jct with the *Trace Ridge Trail* described above. When going downstream from its jct with *Fletcher Creek Trail,* the *Spencer Branch Trail* crosses Fletcher Creek at 0.6 mi, passes a large rock overhang, L, at 0.7 mi, and ends at a jct with *Big Creek Trail* at the reservoir at 0.9 mi. It is 1.5 mi L on FR-142 to the parking lot.

The orange-blazed *Middle Fork Trail* is moderate in its ascent and is accessed from the *Fletcher Creek Trail.* A popular trail for bikers and equestrians, it follows an old RR grade from side to side of Middle Fork. When the *Fletcher Creek Trail* makes its jct with the *Spencer Branch Trail,* cross Fletcher Creek, bear L a few yd on *Spencer Branch Trail,* then turn R up Middle Fork. (There may be a bridge for hikers and bikers across Fletcher Creek. If so, follow that route to jct with the *Middle Fork Trail.*) After 0.5 mi cross Middle Fork; enter wildlife clearings at 0.6 mi and 1.0 mi. Cross FR-5097 and rock-hop the stream at 1.5 mi. Rock-hop a tributary at 1.7 mi and follow between streams until the trail's end at FR-5097. Backtrack, or turn L on FR-5097 for a return to the trail's crossing of FR-5097, or continue to *Fletcher Creek Trail* or *Spencer Branch Trail* or all the way to the parking lot on FR-5097.

To reach yellow-blazed *Big Creek Trail,* follow FR-142 1.5 mi to the Hendersonville Reservoir from the *Trace Ridge Trail* parking lot. Jct with the *Spencer Branch Trail* and after a few yd turn L. Follow around the back side of the reservoir and go upstream (SW and W) on an old RR grade. A number of good campsites are along the route in a cove hardwood area of birch, poplar, oak, and rhododendron. Big Creek will be crossed a number of times; wading or rock-hopping is necessary. A strenuous trail, the climb is 2,400 ft in elev. At 2.5 mi cross Bee Branch and begin an ascent on an old timber road with switchbacks on a S slope. At 3.5 mi follow a footpath, steep in sections, among oak, maple, laurel, and locust along Little Pisgah

Ridge. Reach the trail's terminus at BRP mp 406.9 at the S end of Little Pisgah Ridge Tunnel and service road. There is not a parking area here. Backtrack, or arrange to be picked up. (The trailhead may be difficult to locate from the BRP, but cues are to cross a rock landfill E for 0.1 mi to steps and a more obvious trail route.) (*USGS-FS Map:* Dunsmore Mtn)

SUPPORT FACILITIES: The North Mills River Rec Area has a campground with tent/trailer sites (no hookups), flush rest rooms, picnic tables, and sewage disposal. Facilities are fully open from the last of April through November. A fee is charged, but during the other times of the year camping is free. Groceries, restaurant, svc sta, and other services are at Mills River, 6.0 mi E from the campground.

BENT CREEK AREA (Buncombe County)

Northeast and across the BRP from the North Mills River Area is the Bent Creek drainage. It flows NE to empty into the French Broad River close to the BRP jct with NC-191 about 8.0 mi S of Asheville. The area is known for its beautiful Lake Powhatan Recreation Area with a system of connecting trails and a campground with 96 sites (no hookups), flush toilets, sewage disposal, picnic tables with grills, central water sources, and hot showers. The season is usually April through November. Swimming is allowed and lifeguard is on duty during open hours; boats and canoes are not allowed on the lake; and a parking fee is required of noncampers.

There are at least six loop options for hikers. Only hiking (and some biking) are allowed between the BRP and through the recreation area to FR-479. More trails are being developed near Stradley Mtn area NW of Lake Powhatan. Some have been forest roads, used mainly by equestrians. An **314** example is *North Boundary Trail* (3.8 mi, USFS #485) (F, B, H). Other trails **315-** may be *Side Hill Trail* (2.1 mi, USFS #145) (F, B, H); *Little Hickory Top Trail* **317** (1.8 mi, USFS #136) (F, B, H); and *Ingles Fields Gap Trail* (1.5 mi, USFS **318** #150) (F, B, H). Adjoining the latter is *Upper Side Hill Trail* (2.0 mi, USFS #137) for only hikers, or hikers and bikers. All these trails may be accessed from gated forest roads 479C, F, and E, reaching out like tentacles NW up Stradley Mtn from FR-479 near Lake Powhatan. As you drive from NC-191, past the entrance to the Western North Carolina Arboretum, there is a shel- **319** tered signboard, R. It provides information on the *Ledford Branch Demonstration Trail*, which has interpretive signs to guide visitors on a 4.6-mi tour into the Bent Creek Demonstration Forest. The emphasis is on forest regeneration methods and Southern Appalachian hardwoods. The former Southeastern Forest Experiment Station, now known as Southern Forest Experiment Station, has moved to Asheville from its location on NC-191 near the entrance to Lake Powhatan. The Bent Creek Area has long been significant in forest history and research. An example is the Bent Creek Experimental Forest, where 10 state champion big trees are located (white walnut; northern white and Port Orford cedars; sweet cherry; ponderosa, red, and Scotch pines; spicebush; and white and Norway spruce). The arboretum, fenced and gated, but open daily, is planning botanical trails and special trails for people with disabilities (PWD).

ACCESS: From the jct of I-40/26 in SW Asheville, take I-26 1.5 mi to jct with NC-191, turn L, and follow NC-191 2.1 mi to the Lake Powhatan sign, R. Go 0.3 mi on SR-3480, turn L on Wesley Branch Rd (SR-3484, which becomes FR-479), and go 3.0 mi. (From BRP mp 393.6, turn at the French Broad River bridge and drive 0.3 mi to NC-191; turn L and go 0.3 mi to entrance road, L. Another access is off the BRP on FR-479 (under the BRP bridge) at Bent Creek Gap Rd, mp 404. There are not any access signs on the BRP.

Homestead Trail (1.1. mi; USFS #333) (F, B); Small Creek Trail (0.4 mi, **320-**
USFS #334) (F, B); Deerfield Loop Trail (0.6 mi; USFS #335) (F, B); Pine **326**
Tree Loop Trail (1.8 mi; USFS #336) (F, B); Explorer Loop Trail (3.0 mi;
USFS #337) (F, B); Grassy Knob Trail (0.5 mi; USFS #338) (F); Sleepy
Gap Trail (1.0 mi; USFS #339) (F, B)

LENGTH AND DIFFICULTY: 8.4 mi combined, easy to moderate

TRAILHEADS AND DESCRIPTION: The trails are marked and color-coded, but a map from the campground office may clarify the original trails and the spur trails made by hikers, bikers, and campers. From the beach parking area at Lake Powhatan follow E on the orange-blazed *Homestead Trail* at a hiking sign, and go around the lake through a hardwood and white pine forest. Pass an area where Carl A. Schenck (see *Cradle of Forestry Trail* in this section) had a lodge from where he managed the Biltmore Forest. Cross Bent Creek at FR-480 and return around the lake at 1.1 mi. The red-blazed *Small Creek Trail* is a 0.4-mi connector from the yellow-blazed *Deerfield Loop Trail* and the *Homestead Trail*.

For the *Deerfield Loop Trail*, leave the beach parking area, follow E (but S of the *Homestead Trail*), and meander through a mixed forest and a wildlife field to a jct with the blue-blazed *Pine Tree Loop Trail* at 0.6 mi. Turn L and at 0.9 mi jct L with the red-blazed *Grassy Knob Trail*. (The *Grassy Knob Trail* crosses South Ridge Rd [FR-479M] and ascends on a ridge 0.5 mi to jct with the *Shut-in Trail/MST*.) After another 0.6 mi jct with the yellow-blazed *Explorer Loop Trail*, but follow a new trail, R, on the S side of Bent Creek in a return to the campground beach area at 2.4 mi.

From the trail sign on Bent Creek Gap Rd (FR-479) parking area (between FR-479F and FR-479C jcts), follow the *Explorer Loop Trail* sign across Bent Creek, and at the fork, turn L. Cross Beaten Branch, jct L with the *Pine Tree Loop Trail,* cross Beaten Branch again, and jct L with the red-blazed *Sleepy Gap Trail* at 0.5 mi. (The *Sleepy Gap Trail* ascends an E slope, crosses South Ridge Rd [FR-479M], and ascends in a forest of hardwoods and rhododendron for 1.0 mi to Sleepy Gap at BRP mp 397.3 and jct with the *Shut-in Trail/MST*.) Continue on the *Explorer Loop Trail* to a jct with Cold Knob Rd (FR-479H) at 1.7 mi. Turn R on FR-479H, and after 0.4 mi (before the gate at Bent Creek Gap Rd [FR-479]) leave the road and parallel Bent Creek to the point of origin after a loop of 3.0 mi. (*USGS-FS Maps:* Dunsmore Mtn, Skyland)

SECTION 4: TOECANE RANGER DISTRICT

The Toecane Ranger District received its name from the Toe and Cane Rivers. According to legend the white settlers shortened the name of an Indian princess, Estatoe, who wished to marry a brave from another tribe, whom her tribe rejected and killed. In her grief she drowned herself in the South Fork of the Toe River.

The district's 76,640 acres are in four major segments: two in the N that border the Tennessee state line and the Cherokee NF, and two in the S that border the BRP and a portion of the Grandfather Ranger District. The most SW section covers the Craggy Mtn Scenic Area in the NE corner of Buncombe County. The most E section is the Black Mtn range, an area with 18 peaks over 6,300 ft in elev, and the South Toe River drainage area in Yancey County. Mt Mitchell State Park, the state's oldest and highest, adjoins the W side of this section. The largest NW segment in Yancey and Mitchell Counties is a remote area through which flows the Nolichucky River in a canyon inaccessible except by whitewater and the Clinchfield RR. The N section of the district is the majestic Roan Mtn Area and its famous gardens in Mitchell County.

The district's first 25,000 acres were purchased in 1913 to protect the South Fork of the Toe River's watershed and for its great supply of timber. Because the major timbering and railroad building were abandoned in 1915, large groves (some of the largest in the US) of red spruce and Fraser fir have remained.

The *AT* route of 74.0 mi follows the ridgeline in and out of North Carolina and Tennessee except in an area near Erwin where it crosses a highway bridge over the Nolichucky River. Another famous trail, the *Overmountain Victory Trail (OVT)* (USFS #308), a national historic trail, enters this district from Tennessee at the Yellow Mtn Gap intersection with the *AT*. It descends for nearly 1.0 mi on the historic footpath, Creek Rd (FR-1132). It was near the state line that the frontier patriots camped September 27, 1780, on their march S. The route of the *OVT* is approximately 315.0 mi, beginning in Craig's Meadow in Abingdon, Virginia, and ending at Kings Mtn National Park battlefield in South Carolina. Except for about 12.0 mi on federal lands, the *OVT* is a motor route. The trail commemorates the route used by the mountain men in their march to find and fight Col Patrick Ferguson, who had pledged to "lay their country waste with fire and sword" if they did not support the British forces. Col Ferguson's death in the October 7, 1780, battle at Kings Mtn was a turning point of the Revolutionary War. In 1980 thousands of hikers, equestrians, and motorists celebrated the bicentennial on a march from Abingdon to Kings Mtn. (For more information on the *OVT* route contact the Regional Office, NPS, 75 Spring St SW, Atlanta, GA 30303; 404-331-4998. The battle trails on Kings Mtn are described in *Hiking South Carolina Trails* by Allen de Hart.)

Recreational facilities include two family campgrounds, one at Black Mtn on FR-472 and Carolina Hemlock on NC-80, both along the South Fork of the Toe River. One group campground is at Briar Bottom, adjoining Black Mtn. Picnic areas are Corner Rock on FR-74 E of Barnardsville, Lost Cove on FR-472 near Black Mtn, Roan Mtn off NC-261, Spivey Gap (also called Bald Mtn) on US-19W near the Tennessee border, and Carolina Hemlock Pavilion on NC-80 at the Carolina Hemlock Campground. Some of the special-interest areas are Roan Mtn, North Fork Ivey Creek, Walker Cove, Big Bald Mtn, Black Mtn, and Craggy Mtn (all described in the 1994 Plan, Amendment 5, of the Nantahala and Pisgah NFs).

The district's TIS lists 42 trails. As in other districts the list is mainly for records of trails formerly and currently in use. Some are overgrown, unmarked, and unblazed. Others are old pioneer roads or logging roads open for multiple traffic. An example is trails off FR-74 and FR-5548 on the W slope of more-than-mi-high Craggy Mtn and Point Misery. Access to this remote area from Barnardsville, off NC-197, is on Dillingham Rd (SR-2731) for 5.0 mi to where the paved road ends and gravel FR-74 begins. (Along Dillingham Rd, after 3.7 mi, is paved Stony Creek Rd, R, by a Presbyterian church. After 1.7 mi the pavement ends and the gravel FR-63 begins. It ascends steeply up Mineral Creek hollow for 5.0 mi to Craggy Gardens Picnic Area, *MST* and BRP mp 367.6.) At the end of Dillingham Rd enter the forest

across a small bridge. At 0.4 mi is Corner Rock Picnic Area, R. At 0.6 mi is
327 foot trail sign R for *Walker Creek Trail* (1.6 mi, USFS #165), and at 1.0 mi is
328 another foot trail sign R for *Elk Pen Trail* (1.9 mi, USFS #166). Both exit ahead
329 on FR-74. Another trail is *Corner Rock Trail (Upper)* (1.4 mi, USFS #173) L off
FR-74 at 1.3 mi in a horseshoe curve. (The trail ascends L of the creek by a
large balancing rock. It exists at the end of FR-5548, accessed by FR-74.)

330   Continuing on FR-74 arrive at *Little Andy Creek Trail* (0.6 mi, USFS
#174) L on the W side of Little Andy Creek at 2.0 mi. (It is a steep trail
among cove hardwoods to exit at FR-5548.) At 4.0 mi on FR-74 is Walker
Falls, L. This scenic area is of special interest because of old-growth upper
cove northern hardwoods in a southern forest. At 5.3 mi and 7.0 mi are short
and steep old roads L up to Walker Ridge to FR-5548, which begins L at a jct
with FR-74 at 7.5 mi. (Secluded FR-5548, which may be gated, winds around
ridges for 6.8 mi to dead-end on a knob SW of Locust Pen Gap. Along the
way are scenic views, particularly in the wintertime, but none as rewarding as
at 4.8 mi at a clear-cutting.) Ahead on FR-74 for 1.2 mi is the dead-end parking lot for accessing *Douglas Falls Trail* (formerly called *Halfway Trail*)
331 described below. (The former 1.0-mi *Bullhead Ridge Trail,* USFS #1005, which
connected with *Douglas Falls Trail,* is no longer in use.)

332   Under development and relocation is *Shinbone Trail* (6.9 mi; USFS
#187) (F, B, H). It will switchback down the mtn from Indian Grove Gap on
FR-214 at the beginning to outstanding overlooks of the Nolichucky River.
It later turns R (N) on switchbacks to end at a gated road in Tennessee. A
relocation will complete a loop; the completion may be in 1997. Access to
FR-124 in North Carolina is 4.5 mi N on NC-197 from the community of
Poplar at the Nolichucky River.

ADDRESS AND ACCESS: District Ranger, Toecane Ranger District, USFS, PO
Box 128, Burnsville, NC 28714; 704-682-6146. Access is on the US-19
E bypass, in Burnsville.

CRAGGY MOUNTAINS AREA (Buncombe County)

333 *Big Butt Trail (USFS #161) (F)*

LENGTH AND DIFFICULTY: 6.0 mi, moderate to strenuous

SPECIAL FEATURES: remote, scenic views

TRAILHEAD AND DESCRIPTION: From Burnsville on NC-197, go SW 16.0 mi
to the top of Cane River Gap, or from Barnardsville on NC-197 go NE 10.0
mi. Begin at a parking area and ascend on a white-blazed trail along the
Yancey/Buncombe county line. Reach Mahogany Knob, after 22 switchbacks,

at 1.7 mi, Flat Spring Knob at 2.4 mi, and Flat Spring Gap at 2.6 mi. Primitive campsite and water are available here. Ramps, a long-lasting, garlicky wild onion, is found in sections along the trail area. Curve around the W side of Flat Spring Knob, dip to a saddle, and then slope to the E side of Big Butt (5,960 ft). Switchback to the S side of the peak and follow a narrow ridge at 3.4 mi where the views of Black Mtn range, Mt Mitchell, and Cane River Valley are magnificent. Reach Little Butt at 3.7 mi for more great views. Descend on steep rocky switchbacks among rhododendron to a long saddle before climbing 10 switchbacks to Point Misery (5,715 ft) at 4.4 mi. Descend to Brush Fence Ridge, climb a knob, and descend again before the last ascent to the BRP Balsam Gap parking lot, mp 358.8 (5,320 ft) at 6.0 mi. Here is a jct with the *Mountains-to-Sea Trail*, which crosses the highway. Backtrack or have a second vehicle. (*USGS-FS Maps:* Mt Mitchell, Montreat)

Douglas Falls Trail (USGS #162) (F)

334

LENGTH AND DIFFICULTY: 5.6 mi round-trip, strenuous

SPECIAL FEATURES: waterfalls, wildflowers, wildlife, old-growth hemlocks

TRAILHEAD AND DESCRIPTION: At the end of FR-74 parking lot enter the white-blazed trail at a sign. Descend easily 0.5 mi to the base of beautiful 70-ft Douglas Falls. Tall hemlock, maple, and oak rise from the misty gorge. Wild hydrangea and witch hazel are on the trail bank. Follow the trail L, steeply, among huge old-growth hemlock among large boulders to 0.7 mi. From here to the trail's end at the *MST*, the steep, rough, wet climb is through a botanical display of ferns, mosses, mushrooms, beds of partridge berry, patches of moosewood and yellow root, merrybells, and umbrella leaf (*Diphylleia cymosa*). The treadway is rocky with snags, tree roots, and logs in a treacherous but scenic passage. On wet rocks the tenacious and mucky clay makes shoes as slippery as soap. Cross a cascading stream at 1.2 mi and arrive at spectacular Cascades Falls R and L at 1.8 mi. Carefully cross the falls. (Power of the cascades has bent the steel posts holding the cable.) Cross another tributary of Waterfall Creek at 2.0 mi. Ascend on swichbacks up Sprucepine Ridge in a forest of yellow birch, beech, and oak. Jct with the *MST* at 2.8 mi R and L. Backtrack. (To the L is 1.5 mi on the *MST* to Graybeard Mtn Overlook on the BRP, mp 363.4, and R is 1.7 mi to Craggy Gardens Picnic Area parking lot, mp 367.7.) (*USGS-FS Maps:* Craggy Pinnacle, Montreat, Mt Mitchell, Barnardsville)

Snowball Trail (USFS #170) (F)

335

LENGTH AND DIFFICULTY: 6.0 mi round-trip, moderate

TRAILHEAD AND DESCRIPTION: An old trail, which once had about 30 switchbacks in its final descent and was abandoned, is now open sans switchbacks. Access is off the BRP, mp 367.7, to the Craggy Gardens Picnic Area. At the second curve, Beartree Gap, Barnardsville Rd (FR-63) begins L at a gate. The road to the picnic area turns R and the *MST* crosses the entrance road here. Park off the intersection and ascend S on the *MST*. Immediately is *Snowball Trail*, R. Ascend the slope of Snowball Mtn in a growth of mountain ash, maple, hawthorne, and locust to the ridge at 0.7 mi. Descend and continue NW on the main ridge through birch and chestnut oak, and rich displays of wildflowers. Avoid all trails on old roads L or R from the ridgeline. The trail undulates, passes over Hawkbill Rock, drops to Snowball Gap at 2.1 mi, curves E of Little Snowball Mtn, and ascends to the site of former Little Snowball Lookout Tower at 3.0 mi, the trail's end. (The trail formerly descended on multiple switchbacks to follow Hawkbill Creek to FR-63.) Backtrack.(*USGS-FS Map:* Craggy Pinnacle)

CAROLINA HEMLOCKS RECREATION AREA (Yancey County)

The Carolina Hemlocks Rec Area has facilities for tent and RV camping (no hookups, but water and comfort sta), picnicking (a shelter pavilion can be rented for groups), fishing, swimming, and hiking. The *Devil's Den Nature Trail* (USFS #192) (F, I) makes a 1.0-mi loop and begins and ends from the campground amphitheater. Two other trails, *Colbert Ridge Trail* and *Buncombe Horse Range Trail,* have trailheads nearby. Season of operation is usually from the middle of April to the end of October.

ACCESS: From Micaville, jct of NC-80 and US-19E, drive 8.6 mi S on NC-80 to the Carolina Hemlocks Rec Area. From BRP mp 351.9 in Buck Creek Gap, drive 5.3 mi N on NC-80.

SUPPORT FACILITIES: A nearby commercial campground is Clear Creek Camping Park with full svc, open May 1 to October 31; 704-675-4510. Access from the Carolina Hemlocks Rec Area is 1.0 mi S on NC-80 to Clear Creek Campground Rd (SR-1199) for 0.5 mi. From BRP mp 344.1 it is 4.3 mi N on NC-80. Another is Mountain Cove Campground and Trout Pond with full svc, open April 1 to October 31; 704-675-5362. Access is on NC-80, 1.5 mi N from the BRP. Groceries are available on NC-80 to Micaville, and 4.0 mi farther W on US-19E to Burnsville are motels, restaurants, and supplies.

337 *Colbert Ridge Trail (USFS #178) (F)*

LENGTH AND DIFFICULTY: 3.6 mi, strenuous (elev change 2,950 ft)

TRAILHEAD AND DESCRIPTION: From the Carolina Hemlocks Rec Area go N 0.4 mi on NC-80, turn L on Colbert Creek Rd (SR-1158), and after 0.5 mi park at the trailhead, R. Follow the white-blazed trail, ascending gently at first. Rock outcroppings provide scenic views of South Toe River Valley, Black Mtn range, Roan Mtn, and Grandfather Mtn. At 2.7 mi ascend switchbacks on the E side of Winter Star Mtn. Reach a spring, L, at 3.3 mi, and jct with the *Black Mountain Crest Trail* at 3.6 mi. (A turn L extends 0.1 mi to Deep Gap [5,700 ft] and the Deep Gap shelters. Space for tent camping is nearby. A return loop can be made from here by going S on the *Black Mountain Crest Trail* for 2.3 mi, turn L for 0.5 mi on the *Big Tom Gap Trail,* turn L on the *Buncombe Horse Range Trail* for 6.0 mi, and go another 0.5 mi to the point of origin on Colbert Creek Rd for a loop of 13.0 mi.) (*USGS-FS Maps:* Mt Mitchell, Celo)

Buncombe Horse Range Trail (USFS #191) (F, B, H) 338

LENGTH AND DIFFICULTY: 16.5 mi, moderate to strenuous (elev change 2,860 ft)

CONNECTING TRAILS:
(Big Tom Gap Trail)
(Mt Mitchell Trail)
(MST)

SPECIAL FEATURES: RR history, Camp Alice, spruce/fir groves

TRAILHEAD AND DESCRIPTION: (This trail is rugged and is used both by horseback riders and hikers. Access is described from the NE trailhead.) From the Carolina Hemlocks Rec Area go N 0.4 mi on NC-80, turn L on Colbert Creek Rd (SR-1158), and proceed 0.8 mi to jct with Aunt Julie Rd (SR-1159). Turn R, go 0.2 mi, and park L near a private home. Follow the white blazes on an old jeep road. Take the L fork at 0.6 mi. Cross rocky Middle Fork at 1.3 mi. At 1.8 mi bear R at the jct to begin steep switchbacks up Maple Camp Ridge in a hardwood forest. Cross Maple Camp Creek at 3.4 mi, and reach a heath bald with good views at 4.8 mi. Arrive at Maple Camp Bald (5,613 ft), R, at 5.3 mi. At 6.0 mi cross Thee Creek and jct with primitive *Big Tom Gap Trail,* R, which leads 0.5 mi to jct with the *Black Mountain Crest Trail.* Jct with the blue-blazed *Mt Mitchell Trail,* R and L, at 7.8 mi near a spring. Reach the former Camp Alice Shelter on Community Hill (5,782 ft) at 8.0 mi. (A spring is nearby.) Continue ahead on the old RR grade to the site of Camp Alice at 8.5 mi, R. (Camp Alice was a thriving logging camp in the 1920s. It later served as a lodge for Mt Mitchell visitors. Only remnants of the stone foundations remain.) Cross Lower Creek at 8.7 mi and a number of small streams that drain into Middle Fork and South Fork before approaching the base of Potato Knob at 11.7 mi. (Here is an access route, R, to NC-128, the road from the BRP to the top of Mt Mitchell.) Turn L and pass through a beautiful spruce/fir grove at 12.6 mi. At 14.0 mi enter a large wildlife habitat clearing with fine views and soon begin to follow an old logging road on long, level switchbacks that descend to the Right Prong of the South Toe River. At 16.5 mi reach FR-472 (3,560 ft), the SW trailhead. (To the R it is 2.0 mi to the BRP on FR-472, and L it is 2.9 mi to Black Mtn Rec Area on FR-472.) (*USGS-FS Maps:* Mt Mitchell, Celo, Montreat, Old Fort)

BLACK MOUNTAIN RECREATION AREA (Yancey County)

The Black Mtn Rec Area has facilities for tent and RV camping (no hookups, but water and comfort sta), fishing, picnicking, and hiking. The Briar Bottom Group Campground (reservation required) adjoins upstream on the **339** South Toe River. The 1.0-mi loop *Briar Bottom Trail* (USFS #189) (F, W) serves both as a handicapped-accessible route for hiking. The trail begins at the gate to the group campground, parallels the river to loop the campground, and crosses two locust footbridges in the process. An unnamed short trail goes up (W) Setrock Creek to a scenic cascading waterfall. Two other trails are accessible from the rec area, *Mt Mitchell* and *Lost Cove Ridge*.

ACCESS: From the BRP mp 347.6 at Big Laurel Gap descend 2.5 mi on FR-2074 to jct with FR-472. Turn L, go 0.7 mi, and cross South Toe River, R. Or, from BRP mp 351.9, descend 4.9 mi on FR-472 and turn L at the campground entrance. The N access is from the jct of NC-80 and FR-472 near the Mt Mitchell Golf Course, followed by a 3.0-mi drive upstream. Support facilities are the same as for the Carolina Hemlocks Rec Area (see above).

340 *Lost Cove Ridge Trail (USFS #182) (F)*

LENGTH AND DIFFICULTY: 3.3 mi, moderate to strenuous (elev change 2,070 ft)

TRAILHEAD AND DESCRIPTION: This trail is also called the *Green Knob Trail.* From BRP mp 350.4 at Flinty Gap (4,782 ft), stop at the parking lot and cross the road to climb switchbacks to Green Knob Lookout Tower (5,070 ft). The 360-degree views are outstanding, particularly of the Black Mtn range. Turn R a few yd before reaching the tower and descend on a white-blazed trail between FR-472 and Big Lost Cove Creek. Trees are hardwoods and scattered conifers. At 2.7 mi the trail descends steeply to FR-472. Cross the road, the South Toe River, and enter the Black Mtn Rec Area at 3.3 mi. (*USGS-FS Maps:* Old Fort, Celo)

Bald Knob Ridge Trail (USFS #186) (F)

LENGTH AND DIFFICULTY: 2.8 mi, easy to moderate (elev change 1,300 ft)

SPECIAL FEATURES: virgin spruce and fir groves

TRAILHEAD AND DESCRIPTION: From the parking area at BRP mp 355 (5,200 ft), descend 0.1 mi on the white-blazed trail to the FS boundary, and follow Bald Knob Ridge N of the Left Prong of South Toe River. At 1.0 mi begin switchbacks. The trail passes through magnificent stands of virgin red spruce and Fraser fir. Reach FR-472 at 2.8 mi. Return by the same route or have a vehicle at FR-472, 1.0 mi down the mtn from BRP mp 351.9 in Deep Gap.

Mt Mitchell Trail (USFS #190) (F)

LENGTH AND DIFFICULTY: 5.6 mi, strenuous (elev change 3,684 ft)

CONNECTING TRAILS:

(Briar Bottom Trail)
Higgins Bald Trail (1.5 mi; USFS #190A, moderate) (F)
(Buncombe Horse Range Trail)
(MST)

SPECIAL FEATURES: rugged, highest point E of the Mississippi River

TRAILHEAD AND DESCRIPTION: (Also see *Mt Mitchell Trail* description in Mt Mitchell State Park, chapter 10.) Begin the hike near the bridge in the Black Mtn Rec Area. Walk across a meadow and pass the amphitheater at the upper level near the campground host's residence. Follow a blue-blazed, well-graded trail past Devil's Den Forest walk at 0.1 mi. Ascend on switchbacks in a virgin hardwood forest. Large banks of meadow rue are passed at 0.9 mi. Jct with *Higgins Bald Trail* at 1.5 mi, L. (The *Higgins Bald Trail* is a 1.5-mi alternate route from Long Arm Ridge to Flynn Ridge where it rejoins the *Mt Mitchell Trail.* At its crossing of Setrock Creek is an outstanding cascade and waterfall.) A forest of conifers predominates for the next 0.4 mi. Jct with the old *Old Ridge Trail,* R, at 1.7 mi. Cross Setrock Creek at 2.6 mi, and jct with the *Higgins Bald Trail,* L, at 2.7 mi. Junction with *Buncombe Horse Range Trail* (described above), formerly the *Maple Camp Trail,* at 3.9 mi. Turn L and at 4.0 mi turn R into the forest. (A spring is nearby.) Ascend steeply over a rough and eroded treadway for 1.6 mi to the summit of Mt Mitchell and the picnic area at the parking lot. Backtrack or use a vehicle shuttle. (*USGS-FS Maps:* Celo, Mt Mitchell)

BLACK MOUNTAINS (Yancey County)

344 *Black Mountain Crest Trail (USFS #179) (F)*

LENGTH AND DIFFICULTY: 12.0 mi, strenuous (elev change 3,550 ft)

CONNECTING TRAILS:

345   *Big Tom Gap Trail* (0.5 mi; USFS #191A, strenuous) (F)
    (*Colbert Ridge Trail*)

SPECIAL FEATURES: rugged, high altitude, solitude

TRAILHEAD AND DESCRIPTION: (Sections of this trail were formerly called *Deep Gap Trail* and *Celo Knob Trail*. A former 3.5-mi access route, *Woody Ridge Trail* [USFS #177] [F] from the community of Celo is no longer in use.) The S trailhead is in Mt Mitchell State Park, and vehicles must be registered with the park ranger if left overnight. The N trailhead is on FR-5578 off Bowlens Creek Rd (SR-1109), 3.0 mi S of Burnsville.

Leave the Mt Mitchell picnic area and parking lot to hike N on what is considered to be the most rugged trail in the district. It is also the highest with a traverse of a dozen peaks over 6,000 ft within 6.0 mi. Follow the orange-blazed trail over rocky terrain and through dense vegetation. Sections of spruce/fir groves are dying from acid rain and woolly aphids. At 1.0 mi ascend to Mt Craig (6,645 ft), the park's second highest peak. It was named in honor of Governor Locke Craig (see Mt Mitchell State Park in chapter 10). Reach Big Tom Mtn after another 0.1 mi (6,593 ft); it was named in honor of Thomas Wilson. There is a jct at 1.6 mi with the primitive *Big Tom Gap Trail*, R. (The *Big Tom Gap Trail* is a 0.5-mi steep connector to the *Buncombe Horse Range Trail* described above.) Continue on the crest among ferns, thornless blackberry, Clinton's lily, moosewood, spruce, and fir to the summit of Balsam Cone (6,611 ft) at 1.9 mi. Ascend to Cattail Peak (6,583 ft) at 2.5 mi. Leave the state park boundary and enter the NF boundary to ascend Potato Hill at 3.0 mi. Reach Deep Gap at 3.9 mi. (Tent camping sites are at the gap, and water is 300 yd down the mtn to the E.) Jct with the *Colbert Ridge Trail*, R, at 4.0 mi. (The *Colbert Ridge Trail* is a 3.6-mi access route from Carolina Hemlocks Rec Area.) Reach the summit of Deer Mtn (6,200 ft) at 4.5 mi. Jct with an old road L at 6.2 mi. Continue ahead on an old road, skirting W of Gibbs Mtn and Horse Rock. Leave the old road at 7.2 mi, and reach the summit of Celo Knob (6,427 ft) at 7.4 mi. Turn L and begin the descent into Bowlens Creek watershed on an old logging road at 7.6 mi. Pass a spring on the R. Cross a small stream at 8.8 mi, pass a dangerous open mine shaft L at 9.5 mi, and go past a gate at 10.3 mi. From 11.0 mi, follow the cascading Bowlens Creek to gated FR-5578, the

N trailhead, and a small parking space. Follow the road through an area of private property and reach Bowlens Creek Rd (SR-1109, also called Low Gap Rd) at 12.0 mi. (It is 2.4 mi N to NC-197 and 0.7 mi to jct of US-19E in Burnsville.) (*USGS-FS Maps:* Mt Mitchell, Celo, Burnsville)

ROAN MOUNTAIN AREA (Mitchell County)

Cloudland Trail (3.0 mi round-trip; USFS #171) (F); Roan Mountain   **346-**
Gardens Trail (2.0 mi; USFS #290) (F, W)   **347**

LENGTH AND DIFFICULTY: 5.0 mi round-trip combined, easy

TRAILHEADS AND DESCRIPTION: Take the Roan Mtn Rd (SR-1348) for 1.8 mi at jct with NC-261 in Carvers Gap on the Tennessee–North Carolina state line (13.0 mi N of Bakersville). For the Cloudland Trail turn R to parking lot #1. Follow the trail sign W on the crest of Roan Mtn through spruce, fir, mountain avens (*Geum radiatum*), rhododendron, and sections of heavy moss on the trees and the ground. Pass parking lots #2 and #3 and climb to Roan High Bluff (6,267 ft) at 1.5 mi for superb views of Bald and Unaka Mtns from a wood platform. Backtrack. For the *Roan Mountain Gardens Trail* begin at parking lot #2, pass an information display board, and follow a triple-loop trail (partially paved) through an extraordinary display of purple rhododendron (*catawbiense*) and flame azalea. One of the trails has 16 interpretive signs, and another loop passes through a large grassy bald with rhododendron—usually at their flowering peak the last two weeks of June. The trail has easy access for the handicapped. (Contact the ranger station for information on the date and events of the Rhododendron Festival.) (*USGS-FS Map:* Bakersville)

SUPPORT FACILITIES: Roan Mtn State Resort Park. From jct of US-19E and TN-143 go 5.0 mi S from the town of Roan Mtn on TN-143 (which becomes NC-261 in N.C. at Carvers Gap). Call 615-772-4178. Full svc, rec fac, open all year.

ELK FALLS AREA (Avery County)

Big Falls Trail (USFS #172) (F)   **348**

LENGTH AND DIFFICULTY: 0.5 mi round-trip, easy

TRAILHEAD AND DESCRIPTION: From Main St in Elk Park proceed N on Elk River Rd (SR-1305), which becomes FR-190, for 5.0 mi to Elk Falls parking area. Begin the hike on a timber access road to Elk River, and descend to the bottom of the 50-ft amphitheater-like falls. Camping is not permitted. Backtrack. (*USGS-FS Map:* Elk Park)

4. Uwharrie National Forest

They say it's older than the Smokies; Uwharries,
my home in the evergreens.
—James H. Price III

In the center of the state, the 49,000-acre Uwharrie National Forest spreads into a patchwork of private and public tracts in three counties, mainly Montgomery but more than 8,000 acres in Randolph and another 1,000 acres in Davidson. Nearly 300 mi of county, state, and private roads form part of that patchwork, and another 185 mi of forest roads give easy access to its streams, recreational areas, and trails. With its mountainous range rarely over 900 ft in elev, it disguises its 400-million-year history. Archaeologists have reported that the composite geography has been eroded by the Yankin, Pee Dee, and Uwharrie Rivers to expose parts of the hard basalt and rhyolite deposits in the oldest known mountain range in North America. Its rocky and worn ridges have been mined for gold, silver, copper, and lead, and the early settlers impoverished an already poor soil with inadequate timber and farm management. In 1931 much of the acreage was identified as the Uwharrie Purchase Unit, and in 1935 it was transferred to the USFS for administration. Finally, in 1961 it became a national forest, the state's youngest. During the 1930s the CCC and subsequently the USFS reforested hundreds of acres with pines and allowed groves of hardwoods to mature in the coves and by the stream banks. Slopes with mountain laurel, dogwood, and sourwood became natural understory gardens with 700 species of plants and abundant wildflowers and ferns. A further preservation was made in 1984 when federal Public Law 98-324 created the 4,790-acre Birkhead Wilderness Area. The Final Environmental Impact Statement of the 1986 Land and Resource Management Plan reported 255 historic sites as "recommended for further testing or preservation." The origin of Uwharrie's name is unclear; perhaps it came from the Suala Indians. As early as 1701 it was spelled Heighwaree, an early map of 1733 lists it as

Uharie, and it is listed as Voharee on a 1770 map.

Recreational facilities include three family campgrounds: Uwharrie Hunt Camp has tent sites with picnic tables, drinking water, and sanitary facilities (access from Uwharrie intersection of NC-109 and SR-1150 is 1.5 mi N on NC-109 to a sharp L on SR-1153 for 0.4 mi, R); Badin Lake Campground (new) has 50 tent sites of which 35 have individual electrical hookups, picnic tables, drinking water, bathhouse, flush toilets, and waste disposal system (access from Uwharrie Hunt Camp is on FR-576 off SR-1153 for 2.9 mi to FR-597, turn R, then the first L on FR-597B); and Badin Lake Campground (old) has tent sites, picnic tables, drinking water, and toilet facilities (access is the same as for the new campground, except farther on FR-597 to FR-597B, L). Another campground, Badin Lake Group Camp, has a large field for tent camping, drinking water, and toilet facilities. (Reservations are required to the group camp.) Access is on the same road to Badin Lake Campground (old), but turns R near the campground entrance. There is a fee for all the campgrounds except Uwharrie Hunt Camp; all of the above listed campgrounds are open year-round. These camping areas have access to boat launching to Badin Lake at Cove Boat Ramp, accessible at the end of FR-597B described above. (A new boat ramp is planned at the old Badin Lake Campground. It already has a floating fishing pier.) The lake has largemouth bass, white bass, bream, yellow perch, sunfish, and catfish.

There are two primitive camps: West Morris Mtn Camp with picnic tables and vault toilets (access is at Uwharrie, 0.3 mi N on NC-109 from its jct with SR-1150, to a R turn on Ophir Rd [SR-1303], then 1.2 mi, R); and Yates Place Camp at the end of a 0.5-mi spur trail E off the Uwharrie Trail (0.1 mi S of Mountain Rd [SR-1146] and FR-6746 jct.)

The district has horse trails on backcountry roads, foot trails (the longest of which is 20.5-mi *Uwharrie Trail*), and 20.0 mi of ORV trails. The latter is confined to an area between Badin Lake W and Uwharrie River E, and accessible S off FR-576. Some of the trails are a section of *Dutch John Trail* (2.1 mi; USFS #90); *Rocky Mountain Loop Trail* (2.8 mi; USFS #92); **349-** *Gold Mine Trail* (1.2 mi; USFS #93); and *Dickey Bell Trail* (3.4 mi; USFS **352** #96A). (A map is available from the district office.)

An interpretive double-loop white-blazed trail, *Densons Creek Nature* **353** *Trail* (0.9 mi or 2.2 mi; USFS #97) (F) begins from the ranger station parking lot. Numbered posts describe flora, fauna, history, and geology. Scattered pines are among the hardwoods, and the predominant rock formations are milky quartz. The *Uwharrie Fitness Trail* (0.4 mi; USFS #397) (F) connects **354** with the *Densons Creek Nature Trail*, but its parking lot is accessed on the first turn R, Page Rd, off NC-24/27, a few yd W of the ranger station. Maps and brochures are available from the ranger's office.

In season, hunting and fishing in the forest are allowed in accordance with state laws and licenses. Forest game animals are deer, turkey, raccoon, squirrel, fox, rabbit, and quail. Numerous species of songbirds, owls, and hawks are here also. Among the species of reptiles are the box turtle, lizards, and snakes (including the infrequently seen rattlesnake and copperhead).

ADDRESS AND ACCESS: District Ranger, Uwharrie National Forest, USFS, Rte 3, Box 470, Troy, NC 27371; 910-576-6391. Access is on NC-24/27, 1.8 mi E of Troy.

SUPPORT FACILITIES: Motels, restaurants, and shopping centers are in Troy, Asheboro, and Albemarle, and hospitals are in the latter two. A store for groceries and outdoor-sports equipment is at Uwharrie, jct of NC-109 and SR-1303/1150.

BADIN LAKE AREA (Montgomery County)

This is a concentrated recreational area with facilities for boating, fishing, camping, picnicking, and hiking as described above. At the new Badin Lake Campground (completed in 1995) plans are for a 1.0-mi paved bike trail to encircle the campground, and an access trail to the lake. (If the former route or new route is used to connect with the *Badin Lake Trail,* described below, campers would have a long loop trail to connect with the other campgrounds.) A new boat ramp is planned near the older Badin Lake Campground.

ACCESS: From the jct of NC-109 and Checking Station Rd (SR-1153) (1.5 mi NW from the community of Uwharrie) go 0.4 mi on SR-1153 and turn R on FR-567 (at Uwharrie Hunting Camp/Picnic Area). Drive 2.9 mi and turn R on FR-597. The first L (on FR-597B) goes to Cove Boat Ramp and new campground. The second L (on FR-597A) goes to old campground and Badin Lake Group Camp.

355 *Badin Lake Trail (USFS #94) (F)*

LENGTH AND DIFFICULTY: 6.5 mi, moderate

TRAILHEAD AND DESCRIPTION: This trail has a diamond-shaped white plastic blaze, and because of a lack of maintenance may require alert attention to its route. Begin the trail at the Cove Boat Ramp parking area (described above) and follow N along the Badin Lake shoreline. Curve around a knoll (on whose top is the new Badin Lake Campground) and jct with the return loop route, R, at 0.4 mi. (The new campground facilities may change this connection.) Continue ahead by the lake and at 0.5 mi arrive in a rocky cove with ferns and wildflowers. Enter another cove at 1.0 mi with white alder, oaks, and pines where the old Badin Lake Campground is up the hill. Stay close to the waterfront and continue around the campground to a cove at 1.8 mi. From here there is less evidence of the campground spur trails. At 2.3 mi enter a cove where the trail leaves the shore and slightly ascends to an old road, R and L, at 2.5 mi. (To the R the old road goes to the Badin Lake Group Camp and FR-597A. To the L the road extends 0.5 mi to the tip of the peninsula.) Ahead is a beautiful open forest and the other side of the peninsula.

Descend slightly to the lake's edge and pass R of a floating fishing pier. Follow the shoreline to a cove at 2.8 mi, ascend, and curve L to cross a long ravine at 3.2 mi. At 3.3 mi reach a large sloping rock on the hillside into the lake. Here are lichens, mosses, wildflowers, scrub pine, and laurel. From here the trail soon ascends on the hillside, then drops to the lake before entering a long and dense cove, a favorite place for spring peepers and bull-frogs. At 4.2 mi jct with a sign that indicates an access to the *Dutch John Trail* ahead. Turn R steeply to the hilltop at 4.3 mi at the NE corner of the Badin Lake Group Camp field.

If continuing on the *Badin Lake Trail* from the sign, descend to the stream and rocky area. Then ascend a ridge, descend, cross a hollow, ascend, and cross FR-597A at 0.7 mi. Arrive at a wildlife field at 0.8 mi and curve R. Cross a woods road at 1.0 mi, pass through a damp area among saplings at 1.1 mi to cross an old road with patches of wild quinine and rabbit's pea Cross another road; descend into more saplings. Before a wildlife field, the trail forks at 1.5 mi. To the L is a faint 0.1-mi trail to FR-597, a few yd N of its jct with FR-597B. To the R the trail goes around the wildlife field and exits at FR-597B at 1.6 mi. To the R is the new Badin Lake Campground where the trail disappears, but if the road and old trail are followed down to the lake it is another 0.7 mi for a total loop of 6.5 mi. (*USGS-FS Map*: Badin)

BIRKHEAD MOUNTAIN WILDERNESS AREA (Randolph County)

ACCESS: From the Asheboro jct of US-220 and NC-49, go W on NC-49 for 5.5 mi and turn R on Science Hill Rd (SR-1163). After 0.4 mi turn L (S) on Lassiter Mill Rd (SR-1107), and go 5.2 mi to a wilderness sign at FR-6532. Turn L and drive 0.5 mi to the parking area at the end of the road. (If arriving from the SW on NC-49 [11.0 mi NE of NC-109 jct], turn R on Mechanic Rd [SR-1170]. After 0.7 mi jct with Lassiter Mill

Rd, turn R, and go 4.3 mi to the wilderness.) If from the S, Uwharrie for example, take SR-1303 for 5.3 mi N to Ophir, SR-1134 and SR-1105 for 2.7 mi N to Eleazer, and SR-1107 5.1 mi N to FR-6532, R.

356- *Robbins Branch Trail (3.2 mi) (F); Birkhead Trail (5.6 mi; USFS #100)*
358 *(F); Hannahs Creek Trail (1.4 mi) (F)*

LENGTH AND DIFFICULTY: 10.2 mi combined, easy to moderate

SPECIAL FEATURES: pioneer history

TRAILHEADS AND DESCRIPTION: (These trails do not receive maintenance; some old white blazes remain.) Follow the trail sign and at 0.4 mi reach a fork where the *Robbins Branch Trail* goes L and the *Hannahs Creek Trail* goes R. If following the *Robbins Branch Trail* proceed through a young forest; ascend gently. At 1.2 mi pass through an open area of sumac and wildflowers with a vista of the Uwharrie Mtns. Descend gradually, enter an older forest at 1.5 mi, and at 1.7 mi pass R of rock erosion barriers left by pioneer farmers. Turn sharply L on a footpath at 1.9 mi. After 92 yd cross Robbins Branch, bordered with Christmas ferns, and continue upstream to cross the branch three times and a tributary once. (In late August cardinal flowers are brilliant near the branch.) Leave the branch headwaters and jct with the *Birkhead Trail* at 3.2 mi.

To the L, the *Birkhead Trail* goes 2.6 mi to Tot Hill Farm Rd (SR-1142), its N terminus. To the R it runs 2.0 mi to a jct with *Hannahs Creek Trail* and another 1.0 mi to its S terminus at the forest boundary. If taking the N route, curve R at 0.2 mi to a shallow saddle for a traverse on the Coolers Knob Mtn crest. Pass Camp #1-B, L, at 0.7 mi. Reach Coolers Knob with a scenic view E on a 50-yd spur at 1.4 mi. Cedar Rock Mtn and peaks from 900 to 1,050 ft are visible from here. Descend, and at 1.5 mi leave the Birkhead Mtn Wilderness Area and cross private land for 0.2 mi before reentering the NF. Cross Talbotts Creek at 2.4 mi and reach SR-1142 at 7.2 mi. (It is 2.0 mi L to NC-49 and 5.1 mi R on NC-49 to Asheboro.) If taking the *Birkhead Trail* R (S), pass patches of wild quinine (*Parthenium integrifolium*) and Camp #5 with a grill at 0.4 mi. Descend gradually in a hardwood forest. Reach the remnants of the Birkhead Plantation at 1.0 mi. (Boy Scout Troop 570 has erected a sign about John W. Birkhead [1858–1933] and his wife, Lois Kerns [1868–1943], and their 10 children. The family later moved to Asheboro where Mr. Birkhead was clerk of court and county sheriff.) At 1.7 mi pass Camp #4, R, with a spur. At 2.0 mi is the site of the Christopher Bingham Plantation (ca 1780) and jct, R, with the *Hannahs Creek Trail*. Ahead the

Birkhead Trail goes another 0.4 mi to cross the North Prong of Hannahs Creek and to a campsite at 0.9 mi. At 1.0 mi arrive at the S boundary of the Birkhead Mtn Wilderness Area and the trail's S terminus. (Ahead it is 1.0 mi on a private jeep road to a crossing of the South Prong of Hannahs Creek and entry to SR-1109 at Strieby Church. From here it is 0.6 mi on the road to jct with SR-1143. To the R [W] it is 2.1 mi to Lassiter Mill crossroads with SR-1107, and L [E] 10.8 mi to Ulah and US-200.)

On the *Hannahs Creek Trail* follow the old woods road, cross a streamlet, and pass a chimney and foundation L at 0.2 mi. Cross another streamlet at 0.5 mi, pass a man-made rock wall, and cross Robbins Branch at 0.9 mi. Ascend to the jct with the *Robbins Branch Trail* at 1.4 mi. Veer L and return to the parking area. (*USGS-FS Maps:* Eleazer, Farmer)

UWHARRIE TRAIL AREA (Montgomery County)

Uwharrie Trail (USFS #276) (F)   359

LENGTH AND DIFFICULTY: 20.5 mi, moderate

CONNECTING TRAILS:

West Morris Mtn Trail (2.2 mi; USFS #95, moderate) (F)   360
(Dutchmans Creek Trail)

SPECIAL FEATURES: Dennis Mtn, Island Creek

TRAILHEAD AND DESCRIPTION: The Uwharrie Trail (a national recreation trail since 1980) is a N-S route, which at the S end forms a reversed S crosses the middle of *Dutchmans Creek Trail* and forms an irregular figure eight. Access to the S trailhead is at a parking lot on NC-24/27, 2.0 mi E of the Pee Dee River bridge and 10.0 mi W from the center of Troy. From the NW corner of the parking space, enter a footpath through small oaks and descend on the white-blazed trail into a more mature forest of hardwoods, pine, and laurel. Pass under a power line at 0.3 mi. At 1.0 mi cross Wood Run Creek in a laurel grove, and at 2.0 mi jct with a 0.3-mi spur, R, to Wood Run primitive campsite. At 2.4 mi pass a spur a few yd R to FR-517. Follow the trail downstream, cross it six times, observe crested dwarf iris, and pass the remnants of an old automobile at 2.5 mi. Cross a timber road at 3.5 mi, ascend steeply to the top of Dennis Mtn (732 ft) at 3.7 mi for views W of Morrow Mtn State Park and Lake Tillery. Descend, join an old woods road R, rock-hop Island Creek at 4.6 mi, turn R on a footpath, and go upstream in a scenic forest with galax and royal ferns. After crossing the creek four times, ascend to and cross the terminus of FR-517 at 5.6 mi. At 5.7 mi arrive at a cross-trail with the yellow-blazed *Dutchmans Creek*

Trail. (Dutchmans Creek Trail goes 5.3 mi L to rejoin the Uwharrie Trail N, and 5.9 mi R [S] to the NC-24/27 parking area. A loop can be formed here for either trail.) Continue on the Uwharrie Trail and jct at 6.0 mi with a 0.3-mi spur, R, the Pond Camp Trail, which goes to a small pond at the headwaters of Clarks Creek. For the next 2.2 mi the trail ascends and descends three hilltops, crosses three old forest roads and four streamlets, and reaches Dutchmans Creek at 7.0 mi. Deer and turkey may be seen in this area. The forest is open in a number of places, but laurel is dense near some of the stream areas. At 8.2 mi ascend from a young forest to jct with the Dutchmans Creek Trail, L, at 8.4 mi. At 8.9 mi jct R with a spur trail of 0.5 mi to primitive Yates Place Camp. At 9.0 mi arrive at Mtn Road (SR-1146) where the trail crosses. (Left it is 2.1 mi to SR-1150; R it is 0.5 mi to Yates Place Camp and then 5.0 mi on Carrol Rd [SR-1147] and NC-109 to Troy.)

Continue ahead on the Uwharrie Trail, and cross a tributary of Cedar Creek at 9.3 mi and Watery Branch at 10.0 mi. Follow downstream, R, for 0.5 mi. Begin a steep rocky climb and reach the hill summit at 10.8 mi. At 11.3 mi make a sharp turn off a logging road and reach NC-109 at 11.9 mi. Cross the road to a parking space. (It is 1.8 mi L on NC-109 to jct with SR-1150 and Uwharrie for groceries, telephone, gasoline, and supplies; R it is 5.0 mi to Troy.)

At 12.4 mi is a spring, L. Cross Cattail Creek at 12.8 mi and cross Spencer Creek hiking bridge at 14.0 mi. Ascend and pass a bed of running cedar at 14.1 mi and intersect with the unblazed West Morris Mtn Trail, L at 14.3 mi. (The West Morris Mtn Trail descends 1.0 mi to the West Morris Campground, a primitive camp with tables, grills, and two vault toilets on Ophir Rd [SR-1303], 1.2 mi N of Uwharrie.) On the Uwharrie Trail ascend and reach the mtn summit at 14.6 mi. Cross an old forest road at 15.0 mi and at 17.0 mi cross two streams on bridges a few feet apart at Panther Branch. Cross SR-1134 at 18.1 mi. Reach a high ridge at 19.2 mi and continue to a rocky peak of Dark Mtn (953 ft) at 19.4 mi. Here is an excellent W view. After a rocky descent, reach a parking area on Flint Hill Rd (SR-1306) at 20.5 mi. Ophir is 1.8 mi L, Flint Hill is 2.8 mi R, and it is 7.0 mi to NC-134. (A former 5.4-mi Uwharrie Trail Extension [USFS #99] from here to SR-1143 has been discontinued because of its traverse on private property.) (USGS-FS Maps: Lovejoy, Morrow Mtn, Troy)

LENGTH AND DIFFICULTY: 11.1 mi, moderate to strenuous
CONNECTING TRAIL: *(Uwharrie Trail)*
SPECIAL FEATURES: reforestation, old mines, remote, Dutchmans Creek

TRAILHEAD AND DESCRIPTION: The S-shaped *Dutchmans Creek Trail* begins, ends, and crosses the middle of the S section of the *Uwharrie Trail* to jointly form the shape of an erratic figure eight. The trailheads are at a parking lot on NC-24/27, 2.0 mi E of the Pee Dee River bridge and 10.0 mi W from the center of Troy. The yellow-blazed trail begins at the NE corner of the parking lot, across FR-517. Cross a natural-gas line at 0.3 mi, then enter a clear-cut at 0.4 mi and leave it at 1.0 mi. Cross a small branch at 1.1 mi and Dumas Creek at 2.2 mi. Ascend steeply to an open area for S views, and at 2.5 mi turn sharply L (N) at a 1978 reforestation project. Leave the clear-cut, dip into a ravine, and at 3.0 mi cross a road in use to the private Piedmont Sportsmen Club. Pass under a power line at 3.1 mi. Ascend gently to the top of a long flat ridge at 4.4 mi and descend to cross FR-517 at 4.9 mi. Cross Island Creek twice; ascend. Cross FR-517 again at 5.5 mi to ascend a rocky ridge. Reach a level area and a cross-trail jct with the *Uwharrie Trail* at 5.9 mi. (On the *Uwharrie Trail* it is 5.7 mi L to NC-24/27 and 3.3 mi R to NC-1146; see description below.) Follow the *Dutchmans Creek Trail* R of a clear-cut, and reach a rocky hill at 6.3 mi. Descend into a grove of laurel and follow Little Island Creek for four crossings before ascending steeply on a rocky scenic mtn of hardwoods, Virginia pine, and wildflowers at 7.3 mi. (In the winter you can see Badin Dam [W] through the trees.) Reach the mtn summit at 7.6 mi. Descend for the next 0.4 mi and notice disturbed earth from old mines. Cross a streamlet three times before climbing another steep mtn to reach the top at 8.6 mi. (Badin Lake area can be seen through the trees in the winter, and Lick Mtn can be seen to the E.) At 9.1 mi descend to a gardenlike area of laurel, galax, trailing arbutus, and wild ginger (*Hexastylis shuttleworthii*). At 9.5 mi rock-hop Dutchmans Creek and go upstream in a scenic area of gentle cascades and clear pools. Pass through a mature forest of tall oak, beech, and poplar with scattered holly. Rock-hop the creek three times before reaching a road at 10.8 mi. Continue straight ahead to reach a jct with the *Uwharrie Trail* at 11.1 mi. It is 0.6 mi L on the *Uwharrie Trail* to SR-1146, and 2.7 mi R to rejoin the *Dutchmans Creek Trail*. (Volunteer assistance for trail maintenance in both the *Uwharrie Trail* and *Dutchmans Creek Trail* is provided by the Central Piedmont Group of the Sierra Club from Charlotte and the Uwharrie Trail Club from Asheboro.) (*USGS-FS Map:* Morrow Mtn)

PART II

5. Appalachian National Scenic Trail

From lonely seas to the mountains high
I'll roam the whole world over,
A vagabond of the wind and sky,
For I was born a rover.
—Earl V. Shaffer

Hikers do not need an explanation for why they hike the *Appalachian Trail,* other than because it is there. But on the menus of reasons are the trail's challenge and magnetic and kinetic appeal. Thousands walk sections of the sacred 2,157.0-mi path in the sky. A continuous scenic corridor through 14 eastern states from Maine to Georgia, it crosses eight national forests, six national parks, more than 60 state parks, memorial sites, and game lands. It is a living, changing masterpiece of incredible dreams, design, and dedication. To hike from end to end, the average number of footsteps is 5,240,000 and the average time is between four and five months.

By 1996 only a few more than 3,000 hikers are known to have walked the entire distance since an unbroken route was completed August 14, 1937. Of those who start with the intent to finish, more than 90 percent drop out. Most run out of will. "How easy it would have been to quit," wrote Earl Shaffer in 1948 when arriving cold, wet, hungry, and exhausted from fighting Nantahala underbrush to Topoco. His spirit sagged lower when the postmaster said there was no mail for him. That night, while writing in his journal, he remembered a poem he had written while serving in the Pacific during WW II. Part of the poem is above. "Get going, Ridgerunner," he wrote in *Walking with Spring.* Shaffer, 29, from York, Pennsylvania, had begun the hike with a degree of sadness; his teenage friend, Walter Winemiller, who had planned to hike the trail with him after the war, was killed on Iwo Jima. At the time of Shaffer's accomplishment, *AT* Conference leaders thought a solo through-hike impossible.

In stories and books by *AT* hikers there is a theme about stamina, mindset, and independence. Shaffer had these qualities, as did the second solo through-hiker, Gene Espry, 24, from Cordele, Georgia, who hiked the trail in 1951. A US Navy veteran of WW II, he traveled light, used ATC guidebooks, and, like Shaffer, did not have caches or anyone to meet him along the way. It took him 123 days, one day less than Shaffer. In some of the shelters Espry read notes and poems left by Shaffer. One poem had the lines "And though it be sun or rain/I walk the mountaintops with spring." Espry told news reporters that he enjoyed the trail in spite of bad weather and being lost on occasion. Maine's *Daily Sun* praised him as a conqueror of the nation's "most exacting thoroughfare."

Four years later, Emma Gatewood (Grandma Gatewood) of Thurmond, Ohio, and mother of 11 grown children, started hiking the *AT* in Georgia May 3, 1955, and finished in Maine September 25. She followed the same route again in 1957, and by 1964, at the age of 77, completed her third trip in sections. In 1959 she hiked the *Oregon Trail*. She was dearly loved by the trail world for many reasons. She inspired hikers with her simplicity (no backpack or fancy gear, no sleeping bag, and no hiking boots—only sneakers), her stamina, her love for people, and her great sense of humor. An example of the latter is an occasion in Maine (before her serious through-hikes) when she became lost. When found by a forest official and reminded of it, she replied, "Not lost, just misplaced."

In 1957 another solo through-hiker, Dorothy Laker, a teenager from Tampa, Florida, began the *AT* in Georgia and finished in Maine. An observant account of her journey is in *Hiking the Appalachian Trail*. She hiked the *AT* again in 1964 and the third time in sections by 1972. "Any memory of worry, frustration, and misery of the 1957 hike flew out of my mind...all I could remember were magic days and friendly campfires."

Solo through-hiking carries with it the risk of loneliness, particularly in members of a close family. Two examples are teenagers who hiked the *AT* in the 1960s. Jeffrey Hancock, 16, from Wenham, Massachusetts, hiked the *AT* in 1969. During the month before leaving he, his father, and his brother buried 28 caches of food along the *AT*'s route from Georgia to Maine. In his diary he wrote of his blistered feet, losing the trail, and severe loneliness. Like hikers before him, he had stamina. "A yearning for the outdoors was born in me," he wrote in *A Long Way Home*. During July of that summer his path crossed with

Rhododendron on Roan Mountain. Bill Russ

Eric Ryback, 17, from Belleville, Michigan, who was hiking solo from Maine to Georgia. "He was really moving, averaging 25 miles a day," said Hancock.

Ryback finished the trail in 80 days because he wished to be back before school started. He wrote about his loneliness and being lost. "Fear crept through me...I was confused." The lonely feeling was painful; "formed into one huge lump," he wrote in his story for *Hiking the Appalachian Trail*. The next summer he hiked the *Pacific Crest Trail*, and two years later he pioneered a hike of the *Continental Divide Trail*, the first hiker to complete such a transnational adventure. "After this I hung up my boots," he said. In a

1995 interview with Peter Olive of *Backpacker* magazine, Ryback discussed mental strength as an ingredient in his success as president of a multi-million-dollar mutual fund company in St. Louis, Missouri: "You have to have a focused mind-set and stay on course, just as you would on a long trail."

Early hikers to complete the *AT* in sections were Myron H. Avery, of Lubec, Maine, from 1920 to 1936; the second was George W. Outerbridge of Philadelphia (usually with hiking companions) from 1932 to 1939. In his writings about trail conditions, Outerbridge emphasized that if the *AT* was made too easy, it "would not be so much fun." Mary Kilpatrick, also from Philadelphia, completed the *AT* in sections by 1939.

Unknown to the *AT* Conference founders, leaders, and experienced hikers until 1993 was a remarkable hike in 1936 from Maine to Georgia by six Boy Scouts, ages 15 to 17, from the Bronx in New York City. Harry (Pop) O'Grady, a Scout leader, and a group of WW I veterans organized and shaped the hike with a support truck that took food to the boys at regular intervals. "At the time, we really didn't know what a feat this had been," said one of the group, Max Gordon, who now lives in Beverly Hills, Florida. The US Army veterans and the truck were their lifeline. "We were poor kids. We couldn't have done it without them," he said to Judy Jenner, editor of *Appalachian Trailway News*, the newsletter of the *AT* Conference. Some of the boys were ready to quit after the snow and drifts in Maine, but they stayed together, determined to finish.

The highly publicized father and son team of Chuck Ebersole (a retired US Navy chief) and his 17-year-old son Johnny hiked the *AT* in 1964 with Snuffy, their beagle. Their diaries are heartwarming adventure stories to be appreciated by all families. Only once, in a dangerous storm near Standing Indian Mtn, in their Georgia-to-Maine journey did the question of continuing arise. "We came within a snap of the fingers of quitting today," Johnny said. Chuck hiked the *AT* again in 1966 with his youngest son, Mike.

Some of the outstanding hikers of the *AT* whose journeys have received considerable national recognition since the 1970s are Edward Garvey (1970), an ATC leader and author of *Appalachian Hiker: Adventure of a Lifetime* and *Hiking Trails in the Mid-Atlantic States;* Warren Doyle (from his first time in 1973 to his 10th time in 1995) who with a group of other *AT* hikers founded the Appalachian Long Distance Hikers Association (ALDHA), which holds an annual gathering of experienced hikers and others interested in long-distance hiking; and Dan (Wingfoot) Bruce, who has hiked the *AT* seven times (1985, and 1987 through 1992). In his 1987 Golden

Anniversary Expedition hike, the 50th year since the *AT* had become one continuous link, his leadership brought unparalleled public attention to the *AT* and the ATC. He is author of *The Thru-Hiker's Planning Guide* and annually *The Thru-Hiker's Handbook*. He plans a network project to survey and publish information on all the common wildflowers seen along the *AT*. He is founder of the Center for Appalachian Trail Studies in Hot Springs, North Carolina (see information sources in the appendix). Bill Erwin from Burlington, North Carolina, with help from his friends and Seeing Eye dog, Orient, completed the *AT* in 1990. Among his current interests are the Irwin Ministries, founded in 1994, and hostels for *AT* hikers in remote locations of the trail. He is author of *Blind Courage* and a children's book, *Orient*. His newsletter is *The Orient Express*.

The first known hikers from North Carolina to complete the *AT* were Joseph Marion, from Winston-Salem, in 1972 and Marjorie Fowler, from Pittsboro, in 1974. Between 1974 and 1995, 145 North Carolinians made the journey. They represent 77 different cities and towns in a wide cross section of the state.

The name and the concept of this supertrail belong solely to Benton MacKaye, a forester and author from Shirley Center, Massachusetts. He has said that he thought of it in the early 1900s, before the *Long Trail* was begun in Vermont in 1910. It was in that year that James P. Taylor, a Vermont schoolmaster, established the Green Mountain Club and the concept of the *Long Trail* from Canada to Massachusetts. Others who had long-trail and connecting-trail concepts were Philip W. Ayers, a New Hampshire forester, and Allen Chamberlain, a Boston newspaper columnist and early president of the Appalachian Mountain Club (founded in 1876). They formed the New England Trail Conference in 1916. One of the conference's goals was to connect the New England trails, a linkage that remarkably resembles the later path of the *AT*.

Two other founding fathers were US forester William Hall, who envisioned a link with the southern Appalachians, and Will S. Monroe, professor and seer of the Green Mountain Club. Monroe's concept was to connect the New England trails to trails in New York and New Jersey. In December 1921, Monroe's friend, J. Ashton Allis, proposed connecting the trails as far as the Pennsylvania state line. Two months before Allis's proposal the *Journal of the American Institute of Architects* carried MacKaye's article "An Appalachian Trail: A Project in Regional Planning." The response to a singular name for the trails was immediate, and within a year the Palisades Trail Conference (which later became part of the New York–New Jersey

Trail Conference) began construction of a 6.0-mi section between Lake Tiorati Circle and Arden to connect with another trail in Palisades Interstate Park. The trail opened on Sunday, October 7, 1923, the first and original section of the AT. (The entire AT design was initially completed on August 15, 1937, but considerable relocation was to follow.)

In 1926 the leadership of Arthur Perkins of Hartford, Connecticut, began to translate MacKaye's dream and proposal into reality, but it was Myron H. Avery of Lubec, Maine, who probably more than any other leader was instrumental in implementing MacKaye's proposals. He worked and coordinated agreements with government agencies, including the important CCC, and thousands of volunteers to complete the AT. He was the first president of the Potomac Appalachian Trail Club, formed in November 1927 in Washington, DC, and served as chairman of the Appalachian Trail Conference from 1930 to 1952. In his final conference report he gave what has since become a classic definition of the AT: "Remote for detachment, narrow for chosen company, winding for leisure, lonely for contemplation, it beckons not merely north and south but upward to the body, mind, and soul of man."

Congress created the National Trails System Act in 1968 and gave further protection to the AT with the Appalachian Trail Act in 1978. In 1996 less than 45.0 mi of the AT remain unprotected. Affected are about 19,000 acres mainly in Maine, Vermont, Massachusetts, Maryland, Virginia, Tennessee, and North Carolina. Congressional appropriations to the NPS for this purpose will determine additional protective purchases.

AT mileage in North Carolina is 305.1 mi, most of which (209.5 mi) frequently weaves back and forth on the Tennessee border between Doe Knob in the Smokies and Elk Park NE of Roan Mtn. The AT is jointly maintained by private clubs of the ATC, USFS, and NPS. The Nantahala Hiking Club maintains 58.7 mi from the Georgia–North Carolina state line to the Nantahala River at Wesser on US-19. From there the Smoky Mountains Hiking Club maintains 99.9 mi to Davenport Gap at NC-284/TN-32. For the next 91.5 mi, the Carolina Mountain Club maintains the AT to Spivey Gap, US-19W. At that point the Tennessee Eastman Hiking Club maintains 55.0 mi to Elk Park (and 65.5 mi exclusively in Tennessee, which takes the AT to the Virginia state line 3.5 mi S of Damascus). (See club information in the appendix.)

Hikers on the AT should acquire the latest edition of the AT Guide to Tennessee–North Carolina and AT Guide to North Carolina–Georgia. If not available in the local bookstore, the guidebooks can be ordered from the ATC, PO Box 807, Harpers Ferry, WV 25425; 304-535-6331.

ACCESS: To reach the *AT* at the Georgia–North Carolina state line at Bly Gap (3,840 ft), begin in Georgia at US-76, Dicks Creek Gap (2,675 ft), 11.0 mi E from Hiawassee and 18.0 mi W from Clayton. After 4.3 mi arrive at Plumorchard Gap Shelter, and at 8.6 mi arrive at the state line at a cleared crest. If beginning at the N end of the *AT* in the state, follow US-19E 1.6 mi W from Elk Park, NC, or 16.0 mi E from Hampton, Tenn.

The following information is a condensed listing of the major locations and prominent features of the *AT* through North Carolina. Water is at all shelters except No Business Knob and Apple House shelters, and the letter *w* follows other places with water listed. Milepoints are listed north to south and south to north. Features include shelters, post offices, highway crossings, support services, and other trail connections. Bold type numbers (the first is **362** for *Betty Creek Gap Trail*) are for the purpose of matching trails in the book to the pocket maps. Beginning with *Russell Field Trail,* **363**, they run W into Tennessee and are not described in this book. The other connecting trails (that are not numbered here) run E into North Carolina. They are described and numbered under GSMNP, chapter 7.

Appalachian National Scenic Trail

Milepoints		Location and Prominent Features
N to S	S to N	
		The first 75.4 mi of the AT are in Ga., beginning at Springer Mtn.
305.1	0.0	Bly Gap, N.C.-Ga. state line (3,840 ft). Nearest all-weather road is 8.6 mi S on US-76 in Ga. (w)
303.6	1.5	Court House Bald (4,650 ft).
302.1	3.0	Muskrat Creek Shelter.
301.4	3.7	Whiteoak Stamp, spring E. (w)
301.1	4.0	Jct W with *Chunky Gal Trail* (5.2 mi to US-64).
298.1	7.0	Deep Gap (4,330 ft). FR-71 leads 6.0 mi W to US-64. (w)
297.3	7.8	Standing Indian Shelter.
295.7	9.4	Standing Indian Mtn (5,490 ft). A rocky heath bald with excellent views of Ga. and the Tullulah River gorge. (w)
292.8	12.3	Beech Gap (4,508 ft). (w)
289.6	15.5	Carter-Gap Shelter (4,550 ft).

Milepoints		Location and Prominent Features
N to S	S to N	
285.9	19.2	*Betty Creek Trail* (USFS #367) (0.3 mi to FR-67). (w) **362**
285.0	20.1	Mooney Gap, FR-67-2 (8.0 mi W to Standing Indian Campground).
283.4	21.7	Albert Mtn (5,280 ft) (named for the grandfather of A. Rufus Morgan). Fire tower and outstanding views of Coweeta Experimental Forest.
282.8	22.3	Big Spring Gap Shelter.
277.5	27.6	Rock Gap Shelter (3,750 ft).
276.8	28.3	Wallace Gap (3,738 ft). Old US-64. Town of Franklin: lodging, groceries, campground, 15.0 mi E.
273.7	31.4	Winding Stair Gap, US-64. Town of Franklin: lodging, groceries, restaurant, PO, 10.0 mi E.
272.8	32.3	Campsites. (w)
270.0	35.1	Siler Bald Shelter and Siler Bald Mtn (5,216 ft) (named in honor of William Siler, great-grandfather of Rufus Morgan).
267.8	37.3	Wayah Gap (4,180 ft). Cross SR-1310.
265.5	39.6	Jct W with yellow-blazed *Bartram Trail* and Wine Spring.
263.6	41.5	Wayah Bald Observation Tower and John B. Byrne Memorial.
263.0	42.1	E jct with *Bartram Trail*.
261.4	43.7	Licklog Gap (4,408 ft). (w)
259.1	46.0	Burningtown Gap, SR-1397.
257.9	47.2	Cold Springs Shelter.
257.2	47.9	Copper Bald (5,249 ft), scenic view of Nantahala River Valley.
256.8	48.3	Tellico Bald (5,130 ft), laurel.
256.4	48.5	Black Bald (5,000 ft), rhododendron.
256.0	49.1	Rocky Bald (5,180 ft), heath bald of rhododendron and azaleas.
254.3	50.8	Tellico Gap (3,850 ft), FR-Otter Creek, leads E to SR-1310.
252.9	52.2	Wesser Bald Fire Tower (4,627 ft).
252.1	53.0	Wesser Creek Trail, E.

Milepoints		Location and Prominent Features
N to S	S to N	
247.2	57.9	A. Rufus Morgan Shelter.
246.4	58.7	US-19, Wesser, N.C. (1,650 ft), lodging, groceries, and restaurant.
246.3	58.8	Cross Nantahala River bridge.
244.2	60.9	Tyre Top (3,760 ft).
243.3	61.8	Grassy Gap (3,050 ft). (w)
239.5	65.6	Sassafras Gap Lean-to.
238.3	66.8	Cheoah Bald (5,062 ft), magnificent panoramas.
232.8	72.3	Stekoah Gap (3,165 ft). Jct with Sweetwater Creek Rd (NC-143).
230.4	74.7	Brown Fork Gap Shelter.
228.4	76.7	Jct W with *Wauchecha Bald Trail*, 1.2 mi to Wauchecha Bald (4,385 ft).
225.2	79.9	Yellow Creek Gap. Tuskeegee Rd (SR-1242) E to NC-28.
224.3	80.8	Cable Gap Shelter.
223.3	81.8	High Top (3,786 ft), highest in Yellow Creek range, no vistas.
221.5	83.6	Walker Gap (3,450 ft). Jct with *Yellow Creek Mountainn Trail*, W.
218.8	86.3	NC-28, Fontana Dam, NC, lodging, groceries, restaurant, recreational facilities, PO. (Permit required for camping in the Smokies.)
217.7	87.4	Fontana Dam Shelter.
217.4	87.7	Fontana Dam Visitor Center.
217.0	88.1	Cross Fontana Dam.
213.0	92.1	Shuckstack Mtn (4,020 ft). Shuckstack Tower for scenic views.
211.8	93.3	Birch Spring Shelter (3,830 ft).
209.5	95.6	Doe Knob (4,520 ft). Jct with *Gregory Bald Trail* into Tenn.
207.2	97.9	Mollies Ridge Shelter (4,600 ft). 0.1 mi ahead to Devils Tater Patch.
363 204.6	100.5	Russell Field Shelter (4,400 ft). *Russell Field Trail* descends W 3.5 mi toward Cades Cove Campground, Tenn..

Milepoints		Location and Prominent Features
N to S	S to N	
202.1	103.0	Spence Field Shelter (4,890 ft). *Eagle Creek Trail* descends E leading to Fontana Lake. Bote Mtn Rd leads W 6.6 mi to Cades Cove Rd in Tenn.
201.7	103.4	Side Trail E, *Jenkins Ridge Trail* leading S in N.C.
201.1	104.2	Rocky Top (5,440 ft).
200.3	104.8	East Peak of Thunderhead (5,530 ft).
200.0	105.1	Beechnut Gap (4,840 ft). (w)
198.2	106.9	Starky Gap (4,530 ft).
195.8	109.3	Derrick Knob Shelter (4,880 ft).
195.6	109.5	Sams Gap (4,840 ft). *AT* goes E, *Greenbrier Ridge Trail* descends W 5.1 mi to Tremont Rd, Tenn. (w) **364**
193.6	111.5	Cold Spring Knob (5,240 ft).
193.3	111.8	*Miry Ridge Trail* exits W to Elkmont Campground, Tenn. **365**
193.0	112.1	Buckeye Gap (4,820 ft). (w)
190.3	114.8	Silers Bald Shelter (5,440 ft) (named after Jesse Siler, great-great uncle of A. Rufus Morgan). Two shelters. Scenic view of Mt LeConte NE.
189.9	115.2	*Welch Ridge Trail* descends E to High Rocks and connects with Hazel Creek trails in N.C.
188.6	116.5	Double Springs Gap Shelter (5,590 ft). *Goshen Prong Trail* exits W to Little River Rd in Tenn. **366**
186.3	118.8	Mt Buckley (6,580 ft).
185.7	119.4	Clingmans Dome (6,643 ft), highest elevation on the entire *AT*. Tower provides panoramic views, 0.5 mi to parking area and Clingmans Dome Rd (named for Thomas L. Clingman, US Senator, explorer). (w)
182.3	122.8	Mt Collins (6,190 ft) and Mt Collins Shelter. *Sugarloaf Mountain Trail* exits W in Tenn. *Fork Ridge Trail* exits E in NC. **367**
179.5	125.6	Indian Gap. *Road Prong Trail* exits W 3.3 mi to Chimney Tops parking area in Tenn. **368**
177.8	127.3	Newfound Gap (5,040 ft) and highway (formerly US-441). GSMNP headquarters W and Gatlinburg; Cherokee E. (w)

Milepoints		Location and Prominent Features
N to S	S to N	
176.1	129.0	*Sweat Heifer Trail* exits E 3.6 mi to Kephart Prong Shelter (5,830 ft).
369 175.1	130.0	*Boulevard Trail* (6,030 ft) exits W to Mt LeConte and the Jumpoff, outstanding vistas.
174.8	130.3	Ice Water Spring Shelter (5,900 ft).
173.9	131.2	Charlies Bunion (5,400 ft). Outstanding view of the Smokies and Mt LeConte. Crowded by visitors, dangerous in icy weather.
173.6	131.5	Dry Sluice Gap (5,380 ft). *Dry Sluice Gap Trail* exits E to connect with *Bradley Fork* and *Kephart Prong Trails* in N.C.
168.7	136.4	Bradleys View (5,800 ft) provides excellent vistas into Bradley Fork gorge.
167.4	137.7	Pecks Corner Shelter (5,850 ft), 0.4 mi E, *Hughes Ridge Trail* exits E, 11.8 mi to Smokemont Campground in N.C.
164.7	140.4	Mt Sequoyah (5,980 ft).
163.2	141.9	Mt Chapman (6,220 ft), forests of balsam and spruce.
162.2	142.9	Tri-Corner Knob Shelter (5,920 ft). *Balsam Mountain Trail* exits E 5.8 mi to Laurel Gap Shelter in N.C.
160.3	144.8	Mt Guyot Spur (6,180 ft) leads to summit of Mt Guyot (6,621 ft).
158.4	146.7	*Maddron Bald Trail* exits W to *Snake Den Mountain* and *Indian Camp Creek Trails* in Tenn.
157.0	148.1	Camel Gap (4,700 ft). *Yellow Creek Trail* goes E 5.2 mi to Walnut Bottoms in N.C.
154.5	150.6	Cosby Knob Shelter (4,800 ft).
152.2	152.9	Low Gap (4,240 ft). *Low Gap Trail* exits E 2.3 mi to Walnut Bottoms in N.C. *Cosby Creek Trail* exits W 2.5 mi to Cosby Campground in Tenn.
151.7	153.4	Mt Cammerer side trail goes W 0.6 mi to summit (5,025 ft), spectacular 360-degree panorama.
370 148.4	156.7	*Chestnut Branch Trail*, E 2.0 mi to Big Creek ranger sta and campground.
147.4	157.7	Davenport Gap Shelter (2,200 ft).
146.5	158.6	Davenport Gap, TN-32, NC-284 (1,975 ft), groceries E 2.0 mi, camping another 0.5 mi.

Milepoints		Location and Prominent Features
N to S	S to N	
144.9	160.2	Big Pigeon River bridge (1,400 ft) and I-40, 15.0 mi W to Newport, Tenn.
141.8	163.3	Painter Branch, camping. (w)
139.4	165.7	Snowbird Mtn (4,263 ft), excellent scenic views.
136.9	168.2	Deep Gap, 0.2 mi E to Groundhog Creek Shelter. *Ground Hog Creek Trail* leads E 2.3 mi to I-40.
134.6	170.5	Harmon Den Mtn (3,840 ft), *Rube Rock Trail* E, 4.0 mi to I-40.
134.0	171.1	Brown Gap, campsites. Jct with FR-148A, 1.3 mi. SE to FR-148 and S to I-40, exit 7, 4.4 mi. (w)
131.3	173.8	Max Patch Rd (SR-1182) 1.6 mi E to FR-148.
130.5	174.6	Max Patch Mtn (4,629 ft). Panoramic views of the Smokies, Tenn. Valley, Mt Mitchell.
125.6	179.5	Roaring Fork Shelter.
125.1	180.0	Lemon Gap, SR-1182 and TN-107 (3,550 ft).
123.8	181.3	Walnut Mtn Shelter.
121.4	183.7	Bluff Mtn (4,686 ft).
117.7	187.4	Garenflo Gap (2,500 ft), FR, E; *Shut-in Trail,* NW, 2.0 mi to SR-1183.
114.3	190.8	Deer Park Mtn Shelter.
111.4	193.7	Jesuit Hostel for *AT* hikers, Hot Springs, N.C.
111.1	194.0	Hot Springs, N.C. (1,326 ft). Lodging, groceries, PO, restaurant, Laundromat. Roads US-25/70 and NC-209.
109.7	195.4	Lovers Leap Rock. Scenic view of the French Broad River.
107.8	197.3	Pump Gap. *Pump Gap Trail* leads W as alternate *AT* route to French Broad River.
105.2	199.9	Tanyard Gap (2,278 ft). Cross US-25/70.
102.8	202.3	Rich Mtn Fire Tower (3,643 ft). Panoramic views of Black Mtn range and the Smokies. (w)
100.1	205.0	Spring Mtn Shelter (3,300 ft).
96.4	208.7	Allen Gap (2,234 ft). Roads NC-208 and TN-70, groceries.
91.5	213.6	Little Laurel Shelter.

Milepoints		Location and Prominent Features
N to S	S to N	
90.2	214.9	Camp Creek Bald (4,844 ft). Jct with *Pounding Mill Trail*, S 6.4 mi to NC-208, 0.2 mi NW to fire tower, scenic.
88.2	216.9	Blackstack Cliffs, superb views of N and W Tenn.
88.0	217.1	Bearwallow Gap.
87.3	217.8	Spring. (w)
85.0	220.1	Jct *Fork Ridge Trail*, S, 2.0 mi to FR-111.
84.8	220.3	Jerry Cabin Shelter.
82.9	222.2	Big Butt (4,838 ft) campsites. (w)
82.4	222.7	Shelton gravestones. Great-great nephew and other relatives live S of here in Big Creek and Laurel Creek valleys.
76.2	228.9	Devil's Fork Gap (3,107 ft), NC-212, N to US-23.
70.2	234.9	Hogback Ridge Shelter.
69.7	235.4	High Rock (4,460 ft).
68.0	237.1	Sams Gap (3,800 ft). Road US-23, groceries, restaurant 3.0 mi E.
61.7	243.4	Big Bald (5,516 ft). Grassy bald with spectacular views.
60.6	244.5	Bald Mtn Shelter.
59.2	245.9	Little Bald (5,185 ft).
55.5	249.6	Campsites. (w)
55.0	250.1	Spivey Gap (3,200 ft). Road US-19W. (w)
50.5	254.6	No Business Knob Shelter. (no water)
48.1	257.0	Temple Hill Gap (2,850 ft).
44.8	260.3	Nolichucky River (1,700 ft). Erwin, Tenn. Lodging, groceries, restaurant, PO, 1.8 mi W.
43.5	261.6	Nolichucky Whitewater Exp., lodging, groceries, restaurant, campsites.
40.6	264.5	Curley Maple Gap Shelter (3,080 ft).
36.5	268.6	Indian Grave Gap (3,360 ft). 3.0 mi W to USFS Rock Creek Rec Area.
35.4	269.7	FR-230, N. 50 yd to spring. (w)
34.2	270.9	Beauty Spot (4,337 ft), grassy scenic bald. (w)
32.1	273.0	FR-230, W.

Milepoints		Location and Prominent Features
N to S	S to N	
31.1	274.0	Unaka Mtn (5,180 ft), summit of conifers.
28.4	276.7	Cherry Gap Shelter.
25.7	279.4	Iron Mtn Gap. TN-107/NC-226 roads (3,723 ft), groceries 0.5 mi E.
21.6	283.5	Greasy Creek Gap, campsites. (w)
19.7	285.4	Clyde Smith Shelter.
17.6	287.5	Hughes Gap (4,040 ft). Accommodations 2.0 mi E; town of Buladean E on NC-26, 5.3 mi. Town of Burbank W, 3.2 mi.
14.9	290.2	Roan High Knob (6,285 ft). Cloudland Rhododendron Gardens. Summit forested with evergreens.
14.3	290.8	Roan High Knob Shelter.
13.0	292.1	Carvers Gap (5,512 ft). TN-143/NC-261 roads. (w)
10.0	295.1	Roan Highlands Shelter in Low Gap (5,050 ft).
8.3	296.8	Yellow Mtn Gap (4,682 ft). Site of John Sevier's "Overmountain Men," historic Bright's Trace, and *Overmountain Victory Trail*. Overmountain Shelter 0.3 mi E.
6.6	298.5	Big Yellow Mtn (5,459 ft). Grassy balds with extraordinary views.
5.0	300.1	Hump Mtn (5,587 ft). Superb panorama of Doe River Valley NW, Whitetop and Mt Rogers in Va , Beech Mtn to NE, and Grandfather Mtn to E.
0.5	304.6	Apple House Shelter. (no water)
0.0	305.1	US-19E, Elk Park, N.C. Lodging, groceries, restaurant, PO, 2.3 mi E. (*AT* continues 69.0 mi NW through Tenn. to Damascus, Va.)

6. Blue Ridge Parkway

This road will be the greatest scenic road in the world and will attract millions of tourists.
—Senator Harry F. Byrd, October 7, 1936

The Blue Ridge Parkway (BRP), a two-lane 469-mi highway described as the most scenic in America, averages 3,000 ft in elev and runs along the majestic crest of the Blue Ridge Mtns. In the beginning it was a trail made by surveyors, landscape architects, and naturalists. "They stamped out a trail with their hobnailed boots/ Cutting blazes on trees as they went/ Over ridges and hollows they marked the way/ For the men and machine that would follow," wrote Albert Clarke Haygard Jr, in his 1959 *The Skyline Saga*. It is a link between Shenandoah National Park at Rockfish Gap in Virginia and Cherokee at the edge of Great Smoky Mtns National Park in North Carolina. It is a "road of unlimited horizons, a grand balcony," wrote Harley E. Jolley in 1969 in *The Blue Ridge Parkway*. It is also a classic piece of engineering that has preserved the physical and cultural aspects of the Blue Ridge.

Although the NPS archives have not identified a single originator of the BRP idea, a number of historians give the credit to Harry F. Byrd, a US senator from Virginia. (Another claim for the credit is from Theodore E. Straus of Maryland, a member of the Public Works Administration [PWA], who said in 1962, "I am the originator of the mountain road connecting the Skyline Drive to the Smokies." Fred L. Weede, from Asheville and one of the leaders in the routing of the BRP through Asheville, said in 1954 that he recognized Straus as "the father of the idea.") Senator Byrd accompanied President Franklin D. Roosevelt on an inspection tour of the CCC camps in the Shenandoah National Park in August 1933. When the president expressed his enjoyment of such natural beauty, Byrd suggested an extension of the mountaintop route to the Smokies. President Roosevelt liked the suggestion, even stated that it should begin in New England. Senator Byrd later stated that the president said, "You and Ickes [Harold L. Ickes, Roosevelt's secretary of the interior, who was with them on the CCC tour] get together for the right of way." It was not that simple. Not only did a political controversy arise over the routing through North Carolina and Tennessee, but a final right of way was not deeded until October 22, 1968. (The original construction route was long opposed by the owners of Grandfather Mtn.) Initially the plan called for the BRP to be a toll road, something North Carolina Governor J. C. B. Ehringhaus opposed. After considerable political debate, Secretary Ickes decided in 1934 to eliminate any Tennessee routing, probably due to the strong influence of Ambassador Josephus Daniels, a North Carolinian and close friend of President Roosevelt and Secretary Ickes.

On September 11, 1935, the first rocks were blasted on the BRP near the Cumberland Knob area, and 52 years later the missing link (6.5 mi that included the engineering wonder of the Linn Cove Viaduct on the E slope of Grandfather Mtn.) was completed and dedicated September 11, 1987. The day of dedication was one of great pride for those who had spent a lifetime as part of this innovative dream. Many had not been aware of the political perils in its construction. Once begun, Virginia and North Carolina were determined to complete it with or without federal assistance. Congress debated the management of the parkway as much as or more than its financing. In July 1934, Secretary Ickes notified the NPS that he desired that agency to maintain and administer the parkway. But Congress had to approve this idea, and on April 24, 1936, N.C. congressman Robert Lee Doughton introduced the bill. "I think that this is the most ridiculous undertaking that has ever been presented to Congress... a colossal steal," argued Jesse P. Wolcott, a congressman from Michigan. The bill barely passed on June 20, 1936 (145 for, 131 against, and 147 abstaining). It was approved quickly by the Senate, and President Roosevelt signed the bill into public law (#848) on June 22, 1936.

The BRP is a popular tourist attraction (nearly 20 million visitors in 1993 for example) with a wide range of cultural and recreational facilities. There are more visitors in July than other months, and October is second. Its 241.0 mi through N.C. begin at milepost 217 in Cumberland Knob Park. Along the way are facilities for camping, fishing, bicycling, picnicking, horseback riding (Cone Park), hiking, and cross-country skiing. In addition there are lodges, historic exhibits, museums, parks, and mountain-culture preserves. Campgrounds are at Doughton Park, Price Park, Linville Falls, Crabtree Meadows, and Mt Pisgah. There are more than 60 trails: some are graded, manicured, and short; some are simple pathways for views of valleys below; others are rugged and natural into deep coves or high jagged rocks. Long segments of the *MST* follow its narrow corridor, and its newest and most expensive trail, the *Tanawha Trail,* is a crown jewel of design and natural beauty of the E slopes of Grandfather Mtn. A number of BRP trails join a network of trails in the adjoining national forests.

Bicyclists are allowed to travel the entire distance of the parkway. For long journeys, planning is essential. Bikers should contact the BRP office in Asheville (704-298-0398) for information on regulations, safety, emergencies, camping, and services. No horse traffic is allowed on the parkway or its shoulders. (The only exception is for crossing the BRP at Basin Creek Fire Rd, mp 243.8.) All trails are foot trails only, unless otherwise indicated.

Tanawha Trail and Linn Cove Viaduct, Blue Ridge Parkway.
Allen de Hart

Because of the density of visitors and user damage to the natural environment, the NPS has a number of regulations for the benefit of all. Some of them are listed here to assist hikers in their planning. Camping is not allowed on any BRP trail—only in the campgrounds or in primitive camps with a permit. No alcohol or open containers of alcohol are allowed in passenger compartments of vehicles. Pets must be kept on leashes. Quiet hours in the campgrounds are 10 PM to 6 AM. Weapons are unlawful (including bows, air guns, and slingshots). Fires are allowed only at designated campgrounds. All plants and animals are protected—berries, nuts, and edible fruits may be gathered for personal consumption. Maximum speed is 45 mph. No vehicles may be parked overnight on the BRP without advance notice to and permission from a ranger (see district telephone numbers below). No swimming in lakes or ponds and no rock climbing unless permission is obtained from a ranger of the NPS. Emergency dispatch telephone number is 800-PARKWATCH (800-727-5928).

Information: For general BRP information call 704-298-0398; for dispatcher, 704-298-0358; for district ranger offices (may be weekdays only): Bluffs at Laurel Springs (mp 216.9 to 298.6), 910-372-8568/704-295-7591; Gillespie Gap at Gillespie Gap (mp 298.6 to 359.8), 704-765-6082; and Asheville at Oteen and Balsam (mp 359.8 to 469), 704-298-0262 at Oteen and 704-456-9530 at Balsam. For personnel at the main office, 704-271-4739; for emergencies, accidents, fires, and criminal activities, 800-PARKWATCH (800-727-5928); and for facilities at specific BRP places call 704-271-4789.

For written information ask for, or pick up at visitor centers, the "Strip Map" or Blue Ridge Parkway Directory. In addition, the Blue Ridge Park Association provides an "Info Pack," also free, by writing BRPA, PO Box 453BRD, Asheville, NC 28802.

The most detailed description of trails on the BRP, available at bookstores and BRP visitor centers, is in *Walking the Blue Ridge* by Leonard M. Adkins.

CUMBERLAND KNOB RECREATION AREA (mp 217.5)

The Cumberland Knob Recreation Area is a 1,000-acre forest and park, 1.0 mi from the Virginia state line. It is the first recreation area constructed as part of the first 12.7 mi of the BRP in 1935–36. It is probably named for William Augustus, Scottish Duke of Cumberland (1721–65). Picnic areas and a visitor information center are open May 1 to October 31. Camping is not available. Elev 2,740 ft. Galax, VA, is 8.0 mi N on NC/VA-89. (*USGS Map*: Cumberland Knob)

371- *Cumberland Knob Trail (0.6 mi); Gully Creek Trail (2.5 mi)*
372 LENGTH AND DIFFICULTY: 3.1 mi combined, easy to strenuous
TRAILHEADS AND DESCRIPTION: Follow the signs to the information center, turn R, and reach the summit (2,855 ft) at 0.3 mi. Circle the knob and return through picnic areas, or descend on the *Gully Creek Trail*. Follow the *Gully Creek Trail* L of the visitor center, descending on a well-graded trail with switchbacks to Gully Creek at 0.8 mi. Trail crisscrosses the stream and begins ascent on switchbacks at 1.3 mi. A scenic knob is at 1.9 mi. Return by the Cumberland Knob, or take a shorter trail, R, to the parking lot.

373 FOX HUNTERS PARADISE TRAIL (mp 218.6)
The trail is an easy 0.2-mi path that provides a scenic view of forests in western Surry County where fox hunters once listened to their hounds from High Piney Knoll.

374 LITTLE GLADE POND TRAIL (mp 230)
The trail is an easy 0.3-mi loop around the site of a turbine-type mill operated about 1895 to 1915.

DOUGHTON PARK (mp 238.5–244.7)
Doughton Park is named in honor of Robert Lee "Muley Bob" Doughton, an enduring congressman (1911-53) from NC's 9th district, and a leader and advocate for establishing and developing the BRP. The 6,000-acre park has Bluff Lodge (open May through October), svc sta, camp store, campground, backcountry camping, picnic area, nature studies, special exhibits, fishing, and more than 30
375 mi of trails. Its most frequently used trail is the scenic *Fodder Stack Trail*. It goes 0.7 mi NE from the parking lot at the lodge to Wildcat Rock and to Fodder Stack outcropping. From here are impressive views of the Basin Creek watershed and the pioneer cabin of Martin and Janie Caudill seen deep in the valley. Along the trail are Fraser magnolia, hemlock, rhododendron, minnie-bush, white moss, and, for this far S, a rare grove of bigtooth aspen. All other trails are interconnecting; they form loops that converge as a funnel into Basin Cove. Backpack camping is allowed near the confluence of Basin and Cove Creeks, but a permit is required from the ranger's office. There is a trail system signboard at Alligator Back Overlook, mp 242.2. (*USGS Map:* Whitehead)
ADDRESS: District Ranger, Rte 1, Box 263, Laurel Springs, NC 28644; 910-372-8568.

LENGTH AND DIFFICULTY: 7.5 mi, easy to moderate
CONNECTING TRAILS:
SPECIAL FEATURES: Brinegar and Caudill cabins, Bluff Mtn

TRAILHEAD AND DESCRIPTION: Park at the Brinegar Cabin parking lot, mp 238.5 (3,508 ft). The Brinegar Cabin has a handicraft exhibit. The cabin was the home (begun in 1885) of Martin Brinegar (1856–1925), his wife, the former Caroline Jones (1863–1943), and their children. From the parking lot follow the trail sign 0.2 mi to the trailheads of *Bluff Mtn Trail*, R, and the *Cedar Ridge Trail*, L. A long loop of 16.5 mi can be made by going in either direction to include the *Flat Rock Ridge Trail*, or a shorter loop of 12.9 mi if using the primitive *Bluff Ridge Trail*. The description below follows these trails in a counterclockwise route. (The *MST* follows the *Bluff Mtn Trail* S to Basin Cove Overlook, mp 244.7, but it will go N on a separate route before leaving the BRP on its E route through Stone Mtn State Park. See chapter 16.)

Begin the yellow-blazed *Bluff Mtn Trail* on an easy grade of grassy fields, wildflowers, and groves of white pine, and after 1.0 mi enter the campground for long RVs. Cross the BRP and briefly parallel the tent and small RV section of the campground. Cross the BRP at Low Notch (mp 239.9) at 1.7 mi and ascend slightly to open and more level areas. Cross the BRP again to arrive at the restaurant and svc sta at 2.6 mi. From here go past the souvenir shop into the forest, come out to the BRP, and cross. Immediately cross the picnic road and follow the trail through the heath and grassy meadows of Bluff Mtn (3,792 ft) to the picnic parking area at 3.9 mi. Continue ahead to the jct of primitive *Bluff Ridge Trail*, L at 4.2 mi.

(The primitive *Bluff Ridge Trail* passes a picnic shelter after 240 ft and follows the ridge of the Alligator Back escarpment. There are views of the Cove Creek drainage and Flat Rock Ridge. Descend on the red-blazed trail to a gap after 0.5 mi, ascend to Brooks Knob at 0.7 mi, and consistently descend for 1.2 mi to the trail terminus and jct with the *Grassy Gap Trail* [fire road] R and ahead, and the *Basin Creek Trail*, L. The *Grassy Gap Trail* goes 4.7 mi up Cove Creek to the *Bluff Mtn Trail* and the BRP at mp 243.9 near Grassy Gap. The *Grassy Gap Trail* also goes downstream from the jct with *Basin Creek*

Trail for 1.8 mi to jct with *Cedar Ridge Trail, Flat Rock Ridge Trail,* and a parking area at Long Bottom Rd [SR-1728]. If hiking the *Basin Creek Trail,* follow the dark-blue blazed old wagon road 3.3 mi up Basin Creek. Rock-hop the creek frequently in a lush valley of poplar, oak, maple, and rhododendron. Pass L of the mouth of Caudill Branch at 1.5 mi. Reach Wildcat Branch, which flows from the L at 3.2 mi. Turn R from here and ascend 0.1 mi to an open area and the one-room cabin of Martin and Janie Caudill. Although the Caudill family had 16 children, only a few were born here. In 1916 a flood washed away most of the houses downstream and drowned some of the residents. The Caudill cabin was not damaged. Backtrack.)

Continuing on the *Bluff Mtn Trail,* descend from the jct with the *Bluff Ridge Trail,* in the picnic area, on switchbacks to Alligator Back Overlook (mp 242.2) at 4.7 mi. Bear L and parallel the BRP to reach Bluff Mtn Overlook (mp 243.4) at 5.8 mi. Here are views of the rock wall and cliffs of Bluff Mtn. Join the *Grassy Gap Trail* (fire road) and follow it 0.1 mi before leaving it R, at 6.3 mi.

(The *Grassy Gap Trail* descends on a green-blazed winding road to jct with *Bluff Ridge Trail* and *Basin Creek Trail* at 4.7 mi. Thirty yd L of the jct is the grave site of Alice Caudill, a child bride, who was drowned in the 1916 flood. Downstream after 0.1 mi is the primitive campsite, and beyond the trail crosses Basin Creek to end at Long Bottom Rd at 6.5 mi.)

Proceed on the *Bluff Mtn Trail* and pass through white and table mtn pine. At 7.4 mi jct with light-blue-blazed *Flat Rock Ridge Trail,* L. Continue R to a grassy area, go through a stile, and ascend to the Basin Cove Overlook at 7.5 mi (mp 244.7).

The *Flat Rock Ridge Trail* descends on a scenic ridge in a hardwood forest with scattered pines, two species of rhododendron, and a number of open rocky outcroppings. At 1.6 mi and 1.7 mi are some of the best views of Bluff Mtn and the Cove Creek drainage area. At 5.0 mi reach the end of the trail at Long Bottom Rd and jct with the *Cedar Ridge Trail* and the *Grassy Gap Trail.* Vehicle access to this point is from the jct of the BRP and NC-18, 7.0 mi SW on the BRP from Doughton Park. Turn S on NC-18, go 5.9 mi to McGrady, turn L on Long Bottom Rd (SR-1728), and drive 7.1 mi to the parking area and gated road L. (Long Bottom Rd becomes SR-1730 en route.) (Absher is 2.5 mi ahead on Long Bottom Rd, and 3.0 mi farther is the W entrance to Stone Mtn State Park.)

To complete the loop begin the orange-blazed *Cedar Ridge Trail* (90 yd inside the gated *Grassy Gap Trail* gate) on a series of switchbacks for 0.6 mi. Ascend gradually along the ridgeline and park boundary in a forest of hardwoods, conifers, and laurel. At 3.5 mi begin another series of switchbacks, and at 4.3 mi return to the *Bluff Mtn Trail* jct and Brinegar Cabin parking lot.

JUMPINOFF ROCKS TRAIL (mp 260.3)   **382**
Follow the easy trail 0.5 mi through a forest with beds of galax and tufts of arbutus to rocky cliffs (3,165 ft) for scenic views. Backtrack to complete 1.0 mi.

THE LUMP TRAIL (mp 264.4)   **383**
The trail leads 0.3 mi to a grassy bald with 360 degree scenic views, particularly of the Yadkin Valley.

E. B. JEFFRESS PARK (mp 271.9)
The park has rest rooms, drinking water, and picnic tables. It is named in honor of the 1934 state highway commission chairman who crusaded for the BRP. The moderate *Cascades Nature Trail* loops through a forest of hardwoods, **384** laurel, and hemlock to cascades on Falls Creek. Complete the loop after 1.0 mi.

TOMPKINS KNOB TRAIL (mp 272.5)   **385**
The trail is an easy 0.6-mi loop from the parking lot around the historic (log) Cool Spring Baptist Church and the Jesse Brown Cabin.

MOSES H. CONE MEMORIAL PARK (mp 292.7–295)
The 3,517-acre mountain estate of Moses H. Cone (1857–1908), textile "denim king," was donated to the NPS in 1950 as a "pleasuring ground" for the public. The Southern Highlands Handicraft Guild occupies part of Cone Manor. A stable is nearby and down the mtn in front of the mansion is the 22-acre Bass Lake. To the L (W) of the manor is the *Craftsman's Trail* (F), a **386** 0.6-mi figure-eight self-guiding trail with medicinal herbs. There are more than 22 mi of old carriage trails that provide one-way trips, loops, and cross-trail connections for hikers, equestrians, and cross-country skiers. High pastureland, deep and damp coves, and a forest with plenty of wildlife make this area ideal for an all-day hike. Access to the network of trails (carriage roads) is from the parking area to the paved road in front of the manor and E to the gravel road at the stable. Three of the trails are N of the BRP; all others are S. The *MST* follows two of the trails—*Rich Mountain Trail* and *Watkins Trail*—(see chapter 16). The shorter trails that connect S of the manor are the 2.5-mi *Duncan Trail* (F, H), the 0.5-mi *Black Bottom Trail* (F, **387-** H), the 1.7-mi *Bass Lake Trail* (F, H), the 2.3-mi *Maze Trail* (F, H), and the **391** 1.7-mi *Rock Creek Bridge Trail* (F, H). The three longest trails are described

below. For the most detailed description of the carriage/horse trails at the park see *Walking the Blue Ridge* by Leonard M. Adkins. (*USGS Map:* Boone)

392-
394 *Rich Mountain Trail (4.3 mi) (F, H); Flat Top Mountain Trail (3.0 mi) (F, H); Watkins Trail (4.0 mi) (F, H)*

LENGTH AND DIFFICULTY: 11.3 mi combined, moderate

SPECIAL FEATURES: Cone Manor and cemetery

TRAILHEADS AND DESCRIPTION: From the parking area, walk E to the gravel road behind the stable. To the L follow the road and enter the BRP underpass to a fork at 0.1 mi. To the L is the *Rich Mountain Trail*, to the R is the *Flat Top Mountain Trail*. If hiking L, descend to a crossing of Flannery Fork Rd (SR-1541, also called Payne Branch Rd) at 0.7 mi. Follow E of Trout Lake (may be drained) to the dam, turn L, and follow switchbacks up a stream under tall hemlocks. Pass a gate at 2.2 mi. After ascending to a scenic open pasture, turn R at the curve at 2.6 mi. Reenter the forest. At 3.2 mi the *MST* turns sharply L off the road. (The *MST* descends W on its route to Price Park. See chapter 16.) Continuing on the road reach a scenic circle and advance to the top of Rich Mtn (4,370 ft) at 4.3 mi. Backtrack to the BRP underpass.

On the *Flat Top Mountain Trail* ascend in a pasture. At 0.8 mi take a spur trail L and enter an avenue of Fraser fir to the Cone family cemetery. Continue on the ascent with switchbacks and reach the scenic summit of Flat Top Mtn (4,558 ft) at 3.0 mi. Backtrack to the stable. Begin the *Watkins Trail* here. From the stable go S, but turn sharply L in front of the manor (at 0.2 mi from the BRP). Descend into a forest of hemlock and white pine; go straight at a curve at 0.7 mi. Follow the well-graded switchbacks through large rhododendron slicks and groves of hemlock. At 2.8 mi keep L in a curve. (The road R is *Black Bottom Trail*, which leads to the *Maze Trail* and the *Bass Lake Trail*.) Pass L of a lake and spillway, and at 3.8 mi cross Penley Branch in a forest of exceptionally tall maple, oak, and hemlock. Turn R at a road used by residents and arrive at US-221 at 4.0 mi. Across the highway is the New River Inn. (It is 1.0 mi R on US-221 to Blowing Rock, 0.2 mi L to the BRP, and 2.3 mi L on the BRP to Cone Manor.)

JULIAN PRICE MEMORIAL PARK (mp 295.5–300)

Julian Price purchased this land in the early 1940s to develop it into a resort for the employees of Jefferson Standard Life Insurance Company. Because of his unexpected death in 1946, the company gave the property to the NPS with an agreement that a lake and park would bear his name. Although the area had been logged in the early part of the century, few settlers ever lived here. One early settler, probably between 1810 and 1817, was Jesse Boone, nephew of Daniel. Boone Fork, which flows N from the lake, bears his name. The

4,344-acre plateau has a developed campground with 134 tent sites (some open all year) and 60 sites for trailers (no hookups). The park is usually fully open from May 1 through October; 704-963-5911. There is also a large scenic picnic area, trout fishing, boat rentals, and hiking. The *MST* follows part of the *Boone Fork Trail.* (*USGS Maps:* Boone, Valle Crucis, Grandfather Mtn)

Green Knob Trail 395

LENGTH AND DIFFICULTY: 2.3 mi, moderate

TRAILHEAD AND DESCRIPTION: From the Sims Lake parking lot (E of the picnic area on the BRP) descend to the lake, cross the bridge, and circle L. Follow up the side of Sims Creek and cross under the BRP bridge at 0.7 mi. Cross the stream in a forest of hemlock, poplar, birch, and oak to ascend Green Knob. Reach the top (3,930 ft) at 1.5 mi, and descend to the BRP parking lot.

Price Lake Loop Trail 396

LENGTH AND DIFFICULTY: 2.4 mi, easy

TRAILHEAD AND DESCRIPTION: Follow the signs counterclockwise around the lake from any beginning point in the lakeside camping area. Cross Cold Prong stream at 0.7 mi, Boone Fork stream at 0.9 mi, and Laurel Creek at 1.6 mi. The trail is well graded and wet only in a few spots near the upstream marshes. Parts of the trail are arbored with rhododendron. Return at the dam and the parking lot to reenter the campground at 2.4 mi.

Boone Fork Trail 397

LENGTH AND DIFFICULTY. 4.9 mi, moderate

TRAILHEAD AND DESCRIPTION: From the picnic area parking lot, cross Boone Fork on a bridge to the trail system sign and enter the woods ahead for a clockwise loop. Ascend gently to the campground and pass through Section B (between campsites) at 0.6 mi to enter a low area. Ascend through a rhododendron grove and jct, R and L, with the *Tanawha Trail* (described below) at 0.7 mi. Turn R and jointly follow the *Tanawha Trail* to a stile and pasture at 1.1 mi. After 35 yd the *Tanawha Trail* turns L, but the *Boone Fork Trail* picks up the *MST* that has come up from the S on the *Tanawha Trail.* Continue on the *Boone Fork Trail,* jointly with the *MST,* on an old farm road through the pasture. Keep straight at a road fork at 1.3 mi, ascend slightly in a patch of woods, and at 1.4 mi turn abruptly R at a signpost. Descend 40 yd to a stile and enter a dense forest to the headwaters of Bee Tree Creek. Cross it 16 times, sometimes on a footbridge. At 2.6 mi turn sharply R off the old RR grade, cross Bee Tree Creek for the final time, and reach Boone Fork at

2.7 mi. Stay on the high N side of the mtn in dense rhododendron, birch, and hemlock. Ascend in a large rocky area at 3.2 mi, elevated from the cascades. Reach an old dam site, L, at 3.6 mi. Pass a large scenic rock slope to immediately leave the *MST* at 3.8 mi. (The *MST* requires rock-hopping Boone Fork on its journey upward to Rich Mtn. See chapter 16.) Continue upstream on an old RR grade and exit into a partial field that has copious patches of blackberries and wild pink roses at 4.6 mi. (This is a good area for birders.) Pass a fence and return to the picnic area at 4.9 mi.

398 *Tanawha Trail*

LENGTH AND DIFFICULTY: 13.4 mi, moderate
CONNECTING TRAILS:
  (*Boone Fork Trail*)
  (*MST*)
399 *Cold Prong Pond Trail*
400 *Upper Boone Fork Trail*
  (*Grandfather Trail*)
401 *Grandfather Mountain Access Trail*
  (*Daniel Boone Scout Trail*)
  (*Beacon Heights Trail*)

SPECIAL FEATURES: trail design, Rough Ridge boardwalk, Linn Cove
TRAILHEAD AND DESCRIPTION: This exceptional trail has been designed, constructed, and supervised at the cost of $700,000. There is not a similar trail elsewhere in the state. The Cherokee Indian name means "fabulous hawk," the name they gave the mtn now called Grandfather. Markers with a feather logo are placed at strategic points on the trail. The trail parallels the BRP from the Price Lake parking area (mp 297.3) to the Beacon Heights parking area (mp 305.3). In the process it passes through pastureland and deep forest coves, ascends to rocky outlooks, crosses cascading streams, and goes under the engineering marvel of the Linn Cove Viaduct. It is a trail for day hikes; no camping is allowed. Camping options are either in Price Park or outside the BRP boundary with fee permits for designated campsites from Grandfather Mtn, Inc (see chapter 14). The trail is described N to S, beginning at the Price Lake parking area. Except for the first 0.7 mi, the trail is also the *MST* route (see chapter 16). (*USGS Maps:* Grandfather Mtn, Valle Crucis, Boone)

Follow the trail sign and cross the BRP to Section B of the park's campground. Bear L of the campsites and enter a rhododendron grove. At 0.3 mi jct R with the *Boone Fork Trail* (described above). Arrive at a pasture and stile at

0.7 mi. Go 35 yd and turn sharply L into the woods. (The *Boone Fork Trail* continues ahead.) Cross two small footbridges and exit from the woods into the pasture at 0.9 mi. Ascend gently to enter the woods again, and pass through three more stiles before crossing Holloway Mtn Rd (SR-1559) at 1.7 mi. (It is 1.0 mi L on the road to BRP mp 298.6.) Enter another stile across the road to ascend a scenic pasture. Views of the Grandfather Mtn range can be seen ahead. Enter another forest and another pasture before passing the last stile at 2.8 mi. Descend gently into a low area of poplar, ash, and white snake-root at 3.0 mi. Pass through a forest of tall hardwoods and groves of rhododen dron to reach at 3.7 mi a jct with *Cold Prong Pond Trail*, L. (It goes 0.2 mi to the Cold Prong parking area and Cold Prong Pond at mp 299.2. Backtrack.) For the next 1.0 mi cross small streams and pass through a mature forest deep into Price Park. Upon coming out around a ridge, leave the Price Park bound-ary (but the trail continues unchanged within the BRP corridor). Pass a rich display of rosebay rhododendron, witch hazel, and at 5.5 mi a patch of flame azalea. Follow an old RR grade a short distance before arriving at an access to Boone Fork parking at 5.6 mi. (A sharp L goes 135 yd to Boone Fork parking, mp 299.9. Along the way, the 0.5-mi *Upper Boone Fork Trail* forks R and fol-lows the Boone Fork under the BRP to scenic Calloway Peak Overlook at mp 299.7.) Immediately after the jct cross a high footbridge over cascades and pools of Boone Fork. Within 100 yd, L is the 0.4-mi *Grandfather Mountain Access Trail,* which is also the *Daniel Boone Scout Trail* access. (It descends on an old road under the BRP bridge to a parking area on US-221. This route is recommended for hikers with required fee permits to the trails of Grandfather Mtn, Inc.) At 5.9 mi jct R with the *Nuwati Trail,* and at 6.0 mi the *Daniel Boone Scout Trail,* R. (Both trails require fee permits and are described in chapter 14.) Descend to a stream crossing at 6.2 mi, curve around a ridge, and descend to a footbridge over Dixon Creek at 7.1 mi. Pass through a lush cove of tall hard-woods, jewelweed, and black cohosh at 7.4 mi. At 8.6 mi jct L with the 0.1-mi access route to Raven Rocks Overlook, mp 302.3 on the BRP. Cross a foot-bridge over a fork of cascading Little Wilson Creek at 9.0 mi. A 60-yd access trail to Rough Ridge parking on the BRP, mp 302.9, is at 9.3 mi. Immediately cross a footbridge over a fork of Little Wilson Creek. Curve around and up the ridge to the spectacular views form the Rough Ridge boardwalk at 9.5 mi. In late September and early October the rocky mountainside turns multiple hues of red from the blueberry bushes. Other plants here are turkey grass, Alleghe-ny sand myrtle, red spruce, and mountain ash. This scenic area is environmen-tally fragile; trail users are urged to stay on the trail and boardwalks. Descend into a scenic area of rocky overhangs at 10.4 mi, and after 0.2 mi cross a footbridge over the cascading Wilson Creek. To the L is a 70-yd access trail under the BRP to the Wilson Creek Overlook at mp 303.7. Reach a pedestrian overlook at 11.4 mi, descend to cross Linn Cove Branch, and pass under the Linn Cove Viaduct to an observation deck at 11.6 mi. After 200 yd arrive at the Linn Cove parking area, mp 304.4. Reenter the forest to a section of huge boulders, descend to cross a footbridge over cascading Stack Rock Creek, and reach Stack Rock, L, at 13.2 mi. Reach the BRP Stack Rock parking area, R, mp 304.8, at 12.5 mi. Cross small Andrews Creek, follow a boardwalk alongside the BRP, and cross US-221 at 13.1 mi. (US-221 is a serpentine route of asphalt between Blowing Rock and Linville. It follows the route the Cherokee called the *Yonahlossee Trail*. There is an overlook on the BRP, mp 303.9, which gives a view of part of the route.) At 13.4 mi jct R and L with the *Beacon Heights Trail* and the end of the *Tanawha Trail*. (A turn L goes 0.2 mi to Beacon Heights [described below], and the *MST* goes with it nearly to the top before forking R to descend to Old House Gap in the Pisgah National Forest. See Chapter 16.) Turn R and after 130 yd arrive at the Beacon Heights parking area, mp 305.3.

402 GWYN MEMORIAL TRAIL (mp 298.6)

This 91-yd garden trail honors Rufus Lenoir Gwyn (1877–1963), whose efforts were influential in the location of the BRP through the Blue Ridge. The trail is at a jct with Holloway Mtn Rd 1.0 mi from US-221.

403 BEACON HEIGHTS TRAIL (mp 305.3)

An easy 0.3-mi graded trail ascends to a bare quartzite summit (4,205 ft) for spectacular views of the Pisgah National Forest, Hawksbill and Table Rock Mtns, and Grandfather and Grandmother Mtns. Along the way the trail jct with the *Tanawha Trail*, L, and the *MST* running jointly L and R. The summit was named by A. M. Huger, poet and trailblazer at the turn of the century.

404 GRANDMOTHER MOUNTAIN TRAIL (mp 307.4)

From the Grandmother Mtn parking lot ascend 0.2 mi on a moderate trail arbored with rhododendron to the NP boundary.

405 FLAT ROCK TRAIL (mp 308.2)

The easy 0.7-mi trail is a well-graded, self-guiding loop. Signs provide geological and biological information. The summit supplies outstanding views of Grandfather Mtn, Linville Valley, Black Mtn, and Roan Mtn. The quartzite outcropping is weather sculpted.

CAMP CREEK TRAIL (mp 315.5)

An easy leg stretcher, this short walk through rhododendron is to the cool banks of Camp Creek for a round-trip of 0.1 mi from the parking lot.

LINVILLE FALLS RECREATION AREA (mp 315.5–316.5)

The 440-acre Linville Falls Rec Area was acquired by the NPS from the philanthropy of John D. Rockefeller Jr, in 1952. It is named for explorer William Linville and his son, who, according to a legend, were killed by Indians in 1766 while they slept near the headwaters of Linville or Watauga River. Sixteen-year-old John Williams, left for dead, survived. At the major falls the Linville River cuts through quartzite to plunge dramatically into a hidden drop before it thunders from a lower open level. The area has 100 picnic sites, two campgrounds (190 sites), trout fishing, and an information shelter. There are four nature trails, but other trails, such as the *Linville Gorge Trail*, are in the Linville Gorge Wilderness Area under the jurisdiction of the Pisgah National Forest and do not make a connection (see chapter 3, section 2). The 0.2-mi round-trip *Linville River Bridge Trail* is separate from the parking area of the four trails described below. It is at mp 316.4, 0.1 mi farther S on the BRP than the entrance road to the falls. However, the trail connects with the picnic area from the entrance in its descent to the riverbank for viewing the architecturally significant stone bridge. (*USGS Map:* Linville Falls)

Linville Falls Trail (2.0 mi, round-trip); Plunge Basin Overlook Trail (0.5 mi, round-trip); Linville Gorge Trail (1.4 mi, round-trip); Duggers Creek Trail (0.3 mi)

LENGTH AND DIFFICULTY: 4.2 combined round-trip, easy to moderate

TRAILHEADS AND DESCRIPTION: To hike the *Linville Falls Trail*, begin at the parking lot and cross the Linville River bridge to follow a wide and heavily used trail to Upper Falls. Ascend from the Upper Falls through hemlock and rhododendron to a choice of three lookouts for outstanding views of the 90-ft (total) Linville Falls. (This trail is also known as *Erwins Trail* and goes to Erwins Lookout at 1.0 mi.) Backtrack. For the *Plunge Basin Overlook Trail* and the *Linville Gorge Trail*, leave the parking lot, L. Ascend through rhododendron to jct with *Plunge Basin Overlook Trail*, R. Turn R and descend to the overlook for a superb view of the Lower Falls. Carolina, catawba, and rosebay rhododendron bloom on the weather-sculpted walls of the gorge. Return to the jct with the *Linville Gorge Trail* and turn at the sign to descend steeply on a rocky slope to the basin of the Lower Falls at 0.9 mi. Backtrack. For the *Duggers Creek*

Trail, follow the signs E of the parking lot for an interpretive loop trail over a rocky area with thick mosses and fern patches. Return to the parking lot.

412 CHESTOA VIEW TRAIL (mp 320.8)

This scenic, short, and easy 0.8-mi route to Chestoa View was named by A. M. Huger. (Chestoa is the Cherokee Indian word for rabbit.) From the parking lot enter a paved trail and follow the loop through mature hardwoods and numerous wildflowers, including large clusters of Bowman's root. Take the gravel trail to return and pass scenic views of the Linville Gorge Wilderness Area and Grandfather Mtn.

CRABTREE MEADOWS RECREATION AREA (mp 339.5–340.3)

The 253-acre Crabtree Meadows has a restaurant that is open from May through October and a gift shop, camp store, and svc sta. Adjoining are an amphitheater and campground with tent and trailer sites (no hookups). The picnic area is on the S edge of the park on the BRP. Crabtree Falls is the central feature of the campground, but the more than 40 species of wildflowers and 35 species of songbirds are significant also. (*USGS Map:* Celo)

413 *Crabtree Falls Trail*

LENGTH AND DIFFICULTY: 2.5 mi, moderate

TRAILHEAD AND DESCRIPTION: From the campground parking lot follow the posted directions N to 0.4 mi and begin at the steps. Reach the waterfalls at 0.8 mi and cross the bridge to begin a return climb. At 1.4 mi cross the stream and walk through spreads of trillium and wild orchids at 1.7 mi. Follow L at all trail jcts until the jct with the original trail.

414 WOODS MOUNTAIN ACCESS TRAIL (mp 344.1)

This is a moderate walk on an old dirt road from mp 342 to mp 344.1. It passes a few other dirt roads from the L and passes a cemetery at 0.5 mi. In a hardwood forest with a rhododendron understory, it descends to Hazelnut Gap at 1.3 mi. To the L is the W end of *Woods Mountain Trail* (USFS #218) opposite a large white oak tree. (The *Woods Mountain Trail,* now part of the *MST,* follows a ridgeline for 5.3 mi to a former fire tower, but the *MST* continues for 7.9 mi to US-221 N of Marion at Woodlawn Picnic Area.) Continue on the old dirt road and descend to Buck Creek Gap parking lot at NC-80 (mp 344.1) at 2.0 mi. (See chapter 3, section 2.)

GREEN KNOB TRAIL (mp 350.4)

From the Green Knob Overlook (4,761 ft) follow the trail N and across the parkway and up switchbacks to reach the fire tower at 0.6 mi for outstanding views of the Black Mtn range. (The trail R at the ridgeline is *Lost Cove Ridge Trail* [USFS #182], Pisgah NF; it descends 3.3 mi to Black Mtn Recreation Area. See chapter 3, section 4.)

DEEP GAP TRAIL (mp 351.9)

The BRP has 0.1 mi on this unmaintained trail (USFS #210) (listed as *Newberry Creek Trail* by Pisgah NF of the USFS). It descends S on switchbacks in a hardwood forest with rhododendron and laurel for 1.9 mi to the headwaters of Newberry Creek and a jct with FR-482A. (The road may be gated farther downsteam before its jct with FR-482.) Backtrack.

BALD KNOB RIDGE TRAIL (mp 355)

This is a terminus point (0.1 mi) of the *Bald Knob Ridge Trail* (USFS #186), Pisgah NF, which descends 2.8 mi toward Black Mtn Rec Area on a white-blazed trail to FR-472.

BIG BUTT TRAIL (mp 359.8)

The BRP claims only the first 0.2 mi of this 6.0 mi Pisgah NF trail (USFS #161). Here at Balsam Gap (5,676 ft), the highest point on the BRP N of Asheville, is a crossing of the *MST*. Its N route ascends on switchbacks to curve around scenic Potato Knob and to NC-128 (entrance road to Mt Mitchell SP). Its S route is seen again at mp 361.2 in Cotton Tree Gap (Glassmine Falls Overlook). The white-blazed *Big Butt Trail* goes W to descend and ascend on a ridgeline of wildflowers and ramp for magnificent views of the Black Mtn range. The trail drops on numerous switchbacks to NC-197W (see chapter 3, section 4).

CRAGGY GARDENS RECREATION AREA (mp 364–367)

The 700-acre Craggy Gardens (5,220 ft) has a grassy picnic ground in Bear Pen Gap with tables, grills, water, and comfort sta. The visitor center has exhibits and BRP information. Although this area is colorful during all seasons with wildflowers, mountain ash, and wild crab apple, the highlight of color is in mid-June when the Craggy summits turn purple with catawba rhododendron. The Craggy Gardens visitor center and picnic area are usually open from April 1 through October.

418   To hike the *Craggy Pinnacle Trail* (1.2 mi round-trip), follow the signs
from the parking lot at Craggy Dome Overlook up switchbacks to the sum-
419 mit (5,840 ft) with 360-degree scenic views. For the *Craggy Gardens Trail*,
follow signs from the parking lot of the visitor center to the picnic area, a
420 one-way distance of 1.0 mi. The *Bear Pen Gap Trail* is 0.2 mi long and runs
through the picnic area. (The *MST* route follows the E side of the parking
lot.) (*USGS Map*: Craggy Pinnacle)

421 RATTLESNAKE LODGE TRAIL (mp 374.4)

The strenuous 0.4-mi *Rattlesnake Lodge Trail* is accessed from a parking area at
the S end of the Tanbark Tunnel. Ascend steeply on an orange-blazed trail to
connect with the *MST* and the ruins of the summer home of Dr. Chase P.
Ambler, an Asheville physician who built the lodge in 1900. To the R of the jct
is a spring and the N route of the *MST*. To the L it is 10.0 mi on the *MST* to
the Folk Art Center (mp 382). (See chapter 16.)

422 SHUT-IN TRAIL (mp 393.6–407.7)

LENGTH AND DIFFICULTY: 16.4 mi, strenuous (elev change 3,611 ft)

TRAILHEAD AND DESCRIPTION: A national rec trail and the *MST* route, it follows mainly a former horse trail named and constructed in the 1890s by
George Vanderbilt as an access route from Biltmore to his Buck Spring Hunting Lodge. It was originally 20.0 mi long and included a fording of the
French Broad River. With the creation of the BRP, parts of the trail were oblit-
erated and the remainder became overgrown. But in the 1970s Pop Hol-
landsworth of the Asheville School, Jack Davis and Arch Nichols of the CMC,
and others cleared sections of the old trail and relocated others. It is listed on
the inventories of both the BRP and the Pisgah NF because it weaves in and
out of the boundaries. Water is infrequent. Tree species are diverse because of
the high altitude changes. Among them are beech, red oak, cucumber tree,
hemlock, yellow poplar, maple, locust, chestnut oak, and birch. Wildflowers
include trillium, mandrake, wild orchids, wild geranium, gold star, galax, and
trailing arbutus. Cancer root, a parasitic leafless yellow brown stalk, is commonplace in the springtime. Game animals likely seen or heard are turkey,
grouse, deer, and squirrel (no hunting is allowed on the BRP).

For the NE access, turn off the BRP ramp at the NC-191 jct (sign for I-
26), and immediately turn L to park at gated entrance of FR-479M. Access
the *MST* by walking back and up the BRP access road to the R at an embankment. It follows a tunnel of rhododendron, passes through a gated fence of
the North Carolina Arboretum, and at 0.5 mi curves L. Here is a former park-

ing area access, R, 125 ft to FR-479M. (An access to this point can be made by walking 0.3 mi on FR-479M from where you parked your car to a L turn to cross Bent Creek bridge for 0.1 mi.) Starting at the former access, ascend on switchbacks through rhododendron thickets and reach an old road at 0.4 mi. Jct with a gravel road at 1.7 mi; turn L. Leave the road and begin an ascent at 1.8 mi. Reach a crest at 2.4 mi and the W side of the BRP at 3.1 mi. Walnut Cove Overlook (2,915 ft) (mp 396.4) is on the E side of the BRP.

Ascend and skirt NW of Grassy Knob, but at 4.4 mi intersect with *Grassy Knob Trail* (USFS #338), Pisgah NF, which goes L 0.3 mi in an ascent to the top of the knob (3,318 ft) and R for 0.2 mi to FR-479M in the Bent Creek Experimental Forest. Pass through tall hardwoods and dense sections of rhododendron to reach Sleepy Gap and Overlook (mp 397.3) at 4.7 mi. To the R (SW) is 1.8-mi *Sleepy Gap Trail* (USFS #339). It descends to a network of trails in the Bent Creek Experimental Forest (see chapter 3, section 3).

Continue to ascend through hardwoods and laurel to the ridge top of Truckwheel Mtn and then descend to Chestnut Cove Gap and Overlook (mp 398.3) (3,035 ft) at 5.8 mi. From here begin a long descent that takes the trail away from the BRP. Cross a small stream at 6.3 mi and make a L turn on an old road at 6.8 mi. Cross Chestnut Creek at 7.1 mi. Ascend through dark passages of rhododendron and laurel to swing around the ridge of Cold Knob. In an ascent from a hollow reach FR-479 in Bent Creek Gap (mp 400.4) at 8.6 mi. (To the R, down the mtn, FR-479 goes to Lake Powhatan Rec Area [and campground], and a network of trails in the Pisgah NF. To the L [under the BRP bridge] the road becomes FR-5000 and descends to the North Mills River Rec Area [and campground] also in the Pisgah NF. A few yd up the access ramp from the BRP, on the R, is the trailhead for 1.8-mi *Bad Fork Trail* [USFS #323].) (See chapter 3, section 3.)

Cross FR-479 and curve away W from the BRP to ascend. At 8.5 mi are excellent views of the city of Asheville and Craggy Mtn. (Views are easier to notice if hiking N rather than S.) Reach the summit of Ferrin Knob after a long switchback, to the site of an old fire tower (4,064 ft) at 9.7 mi. Descend on a ridge through oak and locust to reach Beaver Dam Gap Overlook (3,570 ft) (mp 401.7) at 10.2 mi. Ascend and descend knobs among chestnut oak, maple, and wildflowers to reach Stoney Bald Overlook (3,750 ft) (mp 402.6) at 11.0 mi. Cross the BRP to Big Ridge Overlook (3,815 ft) (mp 403.6). Continuing to ascend among hardwoods, blueberry patches, mosses, and gold star, reach River Valley Overlook (4,085 ft) (mp 404.5) at 13.4 mi. Cross the BRP at Elk Pasture (also called Cutthroat Gap) (4,235 ft) (mp 405.5) at 14.6 mi for a jct with NC-151 (known as Pisgah Highway), R. (It descends to Candler for a jct with US-19/23/74.)

Climb to a plateau through large oaks with a dense understory. Reach the crest of Little Pisgah Mtn at 16.1 mi. (A side trail is R for 1.2 mi to Mt Pisgah [see below].) Continuing on the *Shut-in Trail* descend slightly to Buck Spring Gap parking area at 16.4 mi (4,980 ft). Across the parking space the *MST* continues with the *Buck Spring Trail* for 1.1 mi at arrive to Pisgah Inn. (*USGS-FS Maps:* Asheville, Dunsmore Mtn)

MT PISGAH AREA (mp 407–409)

The mile-high Mt Pisgah complex has a modern motel and dining hall at the 52-room Pisgah Inn. It is open by May 1 through October. There are sweeping views over the Pisgah NF that melt away toward South Carolina. Writer William G. Lord has said that "sleep is quiet as a moth's wing" at the inn. The area is part of the original 100,000-acre estate owned by the late George W. Vanderbilt. (George Weston, who was Vanderbilt's farm superintendent, built and opened the first inn in 1920. In the 1940s it fell into disrepair but was reopened in 1952 by Leslie and Leda Kirschner of New York. The current inn was opened in 1967 and operates under a concession contract with the NPS.) There is a svc sta, a picnic area, and a large (140 sites) campground for trailers and tents (no hookups), with water and flush toilets. Information: Pisgah Inn, PO Box 749, Waynesville, NC 28786; 704-235-8228 (usually open from April 1 to November 1). (*USGS-FS Maps:* Cruso, Asheville, Skyland, Dunsmore Mtn)

423- *Buck Spring Trail (1.1 mi); Mt Pisgah Trail (1.2 mi); Mt Pisgah*
425 *Campground Trail (1.0 mi); Frying Pan Mountain Trail (2.0 mi)*

LENGTH AND DIFFICULTY: 6.5 mi round-trip, combined, easy to strenuous

SPECIAL FEATURES: Mt Pisgah and Frying Pan Mtn vistas

TRAILHEADS AND DESCRIPTION: To hike the *Buck Spring Trail,* a national recreation trail, begin at a signboard at the NE corner of the Pisgah Inn parking lot. (There is a connection here for the *Buck Spring Trail* in the Pisgah NF [6.2 mi, USFS #104] and *Pilot Rock Trail* [3.6 mi, USFS #321]. Follow the easy trail through a natural garden of laurel banks and bluets [*Houstonia caerules*] and weather-formed chestnut oaks. At 0.7 mi jct R with the *Laurel Mountain Trail* [7.4 mi, USFS #121], which descends into the Pisgah NF.) At 1.0 mi visit the historic site of Vanderbilt's Buck Spring Hunting Lodge. Reach the Buck Spring Gap parking overlook at 1.1 mi (The *Shut-in Trail* begins on the N side of the parking area, and the *MST* follows both of these trails.)

Biltmore Estate®

Join us at Deerpark Restaurant for
our delicious buffet any day between
11:30 A.M. and 3:00 P.M. and receive
10% off our regular buffet price
for everyone in your party.

Certificate valid only at Deerpark through November 30, 1996.

To hike the *Mt Pisgah Trail* follow the paved access road N 0.2 mi to the Mt Pisgah parking area. Enter at the trail sign and into the Pisgah NF to begin a strenuous climb at 0.4 mi. After a rocky route to the summit (5,721 ft) reach an observation deck for panoramic views of the Pigeon River and the Blue Ridge range. Backtrack. An easy return to the Pisgah Inn is on the *Mt Pisgah Campground Trail* from the Mt Pisgah parking area. Descend, parallel W of the BRP, pass through the picnic area, and reach the campground at 1.0 mi. From the campground entrance gate there is a sign for the *Frying Pan Mountain Trail*. Ascend to Big Bald where azaleas, filbert, mountain ash, and leatherflowers (*Clematis viorna*) thrive. Reach Frying Pan Gap (4,931 ft, mp 409.6) at 1.3 mi. (The gap was named by pioneer livestock herders.) Follow FR-450 to the fire tower at 2.0 mi for panoramic views. Backtrack.

GRAVEYARD FIELDS OVERLOOK (mp 418.8)

LENGTH AND DIFFICULTY: 3.2 mi easy

TRAILHEAD AND DESCRIPTION: From the parking overlook examine the *Graveyard Fields Trail* design board. Enter a paved trail in the Pisgah NF and through a dense section of rhododendron to the Yellowstone Prong of the East Fork of the Pigeon River at 0.2 mi. Cross a bridge, turn R to view Second Falls, and return to the bridge, but keep R. (A section of the trail is planned for relocation.) Immediately jct R with the *Graveyard Ridge Trail* (USFS #356) that ascends 3.4 mi to Ivestor Gap (see chapter 3, section 3). Continue upstream among open places, near pools, and through grasses; jct at 0.6 mi with a return loop, but continue ahead another 0.5 mi to the scenic Upper Falls. Backtrack for a loop of 3.2 mi (including the round-trip distance to the Upper Falls). (The area received its name from moss-covered fallen spruce trunks and stumps that resembled a graveyard. The trunks were destroyed by a fire in November 1925 that burned 25,000 acres of prime timber.) (*USGS-FS Map:* Shining Rock)

DEVIL'S COURTHOUSE TRAIL (mp 422.4)   426

From the parking lot and signs (5,462 ft) follow the paved trail 0.1 mi toward the BRP tunnel and ascend on a steep but moderately difficult trail. At 0.3 mi jct L with a 0.1-mi spur to the *MST*. Turn R and reach the summit (5,720 ft) at a stone observation deck and disk directors at 0.4 mi. (According to the Cherokee Indian legend, Judaculla, a slant-eyed giant devil, had his legal chambers inside this mtn.) Views from this point are spectacular; on clear days you can see North and South Carolina, Georgia, and Tennessee. The SE side of the rock face is used by rock climbers. Backtrack. (*USGS-FS Map*: Sam Knob)

427 TANASEE BALD/HERRIN KNOB TRAIL (mp 423.5)

From the jct of the BRP and NC-215 go S on the BRP for 0.3 mi to the Courthouse Valley parking overlook (5,362 ft), L, and park at the second parking area. The trail begins at the SW corner behind a picnic table. Follow an unmarked, narrow (perhaps overgrown) trail under beech, fir, hawthorne, arrowwood, and birch. The ground cover is ferns, galax, and wood sorrel. Pass R of Tanasee Bald at 0.4 mi and turn R at a fork at 0.5 mi. After a few yd enter a natural summertime garden of fragrant wildflowers, birds, butterflies, and blueberries. At 0.7 mi climb steeply to the SW slope of Herrin Knob (5,720 ft), named for James P. Herren (correct spelling), a prominent timberman. This rocky bluff is naturally landscaped with laurel, orchids, and multiple moss species. Descend to BRP, mp 424.2, at 1.2 mi. Backtrack, or hike the BRP for 0.8 mi as a loop. (*USGS-FS Map*: Sam Knob)

428 GRASSY RIDGE TRAIL (mp 424.2)

The *Grassy Ridge Trail* (across the BRP from the *Tanasee Bald/Herrin Knob Trail*) begins on the R (N) side of the BRP at Mt Hardy Gap. (There is no designated parking place here.) Enter the forest in a dense stand of beech and yellow birch to climb rocky switchbacks on the N side of Mt Hardy. At 0.6 mi reach a faint trail, R, on open Fork Ridge. (Fork Ridge is in the Middle Prong Wilderness Area of the Pisgah NF with a number of bald areas.) Turn L up the ridge to a partially bald summit of Mt Hardy (6,110 ft) at 0.8 mi. (Formerly called Black Mtn, it was named in honor of Dr. James F. E. Hardy, Asheville Civil War physician, by the United Daughters of the Confederacy [UDC] in 1942.) Backtrack. (An old unmarked trail follows the ridgeline W through a fir/spruce forest with plush carpets of moss and wood sorrel for 1.1 mi to jct with an access trail to the *MST*. A left turn leads a few yd to Rough Butt Bald Overlook, mp 425.4. A turn R on the access trail leads 100 yd to the *Buckeye Gap Trail* [USFS #126].) (*USGS-FS Map*: Sam Knob)

429 BEAR PEN GAP TRAIL (mp 427.6)

The trailhead is at the SE corner of the parking lot (5,560 ft). It is only 0.1 mi within the BRP boundary, but it is an excellent access route to the *MST* and to an open grassy plateau with wildflowers at 1.3 mi in the Wet Camp Gap of the Nantahala NF (see chapter 16).

RICHLAND BALSAM TRAIL (mp 431.4)

At the Richland Balsam Overlook the BRP attains its highest point (6,053 ft). To hike the 1.4-mi round-trip trail, begin at the NW corner of the parking area and follow an interpretive sign. The trail runs through a damp Canadian-zone type of forest, chiefly of fir and spruce. (The Fraser fir has been devastated by the balsam woolly aphid in this area.) Other vegetation includes mountain ash, Rowan tree, birch, pin cherry, witherod, wood sorrel, golden moss, and blueberry. Reach the summit (6,292 ft) at 0.6 mi and return on the loop. (An old trail, *Lickstone Ridge Trail,* is heavily overgrown from the summit.) (*USGS-FS Map:* Sam Knob)

ROY TAYLOR FOREST TRAIL (mp 433.8)

This overlook (5,580 ft) has a 75-yd asphalt walk to an observation deck in honor of Congressman Taylor, a conservationist who said "Next to preservation of liberty and security, government's greatest responsibility is the stewardship of natural resources." (See chapter 2, sec. 2.)

WATERROCK KNOB TRAIL (mp 451.2)

A plaque here honors H. Getty Browning (1881–1966), a leader in the location of the North Carolina BRP route. From the parking area's E side, enter the paved trail (which becomes a rocky path) for a moderate climb to the summit (6,400 ft) at 0.6 mi. Here are superb views of the Smokies and Pisgah and Nantahala NFs. (A faint trail L of the summit follows the ridge for 2.5 mi to private Mt Lyn Lowery, and NE on the high Plott Balsams to Oldfield Top after another mi.) Some of the vegetation is fir, birch, gooseberry, bush honeysuckle, turtlehead (*Chelone lyonii*), meadow parsnip, and mountain lettuce (*Saxifraga micranthidifolia*). Views from the summit are panoramic. Backtrack. (*USGS-FS Map:* Sylva North)

BLACK CAMP GAP TRAIL (mp 258.2)

On the Heintooga Rd (a spur from Wolf Laurel Gap) drive 3.6 mi to the 66-yd trail R. It approaches a Masonic plaque, but its name is from the black ashes of a long-ago forest fire.

7. Great Smoky Mountains National Park

To conserve the scenery and the natural and historic objects and the wildlife therein...
—from an Act of Congress, April 25, 1916,
   establishing the National Park Service

One of the oldest uplands on earth, the magnificent Smokies cover 520,004 acres, of which 275,895 are in North Carolina, the rest in Tennessee. Authorized by Congress in 1926 and dedicated in 1940 by President Franklin D. Roosevelt, the Great Smoky Mtns National Park (GSMNP) receives more than 10 million visitors annually and is the nation's most heavily used national park. The property was not acquired easily. Initially, Congress did not appropriate federal funds for land purchase, and 85 percent of the proposed land was owned by timber industries, most of which were initially unwilling to sell. Although state legislatures appropriated funds and local fund-raising campaigns were widespread, it was not enough. The turning point came in 1928 when John D. Rockefeller Jr, donated $5 million. By the early 1930s Congress had appropriated another $3.5 million. Finally, after 14 years of negotiations (and some litigation) with 18 timber companies and the purchase of more than 6,000 separate tracts, the park became a reality; a former domain of the Eastern Cherokee would be preserved forever.

More than 70 percent of the luxuriant virgin forest had been cut by the timber companies prior to the land sales. Today the second-growth forests are maturing and blending in natural succession. Since 1966, the beginning of wilderness hearings about the Smokies, there has been public demand to protect the wilderness character. With this trend it is likely that the 50-mi North Shore road between Fontana Dam and Bryson City, promised by the NPS in 1943, will never be completed. (The road is also called Lakeview Drive and the Road to Nowhere.) Six mi have been constructed from Bryson City to Forney Ridge (also called Tunnel Ridge because the road dead-ends after passing through a tunnel). An editorial in the *Raleigh News and Observer*, March 12, 1987, stated that a US Senate bill to designate 90 percent of the park as wilderness (and compensate Swain County with $11 million for a broken promise) would be a "reasonable compromise between competing goals of public use and environmental preservation." In 1996 the state and national political attitude was even less friendly to wilderness designation. The future of a North Shore road remains controversial.

For the naturalist, the park is a paradise with more than 1,400 varieties of flowering plants, 130 species of trees, 205 mosses, and more than 2,000 fungi. There are more than 200 species of birds, 65 species of mammals, 38 species of reptiles, and 58 different kinds of fish. Because the park is a wildlife sanctuary, it is forbidden to disturb any of the plants or animals. The park has 10 developed campgrounds, 5 of which are in North Carolina. In addition to camping as a recreational activity, the park has 600 mi of streams for fishing. The park is famous for its hundreds of miles of trails for hiking, horseback riding, and cross-country skiing.

The highest mountain in the park is Clingmans Dome (6,643 ft), accessible within 0.5 mi by auto road or by hiking the *AT*. There are 16 other peaks that tower over 6,000 ft. Geologists estimate that the original peaks in the Smokies were over 15,000 ft in elev when formed 250 million years ago. It is to these high peaks and ridges and into the lower coves that more than 800 mi of hiking and horse trails (of which approximately 510 mi are in North Carolina) form a vast network of highly visible backcountry routes. The longest trail is the 69-mi *AT* from Fontana Dam to Davenport Gap, which follows the Tennessee/North Carolina state line from Doe Knob in the west to near the park boundary at NC-32. The second longest is the combined routes of the 41.8-mi *Lakeshore Trail* on the N shore of Fontana Dam. Only the trails on the North Carolina side of the park are described in this book.

During the 1930s the CCC operated 16 camps in the Smokies. As a result numerous trails were regraded from old RR grades or roads, and others were rerouted. Trail usage declined during the WW II years, but hiker and horse traffic has continuously increased since the 1960s. The increase has made permits and reservations necessary for those who stay overnight in the backcountry. By 1995 the impact of horse traffic was serious enough for park officials to consider closing the *Appalachian Trail* to horses. Damage was on more than half of the AT's nearly 70.0 mi through the park. In a news article in the *Asheville Citizen-Times*, March 6, 1995, the problems were addressed by Peter Williams, a Virginia Tech consultant. He outlined solution methods for both hikers and equestrians to work together for maintenance management.

There are a number of rules and regulations for hiking the backcountry; they are designed to protect both the quality of the natural environment and the quality of the backpacking experience. "It is our attempt to enable you and others to love this wild place without loving it to death," say park officials. Overnight trips require a free permit. Self-registration permits are allowed at any ranger station by following the posted instructions, but some campsites are rationed due to heavy use and require reservations. On the North Carolina side they are Upper and Lower Walnut Bottom (#36 and #37); Mt Sterling (#38); Lower Chasteen Creek (#50); Pole Road (#55); Bryson Place (#57); and Bone Valley (#83). Hikers must telephone the Backcountry Reservation Office (615-436-1231, Monday through Friday from 8 AM to 5 PM EST) to obtain permission. Also, all shelters are rationed. Reservations are recommended up to a month in advance. If desiring a detailed trail map of the park (which includes both Tennessee and North Carolina), purchase one from the visitor centers or call Great Smoky Mtns Natural History Association; 615-436-7318.

The following rules listed by the park are backcountry ethics: Maximum size of party is eight; only one consecutive night at a shelter and three at a campsite; campers must stay in designated sites of the itinerary; do not reserve more space than you intend to occupy; do not damage animal or plant life; carry out all food and trash; use toilet at least 100 ft from campsite (bury all solid waste); do not wash dishes or bathe with soap in a stream; use only wood that is dead and on the ground; practice minimum impact on campsites; no pets, motorized vehicles, or bicycles; no firearms or hunting of animals; feeding of wildlife is prohibited; and notify the ranger of a change in plans.

Bears are more prominent in the park than anywhere else in the state. Remain watchful for them and report all bear incidents to the ranger. The most dangerous bears in the park are the solitary males, but that does not mean a female (with or without her cubs) will not be aggressive. Because the bears are generally shy and secretive and have a keen sense of detecting people, the average hiker will probably not see them. The best way to avoid any bear problems is to avoid attracting them with food. Proper food storage is a necessity, so do not keep food in tents or sleeping bags and do store it in an odor-proof bag tied with a rope at least 4 ft from the nearest limb and 10 ft above the ground. Also, refrain from throwing any food to a bear or leaving food for the bear to eat. Bears are more likely to visit campsites and shelters from June to October.

For the purpose of grouping trail network areas, the descriptions begin in the NE with Big Creek and follow west to Cataloochee, Balsam Mtn, Smokemont, Deep Creek, North Shore, and Twentymile Creek.

ADDRESS AND ACCESS: The park has three visitor centers: Oconaluftee, 2.0 mi N of Cherokee on the Newfound Gap Rd (designated US-441 outside the park); Sugarlands, 2.0 mi SW of Gatlinburg; and Cades Cove, 12.0 mi SW of Townsend, Tenn. (The centers are open daily except December 25.) Headquarters address: GSMNP, 107 Park Hqs Rd, Gatlinburg, TN 37738; 615-436-1200; District Ranger Office, Box 4, Park Circle, Cherokee, NC 28719; 704-497-1902. Other addresses for the ranger stations are listed at the end of each park area introduction.

BIG CREEK AREA (Haywood County)

The Big Creek Area is the most northern corner of the park. The area comprises the Big Creek drainage from Balsam Mtn (SW), Mt Sterling (SE), Mt Cammerer Ridge (N), and Mt Guyot (W) along the state line. The area was logged in the early 1900s, and a logging town was established at Crestmont, the site of a CCC camp in the 1930s. The site is now Big Creek Campground, a developed fee camp of 12 campsites for tents only. It has flush toilets, grills, and tables. A pay telephone is nearby at the ranger station. Big Creek, which flows on the E side of the camp, is a good rainbow trout stream. Bear, rattlesnake, deer, raccoon, grouse, and squirrel are in the area. Spring wildflowers are prominent.

ADDRESS AND ACCESS: From I-40 at the state line at Waterville, take exit #451, cross the Pigeon River bridge, turn L on Waterville Rd (SR-1332), pass the Waterville Power Plant, and at 2.0 mi intersect with Old NC-284 Rd (SR-1397, also called Mt Sterling Rd). (It is 2.5 mi R to Davenport Gap and the AT at the state line; L the road passes through the Mt Sterling village and ascends to Mt Sterling Gap for a descent to the Cataloochee area after 16.0 mi.) Cross the road to the ranger station. Address: Big Creek Ranger Station, GSMNP, Star Route, Newport, TN 37821.

SUPPORT FACILITIES: There is a general store at the crossroads near the ranger station. Shopping centers, motels, and restaurants are in Newport, TN, 15.0 mi W on I-40.

Big Creek Trail (F, H)   434

LENGTH AND DIFFICULTY: 5.3 mi, moderate (elev change 1,375 ft)

CONNECTING TRAILS:

Swallow Fork Trail (4.0 mi, strenuous, elev change 2,180 ft) (F, H)   435
Low Gap Trail (2.5 mi, strenuous, elev change 1,240 ft) (F, H)   436
Gunter Fork Trail (4.1 mi, strenuous, elev change 2,430 ft) (F)   437
Camel Gap Trail (4.0 mi, moderate, elev change 1,611 ft) (F, H)   438

SPECIAL FEATURES: historic, waterfall

TRAILHEAD AND DESCRIPTION: From the ranger station follow the gated road 0.5 mi to the camping/parking area. *Big Creek Trail* goes to Walnut Bottom where the other four trail connections begin. Go R of the campground to a jeep road and go upstream of Big Creek. Pass Mouse Creek Falls (on the far L of the river) at 2.0 mi, and at 2.9 mi pass Brakeshoe Spring. Forest vegetation includes maple, oak, hemlock, butternut, rhododendron, phacelia, and ramps. Cross Flint Rock Cove Branch at 4.5 mi and jct with *Swallow Fork Trail*, L, at 5.0 mi, at the lower edge of Walnut Bottom. It is a former logging camp and now backcountry campsite #37. (*Big Creek Trail* ends at 5.3 mi upstream at Upper Walnut Bottom campsite #36, but the *Camel Gap Trail* begins here.)

The *Swallow Creek Trail* leaves Walnut Bottom and ascends dramatically to Pretty Hollow Gap. At 0.4 mi pass a spring, R. Ascend and follow an old RR grade for a short distance. At 0.9 mi cross Swallow Fork. Cross a number of small tributaries, the last of which is at 2.5 mi on the ascent. After another 0.5 mi make a switchback and ascend to Pretty Hollow Gap at 4.0 mi to jct with the *Mt Sterling Ridge Trail* and the *Pretty Hollow Gap Trail*. (The *Mt Sterling Ridge Trail*, L, goes 1.4 mi to jct with the *Mt Sterling Trail* and the Mt Sterling fire tower. To the R it goes 4.0 mi to Laurel Gap to jct with the *Balsam Mountain Trail*.)

The *Camel Gap Trail* joins the *Gunter Fork Trail* 0.8 mi from its origin at the end of the *Big Creek Trail* in Walnut Bottom (near Upper Walnut Bottom campsite #36). Follow the *Camel Gap Trail* straight ahead on an old RR grade along the N side of Big Creek. Turn sharply R from the creek at 3.2 mi (near the confluence with Yellow Creek). Ascend steeply and at 4.3 mi begin scenic views of the valley. Reach Camel Gap at the state line to jct with the *AT* at 4.9 mi. A loop can be made here, R, on the *AT* for 2.4 mi to *Low Gap Trail* described below.

The *Gunter Fork Trail* forks L from the *Camel Gap Trail*, crosses Big Creek, and ascends by cascades of Gunter Fork. At 2.3 mi cross the base of a major cascade that drops nearly 200 ft. At 2.5 mi leave the stream and ascend steeply on a ridge with laurel, rhododendron, oak, and hemlock where there are scenic views of the Big Creek Valley. Continue ascent in an evergreen forest and thick mossy duff. Arrive at the crest of the Balsam Mtn range and jct R and L with the *Balsam Mountain Trail*. (From here, R, it is 5.6 mi to the *AT* and Tricorner Knob. To the L it is 0.9 mi to Laurel Gap and jct with the *Mt Sterling Ridge Trail*.)

The *Low Gap Trail* leaves Big Creek at the lower end of the Walnut Bottom campsite (0.2 mi before the upstream end of *Big Creek Trail*). On the W side of

Big Creek turn R and parallel downstream with Big Creek. Pass R of an old cemetery at 0.4 mi, and at 0.8 mi leave the Big Creek area at the mouth of Low Gap Branch. Turn L upstream and cross the branch at 1.8 mi, the last water on the ascent to Low Gap and the *AT*. To the R it is 7.3 mi on the *AT* to Davenport Gap. Left it is 0.8 mi to the Cosby Shelter and another 1.6 mi to *Camel Gap Trail* in Camel Gap. (A loop of 12.0 mi back to Walnut Bottom is possible using *Camel Gap Trail*.) (*USGS Maps:* Cove Creek Gap, Luftee Knob, Waterville)

Baxter Creek Trail (F)   439

LENGTH AND DIFFICULTY: 6.2 mi, strenuous (elev change 4,142 ft)
CONNECTING TRAIL:
   Mt Sterling Trail (2.8 mi, strenuous; elev chang 1,952 ft) (F, H)   440
SPECIAL FEATURES: Mt Sterling (5,842 ft), scenic views

TRAILHEAD AND DESCRIPTION: From the Big Creek picnic area, cross the swinging bridge near the lower end of the picnic area, turn R upstream, and follow through a former area of old fields and homesites. With a cliff on the L and through rhododendron, veer away from Big Creek and ascend on the E side of Baxter Creek by 0.7 mi. Cross tributaries and after a final crossing of the streams turn W on a rocky slope. There are views of Big Creek and Pigeon River valleys, R, and Mt Cammerer ahead. Through a rocky section and among oak, maple, hemlock, and rhododendron, ascend steeply on switchbacks. At 4.0 mi reach Mt Sterling Ridge and ascend. By 4.5 mi spruce and fir become dominant. There is a spring at 5.8 mi. At 6.2 mi reach the summit of Mt Sterling to a grassy spot at rationed backcountry campsite #38. Here is a fire tower from which are spectacular views of Mt Cammerer (NW), Clingmans Dome (SW), Snowbird Mtn range and Max Patch (NE), and Mt Pisgah (SE). Backtack or use *Mt Sterling Trail*.

The NW trailhead of *Mt Sterling Trail* is here. It descends steeply and after 0.5 mi jct with *Mt Sterling Ridge Trail*, R. Continue to descend on an old road also used by equestrians. There are switchbacks at 1.5 mi, after which there are fewer conifers and more oaks and maple. At 2.3 mi jct with *Long Bunk Trail*, R. (It descends 3.7 mi to *Little Cataloochee Trail*.) Arrive at Mt Sterling Gap at Old NC-284 to a small parking area at 2.8 mi. Across the road is *Asbury Trail* (see *Cataloochee Divide Trail* ahead). It is 6.7 mi L (N) on Old NC-284 to the community of Mt Sterling and access to the Big Creek picnic area, L.

A loop can be made by taking the *Mt Sterling Ridge Trail* for 1.4 mi to *Pretty Holly Gap Trail*. Turn R (N) on *Swallow Fork Trail*, follow it 4.0 mi to *Big Creek Trail*, R (described above) for a return descent to the point of origin for a loop of 17.1 mi. (*USGS Maps:* Cove Creek Gap, Waterville)

CATALOOCHEE AREA (Haywood County)

In Cherokee, Cataloochee means "waves of mountains or ridges." This area has ridges, a picturesque valley, and a history of the model pioneering spirit of endurance and resilience. Descendants of the early settlers lived in the basin into the 1960s. Since then, they return each summer to special home-comings and dinner on the grounds at the chapel. A number of the original buildings are preserved by the NPS. An example is the Palmer Chapel, built in 1898. The drainage, like the Big Creek drainage, flows N into the Pigeon River, and except for the Cataloochee Creek that flows into Waterville Lake the basin is surrounded by mtn ridges. The Balsam Mtn range is on the W edge, Mt Sterling Ridge on the N, and the Cataloochee Divide on the S and E. Only two roads, one over Cove Creek Gap (SR-1395) and the other over Mt Sterling Gap (SR-1397), connect with the outside world. Plans by the NPS in the 1960s to construct a fast route from I-40 to the heart of the basin were only partially completed, and conservationists stopped a recreational devel-opment that would have destroyed the valley's peaceful character. The valley has a developed campground with flush toilets for tenting, and a ranger sta-tion is nearby. All trails in the area are horse/hiker trails except the *Asbury Trail* and *Boogerman Trail,* which are for hikers only. Fishing is popular in Cataloochee Creek. Flora and fauna are similar to the Big Creek Area.

ADDRESS AND ACCESS: On US-276 (on the W side of the bridge) before its jct with I-40 (exit 20) in Cove Creek, turn N on Little Cove Rd (SR-1331). (There may be a Cataloochee sign here.) Drive 1.3 mi and turn R on Old NC-284 Rd (SR-1395, also called the Cataloochee Rd). After 4.5 mi reach Cove Creek Gap, the park boundary. Descend 1.8 mi to a paved road, turn L, and after 2.7 mi bear L across the Cataloochee Creek bridge and jct with the Cataloochee Rd, R. (It is 7.0 mi to Mt Sterling Gap and another 7.0 mi to the Big Creek Ranger Station described above.) From the jct it is 0.7 mi on the paved road to the Cataloochee ranger station, R. Address: Cataloochee Ranger Station, GSMNP, Rte 2, Box 555, Waynesville, NC 28786.

SUPPORT FACILITIES: Shopping centers, motels, restaurants, and commer-cial campgrounds (some open all year) are in Maggie Valley, 6.5 mi S from Cove Creek on US-276 and W on US-19.

Mt Sterling Ridge Trail (F, H)

441 LENGTH AND DIFFICULTY: 5.4 mi, strenuous (elev change 1,950 ft)
CONNECTING TRAILS:
(Mt Sterling Trail)

(*Asbury Trail*)
(*Baxter Creek Trail*)
Long Bunk Trail (3.7 mi, moderate) (F, H)   **442**
(*Swallow Fork Trail*)
(*Pretty Hollow Gap Trail*)
(*Balsam Mountain Trail*)

SPECIAL FEATURES: Mt Sterling, spruce/fir forest

TRAILHEAD AND DESCRIPTION: The trail can be accessed from two directions. In the Cataloochee basin at the jct of the paved road and the graveled Cataloochee Rd (0.7 mi N of the ranger station), drive 7.0 mi N on the Cataloochee Rd to Mt Sterling Gap. The other access is 7.0 mi S on the same road (usually called Old NC-284 Rd) from the Big Creek ranger station to Mt Sterling Gap. In the gap, the trailhead of the *Asbury Trail* is SE and the *Mt Sterling Trail* goes W. On an old road ascend on the *Mt Sterling Trail* 0.4 mi to jct L with the rarely used *Long Bunk Trail*. At 0.7 mi begin switchbacks. Enter a spruce/fir forest, and reach the ridge top to the *Mt Sterling Ridge Trail* at 2.3 mi. (To the R is a 0.5-mi spur to connect with *Baxter Creek Trail*, backcountry campsite #38, and panoramic views from the Mt Sterling fire tower.) Continue along the ridge. Reach Pretty Hollow Gap and cross trails at 3.7 mi. *Pretty Hollow Gap Trail* goes 5.3 mi L, down the mtn to Cataloochee Rd, and the *Swallow Fork Trail* goes R 4.0 mi to join the *Big Creek Trail*. Continue on the ridge and pass Big Cataloochee Mtn (6,122 ft) on the S slope. Cross streamlets at 6.0 mi and 7.0 mi. At 5.4 mi the trail ends at a jct with the *Balsam Mountain Trail*, R and L. (Left it is 0.1 mi to the Laurel Gap Shelter and R it is 4.9 mi to the *AT*.) Backtrack, or make a 21.5-mi loop by using the *Balsam Mountain Trail*, R, to the *AT*, followed by *Gunter Fork Trail* and the *Swallow Fork Trail*. If turning L, a 23.9-mi loop can be made by using the *Balsam Mountain Trail*, the *Palmer Creek Trail*, and the *Pretty Hollow Gap Trail*. (*USGS Maps:* Cove Creek Gap, Luftee Knob)

Pretty Hollow Gap Trail (F, H)   **443**

LENGTH AND DIFFICULTY: 5.3 mi, strenuous (elev change 2,190 ft)

CONNECTING TRAILS:
Little Cataloochee Trail (5.2 mi, moderate) (F, H)   **444**
Palmer Creek Trail (3.3 mi, strenuous) (F, H)   **445**
(*Mt Sterling Ridge Trail*)
(*Swallow Fork Trail*)

SPECIAL FEATURES: pioneer history, wildlife

TRAILHEAD AND DESCRIPTION: On the Cataloochee Rd, 1.1 mi upstream from the ranger station, park near the trail sign at Palmer Creek. Hike up the road that parallels the scenic stream. At 0.8 mi jct R with the *Little Cataloochee Trail*.

(The *Little Cataloochee Trail* follows an old road alongside a creek 1.2 mi and reaches Davidson Gap at 1.8 mi. Pass through Noland Gap at 2.2 mi, cross Coggin Branch, and pass the foundations of what was once the Daniel Cook house [1856]. Cross Coggin Branch again and at 3.0 mi pass L of the Little Cataloochee Baptist Church [1889] with its tall belfry. Cross Little Cataloochee Creek and a bridge at 3.5 mi. At 4.2 mi pass R of the John Hannah cabin [1862] built of logs hewn on location. Ascend and jct with the rarely used *Long Bunk Trail*, L at 4.0 mi. [The *Long Bunk Trail* ascends 3.2 mi as a connector to the *Mt Sterling Ridge Trail*.] Continue on the dirt road and cross Dude Branch to terminate at Cataloochee Rd at 5.0 mi. It is 5.2 mi R on Cataloochee Rd to the ranger station.)

To continue on the *Pretty Hollow Gap Trail*, enter a partially cleared area at 1.3 mi and jct with the *Palmer Creek Trail* L. (The *Palmer Creek Trail* crosses Pretty Hollow Creek on a footbridge and begins an ascent. Named after pioneer settler and bear hunter Turkey George Palmer, the trail parallels the cascading trout stream. Poplar, maple, and hemlock tower over rhododendron, ferns, and trillium among rock formations. Cross Lost Bottom Creek at 1.1 mi and Beech Creek at 1.7 mi. Ascend through an oak-hickory forest with rhododendron to reach at 3.3 mi Balsam Mtn Rd. It is a one-way vehicle passage from Heintooga campground-picnic area to Round Bottom where it becomes two-way. To the L on the road it is 1.8 mi to N terminus of *Spruce Mountain Trail* and 0.7 mi R on the road to the S trailhead of *Balsam Mountain Trail*. Either trail can be used for connections with other trails to form long loops in rejoining the *Palmer Creek Trail* and *Pretty Hollow Gap Trail*.)

The *Pretty Hollow Gap Trail* goes ahead on the E side of Pretty Hollow Creek after its jct with *Palmer Creek Trail*. It passes heavily used Turkey George campsite #39 at 1.5 mi. Cross the stream three times and at 4.3 mi cross Onion Creek. Ascend through the narrow valley among hardwoods, but in the climb the forest becomes partly hemlock, then spruce-fir near the end of the trail. Arrive at the N terminus at 5.3 mi to a cross-trail jct with *Mt Sterling Ridge Trail*, R and L, and *Swallow Fork Trail* down the other side of Mt Sterling Ridge. Backtrack, or use *Mt Sterling Ridge Trail* R to other trails for a loop of 11.1 mi. If going L on *Mt Sterling Ridge Trail*, a loop of 12.3 mi can be made with 0.7 mi of the route on Balsam Mtn Rd. (*USGS-Maps:* Cove Creek Gap, Luftee Knob)

446 *Cataloochee Divide Trail (F, H)*
  LENGTH AND DIFFICULTY: 11.5 mi, moderate

SPECIAL FEATURES: scenic, historic

TRAILHEAD AND DESCRIPTION: The *Cataloochee Divide Trail* follows the Cataloochee Divide and is a ridge trail with a road access at either end. If beginning in the N, park at Cove Creek Gap on the Old NC-284 Rd (SR-1395) at the park boundary (see access directions in the introduction). Follow the sign and reach Panther Spring Gap and a spring at 2.0 mi. Jct R with the *McKee Branch Trail* at 4.6 mi. (To the L, on private property, is a short trail to Purchase Knob, 5,086 ft.) At 6.4 mi jct R with *Hemphill Bald Trail* where a water source is a few yd downhill. Ascend along the ridge and at 7.0 mi reach scenic Hemphill Bald (5,540 ft) with vistas of the Plott Balsam range, the highest point of the trail. Descend the Pine Tree Gap at 7.5 mi, ascend to the N side of Sheepback Knob, and reach Maggot Spring Gap at 9.0 mi. At Garrett Gap follow an old RR grade to reach Polls Gap at 11.9 mi and jct with the *Rough Fork Trail* and *Spruce Mountain Trail,* R. Here also is a connection with the BRP Heintooga Ridge Rd (2.4 mi S of the Balsam Mtn Campground).

The *Asbury Trail* begins R (N) at Cove Creek Gap. A foot trail, it is usually not maintained except by Boy Scout troops. Follow the trail 1.0 mi through a forest of white pine and hardwoods to Hogan Gap (where the incomplete new highway to I-40 ends), and after another 1.2 mi on the ridgeline of Whiteoak Mtn turn L on a spur ridge. Descend and ford Cataloochee Creek (2,474 ft), or go upstream 0.2 mi to cross the Cataloochee Rd bridge at 3.6 mi. Go R 0.2 mi, leave the road, R, after a horseshoe curve, and ascend to Scottish Mtn (4,287 ft) at 5.4 mi. Follow the park boundary to Mt Sterling Gap at 7.0 mi. From here the trail/road follows SR-1395 to Davenport Gap. (*USGS Maps:* Bunches Bald, Cove Creek Gap, Dellwood)

Caldwell Fork Trail (F, H)

453   *Rough Fork Trail* (6.5 mi, strenuous, elev change 2,380 ft) (F, H)

SPECIAL FEATURES: historic, fishing, "Big Poplars"

TRAILHEAD AND DESCRIPTION: The *Caldwell Fork Trail*, named after the valley's Caldwell families, begins 0.1 mi SW of the Cataloochee Campground, a good base camp. (The trail is also a horse trail; the route has wet and muddy sections.) Cross a footbridge and go upstream in a forest of hemlock, beech, birch, and rhododendron. At 0.8 mi jct L, with the *Boogerman Trail* near Den Branch. (The *Boogerman Trail* follows an old rough road built by Robert Palmer, who built his cottage on the mountainside, a clearing at 2.0 mi on the trail. Huge oak and poplar seen on this trail are there because Palmer never allowed logging. At 2.9 mi descend near Smoke Branch to return to the *Caldwell Fork Trail* at 3.8 mi.)

Continue on the *Caldwell Fork Trail*; cross the creek a number of times. At 2.8 mi jct with the returning *Boogerman Trail*, L, and after another 0.5 mi jct R with the *Big Fork Ridge Trail*. (The *Big Fork Ridge Trail* descends to the Caldwell Fork to cross on a footbridge and ascend on an old jeep road to the site of a former Caldwell Fork schoolhouse at 0.3 mi. It reaches the crest of the Big Fork Ridge at 1.2 mi and descends gradually to cross Rough Fork on a footbridge to jct with the *Rough Fork Trail* at 3.1 mi. Here is the gated Cataloochee Rd and parking area for the *Rough Fork Trail* N trailhead.) (It is 2.4 mi R on the road to the N trailhead of the *Caldwell Fork Trail* for a loop of 8.2 mi.)

On the *Caldwell Fork Trail* it is 0.1 mi from *Big Fork Ridge Trail* to jct with the *McKee Branch Trail*, L. (The *McKee Branch Trail* ascends 2.3 mi, steeply, to Purchase Gap on the Cataloochee Divide to the *Cataloochee Divide Trail* and the park boundary. This grassy horse trail route was used by the early settlers to get over the mtn to Maggie Valley.)

At 4.4 mi on the *Caldwell Fork Trail* jct with the *Hemphill Bald Tail*, L. (The *Hemphill Bald Trail* ascends for 0.4 mi before crossing a stream. At 1.9 mi, R, is a huge black cherry tree. Continue to ascend steeply to reach the *Cataloochee Divide Trail* at 3.0 mi.)

Ahead on the *Caldwell Fork Trail* cross Double Creek to Caldwell Fork backcountry campsite #41. Ahead enter a forest of tall hardwoods and exceptionally large "Big Poplars" to the R (similar in size to some seen in Joyce Kilmer Memorial Forest). Ascend gradually to the trail terminus at 6.5 mi and jct with *Rough Fork Trail*, L and R. (If turning R on the *Rough Fork Trail*, descend 1.5 mi to Big Hemlock backcountry campsite #40. Pass through a grove of large trees and at 2.0 mi arrive at a well-preserved log house (now a larger frame building), which was the original home of Jonathan Woody and his family in the 1860s. From here follow the NPS road downstream in a forest of rhododendron, birch, and white pine to the road gate and parking area. Another 2.4 mi on the road to the N trailhead of *Caldwell Fork Trail* is a loop of 11.1 mi. If taking the *Rough Fork Trail* L from the jct with the *Caldwell Fork Trail*, ascend steeply for the first 0.7 mi before joining an old RR grade that leads another 2.8 mi to a jct with the *Hemphill Bald Trail* in Polls Gap. Here is a connection with the BRP Heintooga Ridge Rd (2.4 mi S of the Balsam Mtn Campground and 6.2 mi N of the BRP.) (*USGS Maps:* Bunches Bald, Cove Creek Gap, Dellwood)

BALSAM MOUNTAIN AREA (Swain County)

The Balsam Mtn Ridge is the only ridge that connects the Smokies with the Blue Ridge Mtns. Much of the Heintooga Ridge area with its dark green forest of fir (balsam) and spruce can be seen from the BRP, but a special paved spur road, Balsam Mtn Rd, takes the visitor 9.0 mi into a section of the ridge. Wildlife is frequently seen, and wildflower species are numerous. The Balsam Mtn developed campground has 46 campsites, usually open from late May to late September. There are flush toilets and water but no hookups and no showers. (This is black bear habitat and food storage regulations are strictly enforced.) The 0.5-mi *Balsam Mountain Nature Trail* begins R, soon **454** after entrance. It descends into a forest of fir, birch, white snakeroot, and rhododendron. The Heintooga Picnic Area, 0.6 mi beyond the campground, has 41 picnic sites and a loop parking area. From here the easy *Flat Creek* **455** *Trail* begins at a gated access. Follow a sign to the Heintooga Overlook (5,335 ft) for exceptional vistas of the ridges and the Raven Fork drainage. Follow the trail through spruce, birch, and rhododendron for 2.6 mi to the Heintooga Ridge Rd. Along the way (at 1.8 mi) is a side trail, R, 0.2 mi to Flat Creek Falls. At the road it is 3.7 mi back (L) to the picnic area.

ACCESS: From BRP mp 458.2, turn onto Heintooga Rd (closed in winter) and go 8.4 mi to the Balsam Mtn Campground. From there it is 0.6 mi to the Heintooga Picnic Area. (A one-way, 14.0-mi gravel road continues N to Round Bottom where the road becomes open for two-way traffic as Straight Fork Rd. No trucks, buses, or trailers; gates are closed at night.)

SUPPORT FACILITIES: All provisions and other camping needs are 20.0 mi in either direction of the BRP to Cherokee or Maggie Valley.

Polls Gap Trail (4.5 mi) (F, H); Spruce Mountain Trail (2.0 mi) (F, partly **456-** *H); Balsam Mountain Trail (10.1 mi) (F, H)* **458**

LENGTH AND DIFFICULTY: 16.6 mi, moderate to strenuous (elev change 1,650 ft)

SPECIAL FEATURES: spruce/fir forest groves, geology

TRAILHEADS AND DESCRIPTION: Although separated by 2.5 mi of road, the descriptions of these three trails are combined because they cover the same major ridgeline and have similar terrain and vegetation. Begin the *Polls Gap Trail* at Polls Gap, 2.4 mi S of the Balsam Mtn Campground. (At the parking area, *Rough Fork* and *Hemphill Bald* trailheads are R.) Ascend in a mixed hardwood and spruce/fir forest to the highest point of the trail, the top of Cataloochee Balsam Mtn (5,970 ft) at 1.7 mi. Descend and ascend to Chiltoes Mtn at 3.2 mi. At 4.4 mi is Spruce Mtn backcountry campsite #42 (5,480 ft), which has a spring in an area of red spruce. Ahead it is 0.1 mi to the end of *Polls Gap Trail* and jct with *Spruce Mountain Trail*, R and L. To the R the trail ascends among Fraser fir, red spruce, and blackberry bushes to the top of Spruce Mtn at 1.0 mi and the site of the dismantled Spruce Mtn fire tower. Backtrack to the jct with *Polls Gap Trail* and descend on the other 1.0 mi of the *Spruce Mountain Trail*. It drops steeply near a cascading stream on a rocky treadway and switchback. The forest is both hardwoods and conifers. Exit at the N side of Balsam Mtn Rd (5.9 mi E on the road to the picnic area). Otherwise, turn R (W) on Balsam Mtn Rd to continue a hike to *Balsam Mountain Trail*.

To reach the *Balsam Mountain Trail* follow Balsam Mtn Rd N for 2.5 mi to Pin Oak Gap (8.3 mi from Heintooga Picnic Area). Jct with *Palmer Creek Trail* along the way at 1.8 mi. Ascend to Ledge Bald (5,184 ft), descend to Beech Gap at 2.3 mi, and jct L with the *Beech Gap Trail,* a 3.0-mi steep and rough access trail from Balsam Mtn Rd in Round Bottom. Ascend in a spruce/fir forest to Balsam High Top (5,640 ft) at 3.6 mi; descend to Laurel Gap at 4.1 mi. A shelter (space for 14) and a spring are here. At 4.3 mi jct R with the *Mt Sterling Ridge Trail.* At 5.2 mi jct R with the *Gunter Fork Trail.* Continue on a generally level trail in a mixed forest with ferns, mosses, and moosewood. Pass L of Luftee Knob (6,200 ft) and reach Mt Yonaguska at 9.5 mi. Turn R and reach the *AT* and Tricorner Knob Shelter at 10.1 mi. (See chapter 5 for other trails connecting with the *AT*.) (*USGS Maps:* Luftee Knob, Mt Guyot)

SMOKEMONT AREA (Swain County)

The developed Smokemont Campground is on the NE side of the Oconaluftee River and at the confluence of the Bradley Fork in the Oconaluftee Valley. Oconaluftee in Cherokee means "by the riverside." The watershed for this area begins from the high elev near Newfound Gap (N), Mt Kephart (N), Hughes Ridge (NE), Richland Mtn (N), and Thomas Divide (NW). The campground has 150 sites (no hookups and no showers) and three group camps. (This is black bear country and food storage regulations are strictly enforced.) Fully operational from mid-April to the first of November, 35 sites are open all year. There are flush toilets, water, and sewage disposal. Its crowded condition during the summer and fall months is not suitable for a hiker who loves solitude and remoteness, but it is a good base camp for hikers with such multiple interests as hiking, fishing, and horseback riding. Reservations for the campground are made through MISTIX (May 1 to October 31). Call 800-364-CAMP for information and reservations. Hitchhiking is forbidden on Newfound Gap Rd.

ACCESS: From Cherokee drive N 5.7 mi on US-441 (becomes Newfound Gap Rd at the park boundary) to entrance, R.

SUPPORT FACILITIES: Cherokee has shopping and service centers, motels, commercial campgrounds, restaurants, and a hospital.

Hyatt Ridge Trail (F, H)   459

LENGTH AND DIFFICULTY: 4.5 mi, strenuous (elev change 2,065 ft)
CONNECTING TRAILS:

Enloe Creek Trail (3.6 mi, moderate) (F, H)   460
Beech Gap Trail II (2.9 mi, strenuous, elev change 1,860 ft) (F, H)   461
Beech Gap Trail I (2.5 mi, strenuous, 2,010 ft) (F, H)   462

SPECIAL FEATURES: wildlife, old-growth forest

TRAILHEAD AND DESCRIPTION: From the Smokemont Campground drive 3.0 mi S on Newfound Gap Rd and turn L on a 0.6-mi connector road (across the Oconaluftee River) to Big Cove Rd. Turn L and follow Big Cove Rd (which becomes Straight Fork Rd) 11.0 mi to the trailhead, L. (A hiking route to this point is 13.4 mi from the campground on *Hughes Ridge Trail, Enloe Creek Trail,* and *Beech Gap Trail.*) Follow an old trail beside Hyatt Creek and begin a steep ascent at 1.0 mi. Reach Low Gap at 1.9 mi and jct L with the *Enloe Creek Trail,* L.

(The *Enloe Creek Trail* descends on an old trail into a beautiful forest of tall hardwood and hemlock. At 1.0 mi reach Raven Fork, a stream of rapids that would be impossible to cross after heavy rains. Enloe Creek rationed backcountry campsite #47 is near the creek. Continue ahead and after 0.4

mi the treadway is rocky and sometimes muddy from horse traffic. Pass a number of small waterfalls and arrive at Enloe Creek at 2.0 mi. Ford the creek [difficult after heavy rains] and at 2.7 mi ascend on switchbacks to jct with *Hughes Ridge Trail* at 3.6 mi. [To the R it is 4.7 mi to the *AT*, and L it is 7.9 mi to Smokemont Campground.])

Continue on the *Hyatt Ridge Trail*, ascend steeply on the ridge, and jct at 3.6 mi with *Beech Gap Trail II*, R.(*Beech Gap Trail II* descends, steeply in sections, on an E slope of a hardwood forest. After 2.9 mi it emerges at Straight Fork Rd and parking area in Round Bottom. Turn L, wade a cement autoford and turn L off the road to ascend *Beech Gap Trail I*. It ascends through a hardwood forest, crosses Thumber Branch at 1.1 mi, and jct with *Balsam Mountain Trail* in Beech Gap at 2.5 mi. [It is 2.3 mi R to Balsam Mtn Rd, and 2.0 mi L to jct with *Sterling Rigde Trail*.])

The *Hyatt Ridge Trail* continues to ascend and ends at the McGhee Spring backcountry campsite #44 at 4.5 mi. Backtrack. (The continuation of *Hyatt Ridge Trail* and the adjoining *Raven Fork Trail* at McGhee Spring have been deleted from the park's trail inventory.) (*USGS Maps:* Bunches Bald, Luftee Knob, Smokemont)

463 *Hughes Ridge Trail (F, H)*
LENGTH AND DIFFICULTY: 12.6 mi, strenuous (elev change 3,340 ft)
CONNECTING TRAILS:
   (*Chasteen Creek Trail*)
   (*Enloe Creek Trail*)
   (*Bradley Fork Trail*)
   (AT)
SPECIAL FEATURES: historic, wildflowers
TRAILHEAD AND DESCRIPTION: Enter the Smokemont Campground, turn R, and park. Ascend to the chapel and go straight. After 0.1 mi bear L from a horse trail. Turn L again at 0.6 mi with another horse trail jct. At the third horse trail jct at 1.0 mi, bear R. After the switchbacks begin, the route is more certain. Ascend in a forest of white pine, dense rhododendron, laurel, and oak on a climb of Hughes Ridge. Cross a small stream at 4.4 mi, the last source of water on the ridge. At 7.4 mi jct L with the *Chasteen Creek Trail* (which descends 4.0 mi to the *Bradley Fork Trail*). After another 0.5 mi jct R with the *Enloe Creek Trail*. (The 3.6-mi *Enloe Creek Trail* is the only trail route from the Smokemont area to the Raven Fork drainage. It is described below.) Continue to ascend on a wide treadway, mainly on the W side of the ridge in an oak/hickory forest with sections of galax and winter-

green ground cover. At 10.4 mi jct L with the N trailhead of *Bradley Fork Trail* (which descends 7.3 mi to the Smokemont Campground). Ascend and descend into a number of low gaps and reach Pecks Corner Shelter and spring at 12.4 mi. Ascend another 0.2 mi to the *AT* and the state line with Tennessee. (*USGS Maps:* Mt Guyot, Smokemont)

Bradley Fork Trail (F, H) 464

LENGTH AND DIFFICULTY: 7.3 mi, strenuous, elev 2,840 ft)
CONNECTING TRAILS:
   Chasteen Creek Trail (4.0 mi, strenuous, elev change 2,300 ft)   **465**
   Smokemont Loop Trail (3.8 mi, moderate, elev change 1,240 ft)   **466**
   Cabin Flats Trail (1.1 mi, easy)   **467**
   (*Hughes Ridge Trail*)
   Dry Sluice Gap Trail (4.1 mi, strenuous, elev change 2,540 ft)   **468**
   (*Grassy Branch Trail*)
   (*AT*)
SPECIAL FEATURES: wildlife, wildflowers, historic
TRAILHEAD AND DESCRIPTION: On entry to the campground, turn L and go to a gate at the end of the campground. *Bradley Fork Trail* makes connections to provide two circuits from the campground (5.7 mi and 15.4 mi). Pass a hemlock grove at 1.0 mi; at 1.1 mi jct with *Chasteen Creek Trail,* R.

(The *Chasteen Creek Trail* begins as a gated jeep and horse road-trail. After 0.1 mi reach Lower Chasteen Creek rationed backcountry campsite #50, and at 0.8 mi is a waterfall in a forest of poplar, oak, and maple. Parallel the creek and leave the road at 2.3 mi. Pass backcountry campsite #18, and ascend steeply on switchbacks to jct with *Hughes Ridge Trail* at 4.0 mi. (A loop of another 7.4 mi can be made by taking the *Hughes Ridge Trail,* R, to the campground.)

Continue upstream. At 1.6 mi jct with *Smokemont Loop Trail,* L. (It returns to the campground. Cross Bradley Fork on a footbridge, ascend on the lower slopes of Richland Mtn in a hardwood forest mixed with pine, hemlock, and laurel. At 1.7 mi reach the ridge crest, then descend on a long switchback before lesser curves. Return to the stream area, and pass L of the Bradley cemetery at 3.4 mi. Enter a white grove to join a svc rd, cross Bradley Fork on an old cement bridge to the campground. *Bradley Fork Trail* is 0.3 mi L for a loop of 5.7 mi.)

On the *Bradley Fork Trail* pass a waterfall at 2.5 mi, and cross the creek twice on road bridges before a turnaround at 4.0 mi. Ahead (N) begins *Cabin Flats Trail. Bradley Fork Trail* turns R and ascends on Long Ridge to a number of outcroppings with scenic views. Cross Taywa Creek twice, at 5.0 mi and 5.6 mi. Ascend steeply on switchbacks to reach *Hughes Ridge Trail* at 7.3 mi. (It is 2.2 mi L on *Hughes Ridge Trail* to the *AT*, and 8.1 mi R to Smokemont Campground for a loop of 15.4 mi.)

(On the *Cabin Flats Trail* go upstream, cross Bradley Fork and Tennessee Branch before a jct with the *Dry Sluice Gap Trail* [formerly *Richland Mountain Trail*] at 0.5 mi. Ahead, 0.6 mi farther the trail ends at Cabin Flats backcountry campsite #49. Backtrack.)

(*Dry Sluice Gap Trail* ascends and crosses a bridge over Tennessee Branch at 0.1 mi. It crosses the branch three more times and a number of drains to 0.9 mi. Ascend steeply and jct L with *Grassy Branch Trail* at 2.8 mi. Begin an easier gradient and pass views of Thomas Divide L [W]. At 4.1 mi jct with the *AT* near Dry Sluice Gap. [It is 0.4 mi L to the spectacular views of the *AT*'s Charlies Bunion and L 4.4 mi farther to Newfound Gap Rd.]) (*USGS Maps:* Mt Guyot, Smokemont)

469 *Kephart Prong Trail (F, H)*

LENGTH AND DIFFICULTY: 2.0 mi, easy

CONNECTING TRAILS:

470   *Grassy Branch Trail* (2.5 mi, strenuous, elev change 1,740 ft) (F, H)

471   *Sweat Heifer Creek Trail* (3.7 mi, strenuous, elev change 2,270 ft) (F)

SPECIAL FEATURES: historic, wildflowers, fish hatchery

TRAILHEAD AND DESCRIPTION: From the Smokemont Campground drive up Newfound Gap Rd for 3.7 mi to the parking area, R. Cross the Oconaluftee River on a road bridge and pass the remains of an old CCC camp. Cross Kephart Prong on a footbridge and pass the site of an old fish hatchery. Cross Kephart Prong three more times and reach the overused Kephart Prong Shelter (accommodates 14) at 2.0 mi. (The shelter is named for Horace Kephart [1862–1931], authority on mtn lore and author of *Our Southern Highlanders*. Mt Kephart, NW of the shelter, was named in his honor October 3, 1928.) Go R from the shelter to follow the *Grassy Branch Trail,* which parallels Kephart Prong. At 0.8 mi it crosses Lower Grassy Branch near a cascade and crosses the stream again at 2.1 mi. Here are views of the valley and Thomas Divide beyond. Jct with the *Dry Sluice Gap Trail* at 2.5 mi. (On the *Dry Sluice Gap Trail* it is 1.3 mi L to the *AT*; R it descends 3.3 mi to the *Bradley Fork Trail*.)

Left of the shelter is the infrequently used *Sweat Heifer Creek Trail*. Cross a small stream, ascend, and reach an old RR grade at 0.7 mi. Ascend and cross a cascading stream at 1.8 mi and leave the old RR grade at 2.1 mi.

Wildflowers are prominent in a hardwood forest. Reach the *AT* at 3.7 mi. It is 1.7 mi L to Newfound Gap Rd. (The trail's name may derive from the practice of driving livestock over the mtn on the Oconaluftee Turnpike, a wagon road constructed in 1931.) (*USGS Maps:* Clingmans Dome, Mt Guyot, Smokemont)

Kanati Fork Trail (F)   472

LENGTH AND DIFFICULTY: 2.9 mi, strenuous (elev change 2,110 ft)
CONNECTING TRAIL:
   (*Thomas Divide Trail*)
TRAILHEAD AND DESCRIPTION: From Smokemont, drive 3.9 mi NW to the trailhead parking area, L (0.2 mi beyond the *Kephart Prong Trail* described above). Follow the graded trail, parallel to Kanati Fork, in a cove of oak, poplar, maple, and birch. At 1.0 mi leave the cove and ascend on switchbacks in a section of hemlock. Cross a small branch at 1.6 mi and ascend in a forest with rhododendron and laurel to jct with the *Thomas Divide Trail* at 2.9 mi. (To the R it is 1.8 mi to the Newfound Gap Rd, and L it is 10.9 mi to the *Thomas Divide Trail* access in Deep Gap. See the Deep Gap Area descriptions below.) (*USGS Maps:* Clingmans Dome, Smokemont)

Newton Bald Trail (F, H)   473

LENGTH AND DIFFICULTY: 5.4 mi, strenuous (elev change 2,900 ft)
CONNECTING TRAILS:
   Mingus Creek Trail (3.0 mi, moderate) (F, H)   **474**
   (*Thomas Divide Trail*)
SPECIAL FEATURES: wildlife, wildflowers
TRAILHEAD AND DESCRIPTION: Park across the road from the Smokemont Campground entrance. Hike up the Newfound Gap Rd (NW) for 0.1 mi, and turn L on an old woods road. At 0.3 mi join a horse trail, turn R, but leave it, R, at 0.5 mi on a well-graded trail. Ascend steadily on a N slope. Cross a small stream in an area of hemlock and rhododendron at 2.7 mi and another water source at 3.0 mi. Jct L with the *Mingus Creek Trail* at 4.7 mi on the ridge crest of Newton Bald (5,142 ft). Descend slightly and jct with the *Thomas Divide Trail* at 5.4 mi. (The *Thomas Divide Trail* goes R 5.2 mi to Newfound Gap Rd, and L for 9.7 mi to Deep Creek Campground.) (*USGS Map:* Smokemont)

DEEP CREEK AREA (Swain County)

Some of the longest and most scenic trails on the E side of the Smokies are on the ridges and valleys that run N-S in or near the Deep Creek basin. The historic area was home to the Cherokee, who were visited by William Bartram in the early part of the nineteenth century; a Civil War battle; sites of CCC camps; and one of the park's first trails in the 1930s. The *Thomas Divide Trail* is on a high E border, the central *Deep Creek Trail* weaves through a lush valley to its watershed near Newfound Gap, and the *Noland Divide Trail* is a lofty W-side route to Clingmans Dome. The famous conservationist Horace Kephart had a permanent camp, Bryson Place, on Deep Creek, and the stream remains a popular route (eight separate backcountry campsites) for hikers, equestrians, and fishermen. With the exception of the *Noland Divide Trail,* all access routes to the trails begin at the *Deep Creek Trail* parking area N of the Deep Creek Campground. The developed campground has 108 sites for tents or RVs (no hookups and no showers), flush toilets, water, and a large picnic area. The campground opens in mid-May and closes in early November. The ranger station is R after the entrance gate. Waterfalls, cascading streams, outcroppings, and virgin forests provide an area of natural beauty. Unfortunately, the wild hogs wallow in the springs and destroy plant life and the food chain for the native animals. The proposed *MST* is routed through this area from Clingmans Dome to include all of the *Fork Ridge Trail*; parts of *Deep Creek Trail, Sunkota Ridge Trail,* and *Thomas Divide Trail*; and all of *Newton Bald Trail* for 26.4 mi to Smokemont. The E trailhead and 25.0 mi of the 42.7-mi *Lakeshore Trail* are also in the Deep Creek jurisdiction.

> ADDRESS AND ACCESS: From downtown Bryson City on US-19, turn N at the Swain County Courthouse, turn R after crossing the bridge, and follow the signs for 3.0 mi. Address: Deep Creek Ranger Station, GSMNP, 970 Park Rd, Bryson City, NC 28713. All inquiries about the trails in the areas of Noland Creek, Forney Creek, and Chambers Creek should also be directed to the Deep Creek ranger.

> SUPPORT FACILITIES: Bryson City has motels, restaurants, shopping centers, commercial campgrounds, and a hospital.

475 Deep Creek Trail (F, H)

LENGTH AND DIFFICULTY: 14.3 mi, strenuous (elev change 2,820 ft)
CONNECTING TRAILS:

476   *Indian Creek Trail* (3.9 mi, moderate to strenuous, elev change 1,555 ft) (F, H)
477   *Loop Trail* (1.0 mi, easy) (F, H)

Martin's Gap Trail (2.7 mi, moderate) (F, H) **478**
Pole Road Creek Trail (3.2 mi, strenuous, elev change 1,800 ft) (F, H) **479**
Fork Ridge Trail (5.1 mi, strenuous, elev change 2,880 ft) (F) **480**

SPECIAL FEATURES: Bryson Place, virgin hemlock, fishing

TRAILHEAD AND DESCRIPTION: From the Deep Creek Campground and ranger station upstream is a jct L with the *Noland Divide Trail,* and a few yd farther N is the 0.3-mi *Juney Whank Falls Trail.* After the parking area begins the *Deep Creek Trail.* Hike upstream on the gated *Deep Creek Trail.* Pass Tom Branch Falls, R, at 0.4 mi, and pass at 0.7 mi the jct R with the S trailhead of *Indian Creek Trail* and *Thomas Divide Trail.* At 1.7 mi pass Jenkins Place, a former homesite, and jct R with the 1.0-mi *Loop Trail* (which connects with the *Sunkota Ridge Trail* described below). At 2.2 mi reach the end of the road and continue on the *Deep Creek Trail* upstream. Follow the sign to an old jeep road that will follow the E side of the creek up and down spur ridges of Sunkota Ridge for 3.9 mi. Pass the first backcountry campsite, Bumgardner Branch #60, at 3.0 mi. At 3.5 mi is a view of the valley from the highest spur on the route. A spring is 0.2 mi ahead. At 4.3 mi pass McCracken Branch backcountry campsite #59, and Nicks Nest Branch backcountry campsite #58 at 5.8 mi. Emerge at Bryson Place backcountry campsite #57 at 6.0 mi. It is a large grassy area with tables, a horse hitching rack, and a clear stream at the campsite entrance. Before crossing the stream, L, at 200 ft, is a memorial plaque on a millstone honoring Horace Kephart, the "dean of American campers." On the R (E) of the campsite is jct with the *Martin's Gap Trail.*

(The well-graded *Martin's Gap Trail* ascends through a beautiful forest of hardwood, white pine, rhododendron, and fern beds for 1.5 mi to Martin's Gap [3,430 ft] on the Sunkota Ridge and a cross-trail jct with the *Sunkota Ridge Trail.* [To the L the *Sunkota Ridge Trail* goes 4.8 mi to jct with the *Thomas Divide Trail,* and 4.3 mi R to jct with the *Deep Creek Trail.*] Descend rapidly on the E side of the ridge on switchbacks to cross Indian Creek for a sharp R turn downstream at 2.4 mi. Arrive at the end of a road at 2.7 mi and follow it to its entrance gate at Deep Creek Rd at 7.3 mi. Along the way at 5.8 mi pass a 1.0-mi spur trail [*Indian Creek Loop Trail*] R that leads to *Sunkota Ridge Trail* and to the *Deep Creek Trail* at Jenkins Place. At 6.1 mi pass R of the *Stone Pile Gap Trail* S terminus, and at 6.6 mi pass the 50-ft Indian Creek Falls. Jct at Deep Creek Rd at 6.6 mi for a loop distance of 13.3 mi back to the parking area.)

From Bryson Place slightly descend to the riverbank and proceed upstream to pass Burnt Spruce backcountry campsite #56 at 6.3 mi. Jct with

Pole Road Creek Trail, L, at 6.7 mi. (The *Pole Road Creek Trail* crosses a high scenic footbridge over Deep Creek and serves chiefly as a wide connecting trail between Deep Creek and Noland Divide. It crosses Pole Road Creek a number of times, but after 2.0 mi ascends steeply in a forest of tall hardwood and hemlock to reach Upper Sassafras Gap. Here it jct with the *Noland Divide Trail* at 3.3 mi. It is 3.7 mi N to Clingmans Dome Rd and 7.9 mi S to the Deep Gap Campground.)

Continuing upstream, the *Deep Creek Trail* passes Pole Road backcountry campsite #55 at 6.8 mi, and Nettle Creek backcountry campsite #54 at 7.7 mi. Pass banks of Fraser sedge (*Cymophyllus fraseriana*) at 8.1 mi, and ascend R of a precipice at 9.3 mi. At 10.3 mi jct L with *Fork Ridge Trail*. Poke Patch backcountry campsite #53 is here.

(The *Fork Ridge Trail* crosses the footbridge over Deep Creek and ascends steeply but soon more gradually. At 0.9 mi is a scenic view of Clingmans Dome Rd area and Bearpen Ridge. Enter a dense laurel grove at 1.5 mi, one of a number of groves on the route through a forest of maple, birch, cucumber tree, and flame azalea. At 2.6 mi are huge hemlocks. After the final switchback on the ridge at 3.8 mi, the trail turns R on a more moderate grade, passes seeps and springs [the last one at 5.0 mi], and exits at a small parking area on Clingmans Dome Rd at 5.1 mi. [To the L it is 3.5 mi to Clingmans Dome parking area, and R it is 3.5 mi to Newfound Gap Rd.] Across the road it is 125 ft to the *AT*.)

On the *Deep Creek Trail* ascend upstream on a bank and parallel the creek until veering R at 10.5 mi. Ascend steeply in a forest dominated by hemlock before a final ascent on switchbacks that leads to the N terminus at the Newfound Gap Rd and parking area at 14.3 mi. (From here, on the road, it is 1.6 mi L [N] to Newfound Gap and 1.6 mi R [S] to the *Thomas Divide Trail*.) (*USGS Maps:* Bryson City, Clingmans Dome)

481 *Thomas Divide Trail (F, partly H)*
LENGTH AND DIFFICULTY: 13.8 mi, strenuous (elev change 3,310 ft)
CONNECTING TRAILS:
482 *Stone Pile Gap Trail* (0.9 mi, easy) (F, H)
483 *Deeplow Gap Trail* (6.0 mi, moderate) (F, H)
484 *Sunkota Ridge Trail* (8.6 mi, strenuous, elev change 2,640 ft) (F, H)
   (*Indian Creek Trail*)
   (*Newton Bald Trail*)
   (*Kanati Fork Trail*)
SPECIAL FEATURES: wildlife, wildflowers, historic

TRAILHEAD AND DESCRIPTION: From the N side of the Deep Creek Camp-ground take *Deep Creek Trail* and after 0.7 mi turn R at the *Indian Creek Trail*, cross Indian Creek on a bridge, and at 0.5 mi turn R at *Stone Pile Gap Trail*. Cross Indian Creek again and begin ascending on a gradual grade to Stone Pile Gap at 0.9 mi and the intersection with *Thomas Divide Trail*. At 3.4 mi turn sharply R. In a forest of hardwood, laurel, and flame azalea reach a knob at 5.0 mi. Descend to a spring at 5.2 mi and to a jct with the *Deeplow Gap Trail*, R and L, in Deeplow Gap at 5.8 mi.

(The *Deeplow Gap Trail* descends R [E] on the S slope of Thomas Divide and enters a cove to cross Little Creek at 0.5 mi. At 0.8 mi it reaches the base of 75-ft Little Creek Falls. It crosses the creek, follows a series of switchbacks down to a road, and jct with the 0.6-mi *Cooper Creek Trail* at 1.7 mi. Because **485** the park has closed the *Mingus Creek Trail* to the Newfound Gap Rd at Min-gus Mill and the Oconaluftee Visitor Center, use the *Thomas Divide Trail* to the *Newton Bald Trail* for an alternate route. The *Deeplow Gap Trail* goes L [W] from the *Thomas Divide Trail* and descends on switchbacks to a hemlock grove where it joins an old road at 1.8 mi. It crosses Georges Branch at 2.1 mi and Indian Creek on a bridge to jct with *Indian Creek Trail*, R and L. A 12.0-mi loop could be made L on the *Indian Creek Trail* to the parking area at the Deep Creek Campground.)

Continue ahead on the *Thomas Divide Trail* to jct R with the W end of the *Newton Bald Trail* at 8.9 mi. (The *Newton Bald Trail* goes E 5.4 mi to Newfound Gap Rd at Smokemont.) At 9.4 mi jct with the N terminus of the *Sunkota Ridge Trail*, L.

(The *Sunkota Ridge Trail* descends moderately and in some places gently for 4.8 mi to Martin's Gap where it intersects with *Martin's Gap Trail*. Along the way it is on the E slope for almost the entire distance. It has trail banks of trail-ing arbutus, gentian, ferns, and wood betony. Sassafras, flame azalea, and striped maple make up part of the understory. Intermittent springs are at 3.5 mi and 4.3 mi. [In Martin's Gap the *Martin's Gap Trail* goes R 1.5 mi to jct with the *Deep Creek Trail*, and L 5.8 mi to jct with Deep Creek Rd.] From Martin's Gap the trail begins on the E slope among rhododendron and laurel and fol-lows the slope and the ridgeline for another 3.8 mi before beginning a steep descent of 1.2 mi to reach its S terminus and jct with a connector trail, the *Indian Creek Loop Trail* at 9.8 mi. Left it is 0.5 mi to the *Indian Creek Trail*; R it is 0.5 mi to the *Deep Creek Trail* at Jenkins Place. From here it is 1.7 mi back to the parking area at the Deep Creek Campground, a total loop of 21.1 mi using part of the *Thomas Divide Trail* and all of the *Sunkota Ridge Trail*.)

Continue on the *Thomas Divide Trail*. (Although not known just where on this historic ridge, the Cherokee Tsali hid his family from the infamous "Trail of Tears" in 1838 somewhere "on the far side of this ridge." It was William Thomas (1805–93) who located him and requested he turn himself in to the US Army for accidentally killing a soldier. Thomas had been adopted by the Cherokee chief Yonaguska as his son, Little Will, near the age of 12. At the death of Yonaguska in 1839, Thomas became the Cherokee chief. Because Thomas was a white citizen he was able to represent the Cherokee in their land claims. His strong leadership before Congress had a permanent influence on the US government establishment of the Qualla Reservation that adjoins part of the park. Thomas Divide is named in his honor. See introduction and *Tsali Trail* in chapter 2.) Descend to Tuskee Gap and ascend to Nettle Creek Bald at 11.8 mi. At 12.2 mi jct R with the *Kanati Fork Trail* (which descends 2.9 mi to Newfound Gap Rd). At 13.0 mi arrive at Turkey Flyway (5,160 ft) for general views of Mt Kephart and Richland Mtn. Follow a narrow ridge to Beetree Ridge before descending to a gap at 13.6 mi. Ascend to Newfound Gap Rd and trail terminus at 13.8 mi. (On the highway it is 0.3 mi R to an overlook and parking area, and 1.7 mi N to jct L with the N trailhead of the *Deep Creek Trail*.) (*USGS Maps:* Bryson City, Clingmans Dome, Smokemont)

486 *Noland Divide Trail (F, H)*

LENGTH AND DIFFICULTY: 11.6 mi, strenuous (elev change 4,155 ft)

CONNECTING TRAILS:
(*Noland Creek Trail*)
(*Pole Road Creek Trail*)

SPECIAL FEATURES: vistas and botanical variation

TRAILHEAD AND DESCRIPTION: This hiker/horse trail has the highest elev change of any trail on the E side of the Smokies. (Other high elev changes are *Baxter Creek Trail* and *Forney Creek Trail*.) An outstanding display of flora is on the trail, ranging from the tulip tree of the valley to the pine, laurel, and blueberries of the dry ridges and spruce/fir near the trail's highest point. Trillium, galax, asters, ferns, orchids, berries, and lichens are present in great variation. Begin at the sign to the L (W) of the Deep Creek Campground. (To **487** the R of the trailhead and near the parking area is 0.3-mi *Juney Whank Falls Trail*, a scenic 90-ft cascade.) Follow an easy route for 0.4 mi. Ascend to a ridge, but leave it at 1.2 mi to follow an exceptionally steep slope to the headwaters of Juney Whank Branch at a long switchback. Reach Beaugard Ridge at 3.5 mi with vistas of Bryson City and the Alarka Mtns, S, in the Nantahala National Forest. Curve R and ascend steeply on the crest to springs at 4.9 mi, the last water source up the trail. Slope R of Coburn Knob and arrive at the ridgeline of Noland Divide. Reach Lower Sassafras Gap at 7.2 mi and Upper Sassafras Gap at 7.9 mi at cross-trails. (The N end of *Noland Creek Trail* is L; it leads S 9.0 mi to North Shore Rd. On the R the W end of *Pole Road Creek Trail* descends E 3.2 mi to jct with the *Deep Creek Trail*.) Continue the ascent on Noland Divide and at 11.0 mi turn R on a road that emerges at Clingmans Dome Rd at 11.6 mi. (To the L on the paved road it is 1.5 mi to Clingmans Dome parking; to the R it is 2.0 mi to *Fork Ridge Trail*, described above.) (*USGS Maps:* Bryson City, Clingmans Dome)

NORTH SHORE AREA (Swain County)

This large area covers the rugged drainage pattern of Noland, Forney, Hazel, and Eagle Creeks, which flow S and SW into Fontana Lake from the crest of the Smokies. Hiking trails ring its borders and provide an interconnecting web within the loop. The spectacular outer loop of 79.5 mi includes 29.6 mi of the AT from Clingmans Dome to the *Lakeshore Trail* near Fontana Dam, 38.6 mi of the *Lakeshore Trail* to 10.3-mi *Forney Creek Trail*, and a final mi of *Forney Ridge Trail* to the Forney Ridge parking area at Clingmans Dome. Such a loop is one of the most scenic, adventuresome, and unforgettable in the Smokies backcountry. Many of the trails in this area were built by the CCC in the 1930s, and others are old roads used by generations past. A historic area, its lush coves were once populated, predominantly by employees of mining and lumber companies. There are many memories about this vast and beautiful forest and its people. The famous writer of mountain lore, Horace Kephart, author of *Our Southern Highlanders* (published in 1913), lived in a mining cabin in the remote hollow of Little Fork for three years in the early part of the century. Uninhabited since 1943, when the Little Tennessee River was impounded by the Fontana Dam TVA project, the area still has more than 20 cemeteries. They have such family names as Proctor, Bradshaw, Mitchell, Posey, and Welch, and such locations as Fairview and Bone Valley. Of the nearly 600 families removed from the project, more than half were from this area. Descendants are provided regular, free boat access (the easiest route) by the NPS. But the bitter controversy of a North Shore rd and a designated wilderness area continues. "The public value of that park for wilderness preservation is more important than a road for those cemetery people," said Ronald J. Tipton of the Wilderness Society in Atlanta. "We won't give up," said Fred Chandler of the North Shore Cemetery Association. "We got children and grandchildren, they won't give up." (See the introduction to this chapter.)

ACCESS: From downtown Bryson City at the Swain County Courthouse, drive N on Everette St, cross the bridge, and go straight on what becomes Fontana Rd (SR-1364) to the park gate after 3.0 mi. Continue ahead on what is also called Lakeview Dr, 5.0 mi to *Noland Creek Trail* access, L, and another 0.7 mi to an access parking area at the tunnel for all North Shore trails. The W access is at the Fontana Dam parking area where a hike of 1.1 mi on the *AT* (across the dam) connects with the *Lakeshore Trail* for an access to all other trails. Another vehicle access is at Forney Ridge parking area at Clingmans Dome. (Clingmans Dome Rd is closed in winter.) (See chapter 5 for *AT* access points.) Address for the ranger who supervises the trails for Noland, Forney, and Chamber Creeks area is the same as for Deep Creek.

SUPPORT FACILITIES: Bryson City has motels, restaurants, shopping centers, commercial campgrounds, and a hospital. Fontana Village has limited seasonal services; call 704-498-2211 for information. A TVA campground with hot showers is at the base of Fontana Dam, open April 15 to October 1. Boat access, rentals, and shuttle service are available at Fontana Marina off NC-28, 1.6 mi E of Fontana Village.

488 *Noland Creek Trail (F, H)*

LENGTH AND DIFFICULTY: 10.0 mi, strenuous (elev change 2,440 ft)
CONNECTING TRAILS:

489   *Springhouse Branch Trail* (8.3 mi, moderate) (F, H)
    (Noland Divide Trail)
    (Pole Road Creek Trail)

SPECIAL FEATURES: fishing, wildlife, wildflowers

TRAILHEAD AND DESCRIPTION: Follow the access description above, from Bryson City. At the trail sign ascend a few ft to the gate and then descend 0.2 mi to where the trail divides. Left it is 1.0 mi to the edge of Fontana Lake and Lower Noland Creek backcountry campsite #66. Backtrack, and pass under the highway bridge. Cross Noland Creek on a bridge, and follow upstream in a forest of hardwood, hemlock, and rhododendron. At 1.7 mi reach the mouth of Bearpen Branch and the Bearpen Branch backcountry campsite #65, L. Cross Noland Creek on a bridge at 3.0 mi and follow the R bank. Arrive in Solola Valley, an area once inhabited, at 4.0 mi. At 4.2 mi reach the mouth of Springhouse Branch and the Mill Creek backcountry campsite #64.

(The *Springhouse Branch Trail* begins L and ascends gradually up Mill Creek. Evidence of old farms [rock piles] is noticeable at 0.5 mi. Cross Mill Creek at 0.6 mi. Pass a spring at 2.4 mi and reach the crest of Forney Ridge in Board Camp Gap at 2.8 mi. Jct here with the *Forney Ridge Trail*, R. It is

5.4 mi R to Clingmans Dome Rd.) *Springhouse Branch Trail* continues another 5.5 mi to Forney Creek.

After leaving Solola Valley pass a waterfall and cross Noland Creek at 5.0 mi. Ford the stream twice more and ascend. At 5.4 mi is Jerry Flats backcountry campsite #63, and at 6.5 mi is Upper Ripshin backcountry campsite #62. Cross Upper Ripshin Branch at 7.2 mi and immediately cross Noland Creek again. Ascend to and cross Sassafras Branch at 8.6 mi and turn R at the trail fork. To the L is Bald Creek backcountry campsite #61. Ascend steeply by Sassafras Branch for 0.4 mi and turn R to approach Sassafras Gap, the trail's terminus at 9.5 mi and cross-trail jct. (It is 3.4 mi L on the *Noland Divide Trail* to Clingmans Dome Rd and 1.5 mi L on the road to *Forney Ridge Trail*. At Sassafras Gap the *Pole Road Creek Trail* descends 3.2 mi to the *Deep Creek Trail*.) (*USGS Maps:* Bryson City, Clingmans Dome, Noland Creek, Silers Bald)

Lakeshore Trail (F, H)   490

LENGTH AND DIFFICULTY: 41.8 mi, easy to strenuous

CONNECTING TRAILS:

Tunnel Bypass Trail (1.6 mi, easy) (F, H)   491
Goldmine Loop Trail (2.1 mi, moderate) (F, H)   492
Whiteoak Branch Trail (2.0 mi, easy) (F, H)   493
(*Forney Creek Trail*)
(*Hazel Creek Trail*)
Jenkins Ridge Trail (6.5 mi, strenuous) (F, H)   503
(*Eagle Creek Trail*)
Lost Cove Trail (3.1 mi, strenuous) (F, H)   505
(*AT*)

SPECIAL FEATURES: former homesites, secluded, fishing

TRAILHEAD AND DESCRIPTION: Access is described above in the North Shore Area. (Boat access is possible at Chambers Creek, Pilkey Creek, Hazel Creek, and Eagle Creek at normal lake level. The trail follows a contour generally between 1,800 and 2,500 ft. An infrequent brown blaze and trail signs help guide the hiker in and out of scores of ridge spines, coves, and cross-trails. The forest is predominantly hardwood with a mixture of pine, hemlock, rhododendron, laurel, and azalea. Leucothoe and ferns are commonplace near the many streams. Wildflowers are profuse and include orchids, cohosh, arbutus, cardinal flower, turtlehead, and dwarf iris. In some of the former settlements are vines, shrubs, and domestic flowers. Bear, wild hog, deer, fox, beaver, grouse, and turkeys are among the wild animals. Songbirds are prominent.

At the tunnel parking area, the "Portals to the Wilderness," there is a choice of trail directions. The direct route is through the tunnel. A longer route is the 1.6-mi *Tunnel Bypass Trail*. It is accessed across the road from the parking area. (It ascends among evergreens and after 0.5 mi jct with the 2.1-mi *Goldmine Loop Trail*, L. The *Tunnel Bypass Trail* continues R, crosses Tunnel Ridge, and descends to partially follow Hyatt Creek headwaters before rejoining *Lakeshore Trail*.) (The *Goldmine Loop Trail* descends S to Tunnel Branch and mainly in a hardwood forest. After curving W it has backcountry campsite #67 near an old homesite at 1.1 mi. It crosses Hyatt Branch and after 0.3 mi follows Goldmine Branch before ascending to a ridge for its route to a jct with *Lakeshore Trail* at 2.1 mi. [It is 1.0 mi E to *Lakeshore Trail* parking area.])

After passing through the tunnel on the *Lakeshore Trail* pass the W jct with the *Tunnel Bypass Trail*, L, and the *Goldmine Loop Trail* at 1.0 mi, also on the L. Follow a graded treadway and stay L of an unnamed trail. Pass L of *Whiteoak Branch Trail* at 2.2 mi. (The 2.0-mi *Whiteoak Branch Trail* is a shortcut, from this point, to *Forney Creek Trail*. The trail ascends, crosses Gray Wolf Creek, and ascends to cross a ridge saddle among conifers. It descends, crosses Whiteoak Branch, and jct with *Forney Creek Trail*.)

Continue on the *Lakeshore Trail* through former homesite areas with former cleared forests. Cross a bridge over Gray Wolf Creek, pass a cemetery, and at 3.0 mi jct with *Forney Creek Trail* (which follows an old RR grade for most of its 10.3 mi to *Forney Ridge Trail*, 1.0 mi from Clingmans Dome Rd). Here the *Lakeshore Trail* turns L and runs jointly with a former section of *Forney Creek Trail*. After less than 0.2 mi cross an old bridge over Forney Creek to Lower Forney backcountry campsite #74, a popular campsite with both hikers and fishermen. Under a forest cover of white pine and hemlock the campsite has picnic tables and a pit toilet.

Follow a gradual and graded ascent to curve the multiple ridge spines of Pilot Knob. At 5.2 mi is a minor gap and jct with old trails; go straight. Descend slightly, cross small Jenny Branch at 6.1 mi and Gunter Branch at 6.7 mi. At 7.2 mi cross a small branch in a small glade by old walls made by early settlers. For the next 2.0 mi pass through a former settlement with evidence of old homesites. There are some switchbacks among open and mixed hardwood forests. Cross Welch Branch at 8.8 mi. (The McClure cemetery is on a gentle knoll, R, on a 0.1-mi side trail at 8.9 mi.)

Chambers Creek is crossed on a footbridge at 9.6 mi and to the right is backcountry campsite #98. Nearby is a chimney from an old homesite. From this area Fontana Lake is visible for the next 5.0 mi, the best views for the entire route. At 11.7 mi pass an old homesite chimney and arrive at Kirkland Branch backcountry campsite #76. A bridge over the creek is at 11.9 mi. Pass an old rusty antique car at 13.1 mi, one of a number of similar relics seen on trails in the North Shore Area. Where side trails jct at 15.0 mi go straight on an old road. Cross a park bridge over Pilkey Creek at 16.0 mi and follow the creek briefly. From here the trail ascends a ridge for a descent to Clark Branch and backcountry campsite #77, near an old homesite at 16.6 mi. Pines and hardwoods shade the area, and S of the campsite it is only 0.2 mi to the edge of Fontana Lake.

From here the trail continues around ridge spines, rocky sections, and crosses cascading Chesquaw Branch at 18.6 mi. The next backcountry campsite, #81, is at Mill Creek, near an old homesite with a chimney at 21.4 mi. Ascend a ridge, dip to a cove, and reach a gap on Welch Ridge at 22.6 mi. Begin a descent to Hazel Creek Valley. At the mouth of Hazel Creek is a long cove of Fontana Lake and a svc rd from the lake's edge upstream by Hazel Creek. Cross the Hazel Creek bridge at 24.2 mi. The *Lakeshore Trail* descends 0.3 mi to the lake boundary and Proctor backcountry campsite #86. (To the L it is 0.2 mi to the Lower Bunkhouse, a cottage from which the park staff monitors the area.) This area was formerly the community of Proctor. The *Lakeshore Trail* makes a radical change in direction here from W to NE. Follow upstream of Hazel Creek to a long curve called the Horseshoe. At 27.1 mi, R, pass Sawdust Pile backcountry campsite #85. Arrive at a jct L (formerly *Sugar Fork Trail*) and stream confluence at 28.7 mi. Sugar Fork backcountry campsite #84 is R. Here at Sugar Fork, the site of a copper mine in the late nineteenth century, is the former pioneer settlement of Medlin. A preeminent mountaineer and devoted friend of Horace Kephart, Granville Calhoun, lived here.

(At Sugar Fork the *Hazel Creek Trail* continues R on the svc rd for 11.8 mi and ends at a jct with the *Welch Ridge Trail*, 1.8 mi from the *AT*. Up the creek for 2.0 mi is a jct with 3.6-mi *Cold Spring Gap Trail*, R. It leads to 5.8-mi *Bear Creek Trail*, R, which leads to *Forney Creek Trail*. A turn R here for 0.5 mi places the hiker at the *Lakeshore Trail*, and only 0.3 mi from the E terminus of the *Lakeshore Trail*. This route, E or W, would reduce the distance of a hike from the E terminus at the tunnel of the *AT* at Fontana Dam by 14.1 mi. The shorter route, however, has more diversity in elevation. An example is the climb to nearly 5,000 ft in elevation on Welch Ridge.)

To continue W on the *Lakeshore Trail* from Sugar Fork follow parallel with the stream. At 29.2 mi, the Higdon cemetery is L, and at 30.4 mi, R, is the mouth of Little Fork. (Kephart lived more than three years, beginning in 1904, in a simple cabin up in this remote hollow.) Arrive at Pickens Gap at 31.0 mi. Here is a jct R with 6.5-mi *Jenkins Ridge Trail*. (It ascends steeply through hardwoods, white pine, and laurel to Woodward Knob at 1.1 mi and Cherry Knob at 2.2 mi. After a short easy passage on the ridge, it ascends again straight up the ridge to Haw Gap at 3.7 mi. Here are wildflowers, briers, and blackberries. Descend gradually to curve around the W side of the ridge for a rock-hop of an Eagle Creek tributary. Ascend gradually among yellow birch, beech, and rhododendron to jct with the *AT* in a grassy ridge sag. A turn L on the *AT* is 0.4 mi to Spence-Field, a grassy area with outstanding views, and a jct L with *Eagle Creek Trail*.)

Continuing on the *Lakeshore Trail*, descend and follow a beautiful and challenging Pinnacle Creek downstream. Rock-hop or wade the stream at least 14 times before reaching Pinnacle Creek backcountry campsite #88, R, at 33.3 mi. Ahead the treadway may be wet and wading necessary at the stream crossings. At 35.0 mi cross the first of three log bridge crossings. Here is the jct with *Eagle Creek Trail*, R. (To the R the *Eagle Creek Trail* ascends 7.9 mi to the *AT*.) To the L on the *Lakeshore Trail* continue to Lost Cove at 36.0 mi. At the Lost Cove backcountry campsite #90, the *Lakeshore Trail* continues L and the *Lost Cove Trail* goes R. (The *Lost Cove Trail* is the only trail connecting directly from North Shore Area to the Twentymile Creek Area. It gradually ascends by Lost Cove Creek, crossing it at least a dozen times. At 1.4 mi is Upper Lost Cove backcountry campsite #91, L. The trail ascends on switchbacks after leaving the stream and ends at Sassafras Gap on the *AT* at 3.1 mi. Ahead on an old rd begins 4.7-mi *Twentymile Creek Trail*. Left on the *AT* it is 0.3 mi to a 0.1-mi spur for Shuckstack fire tower and fantastic views. Farther down the mtn on the *AT*, it is 4.5 mi to the S side parking lot across Fontana Dam. On the *AT* R, it is 0.9 mi to rationed Birch Spring Gap Shelter.) From here pass through a lush cove and begin a steep ascent on a footpath before a level contour in and out of ridge spines of Snaken Ridge and Shuckstack Ridge. The forest is mixed with pines and hardwoods and scattered sections of rhododendron and ferns. At 41.5 mi the footpath ends and an abandoned road begins. The *Lakeshore Trail* jct with the *AT*, R and L, at 41.8 mi. Follow the *AT* L on the paved road 1.1 mi to cross Fontana Dam and reach the parking area. (*USGS Maps:* Noland Creek, Tuskeegee, Fontana Dam, Thunderhead Mtn, Cades Cove)

494 *Forney Creek Trail (F, partly H)*
    LENGTH AND DIFFICULTY: 10.3 mi, strenuous (elev change 4,030 ft)
    CONNECTING TRAILS:
      (*Lakeshore Trail*)
495   *Bear Creek Trail* (5.8 mi, strenuous, elev change 3,100 ft) (F, H)

TRAILHEAD AND DESCRIPTION: Follow the Lakeshore Dr and the *Lakeshore Trail* descriptions above. (Another access is 1.1 mi on the *Forney Ridge Trail* from Clingmans Dome Rd.) After 4.0 mi (2.9 mi if using the tunnel route) on the *Lakeshore Trail* jct with *Forney Creek Trail*, R. (To the L the *Forney Creek Trail* crosses a bridge to Lower Forney backcountry campsite #74 and the lake after 0.2 mi. The *Lakeshore Trail* continues from the campsite W to Fontana Dam.) Go upstream on the *Forney Creek Trail* on an old RR grade for the first 9.0 mi. It crosses the creek at least 15 times; wading or rock-hopping is necessary. At 0.6 mi jct L with the *Bear Creek Trail* (formerly *Jumpup Ridge Trail*).

(The *Bear Creek Trail* follows an old RR grade near Bear Creek. At 2.8 mi is backcountry campsite #75 at Poplar Flats. From here the trail ascends on curves and switchbacks to the top of Jumpup Ridge at 5.0 mi. The trail terminates on Welch Ridge [4,890 ft] at a jct with *Welch Ridge Trail*. [To the R it is 6.5 mi on the *Welch Ridge Trail* to Silers Bald and the *AT*. To the L it runs 0.8 mi to jct with *Cold Spring Branch Trail* and scenic High Rocks.])

Reach the site of an old CCC camp with scattered old farm artifacts at 2.8 mi. Here is CCC backcountry campsite #71. After crossing the creek, jct with the *Springhouse Branch Trail* (formerly the *Bee Gum Branch Trail*), R. (The *Springhouse Branch Trail* ascends by Bee Gum Branch to leave it at 2.3 mi in a cove. Reach the S end of *Forney Ridge Trail* at 5.5 mi. From here the *Forney Ridge Trail* is 5.7 mi to Clingmans Dome Rd, described below.)

Continue on the *Forney Creek Trail* through cove hardwood and a mixture of rhododendron, hemlock, and white pine. At 4.0 mi arrive at the *Jonas Creek Trail*, L, and Jonas Creek backcountry campsite #70. (The *Jonas Creek Trail* fords Forney Creek and follows an old RR grade up Jonas Creek for 1.5 mi where it becomes a path. After crossing Jonas Creek and Yanu Branch begin switchbacks that end at 2.6 mi. Jct with the *Welch Ridge Trail* on Welch Ridge at 4.2 mi. To the L it is 4.8 mi on the *Welch Ridge Trail* to its S terminus at *Cold Spring Gap Trail*. To the R it is 2.5 mi to Silers Bald and the *AT*.)

Continue on the *Forney Creek Trail*, crossing Forney Creek frequently, and reach the mouth of Huggins Creek and Huggins backcountry campsite #69, L, at 5.3 mi. From here the old RR grade gradually ascends on switchbacks to cross other streams such as Buckhorn Branch and Little Steeltrap Creek. After the old RR grade ends at 9.0 mi, follow an old timber road for 0.5 mi to cross Forney Creek for the last time. Ascend on a footpath with a number of seeps in a damp forest of hemlock, fir, and beech. Terminate the trail at 10.0 mi to jct with the *Forney Ridge Trail*, R and L.

(To the L the *Forney Ridge Trail* ascends 1.0 mi on a rough and rocky footpath in a spruce/fir forest to the parking area on Clingmans Dome Rd. A **498** 0.5-mi spur trail, *Clingmans Dome Bypass Trail*, to the AT goes L 0.1 mi before reaching the parking area. To the R the *Forney Ridge Trail* descends 4.6 mi to jct with the *Springhouse Branch Trail* described above. At 0.7 mi it reaches Andrews Bald, which received its name from mountain-born Andres (not Andrews) Thompson, who built a hand-hewn cabin here in the 1850s. Owning 1,280 acres here and elsewhere in the vicinity, he became a prosperous cattle raiser. A scenic area with views of the Little Tennessee River Valley and beyond, the bald's grassy beauty is enhanced in late June when a concentration of flame azalea and catawba rhododendron is in bloom. Ferns, wildflowers, spruce, and fir assist in the display. Descend to gaps and lower knobs to reach *Springhouse Branch Trail* at 4.6 mi. (The *Springhouse Branch Trail* runs 2.8 mi to the *Noland Creek Trail*, described above.) Reach a scenic area at 6.5 mi and slope R of the knob to jct with *Springhouse Branch Trail*, also described above. From here it is 5.5 mi to the *Forney Creek Trail*, a potential loop of 17.3 mi. (*USGS Maps:* Clingmans Dome, Noland Creek, Silers Bald)

499 *Hazel Creek Trail (F, H)*

LENGTH AND DIFFICULTY: 11.8 mi, strenuous (elev change 3,580 ft)

CONNECTING TRAILS:

(*Lakeshore Trail*)

500 *Bone Valley Trail* (1.8 mi, easy) (F, H)

501 *Cold Spring Gap Trail* (4.1 mi, strenuous, elev change 2,450 ft) (F, H)

502 *Welch Ridge Trail* (7.3 mi, moderate) (F, H)

SPECIAL FEATURES: trout fishing, sites of former communities, High Rocks, Hall Cabin

TRAILHEAD AND DESCRIPTION: The *Hazel Creek Trail*, widely known for its trout fishing, is in the heart of the North Shore Area. Access to it is by other trails or by boat on Fontana Lake. The latter provides the quickest (approx 6.0 mi) route from the Fontana Boat Dock; the AT route from Clingmans Dome Rd is the shortest (4.6 mi) trail route. From the lake trailhead, follow the park jeep road, reach Proctor backcountry campsite #86 at 0.3 mi, and jct R with the *Lakeshore Trail*, described above. (It is 25.2 mi on the *Lakeshore Trail* to its E terminus.) The two trails are adjoined for 4.6 mi to the mouth of Sugar Fork, L. *Hazel Creek Trail* begins at the mouth of Sugar Fork. It is *Lakeshore Trail* from the lake to that point. Along the way on the old RR grade, after about 1.0 mi, is the vanished timber community of Proctor. During its thriving history it is estimated that its population was more than 1,000. At 3.3 mi is Sawdust Pile backcountry campsite #85. Another backcountry campsite at 4.9 mi, Sugar Fork #84, is where the *Hazel Creek Trail* begins R and the *Lakeshore Trail* continues to Eagle Creek.

(The *Lakeshore Trail* passes the confluence of Little Fork at 1.7 mi. Horace Kephart lived up Little Fork while doing his research on mountain culture. Ascend to Pickens Gap at 2.4 mi. Ahead is *Lakeshore Trail*, which descends to jct with *Eagle Creek Trail*. To the R begins *Jenkins Ridge Trail*, which ascends 6.5 mi to the *AT* at Spence Field.)

Continue up the old road, close to Hazel Creek, and reach Bone Valley backcountry campsite #83 at 5.6 mi. Here is the jct, L, with *Bone Valley Trail*. (The *Bone Valley Trail* begins across the bridge and gently ascends by the Bone Valley Creek. Ford the stream four times en route to the Crate Hall Cabin, a national historic site, at 1.7 mi. The Hall cemetery is N of the cabin. Ruins of other buildings are nearby. Backtrack.)

Continue following Hazel Creek upstream and jct R with the *Cold Spring Branch Trail* at 6.8 mi. (The *Cold Spring Branch Trail* ascends by the stream mainly on an old RR grade and passes evidence of former homesites, particularly at 0.5 mi and 1.0 mi. The old RR grade ends at 3.0 mi and trail steepness increases. It reaches Cold Spring Gap at 3.6 mi, the trail's E terminus, and the S terminus of 7.3-mi *Welch Ridge Trail*. [After ascending 0.5 mi on the *Welch Ridge Trail* there is a 0.4-mi spur trail, sharply L, to scenic rocks described below. The *Welch Ridge Trail* passes *Bear Creek Trail* on its way to ending at a jct with the *AT*, 0.2 mi E of Silers Bald.])

On the *Hazel Creek Trail* at 5.3 mi reach Calhoun Place backcountry campsite #82 (named in honor of Josh Calhoun, former homesteader). At 7.1 mi the trail ends and a footpath begins. Also here is the confluence of Proctor and Hazel Creeks. Begin a grade increase and wade or rock-hop the creek a number of times. Pass the old Cascades campsite at 10.0 mi. At 10.8 mi begin a steep incline to reach Welch Ridge at 11.8 mi. The trail ends at a jct with the *Welch Ridge Trail*, R and L.

(The *Welch Ridge Trail* runs 1.8 mi L to the meadows of Silers Bald at a jct with the *AT*. On the *AT*, R, it is 4.5 mi to the Clingmans Dome Rd parking area. The *Welch Ridge Trail* runs R through meadows, rhododendron groves, and mixes of hardwoods and conifers. At 1.0 mi from the *AT* it descends on switchbacks to Mule Gap. At 2.5 mi it meets *Jonas Creek Trail*, L. (The *Jonas Creek Trail* descends 4.2 mi to *Forney Creek Trail*.) At 3.8 mi it passes a rock outcrop and descends to a gap at 4.4 mi. It ascends steeply to Mt Glory at 4.7 mi. It passes R of Hawk Knob at 5.0 mi, a spring at 5.2 mi, and a beautiful open area at Bearwallow Bald before a jct L with *Bear Creek Trail* at 6.5 mi. The *Bear Creek Trail* descends 5.8 mi to *Forney Creek Trail*. At 6.8 mi on the *Welch Ridge Trail* there is a 0.4-mi spur trail, R, to High Rocks (5,188 ft), a scenic sandstone and quartz knob. An old fire tower has been dismantled. Views may be North Shore mtn ranges, the Little Tennessee River Valley, S, and the Stecoah Mtn range, S. At 7.3 mi *Welch Ridge Trail* ends at a jct with *Cold Spring Branch Trail,* described above.) (*USGS Maps:* Fontana Dam, Noland Creek, Thunderhead Mtn, Tuskeegee, Silers Bald)

504 *Eagle Creek Trail (F)*

LENGTH AND DIFFICULTY: 7.9 mi, strenuous (elev change 3,170 ft)

CONNECTING TRAILS:

(*Lakeshore Trail*)

(*AT*)

SPECIAL FEATURES: trout fishing, historic, geology, scenic

TRAILHEAD AND DESCRIPTION: The easiest and shortest trail access is on *Lakeside Trail* for 6.2 mi from the S side parking lot of Fontana Dam. A popular trail with frequent traffic, its disadvantage is having to wade the creek 16 times; some crossings can be swift and risky. Former human inhabitants included Cherokee Indians, loggers, miners, and moonshiners.

Begin the trail N on the E side of Eagle Creek, pass through a hemlock grove, and after 0.2 mi wade Eagle Creek for the first time. At 0.8 mi arrive at Lower Ekaneetlee Creek backcountry campsite #89, then cross Ekaneetlee Creek. Moderately ascend the hollow and reach Eagle Creek Island backcountry campsite #96 at 2.2 mi. At 4.2 mi is Big Walnut backcountry campsite #97. Ascend, follow L of cascading Gunna Creek at 4.7 mi, then cross it at 5.4 mi. At 5.7 mi ascend steeply, cross the creek again, begin switchbacks and rock formations, and go through open woods of maple, oak, beech, and buckeye. Arrive at rationed Spence Field Shelter at 7.7 mi. Ascend to the *AT* at 7.9 mi in a grassy bald with scenic views. To the R it is 0.4 mi to jct R with *Jenkins Ridge Trail.* (Using it could make a loop of 18.4 mi.) (To the L [S] on the *AT,* a loop to *Lakeshore Trail* at Fontana Dam is 27.8 mi.) (*USGS Maps:* Cades Cove, Fontana Dam, Thunderhead Mtn)

TWENTYMILE CREEK AREA (Swain County)

In the W corner of the park, in North Carolina, the Twentymile Creek Area is bordered by the state line N and W, the Twentymile Ridge E, and NC-28 and Cheoah Lake (Little Tennessee River) S. The area received its name from being 20.0 mi downstream from the confluence of the Little Tennessee River and the

Tuckasegee River. (Farther W, into Tennessee, the park extends to Chilhowee.) The *AT* formerly followed the state line from Doe Knob over Gregory Bald, Parson Bald, Sheep Wallow Knob, and down to Deals Gap. Here it crossed US-219 and descended to Cheoah Dam where it crossed the bridge to ascend Yellow Creek Mtn (see *Yellow Creek Mountain Trail,* chapter 2, section 1). High on the mtn balds were the grazing fields for cattle and sheep before the 1930s. It is on these balds that spectacular displays of flame azalea are seen in mid-June.

ADDRESS AND ACCESS: From Fontana Village drive W on NC-28 for 6.0 mi to Twentymile Ranger Station, R. Access to the trails is here. Address: Twentymile Ranger Station, GSMNP, Fontana, NC 28733.

SUPPORT FACILITIES: The nearest developed campground is Fontana Dam Campground at the base of Fontana Dam, 5.0 mi E from the ranger station. It has hot showers (no hookups) and is usually open from April 15 to early October. Groceries, gas, telephone, motel, and restaurant are W on NC-28, 2.8 mi from the ranger station.

Twentymile Trail (F, H)   506

LENGTH AND DIFFICULTY: 4.7 mi, strenuous (elev change 2,355 ft)

CONNECTING TRAILS:

Wolf Ridge Trail (6.4 mi, strenuous, elev change 3,345 ft) (F, H)   **507**
Twentymile Loop Trail (2.8 mi, moderate) (F)   **508**
Gregory Bald Trail (7.2 mi, strenuous, elev change 1,740 ft) (F, H)   **509**
Long Hungry Ridge Trail (4.6 mi, strenuous, elev change 2,240 ft) (F, H)   **510**

SPECIAL FEATURES: heath balds, flame azalea, wildlife, historic

TRAILHEAD AND DESCRIPTION: (These five trails create two loops and a potential third loop by using a segment of the *AT*.) From the ranger station parking lot begin on the *Twentymile Trail* (a svc rd) and pass a park svc barn. Cross a bridge over Moore Springs Branch where the trail forks. *Wolf Ridge Trail* goes L on an old RR bed. *Twentymile Trail* goes R. At this fork a loop of 6.3 mi can be made by taking either route to include *Twentymile Loop Trail.* At either end of the *Twentymile Loop Trail* either *Wolf Ridge Trail* or *Long Hungry Ridge Trail* can be used to ascend and jct with *Gregory Bald Trail* to form a second loop of 13.9 mi.

If following *Wolf Ridge Trail* parallel Moore Springs Branch; cross three bridges and make two wadings in the first 1.0 mi to the mouth of Dalton Branch, L. Here is a jct with *Twentymile Loop Trail* R. (It crosses [must wade] Moore Springs Branch, climbs over Long Hungry Ridge, and descends to wade across Twentymile Creek for a jct with *Twentymile Trail* at 2.8 mi.) On the *Wolf Ridge Trail* ascend upstream on Dalton Branch to Dalton Branch backcountry campsite #95 at 2.0 mi. (There have been bear sightings here.) From here turn E to swing N in a climb up Wolf Ridge. Pass through an open oak/hickory forest. Arrive at Parson Bald among wildflowers, flame azaleas, and grasses at 5.6 mi. For the next 0.8 mi the crest is generally level with easy treadway to jct with *Gregory Bald Trail* R and L. Here is rationed Sheep Pen Gap backcountry campsite #13.

(Half of the *Gregory Bald Trail* descends L, 4.0 mi, to Sam Gap, its beginning on Parson Branch Rd in Tennessee. The road, closed in winter, is a one-way vehicle route S only, 5.6 mi from Cades Cove. It exits at US-129. The other half of the trail, R, follows the main ridge to end at the *AT* in Doe Gap at 3.1 mi. Along the way it is 0.5 mi to Gregory Bald (4,948 ft), a grassy field with incredible views and beauty from groves of flame azaleas. They bloom usually from mid- to late June. It is another 0.6 mi to jct L with the 5.0-mi *Gregory Ridge Trail,* which descends to Forge Creek Rd, 2.3 mi S of Cades Cove in Tennessee. To the R of the jct is *Long Hungry Ridge Trail,* described below.)

If following the *Twentymile Trail* from the fork, parallel the Twentymile Creek upstream in a forest of poplar, maple, oak, hemlock, and rhododendron. Ferns, orchids, and other wildflowers are on the trailside. In a valley of logging history, follow an old RR bed, cross two bridges, and reach Twentymile Creek backcountry campsite #93 at 1.7 mi, near another bridge. Cross Turkey Cove Branch at 2.1 mi. Soon cross a bridge and move away from Twentymile Creek, but follow the N side of Proctor Branch to Proctor Field Gap at 2.9 mi. Jct here with *Twentymile Loop Trail,* L. (If hiking the loop, wade across Twentymile Creek, ascend and descend Long Hungry Ridge, and wade Moore Springs Branch to jct with *Wolf Ridge Trail.*) Ahead, and also L, at Proctor Field Gap is *Long Hungry Ridge Trail.*

It crosses Proctor Branch at 0.1 mi, and goes to a ridge nose to parallel Twentymile Creek upstream. At 1.2 mi pass Upper Flats backcountry campsite #92, R. Cross Twentymile Creek and another stream on the E slope climb of Long Hungry Ridge to the crest at scenic Rye Patch (4,400 ft) at 3.5 mi. Reach *Gregory Bald Trail* L and R at 4.6 mi. To the R it is 2.0 mi to the *AT* at Doe Knob. To the L it is 0.7 mi to scenic Gregory Bald described above.

To complete the *Twentymile Creek Trail,* ascend, cross Proctor Branch at 3.1 mi, and follow switchbacks, steeply near the end, to Sassafras Gap (3,653 ft) at the *AT,* R and L, at 4.7 mi. To the L it is 0.9 mi to rationed Birch Spring Gap Shelter, and to the R it is 0.3 mi to a 0.1-mi spur trail at Shuckstack fire tower. Here are magnificent views of Fontana Lake. Ahead (across the *AT*) begins *Lost Cove Trail* described above. (*USGS-FS Maps:* Fontana Dam, Cades Cove, Calderwood, Tapoco)

8. Other Trails in the National Park System

For every shell that plays a tune of the sea in our ears,
There is another that composes a song of wonder in our hearts.
—Glenn Morris

CAPE HATTERAS NATIONAL SEASHORE
(Dare and Hyde Counties)

Cape Hatteras, a chain of barrier islands E of Pamlico Sound, has 30,318 acres of sandy Atlantic beaches, dunes, and marshlands. It is the nation's first national seashore. Authorized as a park by Congress on August 17, 1937, the islands are havens for more than 300 species of migratory and permanent shorebirds. Major shore fish are flounder, bluefish, and spot, and offshore are marlin, dolphin, mackerel, and tuna. Often referred to as the Outer Banks and the "Graveyard of the Atlantic," the offshore area has two ocean currents near Diamond Shoals that are used as shipping lanes and are hazardous for those navigating the seas. More than 600 ships have fallen victim to the shallow shoals, winds, and storms over the past 400 years.

For hikers and campers on the string of islands, the NPS permits camping at designated campgrounds only. Facilities are limited to cold showers, drinking water, tables, grills, and modern rest rooms. Oregon Inlet, Cape Point, Ocracoke, and Frisco fee campgrounds are usually open from Memorial Day through Labor Day. Sites are rented as available, except Ocracoke where sites may be reserved through MISTIX; 800-365-CAMP. Hikers using tents are requested to use stronger tents and longer stakes than usual for protection against the sand and wind. Protection against sunburn and insects is essential. Also be aware of strong littoral currents, rip currents, and shifting sand when swimming. Tidal currents near inlets are hazardous, and the NPS recommends swimming only where lifeguards are on duty.

Short nature trails are located at the visitor centers at Cape Hatteras, Bodie Island Lighthouse, and near the campground on Ocracoke Island. The *Cape Hatteras Beach Trail* (the E terminal route of the *MST*) follows the park's entire chain of islands. It is described below. In addition to the Cape Hatteras park, the same office administers two other area parks. The Wright Brothers National Memorial (9.0 mi N of the US-64/NC-12 jct at Whalebone Junction) is a 431-acre memorial museum to Wilbur and Orville Wright, who on December 17, 1903, were the first to successfully achieve air flight with machine power. The other park is the Fort Raleigh National Historic Site (8.0 mi W of Whalebone Junction on US-64). Designated a historic site on April 5, 1941, it covers 346 acres and includes parts of the former 1585 and 1587 settlements. The Lindsay Warren Visitor Center displays excavated artifacts, and exhibits tell the story of Sir Walter Raleigh's "lost colony." In addition, the park includes a reconstruction of Fort Raleigh, the Waterside Theatre (which presents Paul Green's symphonic drama of the "Lost Colony" in the summer), an Elizabethan garden main-

511 tained by the Garden Club of North Carolina, Inc, and the *Thomas Hariot Trail*. The trail is a 0.3-mi interpretive loop with signs about the plant life that Hariot found in the area in 1585. It begins at the visitor center.

ADDRESS AND ACCESS: Superintendent, Cape Hatteras National Seashore, Rte 1, Box 675, Manteo, NC 27954; 919-473-2111. To reach the park headquarters turn off US-64/264, 3.0 mi W of Manteo at the park sign.

SUPPORT FACILITIES: In addition to the park campgrounds there are commercial campgrounds to choose from, some open all year. For this and other information, contact the Dare County Tourist Bureau, PO Box 399, Manteo, NC 27954; 919-473-2138. Open M–F, 9–5; Sat 10–3.

512 *Cape Hatteras Beach Trail*

LENGTH AND DIFFICULTY: 75.8 mi, moderate

SPECIAL FEATURES: lighthouses, wildlife refuge, seashore

TRAILHEAD AND DESCRIPTION: (Although the difficulty of this trail is listed as moderate, its classification may be vague. The reasons are miles and miles in sand without refuge from inclement weather, gale winds, hot weather [as much as 10 months of the year], and insects can make the hike anything but easy or pleasant.) This unique trail generally follows the beach line, but in shorter sections it climbs dunes with sea oats and beach holly; winds through forests of live and laurel oaks, pine, and sweet bay; passes salt marshes of sedge and cordgrass; and clings to road shoulders. In a given season the hiker will see scores of bird species—swans, geese, ducks, gulls, egrets, terns, herons, songbirds, and shorebirds—migratory and permanent. The trail crosses the Oregon Inlet bridge, passes historic

Cape Hatteras National Seashore. Bill Russ

Coast Guard sites, and requires a ferry ride to pass the wild ponies on Ocracoke Island. (Through-backpackers should plan camping arrangements and shuttle service well in advance; see introduction above.) The trail is not blazed or signed except at a few key points.

Begin the hike at the jct of US-64/264/158/NC-12 at Whalebone Junction in Nags Head and proceed S on NC-12 for 0.1 mi to the Cape Hatteras National Seashore Information Center (919-441-6644), R. (Hatteras and Ocracoke ferries sign is nearby.) Hike the L shoulder of NC-12 by a border of myrtle, beach holly, bayberry, sedge, and cattails. Pass parking areas on the R at 1.5 mi, 3.2 mi, and observation decks at 3.8 mi and 4.4 mi. At 4.7 mi pass a park maintenance area, L, and at 5.9 mi L is a paved entrance road to a large parking area for the beach. Area facilities for picnicking and rest rooms are available, with showers during the summer season. Also at 5.9 mi the *MST* leaves NC-12 and turns R on a paved entrance road to Bodie Light-house Station and Visitor Center (919-441-5711). Reach the parking area for the lighthouse (built in 1871) at 6.9 mi. (Behind the lighthouse is 0.3-

513 mi, round-trip *Bodie Island Pond Trail.* It enters the wetlands on a boardwalk to an observation deck. Some of the plants are bayberry, *Baccharis,* salt meadow, salt marsh cordgrasses, and black rush.)

From the lighthouse and visitor center go to the S end of the parking
514 loop and enter a gated sandy NPS road to the 0.8-mi *Bodie Island Dike Trail,* which runs jointly with the *MST* to NC-12. After 0.2 mi cross a small cement bridge, and turn L, off the road. Follow a wide trail with numbered markers through wax myrtle, beach holly, cedar, and cordgrasses. Occasion-al views of the lighthouse and lakes are on the L. Jct with NC-12 at 8.0 mi.

Turn R and follow the road shoulder to Oregon Inlet Campground on the L at 8.6 mi. Begin to cross the Herbert C. Bonner bridge on the L, facing traffic at 9.0 mi. Observe traffic carefully because pedestrian walk space on the 2.4-mi bridge is only 45 inches wide. Views from the bridge are spectac-ular. Reach the end of the bridge at the abandoned Coast Guard station at 11.4 mi and enter the Pea Island Wildlife Refuge. Pass a ferry schedule sign, R, at 12.2 mi, and a parking area for beach access at 13.8 mi (125 yd to the Atlantic Ocean). At 14.1 mi turn R off NC-12 to follow a hiking sign on the N dike of North Pond in the Pea Island National Wildlife Refuge. (The 5,915-acre refuge has 265 species of birds, 24 species of reptiles, and 23 species of mammals. The waterfowl numbers are greater in January, but a greater variety of species can be observed during the fall migration of Octo-ber–November. For information contact the Refuge Manager, Pea Island National Wildlife Refuge, PO Box 150, Rodanthe, NC 27968; 919-987-2394.) Reach an observation deck of the impoundment at 14.3 mi. Contin-ue on the trail around the W side of North Pond for 1.7 mi. Turn L at 16.2 mi, pass an observation deck at 16.7 mi, and reach NC-12 parking area. (If the South Pond area is hiked, permission must be granted from the refuge office.) Cross NC-12, follow a cement trail to dunes and then to the beach at 16.9 mi. Hike S on the beach 2.3 mi to exit over the dunes at Pea Island National Wildlife Refuge office on NC-12. (The office may have been relocated since the publication of this book.) Pass an interpretive exhibit area where signs indicate the Pea Island Life-Saving Station was authorized by Congress in 1873. The station's crews rescued more than 600 people by 1915. After a visit to the refuge headquarters return across NC-12 and to the beach at 19.4 mi. For the next 30.0 mi you will be hiking on the beach.

At 24.8 mi, pass an exit over dunes to a parking area at NC-12, near the end of the Pea Island Refuge. At 25.6 mi pass dune exit to old Chicamacomico Coast Guard Station, a historic site, on NC-12, 0.5 mi from the beach. A general store, laundry, and private campground are over the dunes at 25.8 mi, 0.5 mi from the beach. The Rodanthe post office is at 26.1 mi, and a restaurant and fishing pier are at 26.3 mi. The original KOA is at 27.7 mi (125 yd from the beach to the KOA bathhouse and another 0.3 mi to the KOA office near NC-12). Holiday KOA is at 28.1 mi, 125 yd from the beach. Waves post office is at 28.3 mi, 0.4 mi from the beach, and Salvo post office is at 30.5 mi, 0.5 mi from the beach. Salvo NPS campground is closed at 31.0 mi, 0.5 mi from the beach. Beach exit and parking area are at 35.4 mi on off-road vehicle ramp #27. Another beach exit and parking area are at 37.6 mi, another at 41.9 mi. Avon post office and shopping center are at 43.7 mi, followed by a fishing pier. Another ORV ramp exit, #38, is at 45.9 mi. A parking area and beach exit are also here. At 46.8 mi cross over the dune for 100 yd to the parking area at the old beach road; NC-12 is 100 yd ahead. Follow S on NC-12 for 0.2 mi and take an old jeep trail R. Hike this road for 2.6 mi to near Buxton. Cross over NC-12 to the beach at 49.6 mi, turn R, and after 1.4 mi arrive at historic Cape Hatteras Lighthouse.

From the lighthouse go W to the Hatteras Island Visitor Center (919-995-4474) at 51.4 mi. Continue straight on the road to Buxton Woods parking area and picnic area at 51.5 mi. Here is the *Buxton Woods Nature Trail*, R, a **515** self-guided, interpretive, 0.6-mi scenic loop. Ahead pass a maintenance area, L, and at 51.9 mi, R, enter the Open Pond Rd where exists the largest forest on Cape Hatteras. (Camp trailers disposal system is L at this point and the paved road continues L 0.9 mi to ORV ramp #44.) Nearby is the NPS Cape Point Campground, which may be closed.

Follow the sandy road and cross a stream at 53.2 mi; reach a Y in the road at 53.3 mi. Take the R fork where a sign restricts ORVs, and follow the S side of the lake at 53.4 mi. Enter an open area of dunes at 53.5 mi and follow the sandy road to NPS Frisco Campground at 55.8 mi. After the campground go to the gate at 56.1 mi, turn L, and follow the ramp to the beach at 56.3 mi. Turn R on the beach, pass a fishing pier, and after 6.0 mi on the beach turn R at ramp #55 to a parking lot and NC-12. Turn L and after 0.1 mi reach the Hatteras Ferry at 62.6 mi. (From the NPS Frisco Campground it is 1.1 mi on a paved road to NC-12 and the Frisco post office.)

Take the Hatteras Ferry to Ocracoke Island (the time is usually 40 minutes), and after arrival hike 0.7 mi on NC-12 to a parking area L. Go over the dunes to the beach at 63.3 mi. A parking area for the beach is also at 66.5. mi. At 68.1 mi cross the dunes from the ocean for 100 yd to a parking area. A short hike on NC-12 leads to the observation deck for the Pony Pen to view the wild ponies. Return to the beach. At ORV ramp #68 reach NPS Ocracoke Campground at 72.4 mi. The *Ocracoke Boardwalk Trail* is a 0.1-mi walk (with handicapped access) to observe the ocean. Follow either the beach or the road to ORV ramp #70 at the Ocracoke airstrip, which is 0.2 mi from the beach, at 75.3 mi. From here follow NC-12 to the town boundary at 75.8 mi, the trail's terminus. Another 1.3 mi goes to the Ocracoke Island Visitor Center (919-928-1461) and Ocracoke Ferry. Toll ferries leave the port to Swanquarter to US-264, or to Cedar Island to US-70 (919-928-3841). The town has motels, restaurants, a marina, and supply stores. (*USGS Maps:* Roanoke Island, Oregon Inlet, Pea Island, Rodanthe, Little Kinnakeet, Buxton, Cape Hatteras, Hatteras, Green Island, Howard Reef, Ocracoke)

CAPE LOOKOUT NATIONAL SEASHORE (Carteret County)

Across Ocracoke Inlet from the Cape Hatteras National Seashore begins the Cape Lookout National Seashore. These barrier islands are narrow with low dunes, bare beaches at the Atlantic Ocean, and flat grasslands and salt marshes on the sound side. It includes Portsmouth Village (part of the N Core Banks), S Core Banks from Drum Inlet to Cape Lookout, and Shackleford Banks, W of the cape and ending S of Beaufort. Authorized by Congress in 1966 and established in 1976, the 58.0 mi of islands remain uncommercialized and present a fragile natural resource. Although the islands are best known as a fisherman's haven, hikers, campers, and beachcombers use the beach as a trail. There are not any signs or distance markers or campsites or lifeguard-protected beaches (there are sharks and jellyfish in the Atlantic Ocean).

Choose comfortable packs and shoes. Wear a hat, shirt, and plenty of sunscreen lotion. Take plenty of potent insect repellent (insects are worst May through October). Use a strong tent with fine insect netting and, because of the wind, use ft-long tent stakes. Carry in plenty of food and water. Pets are not allowed on the barrier islands of the park. Only drift-wood campfires are allowed. All trash must be carried out.

At Portsmouth Village, the 1.0-mi easy *Portsmouth Village Trail* goes **517** from the dock to the old schoolhouse, homes, cemeteries, Methodist church, and former US Life-Saving Station. From here it is another 1.0 mi to the beach. Now a ghost town, parts of the village are preserved by the NPS. Portsmouth began in 1753 as a trans-shipment point for goods entering Ocracoke Inlet. Its population reached nearly 600 by 1860, but most of the inhabitants went ashore upon federal occupation during the Civil War. (*USGS Maps*: Portsmouth, Wainwright Island, Styron Bay, Davis, Horsepen Point, Harkers Island, Cape Lookout, Beaufort)

ADDRESS AND ACCESS: Superintendent, Cape Lookout National Seashore, 131 Charles St, Harkers Island, NC 28531; 919-729-2250. Access is by private concession ferries that operate from Harkers Island to Cape Lookout and the lighthouse (919-728-3907); from Davis to Shingle Point (919-728-2791); from Atlantic to North New Drum Inlet (919-225-4261); and Ocracoke to Portsmouth Village (919-928-4361 or 919-928-1951). Call for rates and schedules.

SUPPORT FACILITIES: Shopping centers, restaurants, and motels are in Beaufort and Moorehead City. There are at least a dozen commercial campgrounds in the area. Contact the Cape Lookout National Seashore office for a list of the local campgrounds, beach driving permits, fishing information, tide table, and map. Waters forecast can be heard by call-ing the Coast Guard base at Fort Macon (919-726-7550) or a five-day forecast from the National Weather Service in Wilmington (919-762-3240) or Cape Hatteras (919-995-5610).

GUILFORD COURTHOUSE NATIONAL MILITARY PARK (Guilford County)

The park was established March 2, 1917, in honor of the 4,300 officers and soldiers of Commanding General Nathanael Greene's Continental Army in the battle against British Field Commander Lord Charles Cornwallis, March 15, 1781. Although the battle was not a total victory for either side, it was significant in that Cornwallis retreated to Wilmington, practically abandon-ing the Carolinas. The end of the Revolutionary War came seven months later at Yorktown, Virginia, October 19, 1781. The 220.4-acre park has a museum in the visitor center; there are seven tour stops of historical interest. Camping is not allowed. Open daily except Christmas Day and New Year's Day.

ADDRESS AND ACCESS: Superintendent, Guilford Courthouse National Military Park, 2332 New Garden Rd, Greensboro, NC 27410; 910-288-1776. Access is 0.5 mi on New Garden Rd from US-220 N 6.0 mi from downtown Greensboro.

518 *Guilford Courthouse Battlefield Trail*

LENGTH AND DIFFICULTY: 2.5 mi, easy

TRAILHEAD AND DESCRIPTION: From the visitor center follow the paved trail SW of the parking area through a mature forest of oak, hickory, walnut, and poplar with an understory of dogwood, redbud, and sourwood. The first tour stop, the American first line, is at 0.4 mi. Cross Old Battleground Rd and reach a spur trail, L, to the General Greene monument at 0.6 mi. Continue on trails through open fields of large scattered oak and poplar with senna, milkweed, evening primrose, lobelia, and bur marigold among the wildflowers. At 1.3 mi reach stop five at the site of Guilford Courthouse. (At a parking area R, a few yds W on the road leads to a 0.2-mi walking/biking trail into the city's Country Park. See chapter 13.) Return by stop six, American third line, at 1.9 mi for a return to the visitor center at 2.5 mi.

MOORES CREEK NATIONAL BATTLEFIELD (Pender County)

The battlefield was established June 2, 1926, by the War Department and transferred to the NPS June 10, 1933. It has 87 acres and is significant because it is where the North Carolina patriots won a victory February 27, 1776, that notably advanced the American cause against the British Loyalists. On April 12, 1776, North Carolina became the first colony whose delegation at the Continental Congress in Philadelphia voted for independence.

519-
520
The 1.0-mi *Moores Creek Trail* begins on the *Pathway to History Trail,* W of the visitor center, and follows interpretive signs through pine and hardwoods with Spanish moss to a bridge at 0.4 mi. The nature trail part begins at 0.7 mi in the loop. There are facilities for the handicapped. Open daily except Christmas Day.

ADDRESS AND ACCESS: Superintendent, Moores Creek National Battlefield, PO Box 69, Currie, NC 28435; 910-283-5591. Access from the jct of US-421/NC-210 is 3.0 mi to Currie on NC-210; follow the signs another 3.0 mi.

CARL SANDBURG HOME NATIONAL HISTORIC SITE (Henderson County)

Carl Sandburg (1878–1967), poet, author, lecturer, and social philosopher, won the Pulitzer Prize for history in 1940 with his *Abraham Lincoln: The War Years* and the Pulitzer Prize for poetry in 1951 with *Complete Poems*. He lived his last 22 years at "Connemara," a 240-acre farm at Flat Rock. A constant hiker, he refreshed himself by walking the trails designed by the first owner of the property (attorney Christopher G. Memminger of Charleston, South Carolina). On October 17, 1968, Congress authorized the farm as a historic site; it acquired the property from the Sandburg family in 1969 for commemorative purposes, and opened to the public in May 1974. It is open daily, 9 to 5, except Christmas Day.

ADDRESS AND ACCESS: Superintendent, Carl Sandburg Home National Historic Site, 1928 Little River Rd, Flat Rock, NC 28731; 704-693-4178. Entrance is by Little River Rd (SR-1123) off US-25 (near the Flat Rock Playhouse), 3.0 mi S of jct with US-64 in Hendersonville.

Memminger Trail (0.7. mi); Little Glassy Trail (0.2 mi); Big Glassy Trail (1.0 mi); Spring Trail (0.3 mi); Jerusalem Trail (0.3 mi); Loose Cow Trail (0.1 mi); Front Lake Trail (0.5 mi) 521-527

LENGTH AND DIFFICULTY: 3.1 mi combined round-trip, easy

TRAILHEAD AND DESCRIPTION: From the main building parking lot ascend on a trail to the main house and follow the signs (or use a brochure map) to begin on the *Memminger Trail*. It connects with, but circles, the *Little Glassy Trail*, which leads to an outcrop in the circle. From the trail gap and jct with the *Big Glassy Trail*, go 1.0 mi through oak, hickory, hemlock, and white pine to Big Glassy Mtn, a large rock face with scenic views. Backtrack to the woodshed for the *Spring Trail*. The *Jerusalem Trail*, *Loose Cow Trail*, and *Front Lake Trail* are all near the main house and are interconnected. (*USGS Map:* Hendersonville)

PART III

Trails in Other US Government Properties

9. National Wildlife Refuges and the Army Corps of Engineers

Wildlife is not born free if it cannot live and die free.
—Kurst Vancor

The origins of the National Wildlife Refuge System began in September 1937 with passage of the Federal Aid in Wildlife Restoration Act. Its conservationist sponsors were Senator Key Pittman of Nevada and then Representative Willis Robertson of Virginia. It did not come too soon, because the impact of plundered forests and uncontrolled slaughter of wildlife in the early twentieth century had wiped out some species and threatened and endangered others. Some earlier efforts had been made. For example, President Theodore Roosevelt in 1903 signed an executive order protecting wildfowl on Florida's Pelican Island. Later, migratory bird bills were passed in the 1930s, the Fish and Wildlife Act in 1956, and the National Wildlife Refuge System Administration Act of 1966. Other acts have followed, each one a building block of a process to save and protect the nation's native wildlife.

There are more than 400 refuges in the United States and its trust territories that encompass nearly 90 mil acres. They range in size from the smallest (less than an acre), Mille Lacs in Minnesota, to the Yukon Delta (nearly 20 mil acres) in Alaska. All these refuges are under the jurisdiction of the US Fish and Wildlife Service of the Department of the Interior. The regional headquarters for North Carolina is at 1785 Century Blvd, Atlanta, GA 30345; 404-679-7289. There are also many citizen clubs and organizations in the nation whose mission is to conserve natural resources and protect wildlife. One is the National Wildlife Federation, which has 13 regions (Region 3 for North Carolina). Its national headquarters is at 1412 16th St, NW, Washington, DC 20036; 202-797-6800. Other names and addresses of government and citizen groups are listed in the appendix. It is estimated that 28 mil people annually visit the refuges for hunting, fishing, boating, and nature study. In North Carolina there are 9 refuges, two of which (Great Dismal Swamp and Mackay Island) are partly in Virginia. Only the refuges with designated trails are described below. The *Cape Hatteras Beach Trail* passes through the Pea Island National Wildlife Refuge and is described in chapter 8.

ALLIGATOR RIVER NATIONAL WILDLIFE REFUGE (Dare and Hyde Counties)

The 150,000-acre refuge is a peninsula between Albemarle Sound and Pamlico Sound. It is a world of pocosins, brackish marshes, white cedar and cypress swamps, and dry lands with hardwoods—all the habitats of a wide range of wildlife and 145 species of birds, mammals, and reptiles. In its center is 46,000 acres owned by the federal government for US Air Force and Navy bombing practice. There are more than 150.0 mi of old logging roads, many too wet and impenetrable for vehicular use or hiking. Other roads (gated or open) are in good condition and popular with hunters and nature enthusiasts. For hunters, a map and brochure on hunting regulations, permits, and list of game animals are essential. Alligator, bear, and red wolf are protected. (Harassing, harming, or possessing a red wolf carries a penalty of one-year imprisonment or $100,000 fine or both.) Hunting and fishing opportunities are available for the physically disabled. Arrangements can be made in advance by contacting the refuge office.

Creef Cut Wildlife Trail is fully handicapped accessible. The wide, paved **528** 0.5-mi trail has boardwalks over freshwater marshes. There are resting benches, interpretive and directional signs, and a fishing dock with priority use for the physically disabled. In addition to a grand pine border on the trail, there are fragrant garlands of yellow jasmine and wild rose, bunches of wax myrtle, and aquatic strands of cattails. Backtrack. The parking access is on the S side of US-64 at jct with Milltail Rd, 7.0 mi E of Alligator River bridge and 3.0 mi W of US-64/264 jct. There are 13.0 mi of canoe/kayak trails in a channel to Sawyer Lake and wide Milltail Creek. Access is at the end of Buffalo City Rd described below from the *Sandy Ridge Wildlife Trail.* (*USGS Maps:* East Lake; Manns Harbor; Buffalo City; East Lake SE; Wanchese; Engelhard W, E, NW, and NE; Stumpy Point; Fairfield NE)

ADDRESS AND ACCESS: The refuge can be accessed from Columbia (E) on US-64 and from Engelhard (S) on US-264. The office is at 708 N Highways US-64/264 jct. The mailing address is Alligator River NWF, PO Box 1969, Manteo, NC 27954; 919-473-1131 (wildlife violations 800-662-7137).

529 *Sandy Ridge Wildlife Trail*

LENGTH AND DIFFICULTY: 2.2 mi, round-trip, easy

TRAILHEAD AND DESCRIPTION: From the Alligator River bridge on US-64 go E 3.8 mi to Buffalo City Rd, and turn R (3.2 mi W on US-64 from *Creef Cut Wildlife Trail*). Go 1.9 mi to dead-end road to park for both the trail and the canoe/kayak trails. Hike across a channel bridge and follow an old road with soft duff from loblolly pine needles and leaves of cypress, sweet gum, willow, and maple. On the L is a canal (used by canoeists/kayakists). At 0.7 mi cross a low bridge. Sections of the trail have wooden pallets in wet areas to assist in keeping feet dry. Sphagnum moss beds and the sounds of wildfowl are prominent; carnivorous plants (such as sundew) are infrequent. Backtrack.

Sandy Ridge Wildlife Trail. Allen de Hart

MACKAY ISLAND NATIONAL WILDLIFE REFUGE (Currituck County)

The refuge is in the extreme NE corner of the state, with 842 of its 8,055 acres in Virginia. Established in 1960 as a wintering ground for migratory waterfowl, it is at its peak from December to February when flocks of ducks, geese, and swans travel through their Atlantic flyways. The refuge lists 174 species of birds, including many songbirds. Some of the most rare fly-ins are the white ibis, peregrine falcon, red-necked grebe, and cinnamon teal (*Anas cyanoptera*). There are two designated trails. The 0.3-mi *Great Marsh Trail*, **530** used heavily by fishermen, leads to a pond where there are excellent views of the marsh and waterfowl. It is on the S side of the Causeway of the Great Marsh, N 4.8 mi on NC-615 from the ferry dock at Knotts Landing. The other trail is described below. No camping is allowed in the refuge.

ADDRESS AND ACCESS: Refuge Manager, Mackay Island NWR, PO Box 39, Knotts Island, NC 27950; 919-429-3100. At the jct of NC-168/615 in Currituck, take the free auto ferry to the island. Drive 2.7 mi on NC-615 and turn L on Mackay Island Rd. Go 1.3 mi to the gated entrance.

Mackay Island Trail   531

LENGTH AND DIFFICULTY: 3.4 mi, easy

TRAILHEAD AND DESCRIPTION: Begin the hike on an open svc road about 3 ft above sea level. At 0.5 mi arrive at a road fork, where either direction completes the loop. If continuing ahead, go through a forest of loblolly pine, yaupon, bays, and cedar, with cordgrass and cattails at the clearings. At the next road jct, turn L and follow a 1.0-mi dike road. Turn L again, go 1.4 mi, and at another road jct take a R; go 0.5 mi to return to the entrance gate. There is evidence of nutria in the refuge, and waterfowl are prominent, particularly egrets, ducks, grackle, and grebe. (*USGS Maps:* Knotts Island, Barco)

PEE DEE NATIONAL WILDLIFE REFUGE (Anson and Richmond Counties)

Containing 8,443 acres, this refuge was established in 1965 to protect the habitat of resident wildlife and wintering geese and ducks. It is the state's most inland refuge where the rolling hills of the Piedmont level out to floodplains (mostly on the S side) of the Pee Dee River. More than 175 species of birds have been classified, including Canada geese, mallards, wood ducks, herons, owls, hawks, and songbirds. There are 28 species of mammals and 48 species of amphibians and reptiles. There is a 2.5-mi wildlife drive with interpretive management panels that is open April 1 through October 15. The 0.5-mi *Pee Dee Nature Trail* has interpretive history signs about flora and fauna. It passes a photo-blind on Sullivan Pond and is open all year. Both routes are located directly behind the refuge headquarters. No camping is allowed.

ADDRESS AND ACCESS: Refuge Manager, Pee Dee NWR, Rte 1, Box 92, Wadesboro, NC 28170; 704-694-4424. Access is on US-52, 6.0 mi N of Wadesboro and 3.0 mi S of Ansonville.

US ARMY CORPS OF ENGINEERS

Formed during the early years of the nation as part of the Continental Army, the US Army Corps of Engineers had its beginning at West Point, a garrison on the Hudson River. In 1798 the Corps was enlarged, and in 1802 Congress made West Point a military academy for the United States. Since then, Congress has authorized a wide range of Corps projects. Among them have been blazing and building roads, clearing waterways and harbors, building dams for flood control and hydropower, protecting and restoring shorelines, providing natural disaster relief, fish and wildlife development, and multiple recreation opportunities. While emphasizing diversity in recreational usage year-round, the Corps enforces zoning regulations to protect the ecology.

There are four major Corps projects in North Carolina; Falls Lake (Neuse River); Jordan Lake (Haw and New Hope Rivers); Kerr Dam and Reservoir (Staunton/Roanoke and Dan Rivers); and Scott Dam and Reservoir (Yadkin River). All were constructed for the major purpose of preventing downstream flood damage. With the exception of the Scott project, acreage is leased by the state's Department of Environment, Health, and Natural Resources (DEHNR) for recreational purposes and managed by the Division of Parks and Recreation. These properties are described by the DEHNR as state recreation areas (SRAs). The Corps also leases acreage to the state's Wildlife Resources Commission for wildlife management and motorboat registration on all four projects. Examples of other types of leases are Wilkes County Park at the Scott Reservoir project and commercial leases (such as marinas) on all the projects (usually subleased by the DEHNR). All the projects have trails.

FALLS LAKE (Durham, Granville, Wake Counties)

The 38,886-acre (11,620 water and 27,266 land) Falls Lake project has 12 public-use sites, 5 of which are SRAs managed by the Division of Parks and Recreation. They are Beaver Dam, Highway 50, Sandling Beach, Shinleaf, and Rolling View. Boating, water skiing, sailing, fishing, and picnicking are the major activities. Hiking the 23.4-mi *Falls Lake Trail*, described below, is another significant recreational activity. It is being constructed on the S boundary of the lake as a joint project of the Division of Parks and Recreation, Triangle Greenways Council, and the Corps of Engineers. The continuation of the trail is proposed from NC-50 to other recreational areas along the Corps's property. Falls Lake received its name from the Falls of Neuse, a short section of rapids below the dam.

ADDRESS AND ACCESS: Falls Lake SRA Management Office, 13304 Creedmore Rd, Wake Forest, NC 27587; 919-676-1027. From the jct of NC-98/50 drive N on NC-50 1.6 mi, R. The Corps of Engineers Resources Manager's Office address is 11405 Falls of the Neuse Rd, Wake Forest, NC 27587; 919-846-9332. Access is 0.9 mi S from the Falls Lake parking area below the dam.

Falls Lake Trail
Section 1 (Falls of the Neuse to Six Forks Rd)

533

LENGTH AND DIFFICULTY: 13.2 mi, moderate

TRAILHEAD AND DESCRIPTION: This well-designed and well-maintained trail section was designated a state trail as part of the *MST* on April 11, 1987. Through a hardwood forest, it weaves in and out of coves and crosses numerous small drainages. It ascends to a number of gentle ridges and offers occasional scenic views of the lake. The mature forest has a few old-growth trees and some specific evidence of succession. For example, a few places have young growth among former tobacco rows. Holly, laurel, loblolly pine, Christmas fern, wild ginger, and running cedar comprise the winter greenery. Among the ferns are royal, cinnamon, sensitive, resurrection, ebony, southern lady, and bracken. Wildflowers include three species of wild orchids, coral bell, squirrel cups (*Hepatica americana*), mandrake, yellow root, and spring beauty (*Claytonia virginica*). Some of the more evident mammals are deer, beaver, fox, squirrel, and raccoon.

Access to the E trailhead is at Tailwater Fishing Access Area parking lot below the dam on Falls of Neuse Rd (SR-2000) in N Raleigh. (Access from Wake Forest jct of US-1 and NC-98 is 0.7 mi W on NC-98 to Old US-98 L, then follow the signs 2.4 mi to the parking area.) (Other access points will be described along the trail route.) The trailhead may not have signs or blazes, but it is in front of the rest rooms at a two-car parking space. (Do not go up the path to the dam.) Follow an old svc road where white blazes line the route. Pass through loblolly pine, sweet gum, tulip poplar, and oaks with an understory of holly and dogwood. At 0.1 mi turn L on a foot trail and after 110 yd the trail forks near a unique double tulip poplar. Take either route. (The blue-blazed trail, L, goes 0.6 mi to rejoin the main trail.) On the main trail, turn R, cross the paved dam road, and arrive at the parking lot of the Corps's Operational Management Center at 0.3 mi. Follow the lakeside rd and after 0.2 mi reenter the forest that has scattered jessamine and redbuds. Cross a Corps svc rd and jct with the blue-blazed alternate route at 0.9 mi. Turn R. At 1.5 mi cross a pipeline right-of-way and a scenic stream area at 2.0 mi. Cross footbridges over streams at 2.3 mi and 2.6 mi. Pass some fine views of the lake between the streams and the arrival at Raven Ridge Rd (SR-2002) at 3.4 mi. (It is 3.9 mi L on Raven Ridge Rd and Falls of Neuse Rd to the E trailhead.) Turn R and cross the Honeycutt Creek causeway to reenter the woods R at 3.5 mi. Enter a clear-cut area at 4.4 mi, followed by a series of small stream crossings and an old power line clearing at the edge of a residential area. At 5.0 mi pass an old farm pond and old farm area, followed by a cove and large beech trees. Arrive at a residential area and exit to Possum Track Rd at 6.1 mi. (The road R is barricaded, but the road L is a vehicle access back to the trail's origin for 6.2 mi; 1.4 mi to Raven Ridge Rd, L; 2.9 mi to Falls of Neuse Rd, L; and 1.9 mi to the parking lot, L.)

Continuing on *Falls Lake Trail,* cross the road into a grove of loblolly pine. Cross a paved road at 6.4 mi, and enter another pine forest grove at 6.6 mi. Pass lake views at 7.7 mi. Cross a couple of ravines before crossing a footbridge at 8.5 mi. At 8.8 mi reach an old woods road, turn R, and arrive at Possum Track Rd at 9.0 mi. (It is 0.2 mi L to Raven Ridge Rd jct.) Turn R and cross the Cedar Creek causeway. At 9.2 mi turn R into a pine forest with cedar and honeysuckle. Pass remnants of an old homestead, R, at 10.1 mi. Enter a scenic area of large beech trees and cross a footbridge at 10.2 mi. After views of the lake at 10.7 mi, enter a section of laurel for the next 0.6 mi. At 12.0 mi arrive at Bayleaf Church Rd (SR-2003). (To the R is the Yorkshire Center of Falls Lake Rec Area, and to the L, on the gated road, it is 1.0 mi to Bayleaf Baptist Church and jct with Possum Track Rd.) Cross the road at the exit sign of the Yorkshire Center and reenter the forest. Cross a number of small streams in rocky areas and arrive at the end of the guardrail on Six Forks Rd (SR-1005), at the Lower Barton Creek causeway, at 13.2 mi. (To the R it is 2.2 mi to NC-98. To the L it is 7.9 mi back to the parking lot below the dam. The vehicle route is 0.7 mi on Six Forks Rd where a L turn follows Possum Track Rd and Raven Ridge Rd as described above.) (*USGS Maps:* Bayleaf, Wake Forest)

Section 2 (*Six Forks Rd and Blue Jay Point County Park*)

LENGTH AND DIFFICULTY: 3.4 mi, moderate

TRAILHEAD AND DESCRIPTION: From the trailhead on Six Forks Rd (described above) follow the road R (N) across the Lower Barton Creek causeway for 0.3 mi to the end of the road railing at gravel shoulder parking. Turn R and enter Blue Jay Point County Park through the forest. Follow an old woods road for 0.1 mi before descending on a footpath to cross a footbridge. Here are wildflowers and unique roots to a maple tree. Ascend and descend in and out of coves and crossing footbridges. At 0.9 mi are patches of spicebush, wild ginger, and hepatica. At 1.6 mi is the first of four spur trails, color coded, for the next 0.7 mi. They cross or join *Falls Lake Trail* from the recreational areas on top of the peninsula. *Blue Jay Point Trail* **534** (0.2 mi) is the first to cross. *Laurel Trail* (0.2 mi) follows, the next trail leads **535** to a trail for the physically disabled, and the last trail, *Sandy Point Trail* (0.2 **536** mi), originates at the park lodge. There are rock piles left by early farmers at 2.0 mi. Come out of the forest at 2.3 mi to a display board and parking lot between a ball field and the park lodge. Cross the paved road and descend to footbridges; follow the undulating trail through hardwoods and loblolly pine to reach Six Forks Rd at 3.4 mi at a trail sign. Here is the temporary end of this section. (To the R is 1.0 mi to NC-98; to the L is 1.3 mi to the W trailhead of Section 1.) (*USGS Map:* Bayleaf)

Section 3 (*NC-98 to NC-50*)

LENGTH AND DIFFICULTY: 6.8 mi, moderate

TRAILHEAD AND DESCRIPTION: From the intersection of Six Forks Rd and NC-98 drive E 1.5 mi on NC-98 to the W edge of the lake bridge. Here is a gravel parking area on the N side of the road. At 0.1 mi pass under a power line among redbud, sumac, and blackberry. Cross a number of footbridges in coves and at 0.7 mi enter a grove of large beech and tulip poplar. Scattered understory is dogwood, holly, and sparkleberry. Views of the lake are here. At 1.1 mi there is a scenic area with large beech and wildflowers, and at 1.5 mi, near cove waters, is a skillfully designed footbridge. At another scenic lake area are infrequent tawny pine-sap (*Monotropa hypopithus*), and also at 2.6 mi in the same genus is Indian pipe (*Monotropa uniflora*). After a number of footbridges and hilly climbs reach Shinleaf Rec Area, a walk-in campground with central rest rooms and showers at 3.0 mi. (Access by vehicle is 0.5 mi N on New Light Rd from NC-98 jct, opposite the N end of Six Forks Rd.) Across the parking area, enter the forest where to the L is Norwood cemetery. Descend steeply and ascend. At 3.5 mi exit to New Light Rd. (It is 1.5 mi L to NC-98.)

Turn R on New Light Rd and after 0.1 mi turn L up an embankment (watch for sign; may be easy to miss). Enter a low area with large ironwood and spots of yellow root at 3.9 mi. Ascend to cross paved Ghoston Rd at 4.0 mi. Descend to banks of mayapple, foamflower, and crested dwarf iris. Cross the dam of a small pond at 4.6 mi. Pass around a rocky knoll at 5.1 mi; notice former tobacco field ridges on the hillside. At 5.3 mi pass R of an unnamed cemetery near an old homesite. On an old road of red clay approach a jct with a grassy road at 5.6 mi. Turn L (avoid the extreme L grassy road) and leave the road R at 5.7 mi. Because of logging, the next two turns (L and R) may require alertness. After the R turn through young pines follow a grassy open road bordered in section with orange cow-itch vine. Cross two paved roads, the latter for the State Management Center, R, at 6.6 mi. Exit at the edge of a highway railing on NC-50 at 6.8 mi. To the R it is 0.1 mi to a gravel road shoulder parking area. (It is 1.6 mi L [S] on NC-50 to NC-98.) (*USGS Maps:* Bayleaf, Creedmore)

B. EVERETT JORDAN DAM AND LAKE (Chatham, Durham, Orange, and Wake Counties)

The US Congress instructed the Army Corps of Engineers to study the historic Cape Fear River basin in 1945 for flood control. A lake, known then as New Hope Lake, was authorized in 1963 and constructed in 1967. In 1973 it was named in honor of US Senator B. Everett Jordan. Since then the North Carolina Division of Parks and Recreation manages nearly 14,000 acres of the 46,768-acre project as SRAs. Twelve areas are now developed, some of which have trails. The prominent recreational activities are boating, fishing, water skiing, sailing, windsurfing, camping, and swimming.

One of the outstanding areas for nature study is at the Wildlife Resources Commissioner's Wildlife Observation Deck. From here in the summertime bald eagles may be seen, usually early in the morning or later in the day. Access to the observation site is on a narrow road (which has a sign) W off NC-751, 6.1 mi S of I-40, exit 274, or 5.6 mi N of US-64. From a parking lot **537** enter a gated corner on *Wildlife Observation Trail*, a birder's delight. After 0.1 mi begin a 1.4-mi loop. The R turn is 0.6 mi to the observation deck. On its approach is a patch of sweet and succulent blackberries, usually ripe the last week of June. The more remote part of the trail is over former tobacco fields and into damp areas near the lake for observing other wildlife and plant life. Call the recreation management center for information on interpretive bird-watching tours (919-362-0586). (*USGS Map:* Green Level.) As facilities continue to develop, visitors are requested to call in advance for an update on services. The 5.0-mi *New Hope Overlook Trail* is expected to open in 1997. Access **538** will be off US-1 on SR-1700 NW of the Haw River bridge.

ADDRESS AND ACCESS: Superintendent, Jordan Lake SRA, Rte 2, Box 159, Apex, NC 27502; 919-362-0586. Access is off US-64 (S), last road before crossing the causeway/bridge, 3.7 mi W from US-64/NC-751 jct.

At Ebenezer Church SRA are two trails (foot traffic only). Access is off US-64 at Wilsonville jct with Beaver Creek Rd (SR-1008) S for 2.1 mi, R. After entrance, take the first road R and park on the E side of the parking lot at a trail sign. Hike the easy red-blazed *Old Oak Trail* past a bamboo grove at **539** sign about puddle and diving ducks at 0.4 mi. Complete a loop of 0.9 mi through a pine forest and tall oaks. Return to the entry road, drive R, and park at the nearest access at the lake on the L at a picnic area. There is a sign about Ebenezer Church. Follow the red-blazed *Ebenezer Church Trail* (foot **540** traffic only) on an old road. After nearly 0.2 mi is the former site of the historic church, R, but turn L off the road. Walk through a young forest, cross a paved road at 0.4 mi, curve around a tranquil small pond, cross the road again, and return to the parking area at 1.0 mi. (*USGS Map:* New Hope Dam)

At the Seaforth SRA is 1.6-mi *Pond Trail* (foot traffic only). Access is off **541** US-64, the first L after crossing the lake's causeway/bridge W from Wilsonville. Park near the end of the parking area across from the beach bathhouse. Enter the red-blazed trail through an oak forest that becomes mixed with loblolly pine. At 0.2 mi cross a boardwalk for an exceptionally beautiful view of the lake. By the boardwalk are lizard's tail, marshmallow, and fragrant buttonbush. Circle L of a pond with a beaver hutch at 0.6 mi. Pass through a field of lespedeza, cross the entrance road, walk through a loblolly pine forest, pass a former pond site with willows, and exit at a picnic shelter. Cross the parking area for a return to the point of origin.

On a return to US-64, drive W 2.5 mi to Griffins Crossroad (5.0 mi E from Pittsboro), and turn L (S) on Pea Ridge Rd (SR-1700) to Vista Point SRA. After 2.5 mi park on the L before the entrance fee booth. Begin the red-blazed 2.7-mi *View Point Trail* (foot traffic only) through a mixed forest of oak, **542** maple, and pine. (At 0.7 mi is a proposed loop extension. At 0.8 mi is a lake view, L, and at 1.1 mi is evidence of former tobacco rows. For the next 1.2 mi curve in and out of a series of coves, sometimes close enough to view the lake through the trees. Footbridges are over the ravines. Forest growth remains the same with occasional holly, sparkleberry, and fern beds. Pass L of a group RV campground at 2.3 mi and R of a picnic shelter at 2.5 mi. Cross a paved road and at 2.6 mi jct with a blue-blazed trail, L. (It is a walk-in route to campsites where a continuance is to an old barn and well house.) Keep R and exit to the parking area where the trail began. (*USGS Map:* New Hope Dam)

JOHN H. KERR DAM AND RESERVOIR (Granville, Vance, Warren Counties in NC; Charlotte, Halifax, Mecklenburg Counties in Virginia)

The reservoir of 48,900 acres was completed in 1952 and named for the N.C. congressman whose leadership made the project possible. More than three-fourths of the area project is in Virginia. There are 29 rec areas, of which 9 are in NC, including 6,200 land acres leased to the state by the Corps. Chief activities are boating, sailing, skiing, fishing, swimming, picnicking, and camping. There are 850 numbered campsites among the following parks: Bullocksville, County Line, Hibernia, Henderson Point, Kimball Point, Nutbush Bridge, and Satterwhite Point. All campgrounds open April 1 or Easter (whichever comes first) and close as late as November 1. After that date all water sources are cut off. Three campgrounds (Cooper Point at Satterwhite, Nutbush Bridge, and Hibernia) have portions open all year. All campgrounds have portions with electrical and water hookups. Three commercial marinas offer full svc for fishermen, boaters, and campers. Among the special events in the parks is the Governor's Cup Invitational Regatta in June. Only the rec areas with nature trails are covered below. (See *The Trails of Virginia* by Allen de Hart, published by the University of North Carolina Press, for trails on the Virginia side of the reservoir.) (*USGS Maps:* Middleburg, Townsville, John H. Kerr Dam, Tungsten)

ADDRESS AND ACCESS: Superintendent, Kerr Reservoir State Rec Area, Rte 3, Box 800, Henderson, NC 27536; 919-438-7791. At the I-85 jct in North Henderson take Satterwhite Rd (SR-1319) N 6.0 mi.

543-544 The 0.4-mi *Big Poplar Trail* and the 0.6-mi *Henderson Nature Trail* are at Satterwhite Point; the access is described above. Access to the *Big Poplar Trail* is in the J. C. Cooper Campground. It is a linear trail between the washhouse (L of the fork) at campsite section 105–123 and the entrance loop, R, of campsite section 1–15. The wide trail in a mature forest could also be called big beech (tree-carving dates are in the late 1800s) or big white oak. A large tulip poplar grows halfway on the trail at a streamlet. On Satterwhite Rd, across the road from the J. C. Cooper Campground entrance, is the entrance to *Henderson Nature Trail.* It loops from the Henderson kiosk at the Outdoor Lab of the Vance Salt and Water Conservation District sign. The graded interpretive trail is bordered with pieces of old RR cross ties. If following the trail clockwise, reach a cleared area at 0.2 mi, pass the lake shore, and at 0.5 mi pass the Richard Henderson (1735–85) grave site.

At the Nutbush Bridge Campground is the 0.3-mi *Sycamore Springs* **545** *Trail.* Access from Henderson, at the I-85 and NC-39 jct, is 4.5 mi N on NC-39 to Harris Crossroads. Turn R on Harris Rd (SR-1308) and after 1.8 mi turn L at the campground entrance. Park in a pine grove at the first fork. The linear path through mature hardwoods, young pine, and honeysuckle exits on the R fork road 0.1 mi from its origin. The trail gets its name from a spring that feeds a drain into Kerr Lake. (The area has hazelnut bushes, which the Saponi Indians called a "nutbush.")

At Bullocksville Rec Area is the 0.5-mi *Old Still Trail,* a loop trail whose **546** entrance is opposite the baseball field at the ranger sta. At 0.3 mi it turns sharply L to ruins of an old illegal liquor still. Access is 3.3 mi W from Drewry on Bullocksville Rd (SR-1366), and Drewry is accessible 2.3 mi W on Manson Rd (SR-1237) from I-85, exit 223, or 2.4 mi W on Ridgeway Rd (SR-1224) from I-85, exit 226. Both I-85 exits are N of Henderson. To reach County Line Rec Area, use either of the accesses to Drewry and drive N on Drewry Rd (SR-1200) for 3.0 mi. Turn L on Buchanan Rd (SR-1202) and go 2.1 mi to the entrance. Park L of the fork at the ranger sta for *Hollow Poplar Trail.* The 0.4- **547** mi loop trail goes through a mature forest of oak, loblolly pine, sweet gum, and red maple. A large, partially hollow tulip poplar gives the trail its name.

W. KERR SCOTT DAM AND RESERVOIR (Wilkes County)

The project was constructed by the Corps from 1960 to 1962 and named in honor of former US Senator and N.C. Governor W. Kerr Scott (1896–1958). There are 16 recreational areas, one of which has been leased to Wilkes County and another to a commercial establishment. The lake contains 1,470 acres and is surrounded by 2,284 land acres. Popular aquatic sports are boating, skiing, swimming, and fishing. Small-game hunting is allowed at selected areas. Land activities are camping (Bandits Roost Park and Warrior Creek Park have electrical and water hookups and hot showers), picnicking, and hiking. At the manager's office is a 0.3-mi self-guiding loop, *Scott Dam Nature Trail.* It has 27 interpretive points for the local trees, **548**

flowering shrubs, and ferns. Access is described below. Another short trail
549 is the 0.8-mi *Bandits Roost Trail*. It goes from the boat-ramp parking lot of
Bandits Roost Campground in Area B along the shoreline to a terminus
between campsites #25 and #26 in Area A. Access is 1.9 mi W on NC-268
from the dam entrance. A longer trail is described below.

ADDRESS AND ACCESS: Resource Manager, W. Kerr Scott Dam and Reservoir, PO Box 182, Wilkesboro, NC 28697; 910-921-3390. The entrance
road to the manager's office is on NC-268, 3.0 mi SW from the jct of
US-421 in Wilkesboro.

550 *Overmountain Victory Trail*

LENGTH AND DIFFICULTY: 2.7 mi, easy

TRAILHEAD AND DESCRIPTION: Now a national historic trail, this trail was
formerly called the *Warrior Creek Trail*. Warrior Creek is historically significant because the mouth of the creek at the Yadkin River (now underwater)
was where the Overmountain Men of the Wilkes County militia crossed the
Yadkin, September 28, 1780. The army of 350 men continued to Lenoir
where it joined the main patriot army (from the mtns of N.C., Tenn., and
Va.) at Quaker Meadows. Their march to the historic Battle of Kings Mtn in
SC, where Col Pat Ferguson was killed and his Tory army defeated on October 7, 1780, was a turning point in the Revolutionary War. To commemorate this route, the Corps and local citizen groups have established this trail.

From the NC-268 entrance to the dam, continue SW 4.3 mi on NC-268
to Section F, Warrior Creek Park, and turn R. Go 0.6 mi and turn L at the
campground sign. (If the campground is open, usually May 1 to September
30, ask for a campground and trail map and drive the 1.0 mi to the trailhead, following the signs. (If the campground is closed, park outside the
gate and walk to the trailhead. From the trailhead parking lot descend the
steps on a well-graded and well-maintained trail. Pass through a forest of
white pine, holly, and tall hardwoods. Galax, yellow root, ferns, and fetterbush decorate the trail and stream banks. Cross two footbridges and arrive
at Area C camping road at 0.5 mi. Cross the road; pass through Area E
camping at 0.6 mi, and pass a natural spring at 1.1 mi. Pass a picnic area at
1.3 mi. Descend into a lush cove on the lake, and arrive at an abandoned
picnic area at 2.0 mi. Ahead, follow an old woods road and ascend to an
abandoned parking area at 2.5 mi. Turn L and follow the road to a Corps
gate at 2.7 mi. To the L is a parking overlook and picnic shelter with scenic
views of the lake. To the R it is 1.3 mi on the paved campground road to the
E trailhead and point of origin. (*USGS Map:* Boomer)

PART IV

Trails in the State Parks and Recreational System, Forests, Natural Areas, Historic Sites, and Other State Properties

10. The State Parks and Recreation System

The measure of a state's quality of life is known by the parks it keeps.
—Carl Jamison

The Department of Environment, Health, and Natural Resources (DEHNR) has seven divisions in Natural Resources: Aquariums, Forest Resources, Marine Fisheries, Museum of Natural Sciences, Parks and Recreation, Soil and Water Conservation, and Zoological Park. The current administrative form was created in 1989, but a number of reorganizations preceded the change. For example, in 1977 the state legislature combined a number of agencies under the Department of Natural Resources and Community Development (DNRCD), which included the Division of Parks and Recreation. In 1955 the state legislature transferred all the state historic sites from Parks and Recreation to a new Department of Archives and History.

The state park system is divided into six units of management. They are state parks, lakes, recreation areas, rivers, trails, and natural areas. All the trails in the parks are covered in this chapter, the natural areas in chapter 11, and the state recreation areas in the preceding chapter.

Interest and concern about the state's natural resources began in the late nineteenth century. A specific example was the establishment of a state Geological Survey in 1891 to determine the state's mineral and forest resources. State geologist Joseph A. Holmes was appointed to direct and present biennial reports. In 1905, the state legislature reorganized the survey to create the N.C. Geological and Economic Survey. Its duty was expanded to "all other material resources." When the legislature and Governor Locke Craige

Hanging Rock State Park. Bill Russ

learned in 1914 that timber harvesting and forest fires were destroying such valuable areas as Mt Mitchell, the governor (a strong conservationist) went to the area for a personal inspection. The result was a bill passed in 1915 to create the state's first park (cost not to exceed $20,000). The management of Mt Mitchell State Park became the responsibility of the Geological and Economic Survey. The state's second state park, Fort Macon, came in 1924 after director Holmes and the legislature were successful in acquiring the 410-acre Fort Macon Military Reservation from the federal government for one dollar.

In 1925 the legislature expanded responsibility to fire prevention, reforestation, and maintenance of the state parks and forests when the Geological and Economic Survey was phased into the new Department of Conservation and Development. Acquisition was slow; only three of the Bladen Lake areas were added to the list in the 1920s, and unfortunately did not include any land acreage at White Lake. But in the 1930s there was a change when federal assistance programs became available, particularly the CCC. Between 1935 and 1943 the state acquired six new parks: Morrow Mtn, Hanging Rock, Pettigrew, Singletary Lake, Jones Lake, and Crabtree (now Umstead). The congressional Recreation Area Study Act of 1936 became the blueprint for state park systems, but the N.C. state legislature appropriated only sporadic capital funds. From 1945 to 1961 only Mt Jefferson was acquired. Five state parks and a natural area were added in the 1960s, and there was a notable increase in the 1970s with 11 new parks, eight new natural areas, and the first state recreation area (SRA) at Kerr Lake (the facilities had been parks since 1951). This decade of growth was under the administrative leadership of governors Bob Scott and James E. Holshouser. Within a three-year period the park lands nearly doubled (50,000 acres more). Other advances during this period were the beginning of the state zoo, a heritage trust fund (for the natural areas), and in 1973 the State Trails System Act, which created a master plan with procedures for implementing a statewide network of multiuse trails for hikers, bicyclists, equestrians, canoeists, and ORV users. It also created a seven-member citizen's Trail Committee to advise the director of Parks and Recreation.

During the 1980s three SRAs were opened—Jordan Lake, Falls Lake, and Fort Fisher—and one state park—Waynesborough. Legislative appropriations were increased but continued to be inadequate for park maintenance and land acquisition. The *Winston-Salem Journal* editorialized in May 1987 that "North Carolina has a large financial investment and a priceless natural heritage in its parks... it needs a master plan to overcome a starvation diet." The same month the legislature passed the State Parks Act, led by Senator Henson P. Barnes. The act would establish a master plan that "firmly defines the purpose of state parks and requires sound strategy in managing the system."

For many years the state has been in the lowest national percentile of funding for park construction, staffing, and maintenance. Voters responded to this neglect on November 2, 1994, when they passed a $35-million bond referendum for a Parks and Recreation Trust Fund and Natural Heritage Trust Fund. It was a first in the agency's history and the largest single appropriation since its creation in 1915. The recreation fund is divided 65 percent to state parks, 30 percent to matching funds for local park projects, and 5 percent for beach access. Phil McKnelly, the division's director, stated that trail supporters were among the many groups who made the citizens aware of park system needs.

Among the park system's 29 regular parks, 23 have trails for a total of 115 trails and 212.3 mi. All the parks are open all year. An exception is Mt Mitchell, which has to close when snow closes the Blue Ridge Parkway. Other western parks may close temporarily if there are unusually heavy snowstorms. Parks open daily at 8 AM and close at 6 PM November through February; 7 PM in March and October; 8 PM in April, May, and September; and 9 PM June through August (except Carolina Beach at 11 PM). There are exceptions: Boone's Cave closes mid-November to mid-March; Hammocks Beach 8 AM to 6 PM year-round; Lake Waccamaw, 9 AM to 6 PM; and Singletary Lake, open to groups 8 AM to 5 PM.

Park rules are posted conspicuously in the parks. Alcohol, illegal drugs, and firearms are prohibited. Fishing is allowed but a state license is necessary. Camping facilities for individual parks are described in this chapter. Some of the parks without a campground have the nearest commercial campground listed under support facilities. Descriptions are also made about primitive and youth-group camping. When visiting a park, first go to the park office and request brochure and maps available to make your stay a pleasurable and educational experience.

The state's physiographic regions are divided into mts (17 western counties in the Appalachian Mtns chain); Piedmont (42 counties from the Appalachian foothills through the central part of the state to the fall line); and the coastal plains (41 eastern counties from the fall line 150.0 mi E on flatlands to the Atlantic Ocean). (The fall line designates the area that separates the hard, resistant rocks of the Piedmont plateau from the softer rocks and sediments of the coastal plains. This common term also designates where the rivers cease to have falls or rapids.) Geographically, the coastal plains include a series of seven sloping terraces that range in descent from about 275 ft in elev to sea level at the barrier islands. Because Mt Mitchell is the only state park in the mtn physiographic region, parks in the adjoining counties (with elev ranging from 2,305 ft to 4,900 ft) are included in the mountain region for the purpose of this guidebook.

INFORMATION: Division of Parks and Recreation, PO Box 27687 (512 North Salisbury St), Raleigh, NC 27611; 919-733-7275. For information on trails contact the state Trails Coordinator, Division of Parks and Recreation, 12700 Bayleaf Church Rd, Raleigh, NC 27614; 919-846-9991.

SECTION 1: MOUNTAIN REGION

HANGING ROCK STATE PARK (Stokes County)

Hanging Rock State Park, with 6,000 acres in the Sauratown Mtns, has more than 18.0 mi of named and side trails. They go to scenic heights, waterfall areas, rocky ridges, and caves, and in the process provide the hiker with views of as many as 300 species of flora, including the mtn camelia (*Stewartia ovata*). Canadian and Carolina hemlock grow together here, a rarity, and a species of lespedeza is found only in this area. Animal life includes deer, fox, skunk, woodchuck, squirrel, raccoon, owls, and hawks. The park has camping (also cabins), picnicking, swimming, fishing, and mtn climbing. All trails connect except the *Lower Cascades Trail*. It can be reached by **551** going W from the park entrance on Moore's Springs Rd 0.3 mi. Turn L on Hall Rd (SR-2012) and go 0.4 mi to the parking area, R. The 0.6-mi round-trip *Lower Cascades Trail* descends to the scenic falls and pool under a huge overhang. The park is open all year. (*USGS Map:* Hanging Rock)

ADDRESS AND ACCESS: Superintendent, Hanging Rock State Park, PO Box 278, Danbury, NC 27016; 910-593-8480. To reach the park, turn off NC-8, 1.5 mi N of Danbury onto Moore's Springs Rd (SR-1001), across the road from Reynolds Hospital. The W entrance route is off NC-66, 0.5 mi N of Gap, on Moore's Springs Rd.

SUPPORT FACILITIES: The park has a campground with 73 tent/trailer campsites (no hookups) and family vacation cabins. The campground is open all year (water off December 1 to March 15); the cabins are available (with reservations) March 1–November 30. Groceries, restaurant, gasoline, and PO are in Danbury.

Hanging Rock Trail (1.2 mi); Wolf Rock Loop Trail (1.9 mi); Cook's Wall **552-** *Trail (1.1 mi); Magnolia Spring Trail (0.4 mi); Chestnut Oak Nature* **557** *Trail (0.7 mi); Moore's Wall Loop Trail (4.2 mi)*

LENGTH AND DIFFICULTY: 11.4 mi combined, round trip, easy to strenuous

CONNECTING TRAIL:

(*Tory's Den Trail*)

SPECIAL FEATURES: geology, wildflowers, scenic views

TRAILHEAD AND DESCRIPTION: After passing the park office entrance, L, turn L to a large parking lot at the visitor center. Heavily used *Hanging Rock Trail* begins on the R at a sign. Descend on wide cement steps and follow a cement tread for 340 yd before ascending on gravel. At 0.5 mi jct with *Wolf*

Rock Loop Trail, R. At Hanging Rock ascend steeply 200 ft on metamorphic rock to the summit for superb views. Backtrack to form a loop by taking Wolf Rock Loop Trail. Ascend to and remain on a rocky ridge with pine, oak, laurel, and blueberry. Overlooks are L (SE and S). After 1.0 mi jct with Cook's Wall Trail which goes ahead on the rigde. Wolf Rock Loop Trail turns sharply R, descends to join the Chestnut Oak Nature Trail, and ends at the swimming lake's bathhouse. From here through the parking lot and entrance road it is 0.4 mi back to the parking lot for Hanging Rock Trail, a loop of 4.2 mi.

If continuing on the ridgecrest for Cook's Wall Trail ascend among a mixture of hardwoods, pine, and laurel with patches of galax, trailing arbutus, and downy false fox glove. After 0.5 mi jct with Magnolia Spring Trail, R. (Although this name may not be on the trail signs, the trail is a popular connector between the park's two main ridges. It received its name from the magnolia growing in a damp area of the trial's N end.) Arrive at House Rock at 0.7 mi. Here are excellent views of Hanging Rock (NE) and the vicinity of Winston-Salem (S). At 1.1 mi reach Devil's Chimney over rocky Cook's Wall for a view of Pilot Mtn (W). Backtrack, but turn L at Magnolia Spring Trail. Descend steeply through a dense forest to Magnolia Spring at 0.1 mi. Pass through an arbor of rhododendron, cross a footbridge over a clear stream, and jct with Moore's Wall Loop Trail, R and L and 0.4 mi. A turn R goes through a bog with boardwalks. Ferns and purple turtleheads grow nearby. Jct with Chestnut Oak Nature Trail, arrive at the bathhouse, and return to the Hanging Rock Trail parking lot for a loop of 6.4 mi.

If following the Moore's Wall Loop Trail from Magnolia Spring Trail, follow the sign and after 0.6 mi jct with a connector to the former Sauratown Trail and Tory's Den Trail. Turn R and ascend to a rocky area with hemlock, turkey grass, and laurel after another 0.6 mi. An observation tower (2,579 ft) with spectacular views is reached at 1.9 mi. Descend, pass Balanced Rock and Indian Face on an old road. Cross Cascade Creek at 3.0 mi, pass through the camping area, and rejoin the trail's entrance. Turn L and return to the parking lot at the bathhouse at 3.9 mi. If walking from the parking lot to the Hanging Rock parking lot, the loop is 9.3 mi. (If hiking only the Moore's Wall Loop Trail, it is 4.2 mi if beginning at the parking lot at the bathhouse.)

558- Upper Cascades Trail (0.2 mi); Indian Creek Trail (3.7 mi)
559 LENGTH AND DIFFICULTY: 7.8 mi round-trip combined, easy to moderate
SPECIAL FEATURES: waterfalls, wildlife, cliffs

TRAILHEADS AND DESCRIPTION: From the visitor center parking lot and picnic area access *Upper Cascades Trail* at the W side of the parking lot. Part of the trail is asphalt for the physically handicapped. Backtrack. To access *Indian Creek Trail* follow the trail signs at the NE end of the parking lot and picnic area. Descend 0.4 mi to a shady area at Hidden Falls on Indian Creek. Continue downstream, crossing the creek several times. Pass a jct L with a connector trail to a group camping area. Cross the creek to exit at Hanging Rock Rd (SR-1001) at 1.7 mi (0.1 mi E of the park entrance).

Cross the road, descend on an old farm road, cross a cement bridge, pass L of an old tobacco barn, and descend to the creek. Veer away from the creek, ascend a ridge, follow an old forest road, and descend to a scenic overlook from cliffs at 2.9 mi. Descend to the creek's basin near cliff walls, over mossy banks, and through dense rhododendron. After several creek crossings arrive at an old farm road. Turn R, and cross the creek on a footbridge to the trail's end. Ahead it is 0.1 mi to the Dan River Canoe Trail boat launching and parking area. Backtrack, or use a second vehicle. (Access to the river by vehicle from the park entrance is 0.5 mi E on Hanging Rock Rd to Piedmont Springs Rd [SR-1489], L. After 0.9 mi turn L on NC-8/89, go 0.3 mi, turn L on SR-1482, and go 0.4 mi to the trailhead at the creek. River parking area is R.)

Tory's Den Trail

LENGTH AND DIFFICULTY: 4.2 mi, easy

CONNECTING TRAILS:

(Chestnut Oak Trail)

(Moore's Wall Loop Trail)

TRAILHEAD AND DESCRIPTION: From parking lot #2, follow the trail signs on the E side of the bathhouse and lakeshore. Follow the *Chestnut Oak Trail,* but leave it, R, at 0.3 mi and follow the red-blazed trail. At 0.4 mi pass jct R with *Moore's Knob Loop Trail.* Cross a stream and boardwalk and jct L at 1.0 mi with *Magnolia Spring Trail* (which ascends 0.4 mi to jct with *Cook's Wall Trail*). Continue ahead, ascend slightly to a saddle at 1.5 mi, and jct with a blue-blazed trail, L. (The trail R is *Moore's Wall Loop Trail.*) Follow the blue-blazed trail, and after 0.5 mi reach the crest of Huckleberry Ridge near a large rock formation. Descend, and jct with the former *Sauratown Trail* at 2.4 mi R and L. (*Sauratown Trail* is an abandoned 19.0-mi horse trail. Efforts are being made to reopen it with its E trailhead elsewhere in the park.) Turn R, descend, and cross a small stream at 3.5 mi. Ascend to Charlie Young Rd (SR-2028) at 3.6 mi and turn R. Follow the road 0.4 mi to Tory's Den parking lot, L. Follow the trail 0.3 mi to an out-crop, but turn R on the approach. Descend 90 yd near a small cave L and turn R. (Ahead L, it is a few yd to a view of Tory's Den Falls.) Descend 100 yd on the path to the 30-ft Tory's Den. Backtrack, or use a second vehicle for the Tory's Den parking lot. Vehicle access is to drive W from the park entrance on Moore's Springs Rd to Mickey Rd (SR-2011); turn L, and turn L again on Charlie Young Rd, a total of 4.3 mi.

LAKE JAMES STATE PARK (Burke and McDowell Counties)

Named in honor of James B. Duke, founder of the Duke Power Company, Lake James State Park is one of the state's most recent parks. Established in 1987 by the state legislature, it became the first park in the state's system to receive funding for development and operations at the time of its 565-acre acquisition. The land is at the S side of the 6,510-acre lake where NC-126 runs through it. The lake impounds the Catawba River, its North Fork, and the Linville River. From the park launch sites at Hidden Cove and Canal Bridge, fishermen can use the lake to catch large- and smallmouth bass, walleye, crappie, bluegill, sunfish, perch, and catfish. (Information about the best time of day to fish for specific species is at the ranger office.) Other activities include swimming, boating, camping (backpack tent campsites), picnicking, hiking, and nature study. Special facilities have been adapted to provide tent camping and pier fishing for the physically disabled. (*USGS Maps:* Ashford, Marion East)

ACCESS: From I-40, Nebo/Lake James exit #90, follow the park signs N to veer R on Harmony Grove Rd for 1.8 mi to Nebo and US-70 at Kehler's Store. Turn L on US-70, go 0.3 mi, and turn R on NC-126. Go 2.4 mi to the park entrance L.

561- 564 *Sandy Cliff Overlook Trail (0.3 mi); Lake Channel Overlook Trail (0.7 mi); Fishing Pier Trail (0.1 mi); Fox Den Loop Trail (1.9 mi)*

LENGTH AND DIFFICULTY: 4.2 mi combined round-trip, easy to moderate

TRAILHEADS AND DESCRIPTION: All trails can be accessed from the parking lot. The *Sandy Cliff Overlook Trail* goes N on a peninsula of oak, maple, and Virginia pine to the edge of the lake for scenic views. Backtrack to a con-nection with the *Lake Channel Overlook Trail*, L. It parallels the lake's edge through white and Virginia pine, rhododendron, and young hardwoods at the base of a N slope. After a short distance on a gravel road toward the tent campsites, follow a gravel foot trail to a scenic point at the end of the peninsula. Backtrack. From the SW corner of the parking and picnic area follow the paved *Fishing Pier Trail* to a cove. From the pier follow the *Fox Den Loop Trail* into the cove. At 0.6 mi the trail forks to make a loop on a hilly peninsula. Plant life includes oak, hickory, Virginia pine, hemlock, rhododendron, laurel, and flame azalea. Pink lady slippers bloom in late April or early May, and in rich damp soils are white Indian pipe. Deer, fox, woodpeckers, owls, and songbirds are residents of the area.

MT JEFFERSON STATE PARK (now a Natural Area. See chapter 11.)

MT MITCHELL STATE PARK (Yancey County)

Mt Mitchell State Park, extending over 1,677 acres of the Black Mtns ridge, is the state's highest park (6,684 ft), and Mt Mitchell itself is the highest peak east of the Mississippi. This is also the state's oldest park, having been designated in 1915 thanks to the influence of early environmentalists such as Governor Locke Craig and US President Theodore Roosevelt. The park is listed in the National Registry of Natural Landmarks. Mt Mitchell is named in honor of Elisha Mitchell, a clergyman and University of North Carolina geology professor, who fell to his death in a gorge N of Little Piney Ridge (about 2.0 mi from Mt Mitchell summit) while on one of his scientific explorations. A creek and waterfall also bear his name. Geologically, the Black Mtn range is estimated to be more than 1 billion years old, erosion having worn down the summits about 200 million years ago. Fraser fir (damaged by the woolly aphid and acid rain) and red spruce give the crest an alpine look reminiscent of Canada or Maine. Some of the flowering plants are white hellebore, blue-beaded Clinton's lily, and bearberry. Among the forest animals are bear, deer, bobcat, and squirrel. There are 18.0 mi of hiking trails, including Commissary Rd but not including the many connecting trails into the Pisgah NF. The restaurant and observation lounge are open May 1–October 31. (*USGS Maps:* Montreat, Mt Mitchell)

ADDRESS AND ACCESS: Superintendent, Mt Mitchell State Park, Rte 5, PO Box 700, Burnsville, NC 28714; 704-675-4611. Entrance is from NC-218 off the BRP near mp 355, 30.0 mi NE of Asheville and 11.2 mi S from Buck Creek Gap and jct with NC-80.

SUPPORT FACILITIES: Primitive camping is restricted in the park; inquiry should be made at the park office. The nearest campground is Black Mtn Rec Area in Pisgah NF. Access is from the BRP, mp 351.9, at Deep

Gap. Descend 4.9 mi on FR-472 and turn L at the campground entrance. (There are no hookups.)

567- *Mt Mitchell Summit Trail (0.2 mi); Old Mt Mitchell Trail (2.0 mi); Camp*
571 *Alice Trail (1.1 mi); Balsam Trail (0.7 mi); Mt Mitchell Trail (1.6 mi)*

LENGTH AND DIFFICULTY: 5.6 mi combined, easy to strenuous

SPECIAL FEATURES: Mt Mitchell summit, spruce/fir forest

TRAILHEADS AND DESCRIPTION: From the summit parking area, ascend the wide *Mt Mitchell Summit Trail* in a damp forest of conifers and mosses for 0.2 mi to an observation tower and the tomb of the Dr Elisha Mitchell, who after "39 years a professor at the University of North Carolina lost his life in the scientific exploration of this mountain in his 64th year, June 27, 1857." Vistas from the observation tower are magnificent. Along the ascent, other trails branch off. After 140 yd the *Old Mt Mitchell Trail* goes R and the *Camp Alice Trail* branches from it. The *Balsam Trail* and the *Mt Mitchell Trail* branch off L after 0.1 mi. They are described below in that order.

From the *Mt Mitchell Summit Trail,* branch off R on *Old Mt Mitchell Trail.* At 0.3 mi jct L with *Camp Alice Trail.* (It descends steeply on a blue-blazed trail to Camp Alice, an old logging and railroad camp of the 1920s, at 1.1 mi. Regardless of the name, no camping is allowed. Return on the switchbacks to *Old Mt Mitchell Trail.*) Continue ahead, descending easily to a tent camping area at 0.8 mi, the park restaurant at 1.5 mi, and the trail's S terminus at the park office parking lot at 2.0 mi. This yellow-blazed trail is the oldest route to the summit, probably used by explorers in the early 1840s.

For the *Balsam Trail,* branch off *Mt Mitchell Summit Trail* at 0.1 mi, L. Follow the self-guided loop nature trail back to the parking lot, turning L at each jct. The highest spring in eastern America, with an average temperature of 36, is on this trail.

The *Mt Mitchell Trail* also follows jointly with the *Balsam Trail* for the first 0.1 mi, but continues ahead. At 0.3 mi the blue-blazed trail begins a steep descent over rough terrain. Switchbacks begin at 0.7 mi. Reach Commissary Rd and jct with *Buncombe Horse Range Trail* (see Toecane Ranger District, chapter 3), at 1.6 mi. A spring is nearby. Backtrack, or continue for another 4.4 mi on switchbacks to the Black Mtn Campground in the Pisgah National Forest.

572 *Deep Gap Trail*

LENGTH AND DIFFICULTY: 6.0 mi round-trip, strenuous

TRAILHEAD AND DESCRIPTION: This trail is also part of the *Black Mountian Crest Trail* described in the Toecane Ranger District, chapter 3. From the summit parking and picnic area, follow an orange blaze N over rough terrain to Mt Craig (6,645 ft) at 1.0 mi; at 1.1 mi reach Big Tom (6,593 ft), named in honor of Thomas Wilson (1825–1900), who found the body of Dr. Mitchell. Continue over strenuous treadway to Balsam Cone (6,611 ft) at 1.9 mi, and reach Cattail Peak (6,583 ft) at 2.4 mi. Leave the state park boundary and go another 1.5 mi to Deep Gap, the site of a former USFS shelter. Currently there is tent camping space and a spring nearby. (Ahead the *Black Mountian Crest Trail* goes to Bowlens Creek Rd [SR-1109] for a total of 12.0 mi.) (See chapter 3, section 4.)

NEW RIVER STATE PARK (Ashe and Alleghany Counties)

New River State Park is a 26.5-mi scenic corridor of a river claimed to be North America's oldest. For 22.0 mi the park is the river's South Fork to where it joins the North Fork 4.5 mi S of the Virginia state line. Headwaters for the South Fork are in the Blowing Rock/Boone area. After convergence of the forks, the New River (named by Peter Jefferson, father of Thomas) winds its way N through Virginia and into West Virginia before merging with the Kanawha River. This classic and historic river was threatened by the Appalachian Power Company, which was trying to build a dam. In opposition, citizens and government officials prevented it and declared it a state scenic river in 1975. By 1976 it was a national wild and scenic river. Canoeing and fishing are the river's chief appeal. Permits are required for canoe-in camping downstream. Although canoeing can begin at least 50.0 mi upstream, the park has two major access points. The Wagoner Rd Access Area (with park office and primitive camping) is 8.0 mi SE of Jefferson. It is reached by Wagoner Rd (SR-1590) N off NC-88, 1.2 mi E of jct NC-16 and NC-88. At the US-221 access it is 8.0 mi NE of Jefferson (W of the New River bridge). (A third take-out is just across the Virginia state line at VA-93, E of the road jct with US-58.) At the Wagoner Rd access, near the primitive campsites and picnic shelter, is 0.7-mi *New River Nature Trail*. A loop, it has **573** marked stations for information on the area's botany and wildlife. (*USGS Maps:* Jefferson, Laurel Springs, Mouth of Wilson)

ADDRESS AND ACCESS: New River State Park, Box 48, Jefferson, NC 28640; 919-982-2587. Access to park office at Wagoner Rd is described above.

PILOT MOUNTAIN STATE PARK (Surry and Yadkin Counties)

Pilot Mountain State Park covers 3,703 acres in two sections—Pilot Mtn and the S and N side of the Yadkin River—and is connected by a 6.5-mi 300-ft-wide forest corridor for hikers and equestrians. In the park is the Big Pinnacle, rising 200 ft from its base, 1,500 ft above the valley floor and 2,420 ft above sea level. Dedicated as a national natural landmark in 1976, it is geologically a quartzite monadnock. Park activities are canoe camping, picnicking, horseback riding, hiking, and camping. A family type tent/trailer campground is near the base of the N side of the mtn. It has hot showers but no hookups (closed December 1 through March 15). Trails connect easily with the exception of *Yadkin River Trail* on the S side of the Yadkin River. *Sauratown Trail* has its W terminus at the park, and the *MST* will pass through the *Corridor Trail*. (*USGS Maps:* Pinnacle, Siloam)

> ADDRESS AND ACCESS: Superintendent, Pilot Mountain State Park, Rte 3, Box 21, Pinnacle, NC 27043; 910-325-2355. Entrance to the park is at the jct of US-52 and Pilot Knob Rd (SR-2053), 14.0 mi S of Mt Airy and 24,0 mi N of Winston-Salem.

574- *Sassafras Trail (0.5 mi); Jomeokee Trail (0.8 mi); Ledge Spring Trail (1.6*
578 *mi); Mountain Trail (2.5 mi); Grindstone Trail (1.6 mi)*

> LENGTH AND DIFFICULTY: 7 mi combined, easy to strenuous
>
> SPECIAL FEATURES: Big Pinnacle, scenic ledges
>
> TRAILHEADS AND DESCRIPTION: All of these trails connect and can be reached from the parking lot at the top of the mtn. From the parking lot go past and behind the comfort station to a rocky area and a sign for the *Jomeokee Trail*. To the L, 30 yd, is the *Sassafras Trail*. (Follow the *Sassafras Trail* N on a self-guiding loop. It is an interpretive trail among pitch pine, chestnut oak, laurel, and ground cover patches of galax.) At the *Jomeokee Trail* sign descend among rocks and follow a much used access to the Big Pinnacle. (Jomeokee is an Indian word for "great guide" or "pilot.") At 0.2 mi pass the base of Little Pinnacle and jct R with the yellow-blazed *Ledge Spring Trail*. Ahead, after another 0.1 mi, turn R to follow a rocky loop around the Big Pinnacle. The trail walls have caves, eroded rock formations, ferns, wildflowers, lichens, and mosses. Park officials say that ravens nest on the summit. (Climbing or rappelling is prohibited.) On the return from the loop take the *Ledge Spring Trail,* L. Descend on a rocky, rough, and sometimes strenuous base of the ledges. At 1.0 mi reach Ledge Spring, R, 30 yd from the jct with the *Mountain Trail*. (Formerly the *Mountian Bri-*

dle Trail, the *Mountain Trail* is a rough connector trail to the *Corridor Trail* described below. Blazed red, it descends through a hardwood forest with scattered patches of laurel and pine in the beginning. At 1.8 mi it reaches large boulders pushed up in a row from a former clearing. After another 0.4 mi it leaves the row and follows a footpath to an exit at the Surry Line Rd [SR-2061] to jct L with the 1.7-mi *Grassy Ridge Trail* and R with the 6.5-mi *Corridor Trail* at 2.5 mi.) To continue on the *Ledge Spring Trail* turn R and begin a steep ascent over the ledges to jct with *Grindstone Trail*, L, at 1.3 mi. (*Grindstone Trail* follows first on an easy contour, but soon descends in a rocky area with hardwoods and laurel. It crosses a footbridge and small stream at 1.3 mi, an old road at 1.5 mi, and exits at 1.6 mi between camp-sites #16 and #17). Continue the ascent ahead on *Ledge Spring Trail,* pass R of the picnic area, and return to the SW corner of the parking lot at 1.5 mi.

Grassy Ridge Trail (1.7 mi); Corridor Trail (6.5 mi); Horne Creek Trail (1.3 mi); Canal Trail (1.0 mi round-trip) 579-582

LENGTH AND DIFFICULTY: 10.5 mi combined, easy

TRAILHEADS AND DESCRIPTION: (With the exception of *Canal Trail,* these trails are horse/hiker trails.) The N terminus of the white-blazed *Grassy Ridge Trail* is on Pilot Knob Rd (SR-1151) in Surry County, under the US-52 bridge, 0.2 mi E of the park entrance. (At this trailhead is the W termi-nus of planned *Sauratown Trail*). (Vehicular access to the S end of *Grassy* 583 *Ridge Trail* and the N end of *Corridor Trail* from here is E on Pilot Knob Rd, 1.1 mi to jct with Old Winston Rd [SR-1152]. Turn R, go 0.4 mi, and turn R on Old US-52 [SR-1236]. After another 0.4 mi turn R across the RR on Surry Line Rd [SR-1148], which becomes Pinnacle Hotel Rd [SR-2061] in Surry County, and drive 1.6 mi.)

Enter *Grassy Ridge Trail* at a poplar tree and into a hardwood forest. Cross a streamlet at 0.1 mi and reach a jct, R, at 0.2 mi. (To the R it is 0.3 mi on a footpath to the park office.) Continue L, pass an old tobacco barn at 0.4 mi. Cross small streams at 0.5 mi and 1.3 mi. Arrive at Pinnacle Hotel Rd (SR-2061 in Surry County) at 1.7 mi. (To the R, on the road, it is 75 yd to the S terminus of the red-blazed *Mountain Trail*.) Cross the road to a road jct with Culler Rd (SR-2063) and a parking area in the corner of Pilot Mtn State Park Corridor. Here is the N terminus of the *Corridor Trail*. (Vehicular access to the S terminus of the *Corridor Trail* is W on SR-2061 for 2.6 mi to jct with Shoals Rd [SR-2048]. Turn L, and go S 4.0 mi [turning neither R nor L] but partly on SR-2069, also called Shoals Rd, to a fork. Ahead is a dead-end sign. Turn L on gravel Hauser Rd [SR-2072] and go 1.0 mi to the S terminus, L. Ahead it is 0.2 mi, R, to the park's Yadkin River section.)

Begin the yellow-blazed *Corridor Trail* on an old farm road in a grove of Virginia pine and pass under a power line at 0.1 mi. At 0.3 mi is a view (looking back) of the Pinnacles. Cross two footbridges with a meadow of wildflowers and elderberry in between. At 0.7 mi leave the forest and enter a field with another good view of the Pinnacles (looking backward). After 0.1 mi enter a forest of pine and cedar. Pass remnants of an old tobacco barn, L, at 1.2 mi. Cross a small stream bordered with pinxter at 1.4 mi, and another stream at 1.5 mi. At 1.6 mi cross paved Mt Zion Rd (SR-2064). Follow the trail through areas of old farmland and young-growth forest. Descend to rock-hop a tributary of Grassy Creek at 2.6 mi. Pass patches of yellow root and wood betony among the river birch. Exit from the woods into an open area of honeysuckle, blackberry, and poison ivy, and cross paved Shoals Rd (SR-2048) at 3.0 mi. Follow the woods' edge into the forest, cross a stream, cross a number of old woods roads, and descend gently to another stream with beds of sensitive fern at 4.7 mi. Cross a footbridge constructed by the YACC. Cross paved Stoney Ridge Church Rd (SR-2070) at 5.0 mi. Follow the trail through beautiful routes of alternating pine groves and open hardwoods. At 6.0 mi cross a rocky tributary of Horne Creek. (Upstream are two large millstones.) Pass under a power line at 6.3 mi and reach the trail's S terminus at 6.5 mi at Hauser Rd (SR-2072). Across the road begins the *Horne Creek Trail.* (To the L on the road it is 0.2 mi to the entrance, R, of the Yadkin River section of the park at a log shed.) (A vehicular access to US-52 from here is on SR-2072, E, 2.8 mi to Perch Rd [SR-2065]. Turn L, and go 3.5 mi to US-52 in Pinnacle.) (Vehicular access to the S end of the *Horne Creek Trail* is on the park road. Drive in at the park gate by the log shed, ford the small Horne Creek three times, pass through a picnic area, and reach a cul-de-sac on a bluff by the Yadkin River. The *Canal Trail* begins here, on the W side of the cul-de-sac at a wide trail opening, and connects with *Horne Creek Trail,* after 80 yd, at the Southern Railway track.)

At the N end of *Horne Creek Trail* enter a partial field with walnut trees. After 0.3 mi arrive at the park road, turn R, rock-hop Horne Creek, and at 0.5 mi reenter the woods. Ascend and rejoin the park road in a grove of pines at 0.8 mi. Turn R, follow the road, but leave it after 0.2 mi. Descend to the Southern Railway track and jct, L, with the *Canal Trail* (which begins 80 yd up the bank to the cul-de-sac). Cross the RR tracks and after 60 yd reach the Yadkin River, the trail's end. (To the R the *Canal Trail* crosses a footbridge. It goes upstream 0.5 mi between the river and the RR tracks among sycamore, poplar, and river birch. At 0.2 mi pass a long rock wall, R. Backtrack.) Although *Horne Creek Trail* ends at the river, horses can ford the river to two islands and to *Yadkin River Trail* described below.

Yadkin River Trail 584

LENGTH AND DIFFICULTY: 0.7 mi, easy

TRAILHEAD AND DESCRIPTION: To reach this trail take NC-67 to East Bend and follow Old NC-67 (SR-1545) into town. Turn NW on Fairground Rd (SR-1541), go 0.5 mi, turn R on Shady Grove Church Rd (SR-1538) for 0.4 mi, and turn R on Old Shoals Rd (SR-1546) for 2.5 mi to the picnic and parking area. Follow the yellow-blazed trail to the river and return on a loop through a pine forest W of the ranger station. (This is also an area for a bridle trail that crosses the Yadkin River N to *Horne Creek Trail* and *Corridor Trail* described above.) There are two renovated campsites for individual canoeists on the 45-acre islands in the Yadkin River. Group camping is not permitted.

SOUTH MOUNTAINS STATE PARK (Burke County)

South Mountains State Park is an undeveloped, remote park covering 7,400 acres of upper piedmont ecology. Composed of numerous mountain knobs, all under 3,000 ft elev, the area is underlain by a mixture of mica schist and gneiss with quartzite. Mature forests of oak, poplar, hemlock, and pine grow here; they support an understory of three species of rhododendron, mulberry, holly, and laurel. Wildflowers are abundant along the streams. Wildlife includes deer, squirrel, raccoon, timber rattlesnake and copperhead, and 60 species of birds. The major attraction in the park is the 80-foot High Shoals Falls. The area is the site of a former CCC camp. It provides 14.0 mi of fishable trout streams, backpack camping, and picnicking, and it has 9.6 mi of trails exclusively for hiking. There are 32.0 mi of multiuse trails (most of which are old roads) for horses and hikers and 14.0 mi of which include bikers. Loops can be created up to 20.0 mi. The park's shortest trail is 0.5-mi (one-way) *Short Trail*, a foot trail from the parking lot to a knob for views of 585 Jacob's Fork Gorge. It ascends from near the park office. The four backpack campsites are High Shoals (sites 1–4); Shining Creek (sites 5–8); Murray's Branch (sites 9–11); and Little River (sites 12–14). All campers must register at the park office. (*USGS Maps:* Casar, Benn Knob, S Morganton)

ADDRESS AND ACCESS: Superintendent, South Mountains State Park, Rte 1, Box 206C, Connelly Springs, NC 28612; 704-433-4772. Access from Morganton is S on NC-18 from its jct with I-40. Go 10.8 mi to Sugar Loaf Rd (SR-1913), take a sharp R at the Pine Mtn sign, and go 4.2 mi to Old NC-18 (SR-1924) and make a L. After 2.7 mi turn R on Ward's Gap Rd (SR-1901), go 1.3 mi, cross Jacob's Fork Creek bridge, and turn R on South Mtns Park Rd (SR-1904). Proceed for 3.6 mi to the park office.

SUPPORT FACILITIES: Shopping centers, motels, restaurants, and hospitals are in Morganton.

586- 594 *Chestnut Knob Trail (2.0 mi); High Shoals Falls Loop Trail (2.5 mi); Upper Falls Trail (1.9 mi); Cut-Off Trail (0.8 mi); Shinny Trail (2.6 mi); Possum Trail (2.2 mi); HQ Trail (4.4 mi); Fox Trail (4.2 mi); Jacob's Branch Trail (1.2 mi)*

LENGTH AND DIFFICULTY: 11.8 mi or 20.2 mi round-trip or partially combined, moderate to strenuous

SPECIAL FEATURES: Chestnut Knob, High Shoals Falls, backpack camping

TRAILHEADS AND DESCRIPTION: The above combinations of trails have been chosen to provide the hiker an adventurous route to the major scenic places and diversity of altitude, streams, and plant life. All are foot trails except three multiuse trails necessary for connections or loop routes. Only parts of some trails are used; therefore the total length of trails listed above will not be the length of the following descriptions. From the parking lot follow the *HQ Trail* (road, and also jointly running *High Shoals Falls Loop Trail*) 0.2 mi to jct R with the *Chestnut Knob Trail*. (It ascends steeply through mixed hardwoods and pines to a spur trail R for scenic views from Jacob's River Gorge Overlook at 0.9 mi. Continue an ascent to jct R at 1.9 mi with access to *Saw-*

595 *tooth Trail*. Turn L to Chestnut Knob Overlook [2,291 ft] to scenic views of Little River Gorge N and E and Jacob's River Gorge S. Backtrack.)

Continue up the wide and smooth road to cross a bridge over Shinny Creek at 0.4 mi. (*HQ Trail* goes R to jct with *Shinny Trail* and backpack campsites 5–8 after 0.6 mi.) The *High Shoals Falls Loop Trail* bears L. After 0.1 mi the *High Shoals Falls Loop Trail* forks for its loop. (Backpacking campers turn R here to follow an old road with switchbacks to a ridge for a L turn toward campsites 1–4.) If going L, cross a footbridge and enter a cool misty area among hemlock, ferns, rhododendron, trillium, and foamflower. Cross a footbridge, ascend steps, and view High Shoals waterfall from a deck over large boulders at 0.9 mi. At the top of the fall cross a bridge over Jacob's Branch and begin an ascent to a fork at 1.4 mi. Here *Upper Falls Trail* goes ahead, and the *High Shoals Falls Loop Trail* turns R. If returning to the parking area descend R on an orange-blazed old road with switchbacks through a forest of hemlock, black gum, and poplar. Reach the loop connection at 2.0 mi. Return to the parking area at 2.5 mi.

If continuing on the *Upper Falls Trail* ascend 0.2 mi and leave the trail R on *Cut-Off Trail*. Follow it around a ridge and descend by switchbacks into a deep rocky gorge with dense rhododendron and hemlock. Rock-hop Shinny Creek to *HQ Trail,* R and L, and backcountry campsites 5–8 in a meadow at 0.8 mi. Here the *HQ Trail* leads R 1.1 mi to the parking lot, and 3.3 mi L to *Lower CCC Trail*. At the campsites is the E trailhead of *Shinny Trail*. Follow it **596** upstream, rock-hop the creek of cascades and pools at 0.2 mi. Cross a bridge over Shinny Creek again and jct with *Possum Trail* R. (The *Possum Trail* ascends steeply from the toe of a ridge to a knob; it then follows the ridge of oak, hickory, pine, and laurel to jct with *Horseridge Trail* at 2.2 mi. Backtrack.) **597**

Cross Shinny Creek again on a bridge and immediately another bridge over Dark Creek in a forest of hemlock and rhododendron (bridge construction here and other work on this trail were made possible by the Adopt-A-Park program of the Z. Smith Reynolds Foundation and the South Mountains Sierra Group). Continue upstream on an old RR grade. Turn sharply L at a ridge toe; ascend steeply, rocky in sections, among hardwoods, yellow pine, and turkey beard. Reach the ridge crest at 1.9 mi. Follow an old road and arrive at the trail's end and jct with *HQ Trail* (road), R and L, at 2.6 mi.

Turn R on the *HQ Trail* (road). After 0.8 mi jct with *Lower CCC Trail* (road). At this point you have come 5.8 mi from the parking lot. (If you backtrack on *HQ Trail* [road] to the parking lot the round-trip journey is 10.2 mi, and a total of 18.6 mi if you hiked *Chestnut Knob Trail* and *Possum Trail*.) Continue L on the *Lower CCC Trail* (road) 0.4 mi to jct L with *Fox Trail* (old forest road). Follow it 0.3 mi to the first access R to backpack campsites 9–11 in a former wildlife field. After another 100 yd is a second access R to the campsites. After 0.1 mi farther pass the grave site of William Crotts (Confederate States of America) and unmarked graves on the L. Ascend to Grass Ridge, follow it to a side ridge for a jct with *Jacob's Branch Trail*, L, at 1.1 mi. (The *Fox Trail* continues SE for 1.3 mi to jct with *Dogwood Trail*, paved road, **598** horse and bicycle trail.)

Descend on *Jacob's Branch Trail* and curve L off the ridge to cross Jacob's Branch at 0.6 mi. Ascend to the N trailhead of *Jacob's Branch Trail* at 1.2 mi to jct with *HQ Trail*. (It is 0.3 mi L to the W trailhead of *Shinny Trail*.) Turn R on *HQ Trail,* pass a wildlife field R, at 0.9 mi jct with *Upper Falls Trail* R, descend, cross Shinny Creek on a bridge, pass *Shinny Trail* trailhead at 2.2 mi, cross another road bridge at 2.5 mi, pass large cascades and a flume at 2.6 mi, reach *High Shoals Falls Loop Trail* at jct R at 2.8 mi, and return to the parking area for a round-trip of 11.8 mi, or 20.2 mi if including backtrack excursions with *Chestnut Knob Trail* and *Possum Trail*.

STONE MOUNTAIN STATE PARK (Alleghany and Wilkes Counties)

Stone Mountain State Park, with 13,347 acres of forests, trout streams, waterfalls, and rugged medium-grained biotite granite domes, borders the eastern edge of the Blue Ridge Mtns. The largest granite area is Stone Mtn, rising in grandeur 600 ft above its base and 2,305 ft above sea level. The granite is estimated to be 300 mil years old. The park's protected environment provides a habitat for deer, beaver, mink, otter, bobcat, squirrel, bear, and a number of smaller mammals. Spring wildflowers are prominent. The major activities are picnicking, fishing, hiking, climbing, and camping. There is a 37-unit tent/trailer campground (0.8 mi N of the park office on SR-1100) with grills and tables, flush toilets, and hot showers (water off December 1 to mid-March). Walk-in campsites are also available in the backcountry at designated areas. Group walk-in campers must have advance reservations. Climbing is allowed on the S face of Stone Mtn, and climbers are requested to receive information on the regulations and routes from the ranger's office. Access is by way of *Stone Mountain Trail* (described below) to the mtn base where a panel diagrams the 12 climbing routes. The mtn is closed to climbing when the rocks are wet, and all climbers (as well as all hikers) must be out of the area a half hour before closing. (*USGS Map:* Glade Valley)

> ADDRESS AND ACCESS: Superintendent, Stone Mountain State Park, Rte 1, Box 15, Roaring Gap, NC 28668; 910-957-8185. The main access is from US-21 in Thurmond. Follow Traphill Rd (SR-1002) W 4.3 mi to jct with John P. Frank Parkway (SR-1784), and follow SR-1784 N 2.5 mi to the park office, R.
>
> SUPPORT FACILITIES: McGrady Grocery Store is 0.6 mi W on SR-1002 from the park's S entrance (W of Traphill). Shopping centers, restaurants, motels, and other services are in Elkins, 15.0 mi SE on US-21.

599-
605 *Stone Mountain Trail (4.5 mi); Wolf Rock Trail (1.2 mi); Cedar Rock Trail (0.7 mi); Blackjack Ridge Trail (1.4 mi); Stone Mountain Nature Trail (0.5 mi); Middle and Lower Falls Trail (1.6 mi round-trip)*

> LENGTH AND DIFFICULTY: 9.0 mi combined, easy to strenuous

SPECIAL FEATURES: granite domes, waterfalls

TRAILHEADS AND DESCRIPTION: Access to all these trails is at the lower parking lot; they all connect and provide multiple loop options. The longest trail is *Stone Mountain Trail*. It begins and ends at the parking lot. After 107 yd it forks to make a loop. The L route follows switchbacks, steeply in places, for the first 1.0 mi (may be longer after the relocations are complete). The R route from the fork descends to a footbridge among rhododendron, ascends, and forks again, L, at 0.2 mi. It descends, crosses four more footbridges, passes a picnic area and mtn climbing parking area to enter a large meadow and spectacular view of the S face of Stone Mtn after another 0.4 mi. (See continued description below.)

(At the second fork, listed above, the R fork is *Wolf Rock Trail*. From here it ascends on a ridge and switchbacks to jct with an old road at 0.6 mi. [To the R is a connector trail for a descent to a group campsite at East Prong of Roaring River.] Keep L on the *Wolf Rock Trail* where it blends R on another old road at 0.7 mi. Ahead pass a long stone wall, L, and a former homestead area. At 1.0 mi reach a short spur, R, to the pockmarked flat dome of Wolf Rock. Views W are of Little Stone Mtn and SW of Greenstreets Mtn. After another 0.1 mi, jct L with a narrow path that ascends 120 yd to a cement box spring. Descend, pass a seepage L and two old sheds R. At 1.2 mi jct L with *Cedar Rock Trail,* and end *Wolf Rock Trail* to begin *Blackjack Ridge Trail*. At this point you have a choice of two return loops to the parking lot. If taking *Cedar Rock Trail,* ascend 100 yd to a granite slope and outstanding view of Stone Mtn. Follow the yellow blaze painted on the rock. Descend to join *Stone Mountain Trail,* turn L on it, and complete the loop after 2.9 mi. If taking *Blackjack Ridge Trail,* follow the old road in a forest of oak, laurel, and pine to pass Buzzard Rock, R, at 0.2 mi. Leave the ridge, L, at 0.6 mi [at yellow blazes] and soon descend to rock-hop Cedar Rock Creek. Ascend steeply and terminate the trail at a jct of *Cedar Rock Trail* at 1.4 mi. Bear R on *Cedar Rock Trail* to *Stone Mountain Trail,* where a L for 0.2 mi will complete the loop of 3.8 mi.)

To continue on the *Stone Mountain Trail,* pass through the grassy meadow for views of the S face of Stone Mtn. A plaque describes the dome as a registered natural landmark. At 0.8 mi (at the edge of the woods), jct L with *Stone Mountain Nature Trail*. (It crosses the meadow, N, to the base of the mtn. Enter the woods to an information panel of the climbing routes, L. Turn R on a yellow-blazed trail with interpretive signs among the boulders. Cross a small stream and return to *Stone Mountain Trail* after 0.5 mi.) On

Stone Mountain Trail, 25 yd into the woods, jct with *Cedar Rock Trail.* (A sign here may refer to *Stone Mountain Trail* as *Stone Mountain Falls Trail;* they are the same.) Cross Big Sandy Creek twice. Continue downstream on the *Stone Mountain Trail,* and jct R with the *Middle Falls Trail* and *Lower Falls Trail* at 1.5 mi. (Both of the falls trails dead-end. Rock-hop Big Sandy Creek, follow an old road, and after 0.2 mi jct with the *Middle Falls Trail,* R. Follow it for 0.1 mi to a view of the cascades. For the *Lower Falls Trail* continue on the old road and rock-hop or wade Big Sandy Creek twice to see the cascade after 0.5 mi. Backtrack.)

Proceed on the *Stone Mountain Trail,* which becomes a footpath through a rhododendron grove. Arrive at the beautiful 200-ft tumbling Stone Mtn Falls (also called Beauty Falls) at 1.8 mi. Climb carefully the stairway to the fall's summit, pass an old stone chimney at 2.1 mi, turn L at the next fork. Follow the ridge and pass Hitching Rock with its magnificent views of Wolf Rock and Cedar Rock, W at 2.7 mi. Begin a steep incline and reach the summit of Stone Mtn (2,305 ft) at 3.3 mi. Views N are of the Blue Ridge Mtns and SW of Cedar Rock. Large patches of lichens, mosses, and pines cling to the rocks. Follow the yellow blaze painted on the barren granite and begin the descent at 3.9 mi among chestnut oak, pine, and blueberry patches. Return to the parking lot at 4.5 mi.

SECTION 2: PIEDMONT REGION

BOONE'S CAVE STATE PARK (Davidson County)

The park consists of 110 acres of hardwoods—beech, oak, poplar, elm, and hornbeam; laurel, rhododendron, wild hydrangea, and wild pink are among the flowering plants. On the E side of the Yadkin River and generally undeveloped, the park provides picnicking, fishing, hiking, and a canoe rest stop on the 165-mi *Yadkin River Trail.* (For information on the *Yadkin River Trail,* contact the Yadkin River Trail Assoc Inc, 280 South Liberty St, Winston-Salem, NC 27101; 919-722-9346.) *Daniel Boone's Cave Trail* is an easy 0.5-mi route. From the parking lot descend on a gravel trail with steps 100 yd to Boone's Cave, R. (Legends are that Daniel Boone hid from the Indians here, or that he discovered and explored the 80-ft cave, thus the park's name. Cave explorers should be prepared to crawl and have dependable flashlights.) Follow the elevated boardwalks to the riverbank access before following a footpath, L, toward a reconstructed cabin built on the site of an original structure, perhaps that of the Boone family (who, according to leg-

606

end, moved here in 1752 when Daniel was 18). Return to the parking lot on the service road to complete the loop. (*USGS Map:* Churchland)

> ADDRESS AND ACCESS: Morrow Mtn State Park, 49104 Morrow Mtn Rd, Albemarle, NC 28001; 704-982-4402. From I-85 jct with NC-150, halfway between Lexington and Salisbury, go 5.0 mi N on NC-150 to Churchland. Turn L on Boone's Cave Rd (SR-1162) and go 3.8 mi to the parking area.

CROWDER'S MOUNTAIN STATE PARK (Gaston County)

Crowder's Mountain (1,625 ft), named in honor of Ulrick Crowder, a German merchant who settled in the area in the 1780s, is part of 2,713 acres of Crowder's Mountain State Park. In 1987 Kings Pinnacle (1,705 ft) was acquired. Family and group backpack camping is available in separate camping areas. Registration at the park office is necessary. The park has been designated a natural heritage area; some infrequent plants—ground juniper (*Juniperus communis*) and Bradley's spleenwort (*Asplenium bradleyi*) found in acidic rocks—and a wide variety of flora and fauna make it ideal for natural preservation in the future. Recreational opportunities are picnicking, fishing, camping, rock climbing, and hiking. (*USGS Maps:* Kings Mtn, Gastonia)

> ADDRESS AND ACCESS: Superintendent, Crowder's Mtn State Park, Rte 1, Box 159, Kings Mountain, NC 28086; 704-853-5375. One access from I-85 jct is US-74/29 (E toward Gastonia). Turn R on Freedom Mill Rd (at sign) and after 2.5 mi turn R on Sparrow Spring Rd. Reach the park entrance on R after another 0.6 mi.

Crowder's Trail (3.0 mi); Backside Trail (0.9 mi); Tower Trail (2.0 mi);   **607-**
Rocktop Trail (2.1 mi)   **610**

> LENGTH AND DIFFICULTY: 5.2 mi round-trip, moderate to strenuous
>
> SPECIAL FEATURE: views from Crowder's Mtn
>
> TRAILHEADS AND DESCRIPTION: From the park office follow the signs on a well-graded and well-maintained trail N to jct with *Pinnacle Trail* at 0.1 mi. Turn R, follow yellow dot markers through mature hardwood to Freedom Mill Rd (SR-1125) at 0.8 mi. Cross the road, turn L, and skirt the ridge to jct with *Backside Trail* at 2.6 mi. Turn R. (The *Backside Trail* is a 0.9-mi connector trail with *Tower Trail*, which runs from Linwood Rd Access [SR-1131] to Crowder's Mtn. The parking lot for these trailheads is W of Linwood Rd, 200 yd NE of the trails' intersection. It is 1.8 mi round-trip. The *Tower Trail* is 4.0 mi round-trip). At 2.9 mi climb steps and at 3.0 mi reach the summit for

impressive views from 150-ft cliffs. Return SW on *Rocktop Trail,* whose jct with *Tower Trail* loop is at 3.4 mi; continue on rocky quartzite ridge, descend, and reach SR-1125 at 4.4 mi. Return to the park office parking lot at 5.2 mi.

611- *Pinnacle Trail (1.7 mi); Turnback Trail (1.2 mi); Fern Nature Trail (0.7*
614 *mi); Lake Trail (1.0 mi)*

> LENGTH AND DIFFICULTY: 4.5 mi combined, easy to strenuous
> SPECIAL FEATURE: views from King's Pinnacle
> TRAILHEADS AND DESCRIPTION: From the parking lot at the park office go N on a gravel trail 0.1 mi to jct with the *Pinnacle Trail* and *Crowder's Trail.* Take
615 the L (*Bridle Trail* joins the *Pinnacle Trail* for 0.1 mi), and at 0.7 mi pass an access route to walk-in campground. Continue ahead to a rocky ridge tread-way and jct with *Turnback Trail,* L, at 1.1 mi. At 1.3 mi climb gradually along the eastern slopes of King's Pinnacle to the ridge top at a point 1.6 mi S of the summit. Turn N and continue to the terminus at the summit for scenic views of Crowder's Mtn and pastoral scenes, W. Vegetation has blue-berry, scrub oak, pine, sourwood, and sassafras. Backtrack, or take the *Turnback Trail,* R, at the base of mtn, a portion of *Fern Nature Trail* and *Bridle Trail,* in a 1.4-mi return to the park office. The *Fern Nature Trail* is a loop that can be reached either from the office parking area or the picnic parking area. Among the plants are yellow root, sweet pepperbush, pine, and hard-woods. Between the office and the picnic area is a lake parking lot where 1.0-mi *Lake Trail* circles the lake.

DUKE POWER STATE PARK (Iredell County)

Located on the northern shore of Lake Norman, the largest man-made lake in the state, is Duke Power State Park. It has 1,458 acres (mostly donated by Duke Power Company) set aside for swimming, boating, fishing, picnick-ing, camping, and hiking. Norwood Creek and Hicks Creek transect the park. Lake Norman covers 32,510 acres and has a 520.0-mi shoreline. A 33-site campground is open March 15 to November 30 (no hookups) with hot showers, flush toilets, tables and grills, and a sanitary dumping station. The park harbors more than 800 species of plants. The forest is mainly hard-woods with Virginia and loblolly pines. A subcanopy of sweet gum, dog-wood, and sourwood tops numerous ferns and wildflowers. Among the waterfowl are green-winged teal, blue heron, wood duck, and osprey. Black crappie, bass, and perch are the chief fish. After entrance into the park is a
616 parking lot L. The 0.8-mi *Alder Trail* begins at the parking lot of picnic area

#1. It loops around the peninsula among stands of wildflowers, willow, and tag alder to picnic tables and to the swimming area. (*USGS Map*: Troutman)

ADDRESS AND ACCESS: Superintendent, Duke Power State Park, 159 Inland Sea Lane, Troutman, NC 28166 704-528-6350. From the town of Troutman (6.0 mi S of Statesville and 3.0 mi N of I-77 on US-21/NC-115) go 3.6 mi W on State Park Rd (SR-1330).

SUPPORT FACILITIES: Groceries, gasoline, restaurants, and other stores are in Troutman. Statesville has shopping centers, motels, and restaurants.

Lakeshore Trail 617

LENGTH AND DIFFICULTY: 6.7 mi round-trip, moderate

TRAILHEAD AND DESCRIPTION: Begin at the parking lot of picnic area #2, and follow the sign R of the rest rooms to white blazes. At a jct, after 0.5 mi, turn either R or L for a loop. If R, follow to the main park road and cross near a gate. (It is 0.7 mi S on the road to the campground.) At a red-blazed jct, follow ahead by the lakeside to the end of the peninsula. (For a shortcut, the red blazes can be followed for a 3.5-mi loop.) In the process pass the amphitheater and the campground before continuing around the lakeshore on the return trip.

ENO RIVER STATE PARK (Durham and Orange Counties)

Eno River State Park is a popular hiking and fishing area along 12.0 mi of the river between Hillsborough and Durham. Covering 2,304 acres, the park is segmented into four sections (Few's Ford, Cabe's Land Access, Cole Mill Rd Access, and Pump Station Access), but they are similar, with floodplains, rocky bluffs, and some low-range white water. Remnants of mill dams and rock piles illustrate the settlements of pioneer millers and farmers. Sycamore, river birch, and sweet gum are prominent on the riversides. Wildflowers are profuse; it is a park with a million trout lilies. Among the wildlife are deer, beaver, squirrel, fox, chipmunk, and turkey. Anglers will find Roanoke bass, largemouth bass, bream, redhorse sucker, and catfish. Other activities include picnicking and canoeing. Canoe launching points are below Pleasant Green Dam, Cole Mill Rd, Few's Ford, and Guess Rd. Organized group camping is allowed by reservation. All supplies including water and firewood must be packed in for 0.2 mi. Five backpack sites are available on a first-come basis for small groups or individuals. These require a 1.0-mi hike to access. (*USGS Maps*: Durham NW, Hillsborough)

ADDRESS AND ACCESS: Superintendent, Eno River State Park, 6101 Cole Mill Rd, Durham, NC 27705; 919-383-1686. One access to the park office is 5.3 mi from I-85 in W Durham, N on Cole Mill Rd (SR-1401 in Durham County, which becomes SR-1569 in Orange County). West-bound traffic on I-85 has a ramp to Cole Mill Rd, but eastbound traffic must take the US-70 lane, R, 0.4 mi to turn L, and go under I-85.

618- Eno Nature Trail (0.3 mi); Cox's Mountain Trail (3.7 mi); Fanny's Ford
620 Trail (1.0 mi)

LENGTH AND DIFFICULTY: 5.0 mi combined and round-trip, moderate

TRAILHEADS AND DESCRIPTION: All these trails connect and are red-blazed. From the park office drive to the second parking area, R. Follow a well-main-tained trail 0.1 mi to a jct L with the *Eno Nature Trail*. (The self-guiding trail is also called the *Eno Trace;* it loops 0.3 mi through large hardwoods with 12 interpretive posts.) Continue on *Cox's Mountain Trail* to cross the swinging footbridge over the Eno River. Reach the Wilderness Shelter campsite, L at 0.3 mi. At 0.7 mi the trail forks for a loop, L, up the mtn and ahead on the old road. If hiking L, ascend and pass under a power line at 0.9 mi to Cox's Mtn. Descend to a stream at 1.2 mi and follow downstream to the Eno River at 1.6 mi. Turn R and go downriver among river birch and beech. Turn R on an old wagon road at 2.0 mi, pass under a power line, and follow the old road in a forest with beds of running cedar. At 2.8 mi jct with *Fanny's Ford Trail*, L. (*Fanny's Ford Trail* is a 1.0-mi loop by the riverbank and the pack-in primitive campsite. The trail's name comes from Fanny Breeze, a beloved black midwife and hospitable neighbor to the river community during and after the Civil War.) To complete *Cox's Mountain Trail* loop, continue on the old road to the fork at 3.0 mi. Backtrack to the parking lot at 3.7 mi.

621- Buckquarter Creek Trail (1.5 mi); Holden's Mill Trail (2.6 mi)
622 LENGTH AND DIFFICULTY: 4.1 mi combined and round-trip, easy to moderate

TRAILHEADS AND DESCRIPTION: From the park office drive ahead to the first parking lot, R. Walk down to the Eno River, turn R, upriver to a loop fork at 0.1 mi. If hiking R follow an old road, but turn L at 0.2 mi off the road and into a forest of laurel, oak, and pine. Join an old logging road at 0.5 mi. Pass through a cedar grove and curve L to follow downstream of Buckquarter Creek. At 0.8 mi jct R with *Holden's Mill Trail*. (*Holden's Mill Trail* crosses Buckquarter Creek on a footbridge and after 160 yd ascends on an old farm road in a hardwood forest. Pass rock piles from early farm clearings. Pass under a power line and descend to the Eno River at 1.0 mi. (On the descent is a 0.6-mi loop upriver.) To the R is the site of Holden's Mill. Return down-river on a scenic path of rocks and wildflowers near occasional rapids. Rejoin the *Buckquarter Creek Trail* at 2.6 mi.) Continue downriver and complete the trail after another 0.7 mi.

Pea Creek Trail (1.3 mi); Dunnagan's Trail (1.8 mi); Cole Mill Trail (1.2 mi); Bobbitt Hole Trail (1.6 mi)

623-626

LENGTH AND DIFFICULTY: 7.0 mi combined and round-trip, easy

TRAILHEADS AND DESCRIPTION: These trails are at Cole Mill Rd Access, Section 2. Activities are picnicking, fishing, canoeing, and hiking. Access is as described above to the park office, except from I-85 go 3.2 mi and turn L on Umstead Rd (SR-1449). The trails connect, may overlap in parts, and are red-blazed. From the lower end of the parking area follow the sign down to the Eno River at 0.3 mi to *Pea Creek Trail,* L, and *Cole Mill Trail,* R. On the *Pea Creek Trail* pass under the Cole Mill Rd bridge, and at 0.6 mi under a power line. Reach Pea Creek in an area of wildflowers and ferns. At a footbridge is a jct with *Dunnagan's Trail.* Across Pea Creek turn R along the Eno River. Turn L at the river and follow the bank downstream. Just after the stone wall of the old pump station is visible across the river turn L. Go uphill and circle back to Pea Creek on a ridge above the river and pass through two old homesites. Complete the *Pea Creek Trail* on a return to *Cole Mill Trail.*

Hike upriver on the *Cole Mill Trail,* and at 0.6 mi jct with *Bobbitt Hole Trail* which continues upriver, but *Cole Mill Trail* turns R under a power line. This route rejoins *Bobbitt Hole Trail,* L, after 300 yd. (From here, R, it is 0.4 mi on *Cole Mill Trail* to the upper parking lot and picnic area.) If taking the higher elev of *Bobbitt Hole Trail,* follow a beautiful wide trail through pine, oak, and holly on the approach to the river. A turn R for a few yd is to a sharp curve in the river and the large scenic pool called Bobbitt Hole after 0.9 mi. Return downriver, and after 0.6 mi jct with *Cole Mill Trail* for a return to the parking area.

Old Pump Station Trail

627

LENGTH AND DIFFICULTY: 1.5 mi, easy

TRAILHEAD AND DESCRIPTION: This loop trail is the Pump Station Access, Section 4. Access is as above, except after I-85, go 2.3 mi and turn R on Rivermont Rd (SR-1402). Drive 0.6 mi to Nancy Rhodes Creek and park, L. Follow the trail sign to remains of the old Durham Pump Station at 0.4 mi. Turn L upriver of the Eno and make a sharp L at 1.0 mi. Return under a power line and reach Rivermont Rd at 1.3 mi. Turn L and follow the road back to the parking area.

628 *Cabe Lands Trail*

LENGTH AND DIFFICULTY: 1.2 mi, easy

TRAILHEAD AND DESCRIPTION: This loop trail is at Cabe's Land Access, Section 3. Access is as above, except after I-85, go 2.3 mi and turn L on Sprager Rd (SR-1400). Go 1.3 mi, turn R on Howe St (Howell Rd on county maps), and after 0.5 mi reach parking space on R. Follow an old service road to the Eno River, passing carpets of periwinkle, ivy, and running cedar. Reach the river at 0.4 mi, turn L, pass beaver cuts and old mill foundations at 0.4 mi. Cross a small stream and ascend to the point of origin.

MEDOC MOUNTAIN STATE PARK (Halifax County)

The 2,286-acre park is on the granite fall line of the Piedmont where the coastal plain zone begins. The area was named Medoc, for a grape-producing region in France, when a large vineyard was operated here in the nineteenth century. Although locally called a mtn because of its higher than usual elev in the area, it is more a low ridge with the summit at 325 ft above sea level. Winding through the park is Little Fishing Creek with bluegill, largemouth and Roanoke bass; redbreast sunfish; and chain pickerel. Plant life is diverse; it is unusual for laurel to be this far E. Activities include fishing, picnicking, hiking, and tent camping. Camping facilities include tables, grills, tent pads, a central water source, and hot showers. Camping facilities for groups and families are available mid-March through November (reservations for groups required). (*USGS Maps:* Hollister, Aurelian Springs, Essex)

ADDRESS AND ACCESS: Superintendent, Medoc Mtn State Park, PO Box 400, Hollister, NC 27844; 919-445-2280. Park office is on Medoc Mtn Rd (SR-1002), 4.6 mi E of NC-561 intersection at Hollister, and 2.0 mi W of NC-48.

SUPPORT FACILITIES: Groceries and gasoline are in Hollister.

629- *Summit Trail (2.9 mi); Dam Site Loop Trail (0.9 mi)*
630   LENGTH AND DIFFICULTY: 3.8 mi combined and round-trip, easy

TRAILHEADS AND DESCRIPTION: From the park office parking lot follow the trail sign, and after 125 yd turn L to begin the loop of *Summit Trail*. At 0.5 mi cross Rocky Spring Branch, and reach the E bank of Little Fishing Creek at 0.7 mi. Turn R and go upstream. Pass a large granite outcropping, the core of the summit, at 1.4 mi. After a few yd the trail ascends R 0.1 mi to the peak, but to include the *Dam Site Loop Trail* continue ahead, N, and pass an artesian well. Pass the ruins of a dam built by the Boy Scouts in the early 1920s, and the ruins of another dam upstream. Circle back to the *Summit Trail* through groves of laurel at 2.5 mi. Follow a gravel road, but turn from it at 3.1 mi. Pass an old cemetery, L, and return to the parking lot.

Stream Trail (2.2 mi); Discovery Trail (0.1 mi); Bluffs Trail (2.8 mi)

631-633

LENGTH AND DIFFICULTY: 5.1 mi combined, easy

TRAILHEADS AND DESCRIPTION: Access to these connecting trails is 2.2 mi W from the park office on SR-1002 to Medoc State Park Rd (SR-1322). Turn R and follow the park signs 1.0 mi to the picnic parking area. From the parking area go 60 yd R of the picnic shelter to the trail sign. *Stream Trail* is L. (The *Bluffs Trail* is R.) *Stream Trail* is a beautiful, well-designed, and carefully maintained trail. It passes through a forest of loblolly pine, oak, and beech with laurel, holly, and aromatic bayberry part of the understory. Rattlesnake orchid, partridgeberry, and running cedar are part of the ground cover. At 0.2 mi arrive at Little Fishing Creek and go upstream. At 0.4 mi jct with *Discovery Trail*, proceed 0.3 mi L to exit to picnic and parking area. To include the *Discovery Trail* turn R. At 1.2 mi is a confluence with Bear Swamp Creek. Enter an open area with kudzu and trumpet vine at 1.6 mi. Exit the forest at 2.0 mi and cross the picnic grounds to the parking area at 2.2 mi. On *Bluffs Trail*, pass through an old field on a wide manicured trail into a forest. At 0.4 mi turn R downstream by Little Fishing Creek. Pass through large loblolly pine, beech, river birch, and oak. Climb to a steep bluff at 1.0 mi. Reach the highest bluff (over 60 ft) at 1.4 mi. Descend, bear R on a return ridge, cross a stream at 2.6 mi, and return to the parking lot at 2.8 mi.

MORROW MOUNTAIN STATE PARK (Stanly County)

This 4,693-acre park is in the heart of the lower Piedmont region and in the ancient Uwharrie range. More than 500 million years ago it was covered by a shallow sea in which volcanic islands developed; they later became the hard basalt and rhyolite deposits of this area. Established in 1935, the park is on the Pee Dee River and Lake Tillery. Named after J. M. Morrow, a former landowner, the park is scenic and historic. It offers a nature museum, picnicking, boating, fishing, nature programs, swimming, hiking, equestrian trails, and camping. Family camping, with 106 tent/RV campsites, is open all year with water, showers, and rest rooms (no hookups; water off December 1 to mid-March). Backpack camping and youth-group tent camping are also provided, but advance registration is necessary. Rental cabins, available from

March 1 through November, also require advance registration. Historic in its own right (the state's fourth oldest and a former CCC camp), the restored homestead of Dr Francis Kron is another example of the park's effort to maintain cultural resources with its natural resources. (*USGS Maps:* Badin, Morrow Mtn)

> ADDRESS AND ACCESS: Superintendent, Morrow Mtn State Park, 49104 Morrow Mtn Rd, Albemarle, NC 28001; 704-982-4402. An access route from Albemarle is 1.8 mi NE on NC-740 (from jct with NC-24/27/73) to Morrow Mtn Rd (SR-1798) and 2.5 mi to the park entrance.

634- *Laurel Trail (0.6 mi); Morrow Mountain Trail (3.0 mi); Quarry Trail (0.6*
637 *mi); Hattaway Mountain Trail (2.0 mi)*

> LENGTH AND DIFFICULTY: 6.2 mi combined, easy to moderate

> TRAILHEADS AND DESCRIPTION: Park at the Natural History Museum and begin the *Laurel Trail* behind the museum. If going clockwise, stay on the main trail through a mature forest of hardwoods, pine, laurel, and pink azalea for a loop of 0.6 mi. (After 0.2 mi jct L with *Morrow Mountain Trail,* which goes to the top of Morrow Mtn. Ascend W of Sugarloaf Creek and jct with *Sugarloaf Mountain Trail* at 0.7 mi. Follow the *Sugarloaf Mountain Trail* for 0.6 mi and turn L. Cross a small stream and arrive at the E side of Morrow Mtn at 2.5 mi. Ascend steeply on switchback to jct with the *Mountain Loop Trail.* Exit at either the overlook or the picnic area to the Morrow Mtn parking area.)

> For the *Quarry Trail,* hike NW from the museum, past the swimming pool, to the picnic area (or drive to the picnic parking area). The loop of 0.6 mi reveals a man-made gorge where volcanic slate of the Slate Belt can be studied. On the *Hattaway Mountain Trail,* begin at the pool bathhouse and follow the 2.0-mi loop trail up and over dry, rocky Hattaway Mtn, the park's third highest. The mature forest has oak, sourwood, maple, and laurel.

638- *Three Rivers Trail (0.6 mi); Fall Mountain Trail (4.17 mi)*
639

> LENGTH AND DIFFICULTY: 4.7 mi combined, easy to moderate

> SPECIAL FEATURES: Kron House, river views, rhyolite

> TRAILHEADS AND DESCRIPTION: Park at the boathouse near the boat launch. The *Fall Mountain Trail* begins at the S end of the parking lot. If taking the W route, jct L with *Three Rivers Trail.* (*Three Rivers Trail* is a 0.6-mi self-guiding interpretive trail that crosses the boat-launch road and loops by an open marsh of swamp rose and arrowwood. It passes through a damp forest area and to the riverside for views of the Yadkin, Pee Dee, and

Uwharrie Rivers.) Continuing on *Fall Mountain Trail,* twice cross an access path to the youth-group tent campsites. At 1.2 mi pass the historic Kron House, L. (Dr Kron, physician, lived here from 1834 until his death in 1883. His 6,000-acre farm was used for numerous horticultural experiments.) Ascend N to cross the Fall Mtn ridge in a forest of oak, laurel, and scattered pine at 1.7 mi. Descend on a rough area of rhyolite and volcanic outcroppings. There are excellent views of the Falls Dam and the Yadkin River. Silverbell, coneflower, and lip fern are among the flowering plants and ferns. Pass through a crack in a boulder the size of a house. Descend, cross a small stream, and twice cross the road to the group camp for a loop of 4.1 mi. Deer and squirrel may be seen in these areas.

Rocks Trail 640

LENGTH AND DIFFICULTY: 2.6 mi round-trip, easy
TRAILHEAD AND DESCRIPTION: Park at the administrative building and begin at the rear of the building, hiking E. Arrive at the family campground and follow the yellow blazes on *Rocks Trail* (which has parts of a bridle trail). At 0.2 mi from the campground turn L. (Because of numerous campground trails and extra lead-in trails to *Mountain Creek Bridle Trail,* the hiker may need to watch carefully for the yellow blazes.) Pass R of a jct with the bridle trail at 0.6 mi. Continue ahead to an excellent view of the Pee Dee River. Descend over a rock area to trail's end at 1.3 mi. Return by the same route.

Sugarloaf Mountain Trail (2.8 mi); Mountain Loop Trail (0.8 mi) 641 642

LENGTH AND DIFFICULTY: 3.6 mi combined, moderate
TRAILHEADS AND DESCRIPTION: (These trails connect with the *Morrow Mountain Trail,* bridle trails, and Morrow Mtn Rd.) Park at the lot R and E of the staff residences. Follow the trail sign for hikers, bearing L from the bridle trail. Cross two small streams and Morrow Mtn Rd. Ascend and follow the NW ridge side of Sugarloaf Mtn (858 ft). Jct L with *Morrow Mountain Trail* at 1.4 mi. Turn R (jointly with *Morrow Mountain Trail*) and after 2.0 mi continue R (*Morrow Mountain Trail* goes L in its ascent to the top of Morrow Mtn), cross Morrow Mtn Rd at 2.2 mi, cross a stream at 2.7 mi, and enter a field near the parking lot to complete the loop. For the *Mountain Loop Trail,* drive to the top of Morrow Mtn. The trailhead can be found at the picnic shelter or the overlook. It leads to a loop around the peak (936 ft). The trail is graded, with bridges over the ravines. It also connects on the E side with *Morrow Mountain Trail,* described above. From Morrow

Mtn are views E to Lake Tillery and Dennis Mtn (the route of the *Uwharrie Trail*) in the Uwharrie NF (see chapter 4).

RAVEN ROCK STATE PARK (Harnett County)

Established in 1970, Raven Rock State Park is a large 3,300-acre wilderness-type forest. The Cape Fear River runs through its center. A major geological feature of the area is the 152-ft-high crystalline rock jutting out toward the river. Ravens once nested here; thus the park's name. It is unusual for rhododendron and laurel to grow this far E with a diverse and long list of Piedmont and coastal-plain plants. Some of the wild animals and birds are osprey, eagle, owls, squirrel, raccoon, salamanders, and deer. Prominent fish are largemouth bass, catfish, and sunfish. Activities are picnicking, hiking, fishing, and primitive backpack camping. (All gear, including water, must be carried to the camps. Registration is required at the park office.) There are bridle trails on the N side of the river; directions and regulations are available from the park office. (*USGS Map:* Mamers)

ADDRESS AND ACCESS: Superintendent, Raven Rock State Park, Rte 3, Box 1005, Lillington, NC 27546; 910-893-4888. Access to the park is 3.0 mi off US-421 on Raven Rock Park Rd (SR-1314), 6.0 mi W of Lillington.

643 *Raven Rock Loop Trail*

LENGTH AND DIFFICULTY: 2.1 mi, easy

CONNECTING TRAILS:

644   *American Beech Nature Trail* (0.5 mi, easy)
645   *Little Creek Loop Trail* (1.4 mi, easy)
646   *Fish Traps Trail* (1.2 mi round-trip, easy)
647   *Northington's Ferry Trail* (2.2 mi round-trip, easy)

SPECIAL FEATURE: Raven Rock overhang

TRAILHEAD AND DESCRIPTION: From the parking lot follow the Raven Rock sign on the E side of the lot. Jct R with the *American Beech Nature Trail*. (The nature trail descends and crosses a small stream through poplar, sweet gum, red maple, beech, sweet bay, laurel, and oak. It returns on the E side of the picnic area.) At 0.8 mi the *Raven Rock Loop Trail* jct R with *Little Creek Loop Trail*. (It descends downstream by Little Creek for 0.7 mi to a canoe camp.) Downriver it is another 0.5 mi to a group backpack campsite. Reach scenic Raven Rock at 0.9 mi. Descend on stairways to the riverbank and rock overhangs. Return on the steps, but take a turn R at the top. Arrive at a scenic overlook of the Cape Fear River at 1.1 mi. Jct sharply R with *Fish Traps Trail* and *Northington's Ferry Trail* at 1.7 mi. (*Fish Traps Trail* leads to a rock outcropping at 1.1 mi beside the river. [Indians placed trap baskets at the rapids to catch fish. Backtrack.] *Northington's Ferry Trail* follows a wide, easy route to the mouth of Campbell Creek [also called Camels Creek], site of the Cape Fear River crossing. The ferry served as a crossing between Raleigh and Fayetteville as early as 1770. Backtrack.) Continue on the *Raven Rock Loop Trail* on an old woods road to the parking area.

Campbell Creek Loop Trail (5.1 mi); Lanier Falls Trail (0.4 mi) 648-
649

LENGTH AND DIFFICULTY: 5.5 mi combined round-trip, easy to moderate

TRAILHEADS AND DESCRIPTION: At the parking lot follow the old svc road N 45 yd and turn L into young growth that enters an older forest. Descend gradually in an oak-hickory forest to a footbridge over Campbell Creek at 0.7 mi. Here the trail loops R or L. If taking the L route ascend and descend on low ridges through sections of laurel to jct with the former *Buckhorn Trail* at 2.1 mi. (See *Buckhorn Trail* in chapter 14. The section adjoining Raven Rock SP has been abandoned.) A park svc road comes in from the L and joins *Campbell Creek Loop Trail* R. Descend to the primitive campsites at 2.3 mi, L, and *Lanier Falls Trail*, L, at 2.5 mi. (The 0.2-mi *Lanier Falls Trail* leads to a scenic rock outcropping at the Cape Fear River. Backtrack.) Continue the trail to the mouth of Campbell Creek and follow upstream to rejoin the access route at the bridge at 4.4 mi.

UMSTEAD STATE PARK (Wake County)

William B. Umstead State Park covers 5,381 acres: 4,026 in the Crabtree Creek section (N) and 1,355 in the Reedy Creek section (S). Crabtree Creek, which runs W to E through the park, separates the two sections. Among the largest state parks, Umstead is a valuable oasis in the center of a fast-developing metropolitan area. Adjoining on the W is the Raleigh-Durham International Airport, on the N is US-70, and on the S is I-40. A former CCC camp, the park's original 5,088 acres were deeded to the state by the US government in fee simple of one dollar in 1943. It was designated Crabtree Creek State Park, but in 1955 it was named in honor of the former governor. In the Reedy Creek section is Piedmont Beech Natural Area, a 50-acre tract with American beech (*Fagus grandifolia*), some of which are more than 300 years old. The tract is included in the National Registry of Natural Landmarks. Access is allowed by permit only from park officials.

In addition to Crabtree Creek, Sycamore Creek also runs through the park from the NW to the SE to empty into the Crabtree. The park is hilly and rocky with tributaries such as Pott's Branch, Reedy Creek, and Turkey Creek flowing into the main creeks. Quartz rock piles indicate the presence of farmers in the last century and the early part of the 1900s. There are three lakes: Big Lake, Sycamore Lake, and Reedy Creek Lake. Fishing for bass, bluegill, and crappie is allowed, but swimming is allowed only at the park's group campsites. Large stands of mature oak, poplar, and loblolly pine provide a canopy for dogwood, redbud, laurel, and sourwood. Beaver, deer, squirrel, and raccoon are among the mammals found in the park. Recreational activities are fishing, camping, hiking, picnicking, horseback riding, bicycling, and nature studies. There are three organized group camps and a lodge. In both park sections are equestrian and hiking trails for 16.0 mi on gated park gravel roads. Their access points are off Ebenezer Church Rd from US-70 (N), from Reedy Creek Rd off Ebenezer Church Rd (SE), and Old Reedy Creek Park Rd from Weston Pkwy (SW). In the Crabtree Creek section there is a

650 0.2-mi (one-way) paved trail for disabled persons, the *Big Lake Handicapped Trail*, for scenic beauty and fishing. It crosses the dam and a bridge over the spillway to the bathhouse. Access is on the road past the park office to a parking lot R. The 6.0-mi linear *Loblolly Trail* is partly (2.7 mi, one way) in Umstead State Park. Its other mileage is in the city of Raleigh. The park access is at the NE corner of the parking lot at the Reedy Creek section. A signboard shows its direction beginning at a large white oak tree. Its S access is at gate D of Carter/Finley Stadium (see Raleigh in chapter 13). (*USGS Maps:* Cary, Raleigh W, Durham SE)

ADDRESS AND ACCESS: Umstead State Park, Rte 8, Box 130, Raleigh, NC 27612; 919-787-3033. Access to the Crabtree Creek section entrance is on US-70, 6.0 mi W of the jct with I-40. To reach the Reedy Creek section entrance from the Crabtree Creek entrance on US-70, drive W 1.0 mi to Aviation Parkway. Turn L, go 4.0 mi to I-40. Turn L on I-40, go 3.6 mi to exit 287 at Harrision Ave, L (N). If from I-40 jct at Wade Ave in Raleigh drive W 4.0 mi to exit 287 R.

651- *Sal's Branch Trail (2.4 mi); Pott's Branch Trail (1.0 mi); Oak Rock Trail*
653 *(0.7 mi)*

LENGTH AND DIFFICULTY: 4.1 mi combined round-trip, easy to moderate

TRAILHEADS AND DESCRIPTION: In the Crabtree Creek section, park at the lower parking and picnic area (nearest Big Lake). At the lower corner (SW) of the lot descend 110 yd on a wide trail with steps to jct L with orange-diamond-blazed *Pott's Branch Trail*. Another 75 ft down the steps jct R with oranged-circle-blazed *Sal's Branch Trail*. Another 60 ft descends to the paved *Big Lake Trail*, R and L, described in the introduction above.

Follow the *Sal's Creek Trail* through loblolly pine and hardwoods with Christmas ferns and running cedar on the forest floor. Cross a svc road at 0.5 mi; pass a beech grove by the branch at 0.8 mi. Turn uphill sharply at 1.9 mi and complete the loop at 2.4 mi.

On the *Pott's Branch Trail* follow it through tall loblolly pines and undulate to 0.3 mi where the trail turns L away from Sycamore Creek and parallels with Pott's Branch. At 0.5 mi intersect with the *Sycamore Trail*. (It goes up the steps L and 0.2 mi through the picnic area to the parking lot, and to the R across Pott's Branch on its long loop (see description below). Continue on the *Pott's Branch Trail*, notice stone dam remains from CCC work on the R, pass a large observation deck R, and ascend to the upper parking lot at 1.0 mi.

Sycamore Trail

LENGTH AND DIFFICULTY: 6.5 mi, easy to moderate

TRAILHEAD AND DESCRIPTION: Park at the lower parking lot. Follow trail signs up steps to the picnic area. Pass between two large picnic shelters and descend on wide steps to cross *Pott's Branch Trail* and Pott's Branch at 0.2 mi. Follow upstream the blue-blazed trail to cross Sycamore Lake Rd at 0.5 mi. Follow the path through a forest of oak, maple, pine, and running cedar to pass under a power line at 1.5 mi. Ahead is a former homesite in a grove of huge white oaks and wisteria. Exit to a park road and horse trail; to the L is King Cemetery and gate to Graylyn Rd (a spur off Ebenezer Rd). Cross the road, descend among more large white oaks. Cross a horse trail, then at 1.9 mi the *Sycamore Trail* forks for a loop. If turning L descend into a hollow with holly and beech. Cross at least four footbridges at the bank of a rocky bluff among wild orchids, crested dwarf iris, and ferns. Cross more footbridges, curve R, ascend a ridge with quartz footing to parallel Sycamore Creek. Descend to cross park road (used by equestrians and bikers) at 3.4 mi. (To the L, across the CCC-built bridge and immediately R, is a 280-ft spur trail to connect with the *Company Mill Trail*.) After a flat area ascend a rocky hillside, pass the edge of a high bluff, then descend to the creek bank. Pass under a power line at 4.1 mi. Ascend steeply on switchbacks, and on the hilltop cross a park road at 4.4 mi. At 4.6 mi return to the loop for a backtrack to the parking lot at 6.5 mi.

Company Mill Trail (5.3 mi); Inspiration Trail (0.5 mi); Beech Trail (0.4 mi)
LENGTH AND DIFFICULTY: 6.2 mi round-trip, combined, easy to moderate
TRAILHEADS AND DESCRIPTION: From the Reedy Creek section parking lot go
to the NW corner and descend to a display board at the edge of the woods.
At 0.1 mi is a large stone picnic shelter in the picnic area. To the R is the
trailhead for *Company Mill Trail*. To the L is blue-diamond-blazed *Inspiration
Trail*. It descends to a streamlet, turns L, parallels the ravine with laurel,
curves up the hill, and jct L with a blue-circle-blazed *Beech Trail* (which connects the *Inspiration Trail* with the *Company Mill Trail*). Turn R and return to
the picnic shelter and trailhead for Company Mill at 0.5 mi.

The orange-blazed *Company Mill Trail* descends and ascends three
ridges on the descent to the Crabtree Creek steel footbridge at 0.6 mi. On
the way observe quartz rock piles made by pioneer farmers on the rocky
slopes, and pass a jct L with *Beech Trail* at 0.3 mi. After crossing the footbridge turn R or L for a loop. If hiking R, descend between rock ledges L
and the creek R. At 0.7 mi are rapids and remnants of the dam. A millstone
is L of the trail. Turn L at 1.2 mi and follow a tributary, crossing it a number
of times among tall trees, many of them beech. Descend from the ridge to
the S bank of Sycamore Creek and turn L at 2.1 mi. (To the R it is 280 ft to a
park road and L over a bridge to jct with the Sycamore Trail R and L.) Stay
near the creek side, partly on a rim of a former millrace. Maidenhair fern,
buckeye, and black cohosh adorn the trail. There are rock remnants of the
George Lynn Mill Dam to the R. Leave the creek on switchbacks at 2.2 mi to
a ridge. Then descend on switchbacks to a small stream. Ascend; reach the
top of the ridge at 2.7 mi. Cross a park svc road at 3.1 mi, and gradually
descend to the creek bank of Crabtree Creek at 4.2 mi. Pass R of a rock
slope and complete the loop at 4.7 mi. Cross the high footbridge over the
creek and ascend to the picnic shelter at 5.3 mi.

SECTION 3: COASTAL REGION

CAROLINA BEACH STATE PARK (New Hanover County)

The 1,773-acre Carolina Beach State Park is considered a naturalist's delight
with more than 50 species of flora (including the rare Venus's-flytrap and five
other insectivorous plants native to the coastal environment). Its trail system
enables the hiker to study salt marshes, sandhills, rainwater ponds, and
swamplands. One historic sandhill, Sugarloaf, was the settlement area of the
Coree Indians in the 1500s and a navigational landmark as early as 1738. Park

facilities include a tent/trailer campground, picnic area, marina to the Cape Fear River for fishing and boating, and hiking. (*USGS Map:* Carolina Beach)

ADDRESS AND ACCESS: Superintendent, Carolina Beach State Park, PO Box 475, Carolina Beach, NC 28428; 910-458-8206 (office), 910-458-7770 (marina). From Greenfield Park in Wilmington, go S 12.0 mi on US-421 to entrance R, at jct with Dow Rd (SR-1573).

Sugarloaf Trail (3.5 mi); Swamp Trail (0.8 mi); Fly Trap Trail (0.4 mi); Campground Trail (1.0 mi); Snow's Cut Trail (0.4 mi) **658-662**

LENGTH AND DIFFICULTY: 6.1 mi combined, easy

TRAILHEADS AND DESCRIPTION: Trailheads are at Fly Trap parking area, the campground, and the marina parking area. (If Fly Trap parking is chosen, take the first paved road L after the park entrance. The campground trailhead is the second paved road, R.) Follow the road signs to the marina parking area. From here enter the looped yellow-blazed *Sugarloaf Trail* at the trail sign and follow it through a forest of pines, oak, and yaupon. At 0.2 mi the red-blazed *Swamp Trail* is L. Continue ahead along the riverbank to 0.6 mi and turn L in a forest of live oaks, pines, mosses, and pink spiderwort (*Tradescantia rosea*). On white sandhills reach an old road's jct at 1.0 mi; turn sharply L, pass two cypress ponds with white water lilies, and make another sharp L at a lily pond at 1.7 mi, pass a jct with the *Campground Trail,* R, and at 2.3 mi jct with the red-blazed *Swamp Trail,* L. Continue ahead, cross paved road, pass a jct R with the blue-blazed *Campground Trail,* and reach the Fly Trap parking area at 2.8 mi. The *Fly Trap Trail* begins here near a kiosk that describes the Venus's-flytrap (*Dionaea muscipula*). Charles Darwin described it as the "most wonderful plant in the world." Protected by law, it is found only in SE N.C. and NE S.C. After the 0.4-mi loop on the *Fly Trap Trail,* return on the *Sugarloaf Trail,* continue about 20 yd N of the road, and hike NW. Cross a boardwalk, pass through a mixed pine and hardwood forest to the trail's end at the marina parking lot.

If going to the campground from the *Fly Trap Trail* parking area, backtrack on the *Sugarloaf Trail* 0.4 mi and turn L. Blue lupine (*Lupinus perrennis*) grows here. At the N side of the campground loop road enter the woods toward Snow's Cut, and curve L on *Snow's Cut Trail* for 0.4 mi to a picnic area at Marina Rd.

CLIFFS-OF-THE-NEUSE STATE PARK (Wayne County)

Cliffs-of-the-Neuse State Park covers 748 acres, chiefly of forests, on the W bank of the Neuse River. The park's most extraordinary attraction is the 90-ft cliff carved over thousands of years to show countless fossil shells (not for public collection), the remains of other marine species, and sedimentation at what was once the Atlantic shoreline. Spanish moss drapes the oaks and pines. Galax, a more mountainous plant, grows on the N bank of Mill Creek. Picnicking, swimming and boating (in the lake), fishing, and hiking are the activities. Family camping is provided at tent/RV sites that have water, flush toilets, tables and grills, and hot showers (no hookups) March 15–November 30. Tent camps for youth groups are available. (*USGS Map:* Seven Springs)

> ADDRESS AND ACCESS: Superintendent, Cliffs-of-the-Neuse State Park, 345A Park Entrance Rd, Seven Springs, NC 28578; 919-788-6234. Entrance to the park is on SR-1743, E 0.5 mi from NC-111, 13.0 mi SE of Goldsboro.

663- *Spanish Moss Trail (0.5. mi); Galax Trail (0.5 mi); Bird Trail (0.8 mi)*
665   LENGTH AND DIFFICULTY: 1.8 mi combined, easy

TRAILHEADS AND DESCRIPTION: From the parking area follow the trail signs R and descend to a scenic area by the riverbank and Mill Creek. Turn L on red-blazed *Bird Trail* to loop across Still Creek and reach the jct with a yellow-blazed loop, the *Galax Trail,* at 0.8 mi. Follow the *Galax Trail* 0.5 mi and return to the parking lot. The *Spanish Moss Trail* is L of the parking lot but R of the Interpretive Center. Descend and circle back to the parking lot after 0.5 mi. (Campers have made numerous connecting trails in this area.)

FORT MACON STATE PARK (Carteret County)

The Fort Macon State Park is best known for its restored fort at Beaufort Inlet. Emphasis is on its Civil War history. Facilities and services in the 389-acre park include ocean swimming (June 1 through Labor Day), fishing, picnicking, and hiking. A short nature trail and beach hiking provide more than 2.0 mi of
666 walking. The 0.4-mi *Fort Macon Nature Trail* begins R between the parking area and the fort's covertway. Follow the signs on a loop trail through a shrub thicket to Beaufort Inlet and back. Some trees and shrubs are live oak, black locust, Hercules' club (*Zanthoxylum clava-herculis*), and yaupon. Camping is not allowed in the park. (*USGS Map:* Beaufort)

> ADDRESS AND ACCESS: Superintendent, Fort Macon State Park, Box 127, Atlantic Beach, NC 28512; 919-726-3775. To reach the park (which is on the E tip of Bogue Banks), turn S off US-70 in Morehead City to

cross the bridge to Atlantic Beach. At the jct with NC-58 turn L on Fort Macon Rd (SR-1190), and go 2.2 mi.

GOOSE CREEK STATE PARK (Beaufort County)

Goose Creek State Park is a coastal park that covers 1,596 acres on the N side of the Pamlico River. Special features are the tall loblolly pines and live oaks draped with ghostly gray Spanish moss and both freshwater and saltwater fishing. Primitive camping, picnicking, swimming (June 1 to Labor Day), fishing, boating, and hiking are provided in this sandy wilderness. Bogs; sandy natural beaches; excellent freshwater fishing for bass, bluegill, and perch; and saltwater fishing for bluefish and flounder are features of a distinctive recreational area. Native mosquitoes and ticks welcome visitors; a maximum-strength repellent is advisable. (*USGS Map:* Blounts Bay)

ADDRESS AND ACCESS: Superintendent, Goose Creek State Park, Rte 2, Box 372, Washington, NC 27889; 919-923-2191. Access from Washington at jct of US-264/17 is 9.0 mi on US-264 and a R turn on Camp Leach Rd (SR-1334) for 2.4 mi to park entrance.

SUPPORT FACILITIES: Shopping centers, motels, and restaurants are in Washington. A nearby private campground is Whichard's Beach campground, Box 746, Washington, NC 27889; 919-946-1748. From the jct of US-264/17, go 1.7 mi S on US-17 and turn SE on Whichard's Beach Rd (SR-1166) for 3.0 mi. Full svc, rec fac. Open all year.

Live Oak Trail (1.1 mi), Goose Creek Trail (2.9 mi); Ragged Point Trail (0.5 mi); Flatty Creek Trail (0.4 mi); Ivey Gut Trail (1.9 mi) **667- 671**

LENGTH AND DIFFICULTY: 6.8 mi combined, easy

SPECIAL FEATURES: Spanish moss, estuarine wildlife

TRAILHEADS AND DESCRIPTION: A combination trip on the trails, beginning with the *Live Oak Trail,* could be as follows: Begin from the parking lot on the E side of the park and follow the signs for a loop around the riverbank. Pass the swimming area at 1.2 mi. The *Goose Creek Trail* connects near the swimming area but goes W. After 0.2 mi jct, L, with the *Ragged Point Trail.* (This is a boardwalk trail to an observation tower for viewing the Pamlico River and nearby wetlands. Backtrack.) Continue on the *Goose Creek Trail* and at 0.9 mi cross boardwalks over low areas. At 1.5 mi reach a jct with the W parking lot, and at 1.8 mi reach jct with *Flatty Creek Trail.* (This is another boardwalk trail and observation tower. Backtrack.) Continue around the peninsula and return to the W parking lot at 2.9 mi. The *Ivey*

Gut Trail leaves from the W parking area and campground and meanders near Goose Creek to an exit on the park road and parking area at 1.9 mi. (There is a folk legend that the ghost of a Goose Creek pirate walks through these woods after dark looking for a cache of gold.) Some of the plants seen along the trails are prickly pear, blue flag iris, bays, lizard's tail, blueberry, and marsh pennywort. (The park plans to add a 1.0-mi trail through a hardwood swamp with boardwalks. It will be located behind the site of the new Environmental Education Center.)

HAMMOCKS BEACH STATE PARK (Onslow County)

Hammocks Beach State Park with 892 acres occupies all of Bear Island SE of Swansboro. The island is reputed to be one of the most unspoiled and beautiful beach areas on the Atlantic coast. For the hiker there are 3.8 mi of a wide beach trail from Bear Inlet to Bogue Inlet. It is an unmarked trail whose sandy treadway shifts with each change of the tide. There are high dunes; one in the SW section of the island is 60 ft. In addition to hiking, other activities are fishing, swimming, and birding. Vegetation is sparse, but there are sea oats, croton, elder, yaupon, cordgrass, and near the marsh side some live oaks and cedars. A few deer, rabbits, and raccoons live on the island. It is also the nesting ground of the loggerhead sea turtle. The park has a seasonal bathhouse, refreshment stand, and picnic tables. A fee passenger ferry operates daily (9:30–6:00) from Memorial Day to Labor Day. The distance to the park is 2.5 mi through a web of marshy islands. Visitors using private boat service for day use or overnight camping must contact the park office to register for a permit. (*USGS Maps:* Hubert, Brown's Inlet)

ADDRESS AND ACCESS: Superintendent, Hammocks Beach State Park, 1572 Hammocks Beach Rd, Swansboro, NC 28584; 910-326-4881. From the W edge of Swansboro on NC-24, take Hammocks Beach Rd (SR-1511) S to the ferry landing.

JOCKEY'S RIDGE STATE PARK (Dare County)

Jockey's Ridge State Park, better known as a center for hang gliding than for hiking, covers 415 acres of "marching" sand dunes adjacent to Nags Head Woods, a maritime forest of 1,980 acres. Jockey's Ridge is named, according to one among a number of local stories, for its use as a natural grandstand for races of Banker ponies. It has a 140-ft-high dune, the largest and highest on the Atlantic coast. A hike to the top of the ridge presents an outstanding view of both the Atlantic Ocean and Roanoke Sound, particularly at sunset. Activities include hiking, nature study and photography, hang gliding, and kite flying. Hikers on the 1.5-mi self-guided nature trail, *Tracks in the Sand Trail,* are advised to stay on the designated routes to the **672** ridge. Contact the park ranger for information concerning hang glider take-off and landing zones. Facilities include a park office, rest rooms, and picnic shelters with tables and grills. Camping is not available at the park. (*USGS Maps:* Manteo, Roanoke Island NE)

ADDRESS AND ACCESS: Superintendent, Jockey's Ridge State Park, Box 592, Nags Head, NC 27959; 919-441-7132. Access is from US-158 W of Nags Head on West Carolista Dr.

JONES LAKE STATE PARK (Bladen County)

Jones Lake is an example of the Bay Lakes area, where shallow depressions (none deeper than 10 ft) are filled with cool, dark water. Geologically, it is thought that the oval depressions were formed by wind and wave action following a receding Ice Age. Other theories are the ancient ocean springs theory and the ancient ocean lagoons theory. These formations are also found in coastal S.C. and NE Ga. The Bay Lakes area is also known for a wide variety of bay trees and shrubs. The park covers 2,208 acres with facilities for camping, picnicking, swimming, boating, fishing (mainly for yellow perch and blue-spotted sunfish), hiking, and guided nature study (in the summer). The campground has tent/RV sites with drinking water, flush toilets, tables and grills, and hot showers (no hookups). Open March 15–December 1. (Bladen Lakes State Forest is across the road from the park. See chapter 11.) (*USGS Map:* Elizabethtown)

ADDRESS AND ACCESS: Superintendent, Jones Lake State Park, Rte 1, Box 945, Elizabethtown, NC 28337; 910-588-4550. Access is from the jct of NC-53/242 and US-701 on NC-242 N for 4.0 mi.

Jones Lake Trail   **673**

LENGTH AND DIFFICULTY: 3.8 mi, easy

SPECIAL FEATURE: species of bay trees

TRAILHEAD AND DESCRIPTION: Enter from either the campground (if a registered camper) or the picnic area to make the loop around the lake. Follow the signs from the parking lot by the water fountain (70 yd from the entrance). Enter the forest of juniper, pine, gum, and cypress with Spanish moss. Pass sweet bay (a shrub bog plant with large showy leaves and fragrant flowers related to the magnolia); red bay (a small evergreen with a scent of bay rum); the loblolly bay (a member of the tea family with evergreen leaves and white fragrant blossoms); and the bull bay tree (*Magnolia grandiflora,* with large creamy-white petals and scarlet seeds). The trail is sometimes narrow and wet. There are a number of side trails. At 2.5 mi a side trail leads to the parking area. Return to the point of origin at 2.8 mi. Animal life in the park includes deer, raccoons, snakes, bears, and a variety of waterfowl. Yellow perch and blue-spotted sunfish are in the lake, but high acidity makes fishing only fair.

LAKE WACCAMAW STATE PARK (Columbus County)

Lake Waccamaw State Park, with 10,670 acres (1,732 land; 8,938 water), is the second largest state park in the coastal district. The lake, one of the clear lakes of the Carolina Bays, received its name from the Waccamaw Indians. On a remote, gated paved wilderness road, the park offers picnicking, primitive group camping, fishing, and hiking. A boardwalk/pier built into the lake allows for sunbathing and wading. Overnight walk-in campers must register with the park ranger. The park comprises three vegetative communities— white sand ridges, pocosin, and cypress-gum swamps. Among the flora are running oak, Carolina ipecac, queen's delight, and pond pine. Wildlife is abundant; there are bear, swamp rabbit, fox, deer, mink, alligator, snakes
674 (including 3 species of rattlesnakes), and 36 species of fish. The *Sand Ridge Trail* provides an 0.8-mi loop from the parking lot. (*USGS Maps:* Whiteville, Bolton, Juniper Creek)

>ADDRESS AND ACCESS: Superintendent, Lake Waccamaw State Park, 6707 NC-53 Highway, Kelly, NC 28448; 910-669-2928 or 910-646-4748. From US-74/76 (W 3.0 mi from Bolton) on NC-214, turn L on the first paved road, Bella Coola Rd (SR-1947).

MERCHANT'S MILLPOND STATE PARK (Gates County)

Merchant's Millpond State Park is home for more than 190 species of birds in its 2,965 acres. Warblers stop over in their fall and spring migrations and a large number of waterfowl make this their winter home. Wildlife includes deer, raccoon, turtle, beaver, mink, river otter, and snakes. The major fish are largemouth bass, bluegill, chain pickerel, and black crappie. The luxuriant park is a rare ecological community with huge bald cypress and tupelo gum trees in the 760-acre millpond and Lassiter Swamp. The trees are draped with Spanish moss and resurrection fern. Large beech groves, oaks, pines, and holly are in the forest surrounding the wetlands. Activities include fishing, hiking, nature study directed by park staff, canoeing (with rentals), and camping (family tent/RV, group, and primitive). The family campsites contain drinking water, a picnic table and grill, flush toilets, and hot showers (no hookups). Hikers should be alert to a heavy infestation of ticks in the forest during warm-weather months. (*USGS Map:* Beckford)

ADDRESS AND ACCESS: Superintendent, Merchant's Millpond State Park, Rte 1, Box 141-A, Gatesville, NC 27938; 919-357-1191. Park entrance is on US-158, 6.0 mi NE of Gatesville, immediately NE of Merchant's Millpond Rd (SR-1403).

Lassiter Trail 675

LENGTH AND DIFFICULTY: 6.8 mi, easy

SPECIAL FEATURE: ecological study of plant life

TRAILHEAD AND DESCRIPTION: Begin the loop trail NW from the parking lot on Merchant's Millpond Rd (SR-1403). After hiking 0.3 mi across the bridge, turn R at the trailhead and enter a forest of cypress, maple, oak, and pine. At 0.6 mi jct L, with a 0.5-mi access route to the family campground. Cross a boardwalk at 0.8 mi and ascend to a division of the loop at 0.9 mi. Turn R, skirt the millpond, and pass a family canoe camp at 1.2 mi. Pass through a longleaf pine restoration near a fire road, and cross it at 2.4 mi. Reach the backpack primitive camp near Lassiter Swamp at 3.8 mi. Turn L on the return trail and pass through a carpet of running cedar. Cross the park fire road at 4.6 mi. Complete the loop at 6.0 mi, jct R with the family campground at 6.2 mi, and return to the road at 6.8 mi. (A loop trail, 0.3 mi, extends to a peninsula with picnic tables below the canoe rental build ing and parking area on SR-1403.) Also at the parking area for the short loop and the *Lassiter Trail* is another loop in the opposite direction with *Coleman Trail.* It parallels the road for 0.2 mi before a fork. Its vegetation is 676 similar to *Lassiter Trail,* and it returns to the parking area at 1.6 mi.

PETTIGREW STATE PARK (Washington and Tyrrell Counties)

Pettigrew State Park covers 17,743 acres, the state's largest. Of this acreage, Lake Phelps has 16,600 acres; it is the second largest natural lake in the state. The lake is unique because it is not fed by any known surface streams; thus it may be the cleanest lake in the state. Its origin may date to 35 million years ago, and in 1775 it was called the "haunt of the beasts" by hunters. Recently archaeologists have discovered such artifacts of Native Americans as more than 30 canoes, one 37 ft long. The lake has bass, catfish, pumpkinseed, yellow perch, bluegill, and shellcracker. Ducks, swans, and other waterfowl winter here. Exceptionally large cypress, poplar, sweet gum, shagbark hickory, swamp cottonwood, coastal plain willow, and sycamore are in the 1,143 land acres of the park. Another part of history in the park is a state historic site, Somerset Place, the nineteenth-century plantation estate of the Josiah Collins family (named for Somersetshire, Collins's home county in England), and Bonarva, home of Confederate General James Johnston Pettigrew (for whom the park is named). The Pettigrew family cemetery is here. Activities at the park are picnicking, fishing, boating, hiking, and camping. The campsites are tent/RV with table and grill, water, flush toilets, and hot showers (no hookups). (*USGS Maps:* Creswell, Roper S, New Lake NW)

ADDRESS AND ACCESS: Pettigrew State Park, Rte 1, Box 336, Creswell, NC 27928; 919-797-4475; Somerset Place State Historic Site, Rte 1, Box 337, Creswell, NC 27928; 919-797-4560. (Adjoining Pocosin Lakes NWR address is Rte 1, Box 195B, Creswell, NC 27928; 919-797-4431.) Access to Pettigrew SP is off US-64 in Creswell for 6.0 mi following park signs, and the same for Somerset.

677 *Carriage Drive Trail*

LENGTH AND DIFFICULTY: 8.2 mi round-trip, easy

SPECIAL FEATURES: Somerset Place, scenic carriage route, overlooks

TRAILHEAD AND DESCRIPTION: From the parking lot near the park office follow the old carriage road W on a level, wide, grassy trail through virgin stands of cypress, sycamore, and poplar bordered with willows, papaw, and honeysuckle. Views of the lake, through patches of wildflowers such as wood sorrel, are found on the L at 0. 4 mi, 0.6 mi, and 1.2 mi. Reach the Western Canal at 2.2 mi, and the trail terminus at Moccasin Canal at 2.7 mi. Here is a boardwalk where winter waterfowl such as American coot, green-winged teal, tundra swan, hooded merganser, and pintail may be seen. Return by the same route. (A new 4.0-mi trail on a canal berm is being constructed from Moccasin Overlook to the W end of Lake Phelps where there is an access area for a fishing pier and canoe launch. Access to this scenic area of cypress knees and Spanish moss is 2.1 mi W on Lake Shore Rd from the park office to turn R on Weston Rd [SR-1164]. Go 2.3 mi to Newland Rd, turn L, and after 4.9 mi turn L on Keep Rd. Drive 2.7 mi to the access parking area L. [To continue on the road it is 0.4 mi to the refuge office of the Pocosin NWR.]) For the E section, hike past the historic Collins House at 0.4 mi. Pass the Bonarva Canal at 0.7 mi and at 1.1 mi jct L, with a short side trail to the Pettigrew cemetery. Continue ahead, R, to the Bee Tree Canal and overlook at 1.4 mi. Return by the same route.

SINGLETARY LAKE STATE PARK (Bladen County)

Singletary Park is headquarters for the Carolina lakes area—White, Waccamaw, Bay Tree, and Singletary Lakes. The major activity of the 1,221-acre park is organized group camping. Of the two camps, one is open all year. Facilities provide a mess hall and kitchen, campers' cabins, and washhouses. Swimming, fishing, and boating are activities open to the group campers. The easy 1.0-mi *Singletary Lake Trail* makes a loop around the **678** lake. It goes 290 yd from the main road to the lake and follows into a forest, R, with cypress, bayberry, gum, poplar, and juniper. Spanish moss is prominent. At 0.4 mi it crosses a svc road, follows green blazes through groves of scrub oak and longleaf pine, and returns to the point of origin. (*USGS Map:* White Lake)

ADDRESS AND ACCESS: Superintendent, Singletary Lake State Park, 6707 NC-53 Highway, Kelly, NC 28448; 910-669-2928. Access is 12.0 mi SE of Elizabethtown on NC-53.

WAYNESBOROUGH STATE PARK (Wayne County)

One of the state's newest (1986), Waynesborough State Park is located at the site of historic Waynesborough (1787). It has a visitor center with history exhibits, picnic area, a 0.6 mi loop trail on a floodplain, and a boat dock at the Neuse River. There is also a village of nineteenth-century houses, a law office (1868), and a one-room school (1911). A total of 8.7 mi of the signed *MST* circles part of the park, crosses US-117 into the city of Goldsboro, and joins *Stoney Creek Trail* (where it follows downstream to Slocum Rd at an entrance to Seymour Johnson Air Force Base. (See chapter 12 for Goldsboro.) (*USGS Maps:* Goldsboro, Goldsboro SW)

ADDRESS AND ACCESS: Waynesborough State Park, 801 Hwy 117 South, Goldsboro, NC, 27530; 919-580-9391 or 919-778-6234). From jct of US-70 and US-117, drive S on US-117 2.0 mi for entrance R.

11. State Forests, Natural Areas, Historic Sites, and Other State Properties

Come forth into the light of things,
Let Nature be your teacher.
—William Wordsworth

In addition to the state parks, the Division of Parks and Recreation in the Department of Environment, Health, and Natural Resources (DEHNR) administers 12 natural areas, 4 of which have visitor centers and designated trails. They are Theodore Roosevelt Natural Area, Weymouth Woods–Sandhills Nature Preserve, Hemlock Bluffs, and Mt Jefferson (transferred from state park to natural area in 1993). (The other natural areas, in order of acquisition, are Baytree Lake and White Lake, 1929; Chowan Swamp and a tract of Dismal Swamp, 1974; Masonboro Island and Mitchell's Mill, 1976; Bushy Lake, 1978; and a tract of marshland on Baldhead Island, 1979.) An increase in public pressure to preserve the natural areas prompted the state in 1963 to adopt principles for the natural area system. Among the principles are to preserve, protect, extend, and develop the natural areas of scientific, aesthetic, and geological value.

The Division of Forest Resources (another division of the DEHNR) administers five educational state forests. They are Bladen Lakes, Clemmons, Holmes, Rendezvous Mountain, and Tuttle. The locations are diverse, but their purpose and facilities are generally the same. For example, they all have interpretive displays and trails, primitive walk-in campsites, and picnic areas. They serve as outdoor-living and environmental centers that teachers and other group leaders use as classrooms. Arrangements can be made with each ranger station for ranger-conducted programs. Campsites are free but require permits. Open season is March 15 to November 30 with the exception of Bladen Lakes, which is open March 1. All are closed on Mondays and Tuesdays. Also within the DEHNR (as a separate unit and no longer under the Division of Parks and Recreation) is the N.C. Zoological Park. The N.C. Aquariums (another division of the DEHNR) has three aquariums: Pine Knoll Shores; Fort Fisher, and Roanoke Island. Trails at any of these sites are described in this chapter. For information contact N.C. Aquariums, 417 N Blount St, Raleigh, NC 27601; 919-733-2290.

There are 23 state historic sites, administered by the Historic Sites Section, Division of Archives and History, Department of Cultural Resources. The sites provide visitor centers with artifacts, exhibits, and multimedia programs about such historic places as the Duke Homestead, Historic Halifax, and the Thomas Wolfe Memorial. The majority of the sites do not have admission charges. Some of the sites have trails and are described in this chapter. For more information, contact the Department of Cultural Resources, Raleigh, NC 27601; 919-733-7862. Although the majority of trails in this chapter are short, they are ostensibly important walks for educational and cultural purposes.

HEMLOCK BLUFFS NATURE PRESERVE (Wake County)

This 150-acre preserve has received its name from eastern hemlock (*Tsuga canadensis*), a conifer usually not naturally found farther east than Hanging Rock State Park, 100.0 mi NE from Cary. In both locations the ingredients of damp, cool N bluffs favor its survival from the Ice Age period of 10,000 to 18,000 years ago. In varying sizes there are more than 200 of these beautiful evergreens, easily viewed from a trail network with observation decks near Swift Creek. (The 0.8-mi *Swift Creek Trail* on the N side of the stream is part of the Cary greenway system and not part of the Hemlock Bluffs trail network.) The hemlocks, some as old as 400 years, are surrounded by other Appalachian Mtns plant species. Examples are yellow orchids, trillium, and chestnut oak, sometimes found in the western Piedmont.

This valuable and unique preserve was purchased by the state in 1976. Adjoining property is owned by the town of Cary, whose Parks and Recreation Department has developed and managed the entire preserve. Some project assistance has been received by the Wake County Grant-in-Aid Program. At the entrance to the trail system is the Stevens Nature Center, completed in 1992 and named in honor of Col W. W. Stevens and his wife, Emily. The center has a park office, exhibit and classroom space, and a developed wildflower garden. Preserve hours are 9 AM to sunset daily; center hours vary according to seasons. The exceptionally well designed and maintained trail system is described below. (*USGS Map:* Apex)

ADDRESS AND ACCESS: Hemlock Bluffs Nature Preserve, 2616 Kildaire Farm Rd, Cary, NC 27512 (mailing address Box 8005); 919-387-5980. To access from the jct of US-1/64, go NE on Tryon Rd for 0.6 mi and turn R on Kildaire Farm Rd. After 1.4 mi turn R at the preserve entrance.

679- *East Bluff Trail (0.3 mi); West Bluff Trail (0.7 mi); Swift Creek Trail (0.8*
683 *mi); Beech Tree Cove Trail (0.4 mi); Chestnut Oak Trail (1.2 mi)*

LENGTH AND DIFFICULTY: 2.1 mi round-trip combined, easy to moderate

TRAILHEADS AND DESCRIPTION: The trails entrance is behind the Stevens Nature Center where signboards provide trail information on distance (including overlap), direction, and blaze colors. Hiking from one to the other in two main loops, the distance is reduced. There are two trail brochures keyed to post numbers for the E and W trails. If following the *East Bluff Trail,* markers 1 through 4 are about the bluffs and 5 through 14 describe the floodplain/Swift Creek area, wildlife, and wildflowers. The trail guide for the W trail grouping is about the history of the upland forest, biological diversity, forest succession, and ecosystems. Quartz rocks are part of the ground cover and chestnut oak is predominant among the trees. If making a R turn in the W trails, *West Bluff Trail* comes first.

MT JEFFERSON NATURAL AREA (Ashe and Alleghany Counties)

Mt Jefferson Natural Area covers 541 acres and includes the summit (4,900 ft) of Mt Jefferson; it is halfway between the towns of Jefferson and West Jefferson. Now a natural area, the park was initially a state forest wayside in 1952. Later citizens were successful in obtaining funding and acreage to make it a state park in 1956. Panoramic views from the fire tower reveal other mtn ranges in a three-state area—Whitetop Mtn in Virginia, Grandfather and Pilot Mtns in NC, and Cherokee NF mtns in Tennessee. The park has a wide variety of trees, shrubs, and flowers. Its chestnut-oak forest is considered to be one of the finest in the Southeast. In addition, there are maple, ash, oaks, black locust, bigtooth aspen, and poplar. Rhododendron, laurel, and flame azalea are also prominent as are banks of galax and scattered wood lilies and Dutchman's-breeches. Animal life includes fox, groundhog, chipmunk, raccoon, songbirds, and red and gray squirrels. Picnicking and hiking are the major activities; camping is not allowed. From
565 the parking lot the *Summit Trail* passes through the picnic ground and ascends 0.2 mi to a lookout tower for majestic vistas. Near the top the self-
566 guiding *Rhododendron Trail* makes a 1.1-mi lofty sweep on a horseshoe-

shaped ridge to Luther Rock. Here is a scenic outcrop of black volcanic amphibolite. A trail booklet at the trailhead provides information on the preserve's history, geology, plant life, and wildlife. The peak season for purple rhododendron blooming is early June. (*USGS Map:* Jefferson)

ADDRESS AND ACCESS: Superintendent, Mt Jefferson Natural Area, Box 48, Jefferson, NC 28640; 910-982-2587 or 910-246-9653. Access is from US-221 between Jefferson and West Jefferson; turn on Mt Jefferson Rd (SR-1152) for 3.0 mi to the summit.

SUPPORT FACILITIES: The nearest campground is Greenfield Campground at the base of the park, 0.7 mi SW on Mt Jefferson Rd (SR-1149 from the park road). Address is West Jefferson, NC 28694; 910-246-9106. Open March 1 to December 1. Full svc, rec fac. Shopping centers, restaurants, and motels are in nearby Jefferson/West Jefferson.

THEODORE ROOSEVELT NATURAL AREA (Carteret County)

This natural area of 265 acres on the island of Bogue Banks is set aside to preserve a maritime forest of laurel oak and live oak, red bay, red cedar, swamp red maple, and red ash, especially in the swales. Other plant life includes eight species of ferns, wild olive, and the toothache tree (*Zanthoxylum americana*). There are marshes (freshwater, brackish, and saltwater) and bird sanctuaries, particularly for warblers. The *Hoffman Trail*, a 0.4-mi loop, provides a visit **684** over the dunes by the swales and the East Pond. The trail entrance is at the SE corner of the Marine Resources Center. The property was established in 1971 from a gift by the grandchildren of President Theodore Roosevelt. Also here is the N.C. Aquarium at Pine Knoll Shores. It houses exhibits, aquariums, a public library, and meeting facilities. Field trips, boat trips, workshops, multimedia programs, and more are presented. Admission is free; it is open year-round. (*USGS Map:* Mansfield)

ADDRESS AND ACCESS: Superintendent, Theodore Roosevelt Natural Area, c/o Fort Macon State Park, Box 127, Atlantic Beach, NC 28512; 919-726-3775. N.C. Aquarium at Pine Knolls Shores, Atlantic Beach, NC 28512; 919-247-4003. Access is on NC-58, 5.0 mi W of Atlantic Beach.

WEYMOUTH WOODS–SANDHILLS NATURE PRESERVE (Moore County)

The 515-acre woodland preserve is E of the city limits of Southern Pines. Most of the acreage was donated by Mrs. James Boyd in 1963. (The preserve has another 254 acres in two satellite tracts not developed.) There are more than 500 species of plants (including 135 species of wildflowers), including

French mulberry, longleaf pine, turkey oak, and bays. Among the wildlife are deer, squirrel, raccoon, beaver, owls, and numerous songbirds. Butterflies are prominent, for example, black and palamedes swallowtails, painted lady, and hairstreaks. The sandy ridges, popularly known as the Sandhills Region, were formed from sediments of clay, sand, and gravel deposited by streams in the region millions of years ago when the area was part of an inland sea. The preserve has a Natural History Museum, and naturalists provide illustrated lectures and tours. Open daily, seven days a week. (*USGS Maps:* Southern Pines, Niagara)

ADDRESS AND ACCESS: Superintendent, Weymouth Woods–Sandhills Nature Preserve, 400 N Fort Bragg Rd, Southern Pines, NC 28387; 910-692-2167. In S Southern Pines turn off US-1 at Magnolia Drive (SR-2053) and go 1.2 mi to jct with Fort Bragg Rd (SR-2074). Turn L and go 1.7 mi to entrance, L.

685- *Bowers Bog Trail (0.5 mi); Lighter Stump Trail (0.5 mi); Pine Barrens*
690 *Trail (1.0 mi); Gum Swamp Trail (0.4 mi); Holly Road Trail (1.9 mi); Pine Island Trail (0.5 mi)*

LENGTH AND DIFFICULTY: 4.3 mi combined, easy

TRAILHEADS AND DESCRIPTION: *Bowers Bog Trail* is a loop nature trail E of the museum and parking area. On the N side of the loop is *Lighter Stump Trail,* a connector between *Bowers Bog Trail* and *Pine Island Trail.* Begin the *Pine Barrens Trail* W of the museum and follow the white blazes through prominent displays of longleaf pine, turkey oak, bracken, and blueberry. The *Gum Swamp Trail* loop adjoins it at the N side, but it contains chiefly hardwoods. From the *Gum Swamp Trail* begin the 1.9-mi *Holly Road Trail.* After crossing James Creek at 40 yd, turn L or R at 0.1 mi on the yellow-blazed trail. If you turn R, reach a jct with the *Pine Island Trail* loop at 0.2 mi, R. (This area is lush with plant life in a swampy area of James Creek. The trail crosses James Creek twice and some tributaries. On the S side of the loop it jct with *Lighter Stump Trail.*) Continue on *Holly Road Trail,* cross a stream and soon a fire road. At 1.4 mi pass L of a spring. Complete the loop at 1.9 mi, and return on the E or W side of the *Gum Swamp Trail* loop and the *Pine Barrens Trail* loop.

BLADEN LAKES EDUCATIONAL STATE FOREST (Bladen County)

The 32,237-acre coastal forest is spread between South River and the Cape Fear River in the bay lakes area. Within the general boundaries are Salters

Lake, Singletary Lake, and Jones Lake, but the forest office, exhibits, trails, and picnic areas are concentrated near the jct of NC-242 and Sweet Home Rd (SR-1511), across the road from Jones Lake State Park. The primitive walk-in campsites are 3.7 mi SE on Sweet Home Rd. *Smith Swamp Trail* is a slow 3.5- **691** mi auto tour (14 MPH) past exhibit stations, and the 0.4-mi *Turnbull Creek* **692** *Trail* is a manicured interpretive foot trail. An approach to them is on Sweet Home Rd, 0.2 mi E from the forest office. If the gate to the road is locked, walk the sandy road and at 0.2 mi pass the Naval Stores Industry exhibit, L. Turn L at the fork in a pine plantation and reach the picnic area (with exhibits and kiosk), R. *Turnbull Creek Trail* is L, opposite the picnic area. The trail dips to a natural spring and circles through Spanish moss, water and turkey oaks, fetterbush, and fragrant nettle (*Cnidoscolus stimulosus*). Turnbull Creek is on the N side. Fox squirrels (which feed on the large seed cones of the longleaf pine) may be seen here. (*USGS Map:* Elizabethtown N)

ADDRESS AND ACCESS: Forest Supervisor, Bladen Lakes Educational State Forest, Rte 2, Box 942, Elizabethtown, NC 28337; 910-588-4964. The office is on NC-242, 4.0 mi N of Elizabethtown (0.6 mi N of Jones Lake State Park) and 9.0 mi S of Ammons.

CLEMMONS EDUCATIONAL STATE FOREST (Johnston County)

A forest of 307 acres between Clayton and Garner, it has study sites for rocks, trees, wildlife, watersheds, and forest management. Opened in 1976, it represents a transitional zone between the Piedmont and coastal plain. A forestry center and exhibits explain the varied facilities of the area. Picnicking and group primitive camping facilities are available, and sections of the trails can be used by the handicapped. There are 15 ranger-conducted programs for visiting groups to choose from. The 2.2-mi *Clemmons Demonstration Trail* **693** begins at the parking lot. Follow the signs 100 yd to a forest information board and another 100 yd to the forestry center and trail signboard. Turn R, and follow the red blazes. At 0.2 mi cross a stream near a short watershed path. At 0.3 mi pass a shortcut trail and pass it again at 1.3 mi. The 0.8-mi yellow-blazed *Clemmons Talking Tree Trail* loops from the trail signboard. An **694** exceptionally well designed trail, it provides push-button devices for recorded botanical information. All trails have easy treadway. (*USGS Map:* Clayton)

ADDRESS AND ACCESS: Forest Supervisor, Clemmons Educational State Forest, 2411 Garner Rd, Clayton, NC 27520; 919-553-5651. Access is on Old US-70 (SR-1004), 1.5 mi N of Clayton city limits and 4.2 mi N of US-70.

HOLMES EDUCATIONAL STATE FOREST (Henderson County)

The forest named in honor of Canadian-born John S. Holmes (1868–1958), who served as the state's first forester from 1915 to 1945. The forest covers 231 acres, 25 of which are rich bottomland and 206 on steep mountainsides and rounded summits. It was a CCC camp in the 1930s, and it became a state forest in 1972. More than 125 species of flowering plants have been identified. Facilities are available for picnicking, hiking, and nature study. Primitive camping is provided on the mountaintop; it has road access. Approach to the trailheads is 0.1 mi from the main parking lot to the forestry center and trail-system signboard. The exception is the unblazed **695** 0.5-mi *Crab Creek Trail*. Access is W at the parking area where it goes to a tree plantation zone near Crab Creek. (*USGS Map:* Standing Stone Mtn)

696- *Forest Demonstration Trail (3.0 mi); Holmes Talking Tree Trail (0.5*
699 *mi); Wildcat Rock Trail (0.7 mi); Soil and Water Trail (0.3 mi)*

LENGTH AND DIFFICULTY: 4.5 mi combined round-trip, moderate to strenuous

TRAILHEADS AND DESCRIPTION: From the forestry center hike E on the red-blazed *Forest Demonstration Trail* with study sites, and through hardwoods and white pines on switchback. Reach the campground shortcut trail at 1.0 mi. Keep L, pass a small pond, cross a forest road, and jct with the shortcut, R, again. Pass a scenic overlook, L, and begin a descent on switchbacks for a return to the forestry center. Also starting L at the forestry center is the green-blazed *Holmes Talking Tree Trail,* which has push-button devices for information on forest history, use, growth, and values. Cross cascades at 0.4 mi. On the W side of the loop is a jct with *Wildcat Rock Trail,* a steep climb on switchbacks to an overlook with superb views of the Crab Creek basin and W to the Blue Ridge Mtns. Additionally, from the forestry center W to the amphitheater is short unblazed *Soil and Water Trail* loop.

ADDRESS AND ACCESS: Forest Supervisor, Rte 4, Box 308, Hendersonville, NC 28739; 704-692-0100. Access is from Penrose on US-64. Take Featherstone Creek Rd (SR-1528) for 2.6 mi to Little River. Turn L on Crab Creek Rd, which becomes Kanuga Rd (SR-1127), and go 4.2 mi to entrance, R. Another route is from downtown Hendersonville. From jct of US-64E and US-25S go S 0.5 mi on US-25S to jct R with Caswell St, which becomes Kanuga Rd (SR-1127), and go 10.0 mi.

RENDEZVOUS MOUNTAIN EDUCATIONAL STATE FOREST
(Wilkes County)

In 1926 Judge Thomas Finely donated the 142-acre Rendezvous Mtn to the state as a park, but the state never developed it. Thirty years later it became a state forest. It is a scenic hardwood forest with rugged terrain at the foothills of the Blue Ridge Mtns. There are facilities for picnicking, hiking, and nature study (primitive camping is planned). After entering the gate, park at the first parking lot, R. Cross the road (R of the picnic area), and follow the 0.2-mi *Table Mountain Pine Sawmill Trail*. The loop has historic exhibits of timber-cut- **700** ting equipment, logging methods, and a sawmill from the 1950s. At the second parking lot, R, the 0.6-mi *Rendezvous Mountain Talking Tree Trail* loops **701** through a beautiful forest of hardwood, laurel, pinxter, and flame azalea with scattered rhododendron. Descent is moderate to steep. Also, from the parking lot is the 275-yd *Firetower Trail*, which ascends N past the forest office to the **702** old fire tower (2,445 ft) with scenic views. (*USGS Map:* Purlear)

> ADDRESS AND ACCESS: Forest Supervisor, Rendezvous Mtn Educational State Forest, Box 42, Purlear, NC 28665; 910-667-5072. From NC-16 in Millers Creek (5.3 mi NW of Wilkesboro), turn W on Old US-421 (SR-1304) and go 2.8 mi to jct with Purlear Rd (SR-1346). Turn R on Purlear Rd and go 1.8 mi, turn L on Rendezvous Mtn Rd (SR-1348), and ascend to the forest entrance after 1.3 mi.

TUTTLE EDUCATIONAL STATE FOREST (Caldwell County)

The forest honors Lelia Judson Tuttle (1878–1967), a teacher and missionary whose property was deeded to the state in 1973. In the 170-acre forest are facilities for picnicking, hiking, nature study, and primitive camping. An original old schoolhouse called Lingle School is part of the emphasis on education. As at the other state forests, ranger programs are designed for groups from kindergarten to adults. Also, workshops are provided for continuing-education credit. Trail access is from the parking and picnic area. The easy 1.9-mi *Tuttle Demonstration Trail* follows signs past the forestry center to a **703** signboard at 0.1 mi. Turn L on the red-blazed trail through pines (white, Virginia, and shortleaf) and hardwoods. At 0.7 mi jct with a shortcut, R. Pass Sleepy Hollow School site and go through the campsites for a return to the parking area. *Tuttle Talking Tree Trail* loops 0.6 mi on a green-blazed interpre- **704** tive trail from the forestry center. The audio devices play recordings about forest succession and species of trees. (*USGS Map:* Morganton N)

> ADDRESS AND ACCESS: Forest Supervisor, Tuttle Educational State Forest,

Rte 6, Box 417, Lenoir, NC 28645; 704-757-5608. Access is on Play-more Beach Rd (SR-1331), 0.8 mi off NC-18 (near the Burke/Caldwell county line), 6.0 mi SW of Lenoir.

BENTONVILLE BATTLEGROUND STATE HISTORIC SITE (Johnston County)

After the capture of Savannah December 20, 1864, General William T. Sherman's troops turned N to join General U. S. Grant's troops in Virginia. On the way General Sherman continued a swath of destruction, particularly in Columbia, SC, the capital city and seedbed of the Secessionist movement. Every public building in the city was destroyed (whether by accident or design) on February 17, 1865. The Battle of Bentonville is significant because it was the last major Confederate offensive and the largest ever fought in North Carolina. General Joseph E. Johnston's troops, with less than half the number of Union troops, fought bravely but lost during March 19 to 21. They withdrew toward Smithfield with plans to protect Raleigh, the state's capital city, but the Union forces did not pursue them.

ADDRESS AND ACCESS: Bentonville Educational State Historic Site, Box 27, Newton Grove, NC 28366; 919-594-0789. Entrance is 1.4 mi off US-701 on Cox Mill Rd (SR-1008), 3.0 mi N of Newton Grove.

705- *Bentonville Battleground History Trail (0.2 mi); Bentonville*
706 *Battleground Trail (13.4 mi)*

LENGTH AND DIFFICULTY: 13.6 mi combined, easy

SPECIAL FEATURES: 27 history stations

TRAILHEADS AND DESCRIPTION: The *Bentonville Battlefield History Trail* is a self-guiding walk that begins near the field fortifications exhibit and leads to the original trenches dug by Union forces on the first day of the battle. From the historic Harper House, begin the longer route by crossing Cox Mill Rd (SR-1008) between trail markers #3 and #4 and follow the public road. At 0.6 mi turn L on SR-1192. Reach a jct with SR-1008, turn R, and at 2.7 mi see the United Daughters of the Confederacy (UDC) monument to the Confederate soldiers. Turn L on SR-1194, which later merges with Devils Race Track Rd (SR-1009), and arrive at the Bentonville Community Building at 5.6 mi. Continue to marker #23 at 5.8 mi; here Confederate cavalry was halted by the flooded Mill Creek. Return to the Community Building and take the road L, following 0.1 mi and turning R at marker #24. At 7.1 mi turn L at marker #25, pass markers #26 and #27, and turn R on a private dirt field road near a feed bin at 7.9 mi. Continue by the field's edge for 0.7 mi to a paved road and turn L at marker #28. Reach SR-1008 at 9.0 mi; turn R and go 0.6 mi to Ebenezer Church to jct with SR-1009. (A country store is across the road.) Turn R and go 0.5 mi to marker #20, return to SR-1008 at 10.6 mi. Follow it to the UDC marker at SR-1194 jct at 11.6 mi. Return on SR-1008 to the starting point for a total of 13.4 mi.

FORT DOBBS STATE HISTORIC SITE (Iredell County)

Named for Royal Governor Arthur Dobbs, the fort was built (ca 1750s) during the French and Indian War to protect the settlers. Excavations of the vanished fort show a moat, cellar, magazine area, and well. A pioneer cottage has exhibits of the period. The 0.5-mi *Fort Dobbs Nature Trail* goes **707** through a hardwood forest with footbridges over small ravines. Ferns and wildflowers are prominent among the spicebushes.

> ADDRESS AND ACCESS: Fort Dobbs State Historic Site, Rte 9, Box A 415, Statesville, NC 28677; 704-873-5866. From the jct of I-40 and US-21 in Statesville, go N 1.2 mi on US-21, turn L on Fort Dobbs Rd (SR-1930), and go 1.3 mi to entrance, R.

REED GOLD MINE STATE HISTORIC SITE (Cabarrus County)

Gold was discovered here, accidentally, when in 1799 Conrad Reed, son of John Reed, found a 17-pound yellow rock while fishing in Little Meadow Creek, which flowed through the family farm. This was the first documented discovery of gold in the United States. A silversmith in Concord, 10.0 mi away, could not identify the rock, so the Reeds used it as a doorstop. In 1802, a Fayetteville jeweler recognized the rock and purchased it from John Reed for $3.50, a week's pay. The Reeds began surface, or placer, mining that year, forming partnerships with other area miners. Underground or lode mining began in 1831 and lasted until 1912. The state purchased the property in 1971 and developed a large visitor center with mining exhibits, orientation film, and guided tour of the underground. The mine trail goes 50 ft below the surface and through 400 ft of tunnel. Self-guided tours are available around the Upper Hill archaeological area and the *Lower Hill Nature Trail*. It is an **708** easy 0.4-mi loop, which starts from the Upper Hill mining area, goes by the restored Stamp Mill, around Lower Hill, and back to the visitor center. Along the way markers indicate sites of mining shafts and adits. Vegetation includes oak, maple, holly, cedar, ferns, and crane fly orchids. The historic site is open daily from April 1 through October 31, and closed on Mondays from November 1 through March 31. Panning is available during spring and summer for a nominal fee. There is no admission charge.

ADDRESS AND ACCESS: Reed Gold Mine State Historic Site, 9621 Reed Mine Rd, Stanfield, NC 28163; 919-786-8337. From the jct of US-601/NC-200, 6.0 mi S of Concord, take NC-200 E 3.5 mi. Turn R on Reed Mine Rd (SR-1100) and go 2.0 mi. From Locust at NC-24/27, take NC-200 W 4.5 mi and turn L.

NORTH CAROLINA AQUARIUM/FORT FISHER (New Hanover County)

The 25-acre aquarium houses fish tanks, exhibits, conference rooms, research laboratories, and the University of North Carolina Sea Grant offices. It is one of three similar facilities in the state. The Pine Knoll Shore Aquarium is described under the Theodore Roosevelt Natural Area in the beginning of this chapter. Open daily (only afternoons on Sunday); closed on Thanksgiving, Christmas, and New Year's Days. Free admission. Trails are open year-round. The trails are accessible from aquarium grounds but are managed and owned by N.C. Division of Parks and Recreation, 910-458-8206; Fort Fisher, tel: 910-458-5538. At Fort Fisher State Historic Site is a 0.5-mi path among Confederate earthworks. Swimming and fishing are on a 4.0-mi undeveloped beach of the Atlantic Ocean. (*USGS Map:* Kure Beach)

ADDRESS AND ACCESS: N.C. Aquarium, Box 130, Kure Beach, NC 28449; 910-458-8257. Entrance is from US-421, 1.0 mi S of Fort Fisher and 5.6 mi S of Carolina Beach State Park.

709- *Marsh Trail (0.8 mi); Hermit Trail (2 .0 mi)*
710   LENGTH AND DIFFICULTY: 2.8 mi round-trip, combined, easy

TRAILHEADS AND DESCRIPTION: From the parking lot follow the signs, cross a boardwalk among yaupon, catbrier, and wax myrtle to a marsh meadow. Reach a fork; the *Marsh Trail* is L, the *Hermit Trail* is R. If taking the *Hermit Trail,* reach a side trail, R, at 0.7 mi. (The 0.1-mi side trail goes to Hermit's Bunker, named for George Harrill, the "Fort Fisher hermit," who lived off the land in this salt marsh for many years.) For another 0.7 mi round-trip, the trail goes to the Hermit basin. After returning to the main trail, reach a jct with *Marsh Trail* at 1.7 mi. Turn L for a return to the parking lot at 2.0 mi, or turn R to make a loop on the *Marsh Trail* for 0.8 mi. Pass a tidal basin and swales to the Atlantic Ocean and return by the pond to the parking area. Among the shore and marsh birds are brown pelican, willet, egret, and blackbird.

PART V

Trails in Counties and Municipalities

12. County Parks and Recreation Areas

Sing louder around...
While our sports shall be seen
On the echoing green.
—William Blake

Fifty-nine percent of the state's 100 counties have parks and recreation departments. They operate as a separate public unit in each county, usually under a county board of commissioners. A few counties and cities combine their departments or resources to provide joint services or special projects. Examples are Clinton and Sampson, Lincolnton and Lincoln, Henderson and Vance, Mocksville and Davie, and Sanford and Lee Counties. Because of population needs and available funding, each county park varies in size, facilities, and scope from a simple day-use picnic area to complex recreational centers such as Tanglewood in Forsyth County. When the President's Commission on Americans Outdoors reported its findings in 1986, it showed rapid expansion in a number of the state's cities. With an increase in the population and less space in the city for outdoor recreation, the county parks are becoming more vital for green space. The report also showed a demographic trend to a fast-growing older segment of the population and a desire for recreation closer to home. Mecklenburg and Forsyth are examples of counties preparing for this trend. Mecklenburg's diverse park and greenway system, the largest in the state, will become what Elisabeth Hair (former chair of the board of county commissioners) called "Charlotte's green necklace." In Forsyth County, greenways will connect the county's towns to a greenway network in the city of Winston-Salem. A number of county park and rec departments have constructed physical-fitness trails. Others, such as Craven County's rec and parks department, do not own property but maintain exercise trails on public school property. For the addresses and telephone numbers of the state's counties and cities with parks, contact the Division of Parks and Rec, Box 27687, Raleigh, NC 27687; 919-733-PARK for the *North Carolina Parks and Recreation Directory*, or call 919-515-7118 at N.C. State University.

ALAMANCE COUNTY (Cedarock Park)

The 414-acre park contains the Cedarock Park Center (for conferences and workshops in the Paul Stevens homestead); Cedarock Historical Farm (1830s); ropes obstacle course, horseshoe courts; disc golf course; basketball courts; picnic area; playgrounds; fishing; horseback-riding trails; walk-in campsites (primitive with permits); and hiking trails. The trails are color coded and create interconnecting loops. There is also a mountain bike trail that begins at picnic shelter #3. The park is open all year. (*USGS Map:* Snow Camp)

> ADDRESS AND ACCESS: Director, Rec and Parks Dept, 217 College St, Graham, NC 27253; 910-570-6760 or 910-570-6759. From jct of I-85/40/NC-49 in Burlington (exit #145A from the W, #145 from the E), go 6.0 mi S on NC-49 to jct with Friendship-Patterson Mill Rd, and turn L. Go 0.3 mi to park entrance L. The ranger station is at the first house (Garrett homestead), R.

711- *Cedarock Trail (2.2 mi); Ecology Trail (0.5 mi)*
712   LENGTH AND DIFFICULTY: 2.9 mi combined, easy

TRAILHEAD AND DESCRIPTION: From the picnic parking lot, begin at shelter #3 at the trail signboard. Follow the yellow-blazed trail through a hardwood forest with scattered cedars and pines. At 0.2 mi cross Rock Creek on a footbridge and join the brown-blazed *Ecology Trail*. At 0.5 mi the *Ecology Trail* turns L to make a loop. (To the R you have a choice on either a blue-blazed trail or a red-blazed trail to make a loop to a tent campsite before returning to the main trail.) Continue on the *Cedarock Trail*, leave the forest, pass through a meadow, reenter the forest, and reach an old mill dam, L. Cross Rock Creek at Elmo's Crossing and enter a meadow of wildflowers, including the Star of Bethlehem (*Ipheion uniflorum*), at 2.0 mi. Pass a maintenance area to the park road and return to the parking lot at shelter #3.

CABARRUS COUNTY

The county has two parks with trails. Bakers Creek Park has 37 acres with picnic shelters, lighted ball fields, tennis and volleyball courts, primitive **713** camping for organized groups, and a 1.0-mile *Science Trail*. Paved 1.0-mi **714** *Bakers Creek Greenway Trail* connects with Village Park.

ADDRESS AND ACCESS: County PRD is 65 Church St SE, Concord, NC 28026; 704-788-9840, but the park location is off I-85, exit 63, W into Kannapolis on Lane St. Cross US-29 and US-29A. At the first traffic light past US-29A turn R on West A St, and go 1.0 mi to park entrance L.

The other park, Frank Liske Park, consists of 180 acres. Fishing and boating are allowed in the 9.2-acre lake, and a refurbished barn provides facilities for group picnics and social gatherings. There is also a complex of lighted fields and courts for baseball, softball, soccer, tennis, and miniature golf. There are also a swimming pool and amphitheater. The 1.0-mi *Liske Park Nature Trail* has markers identifying plant life in its circle around the **715** lake and its connection with the fitness trail.

ADDRESS AND ACCESS: Frank Liske Park, 4001 Stough Rd, Concord, NC 28027; 704-782-0411. Access from I-85, exit 58, is S on US-29 to Roberta Church Rd, L. At Roberta Mill Rd turn R and then L on Stough Rd; park entrance is L.

FORSYTH COUNTY
Horizons Park

The 492-acre park is one of 10 county rec areas and historic sites that encircle the city of Winston-Salem. The county and the city have been leading the state in parks and recreation with 20 acres per 1,000 citizens. Horizons Park is an example of how well they are serving the public. The facility has a large picnic area (with shelters), a children's playground, softball field, 18-hole flying disc golf course (the state's first), and hiking trails. (*USGS Map:* Walkertown)

ADDRESS AND ACCESS: Director, Parks and Rec, 500 W 4th St, Winston-Salem, NC 27101; 910-727-2946. One access is from the jct of US-52 and NC-8 (N of the city). Follow NC-8 4.2 mi and turn R on Memorial Industrial School Dr (SR-1920) 1.1 mi to the entrance, R.

Horizons Hiking Trail (2.5 mi)   **716**
LENGTH AND DIFFICULTY: 2.5 mi combined, easy

TRAILHEAD AND DESCRIPTION: From the parking area go to the picnic shelter and locate the trail signs. After 110 yd the *Horizons Hiking Trail* goes R and L for a shorter loop (B) and a longer loop (A). If going R, cross a stream at 0.3 mi and reach a jct with loop B, L, at 0.4 mi. If going R, go through a field, cross a bridge (one of a number on the trail), and follow the white blazes. Pass a tree nursery and cross another bridge and begin ascending and descending on rolling hills in a young forest. Redbud, Virginia pine, dogwood, and red cedar coexist with the major hardwoods. At 1.1 mi cross a boardwalk in a damp area. Arrive at the loop-B jct at 2.1 mi, L and R. If continuing R, there is a huge holly tree at 2.3 mi, R. Here also is a nineteenth-century graveyard. Return to the nature trail and complete the loops at 2.5 mi.

Tanglewood Park

Tanglewood is the William and Kate B. Reynolds Memorial Park, an outstanding Piedmont recreation and leisure resort. Facilities include the elegant manor house and lodge, rustic vacation cottages, campground (full svc), restaurant, tennis courts, swimming pool, golf (36-hole championship course and driving range), lake for paddleboats and canoes, picnic areas, arboretum and rose garden, deer park, horse stables and steeplechase course, 0.8-mi exercise-walking trail (near campground entrance), professional summer-stock theater, and the Walden Nature Center. (*USGS Maps:* Clemmons, Advance)

ADDRESS AND ACCESS: Tanglewood Park, Box 1040, Clemmons, NC 27012; 919-766-0591. From I-40 jct (Clemmons), go S 0.9 mi on Middlebrook Dr (SR-1103) to US-158. Turn R, go another 1.7 mi, and turn L (park office is L at 1.3 mi).

717 *Walden Nature Trail*

LENGTH AND DIFFICULTY: 1.5 mi combined, easy

TRAILHEAD AND DESCRIPTION: From the park entrance, go E on US-158 0.4 mi to the park office, R (opposite Harper Rd, SR-1101, and svc sta) for the Walden Nature Center. Approach the *Walden Nature Trail* behind the park office and acquire a pamphlet at the signboard or from the park office. The trail has three sections, each consecutively increasing in difficulty and species

718 variety. *Little Walden Trail* (sec 1, 195 yd) has audio stations for the visually handicapped around a small pond (service by advance reservations); *Emer-*

719 *son's Walk* (sec 2, 0.7 mi round-trip) is a paved old road with 18 tree-interpretive markers and is accessible for the physically handicapped; and *Thoreau's*

720 *Woods Trail* (sec 3, 0.7 mi round-trip) has 28 interpretive markers about the trees. The trail is named after Thoreau's Walden Pond and was completed in 1982 as a memorial to the N.C. Wildlife Enforcement Officers who have died in the line of duty since 1947. Little Walden was built entirely by volunteers and through donations. Major contributors were the Reader's Digest Foundation, Winston-Salem Host Lions Club, AT&T Pioneers, and Girl Scout Troop 437. (There is an exhibit of live wildlife L of the main trailhead.)

Lake Crabtree Trail. Allen de Hart

HENDERSON COUNTY

Henderson County's Parks and Rec Dept office is at Jackson Park where there are expansive recreation facilities: lighted basketball and baseball fields, tennis courts, picnic shelters, amphitheater, and an exceptionally beautiful 1.5-mi *Jackson Park Nature Trail.* After entering the park, drive to **721** the office and main building parking lot on the hilltop and acquire a map of the garden trail. (There is a special parking lot near the creek's bridge and a paved route into the garden part of the trail for the physically disabled.) Markers at the stops, plus the brochure, provide information on the flora and fauna. The natural sounds are chickadees, titmice, scarlet tanagers, and warblers. Begin the hike L of the office among hardwoods on the hill, descend to a wide old road, and turn L alongside the stream. Cross the paved road at the sign for the disabled and turn R across a footbridge at 0.3 mi. There are fragrant white and pink wild roses (at their peak in May), buttercup, fire pink, and ferns. At 0.7 mi is an observation deck. Surrounding the trail are hundreds of species of plants, some in wet or boggy areas where inhabit a number of frog species, vocally active. At marker #16 ascend up a ridge to the entrance road for a crossing to the point of origin.

> ADDRESS AND ACCESS: Henderson County Rec and Park Dept, 801 Glover St, Hendersonville, NC 28792; 704-697-4884. Access from I-26, exit 18, is on Four Seasons Blvd (US-64) W. At the sixth traffic light, turn L on Harris St. Descend 0.1 mi to curve L for park entrance.

LEE COUNTY
San-Lee Park

The park is composed of 125 acres of forest, lakes, old waterworks, trails, picnic areas, family (RV) and group campgrounds. There is also an amphitheater, boat launch (and rentals), volleyball court, and other rec facilities. All the trails are well designed and maintained. The park is open all year; 919-776-6221. (*USGS Map:* Sanford)

> ADDRESS AND ACCESS: Director, Parks and Rec Dept, Box 698, Sanford, NC 27330; 919-775-2107. At jct of US-1 (Bus) and Charlotte Ave (US-421/NC-87/42), take Charlotte Ave E 1.2 mi to Grapeviney Rd (also called San-Lee Dr, SR-1509) and turn R. After 2.2 mi turn R on Pumping Station Rd (SR-1510) and go 0.6 mi to park entrance, R.

722- *Muir Nature Trail (1.1 mi); Gatewood Trail (0.8 mi); Hidden Glen Loop*
725 *Trail (0.2 mi); Thoreau Trail (0.9 mi)*

> LENGTH AND DIFFICULTY: 3.0 mi combined, easy

> TRAILHEADS AND DESCRIPTION: From the parking lot by Miner's Creek, cross the bridge, turn R, and follow the *Muir Nature Trail* signs into the woods (there is a choice of an upper or lower loop). At 0.5 mi turn L at the lake's edge at the steps. Follow through rocks, hard- and softwoods, and wildflowers on the return. Hike a few yd or park at the refreshment stand to hike the other trails. Follow the campground road to Colter amphitheater signs. Turn R on *Gatewood Trail* and at 0.3 mi jct with *Thoreau Trail*, R. Turn L and jct with *Hidden Glen Loop Trail* at 0.5 mi. Pass Aldo Leopold

Wilderness group campground on the return. The *Thoreau Trail* begins at the boat launch near the bridge over Moccasin Pond. Cross the bridge and follow the shoreline L. Cross a bridge over Crawdad Creek and jct with Gatewood Trail at 0.6 mi. Return either L (shorter) or R.

MECKLENBURG COUNTY

Mecklenburg County is rapidly developing into an urbanized county. In 1977 a 10-year park plan was begun, in 1982 a park's bond master plan set a goal of 9,250 acres, and in 1986 a $15 million park bond was passed by county referendum. Then in 1992 the city of Charlotte Park and Rec Dept merged with the county's system. A model for cities and counties planning cooperative efforts, the Mecklenburg County Park and Rec Dept operates and maintains more than 10,000 acres of rural and urban parkland with more than 120 parks and 22 greenways. In 1989 the city/county master plan and the 1990s acquisition assessment called for developing another 24 parks. By the end of this decade a visitor will need to visit 3 different parks a week to see them all within a year.

The recreational and cultural diversity of the parks is divided into nature preserves, recreation centers, community parks, golf courses, district parks, aquatic centers, neighborhood parks, greenways, lake and river accesses, historic sites, and other facilities such as arts and athletic arenas, equestrian center, stadium, or nature museum. The three nature preserves encompass the largest parks (1,000-plus acres) designed to serve all the metropolitan area. Usually about 90 percent of the property is held for passive recreation because of the natural qualities. Two of the preserves have trail networks and are described below. Community parks are designed for serving the public within a 5.0-mi radius and usually have between 300 to 500 acres. They are known for their wide range of athletic activities and tournaments. District parks best serve a closer community with less than 200 acres. They are likely to have athletic fields, picnic shelters, playgrounds, small lakes, pools, and fitness/walking connector trails. An East District park, Idlewild Rd, has a 1.5-mi *Idlewild Nature Trail*. It is located at **726** 10512 Idlewild Rd, Charlotte, NC 28212; 704-545-9486. Another park, in the South District, which has multiuse trails, is McAlpine Creek. It is described in more detail below.

The 76 neighborhood parks serve local areas almost within walking distance. They provide the usual playgrounds, ball fields, tennis courts, picnic shelters, and concessions. Some have fitness or short walking trails.

Lake and River Access areas provide water-based sports at Lake Norman, Island Lake, and Lake Wylie. Six aquatic parks serve the metropolitan area. A flagship facility for aquatic sports is the Mecklenburg County Aquatic Center. It features a world-class swimming and diving pool. There are six greenways, one of which is McAlpine Creek Greenway listed above. Other greenway trails are 1.7-mi (2.3 mi if including side trails such as one to Mallard Creek School) *Clark's Creek Trail* (bike/pedestrian, off Mallard Creek Rd near its jct with Harris Blvd); 0.5-mi *McMullen Creek Trail* (bike/pedestrian, off NC-51 in Pineville); 2.0-mi *Campbell Creek Trail* (bike/pedestrian, off NC-24/27 between W. T. Harris Blvd and Central Ave); and 0.8-mi *Little Sugar Creek Trail* (pedestrian, off Blythe Blvd). Among the historic sites is *McIntyre Nature Trail*, which passes a pioneer gold mine and Revolutionary War site. It is located at 4801 McIntyre Ave, Huntersville, NC 28078; 704-875-1391. Visitors unfamiliar with the city/county should purchase a street/road map and request a copy of *Mecklenburg County Park and Rec Directory of Facilities*. (*USGS Maps:* Lake Norman N & S, Mooresville, Mtn Island Lake, Derita, Harrisonburg, Charlotte W and E, Mint Hill, Midland, Lake Wylie, Fort Hill, Weddington, and Matthews)

ADDRESS AND ACCESS: Mecklenburg County Park and Rec, Hal Marshall Svc Center, 700 N Tryon St, Charlotte, NC 28202; 704-336-3854); (park rangers; 704-336-2884); (facility reservations; 704-336-4200); (24-hour program hotline; 704-336-5800).

Latta Plantation Park

The 1,090-acre nature preserve is named for James Latta, merchant and planter, who with his wife, Jane Knox, lived in a handsome Federal-period plantation house in the early nineteenth century. The house, near the Catawba River (Mtn Island Lake), is restored and open afternoons Wednesday–Saturday. The park also has a visitor center; equestrian center (with two arenas and 80 permanent stalls) and 6.0 mi of bridle trails; canoe access to the lake; picnic areas (with shelters); the 55-acre Carolina Raptor Center; and hiking trails. Entrance to one of the hiking trails, *Beechwood Trail,* is at the horse-trailer parking area, the first R after entering the park. The footpath circles the headwaters of a stream that flows into Beechwood Cove. Tall beech, oak, and poplar are predominant in the 1.1-mi loop. Fragrant honeysuckle and cedar are near the entrance. At the Raptor Center is the 0.3-mi *Raptor Trail* for viewing live birds of prey, such as eagles, owls, hawks, falcons, and vultures, in a pine forest. The center is open weekends noon–5

PM; it is a nonprofit tax-exempt public corporation for rehabilitation, research, and conservation of raptors. (*USGS Map:* Mtn Island Lake)

ADDRESS AND ACCESS: Park District Supervisor, Latta Plantation Park, Rte 3, Box 882, Huntersville, NC 28078; 704-875-1391. Carolina Raptor Center Inc, Box 16443, Charlotte, NC 28297; 704-875-6521. Access from the S: At exit #38 on I-85 in Charlotte, take Beatties Ford Rd (SR-2074) N 7.3 mi to Sample Rd (SR-2125) (opposite Hopewell Presbyterian Church), and go 0.7 mi to the park entrance. From the N: Turn off I-77 at Huntersville on Gilead Rd; go W 0.9 mi, turn L on McCoy Rd (SR-2138), and go 1.6 mi to jct R with Hambright Rd (SR-2117). After 1.7 mi on SR-2117, turn L on Beatties Ford Rd and go 0.8 mi to Sample Rd, R.

Dale Arvey Trail (1.0 mi); Mountain Island Lake Nature Trail (1.0 mi)   **734-735**

LENGTH AND DIFFICULTY: 2.0 mi, easy

TRAILHEADS AND DESCRIPTION: From the picnic area parking lot locate the central signboard on a paved route. For the *Dale Arvey Trail* go L, and enter the woods on a trail of natural turf. At 0.2 mi is a scenic area of the lake. Curve around a peninsula (a side trail L leads to a gazebo) and reach a fork at 0.3 mi. (A turn R leads 0.3 mi on a spur trail through a dense grove of young hardwoods, papaw, and grapevine to a floating dock and boat-access parking lot. Backtrack.) The L fork is a return to the picnic area after another 0.2 mi. From the signboard follow the paved route R, pass the rest rooms, and enter the forest to the *Mountain Island Lake Nature Trail.* After 0.1 mi turn R at a fork on a treadway of wood chips into a mixture of sweet gum, Virginia pine, and cedar. Muscadine grapes hang from some of the trees and yellow senna borders open areas. After the trail makes its final turn, L, at 0.6 mi, there is a side trail, R, to the tip of the peninsula where a large rock faces the lake. Here is a beautiful view of the lake, particularly at sunset. Complete the loop by passing a pier at the picnic area.

McAlpine Creek Greenway

The 350-acre McAlpine Creek Greenway was the first purchase for the greenway system. It has mature forests, floodplains, and open meadows along McAlpine Creek. Facilities include soccer fields, picnic areas, and well-designed biking and hiking rails. (*USGS Maps:* Charlotte East, Mint Hill)

ADDRESS AND ACCESS: Park District Supervisor, McAlpine Creek Greenway, 8711 Old Monroe Rd, Charlotte, NC 28212; 704-568-4044. The park is in SE Charlotte, near Matthews and between Independence Blvd (US-74) and Sardis Rd. If in Matthews, take John St W (which becomes Monroe Rd) and go NW 5.0 mi to the Seaboard RR overpass, R. If downtown, take East 7th St (which becomes Monroe Rd) SE 7.3 mi to the above address, L.

736- *McAlpine Creek Trail (1.9 mi); Cottonwood Trail (1.0 mi round-trip);*
738 *McAlpine Creek Nature Trail (1.8 mi round-trip)*

LENGTH AND DIFFICULTY: 4.7 mi combined and round-trip, easy

TRAILHEADS AND DESCRIPTION: At the parking area (N of the RR bridge) follow the signs to *McAlpine Creek Trail* (a bikeway for bikers and hikers), R of the soccer field. Cross a weir at McAlpine Creek, R, and go under the RR at 0.2 mi. Pass under the Monroe Rd bridge, downstream, where the trail becomes compacted pit gravel in an open meadow. At 0.9 mi a paved jct, R, is an access trail that crosses McAlpine Creek on a cement weir. (Ahead, *McAlpine Creek Trail* goes another 1.0 mi to Sardis Rd, and en route passes through a marsh.) On the access trail it is 0.2 mi to Tara Dr. Along the way, R, after 125 yd is *Cottonwood Trail,* and after another 120 yd, L, is the trailhead of *McAlpine Creek Nature Trail.* The *Cottonwood Trail* is a 0.5-mi interpretive path through a floodplain dominated by large cottonwood trees. (Plans are to extend the trail to Monroe Rd.) The *McAlpine Creek Nature Trail* is a footpath through tall sycamore, cottonwood, elm, sweet gum, and oak. A 300-yd boardwalk covers a low area. Wildflowers, raccoon, squirrel, and owls are part of the preserved area. The trail ends at the McAlpine Creek bank at 0.9 mi. Backtrack.

McDowell Park and Nature Preserve

The park is named in honor of John McDowell, a leader of the county's recreation program in the 1960s and 1970s. The initial rolling land on the E side of Lake Wylie was a 150-acre gift to the county from the Crescent Land and Timber Corp, a subsidiary of Duke Power Co, in 1976. Now with 950 acres, the park is among the county's largest; it is open all year. It has a nature center that emphasizes natural history with exhibits and hands-on nature displays. Activities include camping (full svc), fishing, picnicking, hiking, and boating (rentals also). (A hiker symbol is on the park's entrance sign, and another sign on the main road cautions vehicular traffic that hikers have the right-of-way—a distinctive characteristic of the preserve.) The park is also good for birders; more than 85 species of birds have been catalogued. All the trails can be hiked from the nature center, either directly by access trails, or by connecting trails. (*USGS Map:* Lake Wylie)

ADDRESS AND ACCESS: Park District Supervisor, McDowell Park and Nature Preserve, Rte 1, Box 118, Pineville, NC 28134; 704-588-5224. From jct of I-77 and Carowinds Blvd, go on the blvd for 2.4 mi. Turn L on NC-49 and go 4.2 mi to the park entrance, R.

Creekside Trail (2.1 mi round-trip); Sierra Trail (0.2 mi); Trail for the **739-**
Handicapped (0.3 mi); Pine Hollow Trail (0.5 mi); Cedar Ridge Trail (0.6 **747**
mi); Cove Trail (1.0 mi); Shady Hollow Trail (0.6 mi); Kingfisher Trail
(0.3 mi); Chestnut Trail (1.6 mi round-trip)

LENGTH AND DIFFICULTY: 7.2 mi combined and round-trip, easy

TRAILHEADS AND DESCRIPTION: Park at the nature center parking area and enter the trail network on the L side of the nature center. Immediately jct L with the *Creekside Trail* (may have a nature trail sign), and R with the *Sierra Trail*. (The *Sierra Trail* is a sensory-interpretive loop on a hillside of hardwoods. From its loop is a connector trail to the *Chestnut Trail* and the W terminus of the *Pine Hollow Trail*.) If taking the *Creekside Trail* descend gradually 0.3 mi to a parking area and jct, L, with the *Cove Trail*. Turn R on a wide paved trail, cross a bridge over Porter Branch, and go upstream to partially follow the looped *Trail for the Handicapped*. (The 0.3-mi *Trail for the Handicapped* has benches, displays, side trails [one to the water's edge of Porter Branch], wildflowers [including the cardinal flower], and a huge white oak.) Pass a footbridge R and jct with *Pine Hollow Trail*. (The *Pine Hollow Trail* crosses the bridge into mixed hardwoods and pine, crosses a marshy area and tributary to Porter Branch, and ascends to connect with the *Sierra Trail* after 0.5 mi.) At 0.5 mi on the *Creekside Trail* jct with the *Cedar Ridge Trail*, L. (The *Cedar Ridge Trail* ascends slightly to pass under a power line at 0.1 mi. Ahead is a kudzu path and a forest of cedar, pine, and some large oaks near former homestead sites. Running cedar and periwinkle are ground cover. Pass a deep ravine, R, and descend to rejoin the loop end of the *Creekside Trail* at 0.6 mi.) To continue on the *Creekside Trail*, cross the footbridge, R, ascend to pass under the power line, and descend to the creek where the trail forks for a loop at 0.8 mi. If going L, cross the branch on a footbridge and go upstream to jct L with the *Cedar Ridge Trail* at 1.0 mi. Continue upstream through a beautiful forest of tall hardwoods, redbuds, and spring wildflowers such as trillium and bloodroot. Curve around a steep slope to rejoin the creekside at 1.3 mi. Backtrack to the parking area at the *Cove Trail*, or return L to the nature center.

The *Cove Trail* begins downstream at the *Trail for the Handicapped* parking area and follows a slope on a well-graded trail. At 0.2 mi approach Porter Cove in an area of wild ginger, ironwood, and sugar maple. Follow the waterfront to a peninsula ridge and a paved road. Turn R on the road and descend through the L corner of the picnic area to end the *Cove Trail* at 1.0 mi. Continue ahead and after 75 yd jct L with the *Shady Hollow Trail*. (The *Shady Hollow Trail* is a 0.6-mi access route through a mixed forest to the nature center.) Follow ahead 0.3 mi on the *Kingfisher Trail* to the rest rooms, another picnic area, gazebo on the edge of Lake Wylie, and pedal-boat dock.

Begin the *Chestnut Trail* near the rest rooms and follow it to cross a gravel road, pass a playground L, and at 0.3 mi jct with the trail's loop. If going R, cross a footbridge (where a R turn is an access trail to the campground), turn L, and at 0.7 mi jct with an access R. (It is a 0.1-mi spur to the campground information station.) At 0.9 mi jct R with a connector trail to the nature center. The *Chestnut Trail,* among beech, oak, dogwood, and hickory, curves L and descends to rejoin its access at the gazebo for a total of 1.6 mi. (The 0.2-mi connector trail to the nature center from the *Chestnut Trail* crosses the main road and descends to the *Sierra Trail* for a return to the nature center.)

NEW HANOVER COUNTY

748 Among the beautiful trails in the Wilmington area is 0.9-mi *Summer Rest Trail*. It is a wide asphalt passage through a hardwood forest of oak, maple, holly, sweet gum, and scattered pine. Ostrich ferns and fragrant wax myrtle add to the forest floor landscape. The trail ends at a street cul-de-sac at the bay. Backtrack. Access is from the jct of US-74 and US-17 E 3.2 mi on US-74 (Eastwood Rd) (past Landfall Golf Course) to a small parking area on the L (N) side of the highway (which is 0.3 mi before the Intercoastal Waterway bridge to Wrightsville Beach). (*USGS Map:* Wrightsville Beach)

ADDRESS: New Hanover County Parks Dept, 320 Chestnut St, Wilmington, NC 28401; 910-341-7198.

ONSLOW COUNTY

Among the parks in Onslow County are two with nature trails. One is Onslow **749** County Pines Park with a 0.4-mi *Bicentennial Nature Trail*. It is a wide, smooth, carefully designed route through a forest of bays, pines, oaks, holly, and small shrubs such as inkberry (*Ilex glabra*). Completed and dedicated in 1976 (with the assistance of Raymond Busbee of East Carolina University), it has 18 interpretive sites. A major unique site is that of plant succession. The beautiful park has ball fields, tennis courts, an arena, and picnic areas with a shelter. From the jct of US-258 and US-17 in Jacksonville, drive 3.0 mi S on US-17 to Onslow Pines Rd (SR-1116). Turn R; go 0.7 mi and turn R.

Another park, Hubert By-Pass Park, is at the corner of Hubert Blvd and NC-24, 5.3 mi E on NC-24 from the main entrance to Camp Lejeune Marine Corps Base. After a turn on Hubert Blvd (SR-1745), go 0.3 mi and turn R. The park is clean and well maintained. It has picnic areas, a soccer field, a 0.7-mi jogging trail, and a nature trail. The 0.5-mi *Mitchell Swamp Trail* **750** begins at the most E parking area. There are 27 interpretive sites with the common name, botanical species name, and descriptions on a permanent sign. After 0.2 mi reach a rain shelter at the scenic swamp, a major focus point. Eight species of oak are on the trail; other plants include wax myrtle and sweet leaf (*Symplocos tinctoria*). Under development is Stump Sound Park. A 56-acre semi-passive park, it has ball courts, picnic area, and playground. There is 0.2-mi *Stump Sound Nature Trail,* and more trails are **751** planned. Access is off NC-172, 1.0 mi W of its jct with NC-210 at Sneads Ferry. (*USGS Maps:* Jacksonville S, Hubert)

> ADDRESS: Director, Parks and Rec Dept, 434 Onslow Pines Rd, Jacksonville, NC 28540; 910-347-5332.

ROWAN COUNTY
Dan Nicholas Park

Successful business executive and philanthropist Dan Nicholas donated 330 acres to Rowan County in 1968 for recreational activities. As a result the county commissioners established a park and recreation board to develop and administer the park. Facilities include areas for fishing, picnicking (with shelters), tennis, paddle boating, camping (full svc), and hiking. There are four ball fields; a craft shop; and a nature center with plant, animal, and geological exhibits. There is also a small zoo and the outdoor T. M. Stanback Theater. The park is open all year. (*USGS Map:* Salisbury)

> ADDRESS AND ACCESS: Director, Parks and Rec Dept, Rte 10, Box 832, Salisbury, NC 28144; 704-636-2089. At the jct of I-85 and E Spencer, take Choate Rd (SR-2125) 1.1 mi E. Turn L on McCandless Rd, which becomes Bringle Ferry Rd (SR-1002) after 0.5 mi. Continue E 4.8 mi to the park entrance, L.

Persimmon Branch Trail (2.3 mi); Lake Trail (1.0 mi) **752-753**
> LENGTH AND DIFFICULTY: 3.3 mi combined, easy

TRAILHEADS AND DESCRIPTION: From the concession stand at the dam, walk to the opposite side of the lake and turn R at 0.2 mi on the *Persimmon Branch Trail*. Follow the 32 interpretive markers that identify trees such as oaks, pines, ash, elm, and hornbeam, as well as mosses and ferns. Cross Persimmon Branch at 0.4 mi, turn L, and begin the return loop at 1.0 mi. From the dam the *Lake Trail* circles the lake along its edge through a picnic area and large campground. The lake has a large variety of ducks and other waterfowl.

UNION COUNTY
Cane Creek Park

This is one of the state's largest county-owned natural environment parks; it has 1,050 acres of forest that surround a 350-acre lake. It has a large family-oriented campground (full svc), a group camp, a backcountry tent camp, and a camp store. In addition to camping, there is picnicking (with shelters); fishing (a trophy largemouth bass lake with bluegill and crappie); mountain biking; horseback riding; boating (also rentals for sailboats, canoes, pedal-boats and rowboats); and lake swimming. Almost at the South Carolina state line, the park was constructed as a joint project by the county and the US Soil Conservation Svc for recreation, watershed protection, and flood control of Cane Creek. The park is open all year, and a small entrance fee is charged for each car or other vehicle. The park has about 10.0 mi of horse and mountain bike trails. Although pedestrians may use the trails, the only exclusive pedestrian trails are connector trails from the parking lots to the ball field and beach. Horse trailers must be parked in the gravel lot at the ball field, and equestrians are not permitted to ride along roadways, picnic areas, or in family camping areas. All trails interconnect (may be unnamed) and are color coded; red blazes are used on the longest route, which crosses the earthen dam and has loops at both trail ends. (*USGS Map*: Unity)

ADDRESS AND ACCESS: Cane Creek Park, 5213 Harkey Rd, Waxhaw, NC 28173; 704-843-3919. In E Waxhaw on NC-75, take Providence Rd (SR-1117) S 6.7 mi (crossing NC-200 at 5.8 mi) to Harkey Rd (SR-1121), turn L, and go 0.8 mi to park entrance R. (Providence Rd crossing is 11.0 mi S of Monroe on NC-200.)

WAKE COUNTY
Blue Jay Point County Park

Wake County has two major parks with pedestrian trails. Like Mecklenburg County, Wake is largely urbanized. Raleigh, the capital city, like Charlotte is centrally located. The difference in the two counties is that in Wake the city and county parks are in separate departments. (See Raleigh in chapter 13.) Blue Jay Point County Park is located on a peninsula at Falls Lake. It has ball fields, playground, picnic areas, lodge, and a Center for Environmental Education. The latter was established for the purpose of outdoor education for school-children and training programs. Part of the *Falls Lake Trail* (see chapter 9) passes around the park's lake boundary. Short connector trails *Blue Jay Point Trail* (0.2 mi); *Sandy Point Trail* (0.2 mi); *Laurel Trail* (0.2 mi); and a paved trail for the physically disabled descend to meet the 3.1-mi *Falls Lake Trail*.

ADDRESS AND ACCESS: Blue Jay Point County Park, 3200 Pleasant Union Church Rd, Raleigh, NC 27614; 919-870-4330. Access is off Six Forks Rd, 1.5 mi S from its jct with NC-98 and 1.5 mi N from its jct with Possum Track Rd. Wake County Parks and Rec, Box 550, Suite 1000, Wake County Office Bldg, Raleigh, NC 27602; 919-856-6670.

Lake Crabtree County Park

Bordering I-40 at the W edge of the county, this 215-acre park adjoins 500-acre Lake Crabtree. The park provides picnic areas with shelters, playgrounds, fishing piers, and boat rentals and ramps. It has 0.6-mi *Old Beech Nature Trail* **754** with markers in a damp area, where boardwalks are among oaks, pines, sweet gums, and maple (one with three legs at 0.3 mi). Access is at the first parking lot, R, after entry to the park. Also here, across the road, is a foot route with switchbacks up the hill to *Highland Trail*. It has three loops, two of which are **755** L (loop #2 is 0.5 mi, and farther W is loop #3 with 1.0 mi), and the other is R (loop #1 with 1.3 mi). Biking is allowed in the loops, but access is off the road to the boat ramp, or paralleling I-40 from the Old Reedy Creek Rd at *Lake Crabtree Trail* and *Black Creek Trail* (see below). The sound of traffic from I-40 and the Raleigh-Durham International Airport is prominent. The park's longest hiking trail is *Lake Crabtree Trail*, described below. (*USGS Map:* Cary)

ADDRESS AND ACCESS: Lake Crabtree County Park, 1400 Aviation Pkwy, Morrisville, NC 27560; 919-460-3390. Access is from I-40, exit 285, S on Aviation Pkwy 0.3 mi and turn L.

Lake Crabtree Trail   **756**

LENGTH AND DIFFICULTY: 5.4 mi, easy to moderate

TRAILHEAD AND DESCRIPTION: If parking at the trailhead for the nature trail (the closest to the W trailhead of *Lake Crabtree Trail*) and entering first the E trailhead, walk E on the main park road for 0.3 mi to the road R to the boat rental and fishing dock. At the first parking lot notice the trailhead and signboard L. At 0.2 mi cross a footbridge and turn R on the blue-blazed trail. Among the young pine and oak forest pass through redbud, hazelnut, sumac, and witch hazel. At 0.4 mi is an observation deck. Stay near the lake's edge and avoid routes to the L (which connect with the *Highland Trail*). At 0.8 mi parallel I-40, where cow-itch vine hugs the rocks on the lakeside, and pass through a gated fence at 1.0 mi. Ascend to the top of Lake Crabtree Dam. Here is a signboard of information and to the L is a gate at Old Reedy Creek Rd. (Access to Old Reedy Creek Rd is off I-40, exit 287, S on Harrison Ave for 0.4 mi, turn R on Weston Pkwy, go 0.5 mi, turn R, and go 0.8 mi to shoulder parking at the dam.)

Continue on the trail by following asphalt-surfaced *Black Creek Trail* on top of the dam (part of the Cary greenway system). Uplake views are scenic. (At 1.2 mi is a signpost of the 2.5-mi *Black Creek Trail*. The dam, built in 1987, is part of the Crabtree Watershed Project to create a drainage area of 33,128 acres.) At 1.3 mi, R, is a sandy beach area with seats excellent for watching sunsets. Pass the grassy overflow area, go through a gate, and reach an observation deck for scenic views of the lake at 1.5 mi. At 1.6 mi, L, is an emergency phone and access up the hill to an IBM building, part of the Research Triangle Park. Watch for a sudden turn R leaving the paved trail (may be a white blaze instead of blue) at 1.8 mi. (The *Black Creek Trail* continues upstream, underneath Weston Pkwy, on its meandering route to exit at West Dynasty Dr, off N Harrison Ave. See Cary in chapter 13.)

Rock-hop Black Creek and begin to ascend and descend along the S edge of the lake. On a narrow treadway in and out of coves and past close points to the lake are large hardwoods with buckeye (a species in alluvial wood and swamp forests), lavender monarda, and false foxglove. Cross a wet area at 2.6 mi, enter an old road with a thin passage through grasses and shrubs, and at 3.2 mi use the cement footing for a passage through a swamp. Here are cattails, willows, and a cacophony of frogs. Reach Evans Rd at 3.4 mi and walk on the narrow trail at the base of the road shoulder. Cross a steel arched footbridge over Crabtree Creek at 3.6 mi and turn R (though there may not be signs or blazes for direction). Stay R on an old road, perhaps seeing blue blazes near the lake, and pass through a swampy area to exit at Aviation Pkwy, near an undeveloped parking area at 4.6 mi. Turn R across the causeway and reenter the forest at the edge of the shoulder railing at 5.0 mi. Poison ivy is prominent in the woods. Enter a field of tall grasses and shrubs (wet after rains), then approach a manicured lawn of the park. Complete the loop at the *Old Beech Nature Trail* parking lot at 5.4 mi.

13. Municipal Parks and Recreation Areas

A city without parks and trees is like a lawn without grass and flowers without petals.
—Josephine Neville

More than 135 cities and towns in the state have departments of parks and recreation. Some towns whose boundaries join have formed a joint department, and other cities have teamed with the counties for financial reasons and cooperative services. A few cities are moving swiftly with long-range master plans for greenway systems that will not only serve the inner city but connect with other cities and into the counties. An example is the Raleigh/Durham/Chapel Hill/Cary/Research Triangle greenway plan, influenced strongly by a citizens' group, the Triangle Greenways Council. Winston-Salem has a plan to connect with other towns in Forsyth County. Other cities with plans are Charlotte/Mecklenburg County and High Point/Jamestown/Greensboro/Guilford County. The city of Jacksonville has a master plan for more than 40 trails in its greenway system. Urban trails are usually multiple-use for walking, jogging, biking, and in-line skating. They frequently follow streams, city utility routes, nonmotorized roads, recreational parks, and historic areas. The urban trails provide opportunities for appreciating the city's heritage and culture at a relaxed pace, for meeting neighbors, and for physical and spiritual health. Urban walking clubs are being organized, and books and magazines on urban trails are increasing. Examples are *Walking* magazine (Cowles Magazines, Inc.) and *City Safaris* (Random House). "Trails for day use must be developed in and near urban areas," stated the National Park Service in 1986 when it was developing a national trails system plan. On the following pages are examples of diverse trails whose treadways is city soil, asphalt, brick, and cement that lead into history and remind us that urban trails are heritage trails.

ALBEMARLE (Stanly County)

The city has two trails, one in Rock Creek Park and another in Northwoods Park. Access to Rock Creek Park is immediately R after turning S on US-52 at **757** the jct of NC-24/27/73. Begin *Rock Creek Trail* at the far end of the parking area and pass a number of park buildings, R. Follow a wide, easy, old RR grade 1.0 mi to a dead end. Tall pine and hardwoods comprise a canopy over shrubs and honeysuckle. Rock Creek, R, partially parallels the rail. Backtrack.

To reach Northwoods Park, take US-52 from Rock Creek Park N to US-52 Bypass at 2.2 mi. Turn R, go 1.3 mi; turn R on Centerview Church Rd and turn L immediately. Park at the swimming pool parking lot. Begin the unnamed trail at the edge of the hardwood forest and follow a path for a loop of 1.5 mi in either direction. The trail ascends and descends in a hilly area, both on old woods roads and through a section with physical-fitness stations. (*USGS Maps:* Albemarle SW and NW)

ADDRESS: Director, Parks and Rec Dept, Box 190, Albemarle, NC 28001; 704-983-3514.

BLACK MOUNTAIN (Buncombe County)

758 At Lake Tomahawk Park, 0.6-mi *Lake Tomahawk Trail* circles the lake. Wide and easy, the trail is accessible for use by the physically disabled. From the picturesque path are views of Black Mtn range, including the "Seven Sisters." The park also has picnic facilities, senior citizens center, lighted tennis court, and outdoor swimming pool. (A new park and bike route are in the planning stage.) Access is off I-40, exit 64. Go N on NC-9 to second traffic light at US-70. Turn L, go four blocks, turn R on Cragmont Rd; take R fork on Rhododendron Ave to parking lot L.

ADDRESS: Black Mtn Rec and Parks, 106 Montreat Rd, Black Mtn, NC 28711; 704-669-2052.

BLOWING ROCK (Watauga County)

759 The 2.4-mi round-trip *Glen Burney Trail* is a scenic, strenuous descent into the Glen Burney Gorge. Access is off Main St (US-221) W on Laurel Lane 0.1 mi to Ann L. Cannon Memorial Garden and parking lot, L. From the parking lot observe the trail description board, descend into the gorge, cross New Years Creek twice among rhododendron, hemlock, ferns, witch hazel, and wildflowers. At 0.8 mi is an observation deck at Glen Burney Falls. Descend to the falls' base on a rough and sometimes slippery treadway.

Descend to the base of beautiful Glen Marie Falls at 1.2 mi. Backtrack. The more-than-100-year-old trail is on property donated to the town in 1906 by Emily Puruden. (*USGS Map:* Globe)

ADDRESS: Blowing Rock Parks and Rec Dept, Box 47, Blowing Rock, NC 28605; 704-295-5222.

BOONE (Watauga County)

Boone is county seat, home to Appalachian State University, and the historic site of an outdoor drama on the life of its namesake, Daniel Boone. Nestled in Boone Creek Valley at 3,266 ft elev, it is only 1.0 mi E of the Tennessee Valley Divide and at the base of magnificent Howard Knob (4,420 ft). On the E side of this enchanting town is serpentine South Fork of the famous New River. On its floodplains is an appealing greenway system. The S access is 1.0 mi off US-221 (between US-421 and US-321) on State Farm Rd to Hunting Lane L and the Watauga Swim Complex, L. A parking lot is near the basketball court. For the N access turn off US-421/221 on Daniel Boone Dr for 1.0 mi to turn R on Casey Lane; go 0.1 mi to a parking lot near Humane Society Shelter.

If going downriver from Hunting Lane, walk 0.2 mi to a large parking area for Appalachian State University at a cement-lane road, R. Cross the river on a covered bridge. Follow the wide asphalt *South Fork Trail* (for hikers, bik- **760** ers, skaters, and joggers) through meadows on the R and hardwoods on the riverside, L. At 1.1 mi is a bridge over the river, where *Oakwood Trail* begins L. **761** (It ascends 0.6 mi up the hill on an old cattle path of a former farm. Its N access is at Oakwood Dr in a residential area. Access here is from US-421 on Forest Hills Dr, then R on Appalachian Dr.) At 1.4 mi pass a historic dam site. Jct with proposed *Daniel Boone Trail,* L, up Rocky Knob Creek. Cross the river **762** again on a bridge at 1.6 mi, turn L, exit from the woods, and arrive at the parking lot at 1.9 mi. (Plans by the town are to build another 1.8-mi exten-sion loop of *South Fork Trail* upriver from Hunting Lane.) (*USGS Map:* Boone)

ADDRESS: Planning and Inspections, Town of Boone, 1510 Blowing Rock Rd, Boone, NC 28607; 704-262-4540/4560.

BURLINGTON (Alamance County)

The Burlington Rec and Park Dept and the Burlington Women's Club sponsor the Town and Country Nature Park with its easy 1.5-mi *Town and Country* **763** *Nature Trail.* Access to the park is from I-85/40 and NC-87 (exit 147) N on S Main St in Graham. Turn R on NC-49, follow it to US-70 to Church St, and turn L. Go 0.9 mi; turn R on McKinney St for 0.3 mi, R on Berkley Rd, and go 0.2 mi to Regent Park Lane. Park at the end of the street. Follow the trail signs W on a well-graded trail (with picnic areas at intervals) through oak, birch, Virginia pine, black willow, and wildflowers. Cross bridges at 0.3 and 0.7 mi. Pass the S side of the Haw River at 0.9 mi. Side trails go up and down the river. (*USGS Map:* Burlington)

ADDRESS: Rec and Parks Dept, Box 1358, Burlington, NC 27215; 919-226-7371.

CARY (Wake County)

The Cary Greenways system, begun in 1980, continues to expand within town limits and to connect with greenways elsewhere in the county. Parks and trail systems are dispersed throughout the area with greenways frequently following streams. Examples of greenway diversity are the short 0.4-**764** mi *Higgins Trail* along Swift Creek between Danfort Dr (crescent off W Chatham St) (N) to W Maynard Rd (S) and a 7.0-mi trail system in Bond Metro Park. Unless otherwise marked at the trailheads, all trails are for walkers and bikers. Paved trails are also open to skaters. Camping is not allowed on any of the trails.

765   *Black Creek Trail* is an exceptionally scenic 2.5-mi asphalt linear trail from Lake Crabtree County Park (N) to W Dynasty Dr, 0.1 mi off N Harrison Ave (S). Access to its N trailhead is off Weston Pkwy on Old Reedy Creek Rd for 1.3 mi to a gate at Lake Crabtree Dam, L. From here the trail jointly follows *Lake Crabtree Trail* for 1.0 mi. At 0.5 mi is a sandy beach at the lake. Seats are arranged to provide rest, watch the birds and sunsets, or listen to the lake lapping the shoreline. There is an observation deck, R, at 0.7 mi and an emergency telephone, L, at 0.8 mi. At 1.0 mi the trail divides. *Crabtree Lake Trail* turns sharply R for a rock-hop over Black Creek to a dirt path (see Wake County, chapter 12). *Black Creek Trail* continues ahead under Weston Pkwy and later under Cary Pkwy. The trail parallels the creek through a hardwood forest (elm, poplar, oak, black walnut) and wildflowers (cardinal flower, jewelweed). It leaves Black Creek and veers L up a tributary before crossing the last creek bridge at 2.4 mi.

766   At McDonald Woods Park is 0.8-mi *Hinshaw Trail*. Access is off Cary Pkwy on Seabrook Ave for 0.35 mi, R, for street-side parking. At the park sign are steps for a descent to a children's playground, grassy meadow, and svc rd to a gate for 0.2 mi. Across the street from the park sign is the asphalt trail. It weaves through an almost all hardwood forest (elm, poplar, beech, oak, hickory) to parallel Lynn's Branch, a tributary to Lochmere Lake. The

Strollway Trail, downtown Winston-Salem. Allen de Hart

trail's N terminus is at the jct of SE Maynard Rd and Greenwood Cir at the parking lot of Cary Church of Christ. Nearby the McDonald Woods Park is 0.6-mi *Pirates Cove Trail*. Also a N-S greenway, its N access is off Seabrook Ave on Greenwood Cir E 0.1 mi to the street's dead end. Its S trailhead is a dead end of Kildonan Ct, which is off the crescent-shaped Glenary Dr off Seabrook Ave. This access is between McDonald Woods Park and Glenwood Cir. The trail's treadway is gravel in a hardwood forest and parallels Straight Branch. (Be alert to fenced-in dogs that may lunge at pedestrians.)

768   *Swift Creek Trail* is unique, not because of plant life or history, but because of the composition of its treadway. The wide smooth trail looks like asphalt, but as part of the Swift Creek Recycled Greenway it contains ash from coal-powered electric-generating plants, recycled old asphalt, rubber tires, roof shingles, and plastics. There are descriptive signs. Perfectly landscaped, the 0.8-mi trail crosses three bridges and is from Regency Pkwy W to Kildaire Farm Rd E. A place to park is in the center of the route at Ritter Community Park. Access from Kildaire Farm Rd is 0.2 mi W on W Lochmere Dr, L. The trail goes under Kildaire Farm Rd bridge to a T jct. (A turn R crosses a footbridge over Swift Creek to connect with hike/bike trails in Loch Highland residential development.) A turn L connects with a trail at Lochmere Golf Club, where it parallels Kildaire Farm Rd to Lochmere Dr, R (E), for 2.5 mi. It is a serpentine design to Cary Pkwy. (The trail around Lochmere Lake has a No Trespassing sign; usage is for Lochmere residents only.)

A greenway, White Oak Creek, is planned for the most western area of the city. Access will be from Davis Dr along Park Village Dr to connect with a trail near a lake to Davis Dr School. It will also continue downstream to jct with a private greenway, open to the public, between NC-55 and Parkscene Dr. Below are described two parks with a network of trails.

Address: Cary Greenways, 316 N Academy St (Box 8005), Cary, NC 27512; 919-469-4360.

Annie Jones Park

Located in the SW part of the city, Annie Jones Park serves a residential area with Scottish Hills swimming pool, children's playground, tennis courts, and a lighted athletic field. Nearby is a small tributary to Swift Creek shaded by young and mature hardwoods (sweet and black gum, maple, poplar, and loblolly pine) over ferns and spicebush. Access: From a jct of Cary Pkwy go three blocks N on Lake Pine Rd, turn L (W) on Tarbert St for 0.5 mi to parking lot, R.

769   From the park follow 0.2-mi *McCloud Court Trail* (part asphalt and gravel) upstream to McCloud Ct. Backtrack. Downstream is 0.5-mi *Coat-*
770 *bridge Trail* (natural treadway and gravel), which makes a horseshoe shape in returning to Tarbert Dr between Wishaw Ct, R (E), and Brodick Ct, L
771 (W). Across Tarbert Dr is 0.2-mi asphalt *Tarbert-Gatehouse Trail*. It passes a playground to end at Gatehouse Dr. Backtrack. On the horseshoe curve of
772 *Coatbridge Trail* is a side trail, 0.2-mi *Lake Pine Trail*. It continues downstream to end at the corner of Cary Pkwy and Lake Pine Rd (diagonally opposite a minimart).

Bond Metro Park

On the W side of Cary is Wake County's largest municipal park, 360-acre Fred G. Bond Metro Park, named in honor of a former Cary mayor. A 42-acre lake provides fishing and boating (including boat rentals). Swimming and wading are not allowed. Designed to preserve the environment, the recreation areas are separated within the forest and scattered parking areas. There are four lighted athletic fields and two large picnic shelters, one large enough to accommodate 200 people. There is also a children's playground. The Sertoma Amphitheatre is arranged on a natural slope to seat an audience of more than 350. A color-coded network of trails for hikers and bikers provides multiple loops (described below). For guided nature tours throughout the year call 919-387-5980; for reserving the athletic facilities call 919-469-4062; for reserving picnic shelters call 919-460-4965.

ACCESS: From downtown go W on Old Apex Rd to High House Rd and turn L off High House Rd at the park entrance. From the S follow Cary Pkwy off US-1 to High House Rd, turn R and then R again at the park entrance.

Lake Trail (2.5 mi); Loop Trail (2.0 mi); Bond Nature Trail (0.5 mi); **773-** *Parkway Trail (0.8 mi); Oxxford Hunt Trail (1.5 mi)* **777**

LENGTH AND DIFFICULTY: 7.3 mi combined, easy

TRAILHEADS AND DESCRIPTION: The trailheads are accessible from any of the parking areas, because they are all connected. None of the trails is paved and camping is not allowed in the park. The trail system is designed to provide short loop walks or longer combinations. Linear trails (*Parkway Trail* and *Oxxford Hunt Trail*) can be backtracked or a second vehicle used. An example of a loop arrangement is to begin at the parking area near field #1. Enter the woods at Par exercise #5 on the physical-fitness course (may be yellow blazed), which at this point runs R and L with the red-blazed *Loop Trail*. Turn L and after 0.2 mi cross the park's entrance road. At 0.4 mi join the *Bond Nature Trail*, which has markers about the variety of plants, such as blackjack oak (*Quercus marilandica*), whose wood is used commercially for charcoal.

Cross a paved road (which leads R to Pkwy Athletic Complex) at 0.6 mi. At 0.8 mi come out of the woods to a field at the base of the dam, but stay L until the trail markers show a R turn. Reach a jct with the blue-blazed *Lake Trail*, R and L, at 1.1 mi. (The *Loop Trail* [red] and *Bond Nature Trail* [green] goes L.) Turn R on the *Lake Trail* across the dam, one of the most scenic views of the hike. At the other end of the dam to the R are steps that descend to white-blazed *Parkway Trail.* (It follows downstream to cross under Cary Pkwy and end in a private greenway open to the public.) Turn L and continue around the lake. For the next 1.2 mi the trail dips into ravines and over bridges and boardwalks, sometimes close to the lakeshore. On the hillside slope it meanders into the backyards of residents who may watch you pass by their azalea beds and lawn decks. Cross a footbridge over a stream at 2.6 mi and jct with white-blazed *Oxxford Hunt Trail* near another bridge. (It follows 1.5 mi upstream and across W Chatham St to a private greenway open to public use.) Continue L on a svc rd. At 2.9 mi rejoin the yellow and red markers R and L. Turn R and notice Par #17. Pass athletic fields #3 and #2, and return to Par #5, the point of origin, L, at 3.4 mi. (*USGS Map:* Cary)

CHAPEL HILL (Orange County)

The Chapel Hill Parks and Rec Dept maintains 13 park areas, 2 of which have nature trails; others are part of the Chapel Hill Greenway system. For access to Umstead Park, turn off Airport Rd (NC-86) W at Umstead Dr (between down-**778** town and the airport). The *Umstead Park Nature Trail* is an easy 1.1-mi route from the parking lot. Follow it across a bridge, and turn R or L. If R, connecting trails (some from private homes) come in near the athletic facilities. Pass **779** large sycamores beside the stream. For the 0.4-mi *Tanyard Branch Trail,* locate the Umstead Rec Center from the parking lot. Follow R of the building and along the stream to wooden steps that lead to Caldwell St. For another 0.2 mi walk along Mitchell Lane to Hargraves Community Ctr.

To reach Cedar Falls Park, turn off NC-86 E at Weaver Dairy Rd (SR-1733) (N of the airport) to Cedar Falls Park. The 0.7-mi red-blazed *Cedar* **780** *Falls Park Trail* leaves the parking lot through hardwoods around the tennis court. At 0.5 mi pass ruins of an old homestead, and return.

781 *Battle Branch Trail*

LENGTH AND DIFFICULTY: 1.6 mi, easy to moderate

TRAILHEAD AND DESCRIPTION: The W trailhead is at Country Club Rd at the University of North Carolina, Chapel Hill (no parking except a pull-off at picnic tables), and the NE trailhead is at Sugarberry Rd (street-side parking only). Parking may be more practical at the Community Ctr Park parking area, off E Franklin St on Plant Rd. If beginning from the W (across the street from Cobb dormitory), descend by the Forest Theatre to Battle Branch. After 0.2 mi there is a jct L with the corner of Boundary and Park Sts. The rocky and rooty double trails (one following a city waste system road and the other a pathway) crisscross each other and a stream. Towering loblolly pine, oak, and poplar are the principal trees, some of which are entangled with wisteria. Ground beds of ivy and ferns provide diversity in the subcanopy. At 0.5 mi is a steep bluff and at 0.7 mi is a jct with an access R to Sandy Creek Trail (street) and Greenwood Rd. Cross a branch bridge at 1.0 mi near an access L to Glendale Rd. A number of boardwalks, steps, and bridges follow where a path stays close to the stream and a city svc rd parallels on a higher contour. At 1.5 mi the trail forks. A turn L is to Valley Park Dr where a turn L at 0.2 mi accesses Community Ctr Park. On the R fork cross a boardwalk among honey locust and privet to ascend steps at Sugarberry Rd at 1.6 mi. (*USGS Map:* Chapel Hill)

ADDRESS: Parks and Rec Dept, 306 N Columbia St, Chapel Hill, NC 27514; 919-968-2700.

DURHAM (Durham County)

The Durham Rec Dept maintains more than 62 developed parks and 7 undeveloped parks in the city park system. Two of the parks have trails; they are described below. The city also has the Durham Open Space and Trails Commission with master plans for nearly 170 mi in the city and county. An example is the current construction of a mixed pedestrian/bike trail of about 2.5 mi of continuous paved urban trail. Perhaps called the *North/South Trail,* **782** it will extend from Dacian St at its S end to Broad St at the Ellerbe Creek bridge at its N end. It will pass through Northgate Park and Rock Quarry Park, past the Edison Johnson Community Ctr, and the N.C. Museum of Natural History. Access to the trail will be at various locations along its length. It will pass through a variety of landscapes, largely naturalistic wooded areas and parkland, with some portions adjacent to existing streets.

ADDRESS: Director, Parks and Rec Dept, 101 City Hall Plaza, Durham, NC 27701; 919-683-4355.

West Point on Eno

This 373-acre city park emphasizes the history and rec potential of the West Point Mill community (1778–1942). Restored and reconstructed are the McCown-Mangum farmhouse, mill, blacksmith shop, and gardens. There is also the Hugh Mangum Museum of Photography. Facilities in the park allow picnicking, fishing, rafting, canoeing, and hiking (no camping or swimming). The park is supported by Friends of West Point Inc, 5101 Roxboro Rd, Durham, NC 27704; 919-471-1623. (*USGS Map:* Durham NW)

783- 785 *Buffalo Trail (0.5 mi); South Eno River Trail (1.7 mi); North Eno River Trail (1.7 mi)*

LENGTH AND DIFFICULTY: 3.9 mi combined, easy to moderate

TRAILHEADS AND DESCRIPTION: From I-85 in Durham, take US-501 Bypass N (N Duke St) 3.4 mi and turn L into the park (across the road from the Riverview Shopping Ctr). Follow the park road to a small parking area, R, at the trail signboard (across the road from the picnic shelter and rest rooms). *Buffalo Trail* ascends a ridge and descends to jct with *South Eno River Trail* after 0.5 mi. If taking *South Eno River Trail,* walk down the park road to the mill. Cross the millrace bridge and turn L to the dam. Ascend in a forest of hardwoods and laurel. At 0.2 mi and 0.3 mi are spur trails L to *Buffalo Trail.* At 0.6 mi jct with *Buffalo Trail* L. Turn R, rock-hop a stream, and arrive at Sennett Hole (the site of the first gristmill on the river) for scenic views at 0.7 mi. Continue upriver on rocky ledges among laurel, rhododendron, yellow root, trillium, spring beauty, wild ginger, river birch, and sycamore. At 1.7 mi reach Guess Rd. Backtrack, or cross the bridge and locate an old road R that leads to a footpath downriver, the *North Eno River Trail.* Follow the N bank to a cement high-water bridge below the dam. Cross the bridge to the mill and return to the point of origin at 1.7 mi.

Rock Quarry Park

The park is on Stadium Dr, 0.3 mi from N Duke St (0.9 mi from I-85). It has athletic fields and tennis courts. From the parking lot at the softball field, begin the **786** *Quarry Trail* at the woods' edge. Turn L at the first fork, pass the old rock quarry, and reach at 0.3 mi a 90-yd side trail L to the Edison Johnson Rec Ctr. Cross the Ellerbe Creek bridge on Murray St and make an immediate L on a wide paved trail. After 125 yd pass a replica of a brontosaurus, L (part of the N.C. Museum of Life and Science). At 0.7 mi pass the Jaycee softball field. Cross Lavender St and jct L with a side trail and footbridge over Ellerbe Creek to a picnic and parking area of Northgate Park. The trail ends at Club Blvd at 1.2 mi. (Plans are to join **787** the trail with the 0.5-mi *Pearl Mill Trail* for connections downtown.)

EDENTON (Chowan County)

The town of Edenton, surveyed in 1712 and incorporated in 1722, is one of the state's oldest communities. It is often referred to as a "stroller's paradise." Three centuries of outstanding architecture (particularly Georgian, Federal, Greek Revival, and Queen Anne) make this national recreational trail a unique educational experience.

LENGTH AND DIFFICULTY: 1.5 mi, easy

TRAILHEAD AND DESCRIPTION: The visitor center is open April–October: Mon–Sat 9 AM–5 PM, Sun 1–5 PM; November–March: Tues–Sat 10 AM–4 PM, Sun 1–4 PM, closed Mon. Maps are available at the visitor center, but if you do not have a map, the following will guide you past the 28 designated sites. From the visitor center, go L (S) on Broad St, turn R onto W Church St. Pass St Paul's Episcopal Church (begun 1736) R, before turning L on S Granville St. Turn R on W Eden St, but L after one block on Blount St (which becomes W King St). At the jct with S Broad St turn R. Pass the Cupola House (1758) R. Proceed to the waterfront where the Barker House (ca 1782) is located. From the Barker House go R on E Water St to the cannons of Edenton Bay and turn L on the Courthouse Green. Pass the Tea Pot, which commemorates the Edenton Tea Party of October 25, 1774, one of the earliest political actions by women in the American colonies, before turning R on E King St. Pass the Chowan County Courthouse (1767) L, but backtrack after the Coffield House to S Broad St and turn R. Turn R on E Church St. Pass the James Iredell House State Historic Site (1800) L, but backtrack after the Blair House (ca 1775). Turn R on N Broad St for a return to the Historic Edenton Visitor Center.

ADDRESS AND ACCESS: Historic Edenton Visitor Center, 108 N Broad St, Box 474, Edenton, NC 27932; 919-482-2637, fax 919-482-3499. Parking available at the visitor center.

ELIZABETH CITY (Pasquotank County)

Settled in the 1660s, the town, like Edenton described above, has numerous historic buildings. Its 30-block historic district contains the state's largest number of antebellum commercial buildings. A sidewalk trail offers unforgettable views of vintage homes with marble window sills, stained glass windows, aesthetic woodwork, and spacious gardens. In contrast, a nature trail in Knobbs Creek Park shows the unchanged swamp.

Elizabeth City Historic Trail   **789**

LENGTH AND DIFFICULTY: 1.6 mi, easy

TRAILHEAD AND DESCRIPTION: Access is from US-158 (Elizabeth St) on Water St, S (at the W end of the Pasquotank bridge). Park at the riverfront of the Pasquotank River (corner of Water and Fearing Sts). This is the former site of Elizabeth "Betsy" Tooley's Tavern (ca 1790). (If you do not have a guide map the following will direct you past the 32 historic sites.) Follow Fearing St for six blocks, passing Christ Episcopal Church (ca 1856). At the jct of Fearing and South Rd, turn L at the Grice-Fearing House (ca 1800), R (probably the oldest structure on the hike). Turn R on Church St, and after another six blocks turn R on the original brick pavement of Selden St to Main St. Turn R and pass 19 historic buildings (including the courthouse) on your return to Water St. Turn R, one block to the point of origin.

ADDRESS AND ACCESS: Chamber of Commerce, 502 E Ehringhaus St (Box 426), Elizabeth City, NC 27909; 919-335-4365.

Knobbs Creek Park

From US-17 Bus (near the N Bypass jct), take E Ward to the park entrance, L. **790** At the parking area follow the trail sign. The 0.7-mi *Knobbs Creek Nature Trail* meanders through a dark watery area of cypress, black cherry, sweet gum, and beech. A group of Alabama supplejack (*Berchemia scandens*) hangs like lengthy jungle serpents over the cypress knees. Boardwalks built by the YCC in 1976 offer observation decks. Backtrack, or make a loop on the park meadow.

ADDRESS: Director, Park and Rec Dept, 200 E Ward St, Elizabeth City, NC 27909; 919-335-1424.

ELKIN (Surry County)

791 At Elkin Municipal Park there is 0.8-mi (round-trip) *Big Elkin Nature Trail*. Access to it is from the most NW parking area of the park. First follow the paved walking/jogging trail in the park upstream to W Spring St (NC-268) bridge. Go underneath the bridge, pass rapids and the site of an old dam, L ,at 0.3 mi. Follow the curve of the creek to a dead end near an old brick shed. Backtrack. Flora on the trail include sycamore, walnut, cherry, rhododendron, trout lily, and blackberry.

ADDRESS AND ACCESS: Elkin Rec and Parks Dept, Box 345, Elkin, NC 28621; 910-835-9814. Also, Foothills Nature Science Society, Box 124, Elkin, NC 28621. Access from I-77, exit 82, is W on NC-67 1.6 mi to US-21. Turn R, follow US-21 0.7 mi to jct L with W Spring St (NC-268) and go 0.8 mi to park, L.

FAYETTEVILLE (Cumberland County)

Clark Park was established in 1959. It is best known for the J. Bayard Clark Nature Center with its nature exhibits and live animals. (A historical center is proposed.) The park is 70 acres between a RR and the Cape Fear River. A waterfall on a tributary is near the center. The park has three nature trails: 0.3-mi *Laurel Trail* among hardwoods, loblolly pine, and laurel; 0.6-mi *Bear Trail,* which loops to a river overlook among tall trees; and 0.4-mi *Wetlands Trail,* which crosses two streams among sweet gum, pine, ferns and swamp cane. All trails are accessible from the parking area toward the center. **792-** **794**

ADDRESS AND ACCESS: Clark Nature Center, 631 Sherman Dr, Fayetteville, NC 28301; 910-433-1579. Also, Fayetteville Parks and Rec Dept, 433 Hay St, Fayetteville, NC 28301; 910-433-1547. Access to the park is off US-401 on Sherman Dr (E), two blocks S of Veterans Hospital.

GASTONIA (Gaston County)

The Schiele Museum of Natural History and Planetarium is a facility of the city of Gastonia. The 28-acre park is an example of how history can be preserved. Habitat settings in the museum show more than 25,000 mounted birds, mammals, and reptiles. The wide, well-groomed, 0.7-mi *Trail for All Seasons* introduces the visitor to natural and human history through the colonial period. There is a smokehouse, molasses boiler, log cottage, sorghum cane press, mill, and barn. The exceptional trail crosses Kendrick Creek (also known as Slick Rock Branch) twice, and passes 19 markers. The markers indicate the process of forest succession, wildflowers, shrubs, wildlife, and pioneer history. **795**

ADDRESS AND ACCESS: Schiele Museum of Natural History, 1500 E Garrison Blvd (Box 953), Gastonia, NC 28053; 704-864-3962. If approaching from I-85, take New Hope Rd S for 1.1 mi, and turn R on Garrison Blvd for 0.7 mi to the 1500 block.

GOLDSBORO (Wayne County)

A combination of city parks and greenway planning provides a route for the *Stoney Creek Trail* to begin at Quail Park and eventually extend to the Neuse River. To approach Quail Park, turn off Bypass US-70/13 at Wayne Memorial Dr, S, to the first street L, Newton Dr. Turn L again on Quail Dr to the park. Walk past the picnic shelter to Stoney Creek and turn downstream through the Kemp Greenway. Trail blazes may be yellow or white. Plant life includes tall river birch, poplar, maple, laurel oak, ironweed, cardinal flower, day flower, beauty bush, and sensitive fern. (This trail is also good for bird watching.) Cross Royall Ave and go under the RR trestle at 0.3 mi. At 1.1 mi cross Ash St and enter Stoney Creek Park. At 1.8 mi cross Elm St (entrance gate L to Seymour Johnson Air Force Base). Go 130 yd to a dead-end street **796** for parking space. (See chapter 16 for *MST* continuance downstream.) (*USGS Maps:* Goldsboro NE and SE)

ADDRESS: Director, Parks and Rec Dept, Drawer A, Goldsboro, NC 27530; 919-734-9397.

GREENSBORO (Guilford County)

The city of Greensboro operates 37 parks and rec areas. It also includes the Natural Science Center of Greensboro on Lawndale Dr, and a five-lake, 137-acre municipal nursery at Keeley Park for the production of trees, shrubs, and flowers for the city. The Natural Science Center has a zoo of 123 species, a planetarium, and a museum in a 30-acre complex. It is open daily.

797 It has 0.6-mi *Zoo Trail* (which passes by wildlife of chiefly North and South
798- America) and three connecting botanical trails—*Wildwood, Salamander,* and
800 *Muskrat*—for 0.3 mi. Bioluminescent mushrooms grow on a bank near the trail stream. The center is located at 4310 Lawndale Dr, 2.5 mi N from its jct with US-220 (Battleground Ave) in the NW part of the city (910-288-3769). (It adjoins County Park described below.) The city has a 50.0-mi labyrinth of bicycle trails (some of which are used for hiking, birding, skating, and jogging). A number of parks have unnamed paths (such as Fisher Park Circle, traditional and beautiful), and others only physical-fitness courses. Some areas, such as Hamilton Lake, may have a path nearby, but not around

801 the lake. The 0.9-mi *Hamilton Lake Trail* begins at the corner of Starmount Dr and E Keeling Rd at Lake Hamilton. It follows R of Starmount Dr on pea gravel through an open forest of tall and magnificent hickory, oak, poplar, pine, and beech—excellent to view for autumn foliage. The trail ends at the corner of Kemp Rd and Starmount.

Barber Park is an ultramodern and spaciously landscaped facility with an Indoor Sports Pavilion dome for tennis and volleyball. It has sheltered picnic

802 platforms, athletic fields, and remarkable 1.0-mi *Barber Park Trail.* The cement loop is designed for the physically disabled. It passes through the forest on the NW side and sweeps around a grassy area elsewhere. Wild roses, cow-itch vine, wild grapevines, and honeysuckle garnish the E fence line. Access is off I-40, exit 128, W on E Lee St to Florida St L, and park entrance L.

Bur-Mil Park is an expansive and popular facility of 247 acres in the NW edge of the city. The park is off US-220 on 5834 Owl's Roost Rd E, where the entrance is L (N). It is bordered on the N side partly by Lake Brandt and Brush Creek from Lake Higgins on the NW. Facilities include swimming pools, golf courses, tennis courts, two fishing ponds, picnic shelters, athletic fields, volleyball courts, children's playground, clubhouse, restaurant, and two multiple-use trails. They are connected by 0.4 mi of the *Owl's Roost Trail* (see Greensboro Watershed Trails below). The park's 2.0-mi *Big Loop Trail* makes a circuit on the W side of the park. The most convenient access is at picnic shelter #1 at a parking lot off Owl's Roost Rd, L, before the park entrance road. Follow it through a forest of tall poplar, pine, sweet gum, and running cedar. Cross a number of bridges over small streams, the last of which is 0.2 mi before a jct with *Owl's Roost Trail*. (To the L on *Owl's Roost Trail* is a bridge over a narrow part of the lake.) Turn R and follow it to a pier L, and access parking lot, R, near picnic shelter #6. Follow the gravel road past the shelter to the swimming pool and picnic shelter #3 to complete the loop, or continue on the *Owl's Roost Trail* 0.1 mi to fork R and jct with the 1.0-mi *Little Loop Trail*. Follow it around Fishing Lake and return to the club **803** by picnic shelter #7. To complete the *Big Loop Trail* follow it S from picnic **804** shelter #3 to the point of origin. The park's phone is 910-545-5300.

Country Park, also in the NW part of the city, adjoins Science Center/Planetarium on the NW (only 110-yd between their parking lots), Lewis Rec Center on the S, and Guilford Court House National Military Park on the N. Access is off US-220 on Pisgah Church Rd, R, for four blocks to turn L on Lawndale Dr N. Turn L on Nathanael Greene Dr to park's parking area and office. Facilities include a lake for fishing, picnic shelters, volleyball courts, rental boats, and a special 0.5-mi trail for the visually impaired. Another trail, 1.6-mi *Country Park Trail*, is a paved loop around the park. There is a **805** 0.2 mi connector bike/hike trail between the park's parking lot N to stop #5 on the hike/bike trail in Guilford Court House National Military Park. There is also a trail for mountain bikes. One of the city's oldest parks (1924), it has an impressive history. Some of the special events are: Carolina Cup Bicycle Road Race (one of the largest cycling events in the US); December Candlefest involving 2,500 Girl Scouts; Wild Turkey Fat Tire Festival (mountain bike race); and Farmer's Market (vegetables and homemade crafts). Park office phone is 910-545-5342/5343, and shelter reservations is 910-545-5300.

Oka T. Hester Park is a more recent facility SW in the city E of the Sedgefield Country Club. The park has a large center for community activities, a lake with paddleboats, picnic area, children's playground, tennis and volleyball courts, and a physical-fitness trail. The 1.3-mi *Hester Park Trail* **806** loops the beautiful lake. Access from I-40 and US-29A/70A, exit 217, is 1.8 mi W on US-29A/70A to Groometown Rd. Turn L, and after 0.9 mi turn L to Ailanthus St and Hester Park.

Lake Daniel Park has an easy 3.5-mi asphalt biking, hiking, and exercise
807 trail between Lake Daniel Park complex and Latham Park. On *Lake Daniel Trail* the mileage is marked. Entry can be made at a number of streets between the points of origin. To walk the distance given above, begin on Lake Dr near Battleground Ave and proceed W (near an E-flowing stream) to N Elam Ave near Wesley Long Community Hospital. Meadows are open and grassy, with scattered trees of oak, ash, poplar, and pine. (A city bike map is advisable.)

With Guilford County the city has an expansive long-range plan to have greenways, bike and hiking trails to encompass the entire county. The bike trails currently within the city proper will have at least 10 new access routes to connect with the Mountains-to-Sea (*MST*) bike route #2, which passes through the S side of the county. When completed, the outstanding *Bicentennial Trail* will be the longest trail in the state to connect multiple cities. Currently, a 6.2-mi section is completed as a greenway from High Point Lake at High Point/Jamestown N to Regency Rd near I-40 (see High Point in this chapter). The N section will cross I-40, pass E of the Piedmont Triad International Airport, go NE near Horsepen Creek, turn E, then SE along Old Battlefield Rd, and jct with existing greenways at Guilford Court House National Military Park. From there it connects with Jaycee Park and Country Park. A master plan shows the potential for its route N to connect with the lake system of trails, including the *MST* foot trail.

ADDRESS: Parks and Rec Dept, Box 3136, Greensboro, NC 27402; 910-373-2574.

Gardens of Greensboro

The city has three major gardens, Bicentennial Garden, Arboretum, and Bog Garden, all in the heart of the city within a few blocks of, or adjoining, each other. The day-use gardens are open all year and admission is free. They are made possible by the partnership of Greensboro Parks and Rec Dept and Greensboro Beautiful, a nonprofit organization of volunteers affiliated with Keep America Beautiful Inc. Brochures as elegant as the gardens are available on location. Visits to these parks lift the human spirit. Poetic expressions on one of the brochures are inspiring: "I want to surround myself with the symmetry of nature, rejoice in its beauty... I'm feeling a little wild with boundaries undefined... the world is wide and bright and wonderful... I can indulge exotic fantasies of far away places... "

ADDRESS: Greensboro Beautiful Inc, Box 3136, Greensboro, NC 27402; 910-373-2558 (other visitor information, 800-344-2282).

The Greensboro Arboretum is located within Lindley Park, accessed off W Market St on Green Valley Rd (S), then immediately R on one-way Starmount Dr to a parking area. From the end of the parking area (near a basketball court), walk to an arched bridge over a stream. A 1.3-mi *Greensboro Arboretum Trail* loop can be made, but the distance is longer if using spur **808** trails for closer examination of the collection areas and off the trail to the dancing fountain. Hundreds of species in such collections as conifers, sun shrubs, wildflowers, small trees, hydrophytic plants, vines, shade shrubs, and ground covers make this an alluring horticultural delight. Birds and butterflies are prominent visitors.

To locate the Bicentennial Garden turn off Friendly Ave N to 1105 Hobbs Rd. The park is meticulously maintained and specializes in mass regimented plantings of bulbs, annuals, perennials, and roses. Follow the 0.5-mi *Bicentennial Garden Trail* to the bridge over a small stream and into a lightly **809** wooded garden where more than 100 plants are found in a fragrance garden and herb garden. (Labels are also in braille). The area is part of the Caldwell Memorial Park, in honor of David Caldwell (1725–1824), patriot, statesman, clergyman, physician, and founder of Caldwell Log College in 1767.

Nearby the Bicentennial Garden is Bog Garden, E of Hobbs Rd between Starmount Farm Rd (N) and Northline Ave on the S side. It features aquatic plants (such as cattails, iris, lilies, sedges, arum) that need wet, spongy, acidic soil. Additionally, the bog entices ducks, geese, and herons. Paved *Bog Garden Trail*, usable by visitors with wheelchairs, is around the lake. There **810** are boardwalks and a hillside path.

Hagan-Stone Park

The park has 409 acres of forest, fields, and developed areas. Facilities include a tent/RV campground (with full svc), hot showers, picnic tables, and public phone. (Among the rec activities are swimming, boating with rentals (no motors), fishing, picnicking, nature study, and hiking. There are two unique museums: one for tobacco and the other is Oakgrove School House.

ACCESS: From the jct of I-85 and US-421, go SE on US-421 for 3.4 mi to NC-22 jct. Turn R and go 4.1 mi on NC-22 to Winding Rd (SR-3411). Turn L and go 0.4 mi to entrance, L.

Dogwood Trail (0.5 mi); Indian Head Trail (1.4 mi); Hagan-Stone Hiking **811-**
Trail (3.4 mi) **813**
LENGTH AND DIFFICULTY: 5.3 mi round-trip combined, easy

TRAILHEADS AND DESCRIPTION: From the parking lot enter the forest (near the maintenance area) and follow the yellow arrow to the beginning of the loop trails. The *Dogwood Trail* makes a short loop, but the *Indian Head Trail* turns R at 0.6 mi to circle the campground. Continue ahead on the *Hagan-Stone Hiking Trail* to circle the perimeter of the park. Reach the Oakgrove School House at 1.2 mi, and soon enter an open field with pine and cedar borders. Pass a picnic area at 2.4 mi, R, and enter a field L at 3.4 mi. Return to the parking area near a young forest and log cottage at 3.4 mi. The trail is exceptionally well maintained over duff in the forest and grassy avenues in the fields.

Greensboro Watershed Trails (Lake Brandt)

Lake Brandt, between Lake Higgins and Lake Townsend, is one of the city's watershed lakes. It has a marina on the S side that provides fishing and boating (no swimming). Cooperative efforts between the city, county, and private citizens have created and maintain the five hiking trails at Lake Brandt and
814 the two at Lake Townsend. At Lake Higgins Marina is 0.4-mi *Nature Trail*. It begins near the boat ramp, partially follows the lake, and loops through hardwoods, Virginia pine, sparkleberry and clubmoss. Access is 0.4 mi off US-220 on Hamburg Mill Rd (0.9 mi N of Bur-Mil Park entrance on US-220). (*USGS Maps:* Lake Brandt, Summerfield, for both lakes)

ADDRESS AND ACCESS: Lake Brandt Marina, 5945 Lake Brandt Rd, Greensboro, NC 27455; 910-545-5333. From the NW section of the city at the jct of US-220 (Battleground Ave) and Lawndale Dr, follow Lawndale Dr (which becomes Lake Brandt Rd) 5.3 mi N to the dam and park on available road-side space.

815- *Nat Greene Trail (3.5 mi); Owl's Roost Trail (4.4 mi); Piedmont Trail*
819 *(2.8 mi); Reedy Fork Creek Trail (3.7 mi); Laurel Bluff Trail (3.3 mi)*
LENGTH AND DIFFICULTY: 17.7 mi combined, easy
CONNECTING TRAILS:
(*Big Loop Trail*)
(*Peninsula Trail*)

TRAILHEADS AND DESCRIPTION: At the dam, hike back (S) on the road 0.1 mi to enter the forest, R, on the *Nat Greene Trail* (a state trail designated in honor of Nathanael Greene, who led the colonial army against Lord Cornwallis at Guilford Court House, March 15, 1781, and for whom the city is named). Pass the parking area of Lake Brandt Marina at 0.2 mi in a forest of poplar, beech, and Virginia pine. Weave in and out of coves for periodic views of the lake. Cross a small stream at 1.6 mi and jct with *Owl's Roost Trail*, R, on an old RR grade, at 2.8 mi. Cross the old RR grade and after 0.2 mi enter a marsh. Cross a wide 225-ft-long boardwalk at 3.4 mi and through a floodplain to Old Battlefield Rd at 3.5 mi, the end of the trail. (It is 0.7 mi R to US-220.)

To continue on the loop, backtrack to *Owl's Roost Trail* and follow it on the old RR grade N, cross a RR bridge at 0.3 mi, and leave the RR grade, R, into a pine grove. After a few yd enter a forest of oak, hickory, ironwood, tag alder, running cedar, and scattered crane fly and rattlesnake orchids. Cross a small stream at 1.0 mi and at 1.6 mi reach an excellent view of the dam and marina across the lake. At 3.1 mi enter a boggy area. Rejoin the old RR grade at 3.5 mi, pass through the NE corner of Bur-Mil Park at *Big Loop Trail,* and cross a 295-ft RR bridge at 3.8 mi, where traffic can be seen, L, on US-220. Enter a pastoral area at 4.0 mi and jct R with the *Piedmont Trail* at 4.2 mi. Continue ahead for 0.2 mi to jct with Strawberry Rd (SR-2321) and a small parking area. (It is 0.2 mi L to US-220.)

Backtrack on the trail to the *Piedmont Trail*, L, and enter a grazing field with cedar, honeysuckle, wild plum, and blackberry. At 0.5 mi descend into a seepage area at the base of a farm pond and lake edge. Enter another open area, cross a small stream at 1.0 mi and at 1.2 mi. Cross a boardwalk at 1.6 mi and a bridge over a stream at 2.6 mi. Reach Lake Brandt Rd (SR-2347) at 2.8 mi. (To the R it is 0.3 mi across the bridge to parking area for *Nat Greene Trail.*)

Across the road from the *Piedmont Trail* begin the *Reedy Fork Creek Trail.* Enter a forest of oak, river birch, sycamore, and sweet gum to follow downstream. Cross a gas pipeline at 0.5 mi and a footbridge (built by Boy Scout Troop 275) over a stream. Enter a laurel grove. At 1.3 mi turn sharply L from Reedy Creek (the backwaters of Lake Townsend). Briefly join, R, an old woods road at 2.1 mi. Pass through wildflowers such as firepink, black cohosh, blood root, wild geraniums, and buttonbush before arriving at Hendricks Rd (SR-2324) at 3.2 mi, near the guardrail. Turn R on the road and cross a scenic marsh causeway, frequented by waterfowl. At 3.7 mi jct with Church St (SR-1001). (It is 6.4 mi R on Church St and Pisgah Church Rd (W) to US-220.) Turn R, cross the bridge over the lake, and after 0.1 mi jct, R, with the *Laurel Bluff Trail.* (To the L, across the road, is the N trailhead of *Peninsula Trail* at Townsend Lake, described below.)

Laurel Bluff Trail (which runs through the Roger Jones Bird Sanctuary) enters a river birch grove at 0.1 mi. Follow an old woods road for a short distance and pass the boundary of a field at 1.6 mi. Among the trees are willow oak, shagbark hickory, black gum, maple, and poplar. Shrubs and wildflowers include wood betony, beauty bush, arum, laurel, redbud, dogwood, and filbert. Cross a small brook near the edge of the lake at 2.0 mi, and reach a boggy area at 2.1 mi. Bear R at a fork at 2.3 mi and pass a spur trail, L, at 2.7 mi. Pass through a large beech grove at 2.8 mi, and cross a gas pipeline at 3.1 mi. Pass by an old barn and reach former Dillard's Store on Lake Brandt Rd at 3.3 mi. To the L, across the road, is *Nat Greene Trail.*

Townsend Lake

Townsend Lake is fed by Lake Higgins, Lake Brandt, and Richard Lake. All waters flow E, and at the E end of Townsend Lake is its dam. Adjoining the lake/dam area is Bryan Park, one of the city's largest and known for its golf courses. Three Townsend Lake area trails are described below.

820- *Peninsula Trail (1.2 mi); Osprey Trail (2.5 mi); Townsend Trail (4.2 mi)*
822 LENGTH AND DIFFICULTY: 7.9 combined, easy
CONNECTING TRAIL:
(*Laurel Bluff Trail*)
TRAILHEADS AND DESCRIPTION: From the jct of Pisgah Church Rd (its NE end where it becomes Lees Chapel Rd) and Church St (Rd) (N), go 2.0 mi to a roadside parking area R, for the *Osprey Trail,* R. Ahead, across the causeway, it is 1.0 mi to the N trailhead of *Peninsula Trail.* Across the road, L, is the trailhead for *Laurel Bluff Trail.* For the E trailhead of *Osprey Trail,* it is 2.1 mi N on Yanceyville Rd from Lees Chapel Rd. Here is the W trailhead of *Townsend Trail.* Its E trailhead is accessed by taking Lees Chapel Rd NE to Southshore Rd and Townsend Rd jct.

Enter the white-blazed *Peninsula Trail* through young Virginia pines. At 0.6 mi is an observation spot of Townsend Lake. After a wet runoff area is a mixed pine and magnolia grove at 0.9 mi. Exit at N Church Rd at 1.2 mi, turn L, and cross the causeway for 300 yd to a roadside parking area, L (E). The *Osprey Trail* begins here. Follow the white-blazed trail past remains of an old cabin at 0.2 mi. At 0.3 mi pass close to the lake's lapping shoreline. Ascend a slight ridge of oak and pine and descend to parallel a cove before rock-hopping a stream at 0.8 mi. Return to the lake's edge, then cross under two power lines to follow a rim of a former pond. At 2.1 mi is an excellent view of the lake. Arrive at Yanceyville Rd at 2.5 mi. Backtrack, or have a second vehicle. It is 5.9 mi on the roads for a return to the point of origin.

The white-blazed *Townsend Trail* begins across the road at a gate opposite the *Osprey Trail*. Pass through a grassy slope by the lake for 113 yd to enter the forest at a berm. At 0.4 mi, L, is an old well in a forest of oak, beech, and dogwood. Curve around a long cove, cross a stream, and return to the lakeside at 1.0 mi. At 1.6 mi walk on the sandy edge of the lake to avoid dense growth under a power line. Here are buttonbush, filbert, and tag alder. Reenter the forest and follow the edge of another cove. Cross a footbridge, enter a grove of Virginia pine and club moss. At 2.7 mi are ridges on the treadway, indicating a former tobacco field. Pass under a power line at 3.1 mi and 3.4 mi. Curve R of a farm pond to ascend at 3.7 mi. At 3.8 mi cross Southshore Rd to reenter the woods. Come out to a field with bluebird houses in Bryan Park. Cross the field and turn R at a fence. After a few yd enter the fence opening and arrive at paved Townsend Rd at 4.2 mi. To the L are Bryan Park's golf courses. Turn R, go 0.2 mi on the road to a park gate, and exit at the corner of Southshore Rd and Townsend Rd by the RR track. Backtrack, or have a second vehicle parked at the open space outside the gate and between Townsend Rd and the RR to avoid being locked inside the park. (*USGS Maps:* Lake Brandt, Browns Summit)

GREENVILLE (Pitt County)

The city operates 19 parks, and at least 2 have trails. The city is currently constructing the first phase of a greenways corridor. Eventually it will follow Green Mill Run through most of the city. (For an update call 919-830-4474.) Green Spring Park on 5th St (across the street from St Peter's Catholic Church) has an excellent 20-sta 1.2-mi physical-fitness trail that is popular with joggers and walkers. The *Green Spring Park Trail* begins at a picnic area **823** and passes under tall cypress, sweet gum, and ash, many of which are draped with Spanish moss. Another park, River Park North, has nature trails.

ADDRESS: Parks and Rec Dept, Box 7207, Greenville, NC 27834; 919-752-4137 (919-758-1230 at River Park North).

River Park North

The park was opened to public use in 1983 and currently has 324 acres, with at least 190 acres of rich bottomland forest by the Tar River. It has four lakes for fishing, rental boats, boat ramp, organized group camping area, picnic shelter, and a natural science center. The park is open each day except Monday and the major holidays.

River Park North Trail (1.1 mi); Willow Branch Trail (0.3 mi)
LENGTH AND DIFFICULTY: 2.8 mi round-trip combined, easy

TRAILHEADS AND DESCRIPTION: Access to the park from downtown at 5th St and Green St is to go N on Green St 1.5 mi (across the Tar River bridge) and take a R on Mumford Rd for 0.8 mi to the park, R. From the parking area follow the wide svc rd S toward the lakes. Near the picnic shelter a L beyond the pedal-boat dock is the trailhead for the 0.3-mi *Willow Branch Trail*. It follows the lake bank with 12 interpretive posts for plants such as water oak, red mulberry, and black willow. It has a forest observation deck. It rejoins the svc rd in an open area with swamp rose, passion flower, rose mallow, and pinkweed. The *River Park North Trail* follows the svc rd, passes between the lakes and under a power line at 0.3 mi and 0.5 mi. In a scenic forest of tall river birch, ash, cypress, and sycamore turn L at 0.6 mi. This route forms a loop, and bridges and boardwalks were donated by Contentnea Creek Ducks Unlimited. At 1.0 mi reach a tributary and turn R to rejoin the svc rd at 1.2 mi. Turn R, follow the Tar River among cottonwood and water and willow oaks. Return to the parking lot at 2.2 mi.

HENDERSON (Vance County)

Fox Pond Park has lighted tennis courts, picnic area with shelters, children's playground, youth baseball field, fishing (no swimming), and trails. From the parking lot near the tennis courts, begin the 1.4-mi *Fox Pond Trail* on the E side of the lake and go counterclockwise. Cross a floating bridge at the lake's headwaters at 0.5 mi. Cross a svc rd near a cement bunker at 0.9 mi, cross over the stream (near the dam) on a swinging bridge at 1.3 mi, and return to the parking lot. E of the parking lot is the 0.6-mi *Conoconors Trail*, which loops through sweet gum and poplar trees around the tennis courts. *Quarry Trail* and *Sutton's Island Trail* are short loops of 0.2 mi each in the rec area. Park is open all year.

ADDRESS AND ACCESS: Director, Rec and Parks Dept, Box 1556, Henderson, NC 27536; 919-492-6111. On NC-39 (0.4 mi E of Bypass US-1) turn on Huff Rd (SR-1533) and go 0.5 mi to the park, L.

HENDERSONVILLE (Henderson County)

Northeast of Jackson Park, a Henderson County park described in chapter 12, is *Mud Creek Wetlands Nature Trail*. An asphalt surface accessible to all, it is 1.0 mi, of which 235 yd is boardwalk through a swamp. In an appealing 40-acre preserve, the major emphasis is on environmental education.

Unique to the area is the large wood duck population. Other wildlife are teal, owl, hawk, turtles, and chipmunk. Plant species are identified. Dogs must be kept on a leash.

ADDRESS AND ACCESS: City of Hendersonville, Box 1670, Hendersonville, NC 28793; 704-697-3079. From I-26, exit 18, go W on US-64 to Duncan Hill St; turn R, go one block, and turn L on 7th Ave E to parking area near Mud Creek.

HIGHLANDS (Macon County)

One of the most unforgettable towns in the state, Highlands, the "Land of the Sky," is 4,118 ft in elev. It is part of and surrounded by cool fresh air and water and some of nature's magnificent wonders: spectacular waterfalls, rocky knob overlooks, wilderness whitewater, precious gems, and vascular floral gardens. Its accommodations, dining, fishing, cultural activities, and hiking options make it a desirable place for a vacation. Its nearby USFS trails are described in chapter 2, section 2; its *Sunset Rocks Trail* in chapter 14; and the Highlands Biological Station in chapter 15. Within the village, Highlands Rec Park is developing a trail between 4th St and Oak St, and the *Highlands Greenway Trail* is already established.

831

Like a string of jewels it is from Sunset Rocks to Mirror Lake, partly on clean highways and streets, gravel and earthy roads, and soft pathways. The distance is 2.0 mi unless you include the round-trip 1.4 mi of *Sunset Rocks Trail* and 1.0 mi of trails at the biological station. If a second car is used to avoid backtracking, follow US-64 W on Main St and descend to Mirror Lake Rd, R. If beginning at Sunset Rocks return to Horse Cove Rd and the Highlands Biological Station at Ravenel Lake. Follow Horse Cove Rd W to Hudson Library, then an art gallery at the corner of Main St and 5th St. Turn R (N) on 5th St and after two blocks turn L on Pine St to the Chamber of Commerce (where you may receive further descriptions of this walk). From here turn R on N 4th St, but watch for a foot trail, L, after crossing Mill Creek. The trail passes behind the Civic Center, crosses the creek again, and comes out on Oak Lane among hemlock and rhododendron. Follow Oak Lane to Raoul Rd, follow it N to an unpaved road to Mirror Lake Rd and Thorne Park. Here are wood ducks, mallards, and herons and the end of the hike. (*USGS Map:* Highlands)

ADDRESS AND ACCESS: Highlands Park and Rec Dept, Box 460, Highlands, NC 28741; 704-526-3556. Park office is on Cashiers Rd (US-64) W across from Laurel St at Highlands Rec Center.

HIGH POINT (Guilford County)

The city is following the trend of its triangle cities, Greensboro and Winston-Salem, in long-range plans for a greenway system. At present a 1.4-mi section **832** of *Boulding Branch Trail* is completed. Access to its SW trailhead is off N Main St E on Farris Ave to its jct with Forest St. Follow an asphalt trail downstream and go through a cement tunnel at Centennial St at 0.2 mi. Pass through High Point University campus between W College Dr and E College Dr at 0.5 and 0.6 mi. At 1.2 mi reach E Lexington Ave, where to the L is High Point Museum and Historic Park. Ahead and R of the trail is the Little Red Schoolhouse, built in 1930 at Ray Street Elementary School downtown, and moved here in 1987. At 1.3 mi is access W to Welborn Middle School across a footbridge. Continue R on the main trail and exit at the jct of Woodruff and Wiltshire Sts. When the trail (about another 3.0 mi) is completed downstream to Deep River and connected with the *Bicentennial Greenway Trail* at Penny Rd, High Point and Jamestown will be joined by a greenway system. The city also contributes approximately 65 percent of the funding for the Piedmont Environmental Center at High Point City Lake, a 200-acre preserve for natural-science study. One of its services is an outdoor classroom program for public schoolchildren, and it has a special wildflower garden with emphasis on plants from the Piedmont. Picnicking is allowed but no camping or swimming. The center is open daily.

ADDRESS AND ACCESS: Piedmont Environmental Center, 1228 Penny Rd, High Point, NC 27260; 910-454-4214. From the jct of US-29A/70A and Penny Rd (W in Jamestown), go N 1.1 mi on Penny Rd and turn R at the center's entrance. From Greensboro, at the jct of Wendover Ave and I-40, exit 214, go SW on Wendover Ave 4.5 mi to the jct with Penny Rd (at the Deep River intersection). Turn L and go 2.0 mi to the center, L. (The Parks and Rec Dept address is 221 Nathan Hunt Dr, High Point, NC 27260; 910-887-3477.)

Piedmont Environmental Center

833- 840 *Lakeshore Trail (1.8 mi); Fence Row Trail (0.1 mi); Wildflower Trail (0.2 mi); Fiddlehead Trail (0.4 mi); Dogwood Trail (0.6 mi); Pine Thicket Trail (0.3 mi); Raccoon Run Trail (0.7 mi); Chickadee Trail (0.1 mi)*

LENGTH AND DIFFICULTY: 4.2 mi round-trip combined, easy

TRAILHEADS AND DESCRIPTION: All trails can be accessed from the *Lakeshore Trail* (white), which begins at the parking lot or the back porch of the center. If beginning from the parking lot enter at the S side (near the driveway entrance and crossing of *Bicentennial Greenway Trail*). Immediately L is a connector to *Fence Row Trail* (tan), L, and *Chickadee Trail* (green), R. Either way, they connect with the *Lakeshore Trail* after 0.1 mi. If following L pass behind the parking lot and buildings, turn R, and after a few yd jct with the *Wildflower Trail* (purple). (The *Wildflower Trail* has double loops, connects with the *Bicentennial Greenway Trail*, and has a mixed forest of pine and hardwoods, ferns, and wildflowers.)

Continuing on the *Lakeshore Trail*, reach a jct with 0.4-mi *Fiddlehead Trail* (yellow), R. (It descends to jct with *Pine Thicket Trail* [red], L, and down to a cove in High Point City Lake. Here is jct R and L with *Lakeshore Trail*. A turn R on the floating bridge will make a return to the parking lot for a 1.0-mi loop.) If passing by the *Fiddlehead Trail*, go past a spur connector L to the *Bicentennial Greenway Trail*, followed by a R jct with the *Dogwood Trail* (orange). (The *Dogwood Trail* goes through the heart of the *Lakeshore Trail* loop, exposing oak, pine, poplar, and cedar. Along the way it jct R with *Pine Thicket Trail*.)

Staying on the *Lakeshore Trail*, pass through a forest of large trees and arrive at the lake at 0.8 mi. Curve around the peninsulas, where to the interior of the loop is kudzu. Pass the jct R with *Dogwood Trail* at 1.0 mi, and at 1.3 mi jct with *Raccoon Run Trail* (blue) L. (*Raccoon Run Trail* goes briefly on a linear trail before a scenic circle on the peninsula.) Finish the *Lakeshore Trail* by crossing the floating bridge and ascending to the parking lot at 1.8 mi. (Three mi of the *Bicentennial Greenway Trail* are within the center's preserve [see below]. (*USGS Maps:* High Point E, Guilford)

Bicentennial Greenway

Bicentennial Greenway Trail

841

LENGTH AND DIFFICULTY: 6.2 mi, easy to moderate

TRAILHEAD AND DESCRIPTION: The N access is off I-40, exit 210, on NC-68 S for 0.4 mi. Turn L (E) on Regency Dr and park on the R at a parking space (may become another street). Walk 290 yd farther on Regency Dr to trailhead R(S). The S trailhead is at the N end of Deep River bridge on Penny Rd where parking is available 0.35 mi N on Penny Rd to the Piedmont Environmental Center.

Throughout the trail are tall mixed hardwoods of oak, yellow poplar, sycamore, and river birch. Virginia pine thrive on the slopes, mixed with loblolly pine. Grassy trail shoulders are frequently mowed and the width of the landscape provides a flow of breezes. Wild roses, muscadine grape, blackberry, and August olive are prominent. Ferns and wildflowers border the woods' edges.

The multiuse trail is open for biker, pedestrians, skaters, and joggers. Horse traffic and motorized vehicles are not allowed; neither is camping. Dogs must be on a leash. Some sections are easy for the physically handicapped.

If beginning at Regency Dr at Piedmont Centre Office Park, follow the signs on a wide asphalt trail. After steps and a boardwalk in a forest arrive at a meadow of blackberry and honeysuckle. At 0.6 mi is a parking area. A sign indicates the first 2.8 mi of the trail opened in November 1989. Continue along the side of the East Fork of Deep River, occasionally crossing it on cement bridges. Cross a bridge over a stream from Davis Lake, R, at 1.1 mi. At 1.3 mi is a small cascade, L. Cross W Wendover Ave at 2 mi. (The access is under construction, and the trail may go under the road beside the river.)

At 2.5 mi pass through Gibson Park. To the R is Deep River Cabin (ca 1830), rest rooms, and an access on Park Entrance Rd to W Wendover Ave. On the trail is a plaque honoring the history and craftsmanship of the Jamestown Long Rifles. (Here is also a 1.0-mi-loop trail. It has a spur trail to a bluff and cascade.) One of the most scenic areas of the trail is at 3.0 mi where an observation deck juts into a swamp, an excellent retreat for birders. Cattails, arrow arum, buttonbush, swamp buttercups, and willows provide plant diversity. At 3.4 mi is a patch of wild plums. Reach a svc road (Sunnyvale Dr) at 3.5 mi and turn R. After 80 ft red-blazed 4.6-mi *Deep River Trail* (for pedestrians only) crosses the road, L and R. (To the R it follows up a small stream and returns after a crescent to join the main trail. To the L it enters a floodplain and meanders near the W bank of High Point Lake until it rejoins the main trail at E Fork Rd. Along its route it makes a loop, *Hollis Rogers Pine Woods Trail* [under construction] in a loblolly pine forest.)

Continuing on the main trail, follow the road for another 150 yd and turn L, steeply uphill. Cross a pipeline, then under a power line, and arrive at Jamestown Park at 4.4 mi. Here are rest rooms and parking facilities, R, across E Fork Rd. Parallel the road; jct L with the *Deep River Trail* at 4.7 mi. Cross the E Fork Rd. For the next 0.2 mi are a number of boardwalks, bridges, and steps. Enter the Piedmont Environmental Center trail network (see above). At 5.8 mi arrive at the parking area of the center. Beyond the center's entrance the trail descends steeply to High Point Lake and its S end at Penny Rd. Backtrack to the center's parking area. (*USGS Maps:* Guilford, High Point E)

JACKSONVILLE (Onslow County)

The city of Jacksonville's motto is "a caring community." A study of its long-range master plan for trails, greenways, and rail trails shows it cares about

outdoor recreation and how to bring neighbors together on a network of
paths for walking, biking, jogging, and skating. Two bike trails, *Freedom Trail* **844**
(9.7-mi loop downtown near Wilson Bay), and *Jacksonville to Sea Trail* (13.0- **845**
mi linear route from Jacksonville Mall to Hammock Beech Ferry Terminal)
are already established. *Northeast Creek Park Nature Trail* is in progress. **846**
Access is off Corbin Rd. From the parking lot the 2.6-mi trail has eight loops
within an outside circuit. When completed, wildlife on the trail will include
alligator, snakes, snowy egret, blue heron, and deer. Among the tree species
are bald cypress, red mulberry, loblolly pine, and hornbeam. When the ambi-
tious network plan of 40 trails is completed it will represent 106.0 mi.

ADDRESS: City of Jacksonville, Box 128, Jacksonville, NC 28541; 910-
938-5312.

LINCOLNTON (Lincoln County)

In 1982 the Timken Foundation donated funds to construct the *South Fork* **847**
Nature Trail at Betty G. Ross Park. Eagle Scouts of Troop 81 assisted in the
project. Begin the trail S of the swimming pool at a gate. The easy and wide
0.5-mi loop trail is mainly on a floodplain bend of the South Fork. (A primitive campsite is in the loop's center; reservations are required.) Among the
flora are tall water oak, green ash, sycamore, elm, and river birch. Fragrant
japonica honeysuckle covers many understory shrubs. (A physical-fitness
trail adjoins the trail in a grassy meadow.)

ADDRESS AND ACCESS: Director, Rec Commission, Box 25, Lincolnton, NC
28902; 704-735-2671. In downtown Lincolnton at the courthouse, go
W on W Main St (NC-27) and turn S at the first traffic light. Turn R to
the park off S Madison St.

NEW BERN (Craven County)

New Bern, "the land of enchanting waters," is a historic river port at the
confluence of the Trent and Neuse Rivers. Settled in 1710 and named for the
city of Bern, Switzerland, it is one of the most elegantly restored cities in the
state. The colonial assembly met here as early as 1737, and after the completion of Tryon Palace in 1770 it was the colonial capital and the state capital
until 1794. After the Revolutionary War there was a dramatic development
of Federal-style architecture. Examples are the Stevenson House (ca 1805);
First Presbyterian Church (1819); and the New Bern Academy (1806). On
the *New Bern Historic District Trail* are 67 historic buildings (business, gov- **848**

ernment, homes, and churches) within a walking (or auto) route of 4.5 mi. Because the route is divided into four sections (1.2 mi in the palace area; 1.1 mi in the Johnson St area; 1.2 mi in the E Front St area; and 1.0 mi in the downtown area) that may begin or end in irregular patterns (such as in the middle of a block), it is essential that you have a tour map to know which building is in which tour section. Maps are available free of charge from the Craven County Convention and Visitors Bureau (address below). There are guided tours sold through a tour agency or a taped walking tour can be rented from the bureau. Most buildings on the tour have a steel shield (yellow, black, and red) with a bear logo.

ADDRESS AND ACCESS: Craven County Convention and Visitors Bureau, 219 Pollock St (Box 1413), New Bern, NC 28563; 919-637-9400 or 800-437-5767. Open daily. From US-70/17, which passes through on Broad St, turn S on E Front St and go one block to SW corner of E Front St and Pollock St. Turn R and the bureau is the last house on the L on the first block. Tours originate at the SE corner of the Palace Reception Center (George St and Pollock St), across from the Tryon Palace main gate.

RALEIGH (Wake County)

The Raleigh Parks and Rec Dept has a comprehensive system of 131 parks and areas maintained by the department. Part of its program is the Capital Area Greenway (with 245 parcels of land), a model development for municipal planning. The greenway system was begun in 1974 when the city responded to rapid urbanization that threatened its natural beauty. The master plan provides a system of wide trails in their natural state for recreational activities such as walking, jogging, hiking, fishing, picnicking, bicycling, and nature study. The trails mainly follow on floodplains or utility areas of the city's three major streams, Neuse River, Crabtree, and Walnut Creeks, and their tribu-

849 taries. Two singular greenway trails unrelated to those below are *Gardner Street Trail* and *Marsh Creek Trail*. At the Rose Garden and Raleigh Little Theatre, the *Gardner Street Trail* begins at the corner of Gardner and Everette Sts at the greenway sign. (Park entrance on Gardner St.) Descend and pass L of a rest room and basketball court. Cross Kilgore St and follow the sidewalk briefly. After crossing Van Dyke Ave, turn L on Fairall Dr, a gravel road shaded by tall poplar, oak, and loblolly pine. At 0.6 mi enter a forest and arrive at the Jaycee

850 Park on Wade Ave at 0.8 mi. The paved 0.4-mi *Marsh Creek Trail* is at Brentwood Park (at the end of Vinson Ct). The wide trail follows Marsh Creek from

Ingram Dr to a footbridge over the stream at the end of Glenraven Dr. Because the majority of the trails are paved, they can be used by the physically handicapped. Some of the shorter connected or partly connected trails are described below in greenway groups. The five longest trails—*Lake Johnson, Lake Lynn, Loblolly, Neuse River,* and *Shelly Lake*—are described separately. A Raleigh Greenway Map is helpful for locating trailheads.

ADDRESS: Director, Parks and Rec Dept, Box 590, Raleigh, NC 27602; 919-890-3285.

Crabtree Greenway Area

On the Crabtree Creek floodplain and part of the Crabtree Creek Greenway project are the *Alleghany, Lassiter's Mill, Fallon Creek,* and *Buckeye Trails.* They will eventually connect to each other and up Lead Mine Creek to the Shelly Lake trails. The paved 0.4-mi *Alleghany Trail* follows Crabtree Creek **851** in a forest of tall poplar, willow oak, and loblolly pine. It passes under the Yadkin Dr bridge SE and under I-440 bridge NW. (Park on the side of Alleghany Dr either near its jct with Alamance Dr or Buncombe St. Also, access its N trailhead from *North Hills Trail.*)

North Hills Trail is a unique trio of fascinating asphalt routes (two of **852** which may also be called *Ironwood Trail Extension*) in a combined round-trip **853** of 3.1 mi. It can be accessed from the *Alleghany Trail* (see below) off Alleghany Dr, or North Hills Park off Currituck Dr (which is off Yadkin Dr). If proceeding from North Hills Park tennis court parking lot, descend steeply to wetlands thick with elm, ash, yellow poplar, lizard's tail, and jewelweed at 0.2 mi (to the L is the *Alleghany Trail,* downstream under I-440 bridge, and over an arched bridge at Crabtree Creek). For the *North Hills Trail* turn R and after 0.1 mi cross a boardwalk over Lead Mine Creek to a fork. To the R this part of the trail goes 0.3 mi to North Hills Dr. To the L the trail hugs the bank of Crabtree Creek among tall trees for 0.4 mi to North Hills Dr and a temporary dead end (across from a children's day care center). Backtrack on all three parts. (See Shelly Lake trails below.)

The 0.2-mi *Lassiter's Mill Trail* is a paved trail from Lassiter Mill Rd **854** upstream to the dam where Cornelius Jesse Lassiter operated a 1764 grist mill from 1908 to 1958. (Park on Old Lassiter Mill Rd, a few yd from the jct of Lassiter Mill Rd.)

Fallon Creek Trail, a 0.3-mi 21-post interpretive paved trail, goes through **855** tall elm, ash, poplar, and hackberry. A champion river birch (8.5 ft in girth) is near Crabtree Creek. Understory trees are boxelder, hornbeam, holly, and dogwood. (Park at the Kiwanis Park at the end of Noble St or on Oxford Rd, 0.1 mi downstream from its jct with Anderson Dr.)

856   The *Buckeye Trail* is a paved 2.4-mi scenic meandering route in a deep forest of tall river birch, poplar, willow oak, and loblolly pine. If parking at the upstream parking area on Crabtree Blvd, walk 240 yd downstream (E) on the sidewalk, around the curve, to the forest entrance. Pass a picnic area at 0.2 mi, a children's playground at 1.4 mi, and a maintenance entrance from Crabtree Blvd at 1.6 mi. At 1.9 mi, L, is an observation deck (with a ramp for the handicapped) on a knoll with views of the river. Descend and reach the E trailhead parking area at 2.4 mi. Here is access to Crabtree Park and Milburnie Rd off US-64 W of I-440 jct.

Walnut Creek Greenway Area

857- In the Walnut Creek area are the *Lake Johnson Trail* (described below) and
860 *Rocky Branch, Little Rock,* and *Dacian Valley Trails.* (*Walnut Creek Trail* is under construction.) *Rocky Branch Trail* is a paved 1.5-mi route. Begin at the Dix Hospital entrance (Umstead Dr) at Saunders St. (Parking space is 140 yd up Umstead Dr, L, from the trailhead, R.) Descend the steps, pass through an open meadow with large pecan trees and a picnic area. Cross Boylan Ave at 0.3 mi, enter a forest, exit onto a sidewalk of Western Blvd, cross Hunt Dr at 0.6 mi, and cross Rocky Branch bridge. At 1.1 mi cross Bilyeu St and after 0.1 mi follow an old paved roadway to the corner of Bilyeu St and Cardinal Gibbons St (near the S side of Cardinal Gibbons High School).

  Little Rock Trail is a 0.7-mi paved route at Chavis Park. (Park on Chavis Way.) From the corner of Lenoir and Chavis Way, cross the Garner Branch footbridge, pass two picnic areas, cross Bragg St at 0.5 mi, and end at McMackin St. Tall elm, ash, and sycamore shade the trail.

  Dacian Valley Trail is a 0.3-mi loop beginning at a picnic area at the end of Dacian Rd. Pass through tall hardwoods near Walnut Creek. (It will connect with the *Walnut Creek Trail.*)

861   Beautiful *Lake Lynn Trail* is a 2.2-mi asphalt loop, of which 0.5 mi is boardwalk, around the lake bordered with trees, shrubs, and wildflowers in a residential community. On the W side of the lake are a number of footbridges and at the N headwaters/wetlands is a skillfully constructed boardwalk from which to observe waterfowl. An additional 0.5-mi trail is planned N to Lake Lynn Park. Access off US-70 on Lynn Rd is 1.3 mi to parking area L near the base of the dam. Another access is from Crabtree Valley Mall off US-70 on NC-50 for 2.0 mi to Lynn Rd, L, then 0.3 mi to parking lot R.

Durant Nature Park

A former private preserve with emphasis on children's summer camping and nature studies, Raleigh Parks and Rec Dept continues the nature study concept with the Ranoca North Day Camp in sessions during June, July, and August. There are Sawmill and Blind Water Lakes (plus a beaver pond), swimming dock, boathouse, playfield, and training lodge. (*USGS Map:* Wake Forest)

ADDRESS AND ACCESS: Ranoca North Day Camp, Raleigh Parks and Rec Dept, Box 590, Raleigh, NC 27602; 919-870-2872; Main Office, Pullen Community Center; 919-831-6054. Entrance from the S is off US-1 on Greshams Lake Rd to R on Welborn, to R on Spotswood, and park entrance L. North entrance is W off US-1 on Durant Rd for 1.1 mi, L at the sign.

Border Trail (1.5 mi); Lakeside Trail (1.2 mi); Secret Creek Trail (0.5 mi) **862-864**

LENGTH AND DIFFICULTY: 3.7 mi combined round-trip, easy

TRAILHEADS AND DESCRIPTION: From the N parking area enter the *Border Trail* from the SW corner (watch for signs) on an old woods road. Turn R at 0.1 mi. At 0.2 mi follow upstream on Reedy Branch among large loblolly pines and yellow poplar by Sheet Rock Falls. Leave the stream later and enter a preserve of tall trees, running cedar, ferns, wild ginger, and spicebush. Cross a footbridge over Sim's Branch at 1.0 mi. At 1.2 mi is a wisteria grove and remnants of an old homesite. To the L are views of a beaver pond and Blind Water Lake (also called Upper Lake). Jct with *Lakeside Trail* at 1.5 mi. A turn R for a loop is around Sawmill Lake for 1.2 mi over the dam, by the bathhouse, and through the forest to a spillway of Blind Water Lake. Backtrack 0.5 mi the NE corner of Sawmill Lake (at Sycamore Picnic Shelter) to begin *Secret Creek Trail*. Follow it by a rocky streambed, ferns, elm, and wild petunia. Exit near the totem poles, turn R, and return to the parking area for a total of 3.7 mi.

Lake Johnson Nature Park

Lake Johnson Trail **865**

LENGTH AND DIFFICULTY: 3.6 mi, easy

TRAILHEAD AND DESCRIPTION: From Western Blvd (near the WRAL-TV sta and gardens) take Avent Ferry Rd 3.2 mi and park at the lot on the S side (across the causeway) of Lake Johnson. Enter a young hardwood forest to a picnic shelter, and hike counterclockwise. Cross a small stream and pass a small waterfall at 0.6 mi. Wind in and out of coves among tall trees and reach the dam and spillway at 1.6 mi. Cross a bridge over the spillway and across the rim of the dam for scenic views. At 1.8 mi jct with a spur trail R to Lake Dam Rd (no parking here). Continue L and arrive at the picnic and boathouse parking area at Avent Ferry Rd at 2.6 mi. Turn L on a high pedestrian/bike bridge that parallels the lake's causeway for a return to complete the loop of 3.0 mi. (A greenway trail continues across the road from the boat dock at Avent Ferry Rd. The wide wood-chip trail passes N of Lake Johnson in a scenic area. After 0.3 mi bear R and ascend to a parking area at 0.6 mi at William Stadium behind Athens Drive High School.) (Both trails are part of the Walnut Creek Greenway system.) (*USGS Map:* Raleigh W)

Richland Creek Area

866 *Loblolly Trail*

LENGTH AND DIFFICULTY: 6.0 mi, easy

TRAILHEAD AND DESCRIPTION: Take the Blue Ridge Rd exit from Wade Ave, and go S 0.4 mi to Old Trinity Rd; turn R. Park near Gate D at the Carter-Finley Stadium to the L of the gate. Follow a grassy road in a grassy field, NW, pass L of a drain water pool, and enter the forest at 0.2 mi. Follow the old road, cross a rock ditch at 0.4 mi, and confront the base of Wade Ave at a small gate at 0.6 mi. Walk through the square cement culvert (wading may be necessary) under Wade Ave. Follow downstream among river birch. At 1.3 mi enter the North Carolina State University (NCSU) forest management area of conifers and broadleaves, and at 2.2 mi jct with the NCSU 1.2-mi *Frances Liles Interpretive Trail* loop, R. Between the trail accesses is a NCSU weir gauging sta. Arrive at Reedy Creek Park Rd at 2.4 mi. (Wake County Flood Control Lake is L. It is 1.7 mi R to Blue Ridge Rd.) Turn R, and after 150 yd turn off the road, L, to an obscure trail entrance near road shoulder parking. Pass through a damp cove and on a dry rocky lakeside among redbud and young hardwoods. At 3.0 mi enter a fence opening to cross the dam. At the dam's base cross the creek and veer R to enter the forest at another gate opening at 3.1 mi. On an old road pass through young river birch and turn L at 3.2 mi. Ascend in an open forest to enter Umstead State Park at 3.3 mi, where the trail becomes blue blazed. Cross a horse trail at 3.6 mi, descend to a damp hollow; pass R of a pond at 3.8 mi. Cross a park svc rd at 4.2 mi, and after crossing two more small streams (that feed Reedy Creek Lake), cross a high footbridge over Reedy Creek at 5.1 mi. Pass under a power line at 5.7 mi, cross Camp Whispering Pines Rd, and arrive at the Reedy Creek parking area of William B. Umstead State Park at 6.0 mi. Access here is 0.3 mi from I-40 (see chapter 10, section 3). (*USGS Maps:* Cary, Raleigh W)

Neuse River Greenway Area

Neuse River Trail

867

LENGTH AND DIFFICULTY: 4.0 mi, easy

TRAILHEAD AND DESCRIPTION: This linear trail parallels the Neuse River and goes under US-64 on the E side of the city. An access S from the jct of US-64 and New Hope Rd is to drive 0.9 mi E, and turn R on Rogers Ln. After 1.3 mi turn L into parking lot. The N trailhead is to drive 0.9 mi N on New Hope Rd from US-64, turn R on Southall Rd, go 0.8 mi; turn R on Castlebrook Dr, go 0.5 mi; and turn R on Abington Ln to parking lot and dead-end road. If entry is from the S, follow a wide road made from a city waste line. Tall hickory, beech, and loblolly pine are prominent. Birds and butterflies are among the willows, wax myrtle, and wildflowers. At 1.1 mi is a long boardwalk in a wet area inhabited with frogs. Pass under US-64 at 1.5 mi. Turn L at a trail post, then R on Raleigh Beach Rd at 2.1 mi. After 0.1 mi turn L, go up a hill for 130 yd to make a R turn toward the woods. At 2.7 mi is a bridge, a small beaver dam, and wet area with water hyacinths. Pass L of a swamp at 3.3 mi. Curve away from the river, ascend a rocky area, and exit at the parking lot. Backtrack, or have a second car. (*USGS Map:* Raleigh E)

Shelly Lake Park

Shelly Lake Trail (2.2 mi); Snelling Branch Trail (0.6 mi); Ironwood Trail (0.8 mi); Ironwood Trail Extension (0.4 mi)

868- 870

LENGTH AND DIFFICULTY: 4.0 mi combined, easy

TRAILHEADS AND DESCRIPTION: From the jct of US-70 and NC-50 at Crabtree Valley Mall, take NC-50 N 0.8 mi to Millbrook Rd. Turn R on Millbrook Rd (SR-1812) and go 1.0 mi to Shelly-Sertoma Park, L. (Another route to the park follows Millbrook Rd 1.3 mi from Six Forks Rd.) (Parking is both at the Arts Center and below the dam.) If parking below the dam, enter the trail near Lead Mine Creek at the jct L of *Shelly Lake Trail* (a national recreation trail) and *Ironwood Trail,* R. Follow the paved trail to the top of the dam and a fork. If following the paved trail from the dam on the grassy E side of the lake, cross a boardwalk and enter a forest of sweet gum, oak, and river birch at 0.2 mi. At 0.7 mi is an emergency phone, R, and L is an alternate trail to an observation deck near the lake. At 0.8 mi jct with *Snelling Branch Trail,* R. (It goes 0.4 mi to cross North Hills Dr; pass a baseball field, L, and Sanderson High School, R; and ends at the Optimist Club parking lot at 1.0 mi. Access here is off Northcliff Dr.) Continue on the *Shelly Lake Trail,* cross a small stream with banks of yellow root and shade from river birch and yellow poplar. At 0.9 mi cross a wide bridge over Lea Mine Creek among elm and ironwood. Cross a long, high, and wide bridge over the lake at 1.6 mi. This is a favorite scenic spot on the trail to feed and watch the ducks and geese and to fish. Pass an access to the Arts Center R and the boathouse L. Return to the point of origin.

The *Ironwood Trail* follows Lead Mine Creek downstream from the parking area below Shelly Lake Dam. Go under the Shelly Rd bridge, S. Wind through the forest, cross the stream three times, and exit at North Hills Dr in the 5200 block. (The trail will eventually connect downstream with the *Ironwood Trail Extension* to North Hills Park and the *Alleghany Trail* at the Crabtree Creek confluence. At present the connection can be made by walking 0.4 mi on the sidewalk of North Hills Dr. (*USGS Map:* Raleigh W)

ROANOKE RAPIDS (Halifax County)

871 The city has three parks: Emery, Chockoyotte, and Tinsley. *Emery Park Trail* is a wide and neatly groomed 0.5-mi loop. From the parking lot it follows the sign clockwise through a forest of willow, white oak, and loblolly pine. Leaving the forest it passes a lighted athletic field, tennis courts, and a children's playground. Access is from the jct of US-158/NC-48 on NC-48

872 (Roanoke Ave) N to Ninth Ave and a turn L to the park. *Chockoyotte Park Trail* is a 0.7-mi smooth-surface loop similar to Emery. An easy route, it circles all the athletic facilities and can be used for physical fitness. Access is

873 off US-158 on Chockoyotte St for 0.3 mi to a turn L on Third Ave. *Tinsley Park Trail* will be a 0.5-mi nature trail when completed. It is in a natural urban forest island between W and E Arbutus Dr and between Holly Rd and Fifth St. The city's major trail is *Roanoke Canal Trail,* described below.

ADDRESS: Parks and Rec Dept, Box 38, Roanoke Rapids , NC 27870; 919-535-6847.

874 *Roanoke Canal Trail*

LENGTH AND DIFFICULTY: 7.7 mi, moderate

SPECIAL FEATURES: wildlife, river views, Roanoke Aqueduct

TRAILHEAD AND DESCRIPTION: The NW trailhead is at a parking lot at Roanoke Rapids Lake Dam and end of Oakwood Ave, off Fifth St, and the SE trailhead is at the Wildlife Landing parking area beside US-301 in Weldon. The trail has four accesses along the way. Listed on the National Register of Historic Places, the trail is a joint project of the city and the Roanoke Canal Commission. The canal was begun in 1819 and completed in 1823 by hand. Hamilton Fulton, an English engineer, was hired to supervise the construction of the canal around Great Falls. On a natural surface treadway the trail follows the towpath of an old navigational canal. The trail stays on the N side of the canal most of the distance, but crosses many footbridges and ascends and descends steps. It does not have blazes, but has frequent title and distance markers. Principal trees are hardwood, and wildlife includes deer, turkey, fox, beaver, squirrel, and waterfowl.

If beginning at the NW terminus follow the trail's slight descent under power lines in and out of the woods on the L rim of the canal. At 0.6 mi pass the base of Rochelle Pond. At 0.9 mi, R, is an exceptionally large wild grapevine attached to a poplar. To the L are remains of a river lock. Cross NC-48 at 1.6 mi. Here is a minimart, perfect for thirsty summer hikers. To the L are more locks and the Champion paper plant. For a while parallel a RR and go under or near power lines. At 2.8 mi, L, is a bog with arrow arum and white marsh mallow, followed by a dry area with a papaw patch and anise root. Arrive at River Rd E at 3.2 mi. To the L is a parking lot; beyond is a residential area.

Cross the road and after 0.3 mi there are water hemlock in the canal, followed by steps to a footbridge over a stream. At 4.1 mi cross an immaculate lawn between the river and a magnificent home. Within 0.2 mi follow a fence channel to pass under I-95 at the riverbank, then ascend to continue on the canal towpath. At 4.8 mi begin a curve around a pond. After returning to the canal the sound and sight of huge Roanoke Valley Energy Facility is noticeable to the R. Pass a water infiltration plant at 6.1 mi. At 6.2 mi arrive at Aqueduct Rd. (To the R it is 0.3 mi to Ponderosa Campground.)

Follow the canal rim, which parallels a smooth canal base to scenic area of Roanoke Canal Aqueduct at 6.3 mi. An observation deck is at the base of the arch and near Chockoyotte Creek. Continue for a few yd on the canal to return to the canal rim, where the trail goes straight for 0.6 mi to Weldon water treatment plant. Follow the exit road past a warehouse to Walnut St, turn R, and reach First St at 7.2 mi. Turn L, cross the RR, and turn L at an angle on a former RR bed. Pass under a RR bridge among sneezeweed, senna, and wisteria to make a sharp R at the Weldon RR Museum and Weldon Memorial Library at 7.4 mi. At another RR crossing and Washington Ave, turn L on First St. Follow it to the edge of US-301 where a L turn on a sidewalk proceeds to a tunnel under US-301. Exit to the Wildlife Landing and parking area. Complete the trail at an observation platform by the river at 7.7 mi. (*USGS Maps:* Roanoke Rapids, Weldon)

ROCKY MOUNT (Nash County)

The city has proposed the development of a Tar River Greenway. It would connect several major parks and recreational facilities such as City Lake, Sunset Park, Battle Park (see below), Tom Stitch Park, and Talbert Park. (Call Parks and Rec Dept for an update.) Battle Park is a 54-acre recreation park, a gift from the Battle family of Rocky Mount Mills. It has a picnic area with shelters, children's playground, a boat ramp to the Tar River, and a his-
875 tory trail. After parking, follow *Battle Park Trail* on a paved and easy 1.6-mi loop. Pass the Donaldson Tavern site, a stagecoach sta from an overland route. (Near here the Marquis de Lafayette was entertained while on his southern tour in 1825.) At 0.2 mi turn R to the waterfall overlook on the Tar River. Proceed to the children's playground through a picnic area with pine, birch, oak, elm, and dogwood. Cross the driveway at 1.3 mi and pass the site of the first Rocky Mount post office on the return. (The trail is accessible to the physically disabled.)

An additional 0.6-mi paved trail has been added that extends from the loop trail to Church St. Along the way are two fishing piers and overlooks, a boat launch, and several historic sites, including a turn-of-the-century bridge site, a Tuscarora Indian site, and an old dam site.

ADDRESS AND ACCESS: Parks and Rec Dept, PO Drawer 1180, Rocky Mount, NC 27801; 919-972-1151. Access is from the jct of US-64 Bypass and NC-43/48. Take NC-43/48 (Falls Rd) SE 0.5 mi to the parking area near the Confederate monument.

SALISBURY (Rowan County)

The city was founded in 1753 and has a 23-block historic district that is list-ed in the National Register of Historic Places. It is through this area and 20
876 other blocks that the *Historic Salisbury Trail* loop covers 3.9 mi of industrial, commercial, and residential historic sites. A national recreation trail, it is an exceptionally grand tour past tall trees and nineteenth-century architecture. It reflects the pride of the Historic Salisbury Foundation and its dedication to preserve the city's heritage. A map and individual site description can be obtained from the address below. Otherwise, a description of the route and a few buildings is as follows: Begin at the NE corner of N Bank St and S Jack-son St (two blocks W of Main St) at the Josephus Hall House, a large ante-bellum house (1820) with Federal, Greek Revival, and Victorian features. Proceed N on Jackson St to the Rowan Museum (1819), which is open for guided tours. After five blocks turn L on W Kerr St to Water St R, and to the

Waterworks Gallery. Turn R on W Cemetery St one block to Church St, turn L one block, and turn L again on W Franklin St to the Grimes Mill (1896). After two blocks turn L on Fulton St, go six blocks, turn R on W Fisher St, go one block, and then turn L on S Ellis St to the Governor John Ellis House (1851). Go two blocks to the R on Horah St, go one block, turn R for three blocks on S Fulton St, and turn L on Thomas St. Go three blocks to Main St and turn L. To the R is Military Ave and the Salisbury National Cemetery. (Monuments honor the nearly 5,000 Union soldiers who died here in the Civil War.) Continue N on Main St on wide sidewalks for six blocks (passing such sites as the Empire Hotel and the former courthouse square.) Turn L on W Council St for one block to pass L on S Church St for three blocks (to pass Andrew Jackson's well), and R on N Bank St to the point of origin.

ADDRESS AND ACCESS: City of Salisbury, Box 479, Salisbury, NC 28144; 704-637-2200 or 704-636-0103. From I-85 jct with US-52 in Salisbury, go NW 1.0 mi to Main St (US-29/70). Continue ahead on W Innes St two blocks and turn L on S Jackson St two blocks to Hall House at 226 S Jackson.

SHELBY (Cleveland County)

In *The Shelby Star,* May 13, 1995, front-page news was about the option of Cleveland County to purchase 423 acres along the Broad River for a park and preserve. It would preserve "a beautiful part of the county for generations to come," wrote the editor. The property's W boundary would include the E end of *Old College Farm Trail* (an abandoned trail on private property). While **877** progress was being made in the development of a major park for all citizens, the town of Shelby had already established 3.3-mi urban *Historic Shelby Trail.* **878** The downtown area reflects architectural history of pre–Civil War, Colonial Revival, and Gothic styles. Additionally, there is the history of one of the state's most powerful political influences, beginning with Max Gardner as governor in 1928 and lasting until the death of US Senator Clyde R. Hoey in 1954 (a former governor).

The walk in Shelby Central Historic District begins at the former Cleveland County Courthouse on S Washington St, and in a counterclockwise route to Marion St at the Colonial Revival home of Governor Hoey. One block N on Sumter St is the Blanton House, an example of Gothic Revival. A return on Marion St includes historic homesites, markets, and commercial places on W Warren and N Lafayette Sts to S Washington St. The walk then follows S Washington St S in a clockwise manner to Gidney St before returning to Courtsquare, covering a total of 38 sites. Landscaped lawns and floral gardens enhance this stimulating walk. (A detailed map is available.)

INFORMATION: Historic Shelby Foundation;: 704-481-1842. Cleveland County Chamber of Commerce, 200 S Lafayette St, Shelby, NC 28150; 704-487-8521.

SMITHFIELD (Johnston County)

879 The *Neuse River Nature Trail* in the Town Common Park is maintained by the city's Parks and Rec Dept and the Year-Around Garden Club. It is an easy 1.6-mi route on the E banks of the Neuse River, downtown. From the parking lot on N Front St hike 0.2 mi up the E bank of the river to the terminus and return. Hike downriver past the historic site of Smith's Ferry (1759–86) and under the US-70 bridge at 0.5 mi. Continue through a pristine forest of large sweet gum, oak, and green ash. Turn L at 0.7 mi and reach the tennis courts, children's playground, and parking area on E Market and S 2d St at 1.0 mi. Return by the same route or go on N Front St for a distance of 1.6 mi. Vehicular traffic is allowed on parts of the trail.

ADDRESS AND ACCESS: Director, Parks and Rec Dept, Box 2344, Smithfield, NC 27577; 919-934-9721. Access is on N Front St, one block from E Market St (US-70) at the bridge (or the E Church St parking lot).

SOUTHERN PINES (Moore County)

The town of Southern Pines has a trail system in 165-acre Reservoir Park. Its **880** central 2.0-mi loop, *Reservoir Park Trail*, around the lake, has connective trails to Sandhills Community College, NW, and to *Whitehall Trail* at Whitehall Center, NE. (An additional connection is planned to include 3.0 mi of trails S in the Talamore Country Club area.) Forest trees in the park include longleaf pine, sweet gum, maple, and turkey oak.

From the parking lot begin by crossing the arched bridge over the spillway, cross the dam, and turn L at 0.1 mi. (Sharply R is an unmarked 0.8-mi connector on an old road by twin lakes to a gate at the Sandhills Community College Horticultural Gardens. See chapter 15.) Follow the wide-screened gravel trail by the lake, cross a boardwalk in a sphagnum bed at 0.3 mi, and a boardwalk over a stream at 0.6 mi. Cross another boardwalk over a stream at 0.9 mi. Pass L of a golf course and lake to reenter the woods at 1.2 mi. Enter a clearing that exists for 0.4 mi to provide excellent views of the lake. There are spur trails for closer lakeside viewing. Pass through a picnic area and return to the parking lot at 2.0 mi. (From the parking lot is 2.0-mi *Whitehall Trail* loop on private property open to the public. See chapter 14.)

ADDRESS AND ACCESS: Southern Pines Rec and Parks Dept, 482 E Connecticut Ave, Southern Pines, NC 28382; 910-692-2463. From US-1 turn W on Midland Rd, go 0.2 mi, turn R on NC-22. After 1.6 mi turn L at the park entrance.

STATESVILLE (Iredell County)

Among the city parks is 25-acre Lakewood Park, which contains the 1.6-mi *Lakewood Nature Trail*. If approaching from I-40 and NC-115 (N Center St), **881** go S 0.4 mi on NC-115 into the city and turn L on Hartness Rd. After 0.3 mi turn L on Lakewood Dr to the parking area. From the parking area follow the trail signs onto a paved and interconnecting trail system in a mature forest of oak, pine, and poplar. The city also has a physical-fitness trail that is used by walkers in Anderson Park and an unnamed short trail in E Statesville Park.

ADDRESS AND ACCESS: Director, Parks and Rec Dept, 432 W Bell St, Statesville, NC 28677; 704-872-2481.

TARBORO (Edgecombe County)

The *Tarboro Historic District Trail* is a remarkable adventure into history. It is **882** a trail of beauty any season of the year. A national recreation trail, it is a 2.4-mi walking or driving tour within a 45-block area of beautiful downtown Tarboro. More than 100 homes, gardens, churches, and government and business structures are designated as historically or architecturally significant. The trail begins at the tour headquarters on Bridgers St at the Blount-Bridgers House (ca 1808). (A trail map is advisable and is available here. The building is open Monday–Friday, 10 AM–4 PM; Saturday and Sunday 2–4 PM [April–November]; and by appointment; 919-823-4159.) In case you do not have a map, brief directions follow: Within the Bridgers St block, go N (R side of the Blount-Bridgers House) and pass the Pender Museum (ca 1810). Turn R on Philips St; L on St Patrick St; L on Battle Ave; L on Main St; R on Porter St; R on Trade St; R on Baker St; R on St Patrick St (by the Town Common [1760] at 0.9 mi); L on Church St; R on St David St; (by the Calvary Episcopal Church); R on St James St; R on St Andrew St; L on Wilson St; and L on Main St. At 1.8 mi jct with Granville St; turn R and backtrack on Main St to R on Park Ave; turn L on St Andrew St and return to the

Blount-Bridgers House. The Main St section of the trail has received national recognition for expansive restoration.

ADDRESS AND ACCESS: Tarboro Dept of Planning and Economic Development, 500 Main St (Box 220), Tarboro, NC 27886; 919-641-4249. (Chamber of Commerce; 919-823-7241.) Access: turn E on Bridgers St from Main St (NC-33), and go one block.

883   Another trail is 0.6-mi *Indian Lake Nature Trail* in 52-acre Indian Lake Park. The trail has interpretive stations about the vascular flora. The park also provides a picnic area, fishing, boat rentals, nature tours, and camping for special groups or organizations.

ADDRESS AND ACCESS: Tarboro Parks and Rec Dept, 305 W Baker St, Tarboro NC 27886; 919-641-4263. Access to the park is on Western Blvd (US-64A), 0.5 mi S from its jct with N Main St.

TRYON

The Polk County Community Foundation has constructed a 0.6-mi nature trail, **884** the *Woodland Park Trail*, in Tryon. Entry is from Chestnut St. Turn L after crossing old tracks at the RR station on US-176. The trail can also be reached from Trade St (US-176) near the A&P store. The trail is excellent in both design and maintenance. The forest is chiefly hardwoods; no camping is allowed.

ADDRESS: Town Manager, Town of Tryon, Drawer K, Tryon, NC 28782; 704-859-6654.

WASHINGTON (Beaufort County)

The "original Washington, 1776," is the first town in the US to be named for George Washington. Settlements at this jct of the Pamlico and Tar Rivers began as early as the 1690s, but the origin of the present city is traced to the early 1770s. The city's earliest buildings of historic and architectural significance were mainly destroyed by fire, first in 1864 by federal forces and again in the business district in 1900 by an accidental fire. A remarkable restoration and preservation has created a historic district of at least 29 historic buildings and special sites in the downtown area. They can be seen on the **885** 2.0-mi *Washington Historic District Trail* (a national recreation trail), a walking tour among homes, businesses, churches, by the old courthouse, and along streets of magnolia and crepe myrtle. Parking is available at the corner of Gladden St and Stewart Parkway. A map of the tour is available from addresses below, but without a map the following description will assist.

Also, the trail sign, a colorful shield with directional arrows, serves as an excellent guide at each turn.

Begin the trail at the NW corner of Gladden and Main Sts at the renovated Seaboard Coastline RR Depot. On Main St walk W three blocks and turn R on Pierce St. Go one block, turn L on W 2d St for one block, and turn L on Washington St back to W Main St at 0.5 mi. Turn R to see (halfway down the block) the stately 1820s "Elmwood." Return on Main St to pass the Havens Warehouse and Mill to the parking lot at 1.0 mi. Walk R along the Stewart Parkway waterfront pavilion. After passing three eighteenth-century houses on Water St, go N two blocks on Bonner St (passing the 1860s St Peter's Episcopal Church). Turn L for one block on E 2d St, turn L one block to Main St, and turn R for the return.

ADDRESS AND ACCESS: City of Washington, Box 1988, Washington, NC 27889; 919-946-1033. For access to the trailhead, follow US-70 N or S to Main St. Turn E two blocks to the corner of Gladden St.

WAYNESVILLE (Haywood County)

This ideal historic town is in a scenic valley N of the Blue Ridge Parkway's Balsam Gap on US-23/74 and S of Lake Junaluska and I-40. Its quality of life is demonstrated in immaculately clean Main St and sparkling business windows. Friendly, cultural, environmentally concerned, and lovers of the outdoors, its people welcome visitors. Generally, the town reflects Haywood County's charm and natural beauty. The county has 19 mountain peaks above 6,000 ft, streams for fishing, and forests for multiuse trails. Local citizens have produced the detailed color-coded *Haywood County Trail Map*, which reveals nearly 50 hiking, biking, equestrian, cross-country skiing, and canoeing trails. In Waynesville, the county seat, is the 6.2-mi *Volkswalk*. It **886** loops through downtown between historic sites, country club, and residential areas. Additionally, there is 0.5-mi *Richland Creek Trail* in Richland Creek **887** Park. The linear 8-ft-wide trail is part rock dust and pavement for the physically disabled. The paved section leads to a fishing/observation deck with two fishing pads. The trail is also open to bicycles and skates. Other park facilities are a ball field, track field, and picnic area. Access is off Main St on Vance St toward the Southern Railway line.

ADDRESS: Waynesville Parks and Rec Dept, 217 W Marshall St, Waynesville, NC 28786; 704-456-8577. For additional information on *Volkswalk*: Tarheel State Walkers, American VolksSport Assoc, Box 15013, Winston-Salem, NC 27113.

WILMINGTON (New Hanover County)

Greenfield Gardens Park

Greenfield is a magnificent 200-acre city park with trails, tennis courts, picnic areas, rental boats, amphitheater, rec center, nature study area, and fragrance garden. Millions of azalea blossoms provide a profusion of color in April. Additional color and greenery come from camellias, yaupon, magnolias, bays, live oaks, crepe myrtle, water lilies, dogwood, and Spanish moss draped on cypress. (The park is popular during the city's annual N.C. Azalea Festival [first or second weekend in April].) Open daily. No camping or swimming.

> ADDRESS AND ACCESS: Public Services and Facilities Dept, Box 1810, Wilmington, NC 28401; 919-341-7855. The park entrance is reached from US-421, S, at South 3d St to Willard St. Turn L on Willard St, then R to the parking area (the park office is next to the parking area on Willard St).

888- *Rupert Bryan Memorial Trail (4.5 mi); Greenfield Nature Trail (0.3 mi)*
889   LENGTH AND DIFFICULTY: 4.8 mi combined, easy

TRAILHEADS AND DESCRIPTION: The trail (also called *Greenfield Gardens Trail*) is a paved loop for hiking, jogging, and bicycling around the lake and over bridges. (It parallels, with little exception, the auto route on W and E Lakeshore Dr.) If you follow the trail R from the parking area, pass the amphitheater and rec center at 0.9 mi. At 2.4 mi jct L with the *Greenfield Nature Trail* boardwalk, which has interpretive signs. Among the plants are ferns, swamp rose, and Virginia willow. Continue ahead to Jackson Point picnic area, Indian sculpture, and a return to the parking area.

WILSON (Wilson County)

There are more than 26 parks in the city, and many others are proposed. Unnamed walkways are prominent; three areas have designated trails. The wide
890 *Hominy Canal Trail* is a 0.9-mi path between Ward Blvd and jct of Kincaid Ave and Canal Dr. Tall loblolly pine, willow and live oaks, sweet gum, and river birch shade the trail. Access to parking can be had at Williams Day Camp on
891 Mt Vernon Dr. The 1.2-mi *Toisnot Lake Trail* circles the lake; it also extends 0.6 mi into the hardwood forest downstream to the Seaboard Coast RR. Access to Toisnot Park is on Corbett Ave, N, near its jct with Ward Blvd (NC-58/42). Corbett Ave is also the 3.8-mi access route to Lake Wilson and the *Lake Wilson Trail*. Go N 3.3 mi, turn L on Lake Wilson Rd (SR-1327) at Dunn's Cross Rd, and go 0.5 mi to the lake, R.

LENGTH AND DIFFICULTY: 2.3 mi, easy

TRAILHEAD AND DESCRIPTION: From the parking lot go either R or L on the dam. If L, cross the dam/spillway and follow an old road through a forest of river birch, alder, sweet gum, and holly. At 0.8 mi bear R, off the old road, and enter a swampy area to follow the yellow blazes. (Beavers may have dammed the area and prevented crossing.) Cross a bridge on the feeder stream to an old road at 1.3 mi. Among the swamp vegetation are buttonbush and swamp candles (*Lysimachia terrestris*). Turn R and follow the old road (damaged by jeeps and 4WDs) to complete the loop at 2.3 mi. (This is a good bird-watching trail.)

WINSTON-SALEM (Forsyth County)

A city and county planning board has established a growth-strategy program that encourages the development of greenway networks for rec and land-use development. An example is the city's major trail system of *Salem Lake Trail* and *Salem Creek Trail* at Salem Lake, described below. (A loop extension is proposed at the lake's NE cove of Lowery Creek.)

Other metropolitan trails are at Winston Lake, where an easy 0.7 mi is between the Winston Lake swimming pool parking lot and the picnic shelter. From the swimming pool it passes through a playground and gate to enter a mature forest of pine, oak, and poplar near the creek. At 0.3 mi it passes a physical-fitness station. (No camping.) Access: From I-40 (Bus), go on US-311 N for 1.9 mi to turn R on Winston Lake Rd. Go 0.2 mi to Waterworks Rd, turn R, and immediately turn L to Winston Lake swimming pool.

The easy 0.8-mi *Silas Creek Trail* is a wide greenway from the parking **893** lot at Schaffner Park. Access: Off Silas Creek Parkway turn E on Yorkshire Dr for a few yd to the parking lot, R. To the L the trail begins for a parallel of a stream and Silas Creek Parkway. In a mature forest with honeysuckle and wild roses, the trail crosses a footbridge at 0.4 mi. The N trailhead does not have a parking lot. Backtrack, or go E 250 yd on Robinhood Rd to a parking lot at a church.

At Bethabara Park is a longer greenway, *Bethabara Trail*, and side trails **894** to historic sites of the pioneer Moravian settlement. Access: Off Silas Creek Parkway, go W on Bethabara Rd, past the Bethabara Park to a parking lot at the jct of Bonbrook Dr, L. (Mill Creek is nearby.) To access the SE trailhead turn off Silas Creek Parkway E on Bethabara and R on Hayes Forest Dr (a retirement settlement). Descend to the hollow; the gated trail is R and the only parking lot is L (for residential space). If walking the trail from here, ascend ahead 100 yd to a gate R. Descend on the *Bethabara Trail;* cross a culvert into a mature forest. At 0.4 mi pass through a tunnel under Silas Creek Parkway. Ascend on steps, then follow a narrow foot trail to skirt a residential area. Descend through beech grove, and ascend steps to Old Town Rd at 0.9 mi. Turn R for 0.1 mi to turn L. Pass through prominent sycamore and poplar at 1.1 mi. Parallel Monareas Creek and at

895 1.5 mi, L, is *God's Acre Nature Trail.* (It ascends steeply 0.1 mi to a historic hilltop cemetery. Backtrack.) To the R are access points to the meadows of Bethabara Park. Continue downstream to end the trail at Bonbrook Dr at 1.8 mi and the parking lot R.

896   The city's most urban trail is the downtown 1.2-mi linear *Strollway Trail.* Parking at either end is street or business parking. Access: Corner of Salem Ave and Liberty St for S trailhead where it connects with *Salem Creek Trail* (see below), and the N trailhead is on 4th St between Cherry St and Liberty St. If starting from the S trailhead follow the sign at the W side of Liberty St and go N. Called "super greenway," this classic metropolitan trail is landscaped with trees, shrubs, flowers, and bridges. Part of its wide treadway is a mixture of asphalt and pea gravel. Pass by Old Salem, R, and then under I-40 (Bus) at 0.7 mi; reach a drinking fountain at 0.9 mi. To the R are glistening skyscrapers. Reach the N trailhead at a large archway at downtown 4th St. (Plans are to extend the trail S from Salem St to the N.C. School of the Arts.)

   ADDRESS: Rec and Parks Dept, Box 2511, Winston-Salem, NC 27102; 910-727-2063.

Salem Lake Park

The park is a 365-acre city reservoir surrounded by 1,800 acres of land. Activities are picnicking; fishing (bass, bluegill, catfish, crappie); boating (rentals also); horseback riding; biking; birding; and hiking (no skiing or swimming). Open daily, except Thursday; 910-788-0212.

   ACCESS: From I-40 (Bus), go S on US-311/NC-209 at Claremont Ave (which becomes Martin Luther King St). After 0.8 mi turn L on Reynolds Park Rd (SR-2740) and go 1.9 mi to Salem Lake Rd, L.

897- *Salem Lake Trail (6.9 mi); Salem Creek Trail (4.5 mi)*
898   LENGTH AND DIFFICULTY: 11.4 mi combined, easy to moderate
   TRAILHEADS AND DESCRIPTION: Park R on the approach to the second entrance gate. For hiking *Salem Lake Trail,* counterclockwise, begin R (NE)

on a wide svc road through poplar, oak, beech, Virginia pine, and sweet gum. Fern, yellow root, sweet pepperbush, sensitive briar, and wild roses grow in the open coves and lakeside. At 0.9 mi cross a cement bridge and at 2.7 mi a causeway where kingfishers and wild ducks frequent the marsh, R. Arrive at Linville Rd (SR-2662) at 3.4 mi. (To the L it is 0.7 mi to I-40 (Bus), exit 10.) Continue on the trail by crossing the causeway L to a reentrance in the woods. Follow the svc road under a power line at 3.9 mi and to a scenic view by the lake at 5.0 mi.

At 6.0 mi jct L with a causeway and arched bridge over the lake. (To the R is a gravel svc road 0.3 mi to a gate and parking lot at the end of New Greensboro Rd. It goes E 1.2 mi to jct with Linville Rd and its jct with I-40 [Bus], exit 10.) Cross the bridge to a resting bench and scenic view of the lake. Follow near the shoreline to descend at the base of the dam at a jct with *Salem Creek Trail*, R, at 6.5 mi. If making a loop, cross a low-water bridge, ascend to gate and W end of parking lot. (If the gate is locked, follow the paved trail around the fence to the point of origin at 6.9 mi.)

To follow the *Salem Creek Trail*, parallel Salem Creek downstream through tall poplar, river birch, pine, wild grapevines, and wildflowers. Kudzu is smothering trees and shrubs at a few dense sections. Pass a picnic table at a cascade (called gorge by the city) at 0.9 mi. Pass R of Reynolds Park Golf Course and rest rooms at 1.4 mi. Go under Reynolds Park Rd, pass under M. L. King, Jr Dr bridge at 2.0 mi. To the L is the Civitan Park with ball fields and a spur footbridge over the creek to Anderson Center, R. For the next 0.3 mi is a powerful reminder of urbanization: noise from overhead Vargrave St and US-52, high and huge Southern RR trestle, and glimpses of the city skyline.

At 3.0 mi enter the edge of Happy Hills Park, but cross the creek on a footbridge to wide meadows of Central Park ball fields. Cross Waughtown Rd (which goes L to N.C. School of Arts) and jct with *Strollway Trail* at 3.4 mi, R. Follow the sidewalk past a minimart and turn off R from Broad St into the woods. Come out of the woods at 3.9 mi to jct with a fitness trail. Ball fields are on both sides of the creek in Washington Park. Cross an arched footbridge at 4.0 mi, and reach the parking lot at the NW corner of the Marketplace Mall at 4.5 mi. (It is 0.2 mi farther to Peters Creek Parkway and its jct with Silas Creek Parkway.) Backtrack, or have a second vehicle.

PART VI

Trails on Private and Commercial Properties

14. Private and Commercial Trails

Woodman, spare that tree!
  Touch not a single bough!
In youth it sheltered me,
  And I'll protect it now.
—George Pope Morris

Of the 19 million acres of forests in the state, about 13.5 million are owned by private citizens. Named trails on these properties are rare, particularly those trails open to the public. Some landowners have been reluctant to open their properties because of liability and trail abuse. In 1985 there were nearly 200 mi of private trails open to the public; 10 years later there is an 85 percent decrease. The decline continues though the state legislature passed a bill in 1987 (Act to Limit the Liability of Landowners to Persons Using Their Land in Connection with the Trails System) to protect private landowners. At least 45 private organizations, resorts, and clubs have trails for their members and associates only. Nevertheless, corporate and individual landowners have a long history of cooperation with Scout troops, schools, nature-oriented groups, and hunting or fishing clubs to use their properties. Examples are in this chapter. Most private trails are not publicized and the majority have never been named. If all the pathways through farm woodlands, or those favorite forest fishing and hunting routes, or those walks to points of meditation were all counted, they would number in the thousands. There are also private resorts, retreats, and special camps where only paying or invited guests may walk the trails. A popular hiking pastime in the mountain area is to ascend highly publicized mountain peaks (particularly those with a view) on both public and private properties. Some private peak owners object and have placed No Trespassing signs at appropriate places. If you see such signs, they may apply mainly to vehicles. An inquiry to the owners would show respect for their property rights. Frequently, private owners will given an individual, or a small group, permission to walk a path or roadway if the purpose is for education or aesthetics. Access to some mountain peaks requires passage over lands of multiple owners. Bushwhacking or random cross-country hiking on these premises can result in trespassing on one piece of property but not on others. Examples are Blackrock Mtn near Sylva, Sandymush Bald S of Luck, Snake Mtn near Boone, and Wesner Bald near Balsam Gap. Some commercial properties require an entrance fee; for example, Chimney Rock Park and Grandfather Mtn.

BEARWALLOW MOUNTAIN TRAIL (Henderson County) 899

LENGTH AND DIFFICULTY: 2 mi round-trip, moderate

TRAILHEAD AND DESCRIPTION: From the jct of US-74 and Bearwallow Rd (SR-1594) in Gerton (5.0 mi NW on US-74 from jct of NC-9 in Bat Cave), go 2.1 mi on SR-1594 (mostly on a gravel road) to Bearwallow Gap. Park away from the L gate. (No dogs, unless on a leash.) Ascend on a moderate-grade pasture road through oak, hickory, locust, and maple to the fire tower (leased by the state) on Bearwallow Mtn (4,232 ft) at 1.0 mi. Scenic views from the tower are of Sugarloaf Mtn, Bat Cave area, and Little Pisgah Mtn. Flowering plants include bellflower, turtlehead, and phlox. Backtrack. For more information contact the property owner at 704-685-7371. (*USGS Map:* Bat Cave)

BLUFF MOUNTAIN TRAIL (Ashe County) 900

The North Carolina chapter of The Nature Conservancy, a private organization, owns and maintains a controlled-access nature preserve on Bluff Mtn (5,100 ft). The 2.0 mi trail is open only through guided field trip programs offered from spring through fall seasons. Schedules can be requested by contacting the chapter; there is a fee for the hike. During the summer months an intern is stationed at the mtn to assist in the scheduled trips. Described as a "naturalist's dream... with an astonishing concentration of natural diversity," the 758-acre preserve has a fen on top of the mtn. Address: N.C. Nature Conservancy, Carr Mill, Suite 223, Carrboro, NC 27510; 919-967-7007.

BREVARD NATURE TRAIL (Transylvania County) 901

This is a botanical trail system of extraordinary educational value in a 395-acre nature preserve, privately owned and maintained by Charles F. Moore, Box 8, Brevard, NC 28712; 704-884-9614. A clear mountain stream flows through a remarkable diversity of vascular flora. Hiking and nature study permitted with guided tour only.

902 BOB'S CREEK TRAIL (McDowell County)

LENGTH AND DIFFICULTY: 8.0 mi, moderate to strenuous

TRAILHEAD AND DESCRIPTION: From I-40 (S of Marion) turn S on US-221 for 1.9 mi. At Phillips 66 svc sta turn L on Goose Creek Rd (SR-1153) and go 0.5 mi to Old US-221 (SR-1786). Turn L for 50 yd to Glenwood Sta Rd (SR-1766), R, and go 0.5 mi to Huntsville Rd (SR-1790). After 1.8 mi on SR-1790, turn sharply L and ascend a gravel road 1.4 mi to the parking area (near a gated road). Enter the national recreation trail at a sign and go through pine, oak, sourwood, maple, and laurel. The well-designed trail is particularly scenic in the fall. Wildlife includes deer, turkey, owls, songbirds, and squirrel. For the first 3.5-mi loop the trail ascends and descends to Hemlock Falls, Split Rock Falls, Hidden Falls, and Sentinel Rock. If the S fork of the next 4.5-mi loop is taken, pass Poplar Cove Spring, follow a gentle contour, and descend to Big Valley. Halfway around the loop is a backpacking campsite, stream, and rock formations. A number of hemlock groves are on the trail in this 500-acre pocket wilderness. (*USGS Map:* Glenwood)

INFORMATION: Bowater, Public Relations Dept, Box 7, Catawba, SC 29704; 803-329-6615.

903 BUCKHORN TRAIL (Lee County)

Until recently the 45.4-mi white-blazed *Buckhorn Trail* was the longest hiking trail on private property in the state. It was designed and constructed in the early 1980s by volunteers under the leadership of Frank Barringer of Sanford. Assisting him were Boy Scout Troops 906, 907, 941, 942, and 944 in Lee County and Troop 61 in Lillington. Girl Scout leaders were Jane Barringer and Sylvia Adcock. From W to E the trail paralleled generally the Deep River and the Cape Fear River from near the House in the Horseshoe historic site to Raven Rock State Park. The trail, 45.4-mi meandered through floodplains, on steep but low ridges, into tributary coves, and through a remarkable area of natural history, timberland, and segments of remoteness. In addition, a number of individual landowners corporate owners included the Federal Paperboard Co Inc, Har-Lee Farm, and Boise-Cascade Corp. Support and cooperation were given by the hunting clubs of both Lee and Harnett Counties. Campsites were carefully chosen, away from developed areas, roads, or streams. No-trace camping was the rule—the same rules that apply for public wilderness areas (see introduction to national forests). By 1996 the section described below was being maintained by Ralph Meeks Jr. and Eagle Scout

Troop 942. Minor relocations may be necessary. For updated information on the progress of reopening the four sections, see information below.

INFORMATION: Ralph Meeks Jr., 404 Cool Springs Rd (Box 593), Sanford, NC 27331; 919-776-3300/2885 (also, Hal Tysinger; 919-776-2521)

Section A: From Euphronia Church Road to US-421

LENGTH AND DIFFICULTY: 10.7 mi, moderate

SPECIAL FEATURES: ruins of McLeod House, Deep River ledges

TRAILHEAD AND DESCRIPTION: From the jct of NC-42 and Bypass US-1/15/501 in Sanford, take NC-42 W 1.8 mi and turn L on Steel Bridge Rd (SR-1318). Go 7.5 mi W to a R turn on Euphronia Church Rd (SR-1393) and go 0.2 mi to the church parking lot. Begin the trail on the old forest road N, past the church cemetery. At 0.5 mi cross the first of a number of small streams. Ahead is a mixed forest of oak, gum, hickory, poplar, pine, holly, hornbeam, wildflowers, and ferns, through which cross many old pioneer wagon roads and more current logging roads. At 1.4 mi R is the remains of the McLeod House and chimneys. (Here also is an alternate [shorter] yellow-blazed trail, R, that rejoins the main trail at 2.3 mi.) At 1.5 mi cross a stream where trout lilies bloom in profusion in March. When the tree leaves are off, Deep River can be seen from a bluff at 1.9 mi. There are remnants of the Blakley House entwined with yellow jessamine at 2.1 mi. At 2.3 mi the alternate trail rejoins near the ruins of another old house. Reach a cable gate of the Poe Hunt Club and a massive clear-cut, L, at 2.8 mi, but veer R from the clear-cut on an old woods road. Turn off the old road, R, onto a footpath at 3.5 mi (once the Clark Place, now remembered by the escaped jonquils and baby's breath). Follow the trail through an area of hardwoods over a rocky streambed at Smith Creek at 3.9 mi, where switch cane and wild grape provide dense understory. Soon pass L of the edge of a young loblolly pine forest. Cross a Smith Creek tributary with banks of wildflowers at 4.2 mi, and after 0.1 mi pass under a power line to an old road. Turn off the old road, R, onto a footpath at 4.4 mi in a young forest. Old tobacco rows are evident. At 4.9 mi is an abandoned house, L, 50 yd before arriving at NC-42. Turn R to an intersection at 5.0 mi. (On NC-42 W it is 3.0 mi to Carbonton, and 6.7 mi E to US-1/15/501 in Sanford. Road mileage back to Euphronia Church is 3.7 mi on Plank Rd [SR-1007], R, to Steel Bridge Rd [SR-1318], R, for 2.0 mi to Euphronia Church Rd, R.)

Cross the jct diagonally and reenter the forest. Pass rock piles, indicative of pioneer farming. Cross a stream at 5.6 mi, ascend and descend through former tobacco land, now filled with pine, sweet gum, and running cedar. Descend to scenic Little Pocket Creek and follow downstream, L, at 6.0 mi. At 6.7 mi cross a small stream on a living holly tree. Ahead, cross a number of drains and through timber clear-cuts. Follow an old logging road and cross Big Pocket Creek on a large fallen logging bridge at 7.7 mi. Continue on the main road and turn L at a road jct at 8.5 mi. Turn L again on a less used woods road at 9.1 mi. After 0.1 mi reach the end of the road, where a foot trail begins R. (Ahead, 20 yd off the road, is a large and scenic rock ledge with views of the silent and dark Deep River. Hepatica, spring beauty, and trout lilies bloom among the ferns in a natural rock garden.) Turn R on the footpath and over a high bluff above the river through laurel, and return to the road at 9.6 mi. (A clear-cut may have altered the trail across the road.) Turn L and follow the road (formerly Tempting Church Rd, SR-1322). Cross Patterson Creek on an old bridge at 10.5 mi and arrive at US-421 at 10.7 mi. (Gulf is L, 2.0 mi; Sanford is R, 4.0 mi, to US-1/15/501, where a R, 1.8 mi, leads to jct with NC-42. A turn, R, on NC-42 for 4.3 mi returns you to where the trail crossed NC-42.) (*USGS Maps:* Goldston, White Hills)

904 CHAMBERS MOUNTAIN TRAIL (Buncombe County)

LENGTH AND DIFFICULTY: 4.7 mi round-trip, moderate

TRAILHEAD AND DESCRIPTION: From US-19/23 in Clyde, turn onto Charles St, and cross a RR and bridge for the distance of 0.2 mi. Turn L on SR-1513 and Jenkins Valley Rd (SR-1642), and go 0.4 mi to a R turn on Chambers Mtn Rd (SR-1534). Proceed 1.4 mi on a paved road to where a gravel road turns steeply L (NW). Parking space is limited; a resident's permission for parking may be advisable. The summit can be reached by vehicle, but the gate (200 yd up the steep road) may be locked. Respect the private ownership and do not take dogs, unless on a leash. Follow the road to a grassy plateau, then take the switchbacks to reach the summit (4,509 ft) at 2.35 mi. Superb views from the fire tower are of Lake Junaluska, Pisgah Forest, and Newfound Mtn. Backtrack. (For more information contact the property owners, 704-627-2804.) (*USGS Map:* Clyde)

CHEROKEE ARBORETUM (Swain County)

905- *Cherokee Arboretum Trail (0.5 mi); Mt Noble Trail (4.6 mi round-trip)*
906 LENGTH AND DIFFICULTY: 5.1 mi combined and round-trip, easy to strenuous

TRAILHEADS AND DESCRIPTION: From the jct of US-19 and US-441 in Cherokee, turn N on US-441 and go 0.6 mi to a sign for Oconaluftee Indian Village, L. Follow the road to a parking area and locate the trail sign for the *Cherokee Arboretum Trail* near the stockade gate. On an easy loop pass through a forest of pines and hardwoods where more than 150 species of plants are labeled. On the trail are a restored Indian log cabin, a stream, small pool, and an herb garden. A national recreation trail, it is maintained by the Cherokee Historical Association. Access to the *Mt Noble Trail* is from the upper parking lot on the R (E) side. On a moderate to strenuous climb, ascend in and out of hardwood coves, first to the W and then N to headwaters of Owl Branch at 1.4 mi. After curving around a ridge ascend more steeply to the summit of Mt Noble (4,066 ft) and a fire tower at 2.3 mi (elev gain 1,666 ft). Outstanding views are of the Cherokee area (E, SE), GSMNP (NW,N), and Nantahala NF (S). (The village is also home for the Cherokee outdoor drama "Unto These Hills.") (*USGS Map:* Whittier)

INFORMATION: Cherokee Historical Association, Box 398, Cherokee, NC 28719; 704-497-2111.

CHIMNEY ROCK PARK (Rutherford County)

Chimney Rock Park (2,280 ft) is a 1,000-acre scenic private nature preserve with commercial comforts. The first developer was J. B. Freeman in the late 1800s, but the first extensive developers were twin brothers, Lucius and Asahel Morse, from Missouri in the early 1900s. The park continues to be operated by their descendants. One of the park's outstanding features is the giant granite monolith, Chimney Rock, which rises sharply to 315 ft. It is a remnant of 500-million-year-old igneous rock. Another major feature is Hickory Nut Falls, which plummets 404 ft in the gorge. There are a number of special annual events, among them an Easter sunrise service, sports car hillclimb, photography contest, and rope climbing exhibition. Open daily mid-March through November; an entry fee is charged. There is a large picnic area with a pavilion, but camping is not allowed. (*USGS Maps:* Bat Cave, Lake Lure)

ADDRESS AND ACCESS: Chimney Rock Park, Chimney Rock, NC 28720; 704-625-9611. Entrance is on US-74/64/NC-9 in Chimney Rock.

Skyline Nature Trail (0.9 mi); Cliff Trail (0.6 mi); Hickory Nut Falls Trail (1.2 mi round-trip) **907-909**

LENGTH AND DIFFICULTY: 2.7 mi combined and round-trip, easy to moderate
TRAILHEADS AND DESCRIPTION: After entry to the park, drive 3.0 mi to the

parking area and either take the tunnel to the 258-ft elevator to the sky lounge or use the steps on a route past Vista Rock or Needle's Eye. Follow the signs for *Skyline Nature Trail* (and use a brochure for the 28 interpretive stops). Among the trees and shrubs are table mtn pine, wafer ash (*Ptelea trifoliata*), chestnut oak, laurel, and rhododendron. Wildflowers include windflower, wild orchids, and shooting star (*Dodecatheon meadia*). Reach spectacular Hickory Nut Falls at 0.9 mi. Backtrack, or return on the precipitous *Cliff Trail* (which was constructed by Guilford Nanney, a local resident who also designed the intricate series of stairways in the park). Pass Inspiration Point where both Hickory Nut Falls and Lake Lure can be viewed. For the *Hickory Nut Falls Trail*, leave the parking area and walk

Chimney Rock. Bill Russ

through a picturesque and densely shaded forest of hemlock, oak, laurel, and ferns for 0.6 mi to the misty base of the lower falls. Backtrack.

CRABTREE BALD TRAIL (Haywood County)

LENGTH AND DIFFICULTY: 6.7 mi round-trip, strenuous (elev change 2,355 ft)

SPECIAL FEATURE: views of 49 mtns over 6,000 ft elev

TRAILHEAD AND DESCRIPTION: (This route is neither blazed nor signed; the major property owner is Jack Messer, 704-627-6224, who has given his permission for day hikes, though you will see No Trespassing signs. Crabtree Bald, the SW end of a ridgeline called Crab Orchard Fields, is unique in its claim that the state's 49 peaks of 6,000 ft or higher elev can be seen from here.)

From the jct of I-40 and NC-209 (exit 24) go 2.4 mi N on NC-209 to Crabtree-Ironduff School and turn R on Upper Crabtree Rd (SR-1503). After 2.0 mi turn L on Bald Creek Rd (SR-1505) at a James Chapel Baptist Church sign. Drive 3.1 mi along Bald Creek and park off the side of the gravel road near a bridge over Indian Branch with cement curbs. To the L is a cattle chute and pasture gate.

Climb over the gate and follow a distinct jeep road through the pasture with Indian Branch on the R. At 0.2 mi is a second gate; cross Indian Branch and at 0.5 mi reach a road jct at the edge of the woods. Straight ahead is a shorter but steeper route; R is a longer but easier route. If following the shorter route, continue up the valley beside the stream. Cross the stream again at 1.0 mi in an open area and follow the old road. (From this point and for the next 0.9 mi, you can follow any old track that goes in the same direction as the power line [S or SW] because you will reach a number of forks and intersections.) At 2.3 mi reach a bend near the crest of the ridge where you can spot the two antennae on the summit of Crabtree Bald. To shortcut, climb L steeply up the crest of the mountain ridge and generally through open cattle pastures for 0.1 mi to reach a jeep route on the main crest. Bear L and hike through open fields to reach the scenic summit (5,320 ft) at 2.9 mi. If returning on the longer route follow the crest's jeep road NE in open fields for 1.1 mi to a low gap. Bear R on a used jeep road and descend, first through fields and then back into the forest of oak, maple, and locust. Arrive at the road jct for a loop at 6.2 mi, and return to the gate and Bald Creek Rd at 6.7 mi. (*USGS Map:* Fines Creek)

911 DE FLORA NATURE TRAIL (Ashe County)

LENGTH AND DIFFICULTY: 0.7 mi, easy

TRAILHEAD AND DESCRIPTION: At the jct of US-421 and US-221 at Deep Gap (1.0 mi W of the BRP and 12.0 mi E of Boone) go N on US-221 for 2.0 mi, turn R on Pine Swamp Rd (SR-1171). Turn L and go 0.7 mi to a parking area, L. The trail is by marshes, ponds, streams, and through woodland with more than 150 species of flowering plants and numerous species of ferns. Some of the plants are rare. The owner maintains and conducts tours on the trail from May 1 to May 15. For permission at other times and a tour schedule contact Dr F. Ray Derrick, Dept of Biology, Appalachian State Univ, Boone, NC 28608; 704-264-8467.

GRANDFATHER MOUNTAIN (Avery, Caldwell, and Watauga Counties)

Grandfather Mountain is a popular commercial tourist attraction and nature preserve with its mile-high swinging bridge over an 80-ft couloir (dedicated in 1952); natural wildlife habitats (dedicated in 1973); plant and mineral exhibits; hiking trails over rugged terrain; and unspoiled natural beauty (such as the world's largest gardens of pink-shell azalea, *vaseyi*). Geologically, the mtn is unique; its metamorphic sandstone is distinct from all other surrounding mtns. "We have made it inoffensively accessible," said Hugh Morton, whose family has owned the property since his MIT-graduate grandfather, Hugh MacRae, bought it in 1885. Among the annual events are the Highland Games (more than 100 Scottish clans represented in traditional sports and arts) held the second weekend in July; "Singing on the Mountain" (a modern and traditional gospel concert) the fourth Sunday in June; and the Nature Photography Weekend (with contests and lectures) in late May. (Photography is a special interest of Morton, who was a combat newsreel photographer in the Philippines in WWII, and who is internationally known for his filmed wildlife series.) Campground facilities are not available, but picnic facilities are set up at scenic overlooks. An entrance fee is required at the gatehouse on US-221.

One of the reasons Grandfather Mtn is so impressive is because it towers high, 2,100 ft, above the valley floor. The mtn received its name from pioneer settlers who saw a grandfatherly profile northwest of Calloway Peak. The image is of a face looking skyward with a long forehead and a thick beard. It is most recognizable on NC-105 in the community of Foscoe, looking S, between Boone and Linville.

There are 10 trails on the mtn, each connecting to a network of other trails except *Black Rock Trail*. Six accesses provide convenient trail-length options—two on NC-105, one from BRP, one from US-221, one at the visitor center, and one on the entrance road. The access to the visitor center and entrance road is for day hikes only. The short *Under the Swinging Bridge Trail* **912** was constructed in 1995, and a new *Grandfather Trail Access* is under con- **913** struction. Both trailheads originate at the Grandfather Mtn Visitor Center. Overnight parking or walking up or down the entrance road is prohibited. Daily permits (unless you purchase a season hiking pass) and small fees are required on all trails and for camping at the designated campsites. Permits are available at the Grandfather Mtn gatehouse; at Eckerd Drugs at the jct of NC-105 and NC-184; Grandfather Mtn Country Store on US-221 (6.4 mi S of Blowing Rock); High Mtn Expeditions, Main St, in Blowing Rock; and Foot-sloggers, 553 W King St, in Boone. Contact the backcountry manager for a list of additional permit outlets. Permits are also available by mail, directly from the backcountry manager. Before a trip is planned, it is essential to contact the manager and request the free *Trail Map of Grandfather Mountain,* and a flyer on preparation for what to pack and what to do after arrival at the mountain. Examples of the regulations are the limitations of groups to not exceed 12; campfires are not permitted at Hi-Balsam shelter and all high elevation campsites, and no alcoholic beverages are allowed on Grandfather Mtn. The trail map shows all trailheads, campsites, altitudes of the peaks, trail routes, and access points. Other information on the map is about the severe weather condition of the preserve. (Fees for hiking permits are used for trial maintenance, protection and conservation of the ecology, safety, and security patrol.)

Grandfather Mtn is a wilderness area. Some of its 3,087 acres are exceptionally fragile and are protected from visitor exploration. With the cooperation of the N.C. Natural Heritage Area and The Nature Conservancy, there are adjoining areas also protected. In addition, Grandfather Mountain Inc is a member of the Southern Appalachian Man and the Biosphere Reserve. Among the biosphere's objectives is "to build a harmonious relationship between man and the environment." (*USGS Maps:* Grandfather Mtn, Valle Crucis).

ADDRESS AND ACCESS: Grandfather Mtn, Box 129, Linville, NC 28646; office, 800-468-7325; gate, 704-733-4337; backcountry manager, 704-733-2013; maintenance, 704-733-8820. Gatehouse entrance on US-221, 2.0 mi NE from Linville, 1.0 mi W from the BRP.

Grandfather Trail (2.2 mi); Underwood Trail (0.5 mi); Black Rock Trail **914-**
(1.0 mi) **916**

LENGTH AND DIFFICULTY: 3.7 mi combined, strenuous

TRAILHEADS AND DESCRIPTION: From the visitor center parking area locate the trail signs, N, on a high embankment and follow the blue-blazed *Grandfather Trail* through dense rhododendron. At 0.4 mi reach a gap, and at 0.5 mi jct L with the yellow-blazed *Underwood Trail*. (The *Underwood Trail*, which rejoins the *Grandfather Trail* after 0.5 mi, passes Raven's Nest Spring on a rocky treadway. Its purpose is for a route less arduous than the rough climbs of *Grandfather Trail*.) Continuing on the *Grandfather Trail*, ascend steeply and climb ladders to scenic MacRae Peak (5,939 ft). At 1.0 mi jct R with the former *Arch Rock Trail*, now closed.

Continuing on the *Grandfather Trail* reach the Attic Window Peak (5,949 ft) at 1.1 mi, and the Indian House Cave (200 ft off the trail, R) at 1.2 mi. At 1.9 mi jct with the red-blazed *Calloway Trail*, L (described below), and reach a spur trail to Watauga View at 2.2 mi. Here also is the end of *Grandfather Mountain Trail* and the beginning, R, of the white-blazed *Daniel Boone Scout Trail* (described below).

Entrance to the *Black Rock Trail* is on the main entrance road at the Black Rock parking area, near the visitor center. For the first 0.4 mi the yellow-blazed trail is on a level grade. The next 0.4 mi leads to the Black Rocks, followed by 0.2 mi to the cave, which is closed.

917-918 *Profile Trail (2.6 mi); Calloway Trail (0.3 mi)*

LENGTH AND DIFFICULTY: 4.5 mi combined, moderate to strenuous

TRAILHEADS AND DESCRIPTION: Access to the *Profile Trail* is 0.6 mi N of the jct of NC-105 and NC-184 on NC-105. From the parking lot, cross the Watauga River on huge flat boulders and follow a skillfully designed trail on a slope through cherry, maple, birch, beech, Fraser's sedge, ferns, and Indian pipe. Pass benches of impressive stonework. At 0.8 mi cross Shanty Spring Branch in a beautiful area. Pass through a large rock formation at 0.9 mi and begin an ascent on Green Ridge switchbacks to a good view of Snake Mtn, Seven Devils, and the Foscoe Valley at 1.7 mi. At 2.0 mi are three campsites (50 ft L) with intricate rock work for a fireplace and bench, almost under the chin of the Grandfather profile. With good views NW, pass R of Haystack Rock at 2.2 mi. At 2.6 mi jct with the former *Shanty Spring Trail*, R, which is closed. (Here is the last dependable source of water for any of the campsites on the main ridge ahead.) The *Profile Trail* ends at the spring, and the red-blazed *Calloway Trail* begins. After a 0.3-mi climb to the top of the ridge, jct with the blue-blazed *Grandfather Trail*, R and L (To the R it is 1.9 mi to the visitor center parking area, and L it is 0.3 mi to

Calloway Peak, the end of the *Grandfather Trail,* and the beginning of the *Daniel Boone Scout Trail.* The latter trail descends the E side of the mtn to jct with the *Tanawha Trail,* the BRP, and US-221.)

Daniel Boone Scout Trail (2.7 mi); Nuwati Trail (1.2 mi); Cragway Trail (1.0 mi) 919-921

LENGTH AND DIFFICULTY: 4.9 mi combined, strenuous (elev change 2,082 ft)

TRAILHEAD AND DESCRIPTION: These trails can be accessed either from US-221 (1.6 mi S from the Grandfather Mtn Country Store and Motel, and 7.4 mi NE from the Grandfather gatehouse entrance) or from the BRP. The recommended route for overnight parking is from US-221. Begin the hike on the *Grandfather Mountain Access Trail* and after 0.4 mi jct with the *Tanawha Trail* after passing under the BRP Boone Fork bridge. Turn L. (To the R across the Boone Fork footbridge, are two trail accesses to the BRP. The nearest is to Boone Fork parking after 260 yd [mp 299.9], and the other access is at the BRP Calloway Peak Overlook parking area [mp 299.7] on the *Upper Boone Fork Trail* for 0.5 mi. Continue L on the *Tanawha Trail* and go 0.2 mi to a jct, R, with the *Nuwati Trail.* Ahead on the *Tanawha Trail* it is 255 yd to a jct where the *Daniel Boone Scout Trail* begins R. (See Chapter 6 for the details of the *Tanawha Trail).*

If hiking the *Nuwati Trail* follow the old woods road 0.6 mi to a jct L with the *Cragway Trail.* (The 1.0-mi *Cragway Trail* ascends, steeply in sections, to upturned cliffs that offer magnificent views of a geographical cirque, the Boone Fork Bowl. Other views are of the Blue Ridge Mtns and their foothills, NE. Rhododendron, red spruce, Allegheny sand myrtle, and blueberries landscape this beautiful route. It connects with the *Daniel Boone Scout Trail.)* Continue ahead, upstream on the *Nuwati Trail* and cross Boone Fork at 1.0 mi. Ascend to Storyteller's Rock, L, at 1.2 mi for a view of the Boone Fork Bowl and the end of the trail. Nearby are two campsites. Backtrack to either *Cragway Trail* or *Tanawha Trail.*

If continuing on the *Daniel Boone Scout Trail* from the *Tanawha Trail,* ascend on a ridge, eroded in sections, to a campsite L, and jct R with the *Cragway Trail* at 1.3 mi. (A dependable spring is 145 yd to the L.) It is 85 yd R on the *Cragway Trail* to the first of its major scenic views—Flat Rock View.) In a forest of spruce, mtn ash, rhododendron, birch, striped maple, galax, and ferns, ascend on a narrow, rough treadway to Hi-Balsam Shelter, L at 2.3 mi. (The shelter sleeps six; no campfires; use a fire ring near the trail.) A few yd below the shelter from here is a view of the Linn Cove

Viaduct on the BRP. Continue a steep ascent to the Calloway Peak (5,964 ft, the highest elev of the Blue Ridge Mtn range) at 2.7 mi. (Calloway Peak is named for Ervin and Texie Calloway, proprietors of the Grandfather Hotel on the W side of the mtn at the turn of the century.) Panoramic scenery from large boulders provides an awesome view of Beach Mtn and Tennessee (W); Mt Rogers in Virginia (N); Mt Mitchell (SW); and Table Rock (S). (From here it is 2.2 mi on the *Grandfather Trail* to the visitor center.)

GREENCROFT GARDENS (Franklin County)

LENGTH AND DIFFICULTY: 2.9 mi easy

TRAILHEAD AND DESCRIPTION: From Louisburg jct of US-401 and NC-56 W, go S on US-401, 5.5 mi to De Hart Botanical Gardens sign, L at private driveway. (It is 4.4 mi N on US-401 from NC-98 jct.) Park at the designated space and register. Follow the *Greencroft Lake Trail* that winds down to and around a lake, a waterfall, and loops back to the parking area after 0.9 mi. (The 0.8-mi *Crane Fly Orchid Trail* begins at the E end of the lake's cross-bridge.) There is also a 230-ft *Children's Bamboo Trail* near the waterfall, and 275-ft *Trail for the Handicapped* from a parking area. Founded by Allen and Flora de Hart, the gardens have more than 400 wild plant species labeled, the largest private wildflower garden in eastern North Carolina. A prominent species is wild pink (*Silene caroliniana*), a tufted perennial with white, sometimes pink, petals. Open all year without charge or a guide, the preserve is for daytime use only, reserves space for weddings and concerts at the lake amphitheater, and arranges guided tours if requested in advance.

INFORMATION: De Hart Botanical Gardens Inc, Rte 1, Box 36, Louisburg, NC 27549; 919-496-4771 or 496-2521.

LAKE JUNALUSKA ASSEMBLY (Haywood County)

Lake Junaluska Assembly (adjoining the mtn town of Lake Junaluska) is the 1,200-acre conference and retreat complex of the Southeastern Jurisdiction (SEJ) of the United Methodist Church. Named for the Cherokee Indian peace-leading chief, Junaluska, the 200-acre lake covers an area once known as Tusola. Surrounding the lake and valley are mtn ranges. Conference facilities can accommodate individuals, families, and church or educational groups up to 2,500. Recreational activities include ball fields and courts, biking, canoeing, fishing, golf, swimming, and more. The SEJ's Commission on Archives and History and the Boy Scouts of America have a cooperative project for hiking the 27.0-mi *Asbury Trail*. The journey is between Mt Sterling community (accessed on Waterville Rd, off I-40, exit 451) and Cove Creek jct of old NC-284 and US-276 (accessed from I-40, exit 20). The trail route is mainly on the ancient *Cataloochee Trail,* and honors the clergyman Francis Asbury, who covered 275,000 mi as a circuit rider in 45 years. (See chapter 7, *Asbury Trail.*)

Lake Junaluska Trail is a 2.3-mi easy loop that circles the lake. Upon entry **926** to the assembly grounds, park at the first parking lot, R, near the swimming pool. Begin clockwise; pass the Wellth Methodist Center and parallel the rose walk to the Methodist World Council. After passing the Cokesbury Book Center, Auditorium, and Memorial Chapel, enter a gate at 0.6 mi to the *Francis* **927** *Asbury Trail.* It runs jointly with the main trail for 0.2 mi. Here are large pines, oaks, cultivated flowers, and markers honoring distinguished humanitarians. At 0.7 mi cross the dam and bridge to a small health/fitness area, L. From grassy manicured lawns are scenic views of the luminescent lake. Cross a boardwalk-bridge at 2.0 mi, and return to the parking lot at 2.3 mi.

INFORMATION: Lake Junaluska Assembly, Box 67, Lake Junaluska, NC 28745; 1-800-222-4930/704-452-2881; (SEJ Commission on Archives and History, Box 1165, Lake Junaluska, NC 28745).

MONTREAT CONFERENCE CENTER (Buncombe County)

Located in the amicable town of Montreat is Montreat Conference Center, a 4,500-acre compound owned by the Presbyterian Church. Distinctive in mission and services, this outstanding retreat has a conference assembly auditorium, convocation halls, lodges, inn, apartments, retail shops, craft center, child care center, nature center, park, playground, lake, swimming pool, tennis courts, and the most expansive trail system open to the public of any private retreat in the state. Within the center's boundary is Montreat-Anderson College, a four-year liberal arts college. Set like an emerald in the center of this compact community is Lake Susan.

ADDRESS AND ACCESS: Montreat Conference Center, Box 969, Montreat, NC 28757; 704-669-2911 (college: 704-669-8011). From I-40, exit 64, at Black Mtn, drive N on NC-9 for 3.1 mi through the town of Black Mtn to the ranger station R, before Lake Susan.

Piney Ridge Trail (1.4 mi); West Ridge Trail (2.9 mi); Stomping Knob **928-** *Trail (1.0 mi); Graybeard Trail (2.9 mi); Walkers Knob Trail (0.2 mi);* **940** *Rocky Head Trail (0.9 mi); East Ridge Trail (2.3 mi); Buck Gap Trail (0.2 mi); Hickory Ridge Trail (0.2 mi); Lookout Trail (0.8 mi);*

Rattlesnake Mountain Trail (0.3 mi); Horseshoe Loop Trail (0.9 mi); Rainbow Road Trail (1.8 mi)

LENGTH AND DIFFICULTY: 15.8 mi combined, easy to strenuous

TRAILHEADS AND DESCRIPTION: After entering the archway on Assembly Dr there are three parking areas for the trails described below: *Piney Ridge*, *Campground*, and *Lookout*. Other places may be necessary, depending on crowded conditions. It is essential to acquire a trail map at the Assembly Inn or the ranger station. A map will provide an estimated length of time to hike each trail, its connections, and its color code. Some spur trails and connectors are not listed above. Below are examples of possible loops.

To hike the trails to the preserve's highest peak, Graybeard Mtn (5,360 ft), drive from Lake Susan up Graybeard Trail (Rd) to a small parking area L (beside a private drive) to a welcome sign. Walk straight up a gravel rd, pass gate, bear R at sign of orange-blazed, strenuous *Piney Ridge Trail*, and then at 0.1 mi climb up a gravel rd to bear L. After another 100 yd the rd turns R, but the trail goes straight ahead. Descend to a stream at 0.3 mi where a spur trail (50 yd) has a "unicorn tree." Ascend to a main ridgeline in a mixed forest and ground cover of galax. At 1.2 mi arrive at Rattlesnake Rock for views of the town of Black Mtn, Swannanoa Valley, and Blue Ridge Mtns. Arrive at the summit of Brushy Knob (Little Piney Mtn, 4,160 ft) at 1.4 mi. Here is a jct with strenuous gray-blazed *West Ridge Trail* (also known as *Seven Sisters Ridge Trail*), R and L.

(To the L *West Ridge Trail* goes 0.6 mi along a narrow ridge to Stomping Knob (3,970 ft) where it jct with strenuous, yellow-blazed *Stomping Knob Trail*. It descends steeply E to an old woods rd at 0.6 mi, crosses a small stream in a ravine at 0.8 mi, and makes an exit to Harmony Rd. Harmony Rd can be accessed by turning off Assembly Dr between the archway and Lake Susan, on Louisiana Ave.)

Turning R on *West Ridge Trail* from *Piney Ridge Trail*, ascend through a hardwood forest of large oaks and arrive at Big Piney Mtn (4,320 ft) after 0.3 mi. Here are posted signs of Asheville watershed boundary, W. Continue ascending alongside an old wire fence on a sharp ridge crest to Little Slaty Mtn (4,560 ft) and Big Slaty Mtn (4,855 ft). At 3.3 mi ascend between two rocks in a lush craggy area. Jct with *Graybeard Trail*, which comes in from the R, at 3.7 mi. Arrive at the grassy summit of Graybeard Mtn at 4.0 mi (after a 2,560-ft elev gain from the start of the loop). Spectacular views from the summit are of Craggy Mtn W and Black Mtn N.

Returning, descend to the jct with *West Ridge Trail*, but follow L, ahead, on moderate, blue-blazed *Graybeard Trail*. At 4.8 mi is a gap and shelter, R.

Also to the R is a 0.2-mi spur trail, easy orange-blazed *Walkers Knob Trail*, which provides a magnificent view of Flat Creek Valley. Backtrack to the main trail and continue descending; arrive at the headwaters of Flat Creek at 5.0 mi. Cross the creek, enter into a campsite area and follow an old RR grade for 75 yd before turning sharply R. (The old RR grade continues a short distance to connect with the Old Toll Rd. (The Old Toll Rd can be used as a 14.0-mi strenuous hike from the Lookout Rd parking area to Mt Mitchell. Request a directional map from the ranger sta [at Lake Susan], which is open only from early June to mid-August. Otherwise request at the Assembly Inn across the road.)

Arrive at a level spot below a 20-ft flume and campsites across the creek at 5.4 mi. At 5.7 mi reach Pot Cove Gap and turn R back into the watershed. Descend rapidly, crossing and recrossing Flat Creek among hemlock and rhododendron. Arrive near a private home at 6.8 mi. Follow a gravel road downstream L, reach a gate, a small parking area L, for *Graybeard Trail* at 7.0 mi. To complete the loop continue down a paved road to *Piney Ridge Trail* at 7.4 mi.

To access *Rocky Head Trail* from Lake Susan drive ahead past the jct described above for the *Piney Ridge Trail,* and turn R on Calvin Trail (Rd) to a gate at Montreat Campground. Begin strenuous, orange-blazed *Rocky Head Trail* at campsite #21 on the R. Ascend and after 0.3 mi reach a site of old water-holding ponds to make a sharp R on an embankment. At 0.7 mi are views L of Slaty Cliffs and Graybeard Mtn. After rock overhangs and overlooks resume a steep climb. Jct with *East Ridge Trail* at 0.9 mi. A turn L is 60 ft to the rocky summit of Rocky Head Mtn (4,005 ft). (To the L it is 0.3 mi to Long Gap at the Old Toll Rd, the N trailhead of *East Ridge Trail*.)

To the R easy gray-blazed *East Ridge Trail* continues. At 1.4 mi turn L on Trestle Rd; arrive at Sourwood Gap at 1.5 mi, and again jct with the Old Toll Rd. Reach the summit of Brushy Mtn (3,885 ft) at 1.7 mi. Excellent views here are of Rocky Head, Graybeard, Pinnacle, and Clingman's Peak. (The true summit of Brushy Mtn is crowned by a grove of hemlock.) Descend to Buck Gap and jct R with moderate blue-blazed *Buck Gap Trail.* (It goes 0.2 mi to a shelter before Trestle Rd.) Reach the summit of Lookout Mtn (3,520 ft) at 2.5 mi. Bear R (SW) following the ridgeline to jct L with easy blue-blazed *Hickory Ridge Trail* at 2.8 mi. Descend and after 0.2 mi reach the summit of Lookout Rock (3,760 ft) with 360-degree views including Seven Sisters Ridge and Montreat area. Options here are to follow *Lookout Trail* to the Lookout parking lot, or take a longer route on *Rainbow Rd (Trail).*

If choosing the moderate yellow-blazed *Lookout Trail*, descend at times on steps. Bear R on the ridgeline after 0.4 mi, near jct with Trestle Rd. Continue descent on switchbacks and arrive at the E side of the parking lot at 0.8 mi, a total of 3.6 mi from the campground, and 1.4 mi farther back to the campground. If following *Rainbow Rd (Trail)*, leave the jct of *Lookout Trail* on *Hickory Ridge Trail* for 0.1 mi to jct with Old Toll Rd. Bear R and jct with *Rattlesnake Mountain Trail* after 100 yd. Turn L on the Old Toll Rd and soon begin to descend (no blazes on this trail; property belongs to Ridgecrest Conference Center). At 0.5 mi reach the summit overlook of Rattlesnake Mtn where are superb views of South Mtn and the Swannanoa Valley. Backtrack. On the return jct with the Old Toll Rd, turn L, and follow it W. At 0.6 mi jct with *Lookout Trail*, R. Then after 40 yd is jct with Trestle Rd, *Lookout Trail*, and *Rainbow Rd (Trail)*. To follow the easy orange-blazed *Rainbow Rd (Trail)*, it is 1.8 mi to Lookout parking lot. Along the way pass a jct with Old Toll Rd at 0.2 mi and with a strenuous, gray-blazed path at 0.6 mi. (It is steep and rarely used; it exits near [upstream] the arched gate into the conference center.) At 1.0 mi is a jct with a spur trail, R, that leads uphill to Parker Shelter. (It has a door and windows and sleeps 8 to 10 people. A spring is behind the shelter.) Pass a college forest rope course at 1.5 mi. Return to the parking lot after another 0.3 mi. If without a second vehicle, walk down Lookout Rd 0.6 mi to Lake Susan. Turn R on Graybeard Trail (Rd) and Calvin Trail (Rd) for 0.8 mi for a total loop of 6.6 mi to the campground.

For the easy white-blazed *Horseshoe Loop Trail*, begin at the Lookout Rd parking lot and follow a dirt road N to the stables on the E side. After 100 yd cross a small stream, ascend on an old woods road to another stream, and follow a series of switchbacks to a T jct. (To the R is a connection with Trestle Rd.) Turn L, descend on switchbacks, pass posted Foreman property, and return to the point of origin after 0.9 mi. (*USGS Map:* Montreat)

MORNINGSTAR NATURE REFUGE (Martin County)

The 20-acre sanctuary for plants and animals has 5 acres open to the public. In a beautiful biological refuge is a 1.5-mi network of trails: *Morningstar Trail*, *Holly Ridge Trail*, *Blue Heron Trail*, *Buckskin Beech Trail*, *Eagle Spirit Trail*, *Sacred Circle Trail*, *Moon Feather Trail*, and *Marsh Trail*. Access from jct of US-17 and US-64 in Williamston is 4.0 mi S on US-17, turn L (E) on Mill Inn Rd (SR-1521), go 2.0 mi, and turn L on Meadow Branch Rd (SR-1526). (Call Gail Roberson for appointment.)

941-948

INFORMATION: Morningstar Nature Refuge, 1967 Meadow Branch Rd, Williamston, NC 27892; 919-792-7788.

PEARSON'S FALLS TRAIL (Polk County)

Pearson's Falls Trail (0.3 mi) is part of a 250-acre nature preserve maintained and financed privately by the Tryon Garden Club (organized in 1929). Open all year, there is a small fee to view the beautiful 90-ft cascades and botanical display of more than 200 species (one of which is the rare broadleaf coreopsis, *Coreopsis latifolia*). (The club purchased the property in 1931 from the Charles W. Pearson family.) Access to the property is 4.0 mi N of Tryon on US-176; turn L on SR-1102 (3.0 mi S from Saluda). Follow the signs 1.0 mi.

INFORMATION: Tryon Garden Club Nature Preserve, Rte 1, Box 327, Saluda, NC 28773; 704-479-303,1.

PHILLIPS KNOB TRAIL (Yancey County)

LENGTH AND DIFFICULTY: 4.4 mi round-trip, strenuous (elev change 1,520 ft)

TRAILHEAD AND DESCRIPTION: From the town square in Burnsville, drive N on Main St (which becomes Mitchell Branch Rd, SR-1373) and after 0.8 mi park at a fork. Begin the hike, R, on Mica Springs Heights Rd. (Although the road leads to the summit spur, the road is narrow and rough.) It is 0.8 mi to the next jct; turn R on a steep and rough road. Reach the fire tower at 2.2 mi. Views to Big Bald, Table Rock, and Black Mtn ranges are impressive. Backtrack. (*USGS Map:* Burnsville)

SUNSET ROCK TRAIL (Macon County)

LENGTH AND DIFFICULTY: 1.4 mi round-trip, easy

TRAILHEAD AND DESCRIPTION: From the jct of US-64 and NC-28 in Highlands, proceed on E Main St 0.4 mi and park opposite the Highlands Nature Center. Follow the sign and turn R at 0.2 mi over rock slabs through pine, rosebay, rhododendron, hemlock, and locust. At 0.6 mi an 1879 rock engraving indicates that the park area is a memorial to Margaretta A. and S. Prioleal Ravenel. To the R is a large rock outcropping that provides a magnificent view of the Nantahala NF and the town of Highlands. From here can also be seen Satulah Mtn (4,542 ft) about 1.0 mi S, a property owned by the same corporation that owns Sunset Rock, Satulah Summit–Ravenel Park Inc. Backtrack.

INFORMATION: Highlands Chamber of Commerce, Town Hall, Box 404, Highlands, NC 28741; 704-526-2112.

952 WHITEHALL CIRCUIT TRAIL (Moore County)

LENGTH AND DIFFICULTY: 2.0 mi round-trip, easy

TRAILHEAD AND DESCRIPTION: In Southern Pines turn off US-1 W onto NC-2 (Midland Rd), drive 0.2 mi for a R turn on NC-22. After 1.1 mi turn L on Pee Dee Rd; then 0.4 mi to Whitehall Center sign, R. The trail begins here, but ahead on the entrance road at a fork, L is a place to park. (Another place to park is at Reservoir Park. Access is to continue on NC-22 past Pee Dee Rd for 0.6 mi for a L turn to the parking lot.) If beginning at Reservoir Park and hiking counterclockwise, walk up the steps on the bank, W, and turn sharply L on an old road. Follow a white disc through longleaf pine, turkey oak, and scattered patches of goat's rue and tufts of wire grass. Pass R of honeybee hives at 0.6 mi, and soon turn L between fences. At 0.8 mi arrive at a vehicle gate (described above near entrance to the center). At 0.9 mi turn on a road with the sign "Farm Entrance." Leave the road to a footpath at 1.2 mi for a gentle descent to a small bridge over a streamlet. Here is a grove of magnolia bays at 1.5 mi. Complete the loop on a grassy area at the opposite side of the parking lot. The trail is monitored in perpetuity by the Sandhills Area Land Trust. (At the parking area is a 2.0-mi loop trail around Reservoir Lake, described in chapter 13, and a connector trail at the N end of the dam to Sandhill Community College trails described in chapter 15.)

INFORMATION: Whitehall Health Education Center, 490 Pee Dee Rd (Box 1221), Southern Pines, NC 28387; 910-692-6691.

953 WHITE OAK NATURE TRAIL (Wake County)

White Oak Nature Trail is an easy 1.5-mi double loop at Carolina Power and Light Harris Nuclear Power Plant. The skillfully designed and color-coded blazed route begins at a parking and picnic area at the Harris Plant Visitor Center/Energy and Environmental Center. There are interpretive markers about wildlife, trees, ferns, and flowers. The longer part of the loop has boardwalks on the approach to Big Branch, a scenic wetland. (Proposed plans are to have talking-tree markers like those at the state forests' educational centers.) A trail brochure is available either at the trailhead or the visitor center. Access: From US-1 (S of Apex) turn off at New Hill sign to New Hill–Holleman Rd (SR-1127) and drive 1.5 mi SE.

INFORMATION: Harris Visitor Center, Rte 1, Box 327, New Hill, NC 27562; 910-362-3261.

PART VII

15. College and University Trails

Nature teaches more than she preaches.
—John Burroughs

Degree programs in parks and recreation are offered in 21 colleges and universities in the state, and 11 two-year colleges offer preliminary degree programs. Some of the large senior institutions offer degrees in forestry and a variety of environmental fields. Two university medical centers, University of North Carolina at Chapel Hill and Duke University, offer departments in recreation therapy. Although few institutions of higher education have adequate properties for a trail system, all of them require courses in physical education and 60 percent have organizations or clubs that promote or sponsor hiking in outings or outdoor sports programs. Some community colleges have short fitness trails that may serve as nature trails. An example is *Piedmont Community College Trail* in Roxboro. Others have scenic campus walks, such as *Haywood Community College Trail* in Clyde. **954-955**

DUKE UNIVERSITY (Durham, Chatham, Alamance, and Orange Counties)

The 7,700-acre Duke Forest has five major tracts, two of which (Durham and Korstian) have a series of fire roads and unnamed trails for hikers, joggers, bikers, and equestrians. It began with a gift of 4,700 acres from Durham and Orange Counties in the 1920s. In 1931 the university established a Forest Program and appointed Dr Clarence F. Korstian as its first director; he developed the forest into an area of research and a laboratory for forestry students. Once in a rural setting, the Duke Forest now borders an increase in residential and commercial development.

The large Durham tract is located on both sides of NC-751, beginning W of its jct with Bypass US-15/501 (2.0 mi S from I-85), and goes 3.0 mi

NW to US-70. Gate numbers are posted along NC-751 for loop trails and picnic sites. Gates 11 and 12 lead to the tract's highest ridge, Couch Mtn **956** (640 ft) on the *Couch Mountain Trail*. Korstian, another large tract, is between Whitfield Rd (SR-1731) and Mt Sinai Rd (SR-1718), 3.0 mi E of the NC-86/I-40 jct on Whitfield Rd. New Hope Creek flows through, W to E. One trail, through Gate 25 (or 23 on the N side), descends to ford New Hope Creek on a concrete flood bridge. The trail at Gate 26 descends to a cliff and a grove of rhododendron.

The other tracts are less visited. The Blackwood tract is found on both sides of Hillsborough Rd (SR-1009), 5.0 mi N of downtown Carrboro. The Eno tract is on Stony Creek between the triangle of NC-86 (W), Ray Rd (SR-1723) (E), and Old No 10 Rd (SR-1710) (N), 1.5 mi S from I-85 on NC-86. The Hillsborough tract is on both sides of US-70, 1.5 mi W of its jct with NC-86 in N Hillsborough. The Eno River flows through this property.

The forest contains excellent examples of plant succession. A wide range of trees and flowers common to the Piedmont are here, and wildlife (such as fox, deer, raccoon, squirrel, and owls) is protected. Fishing is allowed, but camping, hunting, and use of motorized vehicles on the trails are not permitted. Use of mountain bikes is restricted to graded roads only. There are no facilities for drinking water or rest rooms. More than 20.7 mi of trails are on the fire lanes, and 14.3 mi are possible on all-weather roads. (For walking in a more formal setting, the Sarah P. Duke Memorial Gardens near the university entrance are also open to the public.) (*USGS Maps:* Chapel Hill, Durham NW, Efland, Hillsborough)

INFORMATION: Office of the Duke Forest School of the Environment, Duke University, Box 90332, Durham, NC 27708; 919-613-8013. (Forest brochures and detailed maps can be purchased through the mail or at the office. Access to the office is in the Levine Science Research Campus on Science Dr.

NORTH CAROLINA STATE UNIVERSITY (Wake, Durham, and Moore Counties)

The Carl A. Schenck Memorial Forest is a research laboratory of conifers and broadleaves on the university property between Wade Ave and Reedy Creek Park Rd (SR-1650) in Raleigh. The 6.0-mi *Loblolly Trail* (see chapter 14) goes **957** 1.5 mi through the forest, and the 1.2-mi *Frances Liles Interpretive Trail* is in the forest interior. It has 10 stops that describe the multiple benefits derived from forest land. Redbud groves and pine grafting are prominent on the S side of the loop. Access is either from the *Loblolly Trail* or the picnic shelter. To reach the picnic shelter take Reedy Creek Park Rd off Blue Ridge Rd (1.0 mi N of the state fairgrounds) and go 0.9 mi to the forest entrance sign L. Go 0.1 mi to the entrance gate and park to avoid blocking the gate. Walk on the gated road 0.1 mi to the picnic shelter, R, and the trailhead. (*USGS Map:* Raleigh W)

The Hill Forest is in Durham County and has a network of single-lane access roads that provides 10.5 mi of unnamed trails. Permission for hiking in the forest is required; contact the address below. The forest is on both sides of Flat River, which has some exceptionally steep banks. Dial Creek also flows S through the forest. To reach the forest from I-85 and US-501 in Durham, go 12.5 mi N on US-501 to Quail Roost and turn R on Moores Mill Rd (SR-1601), immediately turning R on State Forest Rd (SR-1614) after crossing the N & W RR. Go 1.0 mi to the forest entrance. (SR-1614 also goes through the forest to jct at 2.2 mi with Wilkins Rd [SR-1613] and Hampton Rd [SR-1603] for a route E to Hampton.) The George K. Slocum Forestry Camp is on the L of the entrance. (*USGS Maps:* Rougemont, Lake Michie)

Goodwin Forest is in Moore County. Although there are no developed trails, there are 4.1 mi of single-lane access roads open to hikers. If approaching from Carthage, go W 1.3 mi on NC-22/24/27 to jct with Bethlehem Church Rd (SR-1261), L. After 1.5 mi enter Goodwin Forest. Follow the first road L or go straight ahead. Permission for the hike is required from the office listed below. (*USGS Map:* Carthage)

INFORMATION: College of Forest Resources, Dept of Forestry, NCSU, Box 8002, Raleigh, NC 27695; 919-515-2891.

UNIVERSITY OF NORTH CAROLINA–ASHEVILLE (Buncombe County)

The 10-acre University Botanical Gardens were set aside by the Board of Trustees in 1960, but the gardens have been developed and maintained by a private board of directors. There are more than 400 native species along an easy 0.6-mi route on grassy and gravelly unnamed trails that cross meadows and into the forest. A log cabin on the trail honors Hubert H. Hayes, author and playwright. The *University Botanical Gardens Trail* returns by Reed **958** Creek from Heath Cove through an area of sycamore, white pine, and oak to cross a stream on a curved bridge. The gardens are open daily; free, but no picnicking or camping is permitted.

ACCESS: From the jct of I-240 and US-19/23/70 in Asheville, turn N on the latter toward Weaverville and Marshall. Go 2.0 mi and turn R off the expressway to Broadway and NC-251 jct. After 0.5 mi turn L on W. T. Weaver Blvd and go 0.1 mi. Park at the entrance. (*USGS Map*: Asheville)

INFORMATION: University Botanical Gardens at Asheville Inc, 151 W. T. Weaver Blvd, Asheville, NC 28804; 704-252-5190.

UNIVERSITY OF NORTH CAROLINA–CHAPEL HILL (Orange County)

The 600-acre North Carolina Botanical Garden is a botanical preserve of southeastern trees, shrubs, plants, ferns, wildflowers, and herbs. Its nature trails are open daily, and the administrative offices are open Mon through Fri. Guided tours of the garden are offered by prior arrangement to groups **959** of 10–60. From the parking lot follow the signs on the *North Carolina Botanical Garden Nature Trail* (a self-guided interpretive trail). Cross a bridge at 0.2 mi and turn R. (Another trail ascends L to connect with other unnamed trails.) Follow a combination of trails under a subcanopy of flowering trees such as dogwoods and return to the parking lot after 1.5 mi. (The Totten Center is across the street.)

ADDRESS AND ACCESS: N.C. Botanical Garden, UNC-CH, CB# 3375 Totten Center, Chapel Hill, NC 27599; 919-962-0522. In E Chapel Hill the location is at Laurel Hill Rd (SR-1901), 0.7 mi S of the US-15/501 and NC-54 jct.

WESTERN CAROLINA UNIVERSITY (Jackson and Macon Counties)

The university has a 300-acre preserve in the Wolf Creek watershed, a state natural heritage area N of Brown Mtn. Access paths are also on private and Nantahala NF properties. One access, frequently used by the university's Biology Club, is 5.4 mi S from the campus. From the jct of the main campus entrance on NC-107 in Cullowhee, go S on NC-107 for 1.3 mi to jct with Speedwell Rd (SR-1001). Turn R and drive 1.1 mi to Cullowhee Mtn Rd (SR-1157) at the bridge over Tilley Creek. Drive 3.0 mi (along Cullowhee Creek, R) to a horseshoe curve in the road and park on a large grassy area beyond the curve. Hike back 50 yd to the center of the curve at Wolf Creek, R. Follow a footpath on private property past a flume with cascades, pools, and falls. Oak, birch, maple, hemlock, and rhododendron shade the gorge. In addition to the common wildflowers and mosses are less-common species such as walking fern and Fraser's sedge. At 0.5 mi jct R with USFS Cherry Gap Rd. Ahead upstream are the university preserve lands and an extended pathway. Backtrack, or follow Cherry Gap Rd out to SR-1157, turn R, and descend 0.6 mi to where you parked. To hike the university and private properties, request permission from the address below. (*USGS Map:* Glenville)

INFORMATION: Dept of Biology, WCU, Cullowhee, NC 28723; 704-227-7244.

In Highlands (Macon County) the university administers the Highlands Biological Station (since 1977), an interinstitutional program of the University of N.C. system. (Serving the station is the Highlands Biological Foundation Inc, a nonprofit organization with 26 member institutions from the SE region who use the facilities for research. Some international studies are also offered.) Highlands (Clark Foreman) Nature Center is part of the station. It has artifacts, minerals, a botanical garden, and local flora and fauna. It is open from Memorial Day to Labor Day, but the station is open all year. The *Highlands Botanical Garden Trail* is through a special garden in memory of **960** Effie Howell Foreman. Established in 1962 and supported by state and private funds, the garden has more than 400 labeled species, most of which are indigenous to the Highlands area and some of which are endemic. Self-guiding, multiple, and connecting, the trails show ferns, azaleas, club mosses, and a bog succession with swamp pinks, lilies, insectivorous plants, and some rare plants. (The *Sunset Rock Trail* is across the road from the Nature Center. See chapter 14.) (*USGS Map:* Highlands).

ADDRESS AND ACCESS: Highlands Biological Station, Box 580, Highlands, NC 28741; 704-526-2602. From the jct of US-64/NC-28 in Highlands, go 0.3 mi on E Main St to 6th St and turn L. Go 0.2 mi to sign and turn R. Pass the station and park at the garden entrance.

SANDHILLS COMMUNITY COLLEGE (Moore County)

The Sandhills Horticultural Gardens and the Landscape Gardening School (established in 1968) at Sandhills Community College are rare among two-year colleges. "There are about 1,500 species in the gardens," said Fred Garrett, coordinator of the Landscape Gardens Program. A citizens support group is the Sandhills Horticultural Society. More than 500 graduates have brought honor and recognition to the college as horticulturists, landscape designers and architects, nurserymen, and managers worldwide.

From the garden's entrance it is 1.5 mi to walk all the circuits and backtracking walkways within the varied collections of the *Sandhills Horticultur-* **961** *al Gardens Trail.* The first garden, R, is the Conifer Garden, with such striking species as weeping blue Atlas cedar, blue weeping juniper, and weeping red pine. The Sir Walter Raleigh Garden is a formal English garden, followed by an herb garden, and the remarkable collection in the Ebersole Holly Garden. To the L of these areas are the Hillside Garden with pools, cascades, and flowers, a rose garden, and even a vegetable and fruit garden. In the

962 cove of twin lakes is the 0.1-mi *Desmond Native Wetland Trail,* a boardwalk through indigenous species and bird sanctuary. (An upland garden is being constructed nearby.) The gardens are open daily without charge; docents for

963 tours are available by appointment. (An 0.8-mi unmarked *Connector Trail* goes beyond the gate at the end of the Ebersole Holly Garden to connect with the 2.0-mi *Reservoir Lake Trail* described in chapter 13. Along the way the connector passes R of the twin lakes, follows part of the college's fitness trail, staying L, and connects at the W end of the reservoir dam.) Access: From US-1 turn W on NC-2 for 0.2 mi, turn R on NC-22, drive 2.3 mi to Airport Rd, turn L and go 1.0 mi to the college, L. Park at the lot at Heutte Hall.

INFORMATION: Sandhills Horticultural Gardens, Sandhills Community College, 2200 Airport Rd, Pinehurst, NC 28376; 910-695-3882.

16. Mountains-to-Sea Trail

We are doing this because it will be something for tomorrow, for everybody.
—Louise Chatfield

After the General Assembly passed the North Carolina Trails System Act of 1973, the Department of Natural Resources and Community Development (DNRCD), now Department of Environment, Health, and Natural Resources (DEHNR), staff began brainstorming about the future of trails. A catalyst was *Resources for Trails in North Carolina,* 1972, written by staff member Bob Buckner. With fresh ideas and concepts about trail purposes and usage, staff planners such as Alan Eaks and Jim Hallsey inspired others to move forward in implementing the Trails System Act. One of the act's statutes explains that "in order to provide for the ever increasing outdoor recreation needs of an expanded population and in order to promote public access to, travel within, and enjoyment and appreciation of the outdoors, natural and remote areas of the state, trails should be established in natural scenic areas of the state, and in and near urban areas." It was also a period when the trend for greenways was on the horizon. Regional councils of government and county governments were proposing canoe trails and trail connections, and Arch Nichols of the Carolina Mountain Club was proposing a 60.0-mi hiking trail from Mt Pisgah to Mt Mitchell. Discussing these and many other exciting ideas with the DNRCD staff was the North Carolina Trails Committee (a seven-member citizen advisory board appointed by the DNRCD secretary and authorized by the Trails System Act).

The committee began functioning in January 1974 with Louise Chatfield (Greensboro) as chair; followed by John Falter (Apex) in 1976; and Doris B. Hammett, MD (Waynesville), in 1977. It was Dr. Hammett who led a planning committee for the Fourth National Trails Symposium, which was held at Lake Junaluska, September 7 to 10, 1977. Among the distinguished state and national guest speakers was Howard N. Lee, secretary of DNRCD (and former mayor of Chapel Hill). Lee's speech was prepared by his speechwriter and director of public relations, Stephen Meehan. Near the end of the speech Lee said, "I think the time has come for us to consider the feasibility of establishing a state trail between the mountains and the seashore in North Carolina." He explained that he wanted the Trails Committee to plan a trail that would utilize the NPS, USFS, state parks, city and county properties, and private landowners "willing to give an easement over a small portion of their land on a legacy to future generations. I don't think we should be locked into the traditional concept of a trail with woods on both sides...I think it would be a trail that would help—like the first primitive trails—bring us together...I would depend on trail enthusiasts for maintenance...Beyond that, how great it would be if other states would follow suit and that the state trails could be linked nationally." After the conference, Curtis Yates of the Department of Transportation sent Lee a copy of the Mountains to Sea bicycle trail map of a route from Murphy to Manteo. Yates inquired if the bike trail could be a part of the proposal.

964   Citizen task forces for segments along the approximately 20.0-mi wide corridor were established to design, negotiate easements, construct, and maintain the "dream trail," whose name became the *Mountains-to-Sea Trail* (*MST*). The "to" was dropped for an easier abbreviation and to avoid the longer *MTST*. Its western trailhead would start at Clingmans Dome as a connector with the *AT* in the GSMNP to its eastern trailhead at Nags Head on the Outer Banks. Between 1979 and 1981 the DNRCD signed cooperative planning agreements with the NPS, the USFS, and the US Fish and Wildlife Service for the *MST* to pass through federal properties. Another agreement was signed in 1985 pledging a cooperative effort to share resources to complete the state's longest trail, estimated to be between 700 and 800 mi long when completed. The *Memorandum of Agreement,* renewable every five years, agreed to "cooperate in developing guidelines for the planning, development, protection, administration and use" of the *MST*.

Plans for the *MST* would use original trails in GSMNP to reach the Cherokee Indian reservation and the Blue Ridge Parkway. It would follow the BRP until reaching the Nantahala NF, where it would alternate between the properties. It would also oscillate between the BRP and Pisgah NF with the exception of a long eastern curve into the Davidson River drainage of the Pisgah district and the Linville River and Wilson Creek drainages in the Grandfather district. On its return to the BRP at Mt Pisgah, it would follow the BRP corridor to the Mt Mitchell entrance road before descending to Black Mtn Campground in the Toecane Ranger District of Pisgah NF. Its return to the

Bodie Island. Allen de Hart

BRP would be a short parallel before following Woods Mtn to US-221. From there the *MST* stays in the Grandfather Ranger District of the Pisgah NF before returning to the BRP at Beacon Heights. Again it would follow the BRP to its final eastern turn at the northern edge of Doughton Park.

From there the *MST* would descend to Stone Mtn State Park, a section to be named in honor of Louise Chatfield (1920–86), a leader in the trails movement and founder of the North Carolina Trails Association in 1978. In her support for trails she had said, "We are doing this because it will be something for tomorrow, for everybody." From Stone Mtn State Park the *MST* route would enter private or public lands to Pilot Mtn State Park, and beyond to Hanging Rock State Park. Continuing SE to Lake Brandt, N of Greensboro, it would pass through Alamance and Durham Counties to approach Eno River State Park in Durham. From there it would connect with the *Falls Lake Trail* system to Raleigh. From Raleigh it would follow the floodplains corridor of the Neuse River through Johnston and Wayne Counties to Cliffs-of-the-Neuse State Park and through Lenoir County. It would leave the Neuse River to enter Croatan NF in Jones, Pamlico, and Carteret Counties. At Cedar Island the hiker would take a state ferry to Ocracoke, the beginning of the final 75.0 mi, and follow the *Cape Hatteras Beach Trail* on the Outer Banks through Cape Hatteras National Seashore. In addition to the main *MST* corridor across the state, regional connecting trails could be planned to major cities, the Uwharrie NF, and other public areas such as state, city, and county parks. A specific route has not been defined. To have a footpath off the road would require purchase or leasing of nearly 400 mi of private property whose cost would make its construction unlikely. A less visionary approach has been discussed among trail leaders since the beginning. It would be multiuse to include bike trails, horse trails, rail trails, and backcountry roads. In metropolitan or urban areas the sidewalks could be used.

Until a foot trail is completed from the mountains to the sea, or a multiuse route, some hikers are choosing to see the state as bikers on the state's bike network. The longest route, Mountains-to-Sea (highway bike #2) is from Murphy to Manteo (700.0 mi). It makes a jct with the *MST* foot trail at Balsam Gap (S) at the US-23/74 and BRP. Bike route #2 follows the BRP to NC-181 E of Linville Falls (and partway down the mountain) where the two mountains-to-sea trails cross for the last time in the mountains. Along the 129.0 BRP mi the *MST* plays tag with bike route #2 in its crisscrossing of the BRP. (Bikers are not allowed on the *MST* footpath if on BRP property, but hikers [pedestrians] may walk the BRP between crossings.) Another cross-state route is North Line Trace (highway bike #4 [400.0 mi]),whose route is close to Stone Mtn SP, the proposed route of the *MST*. This route goes near at least three state parks and a number of county/town parks to Knotts Island. The Ocracoke Option (highway F) (170.0 mi) branches off the Mountain-to-Sea bike route W of Wilson at Christian Rd (SR-1942) and goes to Cedar Island for the ferry trip to Ocracoke, the general route of the *MST* corridor.

The state's bicycle project began in the early 1970s in the Department of Transportation (DOT), the same decade of an enthusiastic awareness for statewide foot trails by the Division of Parks and Rec. In 1974 Curtis Yates wrote a conceptual paper for a network of biking highways in the state, and Mary Meletiou assisted in the final draft to the state legislature. State Senator

McNeill Smith of Greensboro introduced the bill, which easily passed as the N.C. Bicycle and Bikeway Act of 1974. Both Yates and Meletiou have remained on the DOT staff for more than 20 years as leaders of promoting the network project. For hikers who plan to supplement their passage across the state by biking, request information and maps from Office of Bicycle and Pedestrian Transportation, N.C. Dept of Transportation, Box 25201, Raleigh, NC 27611; 919-733-2804. There are 10 routes to choose from for a total of 3,000 mi.

A few hikers have been known to hike across the state on back roads near the MST corridor and to follow short pieces of the state trail system. The first one was Lee Price in 1982, a feat sponsored by the N.C. Trails Association. He began in Murphy and ended on the Cape Hatteras National Seashore. Part of his trek was by bicycling. The most recent through-hike was made by Jeffrey Scott and Jarrett Franklin from October 18, 1994, at Nags Head on the coast to February 9, 1995, at Clingmans Dome in the Smokies. Of the time, 75 days were continuous backpacking. Graduates of Appalachian State University, their hike was part of a project to bring attention to preserving Howard Knob at Boone.

In 1989 the Division of Parks and Rec trail staff produced "Mountain to Sea Trail Proposed Trail Routing and Plan of Action" to incorporate passage across the state to include hiking, biking, horseback riding, and canoeing. The proposal was never fully implemented because priority of energy went to rail trails, greenways, and river trails. At the June 23 and September 15, 1995, meetings of the N.C. Trails Committee, the subject was discussed again. The result was a motion by the committee to reaffirm the MST concept and encourage the state trails staff to open discussions with the staff of DOT on working together in creating a multiuse trail system across the state.

Although the state river trails do not connect for a trans-state journey, they have been discussed as part of the multiuse process. Hikers who also like to canoe could consider the following state-designated river trails, listed in order from W to E: *French Broad River Trail* (67.0 mi) (1979); *Yadkin River Trail* (130.0 mi) (1985); *Dan River Trail* (100.0 mi) (1990); *Lower Lumber River Trail* (96.0 mi) (1984); and *Cape Fear River Trail* (150.0 mi) (1995).

Described below are the sections of the MST that have been completed (some of which are "designated," meaning officially accepted as part of the state's trail system), or in the process of completion. Of the 417.0 mi, 180.7 mi are new trails, constructed entirely for the purpose of the MST route. The sections are supervised by citizen task forces that have the assistance and guidance of the N.C. Division of Parks and Rec and N.C. Trails Committee. Some of the current and active task forces in the mountain area are Balsam

Highlands Task Force, South Pisgah Task Force, Central Blue Ridge Task Force and Sauratown Trails Committee. One in the Piedmont is Triangle Greenways Council, and two in the coastal area are Neuse Trail Association and Cherry Point and Carteret Wildlife Club. The *MST* blaze is a white circle with a three-inch diameter.

Not described in this chapter are the fragmented segments E of the mountains. Because they are described in detail elsewhere in the book, the following is a brief summary of their locations. There are 7.5 mi in Doughton Park (BRP) on the *Bluff Mountain Trail;* 10.5 mi in Pilot Mtn State Park following such trails as *Horne Creek, Corridor,* and *Grassy Ridge;* 22.0 mi at Lake Brandt in Guilford County; 5.6 mi in Eno River State Park; 23.4 mi on the *Falls Lake Trail* in Raleigh; 2.0 mi in Cliffs-of-the-Neuse State Park; 20.9 mi on the *Neusiok Trail;* and 75.8 mi on the *Cape Hatteras Beach Trail.* Of these the *Cape Hatteras Beach Trail* was designated a state trail in June 1982; *Nat Greene Historic Trail* at Lake Brandt in September 1983; 13.2 mi of *Falls Lake Trail* in April 1987; *Neusiok Trail* in 1990; and 8.7-mi *Wayne County Trail* in 1991. There are many trail leaders on these task forces. They have a variety of reasons for working on the *MST,* one of which is adventure. Bob Benner of the Central Blue Ridge Task Force said, "On the trail I always feel a quiet excitement in anticipation of what awaits me around the bend, over the next rise, into the next mile...." If you are interested in being active in one of the task forces, creating a task force, or having your club become a task force, contact the following for more information: State Trails Coordinator, Division of Parks and Rec, Yorkshire Center, 12700 Bayleaf Rd, Raleigh, NC 27614; 919-846-9991. If you find errors in this chapter, please contact the author at Louisburg College, 501 North Main St (or Box 3085), Louisburg, NC 27549; 919-496-2521/4771.

MOUNTAINS-TO-SEA TRAIL

Section 1: Clingmans Dome to Smokemont, GSMNP (Swain County)

> LENGTH AND DIFFICULTY: 24.9 mi, strenuous (4,593 ft elev change)
>
> FEATURES: scenic views, Deep Creek, historic site
>
> TRAILS FOLLOWED: *AT, Fork Ridge Trail, Deep Creek Trail, Martins Gap Trail, Sunkota Ridge Trail, Thomas Divide Trail, Newton Bald Trail;* described in chapter 7
>
> TRAIL CONNECTIONS: *Pole Road Creek Trail, Indian Creek Trail, Mingus Creek Trail*
>
> CAMPSITES: designated by number; permit required
>
> TRAILHEAD AND DESCRIPTION: Vehicular access in GSMNP is on Clingmans Dome Rd, 7.0 mi from Newfound Gap Rd (Clingmans Dome Rd is closed in

the winter). Park at the Forney Ridge parking area and hike 0.5 mi on a paved access trail to the *AT* and Clingmans Dome (6,643 ft), the highest point in the Smokies and on the *AT*. An observation tower here provides spectacular panoramic views of the GSMNP. (Clingmans Dome is named in honor of Thomas Lanier Clingman, Smokies explorer, US senator and Civil War general.) (Foot-trail access is 7.5 mi on the *AT* from Newfound Gap parking area.)

Begin the *MST*, N, on the *AT*. At 1.0 mi reach Old Buzzards Roost in a spruce/fir forest; water is R; descend. Reach Mt Collins Gap at 2.0 mi among moosewood, ferns, mosses; ascend to Mt Collins summit (6,188 ft) (named for Robert Collins in 1858 or 1859) at 3.0 mi. At 3.2 mi jct with *Sugarland Mountain Trail*, L, on which is the Mt Collins shelter after 0.4 mi (bunks for 12; a permit is required for overnight camping from the GSMNP; call 615-436-1231 for information and reservations, daily/24 hrs; see introduction in chapter 7). Jct with a spur trail, R, at 3.5 mi that leads 125 ft to Clingmans Dome Rd. (The *AT* continues ahead for 4.0 mi to Newfound Gap and parking area.) Turn R on the spur trail, cross Clingmans Dome Rd to the small parking area and NW trailhead of *Fork Ridge Trail*. (To the R, on the road, it is 3.5 mi to Forney Ridge parking area; to the L it is 3.5 mi to Newfound Gap Rd.) Follow *Fork Ridge Trail* and descend 2,800 ft in elev for the next 5.1 mi. At 3.6 mi pass a spring, golden Alexander, and white snakeroot. Enter a virgin hemlock forest at 5.6 mi and descend on switchbacks. Galax, a laurel and azalea arbor, and views of Bearpen Ridge, R, are at 7.1 mi. At 8.6 mi cross Deep Creek footbridge. End *Fork Ridge Trail* and jct with *Deep Creek Trail*, R and L, and Poke Patch backcountry campsite #53. (Other campsites downstream are Nettle Creek #54 at 11.2 mi; Pole Rd #55 (rationed) at 12.0 mi; Burnt Spruce #56 at 12.3 mi; and Bryson Place #57 (rationed) at 12.8 mi. Self-assigned permits or reservations are required from GSMNP visitor centers or vehicle campgrounds, or call 615-436-1231.) Hike downstream in forest of tall hardwoods and hemlocks. Jct at 12.1 mi with *Pole Road Creek Trail*, R, scenic creek area, and continue downstream; there are signs of wild hog and deer.

At 12.8 mi reach Bryson Place backcountry campsite #57, jct with *Martins Gap Trail*, L, and ascend on it. (This area is historically significant because here Horace Kephart, often referred to as a principal founder of GSMNP and "dean of American campers," had his last long-term campground. Kephart was killed in an automobile accident near Bryson City in April 1931. There is a plaque on a millstone about 200 ft off the trail, R, if you cross a small stream at the trail jct.) (*Deep Creek Trail* continues downstream 3.9 mi to Deep Creek Campground.) At 14.3 mi arrive at Martins Gap

(3,430 ft) and jct R and L with *Sunkota Ridge Trail*; turn L. (*Indian Creek Trail* goes ahead 3.9 mi to jct with *Deep Creek Trail*.) Ascend gradually on the E slope among hardwoods. Wild hogs wallow in the springs. Jct with *Thomas Divide Trail*, R and L, at 19.1 mi. Turn R. At 19.5 mi leave the *Thomas Divide Trail*, turn L, and begin *Newton Bald Trail* to Newton Bald backcountry campsite #52 at 19.7 mi. Water is 150 yd, R, on a steep slope. At 20.2 mi arrive at Newton Bald Ridge (5,142 ft); jct R with *Mingus Creek Trail*. Elev descent for the next 4.7 mi on *Newton Bald Trail* is 2,900 ft. Cross a small stream and pass a tall hemlock grove at 22.6 mi. At 24.4 mi turn L on horse trail, and turn L again after 0.2 mi. At 24.8 mi arrive at Newfound Gap Rd and turn R (hitchhiking prohibited). Reach the parking area at 24.9 mi, opposite the entrance to Smokemont Campground. (It is 3.1 mi S to Oconaluftee Visitor Center, another 0.8 mi to the BRP, and another 0.9 mi into Cherokee for groceries, restaurants, motels, and other services. (A route change is being proposed from the jct of *Newton Bald Trail* and *Mingus Creek Trail*. The routing on the 5.6-mi *Mingus Creek Trail* would make an exit at the Mingus Mill parking lot at Newfound Gap Rd 0.5 mi N of the Oconaluftee Visitor Center **966** and the N trailhead of 1.5-mi *Oconaluftee River Trail*. Such a change would also provide a greater diversity of plant and animal life in a 3,030-ft drop in elev from dry ridges to the wet hollow of Mudcap Branch after 3.0 mi.) (For updated information call the N.C. Division of Parks and Rec regional trail specialist at 704-251-6208.) (*USGS Maps:* Clingmans Dome, Smokemont)

Section 2
GSMNP and BRP (mp 469.1) on the BRP to Soco Gap, US-19 and BRP (mp 455.7) (14.4 mi plus) (*MST* in planning stage) (Swain and Jackson Counties) (Blue Ridge Motel and food 0.3 mi S on US-19 from Soco Gap.)

Section 3
Soco Gap, US-19, and BRP (mp 455.7) on the BRP to Balsam Gap (S), US-23/74, and BRP (mp 443.1) (12.0 mi plus) (*MST* in advanced planning stage) (Jackson County) (Best Western Motel and food 4.7 mi N on US-23/74 from Balsam Gap.)

Section 4
Balsam Gap (S) (BRP mp 443.1) to Bear Pen Gap (BRP mp 427.6) (Jackson County)
> LENGTH AND DIFFICULTY: 24.2 mi, strenuous (2,245 ft elev change)
> FEATURES: scenic views, wildlife, wildflowers, solitude
> TRAIL CONNECTION: *West Camp Gap Trail*

CAMPSITES: off the trail in Nantahala NF (prohibited on BRP property)

TRAILHEAD AND DESCRIPTION: There are two Balsam Gaps on the BRP. Here is S and the other, N, is in Section 11. (At Balsam Gap S is the W jct of the BRP and the state's longest bicycle route, Mountains-to-Sea, Route #2. To the SW from here on US-23/74 and to US-64 it goes to Murphy, its W terminus. On its way E it follows the BRP from here 129.0 mi to leave the BRP at mp 314 onto NC-1813, L, for 0.9 mi to NC-181 at Jonas Ridge. After 5.3 mi down the mountain on NC-181 it crosses the hiking *MST* for the last time before its next crossing at Falls Lake, N of Raleigh.)

In Balsam Gap (3,370 ft) on US-23/74 (8.0 mi S of Waynesville and 12.0 mi N of Sylva) at 0.2 mi S after the BRP underpass, turn E off US-23/74 at the end of a guardrail. Cross the RR, turn L, and park near the RR in a grassy area. Walk back to the entrance near a school bus stop shelter; a trail blaze and sign precedes the *MST* into the forest with dense understory. Cross a footbridge at 0.1 mi before two switchbacks. Cross a ridge and descend to a series of small stream crossings, all flowing N. Pass near the BRP boundary and R of an old homesite foundation at 1.3 mi. At 1.4 mi cross Hood Rd and a stream before ascending seven switchbacks. Cross Red Bank Rd at 2.4 mi. (Here is an access point L [N] to the BRP; at the R [S] end is a rock overlook). Cross Red Bank Creek at 2.5 mi, then ascend eight switchbacks. Along the way in dense vegetation are logs with shelf fungi and rock tripe. At 3.1 mi is a view L of a BRP overlook below and Waynesville in the valley. A wood vine, Dutchman's pipe, is at 3.7 mi. Cross a variety of Grassy Bald spur ridges, one of which is Pinnacle Ridge where a BRP tunnel (unseen from the trail) is L at 4.9 mi. Arrive at a small clearing (4,920 ft) at 5.6 mi. Views of the BRP are SW and peaks S (R). Wild quinine grows here.

Ascend four switchbacks and gradually climb to a rocky area and yellow birch (5,400 ft) at 7.4 mi. Pass patches of trailing arbutus and galax among beech at 7.9 mi. At 8.2 mi approach a grassy ridge with a spur trail to the L for NE views. For the next 1.1 mi are scattered flame azalea, blue-bead lily, and wood sorrel among hardwoods and conifers. Arrive at Licklog Gap (5,135 ft) at 9.3 mi. Ascend and reach BRP overlook (mp 435.3) Doubletop Mtn at 10.0 mi. (A spur trail L is 145 ft to the S end of overlook parking.) Continue among chestnut oak, Indian snakeroot, and yellow birch to Old Bald Ridge at 11.2 mi. (The above segment was designated a state trail September 1992.) (A spur trail L is 0.1 mi to a curve in the BRP, mp 434.2.) Turn R, follow an old road on Old Bald Ridge into Nantahala NF property; descend. At 11.8 mi turn sharply L at an old road jct. After 0.2 mi leave the roadbed (watch for trail blaze) into a grassy mountainside where there are blueberry patches, evergreens, and wildflowers. There are scenic views S and SW of the Tuckasegee River Valley and Great Balsam Mtns. At 12.3 mi turn L onto an old roadbed. Leave the footpath at 13.0 mi; turn L on an old roadbed in an open forest with fern carpets. Descend among large chestnut oaks. At 13.5 mi turn sharply L. For the next 0.4 mi cross a number of streamlets and R turns on two old roadbeds.

At 14.5 mi leave the old roadbed and enter a footpath through wildflowers and scattered elephant plant, elm, and rhododendron in a cove. Ascend four switchbacks. At 15.4 mi ascend two switchbacks. For the next 0.5 mi is a rocky and damp section with a rough treadway; a botanical paradise. Exit the footpath to an old road at 16.1 mi; take a L turn over a tank trap at 16.4 mi. (Here and elsewhere for the next 8.5 mi may be horse and bike traffic. Some natural campsites are along the way.) Ascend, cross rocky cascading stream at 16.7 mi. Keep R at a road fork. Cross a small stream, the headwaters of Beechflat Creek at 16.7 mi, Chestnut Creek at 17.9 mi, and Bearwater Creek at 19.3 mi. At 19.8 mi begin a descent on a series of switchbacks to jct with a USFS road R at 20.3 mi. Cohosh (both black and blue) and other wildflowers such as baneberry (*Actaea pachypoda*) are on the trail for the next 0.4 mi. Deer, turkey, and squirrel are in the area. Cross Birch Ridge Creek at 21.1 mi and Piney Mtn Creek at 22.0 mi. (Here is an abandoned road, L, steeply up to the BRP.) For the next 1.8 mi the trail is on a generally even contour with 10 streamlets flowing R to Piney Mtn Creek. At 23.4 mi jct with other woods roads; stay L and ascend steeply to jct with *West Camp Gap Trail,* R and L, at 24.2 mi. (The above segment was designated a state trail in August 1994.) (To the R the *MST* continues.) It is 0.6 mi L to Bear Pen Gap parking overlook on the BRP (mp 427.6) (5,560 ft). On the BRP W it is 7.7 mi back to Doubletop Overlook, and another 7.8 mi to Balsam Gap (S). (*USGS Maps:* Hazelwood, Tuckasegee, Sam Knob)

Section 5

Bear Pen Gap (BRP mp 427.6) to NC-215 (BRP mp 423.2) (Jackson and Haywood Counties)

LENGTH AND DIFFICULTY: 8.5 mi, easy to moderate

FEATURES: wildlife, blueberries, songbirds, wildflowers

TRAILS FOLLOWED: *West Camp Gap Trail, Buckeye Gap Trail*

TRAIL CONNECTION: *Haywood Gap Trail*

CAMPSITES: West Camp Gap in Nantahala NF; Pisgah NF 0.2 mi after Buckeye Gap (BRP mp 425.5)

TRAILHEAD AND DESCRIPTION: This section is unique because it stays 1.0

mi high in elev for the entire distance and is the only section where the *MST* passes from the Nantahala NF to the Pisgah NF across the BRP. Access: At the Bear Pen Gap parking lot on the BRP (mp 427.6) (5,560 ft) at the SE corner enter the *Bear Pen Gap Trail,* which becomes the *West Camp Gap Trail* after 0.1 mi to the Nantahala NF. Cross a streamlet at 0.4 mi and by a grove of yellow birch and a jct with the *MST,* ahead and R, at 0.6 mi. (The R access is described above.) Continue ahead, curving L and jointly with the *West Camp Gap Trail* for an ascent on an eroded dirt road (used by ORVs). After 0.6 mi arrive at an open area, the end of *West Camp Gap Trail.* The *MST* abruptly turns L off the old road near a rock and among goldenrod and asters. After 110 ft it reenters the woods. (To the R on the old road is a large grassy plateau, excellent for campsites. Deer, turkey, and songbirds frequent the area.)

After entering the woods begin to ascend the E side of Rough Butt Bald (5,925 ft) on switchbacks at 1.0 mi, in a segment of wildflowers. At 1.4 mi enter a berry field: blueberry, blackberry, strawberry, and gooseberry. On the airy slope are ferns, gentians, fly poison, songbirds, butterflies, and honeybees. Continue among red spruce, hardwoods, and rhododendron to Haywood Gap of the BRP (mp 426.5) (5,225 ft). Cross the BRP and enter a thick mint patch to jct with the *Haywood Gap Trail,* L after 185 ft. (A descent of 0.2 mi on the *Haywood Gap Trail,* into the Pisgah NF, leads to a spring [Sweetwater Spring]). Follow a handcrafted footpath through a beautiful forest of red spruce, birch, rhododendron, maple, and wood sorrel. There are springs along the way. Curve around Parker Knob and an unnamed knob. At 4.1 mi reach Buckeye Gap (BRP mp 425.5), and jct with *Buckeye Gap Trail* L and R. Turn L on an old RR grade. (Up the bank, R, it is 260 yd to Rough Butt Bald Overlook access, BRP mp 425.4.) From here to NC-215 is Pisgah NF property; camping is allowed.

Make a sharp R at 4.8 mi among red spruce, yellow birch, turtlehead, and ferns. At 5.1 mi cross Buckeye Creek, which cascades L. Go 75 yd to a sharp turn R, up the bank, and ascend. (*Buckeye Gap Trail* continues ahead on an old RR grade with RR artifacts. See chapter 3, section 3.) Enter an open area of blueberry and blackberry patches. At 5.6 mi cross the headwaters of Buckeye Creek; ferns, birch, and rhododendron are prominent. Jct with an old trail, R, at 5.8 mi. Keep L and descend easily. Leave the foot trail at 6.5 mi and follow an old RR grade. At 6.7 mi are views of Beech Gap ahead, Mt Hardy R, and more blackberry patches on the trailside. After another 0.2 mi there are views of large cliffs on Fork Ridge, L. Cross a ravine at 7.1 mi and follow R of old RR grade, but rejoin it after 0.2 mi. Turn L sharply to follow another old RR grade. Arrive at the confluence of streams in a rocky streambed at 7.5 mi. Rock-hop and enter an area of rhododendron and fetterbush. Follow an old RR grade to a grazing field. At 8.1 mi reenter the woods, pass a spring R, and follow the old road. Reach NC-215 at 8.3 mi, turn R, up the paved road, and cross a bridge over cascading Bubbling Spring Branch. The *MST* continues L, up an embankment at 8.5 mi. (The parking area is up the road 200 ft, R, and 0.5 mi ahead is the BRP in Beech Gap.) (It is 4.4 mi back on the BRP to Bear Pen Gap parking lot.) This 8.5-mi part of the *MST* was designated a state trail in May 1987. (*USGS Map:* Sam Knob)

Section 6

Beech Gap, NC-215 (BRP mp 423.2) to Mt Pisgah Inn (BRP mp 408.6) (Haywood and Transylvania Counties)

LENGTH AND DIFFICULTY: 37.7 mi, strenuous (3,835 ft elev change)

FEATURES: scenic views, wildlife, Pilot Mtn, Davidson River, botanical diversity

TRAILS FOLLOWED: *Art Loeb Trail, Sycamore Cove Trail, Black Mountain Trail, Buck Spring Trail*

TRAIL CONNECTIONS: *Little Sam Knob Trail, Devil's Courthouse Spur Trail, Farlow Gap Trail, Butter Gap Trail, Cat Gap Loop Trail, North Slope Connector Trail, Grass Road Trail, Thrift Cove Trail, Pressley Cove Trail, Turkey Pen Gap Trail, Pink Beds Loop Trail*

CAMPSITES: two shelters on the *Art Loeb Trail,* one shelter on *Black Mountain Trail;* Davidson River Campground; off Pisgah NF trails (no camping on BRP property or Davidson River bridge area)

TRAILHEAD AND DESCRIPTION: (This section is part of 63.0 mi designated a state trail in September 1985. A new 11.6-mi connector trail has been constructed near or on BRP property. The new connector and the current *MST* can become the longest and most topographically diverse loop [41.0 mi] of any in the state's national forests. For an update on the progress of the loop option call regional trail specialist at 704-251-6208.)

At the parking area described above, at the end of Section 5, descend 200 ft on NC-215 to embankment, R, and enter a rhododendron thicket. At 0.5 mi cross a cascading stream in a grove of yellow birch, and after a ravine crossing begin ascent on six switchbacks. Curve around a low knob to views of Devil's Courthouse at 1.0 mi. At 1.5 mi a short spur, R, provides views of Devil's Courthouse. Enter a dense and beautiful conifer grove. At 2.0 mi jct R with a 0.1-mi spur to *Devil's Courthouse Trail* (and another 0.1 mi to a spectacular overlook). (*Devil's Courthouse Trail* descends 0.3 mi to the BRP.) At

2.2 mi jct L with *Little Sam Knob Trail*. Ahead, 0.1 mi, is a large rock outcropping, L; a climb provides splendid views of Mt Hardy and Little Sam Knob. Curve around Chestnut Bald in patches of large sweet blackberry (ripe the second week in August). Jct with the *Art Loeb Trail*, L and R, near Silvermine Bald at 3.2 mi. Here is the S jct of the *MST*, R, and the new *MST* connector L to FR-816. (The yellow-blazed *Art Loeb Trail* goes L 1.1 mi to FR-816, and beyond 10.9 mi to the N terminus at the Daniel Boone BSA campground.)

(If hiking the new *MST Connector* begin at the jct of the *Art Loeb Trail* and FR-816 [off the BRP mp 420.2]. Descend through a grove of red spruce, then out into the open among grasses and ragwort. Cross a footbridge over cascades [the headwaters of Yellowstone Prong] at 0.5 mi. Ascend on the scenic E slope of Black Balsam Knob in thick grasses, blueberry bushes, and scattered rocks. Descend into a beech grove at 1.3 mi. At 1.6 mi cross *Graveyard Ridge Trail* [old RR bed] [USFS #356, 3.4 mi, whose S trailhead is at Graveyard Fields, BRP mp 418.8; the N trailhead is a jct with the *Art Loeb Trail* at Ivestor Gap]. [See chapter 6 and chapter 3, sec 3.])

Descend on the N side of Graveyard Ridge, join an old RR bed at 2.8 mi, but after 50 yd leave it to enter a beech grove and conifers. Jct R with 0.2-mi spur trail to Yellowstone Falls at 3.5 mi. (The spur trail connects with a bridge over the river to Graveyard Fields Overlook of the BRP, mp 418.8, and *Graveyard Trail*, USFS #358, loop.) Continue on the connector through rhododendron in a descent to a rocky area and cross a ravine at 4.3 mi. Curve around the E end of Graveyard Ridge after switchbacks among cherry and other hardwoods at 4.5 mi. Keep R from side trail L. Cross the skillfully constructed footbridge over Yellowstone Prong of the East Fork of Pigeon River at 5.0 mi. Upstream are cascades and waterfalls, underneath the bridge is a crystal clear pool. Ascend steps, pass a handcrafted wall to prevent erosion, and jct with a spur trail at 5.3 mi. (The spur goes R 150 yd to Looking Glass Rock Overlook on the BRP mp 417 [4,493 ft].)

Continue L, gently descend to Bridges Camp Gap, cross an unmarked trail to the East Fork of Pigeon River at 5.6 mi, and begin an ascent on a ridge. Descend to Tunnel Gap on the BRP, mp 415.6, at 6.7 mi. Follow the W shoulder of the BRP for 0.1 mi to reenter the forest in rhododendron, laurel, and galax on Chestnut Ridge. Descend, cross the BRP at 7.5 mi, ascend a knoll, and descend to cross the BRP in Bennett Gap at 8.0 mi. Ascend gradually to the W side at cliffs of Green Knob, a habitat for wild turkey (5,056 ft) at 8.8 mi. Return to the main ridgeline for a descent on switchbacks. Reach the BRP at Pigeon Gap, mp 412.5, at 9.9 mi. Cross the BRP under a CP & L power line, curve around a knob, and cross US-276 at 10.3 mi (0.4 mi to BRP overpass is L, and 1.6 mi R to S trailhead and parking area for *Buck Spring Trail*, L). Enter a tunnel of laurel and rhododendron on Wagon Rd Ridge and cross small headwater streams at 10.8 mi, 320 yd to another, and a third at 11.3 mi. Descend to steps and jct at *Buck Spring Trail* at a stream at 11.6 mi. (To the L it is 290 yd to jct with the *MST*. To the R it is 0.9 mi to the parking area on US-276.) (*USGS-FS Maps:* Sam Knob, Shining Rock, Cruso)

If hiking the original *MST*, turn R and descend on the *Art Loeb Trail* for the next 18.0 mi, a descent of 3,835 ft. At 3.6 mi cross the BRP and descend into a hardwood forest. At 5.1 mi jct with the blue-blazed *Farlow Gap Trail*, L, and at 6.1 mi arrive at an **A**-frame shelter. (Water is 75 yd NW of the shelter.) Ascend on switchbacks to Pilot Mtn (5,040 ft) for panoramic views at 6.8 mi. Descend on multiple switchbacks and reach Gloucester Rd (FR-475) at 9.0 mi. (To the E, L, it is 6.7 mi to US-276.) At 12.4 mi jct with *Butter Gap Trail*, L, and 0.9-mi *Cedar Rock Trail* ahead; continue R on the *Art Loeb Trail*. Reach the Cedar Rock **A**-frame shelter near a stream and other campsites at 12.6 mi. Pass *Cedar Rock Trail*, L, at 14.0 mi, and *Cat Gap Loop Trail*, L (formerly *Horse Cove Trail*), at 15.0 mi. At 17.6 mi on a N ridge of Stony Knob jct with *North Slope Connector Trail*. (It is a steep 1.1-mi yellow-blazed trail down the mtn to jct with 3.7-mi *North Slope Loop Trail* at Davidson River Campground.) Pass Neils Gap at 17.9 mi. Begin the final descent at 20.0 mi to the Davidson River, cross a footbridge over Joel Branch, pass through a floodplain of tall poplar and oak, and cross the Davidson River swinging bridge at 21.2 mi, the end of the *Art Loeb Trail*. To the R the *MST* continues across US-276.

(To the L is an old road 0.3 mi to a parking lot at an entrance road from US-276, R, to Davidson River Campground, L, across the bridge. Ahead, across the entrance road and for 230 ft on a svc rd is a foot trail R for 0.3 mi to Pisgah Ranger Station Visitor Center on US-276. At the station is an outdoor telephone. The large seasonal campground [full svc April–November] has hot showers, outdoor telephone, but no hookups. The campground is free December–March, phone in season: 704-877-4910/862-5960. East on US-276, 1.2 mi, is a jct with US-64 and NC-280, shopping center, motel, and restaurant. On US-64/276 S toward the town of Brevard at 2.2 mi is V&A Wash House Laundromat [corner of Osborne Rd], which has hot showers for hikers all year [8 AM to 8 PM daily, 9 AM to 6 PM Sunday], phone 704-884-9358.)

To continue on the *MST* from the swinging bridge, turn R, cross a small stream, and turn sharply L at 50 yd to cross US-276 and join *Sycamore Trail*. Follow it jointly on a low area through tall poplar, hemlock, beech, and sycamore. Alder, spicebush, and ferns border the trail. After 0.6 mi the *Sycamore Trail* curves R and the *MST* goes ahead. Jct with the *Grassy Road*

Trail R and the *Thrift Cove Trail* (Rd). (*Thrift Cove Trail* also goes L 0.2 mi to *Black Mountain Trail*.) Walk up *Thrift Cove Trail* (Rd) 230 ft, turn L on a footpath, and descend. Cross streams and jct with *Black Mountain Trail* at 22.2 mi. (It is 0.5 mi L to *Black Mountain Trail* entrance at the parking area near the forest maintenance center.) Turn R and follow the *Black Mountain Trail* for the next 6.5 mi; elev increase of 1,984 ft. At 24.7 mi jct L with the orange-blazed *Pressley Cove Trail,* and jct R with *Turkey Pen Gap Trail* at 25.7 mi. Arrive at Clawhammer Mtn (4,140 ft) at 26.4 mi for superb views. Descend to *Buckhorn Gap Trail* jct, R and L, at 27.5 mi. Ascend embankment and at 27.8 mi arrive at Buckhorn Gap Shelter, R (bunk beds; a spring is nearby). Ascend to Rich Mtn where the MST leaves the *Black Mountain Trail* at 28.8 mi and follows a new trail down the NW slopes of Soapstone Ridge to cross the Pink Beds. (The *Black Mountain Trail* goes 0.8 mi to end and jct with *Club Gap Trail* and *Avery Creek Trail.* See Pisgah Ranger District, chapter 3, sec 3.)

Descend on an old timber road, cross a small stream at 29.5 mi, and at 30.3 mi leave the old road in a curve, L, to descend on a ridge spur. Pass through a grassy open forest; at 31.1 mi jct R and L with the orange-blazed *Pink Beds Loop Trail.* Turn L, go 75 yd, turn R off the *Pink Beds Loop Trail,* and go another 75 yd to cross a log footbridge over the South Fork of Mills River. Pass through a beautiful fern glen of the Pink Beds and cross the N side of the *Pink Beds Loop Trail* at 31.4 mi. Follow an old road through white pine, hemlock, and oak to FR-1206 at 31.9 mi. (Parking area is L 200 ft.) (To the L FR-1206 goes 1.3 mi to US-276.) Cross FR-1206 and at 32.2 mi pass R of cascades and ascend on switchbacks to jct with *Buck Spring Trail,* R and L at 32.6 mi in a hardwood forest of oak, hickory, and maple. (*Buck Spring Trail* goes L 1.1 mi to US-276; 0.2 mi L from here is the jct with the MST connector.) Turn R and ascend on the *Buck Spring Trail* for 5.1 mi to the Pisgah Inn on the BRP at 37.7 mi. (Facilities here are seasonal with a restaurant, motel, campground, and svc sta, but there is an outdoor public telephone.) Pisgah Inn, phone 704-235-8228, is usually open April 1 to November 1; Mt Pisgah Campground is usually open May 1 to November 1. (*USGS Maps:* Sam Knob, Shining Rock, Pisgah Forest, Cruso)

Section 7

Pisgah Inn (BRP mp 408.6) to Folk Art Center (BRP mp 382) (Transylvania, Henderson, Buncombe Counties)

LENGTH AND DIFFICULTY: 31.7 mi, moderate hiking N; strenuous hiking S (3,611 ft elev change)

FEATURES: Mt Pisgah, scenic views, French Broad River

TRAILS FOLLOWED: *Buck Spring Trail* (BRP), *Shut-in Trail*

TRAIL CONNECTIONS: *Pilot Rock Trail, Laurel Mountain Trail, Mt Pisgah Trail, Bad Fork Trail, Sleepy Gap Trail, Grassy Knob Trail*

CAMPSITES: Pisgah NF off trails and Lake Powhatan

TRAILHEAD AND DESCRIPTION: For information on seasonal lodging and food see BRP, chapter 6. Begin at the trail signboard at the NE corner of the Pisgah Inn parking lot to follow the 1.1-mi BRP *Buck Spring Trail*. At the start there is a connection R to *Pilot Rock Trail* (USFS), and at 0.7 mi is a jct R with *Laurel Mountain Trail* (USFS). At 1.0 mi is the historic site of Vanderbilt's Buck Spring Hunting Lodge. At Buck Spring Gap parking overlook, the *Buck Spring Trail* ends, and the *Shut-in Trail* begins. The MST continues on the *Shut-in Trail* (a national recreation trail, like the *Buck Spring Trail*). (The 16.4 mi *Shut-in Trail* oscillates between the BRP boundaries and the Pisgah NF boundaries. Because the boundary lines are not always obvious, camping should be planned for the Lake Powhatan Campground, or off trails and roads on known NF property about 11.5 mi ahead.) (See chapter 3, sec 3.)

To access the *Mt Pisgah Trail* from the Buck Spring Gap parking lot, walk 0.2 mi N on the access road to the Mt Pisgah parking lot. (Also, once on the *Shut-in Trail* hikers may notice a side trail, L, to access the *Mt Pisgah Trail*.) Access points to the MST are at NC-151 (Elk Pastures Gap, mp 405.5) at 2.9 mi; Mills River Valley Overlook (mp 404.5) at 4.1 mi; Big Ridge Overlook (mp 403.6) at 5.1 mi; Stoney Bald Overlook (mp 402.6) at 6.3 mi; and Beaver Dam Gap Overlook (mp 401.7) at 7.2 mi. The forest is chiefly oak/hickory with locust, laurel, rhododendron, and birch. At 7.9 mi is an excellent view of the city of Asheville and Craggy Mtns. Bent Creek Gap (mp 400.3 mi) has a road under the BRP at 9.2 mi. To the N it is Bent Creek Rd and to the S it is Wash Creek Rd. (Under the BRP, S, is the N trailhead of 1.8-mi *Bad Fork Trail*. It begins off the edge of the BRP ramp and descends steeply to a network of trails in the North Mills River headwaters of the Pisgah NF (see chapter 3, sec 3).

The next BRP access is Chestnut Cove Overlook (mp 398.3) at 11.9 mi. Through oak, maple, and dense groves of laurel arrive at Sleepy Gap Overlook (mp 397.3) at 12.6 mi. (*Sleepy Gap Trail* descends L into the Pisgah NF to connect with other trails near Lake Powhatan.) At 13.5 mi is *Grassy Knob Trail*, R and L. (To the L it descends to cross South Ridge Rd [FR-479M] in Bent Creek Experimental Forest. The trail connects to *Pine Tree Loop Trail* for an access to Lake Powhatan Campground. The fee campground has hot showers, flush toilets, swimming, and outside telephone. Open April 15 to November 1.) Continuing on the MST, reach Walnut Cove Overlook (mp 396.4) at 14.4 mi. For the next 3.1 mi the trail descends gradually and skirts E of Hard-times Rd. After curving around the E side of Glen Bald it stays E of Shut-In Ridge. In the descent poplar, dogwoods, ferns, and wildflowers are prominent with oak and maple. Pass through a gate of the N.C. Arboretum and descend to the last switchback in a rhododendron thicket at 17.5 mi. To the L is a spring. (Here is the former parking lot for the N terminus of the *Shut-in Trail*.) Follow the trail through rhododendron and pass through another arboretum gate. Exit at the BRP ramp at 17.9 mi. The *MST* turns R on the ramp to the BRP and S end of the French Broad River bridge (mp 393.6). On the BRP, R (S) it is 0.1 mi to French Broad River Overlook, an excellent parking space (daytime only) for the *Shut-In Trail* or continuing N on the *MST*.

(Hikers may find changes in accessing the *MST* at the ramp in the next few years. The future main entrance road to the N.C. Arboretum will be constructed in the ramp's curve, where current hikers (and bikers on the Bent Creek Rd) are parking. The ramp connects with NC-191, where a L turn is 2.0 mi to a large shopping center, motels, and restaurants.)

After descending the embankment to the BRP entrance road, turn R, walk 0.1 mi to the French Broad River bridge, and turn L. Cross the bridge to the N end at 18.2 mi. Go 35 yd and turn R into an open hardwood forest. Pass under a power line at 18.3 mi, enter a white pine grove but leave it at 18.8 mi. At 18.9 mi cross an old road that goes under the BRP. Ascend and descend on gentle hills, cross the BRP at 19.5 mi, and enter an oak-hickory forest. Join an old woods road and arrive at the I-26 underpass at 19.8 mi (no vehicle access to I-26). Cross the bridge, turn R into the forest at 19.9 mi. Cross a gravel road at 20.2 mi. In a mixed forest pass through wild orchids, galax, arbutus, wild ginger, and laurel. At 20.4 mi pass a man-made spring, R. Cross a number of used roads (that lead to private property) and cross a small stream at 21.0 mi. Pass through a rhododendron and laurel thicket and cross a vehicle bridge over Dingle Creek at 21.2 mi. Pass under tall oaks and white pines. Cross a gravel road at 22.2 mi (L it goes under the BRP) and other woods roads ahead. Cross a vehicle bridge over Fourmile Branch at 22.8 mi, and go under a grove of tall white pine at 23.2 mi. At 23.4 mi arrive at the US-25 bridge (BRP mp 388.8) and access ramps. (It is 2.9 mi L [N] to I-40 and S Asheville, and 16.0 mi R to Hendersonville.)

After crossing the bridge stay on the W side of the BRP for the next 5.7 mi on an easy treadway. The forest is a mixture of hardwoods, white pine, fern, and partridgeberry beds. Cross a Southern RR bridge (mp 388.5), US-25A bridge (mp 388.1) (5.0 mi W to Asheville), US-74 bridge (mp 384.7) (also 5.0 mi W to Asheville), and at 29.1 mi cross under the BRP in a box culvert (mp 384.2). Make a sharp L off a forest rd and ascend a hillside, then coves, before descending on a high bank of steps to an I-40 underpass (mp 383.7) at 30.1 mi. Pass a fence stile at 30.2 mi, cross Southern RR tracks, and after 50 yd cross Swannanoa River bridge and Azalea Rd. Enter a fence stile to a meadow and exit it through another fence stile. Pass between a private residence and the BRP at 30.4 mi. Enter a Virginia pine thicket and poison ivy beds at 30.7 mi. Pass under a powerline and arrive at the BRP to walk on the W shoulder. Cross US-70 on BRP bridge (mp 382.6) at 31.1 mi. (There are shopping centers, motels, and restaurants E and W on US-70.) Cross the BRP ramp at 31.2 mi, go up an embankment into the forest, and approach the Folk Art Center and Visitor Center parking lot at 31.5 mi. On the side of the *MST* is a plaque in honor of Arch Nichols (1907–89), distinguished leader and trail volunteer worker in the Carolina Mountain Club. Arrive at the center's entrance (mp 382) at 31.7 mi. (The center has a major display and sales of traditional and contemporary crafts of the Southern Highlands. There is also a library and museum. Open daily 9 AM to 6 PM; phone 704-298-7928.) (*USGS Maps:* Cruso, Dunsmore Mtn, Skyland, Asheville, Oteen)

Section 8

Folk Art Center (BRP mp 382) to Balsam Gap (N) (BRP mp 359.8) (Buncombe County)

LENGTH AND DIFFICULTY: 22.7 mi, moderate to strenuous

FEATURES: scenic views, historic site, wildflowers

TRAIL CONNECTIONS: *Rattlesnake Lodge Trail* (mp 374.4), *Snowball Trail* (USFS), *Douglas Falls Trail* (USFS), *Big Butt Trail* (BRP and USFS)

CAMPSITES: only on the W side of the BRP boundary in the Toecane Ranger District of Pisgah NF, off the trail

TRAILHEAD AND DESCRIPTION: At the Folk Art Center (BRP 382), which has a major display of traditional crafts of the southern highlands, park at the nearest parking area near the main gate. Begin the trail at the entrance gate, follow the trail sign, and parallel the BRP. Cross a bridge over Riceville Rd (SR-2002) at 0.2 mi. Cross a number of old trails and roads; pass over a water line at 0.5 mi, and cross the BRP at 0.9 mi. Descend and ascend, partly following an old woods road. On an ascent at 2.3 mi is a short spur L for scenic views of NE Asheville. Ascend on a narrow ridge, then a slope, until the mtn top at 2.8 mi in an area of laurel, hardwoods, and gentian. Descend, frequently using old logging roads, cross a streamlet at 3.7 mi, enter a laurel thicket at 4.5 mi and a wildflower patch at 4.7 mi. At 5.2 mi arrive at Craven Gap (mp 377.4) and jct with NC-694. Cross the BRP to a parking area at 5.3 mi, and at the NW corner continue on the *MST*. Ascend on a scenic rocky E slope of Rice Knob in an oak-hickory forest to encounter large banks of wildflowers such as flame azalea, wild geranium, crested dwarf iris, mtn mint, and sedum. At 5.9 mi jct R with a spur trail that descends 0.2 mi to Tanbark Ridge Overlook (mp 376.7). At 6.4 mi cross a streamlet, and at 6.8 mi begin a descent on a ridge. Cross paved Ox Creek Rd (SR-2109) at 7.0 mi. (To the R it is 0.1 mi to the BRP.) Follow the footpath to the end of a ridge and descend on nine short switchbacks to Bull Gap at 7.7 mi. (To the L it is 60 yd to Ox Creek Rd.) At the former carriage entrance to Rattlesnake Lodge, begin on the old carriage road and ascend on nine switchbacks for 0.7 mi. On a scenic route pass through rock formations and gardens of wildflowers in a hardwood forest. Reach remnants of Rattlesnake Lodge at 9.2 mi. A spring is L. Jct here with *Rattlesnake Lodge Trail,* which descends steeply, R, 0.4 mi to the BRP (mp 374.4) and a small parking area (see chapter 6). (The lodge was constructed in 1900–1901 by Dr C. P. Ambler of Asheville for a family summer home. In an article in *Forest and Stream* in 1906 there is a description of the area's wildlife [wildcat, turkey, grouse, rattlesnakes (41 killed the first three years of the lodge)], and many species of birds [scarlet tanager, indigo bird, wood robin, and chewink for examples]).

At 9.3 mi cross a streamlet and pass spur trails R and L. Ascend into a laurel thicket at 9.5 mi and arrive at a spring whose water feeds a patch of bee balm and other wildflowers. A spur trail, L, is on the mountainside. Ascend an old and well-graded trail among hardwoods and wildflowers for the next 0.8 mi to a ridge on Bull Mountain range. Turn I and follow the ridge with undulations. At 11.3 mi pass through a buckeye grove and by a rocky ledge, L, at 11.7 mi. Arrive at the summit of Wolfden Knob at 11.9 mi. Rocky ledges and switchbacks continue for the next 0.8 mi. From the summit area of Lane Pinnacle (5,230 ft) is a scenic view of Beetree Reservoir, R (SE) at 12.7 mi. More rock walls follow with superb views at 13.1 mi. Lichens, mosses, ferns, sedum, and Virginia spiderwort inhabit the rock crevices and ledges. Scenic views are also at 13.3 mi. Descend on switchbacks to a saddle, ascend to a short ridge, and descend again to arrive at the BRP in Potato Field Gap at 14.1 mi (BRP mp 368.2), the Woodfin Watershed. Walk on the W shoulder of the BRP for 100 yd. Reenter the woods, ascend on switchbacks into a hawthorne grove. Reach a scenic view among rocks, phlox, and blueberry bushes, locust, and mtn ash. At 15.4 mi jct L with *Snowball Trail,* and cross FR-63 in Beartree Gap (BRP mp 367.6). Ahead, NE is the entrance road to Craggy Gardens picnic area. Right of the entrance road ascend an embankment, pass a spring, L, at 15.3 mi, and jct with a spur trail, L, to the picnic area parking lot at 15.4 mi.

The MST continues through the picnic area, crosses a svc rd, goes into a rhododendron grove, and descends to an old RR grade at 15.6 mi. Turn R and after 0.5 mi leave the grade on a L turn. Follow a footpath, curve around Craggy Pinnacle on switchbacks through yellow birch, ferns, and white snakeroot. Arrive at jct with *Douglas Falls Trail*, L, at 17.1 mi. (*Douglas Falls Trail* descends 2.5 mi to a scenic gorge and to an isolated entrance road and parking area. See Toecane Ranger District, chapter 3, sec 4.) Continue on the MST around the W slope of the ridge, partially on a rocky treadway to ascend on switchbacks. At 18.2 mi is a spring among rhododendron. Ascend steps to a svc rd, pass a US government building, and reach the BRP at 18.6 mi (mp 363.6) (5,592 ft). Cross the BRP at Graybeard Mtn sign; turn L (N). Follow the blazes in a rocky area, rhododendron arbors, and a dark grove of conifers. Curve W on the slope of Bullhead Mtn.

After coming out on the crest of the Great Craggy Mtns explore the side trails, R, between 19.4 mi and 20.8 mi. From knob to knob are multiple scenic overlooks, naturally landscaped with dense blueberry bushes, laurel, mosses, pungent galax, and pastel-colored lichens. Scattered in rocky apertures are yellow birch and chestnut oaks. Unforgettable as may be the views, camping is prohibited. The views to the SE are of the Asheville Watershed in the valley of the North Fork of Swannanoa River and Burnett Reservoir. East of the lake is the Blue Ridge Mtn range with Graybeard Mtn a landmark. To the W is Ivy Creek Valley and the Walnut Mtn range beyond.

Descend to the BRP parking lot at 21.2 mi (mp 361.2) (5,197 ft). Here is an overlook of Glassmine Falls, E. Follow the shoulder of the BRP, descend on steps to Cotton Tree Gap, then ascend at 21.5 mi. After another knob, descend to begin five switchbacks up the W edge of Walker Knob (5,482 ft); descend on three switchbacks among evergreens and hardwoods to Balsam Gap (N) (mp 359.8) (5,320 ft). Cross the BRP to a parking lot at 22.7 mi. (*USGS Maps:* Oteen, Craggy Pinnacle, Montreat)

Section 9
Balsam Gap (N) (BRP mp 359.8) to Buck Creek Gap (BRP mp 344.1)/NC-80 (Yancey County)

    LENGTH AND DIFFICULTY: 19.6 mi, strenuous (elev change 3,091 ft)
    FEATURES: high altitude, scenic views, wildlife, historic sites
    TRAILS FOLLOWED: *Buncombe Horse Range Trail, Mt Mitchell Trail*
    TRAIL CONNECTIONS: *Big Butt Trail, Higgins Bald Trail*

CAMPSITES: Off the trail in Pisgah NF and at Black Mtn Campground (prohibited on BRP property)

TRAILHEAD AND DESCRIPTION: From the parking lot at Balsam Gap (N) on the BRP (mp 359.8) and S trailhead of *Big Butt Trail,* follow the white circle blazes on a sharp R off the old RR grade. After 75 yd begin to ascend on a series of 22 switchbacks among red spruce and hemlock. On the ascent are wooden steps at 0.7 mi; reach the top of the ridge (6,031 ft) at 0.9 mi. At 1.3 mi, L, is an excellent view of Mt Mitchell, and at 1.5 mi, R, are views of Great Craggy Mtn range (SW). Reach Blackstock Knob (6,325 ft) at 1.7 mi. Descend to views of Mt Mitchell, and a network of radio and TV towers on Clingmans Peak, L. Complete the descent to Rainbow Gap at 2.6 mi. Enter a dense grove of red spruce, some of which are fallen and covered with moss, at 3.1 mi. Arrive at a spring at 3.6 mi. Descend to an open area of grasses and rocks for views of a spectacular landscape on the S side of Potato Knob. To the SW is a sweeping view of the Asheville Watershed. Hug the rocky side of the mtn among rhododendron and laurel to a R turn at 4.0 mi. Descend on a former trail (some call it *Boundary Trail*) among patches of birch, laurel, grasses, and blueberry. At 4.6 mi is a jct ahead and L. Turn sharply L and follow an even contour to Mt Mitchell Rd (NC-128) at 4.9 mi. (If following ahead on the ridge it is 0.4 mi to the BRP in Black Mtn Gap, mp 355.4, the entrance road to Mt Mitchell. From here it is 4.8 mi to Mt Mitchell State Park.)

Continuing on the *MST* cross Mt Mitchell Rd and go 0.3 mi to an old RR grade to jct with *Buncombe Horse Range Trail,* R and L. Turn L on the easy old RR grade, cross Lower Creek at 8.2 mi, and jct with *Mt Mitchell Trail,* L and R, at 9.1 mi on Commissary Hill (5,782 ft). (See Toecane Ranger District, chapter 3, sec 4.) (It is 1.6 mi L on a steep ascent to Mt Mitchell [see chapter 10 for Mt Mitchell State Park].) Unless a new trail is created for the *MST,* continue to follow the *Mt Mitchell Trail,* R, on a 4.0-mi descent to Black Mtn Campground at 13.1 mi. (A partial alternate route is *Higgins Bald Trail.*) The fee campground has drinking water, flush toilets, developed campsites, but no showers. Open April 15–October 30. Vehicle access from BRP (mp 347.6) at Big Laurel Gap is a descent of 2.5 mi on FR-2074 to jct with FR-472. Turn L, go 0.7 mi, and turn R to cross South Toe River. (The campground can also be accessed from FR-472 (BRP mp 351.9), and NC-80 to FR-472.)

(In 1996 the *MST* is under construction from the campground to NC-80/BRP mp 344.1. A proposed plan is to parallel the South Toe River for about 1.0 mi before crossing the river and FR-472 to partially follow a new horse trail on Big Ridge. Ascending, the route would lift S and SE to face the

BRP boundary, where it would turn L (NE) to parallel the BRP on the W side. After at least two crossings of the BRP it would jct with Section 10 on the N side of the BRP bridge over NC-80. The Carolina Mountain Club is working on the S part of the section, and the Central Blue Ridge Task Force is working on the N side until the volunteers meet. Estimated distance is 6.5 mi. Meanwhile, from the campground hike FR-472 downriver 3.0 mi to jct with NC-80, turn R, and follow NC-80 2.2 mi up the valley to Buck Creek Gap at the parking lot.) (*USGS Maps:* Old Fort, Celo)

Section 10
Buck Gap (BRP mp 344.1/NC-80) to Woodlawn Park (US-221) (Yancey and McDowell Counties)

LENGTH AND DIFFICULTY: 13.1 mi, strenuous (elev change 2,016 ft)

FEATURES: wildlife, scenic views, isolation

TRAILS FOLLOWED: *Woods Mountain Access Trail, Woods Mountain Trail*

TRAIL CONNECTIONS: *Armstrong Creek Trail, Woodlawn Trail*

CAMPSITES: in Pisgah NF off the trails

TRAILHEAD AND DESCRIPTION: From the Buck Creek Gap parking lot (BRP 344.1/NC-80) (16.0 mi W from Marion and 14.0 mi E from Micaville) follow the *MST* white blaze up an old BRP svc rd (*Woods Mountain Access Trail*) for 0.7 mi. (See chapter 6.) At a large white oak on the L turn R off the road onto a footpath, the *Woods Mountain Trail*. Skirt S of a knob, leave the BRP boundary, and at 0.2 mi descend to a gap for a jct with *Armstong Creek Trail*, L. (It descends 3.0 mi to Armstrong Fish Hatchery at SR-1443 [see Grandfather Ranger District, chapter 3, sec 2].) Continue on the *Woods Mountain Trail* along Woods Mtn ridge where are scenic views of Table Rock, Hawksbill, Green Knob, Mt Mitchell, Mackey Mtn, Lake Tahoma, and Armstong Valley at 1.2 mi and 1.3 mi. The ridge has chinquapin, turkey grass, laurel, blueberries, pitch pine, and oaks. Wildlife includes, deer, grouse, turkey, and bear.

At 2.4 mi the trail slopes on the N side of the ridge in an arbor of rhododendron, galax, and trailing arbutus. At 2.5 mi is a jct R with an old trail that descends to Singecat Branch. Stay L and ascend to a level area on Timber Ridge at 2.7 mi. Curve R to descend on an old road at 3.0 mi for switchbacks. At 3.3 mi is a shallow saddle, then an open forest. At 3.9 mi is a view, L (N), from an outcrop, showing USFS clear-cuts. Drop to a wide saddle then ascend at 4.3 mi. Pass through tall hemlocks in an open forest; ignore an old road R at 4.5 mi. At 4.9 mi ascend steeply on a rocky ridge for views L of Grandfather Mtn, Table Rock, and Hawksbill at 5.1 mi. Ascend steeply to a knob at 5.3 mi. After another knob descend to ascend at an unused FR-104 jct at 5.8 mi, the end of *Woods Mountain Trail.* (An old road goes L 0.3 mi to former Woods Mtn fire tower, 3,646 ft.) The *MST* continues R (S) for a descent on Betsy Ridge.

In the descent avoid side timber roads and hunter's trails. At 6.6 mi is old road L, abandoned trail ahead, and a turn R for the *MST.* Keep L at 6.9 mi at another jct on easy treadway. At 7.7 mi the road forks; turn L. (Old road R ascends to a knob with views of Mt Mitchell and Lake Tahoma.) Turn L at 8.2 mi, again at 8.6 mi (berm) down the N side of a ridge, and again at 9.6 mi (berm). At 9.7 mi join a used FR; keep L. Cross a number of streams, one with low cement bridge at 10.3 mi. Leave the road, R, at 11.0 mi on a footpath of broom straw and briers to cross Tom's Creek on a foot log after 100 yd. Pass through rhododendron, fetterbush, and running cedar; turn L on an old road. Curve R after ascending to a ridge at 11.9 mi. At 12.2 mi reach a wide road; turn L (blaze may be after the turn) through poplar and white and Virginia pine. Turn L at 12.8 mi, pass R of *Woodlawn Trail* at 12.9 mi, turn R off road in pines at 13.0 mi, and descend to US-221 at 13.1 mi. It is 0.1 mi L to the parking lot at Woodlawn Rest Area, which has picnic tables and a rest room. This section designated a state trail in May 1989. (Vehicles should be parked opposite USFS work center N of the rest area.) (It is 4.6 mi S on US-221 to US-70 and motels, restaurants, and shopping center.) (*USGS Maps:* Celo, Little Switzerland)

Section 11
Ashford (US-221) to Ripshin Ridge (NC-181) (McDowell and Burke Counties)

LENGTH AND DIFFICULTY: 24.1 mi, moderate to strenuous

FEATURES: Pinnacle, Linville River, wilderness, Shortoff Mtn, Table Rock, waterfalls, wildlife

TRAILS FOLLOWED: *Overmountain Victory Trail, Shortoff Mountain Trail, Table Rock Summit Trail, Table Rock Gap Trail, Upper Steels Creek Trail, Greentown Trail, Raider Camp Trail, Harper Creek Trail, North Harper Creek Trail, North Harper Creek Access Trail, Hunt-Fish Falls Trail, Lost Cove Trail, Beacon Heights Trail;* described in chapter 3, sec 2.

TRAIL CONNECTIONS: *Cambric Branch Trail, Little Table Rock Trail, Greentown Shortcut Trail, Persimmon Ridge Trail* (same chapter as above)

CAMPSITES: throughout the Pisgah NF except on private property at Linville River and NF Table Rock Picnic Area.

TRAILHEAD AND DESCRIPTION: This section of the *MST* is incomplete from US-221 to Kistler Memorial Highway (steep gravel road) near Pinnacle.

Although in a planning stage the difficulty is a limited corridor of forest property and the steep ascent to Linville Mtn. A temporary access is described below. If omitting the *Overmountain Victory Trail*, the distance is 19.8 mi from Kistler Rd to NC-181. From the jct of US-221 and Old Linville Rd (SR-1560) in Ashford, drive 2.5 mi S on Old Linville Rd to gated FR-493, L. (If there is a No Trespassing sign on the gate, inquire at the nearest residence to the L or across the road from the gate for permission to walk the first 0.2 mi on private property to the USFS boundary.) Follow the *Overmountain Victory Trail* sign and ascend gradually on a gold-blazed woods road to a ridgeline to cross Dobson Knob Rd at 2.0 mi. Descend on an old road and cross Yellow Fork at 2.5 mi in a rhododendron thicket. Cross another small stream at 3.2 mi, and jct with the gravel Kistler Memorial Highway (SR-1238) at 3.5 mi, the end of the *Overmountain Victory Trail*. Turn L to a parking area. (It is 4.1 mi R steeply down the mtn to NC-126, where with a R turn it is 7.6 mi to Nebo and US-70 jct, or a L turn 16.3 mi to Morganton.) Continue N on SR-1238 and at 4.3 mi turn R on a jeep road that leads 0.2 mi to the Pinnacle. (SR-1238 continues ahead 12.3 mi to Linville Falls.)

A spur trail, R at the Pinnacle, provides a panoramic view of Linville Gorge (E), Lake James (S), Shortoff Mtn (E), Table Rock (NE), and Dogback Mtn (N). Follow the white blaze in a hardwood forest and understory of laurel down the mtn. Turn L on an old logging road at 4.8 mi. Reach a clear-cut at 5.1 mi. Follow an old logging road, cross Sandy Branch twice, 5.5 mi and 5.8 mi. Ascend to a knob and pass through patches of bristly locust. Descend, turn sharply L off the logging road at 6.6 mi, reach a road and gate to private property at 6.7 mi. Turn L and after 0.3 mi turn sharply R off the road in a descent to the Linville River (1,280 ft elev). Vegetation includes ironwood, doghobble, sycamore, hemlock, gums, and yellow root. Wade the 50-ft-wide river, turn R, and go downstream for 0.2 mi. Turn L, ascend through a rhododendron thicket, and cross a ravine at 7.5 mi. Ascend in a forest of oak, pine, laurel, and turkey beard. Jct with an old woods road at 7.7 mi; turn L. Ascend gradually to jct with a foot trail, L and R, at 8.8 mi. (The old road ahead is a longer route to the top of Shortoff Mtn, and the foot trail R is an access route from Old Wolf Pit Rd, a private access.) Turn L on *Shortoff Mountain Trail*. Scenic views of the Linville Gorge Wilderness soon begin along the precipitous W side of the mtn. A small spring is in a crevice at 9.2 mi. (Spring usually has water, but not dependable in long dry summer.) There are more scenic views, L, on short spur trails. There are thick patches of Allegheny sand myrtle, chestnut oak, and blueberry. Reach the old jeep-road entrance (3,000 ft) at 9.3 mi. To the L are spectacular views of Linville Gorge, Table Rock, and Hawksbill. Follow the old jeep road, but turn L on another old woods road at 9.5 mi. Pass a water hole, L, at 9.8 mi. Reach a knob at 12.2 mi in a forest of large white pine and oak. Leave ridge crest, turn R, and at 12.7 mi enter a bed of galax, where to the R is a 60-yd spur to an intermittent spring. Reach Chimney Gap at 13.2 mi. Ascend, steeply in spots, to the Chimneys at 13.8 mi. Pass through dense evergreens on the W side of the Chimneys at 14.1 and to scenic areas for views at 14.5 mi. Chinquapin grow here among the blueberries. Arrive at Table Rock Picnic Area at 14.9 mi. (Area has picnic tables, garbage stand, vault toilets, but no water. Day use only; no camping.) (Access is from NC-181 in Jonas Ridge on Old Gingercake Rd [SR-1264] for 0.3 mi, L on Gingercake Acres Rd [SR-1265], which becomes FR-210 for 5.9 mi and a turn R on FR-210B for another 2.9 mi.)

Cross the parking area and follow *Table Rock Summit Trail*. Jct L with *Little Table Rock Trail* at 15.2 mi. Turn R, ascend 100 yd, and take a sharp L on *Table Rock Gap Trail*. (*Table Rock Summit Trail* continues the ascent of 0.4 mi to panoramic views [3,909 ft].) Follow a rocky treadway, and at 15.9 mi begin a steep descent. Reach an unmaintained road cul-de-sac at 16.1 mi, the end of the wilderness boundary. Cross the road, turn R, descend on an old logging road to gravel FR-210 at 16.3 mi. Turn R on FR-210 and go 0.1 mi to make a L turn off the road. Descend, steeply in spots, on an old woods road in rhododendron, white pine, and oak to reach gravel FR-496 at 16.8 mi. A small stream is R. (It is 5.6 mi L on FR-496 to N terminus of *Upper Steels Creek Trail* and continuing MST.) Turn R on FR-496 and reach a gate and parking area at 16.9 mi. (It is 35 yd ahead to FR-210, and 65 yd R on FR-210 to Table Rock Picnic Rd, FR-210B, L.) Continue on the MST, L, from the gate on an old jeep road over hummocks. Pines, rhododendron, and arbutus are prominent. The headwaters of Buck Creek can be heard from the L. Turn sharply R on a foot trail at 17.4 mi. Follow an erratic trail, partly on footpaths or old logging roads, up and down grades in coves, over streamlets, and over ridges for 2.2 mi to an exceptionally steep descent at 19.6 mi. Arrive at the base of the ridge and trail jct at 20.0 mi in an area of Devil's walking stick, white pine, and ferns. Turn L (R is a fisherman's trail downstream), and rock-hop Buck Creek. Jct with *Upper Steels Creek Trail*, R and L. (To the R, *Upper Steels Creek Trail* crosses the creek and follows an old 4WD route downstream for 0.2 mi to FR-228 and a parking area. From here it is 3.9 mi out to NC-181.)

Continue upstream, jointly with *Upper Steels Creek Trail*, and ascend by rapids and pools. To the R is a waterfall at 20.5 mi. Cross a drainage at 20.6

mi. Turn sharply L at 20.8 mi (easy to miss) and ascend steeply. Follow a logging road and RR grades, cross a deep chasm, and pass cascades and pools. Arrive at a beautiful flat area at 21.1 mi with campsites in fern beds and tall maple, poplar, locust, and hemlock giving shade. Enter a grazing field and follow the E edge to a FR; turn R, rock-hop Gingercake Creek, and after 70 yd rock-hop Steels Creek. Walk on an easy FR amid tall poplar, white pine, and hemlock. At 21.8 mi rock-hop Steels Creek and again at 21.9 mi. Continue on the old FR and gradually ascend to a ridge at 22.6 mi. Enter a cut in the ridge and jct with an old road, R, the *MST* route, at 22.7 mi. (Here the *Upper Steels Creek Trail* goes ahead for 120 yd to the locked gate and access with FR-496. R on FR-496 is 1.3 mi to NC-181.) Follow the *MST* on the old road and cross a scenic and high cascading tributary to Steels Creek at 22.8 mi. Reach a parking area on FR-496 at 23.2 mi; follow R on the road and pass a grassy field at 23.5 mi. Arrive at NC-181 at 24.1 mi, and cross the highway (Mountain-to-Sea bike route #2) to a parking area for *Greentown Trail*. (This section was designated a state trail October 1986.) (To the L, up the mtn on NC-181 it is 4.5 mi to a grocery store, and 4.8 mi farther on NC-183 to motel and restaurants in Linville.) (*USGS-FS Maps:* Ashford, Oak Hill, Chestnut Mtn)

Section 12
Ripshin Ridge (NC-181) to Beacon Heights (BRP mp 305.3) (Burke and Avery Counties)

LENGTH AND DIFFICULTY: 24.2 mi, strenuous

FEATURES: waterfalls, wildlife, wildflowers, fishing

TRAILS FOLLOWED: *Greentown Trail, Raider Camp Trail, Harper Creek Trail, North Harper Creek Trail, North Harper Creek Access Trail, Hunt-Fish Falls Trail, Lost Cove Trail, Beacon Heights Trail;* described in chapter 3, sec 2

TRAIL CONNECTIONS: *Greentown Shortcut Trail, Persimmon Ridge Trail, Timber Ridge Trail*

CAMPSITES: throughout the Pisgah NF off roads and trails; prohibited on BRP property at Beacon Heights

TRAILHEAD AND DESCRIPTION: *Greentown Trail* parking area is 4.2 mi SE of Jonas Ridge community (7.4 mi if from NC-181 jct with BRP mp 312.2) and 21.4 mi NW of NC-818 from US-70 jct in Morganton. (*Upper Creek Falls Trail* parking lot is 1.1 mi NW on NC-181 from *Greentown Trail* parking area.)

For the next 18.3 mi the white-blazed *MST* follows trails described in detail in the Grandfather Ranger District, chapter 3, sec 2. As a result only jct points are listed below. On the *Greenwood Trail* pass a post-gate entrance and descend to Upper Creek. At 2.4 mi jct with *Greentown Shortcut Trail*, R, near the mouth of Burnthouse Branch. At 3.9 mi jct with FR-198R. At 5.8 mi jct with *Raider Camp Trail*, and turn R. (To the L it is 0.2 mi to a superb view of South Harper Creek Falls.) Jct with *Phillips Creek Trail*, R, at 8.0 mi (at two large poplars with initials R. J.). Rock-hop Harper Creek at 8.3 mi and jct with *Harper Creek Trail*, R and L, at 8.4 mi. (*Harper Creek Trail*, R, has an access 1.3 mi out to Wilson Creek Rd, SR-1328.) Turn L on *Harper Creek Trail* and pass cascades and waterfalls. Rock-hop the creek twice before a jct with *North Harper Creek Trail*, R at 10.7 mi, where *Harper Creek Trail* turns L. Rock-hop the creek twice again, and jct R and L with *Persimmon Ridge Trail* at 11.2 mi. Jct with *North Harper Creek Access Trail* at 12.8 mi, and turn R on it. (*North Harper Creek Trail* continues upstream.) Arrive at FR-464 and a parking space at 13.8 mi. Turn R and follow FR-464 0.6 mi to a parking area, L, at the S trailhead of *Hunt-Fish Falls Trail* at 14.4 mi. Descend on *Hunt-Fish Falls Trail* to a beautiful area of falls and pools at 15.2 mi and a jct L with *Lost Cove Trail*, R and L. Turn R and at 16.7 mi jct L with *Timber Ridge Trail*. Follow Gragg Prong upstream by cascades to FR-981 (near Roseborough) and cross the bridge to a parking area, R, at 18.3 mi.

Across the road from the parking area is the S entrance to FR-192. The *MST* follows this narrow and rocky road 3.2 mi upstream, R of cascading Gragg Prong. (Jeep and 4WD are better suited for a vehicular attempt.) Hughes Ridge towers R. At Old House Gap at 21.4 mi, the road improves (to accommodate passenger vehicles coming in from FR-45). To the R is primitive FR-451, and to the L the *MST* continues on an old woods road. Ascend, and turn off, R, at 22.0 mi. Follow an old logging road 0.1 mi to a foot trail, L. Pass a natural rock shelter at 22.3 mi. At 22.4 mi are views of Beacon Heights and Grandfather Mtn. Cross two small streams in a forest of tall hemlock and oak. Cross two ravines and at 23.1 mi enter a 0.1-mi rhododendron arbor. Reach a headwaters stream of Andrews Creek at 23.3 mi under tall hemlock and cucumber trees. Ascend on switchbacks to scenic areas R at 23.8 mi and 23.9 mi. Pitch pine, laurel, witch hazel, and blueberries are here. At 24.0 mi jct with a wide trail; turn R (L it is 35 yd to a small parking area on Gragg Rd, SR-1513). At 24.1 mi jct with *Beacon Heights Trail*. (To the R is a large rock outcropping for panoramic views.) Continue ahead on *Beacon Heights Trail* and jct at 24.2 mi with *Tanawha Trail*, R. To the L, go 130 yd to the Beacon Heights parking area on the BRP (mp 305.3). On the BRP, R, is a jct with US-221, and 3.0 mi S on US-221 into Linville are groceries, restaurant, motel, and supply stores. (This section was designated a state trail October 1986.) (*USGS Maps*: Grandfather Mtn, Chestnut Mtn)

Section 13

Beacon Heights (BRP mp 305.3) to Blowing Rock (BRP mp 291.9) (Avery, Watauga, and Caldwell Counties)

LENGTH AND DIFFICULTY: 24.6 mi, moderate to strenuous

FEATURES: exceptional scenic views, Linn Cove Viaduct, Moses Cone Memorial Park

TRAILS FOLLOWED: *Tanawha Trail, Boone Fork Trail, Rich Mountain Trail, Watkins Trail;* described in chapter 6

TRAIL CONNECTIONS: *Daniel Boone Scout Trail, Nuwati Trail, Grandfather Mountain Access Trail, Upper Boone Fork Trail, Cold Prong Pond Trail, Black Bottom Trail*

CAMPSITES: camping is prohibited on BRP property except at the developed Price Memorial Park Campground (BRP mp 297.1); camping is allowed at designated sites off Grandfather Mtn trails with a fee and permit; 704-733-2013.

TRAILHEAD AND DESCRIPTION: Access to the S trailhead is at the Beacon Heights parking area (mp 305.3) (elev 4,205 ft) at the jct of the BRP and US-221. The *MST* follows the *Tanawha Trail*, an extraordinary example of trail design and construction by the NPS. It is described in detail, N to S, in chapter 6. Therefore, only the access points and trail connections are covered below in a S to N direction. (Camping is not allowed on the *Tanawha Trail* or other BRP properties, except at Price Lake Memorial Park.) Begin at the jct of *Beacon Heights Trail* and *Tanawha Trail,* and follow the signs. (Tanawha means "fabulous hawk" in Cherokee, and the trail is marked with a feather logo.) Cross US-221 at 0.3 mi and at 0.8 mi arrive at the Stack Rock parking area (mp 304.8), L. Approach the Linn Cove parking area (mp 304.4), L, at 1.5 mi, and gently descend to an observation deck of the BRP Linn Cove Viaduct, an engineering marvel. Pass under the viaduct at 1.7 mi and cross Linn Cove Branch. At 2.7 mi arrive at the Wilson Creek Overlook (mp 303.7), R. Ascend to Rough Ridge boardwalk at 3.8 mi for superb scenic views in a natural garden of turkey beard, blueberry, mtn ash, red spruce, and Allegheny sand myrtle. Descend to Rough Ridge parking area (mp 302.9), R at 4.0 mi. (Interpretive board is a story of Andre Michaux and plant communities.) Reach Raven Rocks Overlook (mp 302.3), R at 4.7 mi, and at 5.3 mi Pilot Ridge Overlook (mp 301.8), R. Jct with *Daniel Boone Scout Trail,* L, at 7.3 mi, and *Nuwati Trail,* L, at 7.4 mi. (Both trails are commercial trails of Grandfather Mtn Inc, and a fee registration is required to hike them. Camping is allowed at designated sites. See chapter 14.) Jct R with *Grandfather Mountain Access Trail,* a 0.4-mi access route, to US-221 at 7.6 mi. Cross the scenic Upper Boone Fork bridge and jct R with an access to the Boone Fork parking area (mp 299.9) and *Upper Boone Fork Trail,* which goes 0.5 mi to the Calloway Peak Overlook (mp 299.7). At 9.6 mi jct with *Cold Prong Pond Trail,* R, which leads 0.2 mi to Cold Prong Pond Overlook (mp 299). Continue through a mixed forest with a varied understory of rhododendron, flame azalea, and laurel, and arrive at a large pastoral area (first of three) at 10.5 mi. Cross Holloway Rd (SR-1559) with stiles at 11.6 mi. After a section of forest, enter the third pasture at 12.2 mi and descend gently into a forest. Reach a jct with *Boone Fork Trail* at 12.6 mi, R and L, near another stile, R. (The *Tanawha Trail* follows the *Boone Fork Trail,* R for 0.4 mi before it forks R and reaches the Price Lake parking area [mp 297.3] at 13.3 mi.)

The *MST* turns L and jointly follows the *Boone Fork Trail* 0.3 mi before they turn sharply R to leave the pasture and descend to the Bee Tree Creek headwaters. At 14.1 mi cross Bee Tree Creek for the last time and curve around the ridge R to follow upstream on Boone Fork. After a scenic route through birch and rhododendron and cascades, pass an old dam site, L at 15.1 mi. At 15.3 mi reach a huge rock formation by the river; descend to leave the *Boone Fork Trail* and rock-hop or wade Boone Fork. (The *Boone Fork Trail* continues ahead 1.1 mi to the picnic area at Price Memorial Park, mp 295.5.)

Across the river ascend steeply to a flat knoll at 15.4 mi with laurel, white pine, galax, and running cedar. Follow an old, wide, and level road to Old John Rd at 15.8 mi. Turn R and at 15.9 mi turn L, off the road, and into a large pine plantation (to the R is a chimney from a pioneer farmhouse.) Ascend in a mixed forest and at 16.2 mi pass L of a spring (the last on the climb to Rich Mtn) near a homestead site. Continue ascending the slope of Martin Knob and reach a pasture at the ridgeline at 16.8 mi. Turn R and arrive at Shulls Mills Rd (SR-1552) and gated fence in Martin Gap at 16.9 mi (R, on the paved road, it is 1.7 mi to BRP mp 294.6). Turn R on the road and after a few yd turn L up the embankment to follow the ridgeline. Pass through white pine and then a hardwood area with a grove of flame azalea. Reach a fence and jct with *Rich Mountain Trail,* R and L at 17.4 mi. (To the L the *Rich Mountain Trail* ascends to its W terminus at Rich Mtn summit, 4,370 ft.) Turn R on *Rich Mountain Trail* and follow the carriage road (3.2 mi to the Moses Cone Manor) into a pasture. Turn L at the first curve and descend into a forest. At 19.0 mi take the L fork and go under large hemlocks. Reach a trout lake (may be drained) at 19.2 mi. Cross the dam and arrive at Flannery Fork Rd (SR-1541). Turn R, but after 0.4 mi leave it, L, and ascend on the carriage road with switchbacks to another pasture. Reach the BRP at 20.6 mi, the end of *Rich Mountain Trail*. Go under the BRP (mp 294) and jointly follow *Watkins Trail*. Pass the stables, R, and access steps to the parking area of Moses Cone Memorial Park. Follow a paved carriage trail to the front of the manor, but turn sharply at the first L at 20.8 mi and descend into a forest of white pine and hemlock. Parallel the BRP and stay L of other carriage roads. At 22.2 mi keep L in a curve (the carriage road R is *Black Bottom Trail*, which connects with other carriage trails in the park). Pass L of a lake and spillway at 24.0 mi, cross Penley Branch in a grove of handsome oak, maple, and tall hemlock. At a private road at 24.4 mi turn R, and reach the end of *Watkins Trail* at US-221/321 at 24.6 mi. (The Boone Fork/Cone Manor part of this section was designated a state trail May 1990; the *Tanawha Trail* June 1994.) (Across the road is the New River Inn. To the R it is 1.0 mi to Blowing Rock; to the L it is 0.2 mi to BRP mp 291.9 jct; and ahead it is 6.0 mi to Boone. Both towns have groceries, restaurants, supply stores, and motels. (*USGS Maps:* Grandfather Mtn, Valle Crucis, Boone)

Section 14 from Blowing Rock (BRP mp 291.9) to Deep Gap (BRP mp 276.4) is 15.5 mi on the BRP. **Section 15** from Deep Gap (BRP mp 276.4) to Horse Gap (BRP mp 261.2) is 15.2 mi on the BRP. **Section 16** from Horse Gap (BRP mp 261.2) to Basin Cove Overlook (BRP mp 244.7) is 16.5 mi on the BRP. Here is the S end of *Bluff Mountain Trail* (S edge of Doughton Park) where the *MST* will probably continue N to Brinegar Cabin parking lot (BRP mp 238.5). (See chapter 6.) Preliminary discussions on the routes for these sections (trail distance will be different from the BRP miles) indicate the major need is volunteer groups or clubs to construct and maintain an *MST* route. **Section 17** will pass through Stone Mtn State Park. (See introduction of this chapter for information on plans and routing of other parts of the *MST*.) (Call the author, phone 919-496-2521/4771 for updated information.)

Appendix A

OUTDOOR ORGANIZATIONS AND CLUBS

Without the organizations and clubs in the state there would not be a state trail system. They are the citizen teams of researchers, planners, and workers who are concerned about the natural environment. Some of them are essential watchdogs of properties abused by federal, state, and local governments and commercial developers. In many ways they all form partnerships with government or lobby against or for issues that involve legislative action. The condition of a state's trail system is a barometer of its environmental quality. Some of the groups give purpose, maintenance, and direction to such historic routes as the *AT*, the *Bartram Trail*, the *Foothills Trail*, and more recently the *Benton MacKaye Trail*. (The latter could form a double loop from the *AT* at Springer Mtn, Georgia, to the Cherokee NF in Tennessee, cross the *AT* at Shuckstack Mtn in the *GSMNP*, and follow the park's east edge to Davenport Gap and jct with the *AT*.) In addition, a private equestrian club in Tryon has proposed a new trail on private property that would go from the *Foothills Trail* at Caesars Head State Park in South Carolina N to connect with the *AT* on Roan Mtn. The route would use public property on part of the *MST*. If completed, the trail would provide a long loop using the *Foothills Trail*, the *Bartram Trail*, and the *AT*.

There are other organizations, such as the N.C. Chapter of the Sierra Club, N.C. Nature Conservancy, N.C. chapters of the Audubon Society, N.C. Recreation and Park Society, Friends of State Parks, and the former N.C. Trails Association that not only have a strong interest in trails but also in the preservation of our natural heritage and improving the quality of life. They often have led campaigns separately and collectively to save scenic rivers; protect wildlife habitats; preserve historic places; and promote wilderness areas, clean air, and water. Their work is one of vigilance. They fought to have Congress designate the South Fork of the New River a Scenic River in 1976, only to discover a decade later that this "jewel in the state's scenic crown" was a hollow victory because state and county governments had failed to acquire easements to prevent riverside developments. They won in stopping a road through what is now the Slickrock Wilderness Area (though another road, in spite of classic vigilance, was built within sight of the Joyce Kilmer Memorial Forest).

Nationwide, 40,000 mi of hiking trails in the USFS have disappeared in the past 40 years. Road building has been frenzied, a process one writer called the "roads to ruin." Some private organizations, such as the N.C. Nature Conservancy, are at work "preserving biological diversity by protecting natural lands." The conservancy has acquired 25 areas for a total of 293,000 acres. A few of these properties have trails. One example is Nags **968** Head Woods, whose *Sweet Gum Trail* is on a 680-acre undisturbed preserve that has not changed since the first Englishmen saw it 400 years ago. For days and hours the preserve is open to the public, call 919-441-2521. The Triangle Land Conservancy has 291.5 acres in five tracts in Chatham, Johnson, Orange, and Wake Counties. Some of these tracts have primitive trails open to the public. For information call 919-833-3662. In 1995 the Conservation Trust for North Carolina had 19 active local and regional land trusts, each assisting landowners to protect "the resources and character of their land." For information call 919-828-4199. (For these three and other conservation organizations see addresses under N.C. Citizens' Groups below.)

Although some districts in the USFS place trails low on their budgets and priorities, it does not mean that the trails and preservation of special areas are forgotten by the USFS staff. For example, by 1988 the Pisgah and Nantahala forests had 39 special management areas (40,771 acres, including the wilderness areas). And on the state level, DEHNR has divisions in natural resources and environmental protection for areas of land, water, and forests. Meanwhile, the commercial forests in the state are shrinking at the rate of one million acres every 10 years. (Worldwide, it is 50 acres each minute, equal to the disappearance of all of North Carolina's trees in less than one year.) To preserve our forests and trails, we have a great responsibility. One way to help is by becoming an active member (if not already) of a citizen group. "You don't have to be a hiker to love trails," said Elisabeth Hair of Charlotte. Below is a brief overview of the volunteer organizations that maintain the *AT* and some other local/regional trails.

Carolina Mountain Club

On June 17, 1920, organized mountaineering began in North Carolina when a southern chapter of the Appalachian Mountain Club of Boston was formed tentatively in Asheville. Dr Chase Ambler, originator of the Weeks National Forest Land Purchase Act, was the first president. Three years later, the club withdrew from the AMC and incorporated under the name of the Carolina

Mountain Club with Dr Gaillard Tennent its first president. In 1930 the Carolina Appalachian Trail Club was formed with George Stephens as its first president, but one year later the vigorous hiking club was merged into the CMC. Stephens, like Tennent, hiked actively with the CMC for many years. He published extensive maps and guides, including 100 Favorite Trails, a hiking guide for some of the Smokies and the Blue Ridge Mtns in the state.

During the Appalachian Trail Conference's (ATC) early years, CMC's president Marcus Book was an ATC board member. He was succeeded in 1938 by Arch Nichols (1979 Honorary Member of ATC). In 1940 Nichols engaged the Rev A. Rufus Morgan to work on the Nantahala AT section; Nichols later started the Tennessee Eastman Hiking Club north of Spivey Gap, and helped to establish the Piedmont Appalachian Trail Hikers, a Greensboro-based club (see below). Other accomplishments have been the securing of the Craggy Scenic Area; the naming of Tennent Mtn; marking Mt Craige and Big Top; naming George Masa Mtn; securing the Shining Rock Wilderness Area; establishing the *Art Loeb Trail*; securing the Max Patch properties for the *AT*; and starting the Mt Pisgah to Mt Mitchell Trail System, which will become a section of the *MST*. In 1968 the CMC worked hard for the passage of the National Scenic Trail Act and the Appalachian Trail Act of 1978 by the Congress, and it assisted the USFS in acquiring aerial photos of the *AT* for the *Federal Register*. CMC is the state's oldest trail club, and it maintains 91.5 mi of the *AT* from Davenport Gap to Spivey Gap.

INFORMATION: Carolina Mountain Club, Box 68, Asheville, NC 28802; 704-252-6078.

Nantahala Hiking Club (NHC)

The club was founded in 1950 by the Rev A. Rufus Morgan to assist in maintaining the *AT* in the Nantahala Mountains area. Morgan was the NHC's first president and held that position for 18 years, during which time the membership grew to more than 200 and the club's program expanded to include "pleasure hiking" in northern Georgia, western North Carolina, and eastern Tennessee. As a maintaining member of the Appalachian Trail Conference, the NHC has responsibility for clearing, marking, and constructing 60 mi of the *AT* from the community of Wesser at the Nantahala River south to Bly Gap at the Georgia state line. One of the club's most recent accomplishments was building three new shelters. The club does not have a formal membership requirement other than membership dues. Awards are provided for hours of service, and the club has year-round programs of hiking and meetings. The club holds its monthly meetings at the Nonah Craft House in

Cartoogechay (a few mi W of Franklin) and publishes a bimonthly newsletter and hike listing.

INFORMATION: Nantahala Hiking Club, 31 Slagle Rd, Franklin, NC 28734; 704-369-6802

Piedmont Appalachian Trail Hikers (PATH)

The history of the Piedmont Appalachian Trail Hikers began with the vision of Greensboro, N.C. area conservationists. The idea of forming a regional club with responsibility for maintaining a section of the AT became active in 1965 when volunteers interested in hiking and backpacking were recruited for the club from communities in north central North Carolina. Among the principals in the club's founding were Louise Chatfield, trail leader and hiker; Mrs. Coleman Gentry, who designed the club's logo; and Charles Adams, a librarian at the University of North Carolina. Assisting PATH were Arch Nichols and the Rev A. Rufus Morgan of Asheville, and Tom Campbell, an ATC board member and a member of the Roanoke Appalachian Trail Club.

The Roanoke club relinquished 16.0 mi of the AT from US-21/52 at Walker Mtn to VA-16 in 1965. The following year PATH was assigned an additional 11.0 mi from Groseclose to VA-16 at Mt Rogers NRA Hq, formerly maintained by the Rev A. J. Shumate of Rural Retreat, Virginia, and a troop of Boy Scouts from Grace Lutheran Church. Another 13.0 mi were added in the late 1970s when the AT route was transferred from Big Walker Mtn to the garden rim of the unique and beautiful high basin known as Burke's Garden. In 1987 the Mt Rogers AT Club relinquished 8.0 mi to PATH from VA-16 to VA-670 at the South Fork of the Holston River. Among the club's goals are to maintain its 48.3 mi; promote outdoor activities such as hiking, climbing, and canoeing; protect natural resources; and promote conservation. Current club membership is 240.

INFORMATION: Piedmont Appalachian Trail Hikers, 5113 Woodrun on Tillery, Mt Gilead, NC 27306; 910-723-9819 or 919-967-4449.

Smoky Mountains Hiking Club

By 1924, interest in the development of national park status for the Great Smoky Mtns had progressed, and certain members of the Knoxville YMCA decided a group for adult hikers would be a useful program. It would also "stimulate further interest in the National Park movement." In October of that year, a group of interested hikers from the Knoxville area gathered on top of Mt LeConte and formed the Smoky Mountains Hiking Club. The affiliation with the YMCA was dropped shortly, but the goal of gaining park status for the beloved mountains was never abandoned.

The group began with three major areas of interest. The first was the construction, marking, and mapping of hiking trails. Second, the group set up a hiking program, with hikes held at least once a month. And third, the club worked to publicize the beauty and uniqueness of the Great Smokies in order to convince public officials that the area should be protected by park status. The early goals having been reached, the club now sees itself as a watchdog for the park and the AT, which it helped to construct. It has also been active in the campaign to have the park included under the Wilderness Act for further protection. The club maintains the AT from Wesser (US-19) to Davenport Gap, a distance of 97.4 mi. Mostly from the Knoxville/Oak Ridge area in Tennessee, the club members sponsor day hikes and overnight backpacking trips. There is a membership fee and the club publishes a monthly newsletter.

INFORMATION: Smoky Mountains Hiking Club, Box 1454, Knoxville, TN 37901; 615-558-1341.

Tennessee Eastman Recreation Club

The club is organized under the auspices of the Eastman Recreation Club of the Eastman Chemical Company. Persons other than Eastman employees are also welcome at club activities. Founded in 1946, the club now has an Eastman membership of more than 700. It sponsors a program of both hiking and canoeing, with about 75 trips each year. As a member of the ATC, the club is responsible for maintaining the 125.0 mi of the AT from Spivey Gap to near Elk Park in North Carolina that follows the Tennessee–North Carolina border, after which it goes through Tennessee to Damascus. The trail is maintained by a system of teams within the club (Adopt-A-Trail, arrangements, and special project groups) under cooperative agreements with the Jefferson, Cherokee, and Pisgah National Forests and the Tennessee Valley Authority. These teams generally devote in excess of 3,000 hours each year to clearing, marking, rehabilitation, relocations, signs, shelters, and ensuring the accuracy of guidebook data.

INFORMATION: Tennessee Eastman Hiking and Canoeing Club, Box 511, Kingsport, TN 37662; 615-229-3771.

Appendix B

OTHER SOURCES OF INFORMATION

The addresses of national, state, and local forests, parks, recreation areas, historic sites, gardens, and other areas are provided in the text. The following agencies, organizations, and clubs are also valuable sources of information.

US Congress
Committee on Agriculture (House)
Longworth House Office Bldg,
   Rm 1301
Washington, DC 20515
(202-225-2171)

Committee on Agriculture, Nutrition,
   and Forestry (Senate)
Russell Bldg, Rm 328A
Washington, DC 20510
(202-224-2035)

Committee on Energy and Natural
   Resources (Senate)
Dirksen Bldg, Rm SD-364
Washington, DC 20510
(202-224-4971)

Committee on Environment and
   Public Works (Senate)
Dirksen Bldg, Rm SD-458
Washington, DC 20510
(202-224-6167)

Committee on Resources (House)
Longworth House Office Bldg,
   Rm 1324
Washington, DC 20515
(202-225-2761)

US Executive Branch
Army Corps of Engineers
Pulaski Bldg
200 Mass. Ave NW
Washington, DC 20314
(202-272-0010)

   District Office (Wilmington)
   Box 1890
   Wilmington, NC 28402
   (910-251-4876)

Council on Environmental Quality
722 Jackson Place NW
Washington, DC 20503
(202-395-5750)

Department of Agriculture
14th St and Independence Ave SW
Washington, DC 20250
(202-720-8732)

   Forest Service
   Box 96090
   Washington, DC 20090
   (202-205-0957)

   Forest Service Regional Office
   Suite 800, 1720 Peachtree Rd NW
   Atlanta, GA 30367
   (404-347-4177)

Soil Conservation
Box 2890
Washington, DC 20013
(202-447-4543)

Soil Conservation State Biologist
4405 Bland Rd, Suite 205
Raleigh, NC 27609
(919-790-2888)
(Also same address for state
conservationist)

Department of Commerce National
    Oceanic and Atmospheric Admin.
Hoover Bldg, Rm 5128
14th and Constitution Ave NW
Washington, DC 20230
(202-377-3384)

Department of the Interior
1849 C St NW
Washington, DC 20240
(202-208-1100)

    Bureau of Land Management
    (202-208-5717)

    Bureau of Mines
    (202-501-9649)

    National Park Service
    Interior Bldg
    Box 37127
    Washington, DC 20013
    (202-208-6843)

        Regional Director (Southeast)
        75 Spring St SW
        Atlanta, GA 30303
        (404-331-5185)

US Fish and Wildlife Service
(Southeast Region)
75 Spring St SW
Atlanta, GA 30303
(404-679-7319)

(Washington Office: 202-208-4131)

US Independent Agencies
Advisory Council on Historic
    Preservation
1100 Pennsylvania Ave NW, #809
Washington, DC 20004
(202-786-0503)

Environmental Protection Agency
401 M St SW
Washington, DC 20460
(202-260-2090)

Tennessee Valley Authority
400 West Summit Hill Dr
Knoxville, TN 37902
(615-632-2101)

    Fontana Dam
    Highway 20, Box 1178
    Fontana Dam, NC 28733
    (704-498-2374)

National Regional Commissions
Appalachian Regional Commission
1666 Connecticut Ave NW
Washington, DC 20235
(202-673-7893)

Atlantic States Marine Fisheries
    Commission
1400 Sixteenth St NW
Washington, DC 20036
(202-387-5330)

Marine Mammal Commission
1825 Connecticut Ave NW, Rm 512
Washington, DC 20009
(202-606-5504)

Migratory Bird Conservation
  Commision
Interior Bldg ,
Washington, DC 20240
(703-358-1716)

National and Regional Organizations
Acid Rain Foundation Inc
1410 Varsity Dr
Raleigh, NC 27606
(919-828-9443)

American Bass Association, Inc.
886 Trotters Trail
Wetumpka, AL 36092
(205-567-6035)

American Birding Association
Box 6599
Colorado Springs, CO 80934
(719-634-7736)

American Camping Association
5000 State Rd, 67N
Martinsville, IN 46151
(317-342-8456)

American Cave Conservation
  Association
131 Main and Cave Sts
Horse Cave, KY 42749
(502-786-1466)

American Federation of Mineralogical
  Societies Inc
Central Office, 920 SW 70th St
Oklahoma City, OK 73139

American Fisheries Society
5410 Grosvenor Lane, Suite 110
Bethesda, MD 20814
(301-897-8616)

American Forests
1516 P St NW
Washington, DC 20005
(202-667-3300)

American Geographical Society
156 Fifth Ave, Suite 600
New York, NY 10010
(212-242-0214)

American Hiking Society
Box 20160
Washington, DC 20041
(703-385-3252)

American Littoral Society
Sandy Hook
Highlands, NJ 07732
(201-291-0055)

American Rivers
801 Pennsylvania Ave SE,Suite 400
Washington, DC 20003
(202-547-6900)

Appalachian Mountain Club
5 Joy Street
Boston, MA 02108
(617-523-0636)

Appalachian Trail Conference
Box 807
Harpers Ferry, WV 25425
(304-535-6331)

Boy Scouts of America (National)
Box 152079
Irving, TX 75015
(214-580-2000)
(Call for information on state
   chapters.)

Camp Fire Inc
4601 Madison Ave
Kansas City, MO 64112
(816-756-1950)

Center for Marine Conservation
1725 DeSales St NW, Suite 500
Washington, DC 20036
(202-429-5609)

Clean Water Action
1320 18th St, NW
Washington, DC 20036
(202-457-1286)

Conservation Foundation
1250 24th St, NW
Washington, DC 20037
(202-293-4800)

Cousteau Society
870 Greenbrier Circle, Suite 402
Chesapeake, VA 23320
(804-523-9335)

Defenders of Wildlife
1244 19th St, NW
Washington, DC 20036
(202-659-9510)

Ducks Unlimited Inc
One Waterfowl Way
Long Grove, IL 60047
(708-438-4300)

Environmental Defense Fund Inc
257 Park Ave. South
New York, NY 10010
(212-505-2100)

Friends of the Blue Ridge Parkway
2301 Hendersonville Rd
Arden, NC 28704
(1-800-228-7275)

Friends of the Earth
218 D St SE
Washington, DC 20003
(202-544-2600)

Fund for Animals Inc
200 W 57th St
New York, NY 10019
(Phone 212-246-2096)

Girl Scouts of the USA
420 Fifth Ave
New York, NY 10018
(212-852-8000)
(Call for information on state
   chapters.)

Greenpeace USA Inc
1436 U St NW
Washington, DC 20009
(202-462-1177)

Izaak Walton League of America Inc
1401 Wilson Blvd, Level B
Arlington, VA 22209
(703-528-1818)

National Arbor Day Foundation
100 Arbor Ave
Nebraska City, NE 68410
(402-474-5655)

National Audubon Society
700 Broadway
New York, NY 10003
(212-797-3000)

National Boating Federation
Box 4111
Annapolis, MD 21403
(301-280-1911)

National Geographic Society
17th and M Sts NW
Washington, DC 20036
(202-856-7000)

National Parks and Conservation
  Association
1015 31st NW
Washington, DC 20007
(202-944-8530)

National Speleological Society
Cave Ave
Huntsville, AL 35810
(605-745-4366)

National Wildlife Federation
1400 16th St NW
Washington, DC 20036
(Phone 202-797-6693)

  Region 3 Director
  Box 527
  Ellerbe, NC 28338
  (910-652-5061)

The Nature Conservancy
1815 North Lynn St
Arlington, VA 22209
(703-841-5300)

  Southeast Regional Office
  Box 270
  Chapel Hill, NC 27514
  (919-967-5493)

North American Family Campers
  Association
Box 328
Concord, VT 05824
(802-695-2563)

Rails-to-Trails Conservancy
1400 16th St NW, Suite 300
Washington, DC 20036
(202-797-5400)

Sierra Club
730 Polk St
San Francisco, CA 94109
(415-776-2211)

  North Carolina Chapter
  404 Hillsborough Rd
  Carrboro, NC 27510
  (919-929-6489)

  Southeast Field Office
  1447 Peachtree St NE, #305
  Atlanta, GA 30309
  (404-888-9778)

Smithsonian Institution
1000 Jefferson Dr SW
Washington, DC 20560
(202-357-2700)

Southern Environmental Law Center
137 E. Franklin St, Suite 404
Chapel Hill, NC 27514
(919-967-1450)

Trout Unlimited
800 Follin Lane SE, Suite 250
Vienna, VA 22180
(703-281-1100)

The Wilderness Society
900 17th St, NW
Washington, DC 20006
(202-833-2300)

North Carolina Government Agencies
Department of Commerce
  Travel and Tourism
430 N Salisbury St
Raleigh, NC 27611
(919-733-4171)

Department of Environmental, Health, and Natural Resources
Box 27687
(Archdale Bldg, 512 N Salisbury St)
Raleigh, NC 27611
(919-733-4984)

State Parks and Recreation (director)
(919-733-4181)

Water Resources Commission
(director)
(919-733-4064)

State Parks (Superintendent and trails coordinator have same address and phone)

Yorkshire Center
12700 Bayleaf Church Rd
Raleigh, NC 27614
(919-846-9991)

Department of Transportation
Bicycle Program
Box 25201
Raleigh, NC 27611
(919-733-2804)

Recreation Resources Service
Box 8004, NCSU
Raleigh, NC 27695
(919-515-7118)
(This office offers for a fee a detailed directory, *Parks and Recreation Agencies,* of municipal, county, college and university, military, state park, therapeutic recreation, national park and forest, historic site, DEHNR, and professional organization titles, addresses, and telephone numbers.)

Wildlife Resources Commission
Archdale Bldg, 512 N Salisbury St
Raleigh, NC 27604
(919-733-3391)

North Carolina Citizens' Groups
American Horse Council
N.C. Division
Route 8, Box 80
Fuquay Varina, NC 27526
(919-552-3536)

Ashe County Rail-Trails
Box 6193 Bethlehem Station
Hickory, NC 28603
(704-495-4472)

Association for the Preservation of Eno River Valley
4015 Cole Mill Rd
Durham, NC 27712
(919-382-2722)

Cape Fear River Reserve Committee
711 Princess St
Wilmington, NC 28401
(910-763-8968)

Carolina American Youth Hostels
Box 10766
Winston Salem, NC 27108
(910-661-0444)

Carolina Bird Club Inc
Box 27647
Raleigh, NC 27611
(919-833-1923)

Catawba Lands Conservancy
230 E Independence Blvd, Suite 202
Charlotte, NC 28204
(704-375-6003)

Conservation Council of N.C.
307 Granville Rd
Chapel Hill, NC 27514
(919-942-7935)

Friends of the Blue Ridge Parkway
2301 Hendersonville Rd
Arden, NC 28704
(704-687-8722)

Friends of State Parks
4204 Randleman Rd
Greensboro, NC 27406
(910-885-4249)

North Carolina Nature Conservancy
Box 805
Chapel Hill, NC 27514
(919-967-7007)

North Carolina Rail-Trails
Drawer 124, 703 Ninth St
Durham, NC 27705
(919-493-6394)

N.C. Recreation and Park Society Inc
883 Washington St
Raleigh, NC 27605
(919-832-5868)

North Carolina Wildlife Federation
Box 10626
Raleigh, NC 27605
(919-833-1923)

Outer Banks Audubon Society
Box 1360
Kitty Hawk, NC 27949
(919-261-6850)

Sierra Club (N.C. Chapter)
1715 Park Rd
Charlotte, NC 28203
(704-377-3002)
   Groups: Blue Ridge, Broad River,
   Cape Fear, Capital, Central Piedmont,
   Cypress, Foothills, Haw River, Headwaters,
   Horace Kephart, Medoc, Orange-Chatham,
   Piedmont Plateau, Pinnacle, Pisgah, South
   Mtn, WENOCA.

Triangle Greenways Council
210A Spring Lane
Chapel Hill, NC 27514
(919-942-1265)

Triangle Land Conservancy
Box 13031
Research Triangle Park, NC 27709
(919-833-3662)

Trout Unlimited (N.C. Chapter)
114 Queensferry Rd
Cary, NC 27571
(919-460-0256)

Wake County Audubon Society
Box 12443
Raleigh, NC 27605
(919-834-9573)

Watauga Land Trust
Suite 207, 703 W King St
Boone, NC 28607
(704-264-2511)

Hiking Organizations

Major hiking organizations are listed here
and in Appendix A. For college and university outing clubs in which hiking may be an
activity, call direct. The clubs may be under a
variety of titles, such as Leisure Studies,
Recreational Studies, Physical Education
Department, Outdoor Recreation, Outdoor
Adventures, and Outing Club. For a list of
biking, canoeing, horseback riding, and
motoring organizations contact the state's
trails coordinator office (919-846-9991)
whose address is listed above under state
parks.

ATC Regional Office
Box 2750
Asheville, NC 28802
(704-254-3708)

Balsam Highlands Task Force
103 Surrey Rd
Waynesville, NC 28786
(704-456-3392)

Bartram Trail Society (N.C.)
Route 3, Box 406
Sylva, NC 28779
(704-293-9661)

Carolina Berg Wanderers
2308 Floral Ave
Charlotte, NC 28203
(704-399-3444)

Central Blue Ridge Task Force
122 Crestview Lane
Morganton, NC 28655
(704-437-6635)

Friends of the Mountains-to-Sea Trail
Box 3085
Louisburg, NC 27549
(919-496-4771)

Haywood Knolls Club
Haywood Knolls Dr
Hendersonville, NC 28739
(704-891-8893)

Neuse Trail Association
170 Quail Dr
Dudley, NC 28333
(919-734-1936)

Piedmont Hiking and Outdoor Club
1400 Knightwood Dr
Greensboro, NC 27410
(910-292-7637)

Pinnacle Park Trail Foundation
43 W Main St
Sylva, NC 28779
(704-586-2147)

Pisgah Hikers
#7 Tintill Court
Brevard, NC 28712
(704-883-2619)

Riverlink, Inc
Box 15488
Asheville, NC 28813
(704-252-8474)

Sauratown Trails Association
Route 1, Box 527
Pinnacle, NC 27043
(910-983-3250)

South Pisgah Task Force
Box 68
Asheville, NC 28802
(704-891-4440)

Tar Heel Walkers
Box 15013
Winston-Salem, NC 27113
(919-676-8587)

Triangle Trailblazers
12209 Glenlivet Way
Raleigh, NC 27613
(919-676-8587)

Winston Wanderers
Box 15013
Winston-Salem, NC 27113
(910-766-6446)

Appendix C

FEDERAL AND STATE ENDANGERED OR THREATENED SPECIES

An endangered species is one that is in danger of extinction throughout all or a significant part of a range. A threatened species is one that is likely to become endangered in the foreseeable future.

Fauna

In 1995 North Carolina had 55 endangered species and 51 threatened species. Below are species endangered or threatened in North Carolina *and* throughout the nation. Those *endangered* are listed with an (E); those *threatened* are listed with a (T).

Birds

Eagle, southeastern bald (E)
Falcon, American eastern peregrine (E)
Warbler, Bachman's (E)
Warbler, Kirtland's (E)
Woodpecker, red-cockaded (E)
Falcon, Arctic peregrine (T)
Plover, piping (T)
Stork, wood (E)
Tern, roseate (E)
Woodpecker, ivory-billed (E)

Fish

Chub, spotfin (T)
Shiner, Cape Fear (E)
Silverside, Waccamaw (T)
Sturgeon, shortnose (E)

Mammals

Bat, gray (E)

Mammals

Bat, Indiana (E)
Cougar, eastern (E)
Squirrel, Carolina northern flying (E)
Wolf, red (E)
Shrew, Dismal Swamp southern (T)

Mussels

Mussel, littlewing pearly (E)
Mussel, dwarf wedge (E)
Mussel, Tar River spiny (E)

Reptiles

Turtle, hawksbill (Atlantic) (T)
Turtle, leatherback (E)
Turtle, loggerhead (T)

Snails

Globe, noonday (T)

Flora

In 1994 North Carolina had 80 species as endangered and 36 species threatened. Below are species endangered or threatened in North Carolina *and* throughout the nation. Those *endangered* are listed with an (E); those *threatened* are listed with a (T).

Blue Ridge goldenrod (T)
Bunched arrowhead (E)

Canby's cowbane (E)
Chaffseed (E)
Cooley's meadow rue (E)

Green pitcher plant (E)

Harperella (E)
Heller's blazing star (T)

Michaux's sumac (E)
Mountain golden heather (T)
Mountain sweet pitcher plant (E)

Reflexed blue-eyed grass (E)
Roan mountain bluet (E)
Rough-leaf loosestrife (E)

Schweinitz's sunflower (T)
Seabeach amaranth (T)
Small-anthered bittersweet (E)
Small whorled pogonia (E)
Smooth coneflower (E)
Southern spicebush (T)
Spreading avens (E)
Swamp pink (T)

Virginia spiraea (T)

Appendix D

TRAILS FOR SPECIAL PEOPLE

The following lists of trails are examples of trails suited for three categories of special people: adventurous backpackers (remote, challenging, wilderness-type trails of moderate to strenuous difficulty); families with young children (short walks on easy terrain with natural and historic sites and emphasis on plants and animals); and people with disabilities (PWD)(short and easy paved trails for scenery, meditation, and fishing). Trail users will notice other trails in these categories and in other categories such as group camping trails, multiuse trails, and national recreation trails throughout the book.

Long Distance Backpacking

Appalachian National Scenic Trail (AT) (305.1 mi, linear)
Mountains-to-Sea Trail (MST) (138.2 mi; 72.9 mi; and 71.1 mi continuous, with sections under construction to bring these and other parts of the trail together, linear)
Bartram Trail (BT) (71.1 mi, linear; additional long loops with the AT)
Lakeshore Trail (41.8 mi, linear)
Art Loeb Trail (30.0 mi, linear) (33.0 mi with Cold Mountain Trail)
Slickrock Creek Trail and Hangover Lead Trail, et al (26.6 mi, loop)
Rim Trail (25.0 mi, loop)
Chunky Gal Trail (21.7 mi, linear)
Uwharrie Trail (20.5 mi, linear)
Neusiok Trail (20.9 mi, linear)

Family Day Hikes

All trails with the following italicized words are suggested for parents who wish to use trails for educational purposes with children: *nature* (an example is *Spring Creek Nature Trail*, 1.6 mi); *falls* (an example is *Hunt-Fish Falls Trail*, 1.5 mi); *island* (an example is *Mackay Island Trail*, 3.4 mi); *garden(s)* (an example is *Roan Mountain Gardens Trail*, 1.0 mi); *talking tree* (an example is *Clemmons Talking Tree Trail*, 0.8 mi); *historic* (an example is *Edenton*

Historic Trail, 1.5 mi); and for *animal names* (an example is *Rattlesnake Lodge Trail*, 0.8 mi round-trip). Some other suggested trails are as follows.

Bethabara Trail (1.8 mi)
Cedar Point Tideland Trail (1.4 mi)
Clingmans Dome Trail (1.0 mi)
Cloudland Trail (3.0 mi)
Devil's Courthouse Trail (0.8 mi)
Forest Festival Trail (1.0 mi)
Graveyard Fields Trail (3.2 mi)
Green Knob Trail (0.6 mi)
Greensboro Arboretum Trail (1.3 mi)
John Wasilik Memorial Poplar Trail (1.4 mi)
Joyce Kilmer Memorial Trail (1.2 mi)
Lake Junaluska Trail (2.3 mi)
Lover's Leap Trail (1.2 mi)
Mt Mitchell Summit Trail (0.4 mi)
Oconaluftee River Trail (1.5 mi)
Pickens Nose Trail (1.4 mi)
Price Lake Loop Trail (2.4 mi)
Raven Rock Loop Trail (2.1 mi)
Richland Balsam Trail (1.2 mi)
Sandy Ridge Wildlife Trail (2.2 mi)
Shelly Lake Trail (2.2 mi)
Sunset Rock Trail (1.4 mi)
Table Rock Summit Trail (1.6 mi)
Tracks in the Sand Trail (1.5 mi)
Waterrock Knob Trail (1.2 mi)
Whiteside Mtn Trail (2.0 mi)
Wildlife Observation Trail (1.4 mi)

People with Disabilities
Alleghany Trail (0.4 mi)
Bentonville Battleground History Trail (0.2 mi)
Bicentennial Garden Trail (0.5 mi)
Bicentennial Nature Trail (0.4 mi)
Buckeye Trail (1.9 mi)
Clemmons Talking Tree Trail (0.8 mi)
Creef Cut Wildlife Trail (0.5 mi)
Elizabeth City Historic Trail (1.6 mi)

Emerson Walk (0.7 mi)
Emry Park Trail (0.5 mi)
Fallon Creek Trail (0.3 mi)
Fishing Pier Trail (0.2 mi)
Jackson Park Nature Trail (0.5-mi section)
Guilford Courthouse Battlefield Trail (2.5 mi)
Lake Tomahawk Trail (0.6 mi)
Lassiter's Mill Trail (0.2 mi)
Laurel Trail (0.2 mi)
Little Walden Trail (195 yds)
Maple Springs Observation Trail (220 yds)
Richland Creek Trail (0.5 mi)
Roan Mountain Gardens Trail (1.0 mi)
Summer Rest Trail (0.9 mi)
Trail for the Handicapped (0.3 mi)
Upper Cascades Trail (0.4 mi)
Whitewater Falls Trail (0.4-mi round-trip to overlook)
Wiseman's View Trail (0.2 mi)
Wolf Creek Trail (0.3 mi)

Bibliography

Public Documents

Final Supplement to the Final Environmental Impact Statement, Vol. I and II, Nantahala and Pisgah National Forests, 1994.

Highlights of the Land and Resource Management Plan, Amendment 5, Nantahala and Pisgah National Forests, 1994.

Land and Resource Management Plan, Amendment 5, Nantahala and Pisgah National Forests, 1994.

Land and Resource Management Plan, Croatan and Uwharrie National Forests, 1986.

North Carolina Directory of Secondary Roads, Department of Transportation, 1995.

Outdoors North Carolina, 1990–1995, North Carolina Division of Parks and Recreation, 1989.

Record of Decision, Land and Resource Management Plan, Amendment 5, Nantahala and Pisgah National Forests, 1994.

Supplement to the Final Environmental Impact Statement, Croatan and Uwharrie National Forests, 1986.

Systemwide Plan for the North Carolina State Parks System, Division of Parks and Recreation, 1988.

Maps

Municipal and County Maps (current). Various publishers, coverage, and scale. Examples are *City Map of Greensboro,* H. M. Gousha Maps; *Raleigh, North Carolina,* Universal Map; and *Street Map of Winston-Salem and Forsyth County,* Map Supply. Local chambers of commerce usually have street maps of towns, cities, and counties. *North Carolina County Maps* (with short histories of the counties) is published in atlas format by Thomas Publications.

The Department of Transportation publishes county maps with all primary and secondary road numbers (but not names) and detailed inserts of town and cities.

National Park Service. Maps of the *Blue Ridge Parkway*. Scale is based on mileposts.

Map of *Great Smoky Mountains National Park*, Trails Illustrated Topo Map.

Maps of the *Appalachian National Scenic Trail*, Appalachian Trail Conference.

North Carolina Atlas and Gazetteer Map. DeLorme Mapping Company. Full state map with topographical scale of 1:150,000 with 1 inch representing 2.4 miles.

USFS Maps: *Appalachian Trail in Nantahala National Forest; Chattooga National Wild and Scenic River; Joyce Kilmer Slickrock Wilderness Area; Wilson Creek Area Trail Map; South Toe River Trail Map; Snowbird Area Trail Map; Birkhead Mountains Wilderness Area/ Uwharrie National Forest; Southern Nantahala Wilderness/Standing Indian; Linville Gorge Wilderness Area; Croatan National Forest; Uwharrie National Forest; Nantahala National Forest (Administrative); Pisgah National Forest/Pisgah Ranger District Trail Map; Pisgah National Forest/Grandfather, French Broad, and Toecane Ranger District Maps; Shining Rock/Middle Prong Wilderness*; and *Pisgah Ranger District/Harmon Den Trail Map*.

USGS *Maps of North Carolina*. (Also, modified USFS topographical maps, which show boundaries.) There are 1,075 maps listed with the scale of 1:24,000 with 2 5/8 inches representing 1 mile.

Books and Articles
Allied Recreation

Benner, Bob, and Tom Mc Cloud. *A Paddling Guide to Eastern North Carolina*. Birmingham, Ala.: Menasha Ridge Press, 1995.

Benner, Bob, and David Benner. *Carolina White Water, A Paddler's Guide to Western Carolinas*. Birmingham, Ala.: Menasha Ridge Press, 1993.

Coello, Dennis. *The Complete Mountain Biker*. New York: Lyons and Burford, 1989.

Hargett, Gil Forest. *Great Adventures in the Southern Appalachians.* Winston-Salem, N.C.: John F. Blair Publisher, 1994.

Kelley, Thomas. *The Climber's Guide to North Carolina.* Chapel Hill: Earthbound Inc, 1988.

Skinner, Charlie, and Elizabeth Skinner. *Bicycling the Blue Ridge.* Birmingham, Ala.: Menasha Ridge Press, 1990.

Flora and Fauna

Angier, Bradford. *Field Guide to Edible Wild Plants.* Harrisburg, Pa.: Stackpole Books, 1974.

Bull, John, and John Farrand Jr. *The Audubon Society Field Guide to North American Birds; Eastern Region.* New York: Alfred A. Knopf, 1977.

Catlin, David T. *A Naturalist's Blue Ridge Parkway.* Knoxville: University of Tennessee Press, 1984.

Dean, Jim, and Lawrence S. Early, *Wildlife in North Carolina.* Chapel Hill: University of North Carolina Press, 1987.

Fussell, John O. III. *A Birder's Guide to Coastal North Carolina.* Chapel Hill: University of North Carolina Press, 1995.

Green, Charlotte Hilton. *Birds of the South.* Chapel Hill: University of North Carolina Press, 1995 (Reprint).

Harrar, Elwood S., and J. George. *Guide to Southern Trees.* New York: Dover Publications Inc, 1962.

Justice, William S., and C. Ritchie Bell. *Wild Flowers of North Carolina.* Chapel Hill: University of North Carolina Press, 1987.

Martof, Bernard S., William M. Palmer, Joseph R. Bailey, and Julian R. Harrison. *Amphibians and Reptiles of the Carolinas and Virginia.* Chapel Hill: University of North Carolina Press, 1980.

Potter, Eloise F., James F. Parnell, and Robert P. Tuelings, *Birds of the Carolinas.* Chapel Hill: University of North Carolina Press, 1980.

Radford, Albert E., Harry E. Ahles, and C. Ritchie Bell. *Manual of the Vascular Flora of the Carolinas.* Chapel Hill: University of North Carolina Press, 1986.

Rohde, Fred C., Rudolf G. Arndt, David G. Lindquist, and James E. Parnell. *Freshwater Fishes of North Carolina, Virginia, Maryland, and Delaware.* Chapel Hill: University of North Carolina Press, 1995.

Schmutz, Ervin M., and Lucretia B. Hamilton. *Plants That Poison.* Flagstaff, Ariz.: Northland, 1989.

Simpson, Marcus B. Jr., *Birds of the Blue Ridge Mountains.* Chapel Hill: University of North Carolina Press, 1992.

Stokes, Donald W. *The Natural History of Wild Shrubs and Vines.* New York: Harper and Row, 1989.

Webster, William David, James F. Parnell, and Walter C. Biggs. *Mammals of the Carolinas, Virginia, and Maryland.* Chapel Hill: University of North Carolina Press, 1985.

Zomlefer, Wendy B. *Guide to Flowering Plant Families.* Chapel Hill: University of North Carolina Press, 1995.

History

A Walk on the Wild Side: Croatan National Forest (edited by New Bern Senior High School Coastal Biology Class). New Bern, N.C.: Owen G. Dunn Co, 1987.

Ambler, A. Chase Jr., *Rattlesnake Lodge.* Asheville, N.C.: Friends of Blue Ridge Parkway, 1995.

Bartram. William. *The Travels of William Bartram.* 1791. Naturalist's ed. Edited by Francis Harper. New Haven: Yale University Press, 1958.

Biggs, Walter C. Jr., and James F. Parnell, *State Parks of North Carolina.* Winston-Salem: John F. Blair Publisher, 1989.

Briceland, Alan. *Westward from Virginia: Exploration of Virginia-Carolina Frontier.* Charlottesville: University Press of Virginia, 1987.

Brooks, Maurice. *The Appalachians.* Boston: Houghton Mifflin, 1965.

Jolley, Harley E. *The Blue Ridge Parkway.* Knoxville: University of Tennessee Press, 1969.

Lederer, John. *The Discoveries of John Lederer, 1672.* Reprint, edited by William P. Cumming. Charlottesville: University Press of Virginia, 1958.

Morris, Glenn. *North Carolina Beaches.* Chapel Hill: University of North Carolina Press, 1993.

Pilkey, Orrin H. Jr., William J. Neal, Orrin H. Pilkey Sr., and Stanley R. Riggs. *From Currituck to Calabash.* Research Triangle Park, N.C.: North Carolina Science and Technology Research Center, 1980.

Powell, William S. *North Carolina through Four Centuries.* Chapel Hill: University of North Carolina Press, 1989.

Raeburn, Paul. "Can This Man Save Our Forests?" *Popular Science,* June 1994.

Ritz, Stacy. *Hidden Carolinas.* Berkeley, Calif.: Ulysses Press, 1995.

Roe, Charles E. *A Directory to North Carolina's Natural Areas.* Raleigh, N.C.: North Carolina Natural Heritage Foundation, 1988.

Shaffer, Earl V. *Walking with Spring.* Harpers Ferry, W. Va.: Appalachian Trail Conference, 1983.

Spitsbergen, Judith M. *Seacoast Life: An Ecological Guide.* Chapel Hill: University of North Carolina Press, 1983.

Williams, Ted. "Can the Forest Service Heal Itself?" *Wildlife Conservation,* September/October 1994.

Wilson, Jennifer Bauer. *Roan Mountain: A Passage of Time.* Winston-Salem: John F. Blair Publisher, 1991.

Trail Gear and Supplies

Auerback, Paul. *Medicine for the Outdoors.* New York: Little Brown, 1991.

Axcel, Claudia, Diana Cook, and Vikki Kinmont. *Simple Foods for the Pack.* San Francisco: Sierra Club Books, 1986.

Fleming, June. *Staying Found.* Seattle: The Mountaineers, 1994.

Fletcher, Colin. *The Complete Walker III.* New York: Alfred A Knopf, 1989.

Gorman, Stephen. *Winter Camping.* Boston: Appalachian Mountain Club Books, 1991.

Greenspan, Rick, and Hal Kahn. *The Camper's Companion.* San Francisco: Foghorn Press, 1991.

Kjellstrom, Bjorn. *Be Expert with Map and Compass*. Indianapolis, Ind.: MacMillan Publishing, 1976.

Logue, Victoria. *Backpacking in the 90s*. Birmingham, Ala.: Menasha Ridge Press, 1995.

McDougall, Len, *Practical Outdoor Survival*. New York: Lyons and Burford, l993.

McHugh, Gretchen. *The Hungry Hikers Book of Good Cooking*. New York: Alfred A. Knopf, 1993.

Olsen, Larry D. *Outdoor Survival Skills*. Chicago: Chicago Review Press, 1990.

Randall, Glenn. *The Modern Backpacker's Handbook*. New York: Lyons and Burford, 1993.

Trail Guidebooks

Adkins, Leonard M. *Walking the Blue Ridge: A Guide to the Trails of the Blue Ridge Parkway*. Chapel Hill: University of North Carolina Press, 1991.

Barnes, Lee. *Smoky Mountain Hiking and Camping*. Birmingham, Ala.: Menasha Ridge Press, 1994.

Bruce, Dan. *The Thru-Hiker's Handbook*. Hot Springs, N.C.: Center for Appalachian Trail Studies, 1995.

Chew, V. Collins. *Underfoot, A Geologic Guide to the Appalachian Trail*. Harpers Ferry, W.Va.: Appalachian Trail Conference, 1993.

Coriell, Jack, and Nancy Shofner, eds. *Appalachian Trail Guide to North Carolina–Georgia*. Harpers Ferry, W.Va.: Appalachian Trail Conference, 1994.

De Foe, Don, Beth Giddens, and Steve Kemp, eds. *Hiking Trails of the Smokies*. Gatlinburg, Tenn.: Great Smoky Mountains Natural History Association, 1994.

De Hart, Allen. *Hiking South Carolina Trails*. Old Saybrook, Conn.: Globe Pequot Press, 1994. (Includes connecting trails to North Carolina)

——. *The Trails of Virginia: Hiking the Old Dominion*. Chapel Hill: University of North Carolina Press, 1995. Includes connecting trails to North Carolina.

Edgar, Kevin, ed. *Appalachian Trail Guide to Tennessee–North Carolina*. Harpers Ferry, W.Va.: Appalachian Trail Conference, 1995.

Lord, William G. *Blue Ridge Parkway Guide.* Asheville, N.C.: Hexagon, 1976. Flora and fauna included in addition to history.

Luxenberg, Larry. *Walking the Appalachian Trail.* Mechanicsburg, Pa.: Stackpole Books, 1994.

Meyer, Peter. *Nature Guide to the Carolina Coast.* Wilmington, N.C.: Avian-Cetacean Press, 1992.

Schueler, Donald G. *Adventuring along the Southeast Coast.* San Francisco: Sierra Club Books, 1986.

Silverman, Goldie. *Backpacking with Babies and Small Children.* Berkeley, Calif.: Wilderness Press, 1986.

Wilderness

Doan, Marlyn. *Starting Small in the Wilderness: The Sierra Club Outdoors Guide for Families.* San Francisco: Sierra Club Books, 1979.

Hart, John. *Walking Softly in the Wilderness: The Sierra Club Guide to Backpacking.* San Francisco: Sierra Club Books, 1984.

Hampton, Bruce, and David Cole. *Soft Paths: How to Enjoy the Wilderness without Harming It.* Harrisburg, Pa.: Stackpole Books, 1988.

Hodgson, Michael. *The Basic Essentials of Minimizing Impact on the Wilderness.* Merrillville, Ind.: ICS, 1991.

Oelschlaeger, Max ed. *The Wilderness Condition.* San Francisco: Sierra Club Books, 1992.

Reifsnyder, William E. *Weathering in the Wilderness: The Sierra Club Guide to Practical Meteorology.* San Francisco: Sierra Club Books, 1980.

Schimelpfenig, Tod, and Linda Lindsey. *Wilderness First Aid.* Lander, Wyo.: National Outdoor Leadership School, 1991.

Simer, Peter, and John Sullivan. *The National Outdoor Leadership School's Wilderness Guide.* New York: Simon & Schuster, 1985.

Waterman, Laura and Guy. *Wilderness Ethics, Preserving the Spirit of Wilderness.* Woodstock, Vt.: Countryman Press, 1993.

Trail Index

The trail map numbers in the text are in parentheses. Because the *Appalachian Trail* and the *Mountains-to-Sea Trail* connect with numerous other trails described in the book, page numbers beyond the first mention of the trail in the book are given in italics.

General Index

About the Author

Allen de Hart has been hiking, designing, constructing, maintaining, and writing about trails for six decades. When only five years old, his seventeen-year-old brother, Moir, took him on a hiking, camping, and fishing trip to Smith River Falls, a few miles from their home in Patrick County, Virginia. The experience made an indelible impression and enhanced his interest in natural science and outdoor sports. His first childhood hikes in North Carolina were at Hanging Rock and Pilot Mountain (before they became state parks). In the 1930s he and his two younger brothers, Dick and Willie, built trails on their large farm and the Bobwhite Trail to Woolwine School, a shortcut from a long school bus ride. With the Appalachian Trail being constructed by the CCC at Rocky Knob, he and his brothers were among the first local users before 1940. But it was not until 1978 he hiked the entire length of the Appalachian Trail.

De Hart has a master's degree in American history from the University of Virginia in Charlottesville; did doctoral work at North Carolina State University; and two National Science Foundation grants in psychology, at Florida State University and the University of Georgia. He is a graduate of the Adjutant General Corps of the US Army and served overseas during the Korean War. He is a history professor emeritus at Louisburg College, Louisburg, N.C., where he and his wife, Flora (whose discipline was English), began teaching in 1957. He also served as director of public affairs for 27 years and has taught courses in outdoor recreation for 15 years. Active in state and community service organizations he has received three Governor's Awards.

He has hiked in 46 states and 18 foreign countries. By 1995 he had measured more than 30,000 miles of trails. From his journals he has authored eight books and trail guides for West Virginia, Virginia, North and South Carolina, Florida, and the sea islands of Georgia. Other outdoor sports in which he has participated are mountain climbing, whitewater rafting, biking, canoeing, hunting and fishing, diving, water skiing, and spelunking. He and his wife created the De Hart Botanical Gardens in Virginia and North Carolina in 1969. The preserve in North Carolina (south of Louisburg on US-401) is the largest private wildflower garden in eastern North Carolina.

About the AMC

The Appalachian Mountain Club pursues an active conservation agenda while encouraging responsible recreation. Founded in 1876, the club has been at the forefront of the environmental protection movement. We believe that successful long-term conservation depends on firsthand experience of the natural environment. AMC's 68,000 members pursue interests in hiking, backpacking, paddlesports, bicycling, and other activities and—at the same time—help safeguard the environment.

The most recent efforts in the AMC Conservation program include river protection, Northern Forest lands policy, and support for the Clean Air Act. AMC staff work with its active members and grassroots supporters to promote this conservation agenda.

The AMC's Education department offers a wide range of workshops to members and the general public, from introductory camping to intensive Mountain Leadership School taught in the White Mountains. In addition, volunteers in each chapter lead hundreds of activities and excursions.

The AMC's Research department focuses on the forces affecting the ecosystem, including ozone levels, acid rain and fog, climate change, rare flora and habitat protection, and air quality and visibility.

Another facet of the AMC is the Trails program, which maintains more than 1,400 miles of trail (including 350 miles of the Appalachian Trail) and more than 50 shelters in the Northeast. Volunteers, seasonal crews, and program staff contribute more than 10,000 hours of public service work each summer. Hikers can donate time as volunteers. Contact the AMC Trails Program, Pinkham Notch Visitor Center, PO Box 298, Gorham NH 03581; 603-466-2721.

The club operates eight alpine huts in the White Mountains that provide shelter, bunks and blankets, and hearty meals for hikers. Pinkham Notch Visitor Center, at the foot of Mt. Washington, is base camp to the adventurous and the ideal location for individuals and families new to outdoor recreation. Comfortable bunk rooms, mountain hospitality, and home-cooked, family-style meals make Pinkham Notch Visitor Center a fun and affordable choice for lodging. For reservations, call 603-466-2727.

The AMC's offices in Boston and at Pinkham Notch Visitor Center stock the entire line of AMC publications, including guidebooks and *Appalachia*, the country's oldest mountaineering and conservation journal. To order, call 800-262-4455 or write AMC, PO Box 298, Gorham, NH 03581.